"exercises"

"Ellerslie"

"exercises"

"Ellerslie"

"Valentine's"

Valentine's

perceptual → selection, organization, interpretation

attitudes → emotional

"Valentine's"

cognitive

behavioral

"Ellerslie"

"Rapport"

"open"

"exercises"

"Ellerslie"

"Ellerslie"

"Ellerslie"

exercises

"protestant" court
protest

10/8 1/2 10

Joy - 2
Joy - 3
- 3

protest

MANAGING HUMAN RELATIONS
Concepts and Practices

MANAGING HUMAN RELATIONS
Concepts and Practices

ROBERT E. CALLAHAN
C. PATRICK FLEENOR

Seattle University

Merrill Publishing Company
A Bell & Howell Information Company
Columbus   Toronto   London   Melbourne

Cover Photo: Larry Hamill
Sculptures courtesy of Eric Marlowe

Published by Merrill Publishing Company
A Bell & Howell Information Company
Columbus, Ohio 43216

This book was set in Meridien.

Administrative Editor: Paul Lee
Production Coordinator: Mary Harlan
Art Coordinator: Patrick L. Welch
Cover Designer: Cathy Watterson
Text Designer: Cynthia Brunk

Library of Congress Catalog Card Number: 87-63127
International Standard Book Number: 0-675-20767-3
Printed in the United States of America
1 2 3 4 5 6 7 8 9 — 92 91 90 89 88

For Shirley and Margaret

Robert E. Callahan

C. Patrick Fleenor

Robert E. Callahan, Ph.D., is an Associate Professor of Management at the Albers School of Business, Seattle University. He has authored several books in the field of management and contributes a column in the *Northwest Employment Journal* on human relations practices. He also is a former personnel director of a Fortune 500 company. His interests include managing change, use of quality circles, and creating productive work teams.

C. Patrick Fleenor, Ph.D., is the Robert D. O'Brien Professor of Business at the Albers School of Business, Seattle University, where he has taught management and business policy courses since 1973. He has coauthored a number of management books and has served as a management consultant to private and public organizations in the United States, Canada, and Europe. He holds an affiliate position at the Stockholm School of Economics and has been a guest lecturer at the Singapore Institute of Management.

Preface

This book is about people and organizations. From our own experiences as consultants to and employees of organizations, we are convinced that an understanding of basic human relations concepts can help you increase your effectiveness at every stage of your career, from subordinate to manager. As teachers, we want you to understand some of the problems inherent in organizations and to realize that you can have a positive impact.

Consequently, we decided to develop a book that would help you acquire the necessary knowledge of and skills in human relations and that would present the important concepts in a clear and understandable fashion, without unnecessary jargon. Further, we wanted this text to have a strong applications emphasis—to demonstrate how different organizations have tried to apply these concepts and to show how and why some succeeded and others did not. This presentation from a manager's point of view can help you appreciate the difficulty of translating theory into practice. Finally, we believe strongly that learning aids incorporated throughout a text can make it easier for you to understand the significance of the material.

In short, we have tried to provide some important information about human relations in an understandable, concise fashion, to emphasize a realistic orientation of practicing managers, and to help you learn.

Our specific objectives for a course in human relations are

- [ ] To provide you with information about currently accepted theories of human relations
- [ ] To help you realize that there are many different approaches to a given situation
- [ ] To increase your ability to predict what can happen in organizations, so that you can be more in control of events, both to your benefit and that of your organization
- [ ] To provide an opportunity for you to analyze your assumptions about people and how they behave in organizations and to evaluate the effectiveness of those assumptions
- [ ] To provide some managerial tools and approaches that have proven useful in actual practice

Although you may not think of yourself as a future manager, or intend to become a manager, the approach to human relations that we advocate will allow you to become a more effective *member* of any organization.

In addition to our emphasis on the application of theories and a managerial approach, we have included some topics not found in the typical text on human relations, including career development, organizational culture, stress management, and the impact of computer technology on employees and supervisors. These topics are important now and will gain importance in the future. To ignore them would not help you prepare for the realities of a career in the organizations of today and tomorrow.

This text is intended for a broad range of readers, from students just out of high school to those with many years of practical experience. Whatever your background, you will find that the organization of this book and many of its special features are designed to help you concentrate on the important points and consider their implications. Watch for these elements and features:

☐ **"What's Your Opinion?"**   Preceding each chapter is a brief set of true-or-false questions. Answer these questions before you begin reading the chapter. They not only will give you an idea of the type of material covered in the chapter but also will allow you to identify your present perceptions and attitudes. Some of these questions represent "commonsense" ideas widely believed in organizations but which, in reality, may be myths.

☐ **Opening Story**   Each chapter begins with a story or situation related to the chapter topic. See whether you can identify potential problems or suggest solutions. Additional information about the story is presented at various points later in the chapter, keyed to the discussion of the theories.

☐ **Theory Section**   The first major part of the chapter covers the current and popular theories and their explanations. We have provided a number of examples to clarify what each theory means.

☐ **Human Relations Success or Failure**   Within each chapter's theory section are stories that illustrate the successful application of, or the failure to apply, human relations practices. Answer the questions at the end of each story, then compare your answers to those of other students.

☐ **Marginal Material**   Questions, statements, and definitions of important terms appear in the margins of each chapter. Some of these are focus questions and some are focus statements, intended to draw your attention to important terms and concepts in that section. You can use these to review or outline the chapter material.

☐ **Learning Summary**   This section summarizes the major theoretical material in the form of short statements, which will help you review and remember the critical concepts.

☐ **Answers to "What's Your Opinion?"**   After becoming familiar with the relevant theories, you can check your answers to the true-or-false questions at the beginning of the chapter. Would you now answer these questions differently? Do you understand their implications better?

☐ **Human Relations Applications**   Each chapter presents various examples of how certain theories or concepts have been applied to real situations. This section will help you identify some of the situational factors that can help or hinder the application of theory.

☐ **Personal Guidelines for Human Relations Success**   Following the applications section is a brief unit offering suggestions for applying some of the chapter's concepts to your professional or personal life.

☐ **Discussion and Review Questions**   Questions at the end of each chapter will help you review important concepts and allow you to test your understanding of the chapter's material. Answer each question and check your answers by looking up the appropriate chapter section.

☐ **Human Relations Exercise**   These short exercises were chosen to help you explore personally an important concept from each chapter. Certain of these will be led by your instructor. Were the results what you expected? See if you can explain why.

□ **Human Relations Incident** Each chapter concludes with a brief situation that addresses the chapter material. Identify the major issues raised by the incident and propose some solutions. See how well *you* can apply theory to a specific situation.

Managing Human Relations: Concepts and Practices is supplemented by a comprehensive *Student Resource Guide,* which can be an invaluable learning resource for you. The guide is keyed exactly to the textbook and helps you review the material and test your understanding. The guide has multiple choice, true/false, and essay questions for each chapter, plus a ''mind-map,'' so you can diagram each chapter's contents pictorially. Introductory material in the guide tells you how to study for exams, how to take class notes, and how to develop a more effective and efficient learning style. In addition, the *Student Resource Guide* contains answers to all end-of-chapter questions, as well as to the margin questions from every chapter. Correct answers for all questions are located at the back of the guide.

For instructors, *Managing Human Relations: Concepts and Practices* is supplemented by a comprehensive *Instructor's Resource Manual,* containing additional information, outlines, suggestions for lectures and discussions, class assignments, and answers to text questions, and by a set of transparency masters. A test bank is available in printed form and on diskette for the IBM personal computer.

Acknowledgments

Many people besides the authors are involved in the creation of any book, and we thank all of them for their help. Four people deserve special mention for their creative efforts and contributions: Professor Gary Nelson, Charlotte, North Carolina (Chapter 10, Stress Management and Em-

ployee Counseling); Professor Jack Atkinson, College of Alameda, California (Chapter 11, Career Development); Professor William (Bill) Searle, Enfield, Connecticut (Chapter 12, Working with Unions); and Professor Jayne Colley, Horry-Georgetown Technical College, South Carolina (Chapter 13, Equal Opportunity Issues). We certainly would not have been able to complete the book without their skilled contributions.

We also want to thank all of the people who served as reviewers of various drafts of the text:

Cora Alameda, University of California—Santa Clara; Edward S. Beckstrom, McHenry County College; Charles Beem, Bucks County Community College; Rex Bishop, Charles County Community College; Kathy Eklofe, Indian Hills Community College; Edward W. Friese, Okaloosa-Walton Junior College; Olene Fuller, San Jacinto College North; Jon Gartman, Axtell, TX; Jerry Goddard, Aims Community College; Ron Herrick, Mesa Community College; Charles W. Higginbotham, Jr., Fresno State University; Gail Hotelling, Delhi, NY; Robert F. Kegel, Jr., Buena Park, CA; Jeffrey Keil, Richmond, VA; Betty Ann Kirk, Florida State University; Art Moyer, Stark Technical College; John Neal, Lake-Sumter Community College; Hershel Nelson, Polk Community College; Elaine Olenik, Central Piedmont Community College; Edward Reid, Shelby State Community College; Carla L. Rich, Pensacola, FL; Dick Shapiro, Cleveland; Tom Shaughnessy, Illinois Central College; Marilee Smith, Cedar Rapids; Joan Still-Smith, Kilgore College; Ted Valvoda, Highland Heights, OH; Sandra L. Ward, Halifax Community College; Marc Wayner, Hocking Technical College; and Roger Wohlert, Ellsworth Community College.

Their insightful comments and suggestions enabled us to improve the quality and readability of this text.

The Albers School of Business, Seattle University, provided resources of various kinds, including relief from normal teaching duties, that allowed us to maintain a vigorous writing schedule. Dr. John Eshelman, Executive Vice-President of Seattle University, and Dr. Harriet Stephenson, Interim Dean of the Albers School of Business, especially deserve our thanks.

Our editors at Merrill Publishing Company, Tim McEwen and Pam Budin, deserve much thanks. Mary Harlan, our production editor, showed skill and patience, and her calm authority added immensely to our psychological health.

Finally, we want to thank our wives for putting up with yet another book. Our months of distracted behavior have come to an end, at least until we start another book. Next week.

Survey Respondents

The following individuals participated in a Merrill survey of Human Relations courses and texts. Their contributions to the design and content of this text and its supplements are gratefully acknowledged.

Cora Alameda, University of California—Santa Clara; Dennis G. Allen, Grand Rapids Junior College; Marreese A. Allen, Danville Community College; Harold R. Anderson, Arizona Western College; Jon M. Armon, Muskegon Business College; Neal Aronson, Fox Valley Technical Institute; Paul Aschenbrenner, Hartnell College; Gerald Ashley, Grossmont Community College; B. J. O. Ashwill, University of Oregon; Jack Atkinson, College of Alameda; John T. Atella, Harrisburg Area Community College.

Alvan Bachtell, Milwaukee Area Technical College; Jean Badgley, Brookdale Community College; Mary F. Bales, Walters State Community College; Ernest M. Basile, Moraine Valley Community College; Loretta A. Bates, Donnelly College; Edward S. Beckstrom, McHenry County College; Dan Bellack, Lexington Community College; Estella Bennett, Eastern Oklahoma State College; Alan Berkey, Miami, FL; Larry Berthelsen, Odessa College; Wanda Bilsing, Ankeny, IA; Rex L. Bishop, Charles County Community College; James L. Bliss, Alfred State College; Amy Bollenbach, Anchorage Community College; J. Boyle, Phoenix, AZ; Robert L. Braaten, Tidewater Community College; Suzanne Bradford, Angelina College; Duane Brickner, Maricopa Community College; Pat Brock, Tempe, AZ; Lynn Brokaw, Portland Community College; James

Brother, Ellington, CT; Russell B. Bruce, Thornton, IL; Mark E. Buckley, Barton County Community College; William F. Burtis, Sunnyvale, CA.

Vincent Cain, Rend Lake College; Ronald G. Caldwell, Blue Mountain Community College; Cynthia Calhoun, State Technical Institute at Memphis; Nicholas Campagivone, Maria College of Albany; J. E. Cantrell, De Anza College; Linda Chaparro, Oxnard College; John B. Chism, Truckee Meadows Community College; Maxine Christenson, Aims Community College; Barry S. Coabley, Mountain View College; Debbie Collins, Brevard Community College; Jerry Comingore, Lake Jackson, TX; Paul Concepcion, Chemeketa Community College; George Cooper, Madison Area Technical College; Debra J. Corson, Hawkeye Institute of Technology; Bridget Coughlin, Hocking Technical College; Jerry M. Counce, Paducah, KY; Carol Craig, University of Wisconsin—Eau Claire; Jayne P. Crolley, Horry-Georgetown Technical College; Annabelle Cromwell, Red Rocks Community College; Geoffrey Crosslin, Kalamazoo, MI; Bob Cutler, Los Angeles.

Irmagard K. Davis, Honolulu, HI; Linda Davis, Mount Hood Community College; Richard T. Day, Manchester Community College; Joseph DeFilippe, Suffolk Community College—Brentwood; Rich Dehring, Mukwonago, WI; John C. Dotts, Fresno; Robert Dunbar, City College of San Francisco; Charles L. Dunham, Centralia, WA; Paul F. Dusseault, Herkimer, NY.

Cliff Eisehen, Fresno State University; Kathy Eklofe, Indian Hills Community College; J. Raymond Entenman, Hillsborough Community College.

E. J. Fabyan, Indian Hills Community College; Carol J. Doll-Ferguson, Rock Valley College; David F. Filak, El Paso Community College; Sr. Agatha Fitzgerald, Chatfield College; M. Winona Fleenor, Virginia Highlands Community College; Lee Fleming, El Centro College; Richard E. Foil, Southwest Virginia Community College; Robert Freadenthal, Moraine Valley Community College; Julienne K. Friday, Waldorf College; Edward W. Friese, Okaloosa-Walton Junior College; Olene L. Fuller, San Jacinto College North.

Lawrence Galant, Gaston College; John Gartman, Axtell, TX; Virginia M. Gaustad, Crafton Hill College; Dr. Gava, Richmond, VA; Ben George, Southside Virginia Community College; Thomas Gerry, Hudson, NY; Colleen Gift, Highland Community College; Jerry F. Goddard, Aims Community College; William E. Goetz, Wisconsin Rapids, WI; Clyde A. Goodrum, Martin

Community College; Ann Gregory, South Plains College; Luther Guynes, Los Angeles.

Frank Haeg, Oakland, CA; Charles E. Haley, Lord Fairfax Community College; Sharon L. Hanna, Lincoln, NE; D. David Hanson, Ellsworth Community College; Bernice B. Harshberger, Carteret Technical College; Paul Hegele, St. Charles, IL; John J. Heinsius, Modesto, CA; Ron Herrick, Mesa Community College; J. R. Heran, Westmoreland County Community College; Charles W. Higginbotham, Jr., Fresno State University; Don Hockenbury, Tulsa Junior College; Fayrene Hofer, Visalia, CA; David Holcombe, Horse Shoe, NC; Alan Hollander, Suffolk County Community College; Gail C. Hotelling, SUNY Delhi; Norman Humble, Cedar Rapids, IA; F. L. Hunter, Monrovia, CA.

George Jacobson, Gateway Technical Institute; Margie M. Jefferson, Hillsborough Community College; Tod Johnson, Hoskins, NE; William T. Johnston, Delaware Technical and Community College; W. George Jones, Danville Community College.

Marlene Katz, Menlo Park, CA; Bob Kegel, Buena Park, CA; F. Jeffrey Keil, Richmond, VA; Margot Ann Keller, Lima Technical College; Richard Kellogg, SUNY Alfred State College; R. K. Kellough, Catonsville Community College; Lloyd I. Kenniston, Delhi, NY; Robert A. Kersten, Kirkwood, MO; James Kestenbaum, Rochester Institute of Technology; George Kettleson, Fox Valley Technical Institute; Guadalupe King, Milwaukee Area Technical College; Betty Ann Kirk, Florida State University; Wesley G. Koch, East Peoria, IL; Larry E. Koon, Colby, KS; Bob Kuhnle, Thomas Nelson Community College; Shabse H. Kurland, Catonsville Community College.

Marliss Lauer, Massasoit Community College; Edward J. LeMay, Massasoit Community College; Dorothea L. Leonard, Miami-Dade Community College; William Liebal, Broadview Heights, OH; Hans Lind, Whittier, CA; Walt Lindstrum, Green Bay, WI; Stephen Link, Farmers Branch, TX; Raymond E. Lloyd II, Delaware Technical and Community College; John T. Long, Mount San Antonio College; Marvin Long, New River Community College; Richard Lubinski, District One Technical Institute; Roger J. Lynch, Cottage Grove, MN.

Ricky Maclin, Peoria, IL; Charles Marley, Texarkana, TX; Sue H. Martel, Cleveland, TN; Dennis Martens, El Dorado, KS; John Martin, Mount San Antonio College; Barbara Mase, Lima, Ohio; Haleen Matthews, Appleton, WI; Noel C. Matthews, Northglenn, CO; Robert D.

McAninch, Prestonsburg Community College; Eve McClure, Highline College; Donald Joseph McGee; College of San Mateo; Wilma Jean McLeod, Southwestern College; Marcia McMurphy, St. Louis Community College—Florissant Valley; Bettie M. Meachum, Lancaster, TX; M. K. Meiers, South Lake Tahoe, CA; Jack F. Mercer, Peninsula, OH; Michael C. Metz, Great Mills, MD; Richard F. Michaels, Hamburg, NY; Cecilia Minder, Dothan, AL; Charles A. Moore, Neosho County Community College; Stephen Mozara, Galveston College; Jane Kravitz Munley, Luzerne County Community College.

David T. Nakamaejo, Honolulu, HI; Sandra Nalley, Umpqua Community College; John Neal, Lake-Sumter Community College; Gary Nelson, Central Piedmont Community College; Hershel Nelson, Polk Community College; Robert D. Nelson, Issaquah, WA; David Nickoley, Farmington, NM; Roger C. Noe, Southeast Community College; Timothy D. Nolan, Cincinnati Technical College.

Elaine Olenik, Central Piedmont Community College; Mary Lou O'Phelan, Lakewood Community College; Pat Otto, Racine, WI; Delilah S. Outram, Universal City, CA.

Margaret Park, St. Louis Community College; Mark Parken, DeKalb Technical School; Vera Pearson, Parsons, KS; Sarah Pender, Placerville, CA; Alan Penn, Madison Area Technical College; Jean Perry, Contra Costa College; Ralph Pifer, Sauk Valley College; George P. Pilkey, Fulton-Montgomery Community College; Rosa Preciado, Mount San Antonio College; Ellen Price, Mars Hill, NC; Richard C. Pusz, Sr., West Virginia Northern Community College.

Bill Raeker, Anoka-Ramsey Community College; Sandra Ammons-Rasmus, Big Springs, TX; Paul Rebrovich, Platte College; William A. Reeves, Milwaukee Area Technical College; Ed Reid, Shelby State Community College; William Reinhardt, Moraine Park Technical Institute; Roy Reisinger, Anchorage Community College; Bradford Reynolds, Central Piedmont Community College; Marcia Rhodes, Milford, MA; Carla Rich, Pensacola, FL; J. A. Robbins, Jr., Daytona Beach Community College; Walter Robinton, Hillsborough Community College; Ron Rose, Arapahoe Community College; Judith L. Rotkis, Hocking Technical College; Gerald Rubin, Central Virginia Community College; Dick Rundall, Rock Valley College; Anthony D. Russo, Holland, CT; William T. Ryan, Polk Community College.

Danna Scarlett, Iowa Western Community College;

Prof. Schickler, Southern Ohio College; Paul Schmolling, Kinsborough Community College; Linda Schwandt, University of Wisconsin—La Crosse; Teri Miller Schwartz, Milwaukee Area Technical College; Betty Scott, Overland Park, KS; Bill Searle, Asnuntuck Community College; Richard W. Shapiro, Cleveland, OH; Thomas J. Shaughnessy, Illinois Central College; Vanita Lytle Sherrile, Volunteer State Community College; Connie Sitterly, Texas Woman's University; Peggy Skinner, South Plains College; Joan Still-Smith, Kilgore College; Marilee Smith, Kirkwood Community College; Ed Snider, Mesa, AZ; Ralph G. Soney, Morganton, NC; Cheryl Stansfield, Brooklyn Park, MN; John Storck, Treasure Valley Community College; Robert J. Stout, Clearwater, FL; David Stringer, San Jose, CA; James R. Stuart, Fort Dodge, IA; Shirley M. Sweet, Blackhawk Tech.

Joel C. Tate, Germanna Community College; Mary R. Tauscher, Milwaukee Area Technical College; Louis Taylor, Mission College; W. Robert Taylor, Boone, IA; Rance Thomas, Florissant, MO; Pat Trachy, Gulf Breeze, FL; Murray Turner, Bismark Junior College; Kim J. Tyler, Shasta College.

J. Robert Ulbrich, Champaign, IL.

Ted Valvoda, Lakeland Community College; Kelly VanVliet, Milwaukee, WI; Jacqueline K. Vines, Davenport College of Business.

Sandra L. Ward, Halifax Community College; Judi Warehouse, City College of San Francisco; Marc Wayner, Hocking Technical College; Thomas J. Webb, Lake Land College; Deborah Weber, University of Akron; Blaine Weller, Muskegon Business College; Stephan Y. Werba, Catonsville Community College; L. Westerlin, Cerritos College; Clair Wiederholt, Madison Area Technical College; Roger Wohlert, Ellsworth Community College; P. J. Wolff, Dundalk College; Charles E. Womack, Mattoon, IL.

J. Yeamans, Dayton, OH.

Linda Zaitchik, Newbury College; Rowan Zeiss, Blue Ridge Community College; Lawrence Ziegler, Cincinnati Technical College; Joseph Zielinski, Tarrant County Junior College; Andrew D. Zimmerman, Wilmington, DE; David Zuercher, Huron, OH.

Contents

SPECIAL FEATURES

MANAGING HUMAN RELATIONS
Concepts and Practices

PART ONE

Valentine's

"drop off"

Valentine's Day

INDIVIDUAL ASPECTS OF HUMAN RELATIONS

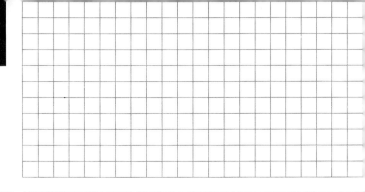

CHAPTER 1
INTRODUCTION

WHAT'S YOUR OPINION? T OR F

_____ 1. Organizations are complex in nature and to understand them properly we must look at their parts.

_____ 2. Other social sciences have had an impact on the study of human relations.

_____ 3. Craft types of work, such as making furniture, are involving in nature and rare in today's society.

_____ 4. Even early civilizations, such as the Egyptians, had to organize human efforts to undertake such complex projects as the pyramids.

_____ 5. Early scientists were surprised that people wanted attention and recognition as well as pay for their work.

_____ 6. Computers have had little impact on people in organizations.

_____ 7. Work force values are changing and today are more closely related to the "Me Generation."

_____ 8. The Japanese management style for top managers is more one of generalists than decision makers. In contrast, top American managers are decision makers.

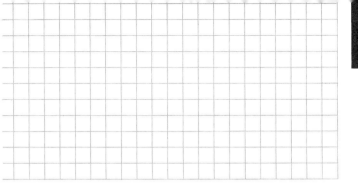

LEARNING OBJECTIVES

☐ Define the term "human relations"

☐ Explain how three major fields contribute to our understanding of human relations

☐ Describe the history of work from the craft era to the present

☐ Understand the historical development of human relations

☐ List and discuss the current trends affecting human relations

☐ Explain how the applications section can be used to understand human relations

Human Relations—Can We Make It a Game?[1]

If you can find Joann's Expressway Lounge in Springfield, Mo., you will find some interesting patrons about 4:30 every afternoon. At this time managers and workers arrive from the Springfield Remanufacturing Center Corp. (SRC), formerly a division of International Harvester.

Here, for example, are Pam Smith and Verna Mae Ross, who assemble fuel-injection nozzles, and general foremen Steve Choate and Joe Loeber. Over there, pounding on a pinball machine is Doug Rothert, the production manager. It's an odd assortment of people, defying normal levels of corporate structure. "The barrier between management and employees just doesn't exist here," says Smith. "I am pretty low in seniority, but I can sit here and shoot the breeze with Jack."

Jack Stack is SRC's president and largest stockholder. Stack can usually be found at Joann's between 4:30 and 6:00 P.M., just in case an employee should want to discuss a problem in less formal surroundings.

This story actually began in 1983 when this division of International Harvester lost $2 million on sales of $26 million. Jack Stack and twelve other employees bought the business from Harvester that year. While an employee buyout is not unique, in this case the resulting management and employee relationship is. Here the employees and managers focus on numbers and how to make them better. The results are impressive. Since the buyout, SRC's sales have grown 40 percent per year, and the appraised value of a share of stock owned by employees has increased from $.10 to $8.45. Meanwhile, absenteeism and employee turnover, once high, have all but disappeared.

Stack gives a quick summary of this success between pool shots, "Look, we're appealing to the highest level of thinking we can in every employee in our company. Why hire a guy and only use his brain to grind crankshafts?"

It is 11:15 on a weekday morning, and—in the company cafeteria—SRC is appealing to the highest level of thinking of the workers on the first shift. They are sitting at Formica tables, eating their lunches. There is just one thing out of the ordinary: high on the wall above the microwave oven sits a red, electronic message board quietly flashing the words, "FUEL INJECTION LABOR UTILIZATION 98%."

As any of the workers can tell you, the message means that the fuel-injection pump assemblers spent 98 percent of their work time on direct labor (rather than overhead) during the first half of their shift. If they keep up that pace, they become eligible for sizable bonuses under a system called "Stop the Praise—Give Us the Raise."

This is just a sample of the numbers that guide the company to success. It's part of Stack's master plan to have some fun while working. "For me, fun was action, excitement, a good game," he says. "If there's one thing common to everybody, it's that we all love to play a good game."

Gamesmanship lies at the heart of Stack's approach to management. The business at SRC is based on the premise that work can be a game for everyone, as long as you make it possible for everyone to play. Everyone must know the rules, receive enough information to play, and have an opportunity to win or lose. To accomplish this, Stack set up an education program for all workers, including accounting and warehousing, to teach the workers how to play "The Game." SRC keeps employees focused on the basics by giving them all the information they need to follow the flow of The Game.

To begin with, everyone—managers, supervisors, administrative personnel, production workers—has access to the company's monthly financial report, a weighty document running to ninety pages. In small group sessions, supervisors or department heads go over the figures, encouraging questions. In addition, every day there are printouts detailing the progress of every job in each supervisor's area.

Managers and supervisors plan a daily income statement listing the key items to be watched. In the afternoon, the supervisors carry the information to plant workers. In one session, Bobby Voelker, a department safety representative, reports that there have been nine accidents, resulting in the loss of 14 days of work. "We've got to do better than that. You must wear safety glasses to and from lunch." The supervisor asks if anyone doesn't understand the income statement for the department. Two workers raise their hands and the supervisor offers to tutor them after work.

In another special program called "Employee Awareness Day," Stack closes the plant and has the employees come to the local Hilton Inn for lunch, supper, and to listen to speakers. They also watch a documentary about Japanese business, which warns that unless the United States improves its productivity, the next generation of Americans will be the first to experience a declining standard of living. After the film, Stack asks, "Do you want this responsibility—to start the decline? We have to do something about it, don't we?" The employees stand and cheer.

To help prevent that decline in his own company, Stack has formed the "Great Game of Business" to conform to the reality that the buyout must work or all employees will lose their jobs. "We had to set up a game, where we couldn't make a $10,000 mistake—or at least where we would know how to correct it right away. And we had to do this without establishing a dictatorship. Systems don't run companies, people do."

THE BASICS OF HUMAN RELATIONS

The opening story relates a unique example of working and managing a company. The principal owner has decided to have fun and still be very serious about the need to win The Game. We chose this story because it contains some ideas that seem contrary to popular beliefs about conducting business. It also suggests that workers and managers can win at the game of business. The story challenges our view of the work world. Human relations should challenge our view of what makes success in the work environment. The world is changing and our "common sense" view of how to be successful, both personally and professionally, needs to be challenged.

What Is Human Relations?

Organizations are social systems that operate to serve some purpose, such as to make a profit or to provide a service. Management is a process of managing the social system so that jobs are accomplished that generate profits or provide services. Simply put, human relations is the study of and application of principles to help organizational members—workers, supervisors, and managers—be effective at their jobs.

But what makes up the organization? Figure 1–1 provides a basic understanding of what we mean by organization.

What are the major parts of the organization? Define them.

The organization is made up of three main components: structure, technology, and people. *Structure* defines the relationships between people in organizations. In an organization, there are many jobs—such as accountants and secretaries—that need to be related in some structured manner so they can be coordinated and performed effectively.

Technology is a term covering a variety of means that people use to accomplish their jobs. It can mean the tools and procedures they use to provide products

FIGURE 1–1
Model of an organization.

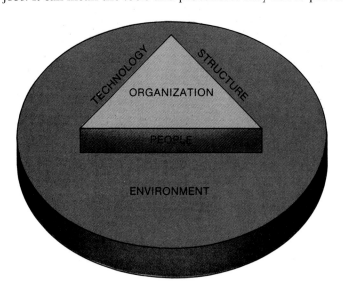

or services. It can mean the machines or plant layout that allows the products to move to completion. Technology is different in the auto industry than in a hospital.

People make up the social system of an organization. People are the means by which organizations try to accomplish their goals. People have their own goals, which may or may not be accomplished by doing their jobs.

The *environment* is the larger context or community in which the organization operates. It contains political, social, and economic factors that influence how the organization will operate.

Now let us return to the definition of human relations. Using this view of organizations, human relations is concerned with understanding, predicting, and influencing individual and group behavior in organizations. In this book we will study many concepts to understand what is meant by human relations: individual and group behavior, organizational culture, conflict, management of change, leadership, motivation, stress management and employee counseling, communication, performance appraisal, unions, equal opportunity issues, computer technology, career development, and future directions of human relations.

Human relations is concerned with understanding, predicting, and influencing both the individual and the group in organizations.

Why Study Human Relations?

We live in a society built around organizations. How many organizations are you a part of today? Family? Church? Sports team? A student club? A business? It's almost impossible to avoid being a member of some kind of organization.

Why do we join organizations? Or why do we leave organizations? We usually join to satisfy individual needs, whether they be social, emotional, physical, or monetary. We depend heavily on organizations to fulfill our own purposes as well as theirs. We will look at our needs and motivations in Chapter 3.

Consider that we will probably work for forty or more years in one or more organizations. Since we spend so much of our lives within organizations, it seems reasonable that learning as much as we can about how they operate might help us be more effective within those settings. By understanding the principles of human relations, we may be able to reduce some of the frustrations that people face in trying to be effective and in meeting their own needs.

Working in organizations means having to work for other people, work with other people, or supervise other people. As supervisors or managers in charge of people and tasks, we need to understand how people react. If we want to be effective as leaders, we need to understand the principles of human relations.

[handwritten margin note: Join to satisfy needs social, emotional, physical, monetary]

What Are the Origins of Human Relations?

The field of human relations is heavily influenced by other behavioral and social sciences, especially psychology, sociology, and anthropology. In a manner of speaking, these disciplines are the underpinnings of human relations. Each contributes to our knowledge of people in organizations. Although each is concerned

(handwritten margin notes: "What factors determine behaviour", "Dynamics two or more interacting", "Origins developments of cultures functioned — continue to function")

with understanding human behavior, each approaches that understanding from a different perspective.

Psychology. This discipline has had the most influence on the field of human relations because of its focus—discovering what factors determine the behavior of individuals. The major areas researched in psychology are motivation and learning. Both are key to being more effective as a worker or as a supervisor.

Sociology. Sociology, while not as prominent as psychology, is nevertheless the basis for trying to understand social behavior. By social behavior we mean the dynamics of two or more individuals interacting. Therefore, sociology focuses attention on groups, organizations, and societies rather than on the individual. This also is critical to workers and supervisors as they strive to function effectively in groups and committees.

Anthropology. Anthropology is a broad discipline that studies the origins and development of human cultures, how those cultures have functioned in the past, and how they continue to function today. While the study of culture may seem to be an indirect approach for today's manager to take, this view is rapidly changing as we deal more directly with other nations that do not share our values and standards of behavior.

In addition, much has been written about corporate culture—a general consensus of values, norms, and ways of doing business that are unique to each organization—as a method of understanding how the organization functions. This will be explored in Chapter 14.

We can see from this brief discussion of the contributing disciplines that human relations draws from a rich array of research. Human relations focuses on

Opening Story Revisited

If we return to the opening story we can see some of the basics of the human relations definition. Jack Stack feels that his employees will be influenced by trying to beat the numbers or by setting goals to win available bonuses. His electronic message board is a direct example of that belief. He is trying to directly tie together what the organization needs—low cost products—with what the employees need—recognition and fair rewards for performance. But Stack goes further by providing support to make that connection. He provides education to know the rules of The Game and information to know the status of The Game.

The description of this organization gives us a unique insight into a corporate culture. Here the culture is seen as a game to win. We can suppose that the opponents are other competitors and *not* management versus workers. This is made even clearer when we see that Stack used the film about Japanese productivity to show the workers that they are responsible for increasing SRC's productivity.

the individual, the group, the organization, and combinations of these elements. For example, an organization in a rapidly changing environment should have a corporate culture in which new ideas are encouraged and valued and a structure in which small work groups are formed, allowing the organization to respond quickly to new demands.

The History of Work

To understand human relations and its importance to living and performing in an organization, we must understand the concept of work. The work experience is one of the most common realities faced in the world. Most of us spend more than fifty percent of our waking life performing work for an organization. And, like other human activities essential to our existence, such as eating, sleeping, and socializing, work is well known by all. Yet if we ask for a definition of work we are likely to hear that work is something one does for money. While this is true for most of us, this definition seems pretty bare in contrast to the richness of experience people can easily relate about their work and jobs.

But what is important to the study of work and human relations is the notion that work is changing over time. Prior to the Industrial Revolution work was extremely physical. With the advent of other sources of energy, work became mechanized and standardized. Now, if we believe current literature, we are entering a new period—a post-Industrial Revolution—which can be called "the Information Society."[2]

Yet to understand and appreciate human behavior we must take a historical perspective to comprehend its richness and inherent dilemmas. Let us first look at one of the earliest forms of work and organization. The ancient Egyptians were masters at organizing people for accomplishing tasks (building the pyramids) that we find hard to duplicate today (as seen in the difficulty of completing some nuclear power plants). Next we look at how the craft-oriented work of the Middle Ages was accomplished. We then compare how the Industrial Revolution changed the concept of work and the organization with which most of us are familiar today. And, finally, we see how the beginning of the information and technology revolution is redefining our present concept of work.

Why is it important to study the history of work?

work is changing over time from physical to mechanized + standardized

Ancient Egyptians. Some of the earliest written records show an awareness of the importance of the organization of work. The organizing problems faced by the early Egyptians in constructing the great pyramids are apparent. One pyramid, for example, required 100,000 men working twenty years to complete. It was constructed of approximately 2,300,000 stone blocks, each weighing an average of two and a half tons.[3] Just planning for and organizing the feeding and housing of 100,000 men over a twenty-year period are monumental efforts in themselves, regardless of the final product. The written records maintained by the Egyptians indicate that their concepts of organization had reached a high level. Indeed, it is

People-Powered Mail-Order Giant's a High-Tech Rarity

Each year about 2.5 million people who are outdoors enthusiasts—or just want to look the part—make a pilgrimage to L. L. Bean Inc.'s famous retail store, a landmark in Maine. Most [of the customers] do not notice the sprawling metal-skinned building that stands unidentified off Route 1, just about a half-mile down the road.

But in recent years, this nondescript building has attracted a different kind of pilgrim: corporate executives from companies as diverse as IBM and JC Penney, Xerox and Eddie Bauer. This 315,000-square-foot building is L. L. Bean's distribution center. From this building, Bean annually sends out 5.8 million packages that contain some 11 million items worth $260 million, or about 86 percent of its total sales.

What these corporate giants have come to study is not merely Bean's remarkable efficiency, but the way Bean has achieved that efficiency: by relying on people rather than robots.

Bean makes no apology for its limited use of modern technology. "Our technology has never been state-of-the-art or on the cutting edge," said John Findlay, a senior vice president. Bean's approach may sound like heresy in an age in which scores of American corporations see automation as the way to regain a competitive edge over the Japanese. But many companies are now discovering that automation alone is not a remedy.

In the last decade, Bean's sales have grown tenfold. But the number of permanent employees rose less than fivefold, to 1,650 from 344.

Bean's performance is especially remarkable in light of not only the tedious nature of many jobs at its distribution center but also the large number of seasonal workers that Bean uses. To be sure, computers—Bean bought its first in 1974—have played an important role in improving productivity and accuracy. But while other companies' most sophisticated warehouses are empires of mechanized racks and robotic carts ruled by computers, the job of machines at Bean is to lend human beings a helping hand. Computers keep track of the location of merchandise, organize orders into batches, suggest the shortest route through the warehouse, and the cheapest way to send each

reasonable to assume that without strong organizational abilities, the pyramids could not have been completed.

However, looking at the human relations concerns of 100,000 workers may have turned up different conclusions. We can assume that the working conditions weren't as comfortable or as safe as they are today. Moreover, the vizier (similar to today's supervisor) did not have to be concerned about worker motivation since most of the labor was forced for the duration of the project. Obviously, the work was efficient from an organizational standpoint (work was completed), but the human relations aspects were missing when compared to today's organizations (worker needs were ignored by vizier).

Craft-oriented Work. Widespread during the Middle Ages, the guild or craft was organized according to specific skill categories, for example, the cobbler guild, the furniture guild, the clothing guild, and the blacksmith guild. Each craft was concerned with control over the learning of and utilization of particular skills

order. This may sound fairly sophisticated, but it is not [in comparison to other companies].

[On the human side,] Bean is a master communicator. All employees—even seasonal workers who might work only a total of 80 hours—receive up to one week of training. This indoctrination includes a film on the history of Bean, whose origins date to the early 1900s, when L. L. came up with the idea of a boot that would keep his feet dry on hunting trips.

Lest the film not make a lasting impression, posters with some of L. L.'s favorite sayings—such as "A customer is not dependent on us, we are dependent on him"—are plastered all over the premises. Bulletin boards are also an important part of the Bean culture. Customer letters—both complaints and praise—are pinned under a section called "messages from the boss."

While "quality circles" have been nothing more than a fad at many corporations, listening to workers' suggestions is just good business at Bean. Bean believes in letting workers know how they are performing. Vital statistics, such as how often customers are sent what they order, are posted and updated daily. Productivity and accuracy records for each picker and packer are also maintained. Bean uses them to decide how much each worker should be paid. . . .

Do not worry about Bean succumbing to high technology. "To a certain extent, some of us hate equipment," Findlay said. Why? "People don't break down."

QUESTIONS

1. What are the elements that make L. L. Bean a successful business? Which elements are technical? Which are human?
2. What are the trends to which L. L. Bean is responding? Are there any trends to which they are not responding?
3. How would you describe L. L. Bean's human relations philosophy?

Source: Condensed from Steven E. Prokesch, "Bean Meshes Man, Machine" (New York Times, December 23, 1985). Copyright © 1985 by The New York Times Company. Reprinted by permission.

---

within the membership. Membership required a lengthy apprenticeship in which the art of the craft was learned from a master. Craft knowledge and work were limited to guild members, who carried out their work with a good deal of freedom and involvement. Once an apprentice mastered the craft, he was able to exert considerable control—deciding upon the type and quality of goods and services to produce; choosing raw materials, tools, and methods of production; marketing the goods; and often developing new products or techniques of production. The performance of these activities allowed total involvement, both mental and physical. The artisan manipulated a few simple tools, guided by his senses and intuition, to turn raw materials into useful and often artistic products.

One need only to observe a modern-day artisan to appreciate the intricate balance that exists between the different parts of the body. Each movement of arms, hands, and fingers is coordinated to produce a slight change in the product's shape. The muscles that control the movement of the eyes contract and expand to allow the artisan to pick up inconspicuous visual clues; the fingers are

Describe what is meant by craft-oriented work

total involvement mental and physical

Membership in a guild required a lengthy apprenticeship in which the art of the craft was learned from a master.

sensitive to slight changes in pressure, heat, and texture; while ears and nose are keyed to sounds and smells that define the quality of the product. Facial expressions and breathing reveal the level of concentration and involvement required to produce a finished product. In many ways, the craft-oriented work allows the individual to decide not only what work will be performed but also how it will be done.

Mechanized Work. James Watt's invention of the steam engine in 1782 revolutionized and displaced craft-oriented work. Once it became possible to replace the individual and beast as the primary source of physical work, people sought ways to mechanize their production processes.

In 1911, Frederick Taylor's scientific approach to analyzing and structuring tasks became the standard for designing work. The scientific approach involved analyzing tasks and combining them into the most efficient method for production. This approach, basically, involved breaking down work into its simplest components, specifying in detail the tasks of each component, and organizing these into an efficient sequence commonly called a "production line."

In contrast to the artisan, the production-line worker was constrained severely. Instead of having control over the work, the worker was limited to a set

The breaking down of each task into its simplest form different method

Describe what is meant by mechanized work.

of highly specified operations. Decisions concerning the type, quality, and amount of goods to produce, the methods of production, the acquisition of raw materials, and the distribution of products were no longer made by production workers, but rather by other specialized "units," such as purchasing, sales, and engineering. Since machines transformed the raw materials into finished products, the individual's contact with the actual product was through controls on a machine. As a result the worker could use only limited physical responses, such as making an adjustment on the machine. The worker became more of an assistant to the machine.

One need only observe a modern day production-line worker to realize the extent to which the individual is *not* fully involved in work. The movement of the body is smooth and rhythmic, yet limited to a few simple operations that are repeated all day long. The operations have been simplified to reduce wasted motion. Raw materials and finished products are brought to and from the work area, allowing the worker to continue working without interruptions. Social contact is limited to one's immediate neighbors or periodic visits from a supervisor closely watching the work cycle for problems. Facial expressions, gestures, and body language reflect the hypnotic effect of the repetitious work cycle. The mind can be blank when the body is called upon to do very little.

The production-line worker's only contact with the product was through controls on a machine.

intrinsic rewards for craft work — personal reward

mechanize cannot identify

What are the differences in motivation for craft/mechanized work?

However, we must point out that this method of controlling and simplifying work made products and services affordable for the general public. This means that one criterion of efficiency was being met. With a broader market for products and services, firms could expand, allowing a higher standard of living for all, including the worker.

However, as production-line workers were limited in the production process, they could not identify with the products or services being offered. Intrinsic motivation stemming from creating a total product was missing. Motivation now depended on extrinsic rewards such as money or on reprimands from supervisors. Thus, the workplace gradually evolved from craft to mechanized work. At the bottom stood the worker, reduced to performing a task that no longer was under the individual's control or used full self-involvement.[4]

Computerized Work. We are again in the process of redefining work through the information revolution sparked by computer technology. Certain concepts and trends need to be examined to appreciate the changing nature of work. Most of us understand that computers increase organizational productivity. What we may fail to realize is that computer technology is to the Information Age what mechanization was to the Industrial Revolution: a threat—because it incorporates functions previously performed by workers. How has this affected the experience of work?

How is computerized work affecting the workplace?

Mechanized work and computerized work have some similarities. First, both types of work control the worker in terms of the tasks having to be completed in a certain way to maintain quality. The information requested by a computer program must be supplied precisely or it will be rejected. Second, the variety of tasks performed are narrow in both computerized and mechanized work. This is especially true in clerical jobs in which paperwork has been computerized without the addition of other responsibilities. Finally, computerized work is no more rewarding than mechanized work. Both provide the worker with feedback that is external to the work performed, such as printout of errors or time spent in routine tasks.

control worker tasks to maintain quality

—variety of tasks narrow

medium mental attention to details

One difference between mechanized work and computerized work is the physical involvement. Instead of limited physical activity, computerized work requires a great deal of mental attention to details—a cause of increased complaints of stress, according to some researchers.[5] Also, this intense mental attention restricts the amount of social contact between workers. We will see that this has some serious consequences for group dynamics in Chapter 6.

Table 1–1 shows the results of both the Industrial Revolution and the "Information Revolution" on the nature and design of work. As we can see from the table, mechanical power replaced wind, water, and animals as the primary source of energy. The development of a steady supply of power made the mechanization of work possible. Mechanized tools and complex machines gradually replaced utensils and tools as methods of production. Through the scientific method the production process was reduced to its simplest components and the work became standardized.

	Craft Age	Industrial Revolution	Information Revolution
Examples	Various guilds	Production lines	Computer termi-nals
Sources of energy	Nonmechanical power (wind, water, animals, human beings)	Mechanical power	Electrical power
Types of technology	Utensils and simple tools	Mechanized tools and com-plex machines	Management in-formation sys-tems, computer programming, and electronics
Task characteristics	Variety, chal-lenge, auton-omy, direct feedback and hu-man contribution	Narrow, quasi-mechanical, indi-rect feedback and human con-tribution	Narrow, quasi-electronic, indi-rect feedback and human con-tribution
Human require-ments	Social, cogni-tive, and physi-cal parts of self	Physical parts of self	Mental concen-tration
Source of control	Self-regulation by worker	External regula-tion by superior or machine	External regula-tion by system and supervisor
Source of motivation	Intrinsic rewards	Extrinsic rewards	Extrinsic rewards
Results	Economic liveli-hood, socially and psychologi-cally rewarding	Economic effi-ciency, mass production, so-cially and psy-chologically in-hibiting	Economic effi-ciency, rapid in-formation pro-cessing, socially and psychologi-cally inhibiting

TABLE 1 – 1
A comparison of craft, mechanized, and com-puterized work

SOURCE: Adapted from Thomas G. Cummings and Suresh Sirvastva, *Management of Work: A Socio-Technical System Approach,* San Diego, CA: University Associates, Inc., 1977. Used with permission.

These scientifically designed jobs were focused on assisting the machines and provided little stimulation for the worker. Instead of engaging the worker's social and mental abilities, as did craft work, mechanized work required only the physical contribution. Since the tasks allowed for little variety, challenge, auton-omy, and individual involvement, the source of control shifted from the worker to the supervisor. As a result, motivation to perform changed from the intrinsic rewards of creative craft work to extrinsic rewards of money and praise.

With the advent of computers, even certain mechanized work was reduced to simpler functions controlled by information and computer systems. The work now demands close mental concentration and can cause stress. Computer tech-

Opening Story Revisited

From our opening story we can see some of the differences between types of work. Despite the fact that assembly work is not craft-oriented but rather mechanized work, we still can see attempts to balance the involvement of the workers. As stated earlier, mechanized work gives the control of work to supervisors and managers. In SRC's situation, management is trying to give some of the control back to the workers through education and decision making. Once a day a master plan is passed down the line and employees are asked to contribute their ideas on how to make it work. This shows an attempt to involve the workers on a higher level of participation rather than merely as extensions of the machines they operate. Stack makes this clear at the end of the story when he says, "And we had to do this without establishing a dictatorship. Systems don't run companies, people do."

nology can also interfere with social interaction between co-workers. The source of control now resides in the information system and its demands for data. The result of this new work revolution is increased speed and accuracy of information processing and greater worker productivity.

Historical Origins of Human Relations

We have already mentioned some of the reasons for the concern of human relations as we viewed the changing nature of work. As work became more standardized and less involving, workers became more separated from the meaning of work, creating tension and boredom.

Beginnings. Frederick Taylor's efforts in 1911 to make workers more efficient was the beginning of the interest in workers' contribution to productivity. Granted that Taylor's "scientific management" was geared toward breaking down the worker's job into simpler tasks, still he helped management to focus on the worker as a neglected resource. During this same period of time, the National Personnel Association was formed (now the American Management Association). This group is devoted to improving the human contribution to organizations at the level of the individual worker as well as at the management level. Also during this period Whiting Williams studied people he worked with. He published a personal interpretation of worker life titled *What's on the Worker's Mind.*[6]

Hawthorne Studies. One of the most significant influences of human relations was a series of studies done by Elton Mayo during the late 1920s at the Hawthorne plant of Western Electric Company near Chicago.[7] To Taylor, human problems reduced the efficiency of machines and should be eliminated through standardization. Mayo also believed that human problems reduced the efficiency of machines, but thought human problems needed to be understood and minimized. Taylor increased production by rationalizing it. Mayo sought to increase production by humanizing it.[8] Thus human problems as a field of study became known as ''human relations'' and the contemporary title used in some places is ''organizational behavior.''

The first study by Mayo investigated the impact physical working conditions had on worker output. Mayo isolated a few workers in a separate room of the plant where they could watch the workers' reactions to changes in the level of lighting. They found that the output went up as the level of light increased. To their surprise, the output also went up as they decreased the level of light, even to the point of being equal to moonlight. After numerous studies to measure and change other working conditions, such as humidity, heat, and work breaks, the researchers interviewed the workers. They learned that the workers were motivated not only by money but also by feeling special and important. The researchers had shown interest in the workers by studying their working conditions and asking their opinions about changes.

What emerged is the conclusion that worker productivity is a more complex issue than originally expected. Worker productivity is influenced not only by technology but also by human interaction and management concern. Thus, humanizing the work place is an effective management tool.

How did the Hawthorne Studies affect the practice of management?

Organizational Development. A modern extension of this concern for increased organizational efficiency through employee involvement in the work setting is called *organizational development*. This field recognizes that organizational productivity is a mutual process of goal accomplishment. Figure 1–2 shows the connections.

Organizational productivity is a joint effort to connect the accomplishment of the organization's goals with those of the employees. To effect this connection some joint problem solving is needed to create a supportive atmosphere of cooperation. With a cooperative atmosphere, new technology is utilized, worker skills are better utilized, workers' needs and contributions to the production process are recognized. This is usually the focus of organizational development.

Current Trends Affecting Human Relations

In today's changing world, an organization is affected by many conditions, both from within and from outside the organization. Some of these conditions make managing more difficult, while others, if properly used, can provide solutions to current management problems. This section, while not all inclusive, should improve our understanding of how the following trends are affecting the practice of human relations.

Work Force Value Changes. One trend that is having an impact on the manager and the organization is the effect of the changing values of today's workers. Much of the literature examines the value changes that result from the workers' search for meaningful, self-fulfilling work. Workers are becoming more inner-directed and now seek and expect, among other things, autonomy in their work,

FIGURE 1–2
Model of organizational productivity

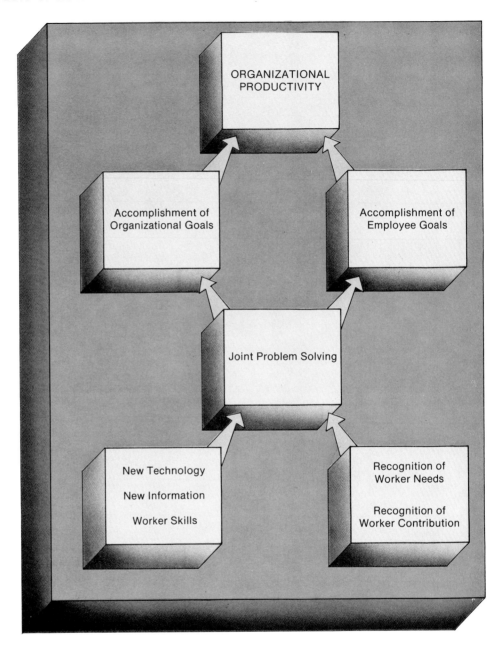

respect from their superiors, open channels of communication, and the opportunity to participate in decision making.[9] What factors have brought about these value changes? Suggested factors include higher levels of education, more leisure time, greater affluence, the effects of today's "instant" culture, and growth of the media.

Most authors agree, however, that the changes are rooted in the social up-heaval of the 1960s. The '60s were characterized by a search for self-fulfillment, self-expression, and personal growth, and by a rejection of such traditional values as materialism and respect for authority. As a result today's workers are left with-out clear directions or goals. They have been forced to look inside themselves for that direction, bringing about the emergence of the "Me Generation."[10]

Author Johanna S. Hunsaker says today's workers see themselves as "total systems." She reports that American workers have "taken to heart the expanded personal freedom that accompanied the social upheaval" and now are focusing on self-fulfillment and personal happiness as ultimate life goals. Hunsaker further suggests that "organizations may find employees harder to manage, but they will also find them highly motivated and committed to tasks they value."[11] The result is that a large group of 1960s baby boomers has arrived on the corporate scene with a new set of values and beliefs about what life should be like. Whether you believe that the problem is a result of such external values changes as those rep-resented by the "Me Generation" or that it is a gradual evolution of worker val-ues, the fact is that there has been a drop in worker morale and productivity.

Before the business world can attempt to deal with the changing demands of its workers, it must clarify what today's employees are looking for. Studies agree that, first and foremost, workers desire to find meaning and self-fulfillment in their work. Work is seen no longer as merely a means of financial support but as a major factor in one's life. As employees have become more concerned with the quality of life in general, they also have become concerned with the quality of life at the workplace. Researcher Marsha Sinetar comments, "Humans today want more than to survive; they want to flourish. They want . . . their work places to be responsive to this need, to assist them in flourishing, to assist them in becoming whole."[12]

As a result workers have come to expect more autonomy in their jobs, more respect from their superiors, open channels of communication, and participation in decision making. In addition, workers expect fair and equal treatment, oppor-tunities for advancement, and employer concern for employees' personal situ-ations. Studies show, however, that employee expectations are not being met. And because these expectations motivate employees to perform well, morale and productivity levels have declined. One study shows that while workers rate tra-ditional motivators such as pay and job security favorably, overall job satisfaction is on the decline. The study shows dissatisfaction in regard to respect from man-agement, opportunities for advancement, and opportunities for upward commu-nication.[13]

> What are today's work-ers looking for in their jobs?

It is clear that organizations must undergo major changes to cope with the demands of changing worker values. First, it is apparent that the traditional hi-erarchical management structure is no longer effective. Workers are looking for upward communication and participation in decision making at all levels. In ad-dition, workers want jobs that are meaningful rather than tedious and boring. They want to feel that they are contributing to the success of the organization and that they will be rewarded for their efforts through recognition and advance-

Can a Company Outgrow a Style of Management?

In its early days, People Express Inc.'s maverick management style inspired admiration and emulation. Executives, consultants, and even academics swarmed to the airline, seeking insight into the methods that were credited with its soaring initial success. At Harvard Business School, students examined its philosophy: minimal bureaucracy, group organization of workers, rotation of staff through a variety of jobs, salaries tied in large part to company profits, and "manager" titles for everyone.

Five years later the airline is in trouble, facing huge losses and the possibility of bankruptcy. The company's board is imposing some of the controls that its managers once eschewed. Outsiders have begun to look at People's experience in a different light. To many observers, the experiment that once demonstrated the potential of an increasingly popular style of management is now betraying its limitations—and the larger lessons are becoming clearer. "The real issue is whether any given style or approach is appropriate for any

organization throughout its lifetime," says William Fonvielle, a management consultant.

Companies such as General Motors Corp. and Cummings Engine Co., as well as many of the newer high-technology companies, have begun experimenting with departures from traditional, top-down management. Innovators have replaced layers of authority with more self- or peer-management; pushed the power to make certain decisions to the lowest possible level; and minimized or dispensed with procedures set by corporate policy in favor of on-the-spot decision making. Such participatory practices, supporters say, can bring increased efficiency, better employee motivation, and greater creativity.

People Express went much further. Each operating group of 250 people decided how it would carry out its assigned tasks. Employees moved from job to job, sometimes daily. Often there would be flight attendants tracking lost bags, or pilots taking tickets and tending computer operations. And everyone had to deal with customers. The next time you fly People Express, your coffee may be served by People's chief financial officer, Bob McAdoo, who is a certified flight attendant and flies weekly. But the loss of specific talents can far outweigh the benefits of flexibility.

ment. Organizations may start with such concepts as quality circles and suggestion systems, take frequent attitude surveys, and make tangible attempts at improving identified problems.

Japanese Management. Publicity about the economic miracles of Japan has been widespread. Recently Japan has outperformed other countries in such areas as electronics, ship building, and production of cameras, watches, video cameras, and cars. While there are many reasons for these successes, including government support, homogeneous population, and a group-oriented culture, credit must be given to the management style of Japanese organizations. Japanese management style has been called Theory Z,[14] in contrast to Theory X or Y (these terms are

"You can make people jacks of all trades and masters of none," says Harvard's Richard Walton. "You lose something from the stability and depth of a person's knowledge."

Some feel that especially for the rapidly growing People Express the lack of tighter organization had detrimental effects. "Their unwillingness to put in a formal management structure was a key element to the current difficulties," says an aviation-industry analyst. Moreover, management specialists say that, while rotating employees through various assignments can make them more well-rounded, it can also reduce their commitment to specific tasks and encourage job hopping.

Another way that People differed from most big companies was the way in which it shunned formal lines of authority and standard reporting procedures. Donald C. Burr, the company's founder and president, once boasted that no People official was more than three levels away from him or a managing director, so that problems could be dealt with in person.

But as any company grows bigger, such a system can get unwieldy. When employees are more numerous, it becomes increasingly difficult to depend on telephone calls and face-to-face meetings to keep information flowing, and on shared ideals to keep company goals in sight. "You go from a pluralistic management to almost an anarchy where you almost don't have anyone in charge,"

says Nicholas J. Radell, a management consultant.

When a loosely managed company is in financial trouble, as in the case of People Express, its problems are often compounded. With a system of shared responsibility for decisions, says Radell, "when things aren't going well, where do you push the button to make it right? You can't push on 500 or 1,000 people."

Management specialists add that one other area needing rigorous attention, even in an informally managed company, is the setting of standards. Companies "have to maintain a certain level of service and have to maintain it with controls. You have to set standards and see where you deviate from them," says James Fonvielle. "If People wanted to remain a small counterculture airline, they could have gotten away with it longer."

QUESTIONS

1. Discuss the major problems facing People Express. Which are issues that an effective human relations program should address?
2. Describe a program you would suggest to reduce or eliminate some of People's problems.
3. Which trends do you feel that People is not addressing?

---

fully defined in Chapter 4) and the art of Japanese management.[15] The co-founder of the Honda Motor Company once remarked that American and Japanese management styles are 95 percent alike, yet differ in all important respects.[16]

Japanese management can be characterized by three basic principles: (1) an emphasis on the group rather than the individual; (2) an emphasis on human rather than functional relationships; and (3) a view of top management as generalists and facilitators rather than as decision makers. Instead of the rugged individualism idealized in the United States, the Japanese relish life in groups. The president of Nippon Steel, describing the difference between American and Japanese management, said that while a U.S. corporation is regarded as a cold, impersonal, economic unit, the Japanese corporation is regarded as a community

Describe the major aspects of Japanese management style.

Japanese management emphasizes the group rather than the individual.

with a common destiny. By focusing on the group instead of the individual, Japanese corporations can unleash considerable energy. Japanese companies seem to elicit worker attitudes similar to school spirit and religious fervor.

Japanese management reinforces the group consciousness through a variety of methods. The first method is to emphasize the permanence of the group. Those recruited into the core of an enterprise enter with the understanding that they are joining for life. Pay and incentives for workers depend partly on company profits or on the financial condition of the firm. Group cohesiveness is supported by morning calisthenics, company songs, and other activities of a group nature, both during and after work. The "us against them" mentality in a Japanese company is likely to refer to the company against its competitors—not the workers against management.

The second major Japanese management principle is the emphasis on human rather than functional relationships. American organizations tend to view people as tools to fill slots that have specific job descriptions. In Japan, however, the permanence of the group forces managers to place more emphasis on people than on the system. This emphasis on human relations can be seen in careful recruitment practices, concern for the employee as a person, and peaceful resolution of conflicts.

In recruiting workers, the president of a Japanese company often personally interviews the candidates to be hired. Virtually all new recruits in Japan are hired directly from schools upon graduation. In addition, firms provide housing and, in many cases, even meals to single employees and families.

The Japanese feel that there should be harmony within and competition without. Japanese people will go to great lengths to prevent the humiliation of a pubic scolding or firing, and as a result emphasize harmony.

Japanese management tends to be generalists and facilitators much like elders in a tribe. Problems are usually solved by middle management after consultation with superiors. Although this makes decision making a very slow process, the implementation is faster because of the full commitment supplied by being involved from the beginning. Another aspect of being generalists is that managers are continually moved between various functions as they climb the corporate ladder. As a result the top management can appreciate problems from manufacturing, sales, financial, and engineering standpoints at the same time.

A summary of the differences between Japanese and American management practices is illustrated in Table 1–2. We can also see that some of their practices

TABLE 1 – 2

Characteristics of Japanese and American management styles

Japanese	American
1. Emphasis on group Permanence of group Same fate shared by all employees Group incentives Group against outsiders	1. Emphasis on the individual Transitory nature of group Own fate determined by each employee Individual incentives Individual against others
2. Emphasis on human relationships "Lifetime" employment and recruitment Harmonious resolution of conflicts Holistic concern for employees Desire for indirection, ambiguity No formal distinctions between managers and workers	2. Emphasis on functional relationships Short-term employment and recruitment Adversarial resolution of conflicts Segmented concern for employees Desire for clarity, brute integrity Frequently sharp distinctions between managers and workers
3. Managers as generalists Manager as social and symbolic leader Manager as facilitator Management by consensus Decisions that come from middle up Centralization Wide dispersion of responsibility Nonspecialized career paths	3. Managers as specialists Manager as professional Manager as decision maker Management by objectives Decisions that come from top down Decentralization Narrow assignment of responsibility Specialized career paths

SOURCE: Adapted from Dick Kazuyuki Nanto, "Management, Japanese Style," in S. M. Lee and G. Schwendiman, eds., *Management by Japanese Systems*, p. 21. Copyright © 1982 Praeger Publishers. Reprinted and adapted by permission of Praeger Publishers.

could have application to our changing work force value changes. If American workers want more say in their jobs, then having managers as generalists and allowing workers to have some say about jobs would benefit both the organization and the worker. Are there other similarities?

Information Technology. In 1982 about one million computers or data terminals were added to the four million already in use by firms in the United States. It is expected that this number will increase by 25 percent each year for the next ten years. There is no doubt that the use of computers will increase and that almost every job will be affected by computers either directly or indirectly. Yet what will the impact be on the behavior of individuals within firms as they adapt to this new technology? What will this change mean for the management of employees? Will this technology affect relationships between individuals on the job? These questions are only the beginning of the concerns felt by workers and management alike. While the answers are not yet known, some effects have been noted as firms begin to introduce computers into employee jobs.

One of the first reactions employees have when they are notified that their jobs are about to be computerized is "Oh, No!" Computers mean change and change means "I have to do something different." But this reaction is typical any time an individual faces change and not necessarily just that of computer technology. More is said about the change process in Chapter 9.

Computerphobia a mental and physical reaction to computer technology

Nevertheless, there does seem to exist a form of reaction termed "computerphobia," meaning fear, distrust, or hatred of computers.[17] Researcher Berkley Rice interviewed and tested several hundred individuals who used computers. Using a galvanic-skin-response-measuring device on the subjects as they worked

---

Opening Story Revisited

In the opening story Jack Stack has intuitively assumed that all employees want to have fun while working. This is similar to the value changes we described; workers want to be more than just extensions of the machines. They want to have a say in their jobs. In SRC, workers have a say in what will happen to the company. They receive financial figures for the entire operation so they can appreciate the impact of their work on the rest of the organization.

Even the SRC management is acting more in the Japanese style of generalists and facilitators by helping the workers to understand the numbers and by resetting new goals with the workers. In another sense the individualism is downplayed in favor of the group. Remember the electronic message that said "FUEL INJECTION LABOR UTILIZATION 98%." To qualify for the bonus, the entire shift must work together to maintain that pace. You need to have a group feeling for that to work properly. Small groups of production workers and their supervisors reviewing the daily operating plan also supports a group orientation. Finally, the employee awareness session focusing on outside competition is similar to the Japanese theme of internal harmony.

at their terminals, he found that nearly one-third of these people had computer-phobia. About five percent of the participants showed the physical symptoms of classic phobia: nausea, dizziness, cold sweat, and high blood pressure. One frustrated worker actually dumped coffee and cigarette ashes into a computer console.[18]

Middle management is another organizational group often cited as fearful of the introduction of computers into its ranks.[19] One factor that contributes to computerphobia seems to be middle management's fear that they don't actually manage anything—that in fact they are not really decision makers but merely "information conduits" who could easily be replaced by the very computers they are learning to use. As we can see from these brief descriptions of the computer's impact, human relations must help firms address these concerns if they are to become more productive using computers.

LEARNING SUMMARY

1. Human relations helps us answer questions concerning the understanding and influencing of individuals and groups in organizations.
2. Studying human relations helps us to cope with frustrations and be more effective as members of an organization.
3. Human relations has a rich foundation from other disciplines, including psychology, sociology, and anthropology. Each gives us a different perspective about organizational life.
4. The history of work spans three periods—craft-oriented, mechanized, and computerized. Each period has a uniqueness that forms the basis of our experience of work.
5. Human relations had its beginnings with Frederick Taylor's scientific management. The Hawthorne studies showed us that humanizing the work place can also increase an organization's productivity. Finally, organizational development is the current concern for increased effectiveness through worker involvement.
6. Today's work world is changed by such trends as work force value changes, Japanese management style, and information technology. For today's supervisors and managers, these trends can provide not only a challenge in understanding but also in applying the positive aspects of each.

ANSWERS TO "WHAT'S YOUR OPINION?"

1. True   Structure, technology, and people make up the major components of the organization.
2. True   Psychology, sociology, and anthropology are the basic social sciences that have influenced the development of human relations.
3. True   Craft-oriented work allows the worker to use his or her whole self in producing a product or service. This is not so for the mechanized and computerized work that predominates in today's work place.

4. True   The Egyptians were highly organized to be able to build the pyramids. We haven't had the opportunity to duplicate that feat because we haven't had a project to use 100,000 workers.

5. True   The Hawthorne studies learned of the need for attention and recognition by accident. They were studying more tangible benefits such as heating and lighting.

6. False   Information technology has lead to "computerphobia" in some situations and a fear of its impact by the middle management personnel.

7. True   Workers seem to be looking for direction and have been forced to look inside for that direction, hence the name, "Me Generation."

8. True   Japanese leaders are generalists and facilitators. They allow the workers and supervisors to make decisions. This is in contrast to a large percentage of American top managers who like to make decisions and see decision making as their responsibility.

KEY TERMS

Anthropology	Information technology
Computerized work	Intrinsic motivation
Computerphobia	Japanese management style
Corporate culture	Mechanized work
Craft-oriented work	Organization development
Extrinsic motivation	Psychology
Hawthorne Studies	Scientific management
Human relations	Sociology
Industrial Revolution	Work force values
Information Revolution	

HUMAN RELATIONS APPLICATIONS

As already noted, most of the chapters in this book consist of two parts: one part describes and explains a widely accepted theory in a specific human relations area, and the other part relates how some of these theories are applied by organizations and managers. Since this is the first of the applications sections, it might be useful to discuss some of the characteristics of these sections so that you can determine how they will be most useful to you.

Purpose of Applications Section

In these applications sections we describe situations in which the application of the theories has been highly successful and situations in which application of the theories has met with failure. We look at the behaviors of managers who support the theory and at the behaviors of managers who oppose the theory and still succeed. In short, we try to get you to look at the theory from the perspective of an action-oriented manager who is responsible for results. This allows you to balance and test the relevancy of the theory to the "real" world and its exceptions.

Several kinds of materials are included in these sections, from a variety of sources:

Popular literature—materials intended primarily for practicing managers and those interested in organizations from a pragmatic viewpoint.

General literature—materials related to human relations and management published in the general press and intended for widespread consumption.

Management experience—information drawn from the actual experiences of managers in organizations.

Consultant experience—information based on the experience of consultants to organizations. We draw on our own consulting practices as well as the experiences of other consultants.

Not every point covered in the theory part of the chapter could, in the interest of space, be covered in the applications section. Criteria for inclusion included that the material be interesting and that it have a managerial emphasis. We were not concerned, for example, that each theoretical point have a corresponding application, or that each point be supported by a description of an organizational practice. We didn't look for items that would either support or oppose our prejudices as they relate to organizations and how they function. We do not intend for the material presented in the applications section to be our suggestion for applying the theory. We know that theory must be balanced in practice with trade-offs of what the situation demands. We always ask you to look at the trade-offs in following a course of action and to decide whether it would be useful based on your analysis of the situation. In other words, place yourself in the situation, analyze it, and then decide what to do. Always remember that theory is based on some constant assumptions, which may not be true in the actual situation. Human relations practices must be oriented to the situation.

A Sample Application: Even Blue-Collar Workers Need People Skills[20]

For many years firms have used various role-playing or psychological tests to decide which managers get promoted. But now more companies are using similar techniques for such entry-level positions as customer-sales representatives and clerks, as well as for blue-collar positions. The trend is most prevalent at companies using participative management styles, giving workers more say in running the day-to-day operations.

"Ten years ago we didn't expect as much from people," says Robert Goehring, manager of human resources development for Kimberly-Clark Corp., the paper products concern. "Now we have participative organizations that foster a high degree of responsibility, even at the operator level." At Kimberly-Clark's newest plants, for example, applicants for nonunion machine-operator jobs are put through ''leadership simulation'' exercises. In one session, the job candidate is asked to play the role of a supervisor directing a seasoned subordinate to switch to a more demanding job. The worker's role is played by a trained supervisor. Says Goehring, ''We're looking for people who can assume work-group leadership, even if they wouldn't have that responsibility initially.''

More companies also say that testing can help them hire better clerical and service representatives to improve customer service and reduce turnover. For example, some insurance agents have begun to use personality tests to hire clerical and customer-service employees. These tests are designed to measure such traits as motivation to please others, organization, desire for detail work, and ''people orientation.''

One test asked the candidates to select from a series of three statements the ones that best and least describe them: ''I don't like to criticize others.'' ''I am considered an interesting conversationalist.'' ''I am more careful with things loaned to me than with my own things.'' Another series asked the applicants to rate on a continuum, from strongly agree to strongly disagree, such statements as: ''Knowing exactly what one is expected to do is essential to getting ahead.'' While endorsing the tests, many companies worry that managers will use them as a crutch for their own hiring decisions. One company vice president says, ''We don't live or die by the test; it's another tool, like a reference check.''

We are beginning to see that selecting the right worker, no matter what the level of entry, is seen as critical. Blue-collar workers are no exception.

PERSONAL GUIDELINES FOR HUMAN RELATIONS SUCCESS

This is the first section presenting some suggestions for you to apply. These are meant as ideas for you to consider to become more successful in human relations situations. Sometimes they are written from the standpoint of a worker and sometimes as a supervisor. From this chapter several suggestions are meant to help you begin the process of becoming more successful.

Stop, Look, and Listen. The world is changing and becoming more complex. From a personal perspective, an effective strategy is to not jump to conclusions about a situation that you are a part of. Instead spend some time listening carefully to what is going on, and form your opinions after you have listened carefully. This suggestion is supported in Chapter 5 on communication. In many situations, it is easy to know our immediate impression but harder to see the situation the way it really is after we have expressed an opinion. Consider that research shows effective managers are good listeners first.

Continue to Learn and Grow. Such trends as information technology and work force value changes are forcing managers and organizations to re-evaluate their efforts and practices. As an employee, you can help in these situations by being knowledgeable about what is happening in the world and making suggestions. Managers and supervisors appreciate employees who not only help define problems but who also make realistic suggestions for improvement. This is not only an attitude but a problem-solving and communications skill. This skill can always be improved.

Many companies have tuition reimbursement programs to help support employee growth and development. Many community colleges offer adult-education programs that are reasonable in cost and worth the effort. Another suggestion is to read management literature and other popular literature to stay current. Many excellent sources are available by subscription or in your library. We recommend the following as a starting list: *Supervisory Practices; Supervision; Training and Development Journal; Personnel; Harvard Business Review; MSU Business Topics; INC.;* and *Success.* This is not meant to be a definitive list but only a starting point for you to establish a regular reading program. Stimulating the mind can stimulate the body and the personality.

DISCUSSION AND REVIEW QUESTIONS

1. Are today's jobs more mechanized or more craft oriented? How do you view the introduction of computer technology in these terms?
2. What characteristics of Japanese management style can we use in the Western world? Which characteristics can't we use? Why?
3. How might you redesign your role as a student in this course using the changes occurring in worker values? What obstacles may prevent you from implementing those changes?
4. If you were asked what you will be studying in a course about human relations, what would you say?

HUMAN RELATIONS EXERCISE

Values

From reading this chapter, you are aware that individual behavior in organizations has evolved over time from craft orientation to more limited task orientation. This means that jobs have less individual decision making attached to them. Yet, a current trend shows a change in workers' values from security to self-actualization. This contrasting picture could present some conflict between the company's needs and the individual's needs. This exercise asks you to collect data from individuals in organizations to see how they view this situation.

Instructions. Organize into small groups of three or four members and identify three individuals in various firms to interview. Try to choose workers and managers from different levels and from union and nonunion firms. An alternative is to see how many of your fellow students are working now or have worked recently and interview them. Using the following questions as a guide, construct your own questionnaire. After you collect the data, present your findings in light of the information in this chapter.

QUESTIONS

1. Tell me about your job responsibilities. What is a typical day like?
2. What are the positive aspects of your job? What excites you about doing your job?
3. What are the negative aspects of your job? What things would you like to change? Who could you tell about those changes? Would they listen and respond? Can you give an example?
4. What are your reasons for working?
5. Is this your first job? If you've had others, how does this job compare to the others?
6. Do you see any differences between why younger and older workers work? What motivates them to work?
7. What advice would you give someone who was considering work in this firm?

HUMAN RELATIONS INCIDENT

Guy Saffold has just been named general manager of a new start-up plant for portable computers. The company has given him a liberal budget to start operations in six months. Part of his task is to hire and staff a 60-person plant. His boss even suggests that he can experiment with new policies and practices since the new plant isn't near any of the old plants and his boss wants the most up-to-date management practices.

Guy is trying to decide what changes are occurring in the work force and how he should set up his new organization. What should he take into account and what are some suggestions for the new organization?

NOTES

1. Adapted from Lucien Rhodes, with Patricia Amend, "The Turnaround," *INC.* (August 1986): 42–48.
2. John Naisbett, *Megatrends* (New York: Warner Books, 1982).
3. William L. Westerman, *The Story of the Ancient Nations* (New York: D. Appleton, 1912): 18–19.
4. Adapted from Thomas G. Cummings and Suresh Srivastva, *Management of Work: A Social-Technical Systems Approach* (San Diego: University Associates, 1977): 5–10.
5. Craig Brod, *Technostress: The Human Cost of Computer Revolution* (Reading, MA: Addison-Wesley, 1984).
6. Whiting Williams, *What's on the Worker's Mind* (New York: Charles Scribner's Sons, 1920).
7. F. L. Roethlisberger and William Dickson, *Management and the Worker* (Boston: Graduate School of Business, Harvard University, 1947).
8. Keith Davis and John W. Newstrom, *Human Behavior at Work: Organizational Behavior,* 7th ed. (New York: McGraw-Hill, 1985): 8.
9. Daniel Yankelovitch, "The Work Ethic Is Underemployed," *Psychology Today* (May 1982): 5–8; and Phillip Grant, "Why Employee Motivation Has Declined in America, *Personnel Journal* (December 1982): 905–9.
10. Ann Howard and James A. Wilson, "Leadership in a Declining Work Ethic," *California Management Review* (Summer 1982): 42.

11. Johanna S. Hunsaker, "Work and Family Life Must Be Integrated," *Personnel Administration* (April 1983): 89.

12. Marsha Sinetar, "Management in the New Age: An Exploration of Changing Work Values," *Personnel Journal* (September 1980): 751.

13. M. R. Cooper, B. S. Morgan, P. M. Foley, and L. B. Kaplan, "Changing Employee Values: Deepening Discontent?" *Harvard Business Review,* vol. 57, no. 1 (January–February 1979): 124.

14. William Ouchi, *Theory Z* (Reading, MA: Addison-Wesley, 1981).

15. R. T. Pascale and A. G. Athos, *The Art of Japanese Management* (New York: Simon & Schuster, 1981).

16. Ibid.

17. Berkley Rice, "Curing Cyberphobia," *Psychology Today* (August 1983): 79.

18. Sanford B. Weinberg, John T. English, and Carla J. Mond, "A Strategem for Reduction of Cyberphobia," presented to the American Association for the Advancement of Science, Toronto, Canada, 1981.

19. *Business Week* (25 April 1983).

20. Larry Reibstein, "More Firms Use Personality Tests for Entry-Level, Blue-Collar Jobs," *The Wall Street Journal* (August 1986): 36. Reprinted by permission of *The Wall Street Journal,* © Dow Jones & Company, 1986. All rights reserved.

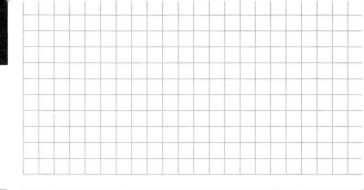

CHAPTER 2
INDIVIDUAL
BEHAVIOR

WHAT'S YOUR OPINION? T OR F

_____ 1. There is always a "right" way to perceive an object or event.

_____ 2. Values are more basic than attitudes.

_____ 3. If you know a person's attitude about something, you can always predict how he or she will act.

_____ 4. Job satisfaction is an attitude.

_____ 5. Satisfied employees work harder than dissatisfied employees.

_____ 6. Dissatisfied workers are absent more often than satisfied employees.

_____ 7. Japanese and American managers have similar values.

_____ 8. Successful managers have somewhat different values than unsuccessful managers.

_____ 9. Salary is more important to older workers than to younger ones.

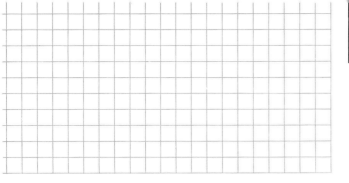

OUTLINE

LEARNING OBJECTIVES

- ☐ Describe the perceptual process
- ☐ Identify the major types of perceptual error
- ☐ Describe the components of attitudes
- ☐ Relate attitudes to behavior and behavior to attitudes
- ☐ Define the major types of value systems
- ☐ See how managerial values affect managerial behavior
- ☐ Have an increased awareness of your own value system

Opening Story: Before[s]You[e]Rush[n]Into[d]the Article, Relax [c]and[a]Enjoy[s]the[h]Nice Headline[1]

SALT LAKE CITY   Utah state legislators expect another round of heated debate over proposed laws concerning certain forms of advertising.

Can you find the word "sex" in the above paragraph? Terry Jessop could. A self-employed management consultant and ballroom-dancing instructor, Jessop is also director of the National Institute for Subliminal Research, which he runs from his home in Provo. For the past five years, the nonprofit group has sought to uncover the hidden messages it claims "a small minority of unethical advertisers" plant in their ads to influence consumers subconsciously.

More recently, the institute has been the principal advocate of three bills now under committee study that would require warnings on ads containing subliminal messages. Failure to comply would constitute an invasion of privacy or unfair trade practice, and consumers could challenge particular ads under outlined procedures. The NISR, which Jessop says has more than 500 members nationwide, is backing similar measures in California, Idaho, New Jersey, New York, and Pennsylvania.

"The average citizen is exposed three to five times a week to various forms of subliminal advertising," he explains. "That is significant exposure that merits a look at this kind of legislation."

Many advertisers disagree. The charge that consumers are manipulated in this way is "absolute stupidity," says Dale Zabriskie, a lobbyist for the Utah Advertising Council, which is opposing the bills on grounds that "subliminal messages exist only in the eyes of the beholder." Part of Zabriskie's arsenal is a poster featuring ice cubes from a liquor ad that Jessop has singled out as "subliminal." The text on the poster concedes that suggestive images may indeed be found in the cubes. It also says that if you look long and hard enough "you might find a portrait of Millard Fillmore, a stuffed pork chop, and a 1947 Dodge."

But lawmakers such as state Rep. Frances Merrill, the Salt Lake City Republican who is sponsoring the bills, remain firmly on Jessop's side. "I don't want anything going into my mind that I'm not aware of," she says.

PERCEPTION

How can people find "hidden messages" in advertising?

The National Institute for Subliminal Research and the Utah Advertising Council could hardly be farther apart. How is it possible for two organizations (or people) to interpret data, objects, and situations so differently? The problem lies in differing *perceptions*.

Factors Influencing Perception

The perceptual process is individual and personal. There is no "right" way to perceive an object or event, although culture, needs, values, and attitudes influence the process. In turn, our perceptions influence our relationships with other people. Differing perceptions lie at the root of many conflicts and tensions between individuals, units, or departments. These conflicts and tensions may reduce both individual and organizational performance.

Of what importance is the eye of the beholder in perception?

The Perceptual Process

The five senses (sight, hearing, smell, taste, touch) bombard us with information from the world around us. The perceptual process allows us to *select, organize,* and *interpret* that information. Figure 2–1 describes the process of perception.

Perception selection, organization, interpretation of stimuli

Perceptual Selection. Have you ever tried to read a magazine and watch television at the same time? It is difficult because, if you concentrate more on the television, you may find yourself reading parts of the magazine article several times. There is too much information (stimulation) from the two sources, so eventually you must either turn off the television set or put the magazine away. By doing so, you have selected one type of stimulus and ignored another. In this example, the choice was conscious. *Perceptual selection* allows us to deal with "relevant" information. It would be physically impossible, and probably psychologically damaging, to react to all of the countless stimuli in daily life.

   Perceptual selection can also operate in a less conscious manner. Workers on a noisy assembly line will "shut out" the normal, continuing noise present at their work stations but may quickly hear a noise that is out of the ordinary. We may also select information based on personal traits and attitudes. It is almost certain that a liberal democrat and a conservative republican will "hear" very different aspects of a presidential State of the Union address.

Perceptual selection does not always occur consciously.

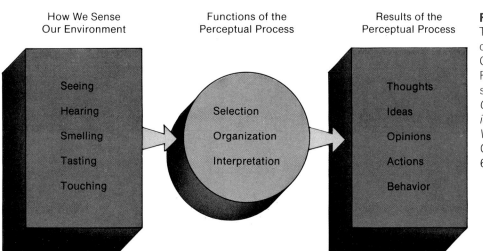

How We Sense Our Environment	Functions of the Perceptual Process	Results of the Perceptual Process
Seeing	Selection	Thoughts
Hearing	Organization	Ideas
Smelling	Interpretation	Opinions
Tasting		Actions
Touching		Behavior

FIGURE 2–1
The perception process (Source: R. E. Callahan, C. P. Fleenor, H. R. Knudson, *Understanding Organizational Behavior: A Managerial Viewpoint* (Columbus, OH: Merrill, 1986): 60.)

Perceptual Organization. What four-letter word can you spell with the following letters: *r g o f?* We assume that your answer is "frog," rather than "forg," "gorf," "grof," or some other combination of letters. To arrive at the correct answer, you had to arrange some random symbols (stimuli) into a recognizable pattern. This process is called *perceptual organization.* To make sense of the world around us, we must relate what we see, feel, smell, taste, and hear to concepts that help us describe or explain our experiences.

Figure/ground objects and background

There are a number of different types of perceptual organization. One, called *figure/ground,* describes our tendency to perceive any scene as consisting of objects (figure) and the space between them as background (ground). As you read this book, you do not see a random collection of colored marks and blank space. Instead, you see words, illustrations, and pictures standing out from a background.

Take a moment to review Figure 2–2. The ambiguous figures allow figure and ground to be readily interchanged, demonstrating our tendency to perceive our surroundings as figure and ground.

Perceptual grouping proximity, similarity, closure, continuity

Another method of organization is *perceptual grouping.* We tend to see stimuli as related when they are next to one another (proximity), when they are similar in some way (similarity), or when a simple pattern can be sensed (closure, continuity). Similarity implies that the more attributes objects share, the more likely that we will perceive the objects as part of a common group. In many hospitals, surgery staff members wear green uniforms, so outsiders frequently assume that anyone wearing a green uniform is part of that staff.

Closure describes a tendency to complete an object or concept, even though only part of the object or concept is present. If neighborhood children regularly play baseball in a vacant lot near your house, and you hear the sound of a bat striking a ball, followed three seconds later by the crash of shattering glass, what do you assume? You probably assume that the children are playing ball, that one of them hit the ball, that the ball went through a window, that the game has abruptly ended, and that most of the children are running toward home.

FIGURE 2–2
Figure/ground illustrations: Concentrate on the colored shapes. Do they form recognizable patterns? Now concentrate on the white spaces between the shapes. This shifting illustrates our tendency to organize the world into figure and ground.

 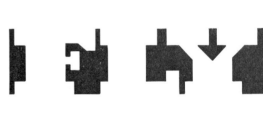

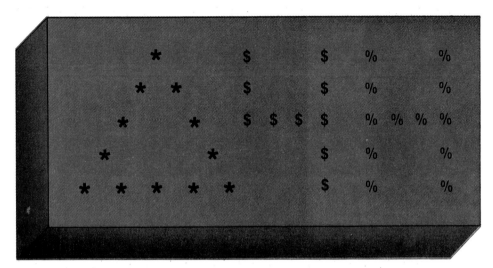

FIGURE 2–3
Closure and continuity

Continuity implies perceiving objects or concepts as continuous patterns. Inflexible managers may not be able to adapt to a new business situation because "we have always done it this way." Such managers may be so rigid and unyielding that they see nothing unusual in the new situation. Figure 2–3 illustrates the processes of closure and continuity.

Instead of seeing a random collection of asterisks, dollar signs, and percent signs, you probably see a triangle, the numeral 4 and the letter *H*.

Perceptual Interpretation. The context in which information appears affects how you interpret it. Consider the statement "Our government supports nuclear disarmament." Does it make a difference whether the statement is made by the president of the United States or the first secretary of the Soviet Communist Party? We submit that most Americans would find the statement more believable if it came from the president. Similarly, many Soviet citizens would believe the statement from the first secretary to be more credible.

Interpretation is also influenced by personal characteristics of the interpreter. Have you ever purchased a new, expensive tennis racket or a pair of skis and suddenly noticed a large number of the same brand on the court or the slopes? It is unlikely that the number of that exclusive brand suddenly increased. Rather, your own purchase influenced your perception so that you were more likely to notice them.

The processes of perceptual selection, organization, and interpretation serve as "filters," in much the same fashion as camera filters—they highlight certain details and suppress others.

Perceptual Errors

How do we explain the fact that individuals can look at the same thing but perceive it so differently? A number of factors shape and sometimes distort our per-

Perceptual errors distort perception.

ceptions. Factors that distort are called *perceptual errors.* The most common errors are stereotyping, selective perception, halo effect, set expectations, emotional state, and projection.

Stereotyping. Stereotyping results in forming an impression of an individual based on assumptions about a group that the person belongs to. Many elements provide a basis for stereotype, including race, sex, nationality, age, and occupation. For example, many people assume that an accountant will be stuffy and uninteresting, or that a Russian will lack a sense of humor. Similarly, women physicians are sometimes assumed to be nurses by new patients.

Selective Perception. Selective perception may lead to error by causing the observer to overemphasize certain aspects of a situation. Recall that the National Institute for Subliminal Research saw some rather novel messages in advertisements—messages not seen by the Utah Advertising Council, among others.

A classic study illustrated how individual background and interests may lead to selective perception. Twenty-three business executives read a lengthy story about a steel company. Six of the executives had a background in sales, five in production, four in accounting, and eight in other departments. Each executive was asked to list the major problem a new president of the steel company should deal with first. Accountants and sales executives were concerned with financial sales problems, while production people would first clarify various production issues. Executives in public relations and industrial relations saw human relations as the biggest problem. In other words, the participants perceived aspects in the situation that related specifically to the activities and goals of the unit to which they were attached.[2]

Halo Effect. The process by which an onlooker evaluates all dimensions of another person according to a single impression is called the halo effect. For example, groups of students viewed videotapes of a college instructor. One student group saw a tape in which the instructor acted in a warm and friendly manner. Another group viewed a tape in which he appeared aloof and arrogant. After watching the tape, the students rated the instructor's likability as well as his physical appearance and mannerisms. As predicted, those who had seen the instructor behave in a warm, friendly manner reported liking him much more than those who had seen him act cold and arrogant. The halo effect of the general trait (likability) carried over strongly to the more specific traits, too. Students who had seen the instructor acting friendly rated his appearance and mannerisms more favorably than those who had viewed the instructor acting coldly.[3]

Which perceptual errors have you committed regarding the instructor of this class?

Halo effect may have serious impact on performance ratings on the job. In many cases, a supervisor observes only a small sample of an employee's work. If for some reason the supervisor samples an area in which the employee does well, the supervisor may judge overall performance to be high in all areas. The reverse can also happen, perhaps leading the employee to be more concerned about avoiding noticeable mistakes than with excellent performance.

Set Expectations. Set expectations distort perception by allowing the observer to see what he or she expects to see. Although the mechanics of set expectations are similar to stereotyping, set expectations derive from personal experience, so the expectations may vary greatly from person to person. By contrast, the assumptions that lead to stereotyping are held by large numbers of people. If our grandparents are forgetful, we may then expect all elderly people to be forgetful—and perceive them that way regardless of their actual behavior. Similarly, if we are short-changed at the corner store, we may conclude that small businesses are not efficient.

A dramatic illustration of set expectations was created in an experiment that manipulated the amount of supervision given to subordinates. A supervisor was required to ensure that the performance of two subordinates was maintained at an acceptable level. In the first round, the supervisor was given almost constant reports on the performance of one employee, but only periodic reports on the other. The experiment was designed to cause the supervisor to have greater trust in the loosely supervised employee. At the end of the first round, the supervisor received summary performance reports that showed identical output for both employees. In the second round of the experiment, the supervisor was free to mon-

In an experiment, set expectations were created that led a supervisor to monitor one employee more than another.

itor either or both employees as much as he wished. The supervisor spent more time monitoring the employee who had been placed under high surveillance during the first round, showing that, despite the equal performance in the first round, the loosely supervised employee was trusted more than the other employee. The set expectations created in the first round resulted in different degrees of surveillance in the second round, even though there was no difference in productivity to justify the different amount of supervision.[4]

Emotional state. "Don't talk to the boss unless you want your head chewed off." Probably every employee has heard that statement from a co-worker. The listener would assume that the boss is in a bad mood—an emotional state. A given emotional state causes us to sense, select, and organize information in a manner consistent with that state. When we are happy and excited, we may be more cooperative than usual. When we are sad and depressed, we may be less cooperative, delay decisions, and react negatively to new ideas.

How can perceptual errors be avoided?

Projection. The tendency to see our own traits in other people is called *projection*. To some extent, this is an efficient practice. After all, people with similar backgrounds and interests often think similarly. In some situations, though, we may project our own feelings inappropriately. For example, a manager may ask a subordinate to redo a report that contains a few errors. Although the manager displays no emotion, the employee may later describe the boss as upset and angry. In fact, the employee was angry at himself and upset that a bad report had been sent to the manager. The subordinate projected anger to the manager.

ATTITUDES

Attitudes valuative feelings about objects, people, or events

Attitudes are valuative feelings about objects, people, or events. They reflect how one "feels" about something. When we say, "I like rock and roll," we are expressing our attitudes toward a type of music. Attitudes differ from perception. Remember that perception involves selecting, organizing, and interpreting information; attitudes involve *evaluation* of information. An example will help illustrate the difference.

Chris Wilson asked his friend Al Vargas to attend a basketball game, but Al replied that he had to study for a test the following day. Chris later changed his mind about going to the ball game and decided to go to a movie instead. Shortly before the movie began, Chris noticed that Al Vargas was sitting six rows in front of him. "The jerk lied to me," Chris thought angrily.

What are the three components of attitudes?

Chris concluded that Al had lied to him (a perception), and responded with anger (an attitude). An attitude is a valuative reaction with three components: emotional, cognitive (belief), and behavioral. The *emotional* component refers to the feelings associated with an object, person, or event. The feelings may be pleasing or displeasing, favorable or unfavorable. In the example, Chris's feelings about Al were clearly unfavorable and displeasing. The *cognitive* or belief component includes the information, beliefs and ideas that a person has about something.

Perception Is a Salesperson

The colors of packages, logos, and signs have always been important to manufacturers, but companies are taking color even more seriously than ever. Consultants are paid huge fees for advice on which colors are most appealing and stand out best on store shelves. Perception researchers flash slides of package displays while a camera and computer track consumers' eye movements to detect what they see first.

Just how seriously is this taken by producers? Consider the Diet Coke can—a simple color design of red lettering on a white background. That "simple" design took six months and the creation of more than 150 different cans before the final version emerged. Some examples of how color affects perception:

☐ The background hue on Barrelhead Sugar-Free Root Beer was changed from blue to beige.

Source: Adapted from R. Alsop, "Color Grows More Important in Catching Consumers' Eyes," *The Wall Street Journal* (29 November 1984): 33. Reprinted by permission of *The Wall Street Journal,* ©Dow-Jones & Company, Inc., 1984. All Rights Reserved.

People swore it tasted more like old-fashioned root beer, though no change was made in the beverage.

☐ Consumers ascribe a sweeter taste to orange drinks the darker the orange shade of the container.

☐ Canada Dry's sugar-free ginger ale enjoyed a 25 percent sales increase when the can color was changed from red to green and white.

According to one package designer, "Color isn't the most important thing; it's the only thing."

QUESTIONS

1. Explain how the color of a soft drink container "changes" the taste of the contents.
2. Many people argue that the color of clothing is important in business. What color suit would you wear to a job interview? Why?
3. Why does the package designer think color "is the only thing"? Do you agree? Why or why not?

Chris, like most of us, holds a belief that lying is not acceptable behavior. The *behavioral* component of attitudes involves a reaction to the object, person, or event. Chris's initial response was a feeling of anger. The behavioral component implies a tendency to behave in a certain way. For example, if Al says hello to Chris the following day, it is likely that Chris will respond in a cool or even hostile manner.

Attitudes and Behavior

Still, we cannot predict with certainty how Chris will react the next time he meets Al. While there is little doubt that attitudes are related to behavior, it has become clear that there is frequently not a simple, direct link between the two.[5] Much work has been done in measuring attitudes and trying to predict later behavior. Prediction of behavior is improved when we remember:

A voter opinion poll is more reliable when taken shortly before the election.

Why are attitudes not
always good predictors
of behavior?

□ The less time elapsed between attitude measurement and behavior, the more
consistent the relationship. In other words, if we have measured someone's
attitude, we will be able to predict that person's behavior in the following five
minutes more accurately than over the next week.

□ Specific attitudes best predict specific behaviors.

□ General attitudes best predict general behaviors.[6]

The first point is clearly understood by public opinion pollsters. Politicians
pay for voter surveys throughout election campaigns, but pollsters are careful to
avoid predicting election outcomes until a day or two prior to an election. Opinions (attitudes) can and do change, and the longer the time between measurement of an attitude and observation of a behavior, the less likely it is that the two
are related.

The contrast between specific and general attitudes can be seen in the choice
of educational level, type of institution attended, and kind of education received.
A generally favorable attitude toward education might allow us to predict that a
high school senior will go on to college, but would not be a good predictor of
specific behavior, such as registering at a large state-supported university on the
West Coast with a major in psychology.

Job Satisfaction: An Important Attitude?

Job satisfaction is defined as the degree of positive feeling one has about one's work situation.[7] This definition clearly identifies the concept as an attitude. Many people assume that the more satisfied workers are, the more productive they are. Yet this common sense notion does not always hold up in practice. In fact, more than forty years worth of research on this topic does not support the hoped-for relationship. The relationship between job satisfaction and job performance is simply too weak to allow prediction. Other factors, including the quality of equipment used and the ability of the worker, have much greater impact on performance than does job satisfaction.[8] This is not to say that job satisfaction is not important. It is, because it clearly relates to absenteeism and job turnover.

Job satisfaction degree of positive feeling about work

     Absenteeism is a major concern to many managers. Covering for absent employees may require reassignment of other employees or costly overtime. Workers who are dissatisfied are more likely to take unauthorized time off.[9] But is the reverse true? That is, will satisfied workers make an extra effort to be on the job? An interesting experiment a few years ago suggests that they will. An unexpected spring blizzard struck Chicago, snarling the transportation system. Getting to

Why is job satisfaction an attitude rather than a perception?

Dissatisfied workers are more likely to be absent from work than are satisfied workers.

work on the day following the blizzard required real effort. Researchers at Sears, Roebuck examined what happened in groups of salaried employees who would not lose any pay even if they did not show up for work. In work units where job satisfaction was high, attendance was high. In units where job satisfaction was low, attendance was much lower. Workers with the greatest job satisfaction were more likely to exert extra effort to get to work.[10]

Turnover involves the loss of an employee and the expensive recruitment and training of a replacement. Workers with low job satisfaction are more likely to leave their jobs, and units with low average job satisfaction generally have higher turnover rates than other units.[11] Of course, other factors can be important in setting turnover rates. In a recession, there are fewer job opportunities and even highly dissatisfied employees may stay on. It should also be noted that not all turnover is undesirable. Managers may want weak performers to leave, and very dissatisfied employees are almost certainly better off elsewhere.

Job satisfaction also has one other interesting relationship—to unionization. Job dissatisfaction is a major cause of unionization,[12] and in unionized organizations it is associated with grievances and strikes.[13]

Attitudes and Change

Whether student, professor, manager, or worker, we exert considerable effort to influence the attitudes of others. In preparation for a job interview, most people will get a haircut, select their best clothes, shine their shoes, and try to be "sparkling" during the interview. Why? To influence the attitude of the interviewer, of course! Managers try to get employees to hold positive attitudes toward work standards, safety practices, and new procedures. The advertising industry exists primarily to influence the attitudes of consumers and potential customers.

Communication is the major tool of attitude change, and we will briefly describe its use here. We look at communication in detail in Chapter 5. Research on attitude change has focused on three factors: the communicator, the message, and the audience.

The *communicator* is more likely to influence attitudes if he or she is perceived to be believable, trustworthy, and similar to the audience. These qualities are not necessarily based on knowledge or expertise. During much of his presidency, Ronald Reagan was famous for his misstatement of facts and lack of depth in certain areas, yet for the most part he received very high public opinion ratings of believability and trustworthiness.

Much of advertising employs the concept of similarity to influence attitudes. The buyers of large Cadillacs tend to be middle-aged or older, while the buyers of Corvettes tend to be younger. It is no accident that people shown in Cadillac advertisements tend to be middle-aged and well-dressed, while people in Corvette ads are generally younger and more casual in appearance.

The *message* can be structured in many ways to increase its persuasiveness. Research indicates that one way for a message to produce attitude change is to create fear or anxiety in the audience. To be effective, the message must create

Stereotyping at Work

Two physicians claimed in a letter to the *New England Journal of Medicine* that U.S. medical schools teach that doctors should use the right hand to examine patients and that the exam should be conducted from the patient's right side. The authors also claimed that some schools actually fail students who use their left hands—an obvious problem for left-handers.

Students in medical schools confirmed that the right-side rule is taught throughout the country, and upperclassmen routinely warn new medical students that they may be failed if they examine with the left hand or from the left side. Medical schools deny that they insist upon examination from the right side, though one medical professor said that medical schools twenty-five years ago flunked lefties. Another professor said that a colleague had recently complained about a student's left-handed technique; he thought the student had not been trained well.

Source: Adapted from F. E. James, "If Sandy Koufax Taught Medicine, Things Would Never Be the Same," *The Wall Street Journal* (30 April 1986): p. 29. Reprinted by permission of *The Wall Street Journal*, ©Dow-Jones & Company, Inc., 1986. All Rights Reserved.

QUESTIONS

1. Does this story reflect halo effect as well as stereotyping? Why or why not?
2. Do you feel that left-handed people are "different"? Why or why not?
3. Thirty years ago, many grade schools in the United States forbade students to write or draw with their left hands. Why?

moderate levels of emotion. If too weak, the message will have no impact; if too strong, it is often rejected. The audience must believe that the dangers cited are real and that the recommended actions will be effective in avoiding the danger.[14] In the 1950s, the U.S. government convinced large numbers of American citizens to build fallout shelters in their backyards. The audience believed that there was a real, but not immediate, danger of nuclear attack and that a backyard shelter would ensure survival. In an organizational example, managers of a lumber mill convinced workers their jobs were in danger if pay rates were not reduced. The work force willingly accepted a reduction in pay in the hope of protecting jobs.

The *audience* is also a factor in attitude change, though research here is less convincing. It appears that people with high self-esteem feel strongly that their attitudes are correct and are less likely to change them. There is also some evidence that highly intelligent people are less affected by persuasive communication than are other people.[15]

To change attitudes, which should be emphasized: the communicator, the message, or the audience?

Is offering a bribe to an official in another country where it is standard practice right or wrong? Is closing down a money-losing plant, which happens to be a small town's major employer, right or wrong? Would you think it right or wrong

VALUES

if your manager requested that you tell callers she is out of the office when she isn't?

People respond to these questions differently, and their answers reflect individual values. Some people might argue that if bribery is an acceptable way of doing business in a country, we will find it impossible to do business unless we follow local custom. Others will argue that such a custom is unethical regardless of the circumstances, and therefore should not be practiced. (In fact, a U.S. law, the Foreign Corrupt Practices Act, makes it illegal for U.S. firms to practice bribery even in countries where the practice is considered usual.)

Values represent basic convictions that "a specific mode of conduct or end-state of existence is personally or socially preferable to an opposite or converse mode of conduct or end-state of existence."[16] In other words, our values tell us generally how things ought to be done. In specific instances, values tell us what is "right" or "wrong" in a given situation. Our values contain a moral structure that provides us with our ideas about what is right, good, and desirable.

Most people in a particular culture share many common values. For example, many Americans espouse the values of competition, fair play, and equal jus-

Values rules of right and wrong

Manipulative people try to reach their goals by manipulating things and other people.

tice. Yet within a culture there are usually value differences between certain subgroups. One researcher has suggested a number of levels to describe different personal values and life-styles.[17] The levels are:

1. *Reactive.* Reactive people are unaware of themselves or others as human beings; they respond only to basic physical needs. These people are rarely found in organizations.
2. *Tribalistic.* These people are highly dependent on others, especially those in authority. They respond to tradition and to the power of a leader.
3. *Egocentric.* These people are aggressive and selfish—"rugged individualists." They respond primarily to power.
4. *Conforming.* Conforming people do not like uncertainty or the unusual. They want others to accept their values and have difficulty in accepting people with different values.
5. *Manipulative.* Manipulative people try to reach their goals by manipulating things and other people. They desire status and recognition and tend to be materialistic.
6. *Sociocentric.* These people dislike materialism, manipulation, and conformity but believe it is more important to get along with others and to be liked than to be successful.
7. *Existential.* Existential individuals easily tolerate uncertainty and people with differing values. They do not like arbitrary use of authority, restrictive policies, rigid behavior, or status symbols.

What is the value level of your closest friend?

Managerial Values and Success

Some interesting research on managerial values has found both similarities and differences among managers from different national cultures. One study surveyed thousands of managers from several countries.[18] Three primary value orientations were found: moral, pragmatic, and aesthetic. If the primary orientation is moral, the person is concerned about having a "right manner of acting." Pragmatics are concerned about being successful and "dealing with only facts or reality," while aesthetics are concerned largely with "achieving a state of pleasure." Figure 2–4 shows the values of managers from five countries. As you can see, pragmatism and moralism are the major value orientations held by the managers, regardless of nationality. Still, there are some interesting differences between the management groups. The highest percentage of pragmatists occurred among Japanese managers, while the greatest proportion of moralists was found among Indian managers.

Managers' values pragmatism and moralism

A related study associated values with success. The study showed that, regardless of nationality, the more successful managers favored pragmatic, dynamic, achievement-oriented values, while less successful managers preferred more passive and static values.[19]

A great deal has been written about the changing nature of values among the American work force. The assumption is that, beginning in the late 1960s,

FIGURE 2 – 4

Values of managers from five countries (Source: G.W. England, "Managers and Their Value Systems: A Five-Country Comparative Study," *Columbia Journal of World Business* (Summer 1978): 35–44. Reprinted with permission.)

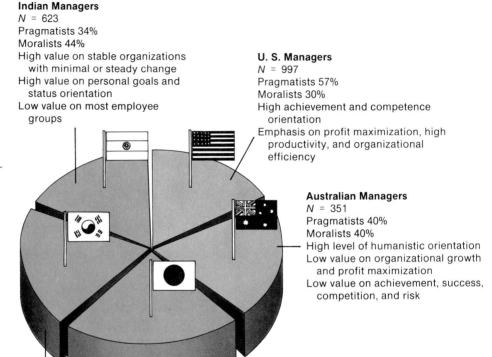

Indian Managers
N = 623
Pragmatists 34%
Moralists 44%
High value on stable organizations with minimal or steady change
High value on personal goals and status orientation
Low value on most employee groups

U. S. Managers
N = 997
Pragmatists 57%
Moralists 30%
High achievement and competence orientation
Emphasis on profit maximization, high productivity, and organizational efficiency

Australian Managers
N = 351
Pragmatists 40%
Moralists 40%
High level of humanistic orientation
Low value on organizational growth and profit maximization
Low value on achievement, success, competition, and risk

Korean Managers
N = 211
Pragmatists 53%
Moralists 9%
Low value on most employee groups as significant reference groups
Self-oriented achievement and competence orientation

Japanese Managers
N = 374
Pragmatists 67%
Moralists 10%
High achievement and competence orientation
Most homogeneous managerial value system of the five countries studied

younger workers have displayed a different orientation toward jobs than older workers. There is some support for the assumption, but other variables, including education and salary level, are also important. To summarize:

Why do young workers value personally rewarding work?

□ Younger workers, especially well-educated, white-collar workers, value self-expression more than older workers.

□ Age made no difference in pride of work, but this value increases with education and income level.

□ The importance of salary decreases with age.

□ Young workers tend to prefer personally rewarding work more than older workers.[20]

Values, Perception, and Attitudes

By now, we should see that values, perception, and attitudes are related. Values are the most basic of the three. Values are learned at an early age and change only slightly, if at all, during our lifetime. Values govern many of our attitudes. For example, the Zhun/twa culture of Zambia considers it normal to kill a newborn twin. While our value system views such an act as both repulsive and illegal, the Zhun/twa have found that there is not enough food to keep two newborns alive. To them, the killing is a humanitarian act—a very different attitude![21]

Attitudes and perception affect one another. As we discussed in the section on perceptual errors, strong attitudes may lead to such errors as stereotyping and set expectations. Similarly, the story about Chris Wilson and Al Vargas demonstrates how perception can influence attitudes.

Values are the basis for attitudes and perception.

LEARNING SUMMARY

1. The perceptual process allows us to select, organize, and interpret the output of our five senses. It is how we "make sense" of the world around us.
2. The major perceptual errors include stereotyping, selective perception, halo effect, set expectations, emotional state, and projection.
3. Attitudes involve evaluation of what we perceive.
4. The three components of attitudes are emotional, cognitive, and behavioral.
5. Specific attitudes are helpful in predicting specific behavior, while general attitudes are helpful in predicting general behavior.
6. Attitudes are not always good predictors of behavior.
7. Job satisfaction is an important attitude, directly related to absenteeism and turnover.
8. Values represent basic convictions—"how things should be done."
9. Personal values and life-styles can be categorized as: reactive, tribalistic, egocentric, conforming, manipulative, sociocentric, or existential.
10. Regardless of nationality, successful managers generally hold pragmatic, dynamic, achievement-oriented values.

ANSWERS TO "WHAT'S YOUR OPINION?"

1. False   The "right" way is strongly influenced by values and attitudes.
2. True   Attitudes stem partly from values.
3. False   Attitudes are a predisposition to act, but circumstances may cause a person to act in a way that is inconsistent with an attitude.
4. True   Job satisfaction is the degree of positive feeling (attitude) about a job.
5. False   They may or may not. The relationship between satisfaction and performance is unclear.
6. True   Dissatisfaction is clearly related to absenteeism.
7. True   Japanese and American managers place importance on pragmatism and moralism.

8. True   Successful managers have pragmatic, dynamic, and achievement-oriented values, while their less-successful peers stress more passive and static values.

9. False   Young workers attach more importance to salary than older workers.

KEY TERMS

Absenteeism	Perceptual interpretation
Aesthetic	Perceptual organization
Attitudes	Perceptual selection
Behavioral component	Pragmatic
Cognitive component	Projection
Emotional component	Selective perception
Emotional state	Set expectations
Halo effect	Stereotyping
Job satisfaction	Turnover
Moral	Value orientation
Perception	Values
Perceptual errors	

HUMAN RELATIONS APPLICATIONS

By now you should have no doubt that our values, perceptions, and attitudes are important factors in the world of work. Let's put some of our perceptions to a test: In terms of quality of life among the world's countries, where would you rank the United States? If you are a U.S. citizen, the chances are that you immediately rated the United States as first. Surprise! In a survey of the quality of life in 107 countries, the United States came in not first, not second, but *forty-second*! The study addressed forty-four factors, including literacy and education, health and welfare provisions for citizens, political participation, women's rights, weather, economic growth, inflation, infant mortality, influence of the military, and per capita income. The top five countries in quality of life were Denmark, Norway, Austria, the Netherlands, and Sweden. The bottom five were Ethiopia (worst), Chad, Uganda, Burundi, and Mauritania. How did the Soviet Union rate? Forty-third—just behind the United States.[22]

What was your reaction when you read the preceding paragraph? Disbelief? Perhaps a little anger? When we receive information that contradicts a strongly held attitude, such a reaction is common. What we must understand is that our own attitudes, perceptions, and beliefs are not shared by everyone in the world, in an organization, or even in the classroom.

Some of the concepts covered earlier in the chapter have been more useful than others in management. Let's look at a few uses and abuses of the concepts in organizations.

Perceptions and Attitudes

In an interesting study of perception, Weis and Fleenor found that managers as a group feel that employees who smoke are less productive than those who don't.[23] Does this perception affect people's lives? More than 53 percent of the 223 managers surveyed indicated that they choose nonsmokers over smokers when faced with a choice between otherwise equally qualified applicants. The other respondents saw the choice as a toss-up. No one would prefer to hire a smoker over an equally qualified nonsmoker. For top executives, the perception was even more clear: 70 percent reported that they would hire a nonsmoker over a smoker, if equally qualified. An increasing number of firms are refusing to hire smokers at all (it is not illegal).

Is this an example of perceptual error? Perhaps, since there is no evidence that smokers are less productive than nonsmokers, but the point is, if managers believe it to be true, smoking can be hazardous to your career.

In another area, over 34 percent of executives in a survey felt that women executives need greater sponsorship than men for promotion. Over 33 percent believed women are less likely to be fired, and more than 19 percent felt that the woman executive is at a disadvantage if she has children. There is a mixture of good news and bad news for energetic women if these perceptions are strongly held by the more numerous male executives.

Attitude Surveys

Attitude surveys are widely used in organizations throughout the world. Many companies use attitude surveys to gather opinions from employees or other groups about some aspect of the organization or its operations. Job satisfaction is a frequent target for surveys. A portion of a survey is shown in Figure 2–5.

Some major businesses survey employees on a regular basis. Xerox Corporation has designated a "Delta Branch." This is not a physical branch but a cross-section of employees selected nationally for periodic data gathering. Whenever there is a specific area of interest, for example job satisfaction, questionnaires are mailed to the Delta Branch employees. Their responses are evaluated and used as one element in decision making.

Many organizations are interested in the attitudes of customers. Marketing research firms specialize in the study of consumer attitudes toward potential and existing products. In recent years, automobile manufacturers and dealers have begun surveying customers about their experience with the purchase. Part of a survey used by Toyota Motors is displayed in Figure 2–6.

Influence of Values

Despite the importance of values in human behavior, few organizations directly address this issue. Texas Instruments is a notable exception, since the company management has developed a program to diagnose the different value types described earlier in the chapter. The object is to match the types with appropriate work situations:

FIGURE 2 – 5
Portion of an attitude survey (Source: L.W. Porter (1961). "A study of perceived need satisfaction in bottom and middle management jobs." *Journal of Applied Psychology, 45,* p. 3. Copyright 1961 by The American Psychological Association. Reprinted by permission of the publisher and the author.)

Instructions: Circle the number on the scale that represents the amount of the characteristic being rated. Low numbers represent low or minimum amounts, and high numbers represent high or maximum amounts.

1. The opportunity for personal growth and development in my management position.
   a, HOW MUCH IS THERE NOW?
      (Minimum)　　1　　2　　3　　4　　5　　6　　7　　(Maximum)
   b. HOW MUCH SHOULD THERE BE?
      (Minimum)　　1　　2　　3　　4　　5　　6　　7　　(Maximum)

2. The feeling of security in my management position.
   a. HOW MUCH IS THERE NOW?
      (Minimum)　　1　　2　　3　　4　　5　　6　　7　　(Maximum)
   b. HOW MUCH SHOULD THERE BE?
      (Minimum)　　1　　2　　3　　4　　5　　6　　7　　(Maximum)

Some individuals, for example, are classified as "tribalistic" people who want strong, directive leadership from their boss; some are "egocentric," desiring individual responsibilities and wanting to work as loners in an entrepreneurial style; some are "sociocentric," seeking primarily the social relationships that a job provides; and some are "existential," seeking full expression of growth and self-fulfillment needs through their work, much as an artist does. Charles Hughes, director of personnel and organization development at Texas Instruments, believes that the variety of work that needs to be done in his organization is great enough to accommodate these different types of work personalities in such a manner that individual and organizational goals are fused.[24]

The values of a single individual can dominate an entire organization, attracting like-minded people. While Edwin Land, the founder of Polaroid Corporation, was still with the company, brilliant scientists and skilled marketers competed for jobs there. The high-risk, rapid growth atmosphere attracted people who valued challenge and innovation. After Land's departure, the new chief executive officer began moving the firm away from its almost exclusive emphasis on consumer products and reduced the amount of research and development funds used for new technology. Many key people left over the next several years, even though analysts felt the company was better managed. As one Polaroid employee described the change: "Polaroid used to be *the* company. Now it's just *a* company."[25]

PERSONAL GUIDELINES FOR HUMAN RELATIONS SUCCESS

As we saw in this chapter, there is much to learn about values, attitudes, and perceptions. A few things you can do to improve your ability to understand and deal with other people include:

□ Remember that different values lead to different behavior. This is especially

TOYOTA
NEW VEHICLE SALES AND DELIVERY SURVEY

FOR EACH OF THE FOLLOWING QUESTIONS, PLEASE CHECK THE BOX THAT BEST REFLECTS YOUR FEELINGS.

I. YOUR PURCHASE EXPERIENCE

1. *When you purchased your new Toyota, how satisfied were you with the performance of the dealer's sales staff on EACH of the following items?*

	Very Satisfied	Somewhat Satisfied	Neither Satisfied Nor Dissatisfied	Somewhat Dissatisfied	Very Dissatisfied
Courtesy and friendliness	5	4	3	2	1
Knowledge of Toyota products	5	4	3	2	1
Professionalism	5	4	3	2	1
Fulfillment of commitments made during sale	5	4	3	2	1
Overall handling of sale by salesperson	5	4	3	2	1

II. YOUR DELIVERY EXPERIENCE

2. *At the time of delivery, did someone at the dealership...*

	Yes	No	Don't Know
Explain the vehicle service maintenance schedule	2	1	9
Explain the new vehicle warranty	2	1	9
Provide information about the dealership's service and parts departments (such as hours open, appointments, etc.)	2	1	9
Offer to demonstrate vehicle features and controls	2	1	9
Give you a copy of the New Vehicle Delivery Checksheet	2	1	9

3. *How satisfied were you with the condition of your new Toyota at the time of delivery on EACH of the following items?*

	Very Satisfied	Somewhat Satisfied	Neither Satisfied Nor Dissatisfied	Somewhat Dissatisfied	Very Dissatisfied
Cleanliness of the exterior	5	4	3	2	1
Cleanliness of the interior	5	4	3	2	1

4. *Did your salesperson or a dealership representative follow-up by contacting you after delivery about your satisfaction with your overall sales experience?*

In Person ☐   By Phone ☐   In Writing ☐   No Contact ☐

III. YOUR OVERALL EXPERIENCE

5. *Would you recommend this dealer to a friend as a place to buy a new vehicle?*

Definitely Recommend	Probably Recommend	Might or Might Not Recommend	Probably Not Recommend	Definitely Not Recommend
5	4	3	2	1

FIGURE 2 – 6

A portion of a Toyota customer attitude survey (Source: Courtesy of Toyota Motor Sales, U.S.A., Inc.)

important to remember when dealing with people from another culture. If you must supervise or work with people from another country, learn what you can about their culture. Talk to them about work customs and expectations in their country. Go to the library for some information about that country.

☐ Concentrate on behavior you can see rather than your impression of another person's attitude or perception. Recall how difficult it is to predict behavior from attitudes. Someone who complains about a job is not necessarily a poor worker.

☐ Try to avoid perceptual errors. When evaluating another's behavior, step back a bit and make sure that you are not over reacting to one good or bad aspect of that behavior (halo effect). Ask yourself whether you are projecting your feelings onto others or whether you are relying heavily on your assumptions about a person's membership in a group (projection, stereotyping, selective perception).

DISCUSSION AND REVIEW QUESTIONS

1. Many think values are the foundation of individual behavior. What is the basis for that belief?
2. "Job candidates for a sales position are more likely to be successful if they hold egocentric values." Discuss your reaction to this statement.
3. Give examples of how people might perceive a situation differently. Explain why.
4. Discuss the importance of attitudes to management of a work group.
5. How might perceptual errors interfere with evaluation of work performance?
6. To change a worker's attitudes about work, should a manager focus primarily on the communicator, the message, or the audience? Why?

HUMAN RELATIONS EXERCISE

Perceptions and Values

This exercise has two goals: to let you identify characteristics in others that are similar to your own and to help you define some of the values within those characteristics.

Instructions. List the names of ten people you know. The list can include friends, family members, work associates, and others. Using the peer perceptions ranking form in Figure 2–7, rank the ten people from the person you think is *most* similar to you to the person you consider *least* similar. Beside each name, list the characteristics of the person that you feel makes them similar to you. Answer the questions that follow the form.

Perceptions Ranking Form

	Your Ranking of Other Individuals	Characteristics You Considered
Most Similar to You	1. _Barbara Bishop_	EVERYTHING.
	2. _____	
	3. _____	
	4. _____	
	5. _____	
	6. _____	
	7. _____	
	8. _____	
	9. _____	
Least Similar to You	10. _____	

FIGURE 2 – 7
Perceptions ranking form

QUESTIONS

1. What values underlie your choice of people as most like you?
2. Why did you classify certain people as least like you? What does this say about your value system?
3. What perceptual processes influenced your view of the top people on the list? What about those on the bottom of the list?

**HUMAN
RELATIONS
INCIDENT**

Space Utilization[26]

Sherman Adder, assistant plant manager for Frame Manufacturing Company, was chairman of the ad hoc committee for space utilization. The committee was made up of the various department heads in the company. The plant manager of Frame had given Sherman the charge to see if the various office, operations, and warehouse facilities of the company were being optimally utilized. The company was beset by rising costs and the need for more space. However, before okaying an expensive addition to the plant, the plant manager wanted to be sure that the currently available space was being properly utilized.

Sherman opened up the first committee meeting by reiterating the charge of the committee. Then Sherman asked the members if they had any initial observations to make. The first to speak was the office manager. He stated, "I know we are using every possible inch of room that we have available to us, but when I walk out into the plant, I see a lot of open spaces. We have people piled on top of one another, but out in the plant there seems to be plenty of room." The production manager quickly replied, "We do not have a lot of space. You office people have the luxury facilities. My supervisors don't even have room for a desk and a file cabinet. I have repeatedly told the plant manager we need more space. After all, our operation determines whether this plant succeeds or fails, not you people in the front office pushing paper around." Sherman interrupted at this point to say, "Obviously we have different interpretations of the space utilization around here. Before further discussion I think it would be best if we have some objective facts to work with. I am going to ask the industrial engineer to provide us with some statistics on plant and office layout before our next meeting. Today's meeting is adjourned."

QUESTIONS

1. What perceptual principles are evident in this case?
2. What concept was brought out when the production manager labeled the office personnel a bunch of "paper pushers"? Can you give other organizational examples of this concept?
3. Do you think that Sherman's approach to getting "objective facts" from statistics on plant and office layout will affect the perceptions of the office and production managers? How does such information affect perceptions in general?
4. What would you suggest Sherman should do instead (that is, if you don't agree with his approach to gather facts)?

NOTES

1. Adapted from C. Psarras, *The Wall Street Journal* (12 March 1986): 37. Reprinted by permission of *The Wall Street Journal*, ©Dow Jones & Co., Inc., 1986. All Rights Reserved.
2. D. C. Dearborn and H. A. Simon, "Selective Perception: A Note on the Departmental Identification of Executives," *Sociometry* (June 1958): 140–44.

3. R. E. Nisbett and T. D. Wilson, "The Halo Effect: Evidence for the Unconscious Alteration of Judgments," *Journal of Personality and Social Psychology*, no. 35 (1977): 450–56.

4. L. H. Strickland. "Surveillance and Trust," *Journal of Personality*, vol. 26 (1958): 200–215.

5. J. Cooper and R. T. Croyle, "Attitudes and Attitude Change," *Annual Review of Psychology*, no. 35 (1984): 395–426.

6. S. Penrod, *Social Psychology* (Englewood Cliffs, NJ: Prentice-Hall, 1983) 345–47.

7. E. A. Locke, "What is Job Satisfaction?" *Organizational Behavior and Human Performance*, vol. 4 (1969): 316.

8. J. B. Herman, "Are Situational Contingencies Limiting Job Attitude-Job Performance Relationships?" *Organizational Behavior and Human Performance*, vol. 10 (1973): 208–24.

9. J. A. Breaugh, "Predicting Absenteeism From Prior Absenteeism and Work Attitudes, *Journal of Applied Psychology*, vol. 66 (1981): 555–60.

10. F. J. Smith, "Work Attitudes as Predictors of Attendance on a Specific Day," *Journal of Applied Psychology*, vol. 62 (1977): 16–19.

11. H. J. Arnold and D. C. Feldman, "A Multivariate Model of Job Turnover," *Journal of Applied Psychology*, vol. 67 (1982): 350–60.

12. J. B. Brett, "Why Employees Want Unions," *Organizational Dynamics* (Spring 1980): 47–59.

13. W. C. Hamner and F. J. Smith, "Work Attitudes as Predictors of Unionization Activity," *Journal of Applied Psychology*, vol. 63 (1978): 415-21.

14. C. R. Mewborn and R. W. Rogers, "Effects of Threatening and Reassuring Components of Fear Appeals on Psychological and Verbal Measures of Emotion and Attitudes," *Journal of Experimental Social Psychology*, no. 15 (1979): 242–53.

15. M. Zellner, "Self-Esteem, Reception, and Influenceability," *Journal of Personality and Social Psychology*, no. 15 (1979): 87–93.

16. M. Rokeach, *The Nature of Human Values* (New York: Free Press, 1973): 5.

17. C. W. Graves, "Levels of Existence: An Open System Theory of Values," *Journal of Humanistic Psychology* (Fall 1970): 131–55.

18. G. W. England, *The Manager and His Values: An International Perspective From the United States, Japan, Korea, India and Australia* (Cambridge, MA: Ballinger, 1975): 1.

19. G. W. England and R. Lee, "The Relationship Between Managerial Values and Managerial Success in the United States, Japan, India, and Australia," *Journal of Applied Psychology*, vol. 59 (1974): 411–19.

20. R. N. Taylor and M. Thompson, "Work Value Systems of Young Workers," *Academy of Management Journal*, vol. 19 (1976): 522–36.

21. S. Worchel and W. Shebilske, *Psychology: Principles and Applications*, 2nd ed. (Englewood Cliffs, NJ: Prentice-Hall, 1986): 415.

22. "Measuring the Quality of Life," *International Herald Tribune* (26 November 1982): 7W.

23. W. L. Weis and C. P. Fleenor, "Cold-Shouldering the Smoker," *Supervisory Management* (September 1981): 31–35.

24. W. C. Hamner and D. W. Organ, *Organizational Behavior: An Applied Psychological Approach* (Dallas: Business Publications, 1978): 187.

25. "Losing Its Flash," *The Wall Street Journal* (10 May 1983): 1.

26. R. E. Callahan, C. P. Fleenor, H. R. Knudson, *Understanding Organizational Behavior: A Managerial Viewpoint* (Columbus, OH: Merrill, 1986): 77.

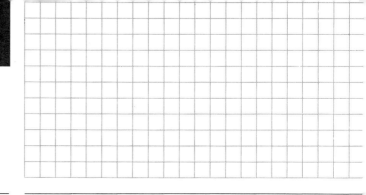

CHAPTER 3
MOTIVATION

_F_ 1. Money is still a key source of motivation for workers.

_T_ 2. It is important to identify internal sources of motivation.

_T_ 3. Salary and working conditions can be a source of dissatisfaction for workers.

_T_ 4. People will compare what they receive for working with what others receive for working.

_T_ 5. Some individuals can view even a promotion negatively rather than as a source of motivation.

_F_ 6. Individuals will be motivated only by realistic goals.

_T_ 7. The environment of individuals is important to understanding motivation.

_F_ 8. Giving praise works best if we allow time to pass for the worker to appreciate the praise when it occurs.

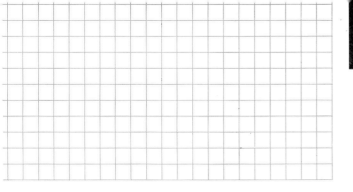

OUTLINE

MOTIVATION CONCEPTS
 Types of Motivation Theories
 Need Theories
 Choice Theories
 Reinforcement Theory

LEARNING SUMMARY

HUMAN RELATIONS APPLICATIONS
 Money as Motivator
 Do Worker/Owners Perform Better?

PERSONAL GUIDELINES FOR HUMAN
RELATIONS SUCCESS

LEARNING OBJECTIVES

☐ Define motivation

☐ Describe the following theories of motivation:
 Need Hierarchy, Two-Factor, Equity, Goal-
 Setting, and Reinforcement

☐ Identify and discuss some human relations
 applications surrounding motivation

☐ Create a personal awareness of your
 motivation

Million Dollar Motivation Plan[1]

During the late 1970s and early 1980s, the employees at Diamond International, a manufacturer of paper egg cartons, faced an uncertain future. The uncertain future resulted not only from stiff competition among styrofoam egg-carton manufacturers but also from the deep economic recession with its high interest rates and high unemployment. This meant that profits were reduced to less than the minimum expected by the parent company. As the director of personnel, Daniel Boyle, says, "Relations between labor and management were strained at best."

Boyle designed and introduced a productivity and motivation system called the "100 Club." The mechanics of the program are simple in nature. Employees receive points for above-average performance. For example, employees get 20 points for no job-related accidents for one year and 25 points for 100 percent attendance. On the program's anniversary date, points are totaled and a letter sent to the employee. An employee who accumulates 100 points receives a light blue jacket with the company logo and a patch identifying the wearer as a member of the "100 Club." Additional gifts can be gained for points over 100.

How is it working? Well, all 325 employees have jackets. Productivity is up 16.3 percent; quality-related errors are down 40 percent; grievances have decreased 72 percent; and time lost from job-related accidents has dropped 43.7 percent. The result of these changes has been a financial return of $1 million to the parent company.

In summarizing what happened, Boyle says, "For too long, the people who got the majority of attention were those who caused problems. The program's primary focus is to recognize good employees."

MOTIVATIONAL CONCEPTS

As in the opening story, managers become concerned about employee motivation as a result of poor financial performance and increased market competition. There are some positive ways of improving the situation, as this story confirms. But, the key question is how? To pursue this question, we will present some basic theories of motivation, give ideas on how to apply them, and describe some conditions that can lead to their successful application in organizations.

Motivation has become an issue of great importance to organizations. Much of this concern centers on improving productivity. In many instances these are called "productivity programs." To appreciate and understand their proper use, we must study their basic premise: People can be motivated.

Other changes in the workplace have made managers aware that motivating employees is an important aspect of their jobs. These changes include the recognition that employees want more from their jobs than just economic rewards, that the work force is more educated and sophisticated than in the past, that external control and authority are not as effective as they were in the past, and that employees are becoming more militant in making demands to have more of their needs satisfied in the workplace. This list was explained more fully in Chapter 1.

Why is it important to understand motivation?

Types of Motivational Theories

People differ not only in their ability to work—that is, their skills and talents—but also in their willingness to use these skills and talents. Motivation is hard to define, much less to understand. The word *motivation* comes from the Latin word *movere,* to move. Yet in most cases a manager is really concerned about worker performance. This means that the manager cares about not only movement but also the direction of the movement. Usually the manager is trying to get the worker to accomplish departmental goals—and not just while the supervisor stands over the worker's shoulder. Therefore, a basic definition of motivation might be the process that causes behavior to be energized, directed, and sustained.[2]

Motivation the process that causes behavior to be energized, directed, and sustained

To explain motivation, we must try to understand the "whys" of behavior. Why does an individual choose to act one way rather than another? Why does the individual stop doing something that needs to be done? In attempts to understand the "whys" of individual behavior, three major categories of motivational theories have been developed: need, choice, and reinforcement. These are summarized in Table 3–1.

What are the three major types of motivational theories?

Need Theories

Need theories of motivation focus on what arouses an individual's behavior—that is, what specific things motivate people. In other words, what does the worker need to be motivated to be productive? An analogy might help. When a machine stops functioning on a production line, the supervisor asks, "What does the machine need? Some power? Oil? Parts? An adjustment?" These questions are aimed at discovering what caused the machine to stop working. In a similar fashion, individuals need something to perform. Various researchers have provided insight by discussing the needs, drives, and incentives that cause people to behave in specific ways. For example, good working conditions, friendly supervisors and co-workers, fringe benefits, and adequate wages are rated in various studies.[3] A model of need theory that indicates its relationship to individual performance is shown in Figure 3–1.

Need theories describe what inspires individuals to perform certain activities.

This basic model shows that the worker feels a particular need that he or she wants to satisfy. If the perceived environment will satisfy that need, then the worker will be motivated to perform the task. As a final step, when the original need is satisfied, the worker may feel a new need to satisfy.

How do need theories work?

TABLE 3 – 1
Types of motivational
theories

Type	Characteristics	Theories	Managerial Examples
Need	Concerned with factors that arouse, start, or initiate motivated behavior	1. Need hierarchy 2. Two-factor	Motivation by satisfying individual needs for money, status, and recognition
Choice	Concerned not only with factors that arouse behavior, but also the process, direction, or choice of behavioral patterns	1. Expectancy 2. Equity	Motivation through clarifying the individual's perception of work inputs, performance requirements, and rewards
Reinforcement	Concerned with the factors that will increase the likelihood that desired behavior will be repeated	1. Reinforcement (operant conditioning)	Motivation by rewarding desired behavior

SOURCE: Adapted from *Organizational Behavior and Performance*, 3rd ed., p. 85, by Andrew D. Szilagyi, Jr., and Marc J. Wallace, Jr. Copyright © 1983 by Scott, Foresman and Company. Reprinted by permission.

Maslow's Need Hierarchy Theory.   The most widely recognized need theory was proposed by Abraham Maslow in 1954.[4] His list of worker's needs is conveniently short, yet it covers most of the dimensions found to be important.

Before we look at specific need levels, there are three basic assumptions to review. First, a satisfied need does *not* motivate. When a need is satisfied, another need emerges to take its place, so people are always striving to satisfy some need. Second, various needs are arranged in a hierarchy such that individuals attempt to satisfy some needs before moving on to others. Third, there are more ways to satisfy higher-level needs than lower-level needs.

Which needs are considered low level?

Lower-Level Needs.   Maslow suggests that human needs can be arranged into five levels (see Figure 3–2). He places the physiological needs first because they tend to have the greatest strength until they are somewhat satisfied. Remember the hunger attacks you have had while studying? Which wins: eating or studying?

Physiological needs food, clothing, and shelter

The physiological needs are those that sustain life itself: food, clothing, and shelter. Until these basic needs are met to some degree of comfort, most of our energy will be devoted to this level. Only when the physiological needs have been sufficiently satisfied will other levels of needs become important and provide motivation.

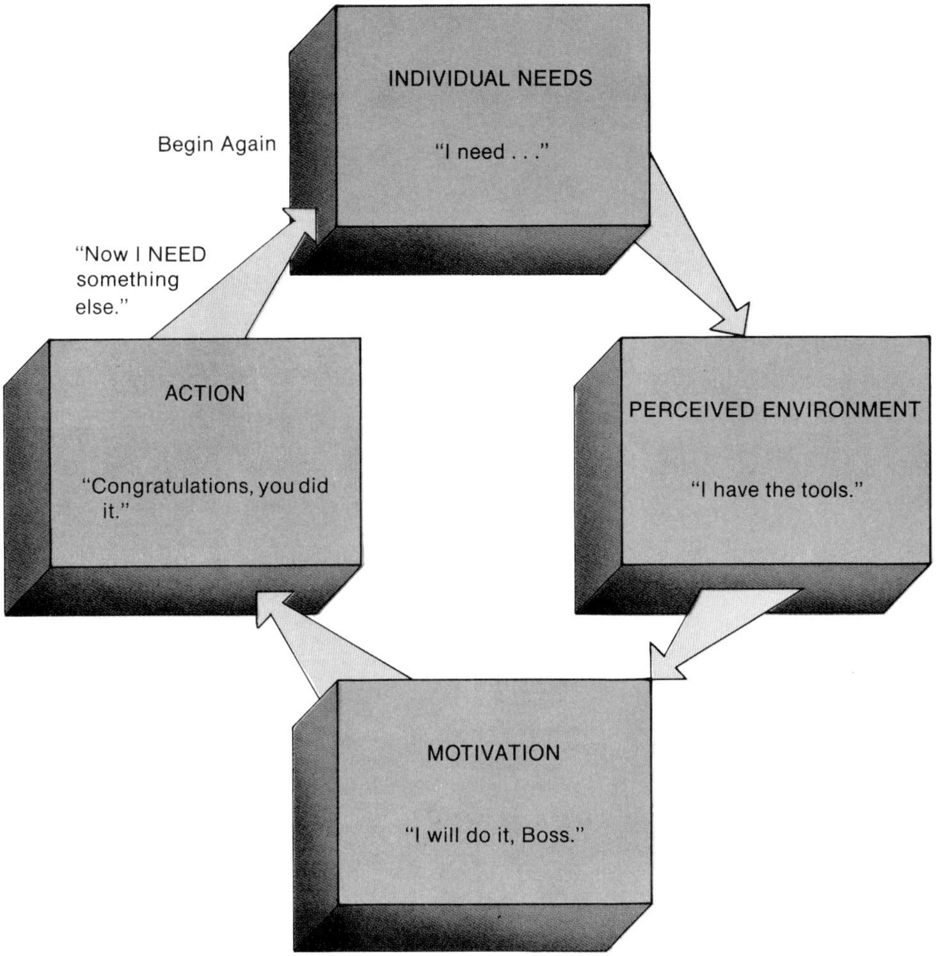

FIGURE 3 – 1
Model of need theory

Common examples of physiological needs are heating and air conditioning, basic wages, cafeteria, and other working conditions. If one of these conditions changes too drastically, for example, if the heating or air conditioning stop functioning in extreme weather conditions, an individual must expend energy to stay warm or cool. As a result this energy is not available to perform a job task.

The next level of needs—safety and security—essentially includes the needs to be free from fear of physical danger and from not meeting basic physiological needs. In other words, this need level involves self-preservation. There is a concern for the future as well as for the present. Will individuals be able to maintain their property and jobs so that they can provide for themselves and their families? This could have been part of the motivation of the Diamond employees as they saw profits decline to the point where the parent company might sell or liquidate the plant. In organizations, this need level can be satisfied by providing safe work-

Safety needs freedom from the fear of not meeting physiological needs

FIGURE 3 – 2
Maslow's five levels
of human needs

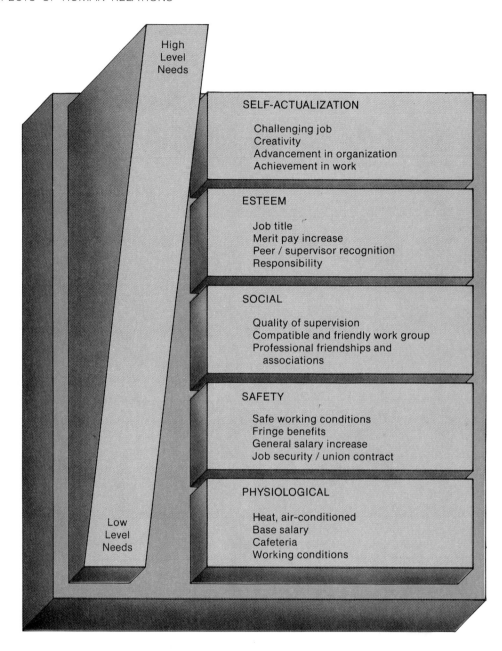

High
Level
Needs

SELF-ACTUALIZATION

Challenging job
Creativity
Advancement in organization
Achievement in work

ESTEEM

Job title
Merit pay increase
Peer / supervisor recognition
Responsibility

SOCIAL

Quality of supervision
Compatible and friendly work group
Professional friendships and
    associations

SAFETY

Safe working conditions
Fringe benefits
General salary increase
Job security / union contract

PHYSIOLOGICAL

Heat, air-conditioned
Base salary
Cafeteria
Working conditions

Low
Level
Needs

ing conditions, adequate fringe benefits, job security, and basic wages to provide day-to-day and future conveniences.

What are the higher-level needs?

Higher Level Needs. After the lower-level needs are fairly well satisfied, Maslow suggests that social or affiliation needs become important. Because people are

Social or affiliation needs can be satisfied in an organization if one has friendly supervisors and co-workers, professional associations, and friendships.

social beings, they have a need to belong and to be accepted by various groups. Do you remember when you felt that it was extremely important to belong to a certain club or group, and you were willing to do what was necessary to become a member? When social needs become dominant, a person will strive for meaningful relationships with others. As the "100 Club" became a reality, with employees beginning to wear blue jackets, we can speculate that others may have begun to see belonging to this group as desirable. Within an organization the individual can satisfy the social level through friendly supervisors and co-workers, professional associations, and friendships.

Social needs striving to belong and interact with others

After individuals begin to satisfy their need to belong, they generally want to be more than just a member of the group. They feel the need for esteem—both self-esteem and recognition and respect from others. Satisfaction of these esteem needs produces feelings of self-confidence, prestige, power, and control. Examples of how organizations can satisfy this level of need include job title, merit pay increase, peer/supervisor recognition of work performed, the type of work, and increased responsibility on the job.

Esteem needs to be valued by oneself or others who are important

Once esteem needs begin to be satisfied, the final higher-level need—self-actualization—becomes important. Self-actualization is the need to maximize

Self-actualization needs to become the best that a person can be; using one's potential to the fullest

one's potential. A welder must weld metal to the best of his ability, a manager must manage people to the best of her ability, and a student must learn as much as possible about a subject. Self-actualization is found organizationally when an individual can have a challenging job, use creativity, advance in the profession or job, and reach some work-related achievement.

Maslow's levels of needs have a commonsense appeal that has gained them wide acceptance. Yet, for such a widely accepted view of needs, Maslow's theory has received little research support. One study showed differences in need levels

FIGURE 3 – 3
Comparisons of satisfiers and dissatisfiers and their effects on job attitudes. (Source: Reprinted by permission of the *Harvard Business Review.* Frederick Herzberg, "One More Time: How Do You Motivate Employees?" (January–February 1967): 57. Copyright © 1957 by the President and Fellows of Harvard College; all rights reserved.)

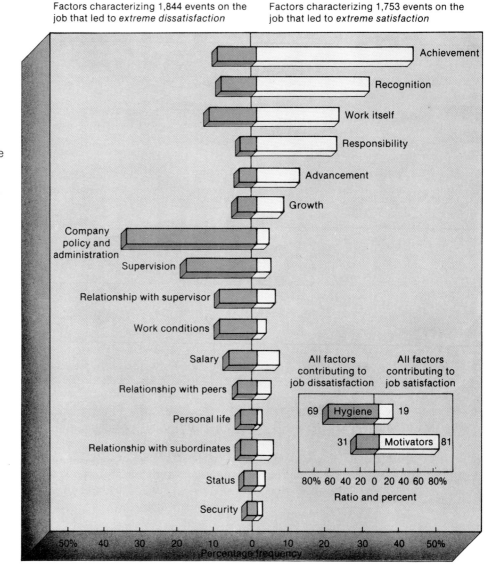

Factors characterizing 1,844 events on the job that led to *extreme dissatisfaction*

Factors characterizing 1,753 events on the job that led to *extreme satisfaction*

between managers in smaller and larger firms.[5] For instance, managers in larger firms placed less emphasis on safety and security needs and more importance on higher-level needs than did managers in smaller firms. This conclusion may be partially explained by assuming that there is more security in a larger organization than in a smaller, less-established firm. How else might you explain this difference?

Herzberg's Two-Factor Theory. Another popular view of human needs that has had a major influence on managerial practice is Frederick Herzberg's Two-Factor Theory.[6] This theory was derived from stories told by people in engineering and accounting professions. These individuals described times on their jobs when they were happy and times when they were unhappy. By studying these stories Herzberg interpreted the existence of two types of needs in the workplace: *hygiene* or *dissatisfiers* and *motivators* or *satisfiers*. The specific conditions that make up these two types of needs and that influence worker's feelings about their jobs are presented in Figure 3–3.

Hygiene factors are those that provide comfort and avoid pain in the workplace, such as the type of supervisor, fringe benefits, company policies, salary, and working conditions. In general, hygiene factors prevent employees from being dissatisfied or unhappy in their jobs. ~~prevent employees~~

Motivation factors meet the needs of employees to use their talents and to grow in their jobs. These factors include recognition, responsibility, advancement, personal growth, and the nature of the job itself. Herzberg considers achievement to be the most important motivator. Motivators make people satisfied with their jobs and may improve their job performance. *meet needs of employees*

Are there any exceptions to Maslow's five levels of needs?

How did Herzberg develop his Two-Factor Theory?

Hygiene factors are geared toward providing comfort and avoiding pain in the workplace.

Motivation factors help employees to use their talents and grow in their jobs.

Opening Story Revisited

The opening story clearly shows that workers were energized to improve productivity. We can imagine that they must have received some direction because errors were reduced and accidents were down. We can also assume that the program was sustained to allow the workers to accumulate enough points to get jackets and gifts and for the firm to earn $1 million.

If we use Maslow's theory we can see that the threat of competition was aimed at the worker's safety level of needs. The patch and jacket could explain the social level and the need to belong. The letters sent to the employees' homes could be a form of recognition.

What about using Herzberg's theory? The letter is a form of recognition and therefore a motivating factor. What about the jacket with the patch? Is it merely a fringe benefit or does it have a more significant meaning of recognition? It is hard to say with any certainty, but it could be a motivator. All the employees have one so it must be important to them. How would you classify these awards?

How to Really Motivate Your Employees!

In the 1970s, Arthur Friedman ran an appliance store in Oakland, California, with his brother Morris. To say that Friedman's approach to employee motivation is unusual is to understate. Consider that Friedman's fifteen employees could set their own wages, determine their own work hours, determine vacation time and schedule, select their own work tasks, and take money from the cash drawer. Friedman did not "phase" the plan in or prepare his employees in any way for the change. He simply announced the new plan at a staff meeting, with immediate implementation.

The idea for the unusual scheme came from Arthur Friedman's approach to his own life. On weekends he taught seminars on such subjects as communication, sensuality, and hexing. The seminars all dealt with trusting other people to be responsible in their behavior. It occurred to Mr. Friedman that he was teaching one thing on the weekend but practicing something different in his business. He concluded that his employees should be made entirely responsible for decisions about their employment.

The initial reaction to the plan was stunned silence. By Friedman's own account, he had to chase the employees down one by one at the end of the first month and demand that they tell him what they wanted to be paid. Most of the employees said that they wanted to be paid what the other employees were being paid, but Friedman forced them to name a figure. None of the employees took an increase in pay, and one serviceman actually settled on a *lower* pay scale since he did not want to work as hard as the other repairman. Friedman also extended his novel plan to part-time and occasional workers.

No employees changed work hours or vacation time. Friedman encouraged employees to take extra time off if they were not feeling well, or even if they didn't feel like working. Without exception, the employees refused to take the extra time off. Friedman insisted that all employees belong to the union, primarily because of the union health and welfare plans. He also insisted that all employees take at least the union scale wages.

Once the plan was well under way, Friedman reported that employee morale was higher and employees had a better understanding of the way the business worked, as well as a new appreciation of an employer's problems. Although sales levels stayed about the same, net profit increased each year, despite inflation, indicating that productivity and efficiency also increased.

What's more, Friedman extended his approach to customers: if bills were not paid, he wrote to the customer saying that the bill would be cancelled if it were not paid! If no payment was forthcoming the bill *was* cancelled, and the customer was asked to write a letter explaining why he or she chose not to pay. The number of delinquent accounts did not increase, and the store no longer had a need for a collection agency.

QUESTIONS

1. Use Herzberg's Two-Factor theory to explain the success in this case.
2. Can Maslow's need theory explain some of the changes in this story?
3. Would Friedman's approach work in a larger organization?

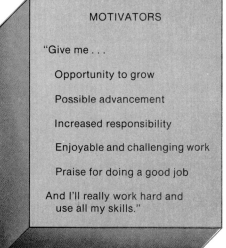

FIGURE 3 – 4
Satisfaction/dissatisfaction relationship

How are these two sets of factors, hygiene and motivation, related? According to Herzberg, the factors leading to job satisfaction are separate and distinct from those that lead to job dissatisfaction (see Figure 3–4). Therefore, managers who seek to eliminate job dissatisfaction can hope only to establish some equilibrium but not to create an environment that motivates employees to use their full potentials. In other words, managers are pacifying their work force, not motivating them. These hygiene factors are *external* to the worker and therefore are *extrinsically* rewarding. To motivate employees, Herzberg suggests emphasizing achievement, recognition, and growth in the job. People find these factors *inwardly (intrinsically)* rewarding and, therefore, will be motivated to use their full range of skills and talents.

Which set of factors does the Diamond "100 Club" represent? Is the gift a fringe benefit or compensation? How do you explain Boyle's comment about the employees who caused problems getting recognition and not being motivated? Questions like these have raised criticism of Herzberg's theory.

One criticism centers on research showing that a given factor, such as pay, may cause satisfaction in one situation and dissatisfaction in another.[7] Other criticism concerns the lack of testing of the direct effect of these factors on worker performance.[8] This merely means that Herzberg was looking at employee satisfaction and not performance. He assumed that these factors were related to perfor-

How are hygiene and motivator factors related?

Motivators: Intrinsic
Hygiene: Extrinsic

What criticism exists concerning the Two-Factor Theory?

mance. While the theory is still criticized by academicians, many business organizations have used the theory as a basis for job redesign.

Choice Theories

Choice theory focuses on the internal decision that an individual makes about how to behave.

In contrast to need theories, "choice" theories focus on the internal decision that an individual makes about a particular work behavior—"Will I finish the extra paperwork today before I go home, or will I relax and start on the paperwork the first thing in the morning?" The matter of choice is central to these theories.

Equity Theory. To understand the equity theory, let us look at the following situation. John Carlson has been working at drafting for Graphics Inc. since he graduated from technical school last year. He was at the top of his class and received $1,100 a month starting salary. He has been ambitious and has proven to be capable with his job responsibilities. His employer, after a year, was extremely pleased with John's performance and gave John a raise of $100 per month. Since the raise, John's attitude seems to have changed and his performance is down considerably. Why? John's employer has just hired another technical school graduate from John's alma mater to perform the same type of job at $1,250 a month—$50 more than John now makes.

How does the equity theory work?

This brief story illustrates the role the equity theory plays in motivation. Equity can mean several things; we use it here as the equivalent of such words as fairness and justice. Individuals in organizations want fair treatment, not only for themselves but for others as well. This is not saying that all people should be treated equally. Pure equality would not take into account various levels of contribution to productivity and other factors that may enter into compensation decisions.

The equity theory involves a social comparison of existing conditions against some standard.[9] The most common example of this is when we compare ourselves with other people and make judgments about the equity or inequity of our present situations. The equity theory uses the relationship between two factors: inputs and outcomes. Inputs represent what an individual gives or contributes to an exchange; outcomes are what an individual receives from the exchange. Table 3–2 presents some typical inputs and outcomes.

How do we use equity theory from the individual's perspective? Each person assigns a value to the inputs and outcomes in the job. This value is based on relative importance of that particular item in the present situation, such as rating a salary increase very high because of buying a new house. As a result of this valuing, three possible conclusions for the person are: (1) there is equity; (2) there is positive inequity; or (3) there is negative inequity. Each conclusion is a personal view and may not be shared by another looking at the same inputs and outcomes. The reason for these differences is the concept of perception covered in Chapter 2. A positive inequity exists when the individual feels that he or she has received more than others in the exchange. A negative inequity occurs when the individual feels that he or she has received less than others.

What are positive and negative inequity? Are the results of both the same?

Inputs	Outcomes
Attendance	Pay
Age	Promotion
Level of education	Challenging job assignments
Past experience	Fringe benefits
Ability	Working conditions
Social status	Status symbols
Job effort (long hours, physical exertion)	Job perquisites (office location, parking space)
Personality traits	Job security
Seniority	Responsibility
Performance	

TABLE 3 – 2
Possible inputs and outcomes regarding jobs

SOURCE: Adapted from D. Belchner and T. Atchinson, "Equity Theory and Compensation Policy," *Personnel Administrator,* vol. 33, no. 3, (1970): 28. Copyright © 1970, The American Society for Personnel Administration, 606 North Washington Street, Alexandria, VA 22314

How do we apply the equity theory to John's situation? Does he view his condition as equitable or inequitable? Figure 3–5 shows the possible inequity to which John is responding. As John views the situation, he may feel that his year of experience is worth more than a new employee with no experience, yet this new employee is receiving $50 a month more. If both were hired at the same time and the other employee was receiving $50 a month more, John could rationalize the difference as a result of performance and thus justify it.

John		New Hire
Job duties	=	Job duties
Technical School	=	Technical School
Experience (1 year)	>	Experience (None)
Salary ($1,200 a month)	<	Salary ($1,250 a month)
Person 1: Outcomes (Pay, status)	? = ?	Person 2: Outcomes (Pay, status)
Input (Job duties)		Input (Job duties)
John: $1,200	<	New Hire: $1,250
Degree + 1 year experience		Degree + no experience

FIGURE 3 – 5
John's view of his situation according to the equity theory

Both positive and negative inequity have motivational consequences because individuals wish to restore a sense of equity. To accomplish this, an individual may engage in any one of the following:[10]

1. Change work input (reduce or increase amount of work performed)
2. Change rewards received (seek recognition from the supervisor for work done if there is no pay increase)
3. Leave the situation (leave job or ask for a transfer)
4. Change the comparison points (reevaluate the worth of the inputs and outcomes)
5. Psychologically distort the comparison (rationalize that the boss doesn't know quality work)

How easy is it to apply the equity theory?

The consequences of managing under the equity theory are fairly clear, yet it is difficult to implement. The mental game of comparing inputs and outcomes with other situations is easily understood by the manager and the employee. The real difficulty is due to the feelings of equity or inequity determined by each party. The manager must not assume that his or her view of the equity will be the same as the employee's.

What should a manager do? The key word in this case is "anticipation." Anticipate employees' viewing the situation from a negative inequity position. Carefully communicate to each individual the evaluation of the reward, the appraisal of the performance upon which it is based, and any comparison points used to make the decision.

Most research of the equity theory has centered on pay levels as the outcome and performance as the input.[11] In addition, the studies tend to look at the issue of underpayment rather than overpayment. Underpayment (negative inequity) seems to lead to absenteeism and turnover.[12] But, remember, overreliance on pay as the key motivator of employee performance isn't consistent with recent trends and the other theories of motivation (see Chapter 1).

Expectancy Theory. Victor Vroom developed another theory based on expectancy.[13] This theory also is based on worker choice. The theory argues that motivation is determined by an individual's beliefs in his or her own efforts, the resulting job accomplishments, and finally the rewards or incentives offered for the job accomplishments. Simply put, the theory is based on the logic that people will do what they can do when they want to do it.[14]

What assumptions underlie the expectancy theory?

We can make certain assumptions to help explain how the expectancy theory works. First, it is assumed that an individual's behavior is voluntary. This simply means that an individual, after considering the options available, can choose between one behavior and another. Second, the theory assumes that people will choose in a rational manner that allows them to gain in a positive way from the situation. In other words, they will try to behave in ways that contribute to their own well-being, either financially or psychologically. Figure 3–6, as well as the following discussion of incentives, expectancy, and valence, should help us understand this theory.

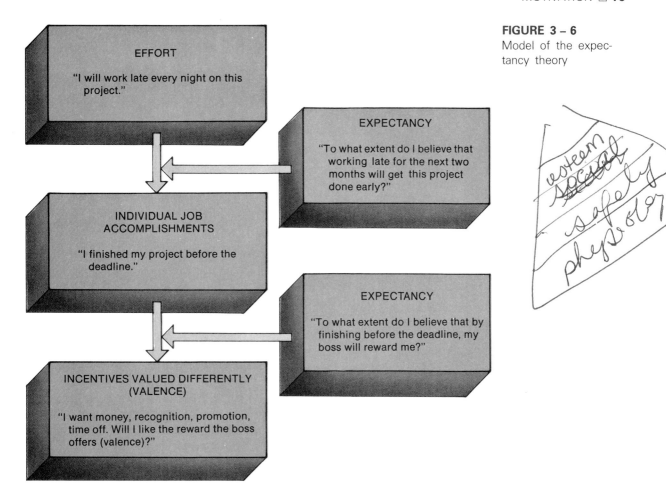

FIGURE 3 – 6
Model of the expectancy theory

Individual job accomplishments are the direct result of expending some effort on the job task—in other words, some level of performance. The performance can be more units per hour, fewer errors on paperwork, or as in the figure, working more hours. Incentives are rewards for meeting performance, such as a raise, a promotion, leaving early, recognition from a supervisor, or simply a good feeling about job performance.

Expectancy affects two parts of the model in Figure 3–6. The first connection is between effort and job accomplishment. Here expectancy is the degree of belief that an individual effort will result in accomplishing the task. Specifically, this means a self-assessment by the worker about whether he or she can actually do the assigned work. This is an important assessment because a lack of self-confidence (especially in a new employee) will result in little or no effort. The theory uses a scale of 0 to 1 to signify the level of belief. For example, a worker can feel certain that working late for the next two months will result in getting the job done before the deadline. This would result in a rating of 1. On the other

Incentives the rewards, both tangible and intangible, for acting in a certain way

Expectancy the degree of personal belief an individual has about how actions are connected

Can a Bonus Be Seen as a Punishment?

Penn Manor School District in Millersville, Pennsylvania, adopted a merit pay plan for its teachers and, at the end of a recent school year, paid $1,000 bonuses to twenty-five of its 233 teachers. District salaries average about $20,000 per year.

The bonus recipients were naturally pleased to get the awards, but some were skeptical of the overall value of the program. Teachers who competed for bonuses and did not win were even more skeptical. Many teachers failed to qualify for a bonus, even though their principals regarded them as worthy of it. One high school, for example, was allotted only ten awards to distribute among ninety-four teachers. Some of the teachers who did not receive awards regarded this failure as personal rejections. No one seemed to know what the precise criteria for selection were. Some school administrators advised losers to sit in on bonus winners' classes, presumably to learn desirable techniques and behaviors.

School administrators could not state what the criteria for selection were. "As a department head, I can't tell my teachers, 'This is what you

can do to get a merit payment next year,' " says the head of one high school's science department. Indeed, the unwillingness or inability of school boards to invest sufficient money in merit pay has contributed to the failure of some such programs, studies show.

The president of the Penn Manor school board isn't certain what the district is getting for its money. It wanted to motivate teachers toward excellence. The teachers' union feels that the program is doomed. The head of the union feels that the problem of motivation is due more to the underpayment of all teachers, which must be addressed before any bonus program can work. The union head feels that the bonus program should be restructured into smaller awards, saying, "Meritorious people should all get the same thing, even if it's only one dollar."

QUESTIONS

1. What were some of the key problems with this motivational plan?
2. Is there any way to salvage the program? How would you accomplish this?
3. Can you use the equity theory to explain some of the events in this story?
4. Use the expectancy theory to describe why some of the rewards did not work to motivate the teachers.

Source: Adapted from Burt Schorr, "School's Merit-Pay Program Draws Gripes From Losers—and Winners," *The Wall Street Journal* (16 June 1983): 31. Reprinted by permission of *The Wall Street Journal,* ©Dow Jones & Company, Inc., 1983. All Rights Reserved.

hand, the worker could feel that no matter how many nights or weekends he or she works late, the work will not be completed on time which would rate a 0.

The second connection, that between job accomplishment and incentives, is also affected by expectancy. Using the same scale of 0 to 1, the worker rates whether he or she believes that finishing ahead of schedule will (1 on scale) or will not (0 on the scale) result in some form of incentive from the boss.

The model does not stop here. The theory says that the worker will do one more mental calculation before choosing to perform. This is simply placing a value (the term *valence* is used in the formal theory) on the incentive being offered by management. Higher value is placed on incentives that are preferred by the worker. These values can range from 0 to 1 and are termed positive values. In a similar fashion, values can be viewed as negative by the worker and range from 0 to −1. Positive values are generally attached to pay increases, recognition, and promotions. Certain incentives may even be viewed as negative by one worker and positive by another. For example, a promotion bringing a relocation to another part of the country may be viewed as negative or positive depending on the worker's viewpoint. Also, a supervisory reprimand may be a negative value for most individuals but a positive value for one seeking attention in any form.

Valence placing worth or value on an outcome

Are all incentives viewed equally by employees?

The importance of this model is its thoroughness. It shows how the motivation of individuals can be sidetracked at various points. Adequate incentives do not guarantee that the worker will be motivated. Problems occur because a worker doesn't think that the extra effort will lead to accomplishing the task. No amount of incentives will help the employee who lacks self-confidence. Futhermore, the concept of valuing helps the manager face the issue that what is important to the manager as an incentive may not be important to the worker.

The concept of expectancy suggests some managerial guidelines. Managers can positively influence employees' motivation by doing the following: First, identify the type and amount of behavior that will be used to judge "good job accomplishment." For example, the manager may spell out that having only two errors per week on certain paperwork and turning in all paperwork within 30 minutes of when it is due will be judged as "good job accomplishment." Second, be certain that the employee has the appropriate skills and knows how to use them. This can be accomplished by asking employees how comfortable they are with handling the job requirements. If there is any indication of apprehension, the manager should provide the needed training. Finally, the manager needs to make incentives contingent on specific job accomplishments and communicate that information. For example, the supervisor might give an employee time off for paperwork with only two errors that is turned in on time.

How would a manager use the expectancy theory to motivate employees?

Goal-Setting Theory.

Like the expectancy theory, goal setting offers another way to energize and direct an employee's effort toward desirable results. A simplified view of this theory is shown in Figure 3–7. This theory is based on the belief that individuals have desires and dreams that result from setting a goal. The goal then directs behavior. Accomplishing the goal can lead to satisfaction and further motivation. Not accomplishing the goal can lead to frustration and low motivation.

What is the basis of the goal-setting theory?

Consider the following example. An employee values a challenge as well as new tasks. The supervisor proposes that the work unit has been missing some critical dates. The interested employee volunteers to conduct a systematic study to prevent this in the future by identifying the causes of past missed dates. The goal is to complete the study and report to the supervisor. Finishing the report becomes the outcome that reinforces the individual to accept future challenges.

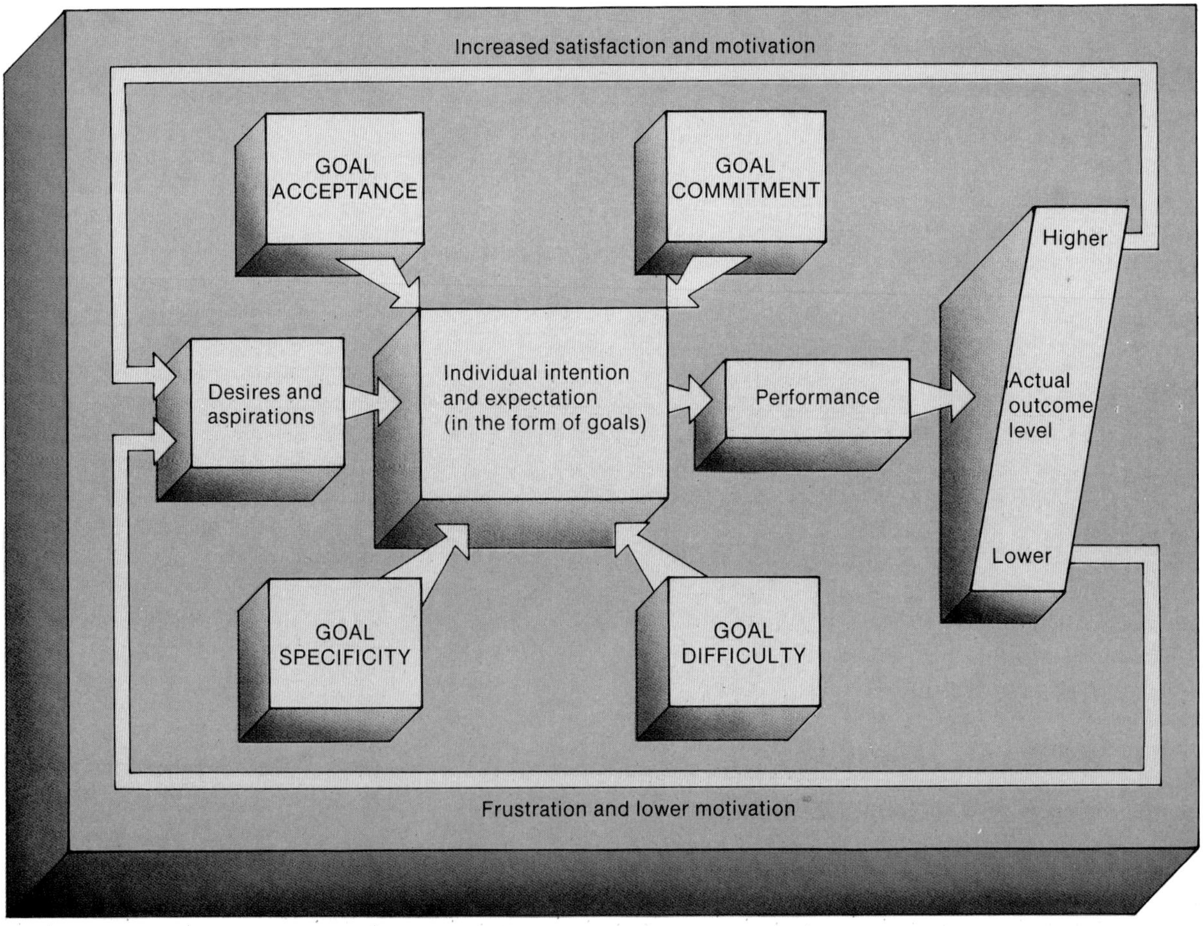

FIGURE 3 – 7
Model of goal-setting theory

Four key aspects help us understand the goal-setting theory and how to apply it.

1. *Goal Difficulty.* There appears to be a direct relationship between goal difficulty and task performance.[15] In fact, the higher the difficulty of the goal, the higher the resulting performance.

2. *Goal Specificity.* It has also been found that specific goals lead to higher performance than general goals.[16] Rather than setting a general goal, such as "I'll do better this term," one might set a more specific goal, such as "I'll read each assignment twice before the test."

3. *Goal Acceptance.* Goal acceptance is the degree to which the employee accepts the goal. To accomplish this, the employee first must perceive some personal benefit from accomplishing the goal—perhaps recognition, a promotion, or

compensation. The employee must feel capable of reaching the goal and must have the knowledge and ability to work on the goal.[17]

4. *Goal Commitment.* Goal commitment is the degree to which the employee is dedicated to accomplishing the accepted goal. Because commitment can change over time, a manager must remain sensitive to the worker's progress. If difficulty arises, the worker may lose commitment. The manager must give encouragement and support when this happens.

Many studies have attempted to measure the effects of goal setting on employee performance. One such study done in the wood-products industry is typical.[18] The workers were independent logger crews who felled trees for a large organization. These workers could work one day a week or a full week—it was their choice. Several problems were identified: The workers were marginal in terms of productivity and attendance, and their safety record was very poor.

Twenty groups of loggers were found who were equal in the amount of physical equipment, terrain on which they worked, productivity, and attendance/safety records. Half of the groups were randomly selected to receive training in goal setting while the other ten groups were used for comparison and were given no training. The trained groups received production tables that helped them determine how much wood could be cut in a given number of hours. With this

Describe the research used to study goal setting in a logging industry.

Logging groups that set specific production goals had higher productivity, lower absenteeism, lower turnover, and fewer injuries.

guide they set specific production goals. In addition, each logger received a counter to wear on his belt to record each time he felled a tree. The other ten groups were simply urged to do their best without any of this support. The groups setting specific production goals had significantly higher productivity, lower absenteeism, lower turnover, and fewer injuries than the groups not setting any goals.

Cutting timber can be a monotonous, tiring job with little or no meaning for most workers. Introducing a goal that is difficult but attainable increases the challenge of the job. It becomes less monotonous. Specific goals also make it clear to the worker what is expected. The goal feedback from the counter and the weekly record-keeping provide the worker with a sense of achievement, recognition, and accomplishment. What other types of jobs could benefit from this simple technique?

Reinforcement Theory

Reinforcement theory focuses on the environment of the individual.

So far we have discussed motivation from the perspective of need and choice, which explains and predicts behavior by considering an individual's "internal" motivations. In contrast, the reinforcement theory avoids looking inside the person or trying to examine the thought processes, but instead focuses on the environment or surroundings. These environmental conditions have consequences for the individual that are the stimulus for individual action or behavior.

How does the reinforcement theory compare to the need or choice theory?

Consider the following situation. While walking down a street a person finds a $5 bill. Thereafter, this person is seen spending more time looking down when out walking.[19] Why is this? The need or choice theories would suggest that this person looks down because of a high value placed on money and the belief

Opening Story Revisited

I t is difficult to use the equity theory to explain the Diamond company's motivation program because the equity theory asks questions about how the situation is perceived from the individual's point of view. We do not have any data about individual perceptions.

We can partially explain what happened using the expectancy theory. The individual job accomplishments were no job accidents and 100 percent attendance. On attaining these, the individual worker would receive points and awards based on points. If the company had not given the rewards as promised, the expectancy would have dropped to zero and the workers would have gone back to their old behavior.

Using the goal-setting theory, the goal specificity is "no accidents" and "100 percent attendance." The goal difficulty was reasonable for the workers. Goal acceptance existed because there were some clearly identifiable rewards for accomplishment—jackets, letters of recognition, and other awards.

that more money may be found by looking down. The individual makes a conscious decision and we as outsiders see the result—looking down.

The reinforcement theory gives a different explanation. When the initial behavior of looking down occurred, it was reinforced by the presence of a $5 bill. Having once been reinforced by this environmental condition (called a consequence), the finding of $5, the behavior is more likely to occur automatically in the future. That is, the behavior is not a conscious decision but has merely been reinforced by the environment. The behavior will continue until another environmental condition (for example, walking into a pole) causes another behavior.

To understand the reinforcement theory we will discuss operant conditioning and types of reinforcement. In addition, we will look at an application of the reinforcement theory called behavior modification.

Operant Conditioning.   Operant conditioning simply means that behavior is a function/result of its own consequences. Individuals learn to behave so they get something they want or avoid something they don't want. Behavior is assumed to be determined from the environment—that is, learned—rather than from within—reflexive or unlearned. If pleasing consequences are created to follow desired forms of behavior, the frequency of that behavior will increase. Individuals will engage in desired behaviors if they are positively reinforced for doing so. For example, if you receive a ''thank you'' for helping a stranger find an address, would you consider helping others? Most of us would probably respond ''yes.'' Rewards, or positive reinforcement, are most effective if they *immediately* follow the desired response. Likewise, behavior that is not rewarded, or is punished, is less likely to be repeated.

> Operant conditioning means that behavior is a function or result of its own consequences.

> Describe how positive reinforcement works.

Types of Reinforcement.   When we use reinforcement to obtain some desired behavior, we are shaping behavior. Suppose an employee's behavior is considered inappropriate by the supervisor, such as taking twice the allowed time for lunch or always being a half-hour late to work. If the supervisor reinforced the individual only when he or she happened to show the desired time orientation, there may be little to reinforce. As a result, the supervisor may apply shaping for better and more timely results.

> How would you use shaping in an organization?

But how do we use shaping to correct the employee who takes one hour for lunch instead of a half-hour? Behavior is shaped by reinforcing each successive step that moves the individual closer to the desired response. If the employee returns after only 50 minutes for lunch, reinforce this improvement by recognition or praise. Continue to recognize each successive step toward the 30-minute lunch. Obviously, this is management by patience.

The three ways to reinforce behavior or to shape behavior are: positive reinforcement, negative reinforcement, and punishment.

Positive reinforcement occurs when a desired behavior is followed by something pleasant, such as when the supervisor praises an employee for a job well done. *Negative reinforcement* is when a desired behavior is followed by the termination or withdrawal of something unpleasant. For example if your classroom instructor asks a question you don't know the answer to, looking through your

> Positive reinforcement occurs when a desired behavior is followed by something pleasant.

> Negative reinforcement occurs when a desired behavior is followed by the withdrawal of something unpleasant.

Punishment is producing an unpleasant condition to eliminate an undesirable behavior.

lecture notes is likely to keep you from being called upon. *Punishment* is producing an unpleasant condition in an attempt to eliminate an undesirable behavior. An employee who receives a disciplinary letter because of poor-quality work has received a form of punishment.

Behavior modification the application of operant conditioning to worker behavior in a planned manner

Behavior Modification.   Behavior modification is the application of operant conditioning to worker behavior in a planned manner. The following production case of a medium-sized industrial plant engaged in light manufacturing illustrates the application of behavior modification.[20]

The plant manager felt the need to increase the plant's performance while maintaining employee morale. Two groups of nine first-level production supervisors participated. One group underwent training in behavior modification while the other group did not. The plant manager described both groups of supervisors as having gone through the "school of hard knocks" to reach their present position in the organization.

What are the major steps in a behavior modification program?

As shown in Figure 3–8, there are five major steps to behavior modification:

1. *Identify the goals and target behaviors of the program.* The plant manager and the production supervisors described and carefully identified the changes they wished to make. In this situation, the supervisors of the work groups were trained to identify behaviors for which reinforcements would be used.
2. *Measure target behaviors.* To provide a baseline for future comparison, the frequency of the desired target behavior is measured or counted. In the production case, work-assignment completions, absences, rejects, quality-control problems, complaints, excessive breaks, leaving work areas, and scrap rates were selected for use.
3. *Analyze the antecedents and consequences of the behaviors.* The behavior to be changed is often influenced by what happens just prior to it (antecedents) and

FIGURE 3 – 8
Major steps in behavior modification

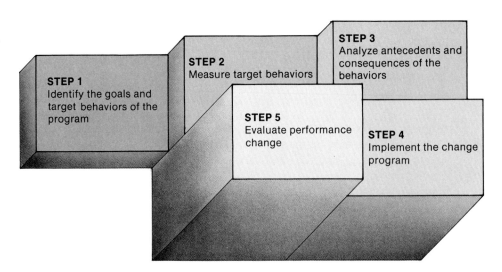

Ignoring complaints but listening to constructive suggestions can serve as positive reinforcement to change the behavior of a chronically complaining worker.

what results from the behavior (consequences). The supervisor decided to study and use antecedents and consequences for a particularly disruptive machine operator. The machine operator often complained bitterly about the production standards to the supervisor (antecedent). In addition, the worker adversely affected the production of co-workers by complaining. In analyzing the situation, the supervisor concluded that paying attention to the complaints was probably serving as a reinforcing consequence. Some people seek attention by complaining.

4. *Implement the change program.* Positive reinforcement, negative reinforcement, or punishment can be used to change behavior. In the production case, supervisors decided to use positive reinforcement by thanking or praising workers for their performance. In the situation with the disruptive employee, the supervisor ignored the complaints but listened attentively to constructive ideas for improvement.

5. *Evaluate performance change.* In the production case, the baseline was compared to the present situation. After six months, the trained group and the untrained group were compared. The overall performance of the trained group had significantly improved—complaints were fewer, scrap rates had decreased, errors had been reduced, and rejects had declined.

LEARNING SUMMARY

1. The need theories, choice theories, and reinforcement theory of motivation are aimed at energizing, directing, and sustaining individual behavior. Need theories are concerned with what arouses behavior. Choice theories focus on the decision individuals make as they choose whether to perform a task. The reinforcement theory centers on the environment of the individual rather than on the internal dynamics.

2. Maslow's theory is based on the concept of partial satisfaction of one need level before moving to a higher need level.

3. Herzberg theorizes that two distinct factors influence motivation—hygiene, which prevents dissatisfaction, and motivators, which are the real source of satisfaction and positive motivation.

4. The equity theory shows how individuals may balance what they put into the job with what they get out of doing the job—incentives—and then compare this ratio with what others give and get out of their jobs.

5. The expectancy theory views motivation as a relationship between the individual's efforts and the associated accomplishments that are rewarded.

6. The goal-setting theory involves matching employee desires with acceptable goals. Selecting difficult but specific goals is more motivating than setting goals that are too easy.

7. Reinforcement theory is not concerned with the internal conditions of the employee, but rather attempts to structure the environment through various reinforcements.

ANSWERS TO "WHAT'S YOUR OPINION?"

1. False   Money is not the most important motivator for today's workers. Using Herzberg's theory, money is only a hygiene factor. Many times money is a symbol for something else the worker really wants. For example, money pays for a new car that means prestige in the eyes of the worker's friends.

2. True   Maslow's theory allows us to visualize some of the internal drives or needs people are trying to satisfy.

3. True   This is the conclusion of Herzberg's theory of dissatisfiers and satisfiers.

4. True   This is the equity view of motivation, a comparison of inputs and outcomes by employees.

5. True   The expectancy theory would call this aspect the value of the reward to an individual. Some people would value a promotion because it may mean a move to a new part of the country; others may view this negatively because they do not want to move away from friends and family.

6. False   Research shows that the mere existence of goals, whether realistic or not, is a motivation for individuals.

7. True   The environment provides a set of reinforcements that can be positive or negative for individuals.

8. False   Feedback and reinforcement should occur as soon as possible after the worker's behavior has occurred for maximum effect.

Behavior modification	Motivation factors
Choice theory	Need theory
Equity theory	Negative reinforcement
Esteem needs	Operant conditioning
Expectancy theory	Physiological needs
Extrinsic rewards	Positive reinforcement
Goal acceptance	Punishment
Goal commitment	Reinforcement theory
Goal difficulty	Safety needs
Goal setting theory	Self-actualization
Goal specificity	Social needs
Hygiene factors	Valence
Intrinsic rewards	

HUMAN RELATIONS APPLICATIONS

The motivational theories we have been dealing with thus far make a great deal of common sense. But what happens when these theories are applied in the real world? As a manager faced with the bottom-line responsibilities, how do you decide which motivational theory to use? How much time do you have to review theoretical procedures when pressure is great and action is required? In this section of the chapter, we deal with some of these practical issues, referring to information taken from the popular press and examples from organizations. We will look at one motivator that has caused considerable debate—money. We will explore what happens when workers become the owners of the organization.

Money as a Motivator

Let's look at the issue of financial reward as a motivating force. Some theories indicate that money does not rank high on a list of motivating factors, but consider the case of Lincoln Electric.[21]

The Lincoln Electric Company of Cleveland, Ohio, is well known for its innovations in employee motivation. The company relies heavily on incentives at all levels of the organization. The basic pay system for the 2,000-plus employees is piecework with performance bonuses. It is not uncommon for the bonuses to exceed regular pay. In mid-1983, the demand for Lincoln's products was down and the workers were on the job only thirty hours a week. Even with the reduced work week, workers would average $30,000 to $35,000 for the year. In 1981, a good year, employees averaged $45,000, including the bonus. Compare this with the average manufacturing wage of $18,000.

How does the company do it? Each employee is responsible for the quality of his or her work. Careful reports are kept on who works on each piece of equipment; defects that get past the worker, to be discovered by quality control or customers, result in a lower merit rating, bonus, and pay.

The employees naturally are fond of high wages, but there is a price that goes with the good pay—hard work. Older workers sometimes want to move to a job with no piecework. Since the company has no seniority system, each employee must compete on a merit basis with all other employees who want the new job.

Each department is allotted a specific number of merit points; thus a very high rating for one person may result in an unhealthy form of competition. Still, turnover is less than 4 percent per year.

Which theory would help to explain Lincoln's success? The reinforcement theory might explain the piecework and quality aspects. Quality reports for the employee can be a form of negative reinforcement or punishment. If the quality reports are eliminated after the employee has had no rejects for a period of time, we could say that these reports are negative reinforcement. On the other hand, if the supervisor presents the report to the employee after a reject or problem, it is considered a form of punishment.

Can you apply the goal setting theory to explain some of Lincoln's success? If you see the workers setting small but increasingly higher levels of production and decreasingly lower levels of rejects, then goal setting is in operation. However, this would have to be a conscious effort supported by the supervisor on a regular basis, such as monthly. The goal specificity would be relatively easy to establish.

Returning to the question of money as a key motivator, this case helps us put financial rewards in a proper perspective. Money is important when it is tied to clear performance measures. But Lincoln does have other forms of feedback that support individual motivation, including quality reports and continual feedback about merit points by the supervisor. We can see that multiple feedback for the worker allows many levels of needs to be met, including financial.

Do Worker/Owners Perform Better?

Another issue that often arises in a discussion about motivation concerns whether individuals have a real interest in a situation. If an employee has a "piece of the action," does that mean more commitment and involvement in the success of the organization? Let's look at what happened in a couple of organizations in which the employees are also owners.

The Great Atlantic & Pacific Tea Company closed all of its stores in the Philadelphia area. The local food workers' union helped twenty-four employees buy one of the stores.[22] Each employee invested $5,000 in the venture, and they opened what is probably the first employee owned and operated supermarket in the country.

Some problems existed initially because of inexperience. Because the new owners did not know how to order goods, the store was frequently overstocked at first. Substitution of wholesale prices for retail prices in an advertisement cost the store money. Becoming managers as well as workers caused problems, too. The owners hired sixteen additional workers but had to lay off two of them during a sales slump. Learning to delegate authority has not been easy, nor has handling union contract talks as the owners are still union members. The owners do not pay themselves when they work longer hours.

Yet, the store has been a success with sales averaging 40 percent higher than other A&P stores. There is a spirit of cooperation and support, with the owners performing tasks throughout the store rather than only within their own departments. Shoplifting and employee pilferage is running at about 17 percent of the usual rate for supermarkets. The union has set up another worker/owner store and is interested in developing others.

Another method of employee ownership is stock ownership. However, most people would agree that this form of ownership does not create the same feeling of involvement and decision making experienced by these former A&P employees. Yet a small airline headquartered in Phoenix, Arizona, seems to have at least partly overcome the lack of ownership felt by most employee-stockholders.[23]

Employees of American West Airlines are required to own company shares equal to 20 percent of their starting salary. The company finances the purchase at reduced prices through a payroll deduction plan. A profit-sharing plan distributes 15 percent of any net earnings to the employee shareholders. Employees currently own only about 6 percent of the company's stock. Base pay for the company's employees is considerably lower than the industry average. Pilots, for example, are paid $32,500 per year, contrasted with an industry average of more than $75,000. Customer service representatives, who also have duties as reservation agents, baggage handlers, and flight attendants, start at $12,600 per year. Rather than resenting the multiple roles, employees report that the job is made more interesting by the opportunity to do different things. Employees also maintain that they understand the company and the industry better through doing several jobs, resulting in better service for the airline's customers.

Again, which motivation theory helps explain the motivation and involvement experienced by these employees? In the worker-owner situation, it is easy to see that higher-level needs are being activated. Owning a supermarket means making many decisions and coming into contact with the other owners. Thus social and esteem needs are being met. In addition, this situation exemplifies one of the criticisms of need theory—lower-level needs not being met doesn't mean that the individual is stuck at that level. Although safety needs seemed to be threatened because of initial inexperience, that didn't prevent the owners from continuing the store. In the airline situation, the multiple jobs held by the workers could easily be satisfying self-actualization needs (Maslow). Even Herzberg's motivators are being activated in this situation. Certainly money is not the primary motivator, as is evident from the salary comparisons.

These two examples would seem to strongly support the argument that involvement has a positive effect on motivation.

PERSONAL GUIDELINES FOR HUMAN RELATIONS SUCCESS

From this chapter you can easily see that motivating individuals is difficult and frustrating work. But, some guidelines will improve your success rate in this area:

☐ Create a sense of involvement for workers in activities that have meaning for them. We know that people like to be included in things that affect them, even if it means just being told personally about what to do next. Involvement can be communicated by spending time with employees—even though certain decisions have already been made—asking how the decisions are impacting their work.

☐ Concentrate on positive aspects of people's lives—even at work. Write down everything positive you can find about an employee. Share that list with the employee and discuss how those things helped to accomplish the job more effectively. (This also works well with friends and spouses.) Send notes on positive deeds to individuals. IBM was famous for sending letters of commendation for just about everything.

☐ Ask individuals what is important to them—it may surprise you. We assume that what is important to us will be the same for others. Having periodic meetings to find out how a worker is doing or hopes to do in the near future may help you create a special motivation system just for that individual. If the program doesn't work, the recognition you give that person will work.

☐ Help set up goal-setting programs for individual workers. Many monotonous plant and office jobs can also be an excellent situation for goal setting. Helping individuals establish specific, measurable targets can make almost any job more interesting.

DISCUSSION AND REVIEW QUESTIONS

1. Which type(s) of motivational theories (need, choice, or reinforcement) do you find most useful in explaining human behavior? Why?
2. Discuss the advantages and disadvantages of operant conditioning as a motivational tool.
3. What words of caution would you give to a manager who was considering the use of behavior modification to improve the motivation of unionized machine-shop workers?
4. What steps would you use to create a goal-setting program among welders in a fabrication plant?
5. Use Maslow's hierarchy of needs to describe various members of your immediate family. How do family members satisfy their needs?

6. Use Herzberg's theory to explain what conditions might incite workers to call a ''wildcat'' strike?

What Motivates You?

People are motivated by different things. Look at the following list of general areas that provide motivation for individuals. As you review the list think about your present job if you are working. If you are not currently working, mentally choose a job for yourself and complete the exercise.

Instructions. Read the list carefully and place a 10 next to the factor that has the greatest work-motivating potential for you. Place a 9 next to the second most important work-motivating factor. Continue until you have ranked all ten.[24]

_____	1. Interesting work
_____	2. Job security
_____	3. Up-to-date equipment
_____	4. A feeling of doing something important
_____	5. Good wages
_____	6. Challenging work
_____	7. Effective supervision by the boss
_____	8. A chance for advancement
_____	9. Pleasant working conditions
_____	10. The opportunity to succeed at what you are doing

Interpretation of What Motivates You. Remember that you gave a 10 to the most important factor and a 1 to the least important factor, so high scores indicate greater motivating potential than low scores. With this in mind, fill in below the number you assigned to each of the 10 factors and then add both columns.

Column A		Column B	
_____	1.	_____	2.
_____	4.	_____	3.
_____	6.	_____	5.
_____	8.	_____	7.
_____	10.	_____	9.
_____	Total	_____	Total

If your total in Column A is higher than that in Column B, you derive more satisfaction from the psychological factors of your job than from the physical side.

Notice that the five factors in Column A are designed to measure how you feel about the job. These factors are internal motivators or are intrinsic in nature. If your score in Column A is more than 30, you are highly motivated to succeed in your job, and jobs with challenge and potential for development and growth will be appealing to you.

If your total in Column B is higher than that in Column A, you derive more satisfaction from the physical side of your job than from the psychological side. The five factors in Column B all relate to the environment in which you work or the pay you receive for doing this work. These factors are external to you and you have limited control over them. These factors are called extrinsic motivators. If you scored more than 30 points on this scale, you are highly motivated by the external rewards, and if they are not present will become dissatisfied with the job and probably move to a job that does provide these types of rewards.

HUMAN RELATIONS INCIDENT

John Kemp is a new supervisor for the school's building cleaning program. He supervises eight individuals who clean all classrooms and bathrooms in a five-building complex. The individuals working for Kemp are moonlighting on this job to make extra money. Because this job is additional work for the people, attendance is very poor and many of the workers are tired from other full-time jobs. Kemp feels that if they have chosen to take on this additional responsibility, they should do it right. Kemp spends several hours after work thinking about how he should address this problem. What should Kemp do?

NOTES

1. Based on an article appearing in *Time* (4 July 1983).
2. R. M. Steers and L. W. Porter, *Motivation and Work Behavior,* 3rd ed. (New York: McGraw-Hill, 1983).
3. D. Yankelovich, "New Rules in American Life: Searching for Self-fulfillment in a World Turned Upside Down," *Psychology Today* (April 1981): 35–91.
4. Abraham Maslow, *Motivation and Personality* (New York: Harper & Row, 1954).
5. Lyman W. Porter, "Job Attitudes in Management: IV, Perceived Deficiencies in Need Fulfillment as a Function of Size of the Company," *Journal of Applied Psychology* (December 1963): 386–97.
6. F. Herzberg, B. Mausnerm and B. Snyderman, *The Motivation to Work,* 2nd ed. (New York: Wiley, 1959); and F. Herzberg, *Work and the Nature of Man* (Cleveland: World Press, 1966).
7. D. A. Whitsett and E. K. Winslow, "An Analysis of Studies Critical of the Motivation-Hygiene Theory," *Personnel Psychology* (Winter 1967): 391–416.
8. John P. Campbell, et al., *Managerial Behavior, Performance, and Effectiveness* (New York: McGraw-Hill, 1970): 354.
9. J. S. Adams, "Towards an Understanding of Inequity," *Journal of Abnormal and Social Psychology,* vol. 67 (1963): 422–36; and J. S. Adams, "Inequity on Social Exchange," in L. Berkowitz, ed., *Advances in Experimental Social Psychology* (New York: Academic Press, 1965): 267–99.
10. Ibid.
11. J. S. Adams and S. Freedman, "Equity Theory Revisited: Comments and Annotated Bibliography," in L. Berkowitz, ed., *Advances in Experimental and Social Psychology* (New York: Academic Press, 1976).

12. M. R. Carrell and J. E. Dettrich, "Employee Perception of Fair Treatment," *Personnel Journal* (October 1976): 523–24.

13. Victor H. Vroom, *Work and Motivation* (New York: Wiley, 1964).

14. Ibid.

15. E. A. Locke, K. N. Shaw, L. M. Saari, and G. P. Latham, "Goal Setting and Task Performance: 1969–1980," *Psychological Bulletin,* vol. 90 (1981): 125–52.

16. E. A. Locke, "Relation of Goal Performance with a Short Work Period and Multiple Goal Levels," *Journal of Applied Psychology,* vol. 67 (1982): 512–14.

17. E. A. Locke and G. P. Latham, *Goal Setting: A Motivational Technique That Works!* (Englewood Cliffs, NJ: Prentice-Hall, 1984).

18. G. P. Latham and E. A. Locke, "Goal Setting—A Motivational Technique That Works," *Organizational Dynamics* (Autumn 1979): 68–80.

19. Edward L. Deci, *Intrinsic Motivation* (New York: Plenum Press, 1975): 7–8.

20. F. Luthans and R. Krentner, *Organizational Behavior Modification,* 2nd ed., (Glenview, IL: Scott, Foresman & Company, 1984).

21. "Ohio Firm Relies on Incentive-Pay System to Motivate Workers and Maintain Profits," *The Wall Street Journal* (12 August 1983): 19. Reprinted by permission of *The Wall Street Journal,* ©Dow Jones & Company, Inc. 1983. All rights reserved.

22. Paul Engelmayer, "Worker Owned and Operated Supermarket Yields Financial Success, Personal Rewards," *The Wall Street Journal* (18 August 1983): 27. Reprinted by permission of *The Wall Street Journal.* ©Dow Jones & Company, Inc. 1983. All rights reserved.

23. "New Airline Surmounting Labor Dilemma," *The Wall Street Journal* (12 September 1983): 31. Reprinted by permission of *The Wall Street Journal,* ©Dow Jones & Company, Inc., 1983. All rights reserved.

24. Adapted from Richard M. Hodgetts, *Modern Human Relations at Work,* 2nd ed. (New York: The Dryden Press, 1984): 36. Copyright 1984 by CBS College Publishing. Reprinted by permission of Holt, Rinehart & Winston, Inc.

PART TWO

INTERPERSONAL ASPECTS OF HUMAN RELATIONS

CHAPTER 4
LEADERSHIP

WHAT'S YOUR OPINION? T OR F

_____ 1. Managers are usually leaders in organizations.

_____ 2. We can identify behaviors that a leader can perform to be effective in most situations.

_____ 3. The power to reward and punish is the most effective source of influence for a leader.

_____ 4. Effective leaders start with subtle methods of influence and evolve to more drastic measures only as required.

_____ 5. Maturity of subordinates can be an influence on a leader's behavior.

_____ 6. When the task of employees is poorly defined, a leader can increase motivation by providing clear instructions on how to do the job.

_____ 7. Being a participating leader works in all situations.

_____ 8. Jobs can be changed to help a leader be more effective.

OUTLINE

CONCEPTS OF LEADERSHIP AND POWER
Leadership or Managership?

THEORIES OF LEADERSHIP
Behavioral Theories of Leadership
Situational Theories of Leadership

POWER AND ITS USAGE
Characteristics of The Power-Holder

LEARNING SUMMARY

HUMAN RELATIONS APPLICATIONS
Become a Dynamic Subordinate
Management by Walking Away
Women as Leaders

PERSONAL GUIDELINES FOR HUMAN
RELATIONS SUCCESS

LEARNING OBJECTIVES

☐ Discuss the differences between managers
and leaders

☐ Identify and define the major behavioral
theories

☐ Describe the situational theories and the
advantages of each

☐ Discuss the chief sources and uses of power

☐ List and define the methods of influence

☐ Identify and discuss the major human
relations applications

☐ Describe a personal approach to more
effective leadership and influence

Can a General Lead a Military Branch to Effectiveness?[1]

In the clear skies over Nevada, a major air battle is raging between fifteen Russian MiGs and F–15s. At another location, an F–15 launches a Sidewinder at a MiG. Finally, a Falcon F–16 opens fire on a column of Soviet tanks.

Obviously the attacks are simulated, but the planes are real, and the score is kept on a big video screen at the Air Force base. On this day the good guys win. But this wasn't the case in 1977. At that time, half the planes were not battle ready and more than 220 planes were classified as "hangar queens"—grounded at least three weeks for lack of spare parts or maintenance. Pilots were losing their skills because they couldn't get the necessary flight time, and the accident rate was soaring.

Into this mess stepped General W. L. (Bill) Creech. In less than seven years, Creech turned those statistics around. But what was most remarkable was that he got no additional money or personnel. His strategy was to force a bottom-up management style on an organization that had been always top-down. He did this by pushing responsibilities down to the lowest possible level. While the previous administration used centralization, Creech pushed for and won a decentralized plan of action. Instead of having one person do one thing before another person could perform his task, Creech formed teams with cross-training to help in crises.

Prior to Creech, a unit consisted of 76 planes; after his leadership the unit size was 24 planes, with repair teams assigned and cross-trained. Instead of a 2,000-person unit, the new group size was 400. The small groups assigned themselves to planes and painted their names on the sides of the planes, just as pilots did. While pilots showed their stuff with low flying "roll-bys" to impress the public and the brass, the maintenance group had its own "roll-bys," displaying its gleaming trucks and vans.

At the same time, Creech mounted a crusade to develop quality in all aspects of the airmen's lives. Barracks, maintenance trucks, tools, and offices were cleaned and painted. Creech said, "My philosophy is that if equipment is shabby looking, it affects your pride in your organization and your performance."

"It's not really that hard to run a large organization," the general explained. "You just have to think small about how to achieve your goals. There's a finite limit as to how much leadership you can exercise at the top. You can't micromanage—people resent that. Things are achieved by individuals, by groups

Reprinted with permission, *INC.* magazine, January, 1986. Copyright © 1986 by INC. Publishing Company, 38 Commercial Wharf, Boston, MA 02110.

of two, five, or twenty, not collections of 115,000. And that's as true in industry as it is in the military.''

Leadership or Managership?

Leadership has long been considered one of the most important influences of organizational performance. For the manager, leadership is the means to accomplish a department's or organization's goals. Why is this so important in human relations? Because it is the leader who affects the attitudes, behavior, and ultimately the performance of individual workers.

In the opening story General Creech is clearly affecting the performance of the Air Force organization. We can appreciate the positive changes. But we still don't have a working definition of what we should do as leaders to ensure employee commitment and performance. In this chapter we will explore the concept of leadership, discuss various theories of leadership, describe the sources of power and influence a leader can use, and see how leadership is applied in some organizations.

Managerial Functions. Before we can define the concept of leadership, we should have a basic understanding of what managers and supervisors do. One difference between the two is the location of the individuals in an organization's hierarchy. Supervision is used to describe people who occupy the first level of managerial responsibility. The term used in many organizations is ''first-level supervisor'' or ''supervisor.'' Managers usually occupy levels above this position. Figure 4–1 illustrates this relationship. At the very top of the organization the managers are called ''executives.''

All levels of management perform certain functions, including leading, planning, organizing, staffing, and controlling. The difference between managers and supervisors is not the actual performance of these functions but rather the amount of time they spend doing each in a typical day. Figure 4–2 shows in a rough manner some of the differences between levels. Supervisors spend more time in leading or directing worker activities than in planning those activities. Plans are usually made at the upper levels of management and carried out by supervisors. For example, upper management decides to enter their product in a new market and informs middle management of this decision. Middle management then prepares various plans for the manufacturing and sales departments to market the product. The supervisor is informed that the new plan involves a different packaging, and in turn instructs workers on new tasks or on how to prepare the machinery to accept the new packaging.

As we can see from this simple example, upper- and middle-level management does more planning, and supervisors carry out those plans on an operational basis. One important element for all levels, as shown by Figure 4–2, is leading. We will focus on this function in this chapter. But since all levels have

Why is leadership important to the study of human relations?

Do managers at all levels of the organization perform the same tasks?

FIGURE 4–1
Model illustrating the relationship of managers and supervisors

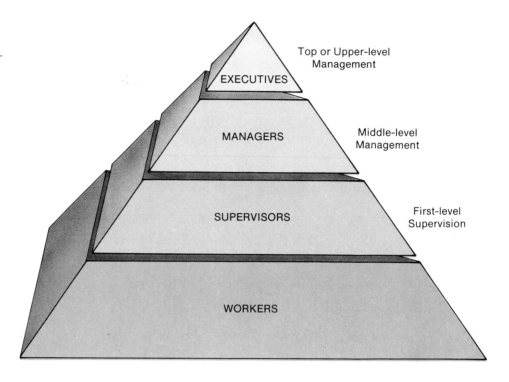

Top or Upper-level Management

EXECUTIVES

MANAGERS

Middle-level Management

SUPERVISORS

First-level Supervision

WORKERS

the responsibility of influencing and leading employees, we will use the terms managers and supervisors interchangeably.

Differences between Leaders and Managers. We have been talking about the functions of a manager. Does this mean that all leaders are managers? In certain respects, yes; but management and leadership are not synonymous: a person can be a leader without being a manager. For example, Henry Kissinger was President Nixon's national security advisor—a staff position with little or no direct authority or supervisory responsibilities. Yet, when he spoke at meetings, people were influenced by his ideas and arguments. Because of his organizational position, his leadership took the form of influencing but not controlling the staff.

On the other hand, a person can be a manager without being a leader. Figure 4–2 shows that managers have a ''lead'' function, but this does not mean that they will exercise this function and the ''right'' to influence. Managers have the *right* to exercise their influence, but they may not *choose* to exercise it. For example, a head nurse in a hospital is the designated manager of other nurses on the staff. Yet, frequently the behavior of the staff nurses is influenced to a greater degree by the directions of doctors than by the head nurse. From this and the previous section we can see that management as a function is a much broader concept than leadership. Leadership is one of the most important activities of a manager or supervisor.

Can an individual be a leader without being a manager?

[handwritten marginal notes:] an individual can be a leader without being a manager / a leader has the right to exercise their influence but may choose not to do so.

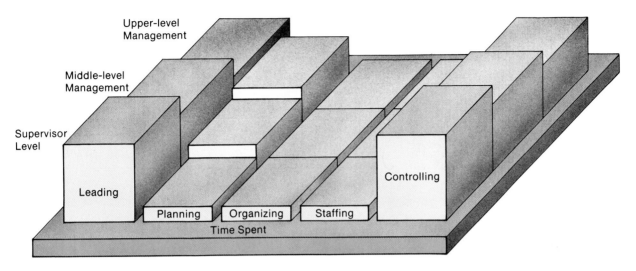

FIGURE 4-2
Time devoted to various managerial functions as related to organizational level

Definition of Leadership. If being a manager does not necessarily mean being a leader, what is leadership? When asked for definitions of leadership, people will respond with such concepts as direction, power, motivation, control, authority, delegation, good communication, honesty, fairness. Leadership encompasses all of these, but the one word that seems to pinpoint the major element of leadership is influence. We can define leadership as a process involving two or more persons in which one party attempts to influence the other to accomplish some task or goal.

Leadership is a process between two or more individuals in which one attempts to influence the other's behavior toward the accomplishment of some task.

leader is the process of two or more individuals who try to influence each other behaviour to accomplish a task.

There are three important implications of this definition. The first is that leadership is a process—a constantly changing phenomenon. Second, leadership involves other people, who may be subordinates, peers, or superiors. Third, the outcome of the leadership process is concerned more with getting results and achieving goals than with procedure and policy.[2]

In the study of leadership, both earlier and current theories have focused on the same objective: identifying the factors that result in effective leadership. That is, can we identify certain behaviors or situations that make some leaders or some types of leadership more effective than others? To answer this question, we summarize the concepts of two major theories of leadership: behavioral leadership and situational leadership. Early theories focused on the style of leadership. The key question was, "Is one leadership style more effective than any other?" Put another way, "How important is what a leader does?"

As researchers failed to clearly identify one effective style of leadership, new models were considered that focused on the situational conditions. These models

THEORIES OF LEADERSHIP

What is the difference between behavioral and situational theories of leadership?

assumed leadership to be a complex process that involved the leader, the subordinates, and the situation. The research asked, "What set of situational determinants explains why certain leaders are more effective than others?" For example, is the time to complete the task or the maturity of the individual being led more critical to the effectiveness of one style or another?

Behavioral Theories of Leadership

Behavioral theories concentrate on what leaders do and how they do it. The underlying assumption is that effective leaders use a specific style to lead others in achieving goals that result in high productivity and morale.

Theory X and Theory Y. One popular explanation for leader behavior was developed by Douglas McGregor, who stated that leaders acted according to two sets of assumptions about subordinates.[3] These assumptions were personal beliefs held by the individual leader about how and why employees behave. One set of assumptions, called Theory X, is found in the more traditional directive style of management. Leaders who subscribe to Theory X assume the following:

1. Most people have an inherent dislike of work and will avoid it if they can.
2. Because they dislike work, most people must be coerced, controlled, directed, and threatened, or else they will not put forth adequate effort toward the achievement of organizational objectives.

Theory X leaders assume that most people dislike work, prefer to be directed, and wish to avoid responsibility.

FIGURE 4–3
Theory X–Theory Y
continuum

THEORY X	COMBINATION OF THEORY X AND THEORY Y	THEORY Y

3. Most people prefer to be directed, wish to avoid responsibility, have relatively little ambition, and want job security above all.

In contrast, leaders who subscribe to Theory Y assume the following:

1. The expenditure of physical and mental effort is as natural in work as in play.
2. External control and the threat of punishment are not the only means for bringing about effort toward organizational objectives. People will exercise self-direction and self-control in the service of objectives to which they are committed.
3. Commitment to objectives is a function of the rewards associated with their achievement.
4. Most people learn, under proper conditions, not only to accept but also to seek responsibility.
5. The ability to exercise a high degree of imagination, ingenuity, and creativity in the solution of organizational problems is widely, not narrowly, distributed in the population.

Theory Y leaders try to integrate the subordinate's goals with those of the department. But this is not to say that Theory Y leaders are never directive, or that Theory X leaders never try to be supportive of their subordinates. Most leaders are some variation of Theory X and Theory Y. Figure 4–3 shows these leadership styles on a continuum, which was the original intention of McGregor.

The Michigan Studies.   In 1940, the University of Michigan began a large-scale program of research on the human problems of administration. Part of this research was concerned with discovering the principles and methods of leadership and management resulting in the best performance.[4] The research compared the style of leadership and select performance variables in the best and the worst units of several organizations. The best and worst units were identified according to such criteria as productivity, job satisfaction, employee turnover, absenteeism, waste, and costs.

The studies identified two basic leadership styles used by both managers and supervisors. The *job-centered style* is characterized by close supervision, negative use of power, emphasis on schedules, and critical evaluation of work perfor-

Describe the two basic styles of leadership identified in the Michigan studies.

*job centered
supervision
negative use
of power.
emphasis on
schedules*

*critical evaluation of work
performance .*

FIGURE 4–4
Comparison of employee-centered leaders with job-centered leaders: How do they affect productivity?

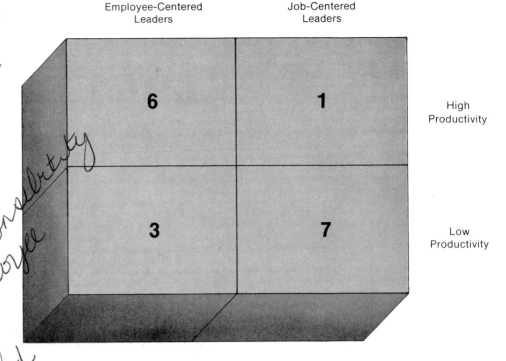

Employee-Centered Leaders | Job-Centered Leaders

6 | 1 — High Productivity

3 | 7 — Low Productivity

employee-centered delegation of responsibility concern for employee welfare; needs advancement personal growth

Does being employee-centered ensure that a supervisor will be an effective leader?

no. guarantee

mance. The *employee-centered style* emphasizes delegation of responsibility and a concern for employee welfare, needs, advancement, and personal growth. A popular title for this approach is the "human relations" style. If you compare the Theory X assumptions with how job-centered leaders accomplish their functions, you will see striking similarity. The same can be said for Theory Y and employee-centered leadership.

Returning to some of the original research (see Figure 4–4), which compared productivity performance with these styles, we begin to develop some interesting questions. When comparing high-productivity units with low-productivity units, we are immediately struck with the conclusion that employee-centered leadership is better. But, look again at the numbers and we can also say that using an employee-centered style of leadership does not *guarantee* that your workers will be high performers. One third of the employee-centered leaders were low performers. One out of eight of the job-centered leaders was a higher performer. What can account for this? Is there another explanation for these results? Could there be another variable that helps or hinders a leader while leading others? These types of questions stimulate researchers to continue to look for answers to the difficult question of "What is effective leadership?"

Three-Factor Theory. Another set of researchers expanded the previous two styles of leadership identified by the Michigan studies.[5] Their model uses a continuum similar to Theory X and Theory Y, but they further identified five points

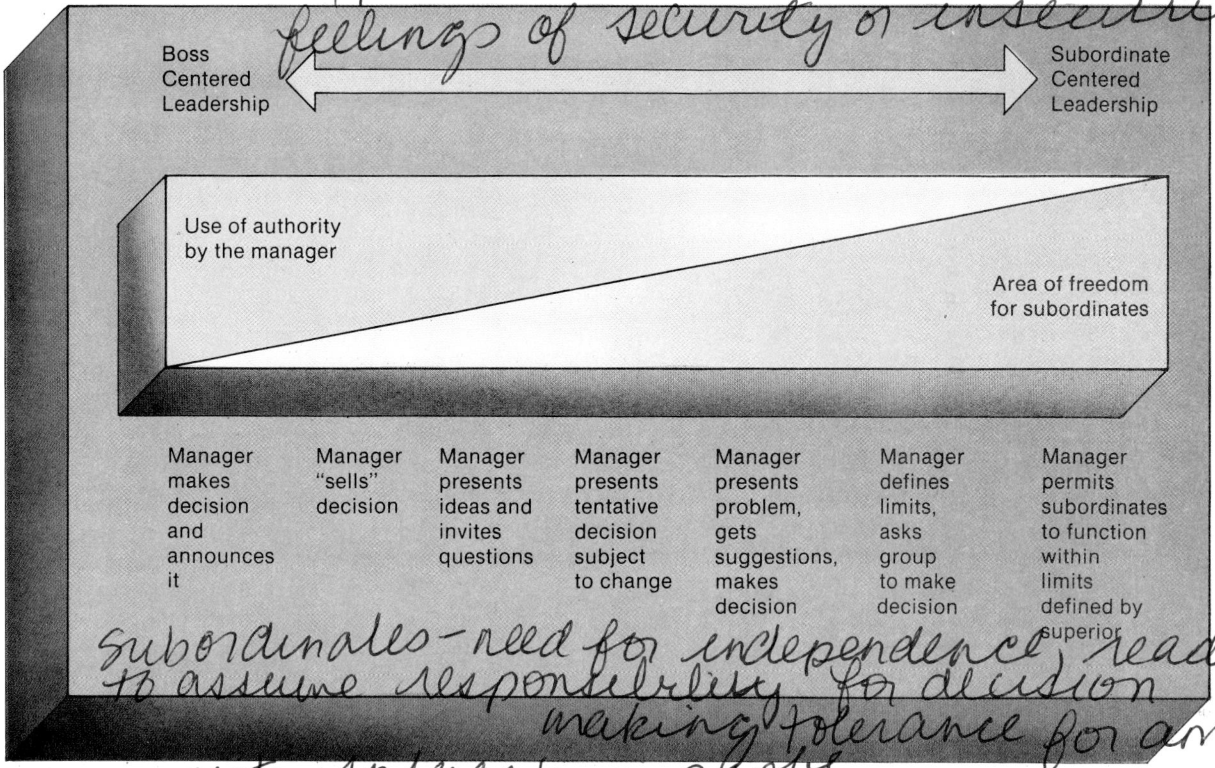

[handwritten annotation: Manager- values, confidence in subordinates, personal leadership tendencies, feelings of security or insecurity]

Boss Centered Leadership ← → Subordinate Centered Leadership

Use of authority by the manager

Area of freedom for subordinates

| Manager makes decision and announces it | Manager "sells" decision | Manager presents ideas and invites questions | Manager presents tentative decision subject to change | Manager presents problem, gets suggestions, makes decision | Manager defines limits, asks group to make decision | Manager permits subordinates to function within limits defined by superior |

[handwritten annotation: subordinates - need for independence, readiness to assume responsibility for decision making tolerance for ambiguity interest in problem]

FIGURE 4–5

A leadership style continuum (Source: Robert Tannenbaum and Warren H. Schmidt, "How to Choose a Leadership Pattern," *Harvard Business Review* (May–June 1973): 164. Copyright © 1973 by the President and Fellows of Harvard College; all rights reserved.)

between the two extremes of boss- and subordinate-centered leadership (see Figure 4–5).

This theory suggests that a wide range of factors determines whether directive leadership, participative leadership, or something in between is best. The factors fall into three groups:

1. Factors relating to the *manager* (values, confidence in subordinates, personal leadership tendencies, feelings of security or insecurity)
2. Factors relating to the *subordinates* (need for independence, readiness to assume responsibility for decision making, tolerance for ambiguity, interest in the problem, understanding of and identification with the departmental goals, knowledge and experience pertinent to the problem, expectations about sharing in decision making)
3. Factors relating to the *situation* (type of organization, the group's effectiveness, nature of the problem itself, time constraints).

What three factors can influence a leader to be either more boss- or more employee-centered?

(handwritten margin note: While Michigan studies were going on the Ohio State studies were going on as well)

These factors form a checklist that a leader can use to analyze a situation to determine which style of leadership will work best. This theory also hints at some of the answers to the questions raised by the employee- and job-centered leadership research. Consider one element of the situation—time constraints. During a crisis period—say, during a strike at a major plant—centralized decision making about schedules and supplies is appropriate. But in a period with no labor unrest, a more democratic approach might be in order.

We now can appreciate that choosing a leadership style is a complex decision. A leader needs to consider each element of a situation to determine which of the five styles shown in Figure 4–5 to choose.

The Ohio State Studies. While the Michigan studies were going on, Ohio State University researchers were also studying leadership styles and their impact on performance and satisfaction.[6]

Initiating structure means that the leader defines how, when, and where employee activities will be performed.

The Ohio State researchers identified two leadership styles similar to those in the Michigan studies (see Figure 4–6). The Ohio group called one style *initiating structure*, meaning the leader initiates the structure of the work group and its activities. This is equivalent to job-centered leadership or boss-centered leadership. Some of the leader's duties under this style of leadership include organizing

FIGURE 4–6

Two dimensions of leadership style

(handwritten margin note: Initiating structure — leader decides how, when, where employee activities will be performed (job-centered or boss-centered equivalent))

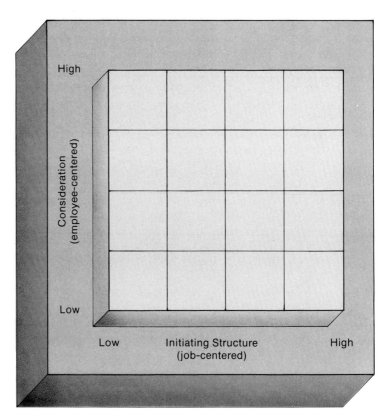

Learning to Lead: The Six-Day Method

Seminars on corporate leadership are the "in" thing now, and the Center for Creative Leadership is in the middle of the action. Last year, 7,600 managers from throughout the nation—80 percent more than the year before—took part in sessions run by the nonprofit organization, which has increased its staff to more than four times its 1975 size to meet demand. "Leadership has become the universal vitamin-C pill. Everybody seems to want megadoses of it," says psychologist David Campbell, a senior fellow.

A group of 24 executives gulped down big doses at a six-day seminar that cost $2,500 per person. As the session got under way, participants talked about what they hoped to get out of it. "I'd like to learn to be less of a dictator and more of a leader," said one manager.

Little time was wasted in helping to find answers to their dilemmas. There were discussions and lectures on such topics as what constitutes a leader and giving feedback to subordinates. Instructor Bob Bailey stressed that leadership means helping others get ahead. "You're not in bricks, auditing, or textiles but in people," he said. "You're in the business to serve those under you."

The executives, whose days began at 7:15 A.M. and ended at 8 P.M., were advised of the importance of balance between corporate and per-

sonal life. "It's not unusual to have a 50-year-old executive say, 'I am a success, but what happened to my family?'" warned instructor Bill Sternbergh.

Exercises to test flexibility, ability to work with colleagues, and other skills were also part of the regimen. In one, participants had to dream up the kind of person they would put in charge of a large number of people leaving an overcrowded Earth for another planet. Then they had to convince colleagues that theirs was the best choice.

Staff members of the center sat behind a one-way mirror and watched the goings-on. Then they talked to the executives about what they observed.

The participants emerged from the seminar pleased with what they had learned. Berlins Murphy, a vice president with Chase Manhattan Bank in New York, discovered when to include others in a decision and when to go it alone: "I'm sure I've done that wrong so many times it isn't funny."

QUESTIONS

1. What would be important subjects to cover in a leadership seminar?
2. Which leadership theory or theories would you use to help these managers do a better job of leading?
3. In the exercise to describe the person in charge of the ship to leave Earth, what characteristics would you use?

Source: Adapted from Linda K. Lanier, "Learning to Lead, The Six-Day Method." Copyright 1985, *U.S. News & World Report*. Reprinted from issue of December 2, 1985.

and defining what activities workers will perform, defining roles within the work group, establishing how employees will communicate, and evaluating work performance.

The other major leadership style identified in the Ohio study is *consideration*. This is comparable to employee-centered leadership. Under consideration, a

Consideration is a leadership style in which the leader tries to gain the employees' trust and respect and create a supportive atmosphere for employee development.

leader would try to develop trust and respect from the workers, create a supportive and stimulating atmosphere for employee growth and development, and help employees generate their own goals for performance improvement, dependent upon their skill level.

One of the most important conclusions of this research was that the two styles, initiating structure and consideration, were independent of one another. That is, the amount of "structure" used by a leader did not automatically predict the amount of "consideration" that the leader will use. A leader can show a high degree of both structure and consideration. Conversely, a leader can show a low level of each characteristic. This is in contrast with the previous theories, which were on a continuum. If a leader was more employee-centered, then he or she *had* to be less job-centered. In practical terms this means that a leader has more possible ways to behave. The Ohio State research gave the leader four possible behaviors while the earlier research used only two styles. Four styles is closer to reality than two styles.

Numerous studies have been conducted to assess the effects of initiating structure and consideration on worker performance and morale. Some studies showed that high ratings in both areas were associated with high performance and worker satisfaction. But other studies indicated that this combination produced the opposite effects of lower worker satisfaction and absences. Some studies showed that these leaders received lower ratings from their superiors.[7] As a result we can't predict which style to use for more effectiveness and performance from our workers.

How consistent is research surrounding the use of one style of leadership?

No one is style is consistant we realize we need a combo - flexible according to situation

Using Ohio State Studies. At this point in our study of leadership styles, we can begin to see some popular terms used to describe various types of leaders. Figure 4–7 points out these four major styles.

Authoritarian work- or job-centered

behavioral

Authoritarian Leaders. These leaders are characterized as mostly work- or job-centered. The authoritarian approach focuses almost exclusively on accomplishing tasks according to the manager's instructions and little on human concerns. With this type of leadership, employees are not offered any input with decision making or even with ways to perform their jobs.

Authoritarian leadership has been used in organizations that have large production facilities with routine work, such as assembly lines. The work and its specifics have been determined by the plant engineer and all that is required is blind obedience to the supervisor's instructions. Authoritarian leadership is effective during a crisis, such as a unionizing attempt or a company takeover. Under these conditions, you need one individual who can call the shots and make fast decisions. In such a situation the workers need to follow instructions and quickly get the job done.

The problem with authoritarian leadership is that organizations are rarely in a continual crisis. When not in a crisis, this type of leadership will lead to a company of "yes men," and employees will not take on responsibility for the leader's decisions. This also limits the amount and type of information needed to

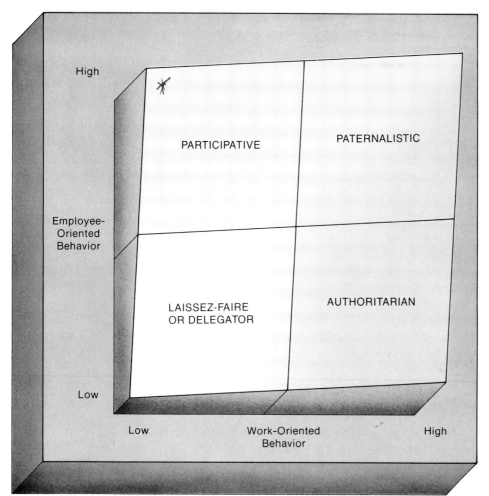

FIGURE 4–7
Four major leadership
styles

make good decisions. In today's complex society, organizations cannot survive without useful and creative information to make their decisions.

Paternalistic Leaders.   These types of leaders are just as focused on work or job-centered activities, but they also have concern for their employees. They reflect the attitude, "Do what I ask and I'll look out for your welfare." This style of leadership was prevalent in the late nineteenth century. Many companies would provide basic living in so called "company towns" to take care of employees. In return the company could expect employees to do as they were told.

Paternalistic job-centered and concerned for the welfare of the employees

behavioral

"Company towns" do not exist in the United States today. However, in Japan this style of leadership is still practiced. The larger organizations offer employees lifetime employment in return for loyalty to perform jobs assigned by management. This style of leadership is fairly consistent with Japanese culture.

Paternalism is still practiced today but it is not common. Most employees resent this form of supervision since it assumes that individuals cannot take care of themselves. Most—but not all—workers want some say in decisions and want to know reasons why certain jobs are assigned to them (see Chapter 1). A situation in which the paternalistic style might be appropriate is when an employee is going through personal difficulties. During a personal crisis an individual needs some certainty in his or her life, even if it is only at work.

Participative Leadership. This form of leadership is characterized more by employee-centered than job- or work-centered leadership. Participative leaders encourage their subordinates to play an active role in conducting the business. They expect the employees to help make decisions about what will affect them, to suggest better methods of doing their jobs, and to take on more job responsibilities as they grow and develop. The participative manager also regularly encourages and praises employees.

In the participative mode, a leader will present employees with a problem or decision and ask for input and discussion of various ideas. After thoughtful

Participative more employee-centered than job-centered

behavioural

Participative leaders expect their subordinates to help make decisions and to suggest better methods for doing their jobs.

Opening Story Revisited

I n the opening story we can see that General Creech is not only a manager because of his position as head of the Air Force base, but he is also a leader who has influenced and changed how planes are handled. General Creech uses Theory Y, which says that workers want to control their activities. This is seen in the decentralization of the activities. While it is hard to say with any certainty which of the four styles he uses, General Creech seems to use delegation leadership. Again, his philosophy is to get the job responsibility to the lowest level in the organization. From the story we see that the workers take pride in their jobs and equipment, so they must be accepting the responsibilities of their jobs.

consideration, the leader will then make a decision. The employees, because they have a say in the decision, are committed to carrying it out. This approach might be used successfully with an engineering or sales group.

Participative leadership looks ideal. Why doesn't everyone use this approach? This is a difficult question to give a complete answer to. Part of the reason is that many managers are suspicious of allowing employees that much involvement. Another problem is that some organizations have excessive rules and regulations that sometimes do not support the freedom to do things differently. Finally, conditions, such as a crisis, may not allow this option.

Laissez-faire or Delegation Leadership.   This style of leadership is best described as very low employee- and work-centered. However, this final style of leadership can be seen from two perspectives. The first, laissez-faire, is based on the French term meaning "to not interfere." If a leader uses this style as the main form of leading others, it can be viewed as giving up responsibility. Not only are the subordinates entirely on their own, but no information about where the company is going is provided for the employees to contribute to the objectives through their efforts.

On the other hand, if the supervisor periodically checks employee progress and makes suggestions about future directions, this style can be viewed as delegation. It can be a challenging environment for the employee. Without some form of feedback and future orientation, however, employees become disoriented and frustrated. Very creative people thrive under these conditions of freedom. For example, research and development scientists like freedom to determine their work habits and activities. They don't need praise from the supervisor because they receive satisfaction from the work itself (intrinsic).

We have taken a brief look at four styles of leadership that are practiced in organizations. At this point we are left with the question of how to choose a style, since all have some conditions under which they are more effective. The next section addresses this reality with the "situational theory."

Laissez-faire/delegation low concern for employee or job

[handwritten marginalia] Two Styles – not to interfere; leader gives up responsibility – no info about where the co. is going

[handwritten notes at bottom] creative people thrive under these conditions; Delegation: supervisor periodically checks with staff; staff reports to supervisor as soon as prob. arise

Situational Theories of Leadership

Because of the questions about how to apply behavioral theory, researchers developed other approaches. Some of this new focus is the result of the model by Tannenbaum and Schmidt. Recall that they included situational factors as a checklist for choosing a style. While this model was on a continuum, the list of situational factors to consider was its strength and richness.

The following theories focus on situational factors. Can we begin to see critical information in the situation that will help us choose a more effective style of leadership?

What variables does Fiedler use in his theory of leadership?

A Contingency Model. One of the first researchers to attempt to look at the complexity of the leader's dilemma was Fred Fiedler. Fiedler argued that the effectiveness of any leadership style is dependent on the characteristics of the situation.[8] An important feature of his model is the leader's influence. Fiedler tried to identify which elements affect a leader's influence. The key factors he identified were *leader/member relations, task structure,* and *leader position power.* Looking at each of these three factors one can conclude that the leader's influence is strong, weak, or moderate. If the leader's influence is either strong or weak, the proper style is task-oriented. If his influence is moderate, then his style should be employee-centered. These relationships are shown in Figure 4–8.

Let us consider each of Fiedler's factors in some detail. *Leader/member relations* refers to the degree of confidence, trust, and respect subordinates have in their leader. This factor is evaluated as either good or poor. The assumption is that if subordinates respect and trust the leader, it will be easier for the leader to exercise leadership. If the employees do not trust the leader, the leader may have to resort to special favors to get good performance from the employees.

Leader/member relations the degree of confidence, trust, and respect subordinates have in their leader

Task structure refers to the nature of the employee's task—whether it is routine (structured) or complex (unstructured). An accounts-payable clerk may work on a fairly structured task, whereas the corporate planner for an electronics firm probably works on an unstructured task.

Task structure the degree of complexity and routineness of a subordinate's activities

Leader position power refers to the extent of the leader's power base—the degree to which the leader can reward, punish, promote, and demote employees. According to Fiedler, position power is either strong (e.g., an operations manager) or weak (e.g., the leader of a volunteer group).

Leader position power the extent of the leader's power and influence

These three factors together determine the leader's influence, or "situational favorableness." The more influence a leader has, the more favorable the situation is for the leader. The greatest favorable situation for a leader is characterized by good leader/member relations, a highly structured task, and strong leader position power, for example the owner of a large automotive retail store who is liked and respected by the employees. This situation would fall into Cell 1 because the tasks are highly structured for the sales clerks and stock personnel, the position power is strong, and the leader/member relations are good. Under these conditions, the leader should be task-oriented to be effective.

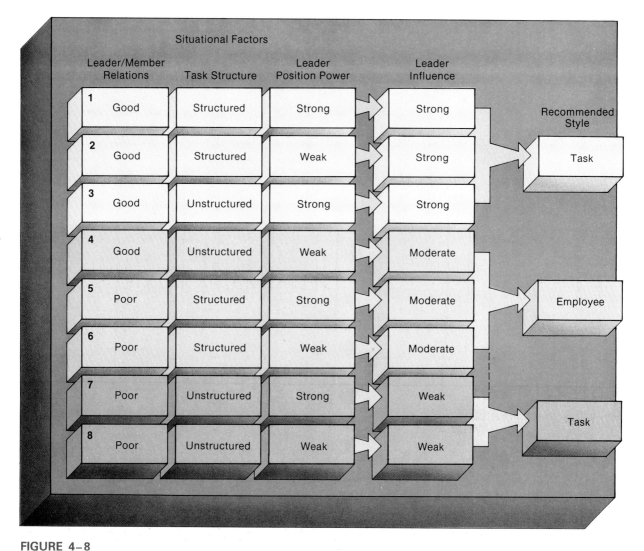

FIGURE 4–8
Fiedler's contingency model of leadership style (Source: Adapted from Fred E. Fiedler, *A Theory of Leadership Effectiveness* (New York: McGraw-Hill, 1967): 37. Used by permission.)

An employee-oriented style is more appropriate when leader influence is moderate. For example, in many research laboratories, the tasks of the scientists are quite unstructured, the leader may have weak position power, but leader/member relations are usually good. This situation is captured in Cell 4 of the model. Because research scientists prefer following their own creative tendencies, an employee-oriented approach is more effective.

An employee-oriented approach may be quite effective in a research laboratory where tasks are relatively unstructured.

A task-oriented or directive leadership style is again preferred when leader influence is weak, such as in Cell 8. A scenario for Cell 8 would be: a volunteer committee meets to plan a picnic for a large company (unstructured task), the leader is not well liked by the other members of the committee (poor leader/member relations), and the leader cannot reward or punish other committee members for lack of participation (weak position power).

This theory brings important implications for leadership and human relations in organizations. This model stresses the fact that successful leaders know the conditions under which they are trying to lead. This knowledge gives power because it allows managers to "engineer" jobs to fit their leadership style. If a basically employee-oriented manager is leading a group like Cell 8, it may be possible to change some of the conditions to make the situation more favorable. For example, the leader could obtain permission to reward the employees by having the meetings over dinner at the firm's expense. This would strengthen the leader's position power and move the situation closer to Cell 7. In addition, the leader could spend time planning the major tasks and ask for volunteers to perform them. This would make the task more structured and move the leader's situational favorableness to Cell 5, which requires an employee-oriented person.

How can one use Fiedler's theory to engineer a job for the leader to be more effective?

Middle Managers and Supervisors Resist Moves to More Participatory Management

Applying a more participatory style of leadership is not easy. When Corning Glass began a program last year to foster a more participatory style of management, some supervisors were dubious. Why? This level of management is sandwiched between workers and upper management. They work hard to get into management and tend to guard their old-style authority jealously. They grew up in a system in which "management has all the answers"—even if it didn't—and they have long been taught that their job is to keep the hourly employees in the dark and the production lines humming.

Now their bosses want more participation from the workers, as well as better management and a steady flow of quality products, says Joseph Propersi, Corning's manufacturing-education manager. Managers in the middle are left wondering, "How do I do both?" Faced with that dilemma, many managers and supervisors dig in to oppose the change. When one big telecommunications company started its program, middle management boycotted an orientation session.

Because of the central role that middle managers and supervisors play in implementing a more participatory management style, attitudes can jeopardize an entire program. "People in the middle are the ones who can make it go or not go," says Mark Arnold, a consultant in the field.

What can be done? At Florida Power and Light Company, middle managers became confused about their new roles, prompting the company to tailor special training sessions to help them along. But while such retraining can be useful, some managers and supervisors never get the message. "The participative manager needs better management skills and people skills. Most of those things aren't trainable," says James Lester, president of Eggers Industries Inc., a building products company. Eggers will even go to the point of reassigning managers and supervisors to jobs that don't involve supervising workers because they failed to change their style.

One of the more difficult changes a manager must make is knowing when to give commands and when to be more diplomatic. "You don't tell people to do something, you ask them to do it," says David Goodfield, a TRW instructor who was a supervisor for six years. Still there are times when the boss has to make a decision without spoiling the teamwork of his group. "Sometimes," says John C. Boldt, a manager at TRW, "you have to call the shots."

QUESTIONS

1. Do you agree with Lester that better management and people skills are not trainable? Which leadership theory in the text would agree with Lester? *Participative*

2. Which theory agrees with Goodfield about *Path-Goal* knowing when to give a command and when *Theory.* to get things done diplomatically?

3. Describe some conditions under which a manager using a more controlling style would be appropriate. *Life Cycle*

2,3. *situational dependent on employee maturity*

From this example, we can see that leaders' tasks can be changed to reflect their styles and as a result make them more effective.

Another implication of this theory is to provide training to managers and supervisors, allowing them to identify situations in which they will be successful and situations in which they might fail. This training should be specific to their individual styles and to the conditions that will ensure success.

Explain how the path-goal theory of leadership and motivation relate.

Path-Goal Theory. The path-goal theory is based on the expectancy theory of motivation covered in Chapter 3. As you remember, expectancy theory states that motivation is the product of the expectation that goal accomplishment will result in certain rewards and the value of the rewards received.[9] The path-goal theory is based on the premise that effective leaders have the ability to motivate employees to reach departmental objectives and to find satisfaction in their work.

The theory can be summarized as follows:

1. A leader can increase the motivation of employees by making the rewards of productivity more attractive to them. For example, a manager can reward high productivity with raises, promotions, and praise, thereby increasing the attractiveness of high productivity.
2. When the task of employees is poorly defined, a leader can increase motivation by clarifying the goal or by giving structure to the path that leads to the goal (e.g., by providing supervision or instructions). Defining the task increases the expectancy of goal accomplishment and, consequently, motivation.
3. When the task of employees is well defined (e.g., assembly-line work), instead of focusing on work-oriented activities, the leader should use employee-oriented efforts to help employees meet personal needs. By introducing structure where sufficient structure already exists, the supervisor may cause a decrease in motivation because employees may feel insulted and resentful.

While research seems to support this theory,[10] there are questions about some of the findings.[11] One example of inconsistency is the amount of structure wanted in an unstructured situation. The theory suggests that employees want more structure; however, certain groups do not.

The path-goal approach to leadership does have advantages in the practice of human relations. First, it begins to tie motivational theory and leadership theory together. Now we can view the attempts to be work-centered as helpful where the structure is unclear, preventing employees from being motivated to do a good job. Second, this theory helps leaders be more specific about what situations should be more task-oriented.

Situational Leadership. A final approach to leadership is provided by Paul Hersey and Kenneth H. Blanchard, who used similar concepts to those of the Ohio State University study on initiating structure and consideration. Hersey and Blanchard identified *task behavior* and *relationship behavior*. Task behaviors are focused on explaining what each employee is to do, as well as when, where, and

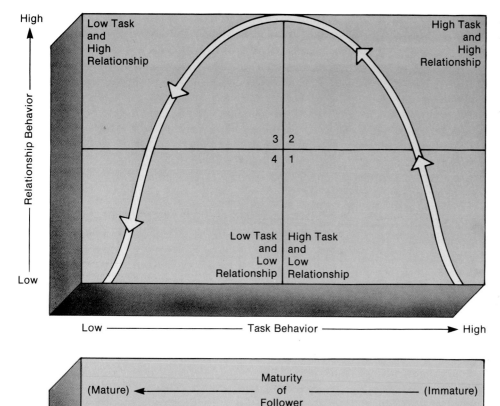

High

Relationship Behavior ────────

Low

Low Task and High Relationship		High Task and High Relationship
	3 | 2	
	4 | 1	
Low Task and Low Relationship	High Task and Low Relationship	

Low ──────── Task Behavior ──────── High

(Mature) ◄──── Maturity of Follower ──── (Immature)

FIGURE 4–9
A model of situational leadership (Source: Paul Hersey and Kenneth Blanchard, *Management of Organizational Behavior: Utilizing Human Resources*, 4th ed., 1982, p. 152. Adapted by permission of Prentice-Hall, Inc., Englewood Cliffs, New Jersey.)

Life Cycle Theory

how tasks are to be accomplished. This is similar to work- or job-oriented behavior.

Relationship behavior refers to the leader engaging in a two-way communication to provide support to the employee. This can be in the form of questions to show concern and emotional support. Since Hersey and Blanchard considered these two behaviors to be independent, the model of their theory is similar to a matrix (see Figure 4–9). In addition, they proposed that another aspect of the situation is the maturity level of the employees being supervised.

A comparison of leadership terms:
Task behavior = initiating structure = job-centered = work-oriented.
Relationship Behavior = Consideration = employee-centered = people-oriented.

Maturity is defined as the capacity to set high but attainable goals, the willingness and ability to take responsibility, and the education and experience of the individual or work group. This maturity variable is considered not just in general terms, but for each specific individual and each specific task. For example, a sales representative may have a high maturity rating for contacting clients but a low rating for writing sales proposals (perhaps due to lack of experience). This theory would recommend that the supervisor spend time—exercising a more directive style of leadership—on how to write proposals. In contrast, the supervisor should delegate the contacting of clients to the employee and praise only that aspect of the employee's performance. This model has received some criticism about its consistency.[12] However, it is appealing to practicing managers because it provides specific yet flexible guidelines for dealing with each subordinate in different situations.

This theory does have practical implications for human relations. First, it clearly identifies the subordinate as the key situational factor a leader must consider. This makes tremendous sense from the perspective of what we know about individual performance in an organization. It also helps the manager to focus on each individual rather than try to develop one style for all situations. Finally, it breaks maturity into two parts: skill/technical maturity and emotional/psychological maturity.

This reflects reality. When we hire new employees, we usually do so on the assumption that they have most of the skills required. This means that their technical maturity is fairly high. However, since they are strangers to others in the organization and do not know how things work yet, they are emotionally immature. Therefore the supervisor will probably be more directive with new employees during the first weeks of their employment. Again, this makes good human relations sense.

How does maturity relate to the practice of human relations?

POWER AND ITS USAGE

We will look at power because this use of the manager's influence is important to the organization and the individual worker. For example, if a manager feels that a more directive management style is appropriate, how should that manager exercise power to be more directive with the employee? Some choices the supervisor must consider are *reward power, expert power, legitimate power,* and *coercive power.*

The concept of power has been around for some time. Many times the terms *power* and *influence* are used interchangeably; however, in our discussion, we distinguish between the two. *Influence* is the act of changing or affecting the thoughts, feelings, or behaviors of others. Influence occurs only in the act of relating to another. *Power* is the capacity to influence others to get things done. Therefore, influence is the application of power. By virtue of position, managers hold power. Whether a manager exercises this power and tries to influence (and therefore lead others) is another question. For example, a vice president of sales has power by her position as the head of the sales division. If she wants to change the advertising budget, she can merely tell the advertising manager to change it (a form of legitimate power based on her position as the boss). Or she can ask

How do power and influence relate to one another?

Power is the capacity to influence others to get things done.

FIGURE 4-10
The concept of
power: An interaction

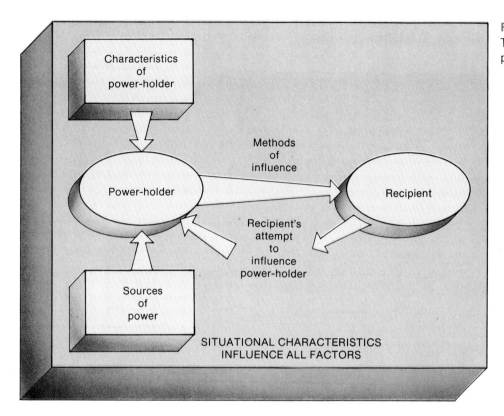

the advertising manager's opinion about the effectiveness of the ad campaign, reaching a mutual decision to change the budget. This approach could be described as using influence.

Power may be used or withheld, depending on the situation or the person who holds the power. For example, the office of the president of United States has power and the ability to influence. President Carter tended to withhold his power even during the Iranian crisis, while President Reagan used his power to get Congress to agree and act upon his economic measures during the recession of the early 1980s.

As with communication, power can be a two-way process. The power-holder can be influenced by the recipient's performance. For example, supervisors show more consideration to subordinates who perform at a higher level. This often leads to higher satisfaction among the subordinates. Figure 4–10 shows elements that make up the power and influence activity of a manager.

Characteristics of the Power-Holder

Earlier we discussed leadership styles and their effects on employee behavior. If the leadership style is perceived by the employee as appropriate for the condi-

Opening Story Revisited

We can use some of the situational theory to explain General Creech's success. The path-goal theory states that motivation can be increased by clarifying the goal of the organization and imposing some structure to get there. General Creech set high standards for the air-worthiness of the planes and refined the structure to small work units that could be held accountable for maintaining air-worthiness of their own planes. He also gave the military more responsibility for arranging equipment and its state of readiness. General Creech recognized the maturity level of his personnel and varied his style to match, in this case delegating more power to lower levels. He was correct in his assessment because his staff responded favorably.

What personal characteristics are important in using power?

tions, the influence attempt will be more successful. Trust, credibility, prestige, and self-confidence are important power-holder characteristics. Without trust and credibility, the power-holder's attempt to influence is viewed with suspicion and will be only partially successful. Prestige can enhance the power-holder because the employee would like to be associated with the supervisor. Finally, the self-confidence of the supervisor is based on the power-holder's past successes and experiences as a user of power. While these are not the only supports for the power-holder's ability to influence, they are the more positive in the eyes of the employee.

Sources of Power.   Additional support for the power-holder comes from various sources of power identified by John French and Bertram Raven.[13] The following are the major sources:

Reward Power.   Managers usually hold power by virtue of their ability to reward, which is one aspect of motivation. The strength of the power differs upon the amount of regard that the manager controls and the strength of the subordinate's desire for the reward, which can include pay increases, bonuses, and promotions.

Coercive Power.   Coercive power is a force held by those who can cause others to have unpleasant experiences, usually a form of punishment for not complying with the power-holder. Examples include discharge, demotion, and other disciplinary actions, as well as threats to act. Managers need to exercise caution because the use of coercive power may bring about the opposite result than the power-holder intends. Some studies have found that the use of coercive power actually decreased productivity as it was applied.[14]

Legitimate Power.   Legitimate power is held by individuals because their position, role, or status in a company provides a right to direct the actions of others.

[handwritten margin notes:] John French, Bertram Raven; Reward – ability to reward, strength of subordinates desire

[handwritten margin notes:] held by those who can cause others to have unpleasant experience; punishment may have opposite effect

[handwritten notes at bottom:] position, role or status in co. provides a right to direct actions of others

Legitimate power is based upon a mutually accepted perception that the power-holder has the right to influence the other. For instance, in an organization the manager has the right to expect certain tasks of the unit to be completed by employees. As a complementary right the subordinate expects to receive certain fair compensation for doing those tasks. *Manager expects that aim things to be done; subordinate expects fair compensation*

Referent Power. The recipient's identification with the power-holder is the basis of referent power. The recipient desires to be like the power-holder and therefore may act, perceive, feel, or think like the power-holder. In a sense, this is a form of charisma that draws respect and attracts others to the power-holder. In an organization, certain top managers may have referent power with young managers who aspire to reach those positions by emulating their success.

Expert Power. Expert power is based on a special ability or knowledge of the power-holder that is needed by the recipient. Accountants, engineers, and computer specialists gain organizational power as a result of information they collect and knowledge they obtain from their professional training. A major problem with expert power as a power base is that it depends on the perceptions of others.[15] As we know from Chapter 3, perceptions are often inaccurate. Futhermore, expert knowledge can quickly be used up as a problem is solved.

To put the sources of power in the proper perspective, we must understand aspects of their usage. First, these sources of power are not equally available to everyone in an organization. For example, the sources of power are different for line managers and staff managers. A line manager can usually exercise reward power with employees, while staff personnel, like engineering, must use expert power with line workers.

Second, these sources of power are not completely independent. The person with legitimate power often has reward power and coercive power. The person with reward power usually has coercive power.[16] And the use of expert power can increase referent power.

Finally, some studies show that expert power is perceived as most effective in inducing workers to accept changes, whereas coercive and legitimate power were least effective.[17] Another study showed that the greater the coercive power—punitive behavior of supervisors—the greater the reported feelings of fear, anxiety, anger, and depression among employees.[18]

Methods of Influence. While there are a multitude of means to influence the worker, they can be classified in two categories: direct and indirect. Table 4–1 shows the methods of influence identified by John Kotter in a study of twenty-six organizations.[19] He classified methods according to whether they involved direct (face-to-face) or indirect influence. He concluded that successful managers are able to, and do, use all the influence methods.

Describe how the sources of power differ in terms of effects and uses.

TABLE 4 – 1
Methods of influence

Face-to-face Methods	What They Can Influence	Advantages	Drawbacks
Exercise obligation-based power.	Behavior within zone that the other perceives as legitimate in light of the obligation.	Quick. Requires no outlay of tangible resources.	If the request is outside the acceptable zone, it will fail; if it is too far outside, others might see it as illegitimate.
Exercise power based on perceived expertise.	Attitudes and behavior within the zone of perceived expertise.	Quick. Requires no outlay of tangible resources.	If the request is outside the acceptable zone, it will fail; if it is too far outside, others might see it as illegitimate.
Exercise power based on identification with a manager.	Attitudes and behavior that are not in conflict with the ideals that underlie the identification.	Quick. Requires no expenditure of limited resources.	Restricted to influence attempts that are not in conflict with the ideals that underlie the identification.
Exercise power based on perceived dependence.	Wide range of behavior that can be monitored.	Quick. Can often succeed when other methods fail.	Repeated influence attempts encourage the other to gain power over the influencer.
Coercively exercise power based on perceived dependence.	Wide range of behavior that can be easily monitored.	Quick. Can often succeed when other methods fail.	Invites retaliation. Very risky.
Use persuasion.	Very wide range of attitudes and behavior.	Can produce internalized motivation that does not require monitoring. Requires no power or outlay of scarce material resources.	Can be very time-consuming. Requires other person to listen.
Combine these methods.	Depends on the exact combination.	Can be more potent and less risky than using a single method.	More costly than using a single method.

Indirect Methods	What They Can Influence	Advantages	Drawbacks
Manipulate the other's environment by using any or all of the face-to-face methods.	Wide range of behavior and attitudes.	Can succeed when face-to-face methods fail.	Can be time-consuming. Is complex to implement. Is very risky, especially if used frequently.
Change the forces that continuously act on the individual: Formal organizational arrangements, informal social arrangements, technology, resources available, statement of organizational goals.	Wide range of behavior and attitudes on a continuous basis.	Has continuous influence, not just a one-shot effect. Can have a very powerful impact.	Often requires a considerable power outlay to achieve.

SOURCE: J. P. Kotter, ''Power, Dependence, and Effective Management,'' *Harvard Business Review* (July–August 1977): 133. Copyright © 1977 by the President and Fellows of Harvard College; all rights reserved.

118

The supervisor's actual choice of methods is constrained by the individual's base of power. Methods based on formal authority are not usable unless the appropriate authority is granted. Giving and withholding information is not possible unless the power-holder has control over information. Indirect influence is difficult if one has no network of contacts that control the worker. A simple conclusion is that the choice of methods of influence is situationally dependent. However, there is some agreement that effective users of power begin with subtle methods, evolving to harsher methods only as required.

Uses of Power and Human Relations. While the conditions of power are not simple to apply, some basic ideas can help managers be effective in using power with subordinates or others. One aspect of using power more effectively concerns the *norm of reciprocity*. This simply means an exchange between individuals, "I'll do something for you if you do something for me." In terms of power-holder and subordinates, this means helping the subordinates meet their needs as they are influenced to perform certain organizational purposes. When individuals are able to successfully arrange "trade-offs," they can build an alliance that may be beneficial for both parties.

Define the term *norm of reciprocity*.

exchange between individuals.

Another aspect of using power is to remember its limitations. For example, expert power works fine when the specific situation relates to that expertise, but many times individuals forget they are dealing with a subject outside their expertise. There also are limitations to coercive power. It is most effective when the threat is constant. In many situations that can mean the physical presence to ensure the pressure of coercive power. A better alternative is the use of reward power, especially if the rewards are valued by the recipient.

---

1. Leadership and management are not synonymous. Leadership is an activity of management that varies with the specific managerial job and situations encountered.
2. Leadership theories are classified as behavioral and situational.
3. There is strong evidence that leadership behavior can be described along two dimensions: job-centered and employee-centered (University of Michigan studies) or initiating structure and consideration (Ohio State University studies).
4. Situational theories add other variables for the supervisor to consider before choosing a style: leader/member relations, task structure, leader position power, subordinate maturity, path-goal clarity.
5. Flexibility in adopting different leadership styles is an important management skill.
6. Power is the capacity to influence, while influence is the application of power.

LEARNING SUMMARY

7. Fundamental sources of power are reward power, coercive power, legitimate power, referent power, and expert power.
8. A leader should use subtle methods of influence before trying harsher methods.

ANSWERS TO "WHAT'S YOUR OPINION?"

1. **True** Managers usually try to influence their employees and others in the organization, which is a sign of leadership. But occupying the managerial position does not guarantee that the individual will exercise this function.

2. **False** We can suggest some behaviors that may work in certain situations, but the manager must stop and consider other important variables, such as limited time for action.

3. **False** Referent and expert power are more effective sources of power. Coercive power can cause the opposite effect if not carefully applied.

4. **True** Managers should use more subtle and indirect means of influence first. If these do not produce the desired results, more direct and confrontative methods may be appropriate.

5. **True** According to Hersey and Blanchard, the maturity level of the subordinate is critical to choosing an effective style of leadership.

6. **True** The path-goal theory uses the expectancy theory and the concept of various rewards to the employee. One aspect of particular importance for the manager is to help clarify the path to that goal (provide some structure).

7. **False** Participative leadership works in some situations, especially those in which there is time and in which employees expect that they will be involved in decisions.

8. **True** According to Fiedler, leadership positions can and should be altered to accommodate the leader. For example, if the rewards are unclear, then the power position is unclear. Management must clarify what rewards the leader can allocate, thus strengthening the power position.

KEY TERMS

Authoritarian leader	Delegation leader
Behavioral theory	Employee-centered leadership
Boss-centered leadership	Expert power
Coercive power	Initiating structure
Consideration	Job-centered leadership
Contingency model	Laissez-faire leader

Leader/Member relations

Leader position power

Legitimate power

Maturity

Norm of reciprocity

Participative leader

Paternalistic leader

Path-Goal theory

Referent power

Relationship behavior

Reward power

Situational theory

Task behavior

Task structure

Theory X-Theory Y

Become a Dynamic Subordinate

HUMAN RELATIONS APPLICATIONS

One area that hasn't received much attention in the leadership literature is how to be a dynamic subordinate. Yet, most managers will quickly state, "If only I had a good employee." If properly approached, subordinates can transfer some of the power and resulting rewards to their side of the balance sheet. There are several guidelines for becoming a dynamic subordinate:

☐ *Know the job*. Develop a clear and basic understanding of the job itself. Know what is expected by the supervisor. In most jobs there are many uncertainties about what needs to be done. Managers appreciate a subordinate who initiates a discussion about the expectations and responsibilities of the job.

By brainstorming and discussing ways to improve job performance, we enhance the possible performance of our boss. Doing a more effective job directly relates to how management sees our boss, and to how the boss respects and seeks our input. To be able to discuss how we can perform more effectively assumes that we have conducted a self-examination of our needs as well as the department's needs. Using this analysis as a basis for discussion with the supervisor is another way to distinguish ourselves as dynamic subordinates from other more passive workers.

☐ *Boss-subordinate relationship*. We all know that there is more to the job than just getting it done, no matter how well we perform it. A critical factor for success is the quality of the relationship with the supervisor. This relationship needs to be developed and nourished. One aspect of this development process is the ability to challenge the boss's ideas and decisions from the perspective of improving and not disproving them. This distinction may be at times difficult to accomplish. One way to challenge a superior's ideas is to do so privately, so the boss can "save face." This is the same rule for supervisors: do not criticize a subordinate in public. The purpose of this challenge is to create better ideas and decisions. It may take time to demonstrate this positive attitude, but once established, a supervisor will seek out this type of employee for an opinion.

☐ *Fully inform your superior.* This suggestion for a dynamic "subordinateship" is a key to developing trust between the two parties. The informing process is a part of the accounting responsibility that makes up any job. Initiating the passing of information shows a boss the follow-through that is so important in any responsible position and prevents unexpected problems from appearing.

☐ *Ask for and give feedback to the manager.* Any part of a relationship is affected by perceptions, and perceptions can be inaccurate because of emotionality. This becomes a problem only if we do not review the relationship. Giving and asking for feedback is one way to clarify job responsibilities and carry them out. It also reduces the building of distrust and suspicion.

These few ideas can, if applied on a regular basis, create a dynamic, active subordinate who helps a manager manage.

Management by Walking Away

Management by walking away is a leadership style practiced by the president of Quad/Graphics of Pewaukee, Wisconsin. For one day each year, known as the Spring Fling, the management of Quad/Graphics walks away and leaves the operation of the company in the hands of employees.[20] The tradition began in the mid-1970s, as president Harry V. Quadracci was looking for a way to get his managers out of the plant for a day of planning and socializing. The original plan was to shut down production for the day, but some unexpected orders came in and, rather than pass them up, the company instructed the employees to run the plant themselves.

Quadracci is known as a fan of management theory. He has created the kind of force from which he can walk away—a company that will literally run itself. A major part of his leadership philosophy is that responsibility should be assumed and shared. Anyone who sees something that needs to be done should assume the responsibility for doing it. In fact, Quadracci often refuses to tell his people what should be done. For instance, when the company needed greater backhaul revenue to finance expansion of its trucking fleet, Quadracci handed each of the drivers the keys to one of the company's large trucks and told them they were now owner-operators in a new division of the company. He made it their responsibility to make the trucks profitable on their return trips. When the drivers asked what they should carry on the backhauls, Quadracci responded that they would have to find out themselves. The truckers rose to the challenge and, in a relatively short period of time, had a profitable operation going.

Quadracci notes that sometimes management by walking away is a difficult leadership style for him, as he has some opinions that he would like to express. But he has found that to be consistent with his philosophy on sharing responsibility and encouraging employees to assume responsibility, often his best action is, in fact, to walk away. Quadracci's style seems to combine important elements of path-goal (increasing the value of goal accomplishment, clarifying goals) and situational leadership (flexibility, developing subordinate maturity).

Women as Leaders

No one doubts that the number of women in leadership positions is increasing, yet there is strong controversy over whether the numbers reflect a real change in our cultural bias toward a ''male business world.'' But numbers and their superficial meaning do not suggest the positive trend that was raised in *Vital Speeches of the Day*.[21]

Anita Taylor uses John Naisbitt's *Megatrends* as a basis to show that overall trends in our country are making women uniquely qualified for leadership positions. Taylor cites two trends in particular: the movement toward high technology with its accompanying need for high touch, and the movement from hierarchical frameworks to informal networks. According to Taylor, women are more com-

According to Taylor, women are more at ease than men are about touching others, and both women and men are more comfortable being touched by a woman than by a man.

fortable using touch than men, and both men and women are more willing to be touched by women than by men. Defining this trend more broadly as the movement to stay in touch, we see that women are more concerned with developing relationships. Therefore, women have unique skills to help work groups develop and grow.

The second trend is more reliance on informal networks rather than formal structures. Again, the socialization of women supports their being able to take advantage of this movement. Women have not been socialized as much as men to accept a hierarchy and its inherent limitations to process information. In the distant past, men were leaders because of strength, but today power and influence lie in information and its control through networks. As a result, women may have an advantage because of less mental resistance about how information should be used.

Finally, Taylor notes that women must guard against three dangers if they are to continue to assume leadership positions in organizations: Apathy—society talks about equality and during schooling all looks well, but the first years on a job can be a shock; anger—some women respond to discrimination with intense anger, which could be to their disadvantage because of the energy it drains and the reaction it elicits from the men it is aimed at; lethargy—this result of constant battling can create exhaustion. If women can overcome these dangers and view the challenges differently, they are more than ready now for leadership positions in all types of organizations, even more so than men.

PERSONAL GUIDELINES FOR HUMAN RELATIONS SUCCESS

In this chapter we looked at a variety of leadership theories that helped illustrate its complexity and diversity. Yet there are some guidelines that enhance our own success as supervisors:

1. *Create an atmosphere of involvement.* One area that can contribute significantly to a supervisor's effectiveness is worker involvement in deciding how to do the job. In most businesses, work seems to be predetermined—"We have always done it this way." In a sense, history determines how we will do a job. But new methods and technology can allow for improvement. Who knows better how to improve the job than the employee? Allowing employees to discover and suggest new approaches to old jobs can create renewed interest and help employees work on other levels of needs besides survival in the job.
2. *Stretch through goal setting.* One of the most powerful ways for a leader to guide employees to greater accomplishments is through the path-goal method. People want to know how they can be a part of something. Showing employees how to set realistic goals for improving job performance can create a challenge to reach and beat the goals. This assumes that the supervisor has shared information about where the department is heading and how the employee's goals fit into the plan.

3. *Personalize your leadership approach.* Several situational theories suggested varying management style to fit the situation. Assuming that you accept this approach to leadership, you need to inform your employees of this decision to use different styles. We tend to assume that employees know what we are doing when we ''baby'' a particular employee. That probably is a wrong assumption; this behavior could be interpreted as favoritism. Make sure that employees know that some people need to be led by the hand through tasks while others do not. Explain this approach at the beginning so they can appreciate that you are trying to personalize your leadership to their needs. Specifically, you should contract with each employee, one by one, to establish which management style will work best for them. Should you direct, support, coach, or delegate? Only some form of discussion periodically will help you be on target.

4. *Share influence and power.* We assume that only leaders have power and therefore the ability to influence. This is true on the surface, but employees also have the ability to influence. In many situations, supervisors need to suppress the natural instinct to use their own power. One way to share power is to allow employees to generate goals for themselves and for the work group. In one sense, this is using the expert power that all employees have because they are closest to the individual jobs.

DISCUSSION AND REVIEW QUESTIONS

1. What is effective leadership?
2. What problems are involved in using one leadership style? What advantages accrue from consistently using one style?
3. Is participation more effective than a more directive style of leadership? Why or why not?
4. Why are the simplified management theories like McGregor's Theory X and Theory Y so popular with managers?
5. Can a person have power without influence? What are the major sources of influence? Which are more effective?

HUMAN RELATIONS EXERCISE

Leadership

Please complete the following questionnaire. For each of the following ten pairs of statements, divide five points between the two according to your beliefs and perceptions of yourself, or according to which of the two statements better characterizes you. The five points may be divided between the A and B statements in any one of the following ways: 5A 0B, 4A 1B, 3A 2B, 2A 3B, 1A 4B, 0A 5B, but not equally (2½) between the two. Weigh your choices between the two according to which one better characterizes you or your beliefs.

Leadership Questionnaire

_____ 1. A. As a leader I have a primary mission of maintaining stability.

_____ B. As a leader I have a primary mission of change.

_____ 2. A. As a leader I must cause events.

_____ B. As a leader I must facilitate events.

_____ 3. A. I am concerned that my followers are rewarded equitably for their work.

_____ B. I am concerned about what my followers want in life.

_____ 4. A. As a leader a primary task I have is to mobilize and provide focus for followers' needs.

_____ B. As a leader a primary task I have is to ensure clarity of responsibility and roles for my subordinates.

_____ 5. A. My preference is to think short-range, what is realistic.

_____ B. My preference is to think long-range, what might be.

_____ 6. A. I believe leadership to be a process of changing the conditions of people's lives.

_____ B. I believe leadership to be a process of exchange between leader and follower.

_____ 7. A. As a leader, I spend considerable energy in managing separate but related goals.

_____ B. As a leader, I spend considerable energy in arousing hopes, expectations, and aspirations among my followers.

_____ 8. A. While not in a formal classroom sense, I believe that a significant part of my leadership is that of teacher.

_____ B. I believe that a significant part of my leadership is that of facilitator.

_____ 9. A. As a leader I must engage with followers at an equal level of morality.

_____ B. As a leader I must represent a higher morality.

_____ 10. A. What power I have to influence others comes primarily from my ability to get people to identify with me and my ideas.

_____ B. What power I have to influence others comes primarily from my status and position.

Source: W. Warner Burke, Teachers College, Columbia University. Used by permission of W. Warner Burke, 1986.

James MacGregor Burns, in *Leadership,* distinguishes between two kinds of leadership: *transformational* and *transactional.*[22] A transformational leader "recognizes and exploits an existing need or demand of a follower. But, beyond that, the transforming leader looks for potential motives in followers, seeks to satisfy higher level needs, and engages the full person of the follower." A transactional leader, on the other hand, is one who views the leader-follower relationship as a process of exchange—rewards for work, jobs for votes, favor for favor, and so on.

In a similar fashion, we can expect the transactional leader to be more likely to initiate structure and be task-oriented, while a transformational leader would probably have a higher regard for consideration and relationship-orientation. Which are you?

Scoring

The questionnaire is constructed according to Burns's two types of leaders—transactional and transformational. In other words, half of the A responses represent one type, and half the other; the same is true for the B alternatives. The key is as follows:

Transformational		Transactional	
1. B	6. A	1. A	6. B
2. A	7. B	2. B	7. A
3. B	8. A	3. A	8. B
4. A	9. B	4. B	9. A
5. B	10. A	5. A	10. B

By adding your responses for each of these two columns, you can determine the relative weight you are giving to one type of leadership as compared with the other. Burns contends that most of us are transactional rather than transformational. Compare your scores with your classmates and see whether Burns is correct. Do you think that one or the other is more effective, given our changing work values (see Chapter 1)?

HUMAN RELATIONS INCIDENT

Patty, an energetic twenty-five-year-old, had just returned from France, where she had completed a special program for those with fluency in several foreign languages. Upon her return, she took a temporary clerical job in the filing department of a huge government office dealing with international trade. She had hoped to use some of her new skills.

After three months, Patty began to come in late to work. This was distressing to her co-workers and her supervisor because she was well liked and her work was exceptionally well done. Her supervisor called her in, explained that this could not be tolerated, and warned her to be on time in the future. For the next several weeks, all was well.

Over a period of time, however, Patty again began to be late to work and took longer coffee and lunch breaks. Her supervisor had several sessions with her and tried to impress upon her the importance of coming to work on time. He even began to write a formal disciplinary letter. After several sessions, he concluded she was basically disorganized in her private life and decided to help her go over bus schedules to plan getting to work on time. Nothing seemed to work, and the rest of the work group became dissatisfied with the amount of attention she was getting. Her supervisor decided that he needed to seriously consider firing her. What would you do?

NOTES

1. Adapted from Jay Finegan, "Four-Star Management," *INC.* (January 1986): 42–51.
2. S. Donnell and J. Hall, "Men and Women as Managers: A Significant Case of No Significant Differences," *Organizational Dynamics,* vol. 8, no. 4 (1980): 60–77.
3. D. McGregor, *The Human Side of Enterprise* (New York: McGraw-Hill, 1960).
4. Rensis Likert, *New Patterns of Management* (New York: McGraw-Hill, 1961).
5. Robert Tannenbaum and Warren H. Schmidt, "How to Choose a Leadership Pattern," *Harvard Business Review* (May–June 1973): 162–80.
6. Edwin A. Fleishman, "The Leadership Opinion Questionnaire," in Ralph M. Stogdill and A. E. Coons, eds., *Leader Behavior and Its Description and Measurement* (Columbus, OH: Bureau of Business Research, Ohio State University, 1957).
7. Edwin A. Fleishman, "Twenty Years of Consideration and Structure," in Edwin A. Fleishman and J. G. Hunt, eds., *Current Developments in the Study of Leadership* (Carbondale, IL: Southern Illinois University Press, 1973).
8. F. E. Fiedler, *A Theory of Leadership Effectiveness* (New York: McGraw-Hill, 1967).
9. R. J. House and T. R. Mitchell, "A Path-Goal Theory of Leadership," *Journal of Contemporary Business,* vol. 3 (1974): 81–99; and M. G. Evans, "The Effects of Supervisory Behavior and the Path-Goal Relationship," *Organizational Behavior and Human Performance,* vol. 5 (1977): 277–98.
10. R. J. House and G. A. Dessler, "Path-Goal Theory of Leadership: Some post hoc and a priori Tests," in J. G. Hunt and L. L. Larson, eds., *Contingency Approaches To Leadership* (Carbondale, IL: Southern Illinois University Press, 1974).
11. C. N. Greene, "Questions of Causation in the Path-Goal Theory of Leadership," *Academy of Management Journal,* vol. 22, no. 1 (1979): 22–41.
12. Claude L. Graeff, "The Situational Leadership Theory: A Critical View," *Academy of Management Review,* vol. 8, no. 2 (1983): 287.
13. J. R. P. French and B. Raven, "The Bases of Social Power," in D. Cartwright and A. F. Zander, eds., *Group Dynamics,* 3rd ed. (New York: Harper & Row, 1968): 259–69.
14. K. Sheley and M. E. Shaw, "Social Power: To Use or Not to Use?" *Bulletin of the Psychonomic Society,* vol. 13, no. 4 (April 1979): 257–60.
15. R. E. Spekman, "Influence and Information: An Exploratory Investigation of the Boundary Role Person's Basis of Power," *Academy of Management Journal,* vol. 22 (1979): 104–17.
16. A. Litman, G. Fontaine, and B. H. Raven, "Consequences of Social Power and Causal Attribution for Compliance as Seen by Power-holder and Target," *Personality and Social Psychology,* vol. 14, no. 1 (April 1978): 260–64.
17. R. J. Myers, "Fear, Anger, and Depression in Organizations: A Study of the Functional Consequences of Power" (dissertation, St. John's University, 1977), *Dissertations Abstracts International— The Humanities and Social Sciences,* vol. 39, no. 7, 4530 (January 1979).

18. J. Pfeffer, ''Power and Resource Allocation in Organizations,'' in B. M. Staw and G. R. Salancik, eds., *New Directions in Organizational Behavior* (Chicago: St. Clair Press, 1977).

19. John Kotter and G. Strauss, ''Tactics of Lateral Relationship: The Purchasing Agent,'' *Administrative Science Quarterly,* vol. 7, no. 2 (1962): 166–67.

20. E. Wojahn, ''Management by Walking Away,'' *INC.* (October 1983): 68–80.

21. Anita Taylor, ''Women as Leaders: The Skills at Which We Are So Uniquely Qualified,'' delivered to the *GROW* Conference of Kentucky Women Researchers, Eastern Kentucky University (23 February 1984).

22. James MacGregor Burns, *Leadership* (New York: Harper & Row, 1978): 4.

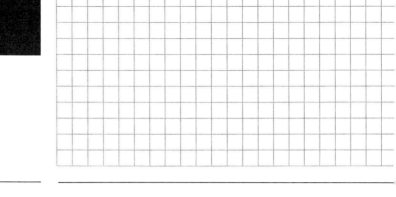

CHAPTER 5
COMMUNICATIONS

WHAT'S YOUR OPINION? T OR F

_F_ 1. When another person hears you, you have communicated.

_T_ 2. Managers spend more than 80 percent of their time communicating with others.

_F_ 3. We always know what we are communicating.

_T_ 4. Communicating upward in an organization is more difficult than communicating downward.

_T_ 5. A good beginning and ending for effective communication is to "stop talking."

_T_ 6. Centralized communication is more effective for complex tasks.

_T_ 7. Our behavior can either help or hinder our communications.

_F_ 8. Feedback should be general so as to not upset the other person.

LEARNING OBJECTIVES

- ☐ Identify the elements of the communication process
- ☐ Explain the barriers to effective communication
- ☐ List six methods of reducing the communication barriers
- ☐ Describe how organizational networks affect the communication process
- ☐ Recognize the impact of nonverbal behavior on communication
- ☐ Identify the major human relations applications aimed at improving communication
- ☐ Describe personal steps to more effective communication

Gossip, Rumor, Innuendo, Libel—It's All Inder Works[1]

A newly hired employee of Snohomish County in Washington state complained to a lonely-hearts columnist that an alarming number of her co-workers were pregnant. The reply wasn't comforting. The columnist cited a "scientific study" by health officials that concluded that static electricity from carpets, polyester knit apparel, and asbestos from light fixtures dramatically increase fertility.

Such tongue-in-cheek advice is usual fare for readers of "Ask Annie Engineer," a regular feature of *Inder Works,* the newsletter for the more than 250 Department of Public Works employees. In the past year, circulation has jumped more than 30 percent to nearly 400. Readers include judges, an East Coast consulting firm, the mayor of a nearby small town, and the employees of neighboring San Juan County. A group of 25 retirees asked to be added.

Why is the newsletter so successful? It could be its unpredictable nature! Whatever a typical employee newsletter is, *Inder Works* isn't.

"We tend to 'slander' people who are going to take it well," *Inder Works* staff writer Jeff Kelly-Clark explains. And no one seems to mind, including the public works director, Jerry Weed. "A lot of times you send things out to employees to read and it goes straight into the garbage can, even if it's attached to their paychecks," Weed says. "This thing gets read."

Inder Works meets its publishing deadline each month, despite the fact that it has no budget. Its four staff members work one or two extra days a month to get it out and also pick up most of the expense.

Inder Works operates by two hard-and-fast rules. "We don't want to embarrass the department," says Kelly-Clark. "At the same time, we don't want to be pablum."

The newsletter pokes fun at a wide range of foibles and a broad range of subjects. Frequent targets are the department's many engineers, who are jabbed at for being overly technical. Management (nicknamed "The Bull") was advised to "never let reality get in its way." Workers in the solid-waste division (Seagulls) fared the worst: "Any feelings of isolation, of being unloved and ignored, are well-founded. Even the stars prefer to keep their distance."

The entries aren't all barbs, however. There are liberal pats on the back, such as the one for biologists in the department's salmon restoration program, who are "constantly swimming against the current." *Inder Works* isn't all frivolity, either. County employees get free classified advertising, profiles of co-workers, and articles to keep them abreast of seminars, services, and events.

Staff member Debbie St. Marie-Eidson calls *Inder Works* "just good communication. It's better for people to keep laughing at themselves than to let

problems stew away unmentioned.'' She says the newsletter is a valuable link for far-flung public works employees, many of whom are stationed at road repair shops in other towns around the county and rarely visit department offices. ''We can't bring people around the table,'' she adds. ''We're too big an organization.''

When a road worker was unable to keep an appointment for an interview, an *Inder Works* staff member talked to an empty chair. The text of the one-sided question-and-answer session, which pointed up how little time road crews have to sit during an average day, ran in the next issue—alongside a picture of the chair.

The Importance of Communication

Communication, like leadership and motivation, is one of the most discussed areas in human relations. Everyone favors improving communications, and no one disagrees that good communications leads to effective and satisfying work and personal life. But how do we measure its impact on corporate profits? How do we know when communications are good or effective?

What Is Communication? To define communication, let us look at one of the consequences of poor communication:

> A plumber wrote to the Bureau of Standards to ask about using hydrochloric acid for cleaning pipes. The bureau replied, ''The efficacy of hydrochloric acid is indisputable, but the chlorine residue is incompatible with metallic permanence.'' The plumber sent a brief note of thanks to the bureau for agreeing with him. The bureau hastily wrote him, ''We cannot assume responsibility for the production of toxic and non-toxic residues with hydrochloric acid, and suggest that you use an alternative procedure.'' Again, the plumber sent a brief note of thanks for the confirmation of his opinion. Finally, the bureau wrote the plumber, ''Don't use hydrochloric acid; it eats the hell out of pipes.'' He understood.[2]

Communication is difficult to define. Everyone ''knows'' what communication is, and yet there is no generally acceptable definition. Some researchers equate communication with ''interaction.'' Thus, communication occurs whenever two or more individuals interact. But have you interacted with someone, such as your boss or friend, and then said to yourself, ''She didn't hear me''? Would you say that you have communicated with the other person in this situation? Probably not.

We have chosen to limit the definition of communication and qualify it. As a result, we have settled on the phrase, *effective communication*.

Communication is more than simply the passing of information between two people. Remember the plumber and the Bureau of Standards! The key to communication is the passage of the *meaning* of the information; yet we must go

Effective communication is the information flow resulting in a shared meaning and a common understanding for both the information sender and the receiver.

information flow resulting in a shared meaning and a common understanding for both info sender, receiver (handwritten note)

FIGURE 5–1
Distribution of managers' time among various communication media (Source: Adaptation of Figure 4 (p. 39) from *The Nature of Managerial Work* by Henry Mintzberg. Copyright © 1973 by Henry Mintzberg. Reprinted by permission of Harper & Row Publishers, Inc.)

further than just transmitting the meaning. If the Bureau of Standards had not continued to communicate, the results might have been disastrous for the homeowner. Therefore, we must add the term *effectiveness* to our definition.

Communication is the information flow that results in a *shared meaning* and a *common understanding* for the sender and receiver of information. A good example of this definition is the last correspondence from the bureau to the plumber, "Don't use hydrochloric acid; it eats the hell out of pipes." It is important to note that "common understanding" and "shared meaning," do not necessarily mean agreement between the two parties. It does mean that both parties understand each other's position on the subject.

Importance to Management. "Poor communications" is often blamed for problems in organizations, because communication is the process by which managers collect information to make a decision. When poor decisions occur, ineffective communication is frequently to blame. For example, an inventory manager will collect information from the sales and manufacturing departments about their

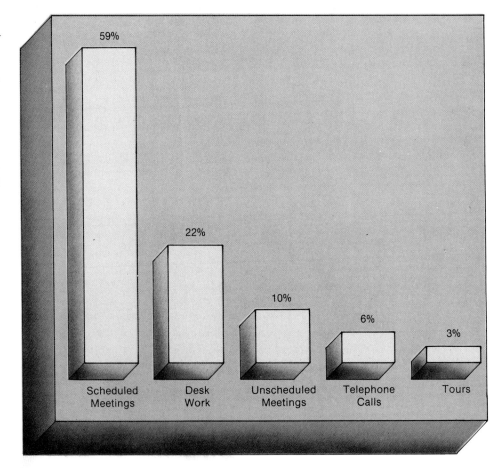

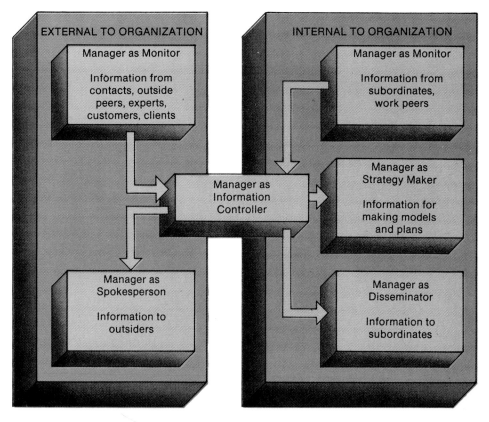

FIGURE 5–2
The manager as an information-processing system (Source: Adaptation of Figure 10 (p. 72) from *The Nature of Managerial Work* by Henry Mintzberg. Copyright © 1973 by Henry Mintzberg. Reprinted by permission of Harper & Row Publishers, Inc.)

needs before planning the appropriate levels of inventory for a selected product. If the sales manager does not understand the request for information, incorrect data may be supplied. If the information is used and the resulting inventory levels are too high or too low, it is clear that a "poor decision" was made. But was the decision poor or was the information used inaccurate because of ineffective communication?

Managers depend on their communication skills to make decisions and to convey the results of these decisions to other people. Research indicates that managers spend as much as 80 percent of their time communicating with others.[3] Figure 5–1 shows how the time of five executives was used in various types of communications: telephone calls, scheduled and unscheduled meetings, plant tours, and desk work. But about what do they communicate? If we visualize a manager as the hub of information (see Figure 5–2), we can begin to appreciate the difficulty of creating effective communication.

We see the manager at the center of control of information flow—at the intersection of information that flows upward, downward, and laterally within the organization's structure. The effectiveness of the communication involved can help or hinder the manager's attempts to maintain or increase the organization's performance. In downward communications, the manager transmits to subordi-

[handwritten margin notes: "make decisions and to convey the results of these decisions to people"]

[handwritten: Why is the communication process so important to management?]

[handwritten: as much as 80% of time is spent communicating]

FIGURE 5–3
The flow of information within an organization

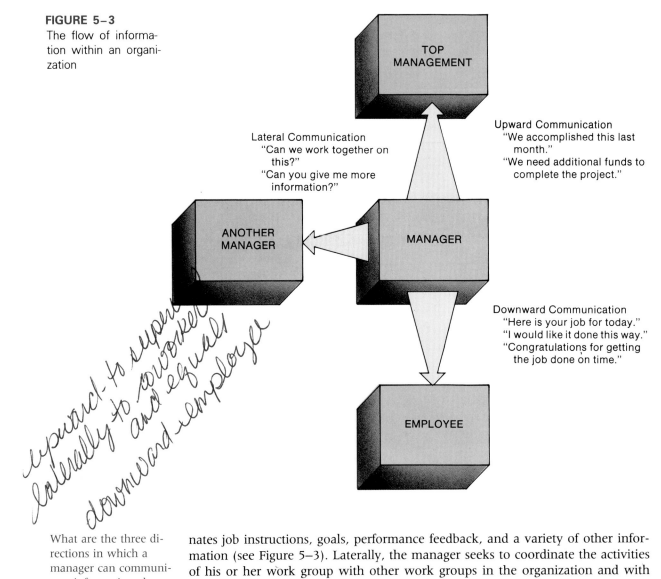

Lateral Communication
"Can we work together on
this?"
"Can you give me more
information?"

Upward Communication
"We accomplished this last
month."
"We need additional funds to
complete the project."

Downward Communication
"Here is your job for today."
"I would like it done this way."
"Congratulations for getting
the job done on time."

What are the three directions in which a manager can communicate information about an organization's performance or tasks?

nates job instructions, goals, performance feedback, and a variety of other information (see Figure 5–3). Laterally, the manager seeks to coordinate the activities of his or her work group with other work groups in the organization and with customers or suppliers. Upward communications provides opportunities for the manager to transmit information on work group activities, problems, or challenges.

Communication Processes

Interpersonal Model. Let us begin by exploring the communication process between two people. The key elements of this process, diagrammed in Figure 5–4, include the sender, the message transmission and reception, and the receiver.

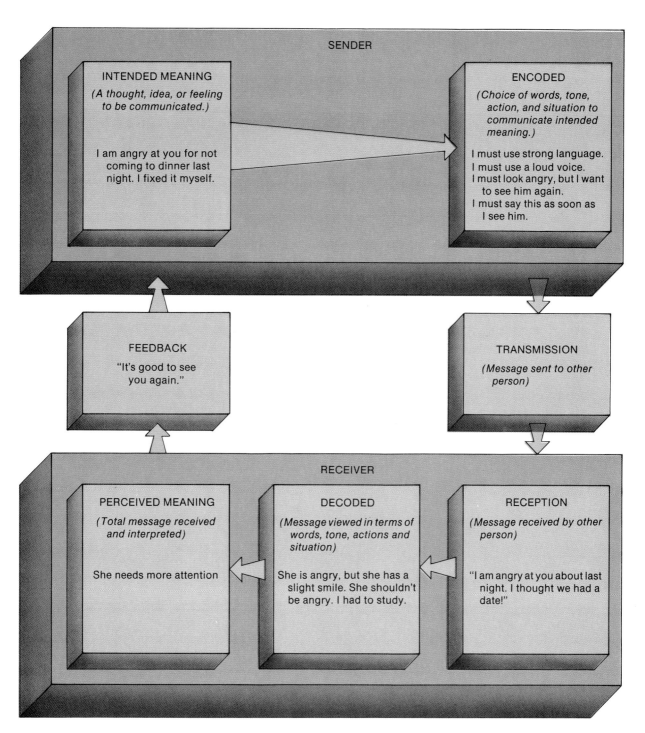

FIGURE 5–4
Interpersonal model of communication

Lines of Communication

As your organization grows, so does what you need to know. After all, if you don't know your employees, do you really know your company? While it would be nice to report that technology has created newer and better ways to deal with communications, it hasn't. It seems that one key to communication is presence. Technology can help but it certainly cannot replace physical presence.

A good example of helpful technology is demonstrated by James Treybig of Tandem Computers Inc., who appears on a monthly television program broadcast over the company's in-house TV station. Employees around the world watch the show and call in their questions and comments. In a similar vein, Tom Monaghan of Domino's Pizza Inc. maintains toll-free numbers for em-

ployees. He also has a monthly "call-in" during which he listens to suggestions and fields complaints for a couple of hours.

But you really don't need technology to communicate with employees, even if they are spread out across the land. For Robert Darvin of Scandinavian Design Inc., it's the suggestion box. He distributes special stationery to every employee at his 21-year-old retail furniture company. The stationery is intended for one purpose: communicating with the boss. And everyone is expected to use it.

Arthur E. Morrissette, president of Interstate Van Lines Inc., found another more dramatic move to communicate—training and sing-along sessions. The training session is a daily affair, from 7:30 to 8:30 A.M., during which managers address the movers and packers on different aspects of the business. The sing-along happens once every couple of weeks. All of the employees meet in the convention hall, under orders to mingle so that they won't think of themselves as sep-

Source: Adapted from Nelson W. Aldrich Jr., "Lines of Communication." Reprinted with permission, *INC.* magazine, June, 1986. Copyright © 1986 by INC. Publishing Company, 38 Commercial Wharf, Boston, MA 02110.

What are the major parts of the interpersonal model of communication?

Intended meaning a thought, idea, concept, or feeling the sender wants to convey to the receiver

Encode to transfer the thoughts, motives, and emotions into symbols for sending to the receiver

From the diagram, you can see that these basic elements have other parts to complete the model.

The first step is to have an *intended meaning* to communicate to the receiver. In our example, the sender wants to communicate that she is angry at the other person for not coming to dinner as expected. She now needs to encode this intended meaning and a feeling of anger. *Encoding* involves transferring the thoughts, motives, and emotions into symbols that convey meaning. For example, in writing this book we needed to organize important information for this chapter by anticipating who the readers would be, how much experience they would have to relate to these ideas, and where in the course this subject would be covered. Our assumptions based on these questions helped us to write (encode) the material so that the reader learns about communication.

Returning to the previous example, we see that the sender needs to encode her meaning. She decides to use strong language and a forceful tone but to not look so angry as to discourage the receiver from future dinners. She decides to send this message the next day when she meets the receiver.

arate camps. It's a time to emphasize the team, Morrissette explains, and to recognize individual achievement with awards, cash prizes, and points toward evaluation.

Another example of trying to communicate within an organization is Stew Leonard's old staple of in-house communication, the newsletter. Leonard is the founder of an $80 million grocery store in Norwalk, Connecticut. The publication is called *Stew's News*. Thirty to fifty pages long, with more photos than text, it appears monthly and carries as much need-to-know information as an oversize bulletin board.

The staff is anyone who wants to be involved, which can mean forty people on the credit line at one time. The initiator of this newsletter was not from the head office, but rather a fellow named Mike Hughes from grocery. One edition introduced Mike to the readers:

Born: Norwalk. Enjoys all *Rocky* movies. Fav. singer, song, entertainer: Lionel Richie, "Penny Lover," Bill Cosby. Fav. book, magazine: *Thesaurus, TV Guide*, Fav. restaurant, meal: Peppermill, lobster and filet. Most enjoyable thing won: $3 lottery. Epitaph: "I did the best I could with the hand of cards life dealt me." Hates people who lie and gossip.

That's quite a lot to know about a fellow worker. But, in *Stew's News,* everyone gets a chance to know and be known.

What these methods of communication tell us is that no one method is correct for every situation. In one sense these methods reflect the company from which they originate, the kind of industry they are from, and the personality of its leader.

QUESTIONS

1. Explain some of the reasons for the success of these various means of communication.
2. Why is presence so important in communication?
3. Use the communication networks to describe how Interstate Van Lines Inc. communicates with its employees.
4. If you were asked to establish an organizational communications program, what would you include and why?

The next two elements of communication are in the transmission and reception of the message between the two parties. In this part of the model, both parties' senses are acting (sight, hearing, touch, smell). The transmission is a physical action by some part of the body. The voice (oral messages), hands (written messages), or body parts (nonverbal messages) may transmit messages. The medium is the means by which the messages travel from the sender to the receiver. The most frequently used media include face-to-face conversations, telephones, written messages, and speeches.

Transmission a physical action by some part of the body

In the example, she says, "I am angry at you about last night. I thought we had a date!" The reception of this message by the receiver involves not only the words spoken but also the tone (rather loud), the body language (hands on hips), the facial expression (a slight smile), and the situation (the receiver's mid-term exam on which he needs a good grade).

Reception the use of one's physical senses (sight, hearing, smell, or touch) to collect data about the message sent

Decoding is the translation of received messages into interpreted or perceived messages. If the communication has been effective, the meaning decoded by the receiver is the same as that encoded by the sender. In decoding a message

Opening Story Revisited

I s there a common understanding and a shared meaning in the opening story? Judging by the number of new readers (up 30 percent) and the 25 retirees who wanted to be added to the mailing list, it appears that some powerful interest is being generated by *Inder Works*. Important information (from management's perspective) may not be read if normal channels, such as memos, are used, as the public works director pointed out, but this newspaper is read by the employees.

Decoding the translation of information received by the senses into perceived messages

the receiver takes into account not only the symbols used by the sender but also personal and situational factors surrounding the sender and receiver. The decoding of the message is also influenced by the motives, emotions, and perceptual tendencies of the receiver. For the decoded message to completely match the coded one, the receiver must be able to align with the sender regarding symbols, motives, emotions, and perceptual processes.

To what extent do you feel that the sender and the receiver in our example have communicated effectively? Do they have a shared meaning and a common understanding? If not, what happened?

Explain why communication between people can be difficult.

One reason for a failure to communicate might be the facial expression (a slight smile), which negates the strong tone and words. What about the receiver's motives? We must remember that he is facing a difficult mid-term exam. Might not this be the main focus of his attention at this time? While we can't say how effective the communication was, we see from this simple example the complexity of two-person communication.

Communication network the pattern and flow of written or verbal messages between individuals

Organizational Communication.   Up to this point we have been discussing the communication process between two people. When communication occurs within large groups, the channels by which information flows become critical. The way a group or organization structures itself determines the ease and effectiveness with which members can communicate. The actual pattern and flow of written or verbal messages between individuals form a communication network.

Centralized networks messages flow through one individual who controls the amount and speed of transmission

Five common networks are shown in Figure 5–5. These five networks can be classified into two major groups: centralized and decentralized. In the centralized networks, one individual acts as the focus or control point for the information flow. The networks with a control point are *chain, wheel,* and *"Y."* In the decentralized networks, there is no control point for information flow. The *circle* and *all-channel* are decentralized networks.

Centralized Networks. The centralized *chain network* is represented by a five-level hierarchy. In this situation, information would flow upward and downward but not laterally. A typical example would be one in which the assembly-line worker reports to the first-line supervisor, who in turn reports to the general

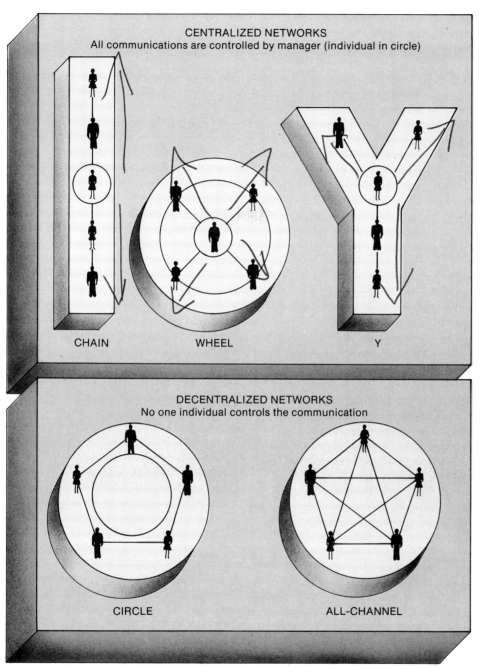

FIGURE 5–5
Communication net-
works

centralized

decentralized

supervisor, who reports to the plant manager, who reports to the divisional manager. Another common example is the organizational "grapevine" that passes information throughout the organization between different departments and orga-

Grapevine the informal communication system that passes information unofficially throughout a company

nizational levels. The grapevine is compared to the chain because the information usually travels in one direction and, since the grapevine is unofficial, the accuracy of messages isn't checked after they are sent.

When we look at the *wheel network,* we can visualize a manager with four supervisors. In this instance, the four supervisors do not communicate with one another but just with the manager in the center of the wheel.

The *"Y" network* is more easily understood if turned upside down. A central manager has two subordinates. The manager then reports to another manager, who in turn reports to another level further up the organization.

Decentralized network no one person controls the flow of information

Decentralized Networks. The circle and the all-channel networks are decentralized. This means that there is no central person through whom communications must flow.

The *circle network* allows members to interact with adjoining members directly but not with the other members of the same group. It is difficult to find such a network in an organization or in other areas of life. The only example might be prisoners in jail cells who can communicate only with adjoining cells.

The *all-channel* network allows each member to communicate freely with all others. The all-channel network has no central position, nor are there restrictions about who talks to whom; all members are equal. This network is best illustrated by a committee in which no one member either formally or informally assumes a dominant or leadership position. All members are free to share ideas, opinions, and feelings.

[handwritten margin note: Potential effects of speed of task completion, accuracy of solution, member satisfaction]

Do centralized and decentralized networks differ in effectiveness in dealing with problems?

[handwritten margin note: yes]

Effectiveness of Different Networks. The importance of these networks lies in their potential effects on three areas: speed of task completion, accuracy of solutions, and member satisfaction. The key issue in determining these effects is task complexity.[4] We will see different results from centralized networks and decentralized networks when groups perform simple tasks (e.g., identifying a symbol common to all cards given to participants) and complex tasks (e.g., solving word problems).

What are the conclusions? Table 5–1 provides a summary. Using complex problems, decentralized networks reached solutions faster and made fewer errors. Looking at simple problems, centralized networks reached solutions faster and made fewer errors.

Can we explain these results? A possible explanation is that the more information any one group member has to deal with at one time, the more likely that person is to become "saturated." A person who is saturated is overloaded with information and finds it difficult to perform effectively. The group's performance will also suffer. This is what seems to have happened when the centralized group performed a complex task. The central person became so overloaded with information that the group was slowed down and errors were made.

However, if we look at a simple task, we can appreciate that the central person could easily solve the simple problem alone after receiving information from the other members. On the other hand, in the decentralized networks, the

Performance Variable	Centralized Networks	Decentralized Networks
Speed (Number of problems solved)		
Simple problems	Faster	Slower
Complex problems	Slower	Faster
Accuracy (Number of errors made)		
Simple problems	More accurate	Less accurate
Complex problems	Less accurate	More accurate
Job satisfaction	Less satisfied	More satisfied

TABLE 5-1
Effectiveness of communication networks

SOURCE: Marvin E. Shaw, "Communication Networks," in L. Berkowitz, ed., *Advances in Experimental Social Psychology*, vol. 1 (New York: Academic Press, 1964.) Reprinted by permission.

group members had no central person to control the flow of information and therefore it took longer to get enough information to one person to solve the simple problem.

Another important conclusion from this study is that members of centralized networks are *less* satisfied with their work than the decentralized members. Why? It appears that members enjoy having an equal say in decisions made in the circle networks and do not like having a central person in the wheel make decisions for them. This makes sense in view of other studies showing that workers are more satisfied with their jobs when they participate in making decisions about them.[5]

Will individuals be happier in centralized or decentralized networks? Why?

Opening Story Revisited

The *Inder Works* newspaper is an example of transmission of information from the staff to the audience. It is the physical aspect of the communication process.

One staff member states, "We don't want to embarrass the department and we don't want to be pablum." This is an example of encoding. The staff members want to establish rules before putting material or information in the newspaper. In a similar fashion, as individuals, we have do's and don'ts about what we will or won't say in certain situations.

We can also use the communication networks to explain how information flows. Is it centralized or decentralized? From the information given, the newspaper incorporates centralized communication. The staff members collect information about the public works department and disseminate that information in the form of a newspaper—one-way flow of information. If there is an editorial column, we could say that a portion of the communication flow is decentralized, but only a small portion.

Implications for Effective Communications

We have defined effective communication as the transmission of information that results in a shared meaning and a common understanding for both parties. We now need to understand what can hinder our attempts to communicate. What are some of the reasons people, managers, or organizations fail to communicate? To appreciate how difficult it is to communicate effectively, we will look at the effects of nonverbal behavior, barriers to communications, and methods to overcome these barriers.

Nonverbal Behavior.   Look at the accompanying drawing of a supervisor and an employee. What is happening?

How will our body language affect our ability to communicate?

Watch a busy supervisor and note the speed of body movements, facial expressions, and posture. It doesn't take much to sense that a rapid pace, furrowed brow, and thrust-out chin mean, "I am harassed and under pressure; don't bother me with trivial matters." Most people communicate something of the sort when feeling overworked. But when this overworked individual is stopped by a concerned friend, asking what is wrong, the usual reply is "Nothing is wrong, I'll see you later."

The verbal message says everything is OK, but the conflicting nonverbal message says things are not OK. This situation shows how we can be unaware of

"Is anything wrong, boss? Can I help?" "Nothing is wrong. I'll see you later."

how our body language communicates another message that can be at odds with our spoken message. The harassed supervisor is unaware of how his body language is communicating the feeling of problems while his verbal message is "everything's OK." What would you do as the employee of this supervisor? You would probably not want to tell him your problems at this time. The importance of this conclusion is that the receiver more often considers body language as more accurate than the words spoken.

How important is our understanding of body language? If we look at some studies in the area, we can appreciate the significance of this form of communication. One researcher, Albert Mehrabian, studied the importance of nonverbal communication as contrasted with verbal communication in producing attitude change.[6] He found that verbal messages produced only a 7 percent change in attitudes. However, facial expressions accounted for 55 percent, and 38 percent was due to the rate of speech, voice inflection, and voice quality.

Managers who use strong nonverbal communication are perceived differently than those who do not. Strong nonverbal communicators are seen as exciting, bold, strong, and hard. On the other hand, managers who use little nonverbal communication are seen as warm, informal, impressionable, and pleasant. Which are you?

It is easy to see how communication involves more than words. But nonverbal communication involves more than just body, facial, and voice messages. The physical arrangements, including spacing between individuals, also affect our ability to communicate effectively with one another.

Look at Figure 5–6. Where is the guest's chair relative to the office holder's desk? Is it positioned beside the desk, directly in front of the desk, or across the

Albert Mehrabian verbal messages produce only 7% change in attitudes

How influential are our words as compared with our actions? *facial expressions 55 percent 38% rate of speech, voice inflection voice quality*

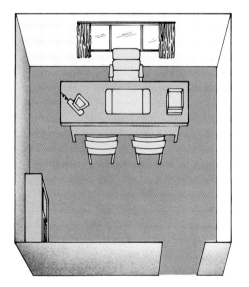
"I'm the BOSS"

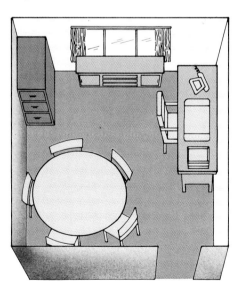
"Forget I'm the boss.
Let's talk."

FIGURE 5–6
Physical location of furniture as nonverbal message

How close people stand when speaking varies by culture. Communications can be awkward when people from different cultures meet.

room? Each position conveys a subtle message about how the office holder wants to interact with the visitor. Which message would you like to convey to your subordinates?

Spacing can also affect communication, especially between people from different cultures. Studies indicate that in some cultures people stand very close together, while in others they stand apart.[7] In South America, the proper distance may be only several inches apart. In North America, it is approximately 18 inches. If we bring the two cultures together, we can have an interesting situation. The South American will try to move closer to talk, while the North American will move farther away. Both are trying to communicate effectively and to use distance to their culture's best advantage. But as the South American moves closer, the North American moves away because he is uncomfortable being so close to a stranger (being close to a loved one would make sense to the North American). As he moves away, the South American interprets the move as an insult, and the North American interprets the South American as pushy.

Barriers to Effective Communication. Organizations cannot avoid creating some barriers to effective communication, simply because they have formal structures. The very existence of a hierarchy creates organizational and perhaps physical distance between people. In addition, the reliance upon clear lines of authority requires that communication be more formal and follow established channels. As a result, messages must pass through many levels before reaching their ultimate destination.

Human nature also hinders effective communication. Instead of listening in a rational, objective manner to what is being said, people tend to become emotionally involved. Personal judgments are imposed in place of facts. As noted in Chapter 2, people inject their own values into what they hear or read and, too often, can lose objectivity in the decoding process as a result.

Some of the most common barriers to effective communication are different frames of reference, filtering, in-group language, information overload, semantic differences, status differences, and time pressures.

Frames of Reference.   A frequent cause of communication problems is the different perception that the sender and the receiver have of the same message. Differing perceptions can be due to the parties having different frames of reference. This simply means they have a different base of experience from which to judge the message. Consider a farm-raised person talking to a city-raised person about the use of insecticides. Some other examples are boss and subordinate, parent and child, and instructor and student.

Filtering.   Another barrier to communication is the filtering that occurs as information is passed from one level to another in an organization. Filtering is the passing of partial information by the sender. The reasons for sending only some of the information are as varied as the individual senders. Filtering can occur when information is passed either downward or upward in organizations.

Downward communication probably receives the greatest attention from managers because they pass job instructions, procedures, and goals to subordinates. Unintentional filtering can occur because of errors in receiving and decoding messages or in encoding a message for the next person. This unintentional filtering is due mainly to differences in experiences, values, and unconscious motives. Deliberate filtering occurs because a manager disagrees with the message or for some reason does not want subordinates to receive it in the form in which it was sent. One study found that the organizational level of vice president received only 63 percent of the information content communicated by their superiors; plant managers received only 40 percent; and workers received just 20 percent of this information.[8] In many cases, messages are simplified or summarized at various levels to speed the flow of information or to add emphasis or clarity. However, the meaning of the message usually changes in the filtering process.

Upward communication suffers even greater problems of filtering than does downward communication. Greater intentional filtering occurs because of the desire of subordinates to withhold information or to change messages that reflect unfavorably on them and may threaten a promotion, pay, or other rewards. In other words subordinates want to look good in the eyes of their superiors.

In-group Language.   Another barrier to effective communication results from specialized words or vocabularies used by occupational groups. This is especially true of certain professional groups, such as accountants, lawyers, doctors, psychologists, or computer specialists. This development of jargon can also develop

Frames of reference the collection of past and present experiences that affect an individual's perception of what is being said

Filtering passage of partial information by the sender

In-group language terms or jargon used by a group of people with a common interest

Grapevines: How Dangerous Are They?

In the communications department of one of Chicago's largest banks, a staff member and supervisor have successfully avoided speaking to each other for eighteen months. Any necessary correspondence is done by memo. They keep unofficial tabs on each other through the office grapevine.

At First Federal Savings and Loan Association of Chicago, the grapevine nearly had a senior executive resigned and out the door before it buzzed across a correction. It was the same first name, a different last one, and a much lower position on the management ladder.

Every company, every organization, every industry has a grapevine. It's the unofficial source of information for everyone from the lowliest clerk to the chief executive officer and the chief executive's spouse. It hums loudest at a company that is autocratically managed or in a state of turmoil. While it nearly always carries negative connotations, the office grapevine can be put to good use. In fact, in some instances, it is absolutely essential to the survival of an organization.

"Despite the stigma of the company grapevine, it can be used to supplement formal communications," wrote Vanessa Dean Arnold in a recent issue of *Management World,* a trade publication. Arnold is an assistant professor of business communications at the University of Mississippi. She added, "In a healthy organization, there will be both formal and informal channels of communications. Managers should listen to and study the grapevine to learn who its leaders are, how it operates and what information it carries."

Despite the best efforts, however, defusing bad situations is difficult when an organization is in turmoil. One executive with a Chicago firm facing an uncertain future sighs over the problems of keeping one step ahead of what he considers the frequently inaccurate company and industry grapevines. "I try to keep one ear to the ground, so I

Source: Adapted from Sally Saville Hodge, "The Old Grapevine Is Doing Fine," *The Chicago Tribune* (28 August 1983): B6. © Copyrighted, Chicago Tribune Company, all rights reserved, used with permission.

in other common-experience groups, such as electricians, welders, actors, or police. The special language or jargon helps these members communicate more effectively among themselves, but it can pose problems for outsiders.

Overload condition in which an individual or department becomes bogged down with too much information

Overload. This problem describes a condition in which any individual or department becomes bogged down with too much information. Remember when you had two mid-term exams, a quiz, and a term paper due on the same day? People in organizations can also have too many things to do at once. Managers can feel overloaded when they arrive back at the office Monday morning after a two-week vacation and face an in-basket full of telephone messages, correspondence, reports, and requests to attend meetings and to make presentations. A new employee can feel overloaded with information during the orientation period.

When faced with this overload, people seem to have several responses: *omit*—fail to process some of the information (for example, discard "junk" or

can act with official communications (in response to the rumors)," he said.

He recalls being in a company elevator recently, carrying a file bearing the name of a firm that, with much publicity, had earlier considered buying his. Inside the file was marketing background information he thought might be of use to a new employee. On the elevator was a passenger, however, who couldn't have known that. "The guy practically bent over backwards trying to read what was on the cover of the file," the executive said with a laugh. "I told him what it was, and he got off the elevator kind of embarrassed, but I can imagine what the grapevine would have made of that if I hadn't told him."

Some executives use the grapevine to their advantage. One executive uses it to expose part of a master plan, so that no one will be surprised later. While Frank Corrado, head of Communications for Management, agrees that this is possible, he insists, "I'd much rather see (my clients) open up their formal lines of communication. Research on employee communications shows that the grapevine is the least desirable way of communicating with employees, but in some instances it is a survival mechanism that has to be used."

Educator Arnold points to a couple of other aspects of the maligned grapevine:

- [ ] Some studies have indicated that the grapevine is 80 to 85 percent accurate, with inaccuracies in the form of incompleteness rather than wrong information. Arnold writes that many researchers believe that much of the grapevine's information may be more accurate than information relayed by formal channels, particularly where managers are less frank and honest than they should be.
- [ ] Despite the generally held idea that women participate more actively in grapevine activity than men, other studies indicate men and women are equally active.

QUESTIONS

1. Why could one argue that having a grapevine is a sign of a communications failure?
2. If a grapevine is strong in your organization, what would you propose to correct the situation?
3. List the advantages and disadvantages of a grapevine.

"occupant" mail); *create errors*—process information incorrectly; *sort or prioritize*—separate important information from less important information; *queue*—level out peaks by saving some for lull periods; *approximate*—use some average response for all requests; *escape*—avoid the information and go on another two-week vacation.[9]

Semantic Differences. *Semantic* relates to the meaning of language or words. "Bear" (to carry) and "bear" (animal) mean different things, although the spelling and sound of the words are the same. To know the correct meaning we must see the word in a context or situation—the grocery store versus the Arctic wilderness.

Semantic problems are common in companies. The terms "profit" and "efficiency" roll off the tongues of managers with warmth and affection, but in the language of the assembly line workers the terms may carry a cold, impersonal

Semantic difference situation in which a word takes on meaning from the context in which it is said

149

Significant differences in status tend to inhibit upward communication.

message of "rip-off," "inflation," and "speed-ups" on the line. Rationally, the two groups may agree upon a dictionary meaning, but in real-life communication, the words carry different emotional overtones for labor and management.

Status difference condition in which an individual feels less important than another person because of titles or positions in the organization

Status Differences.   Significant differences in status tend to inhibit upward communication. Organizations can create status differences through titles, offices, and the amount of other resources they distribute to different levels. But it is the individual who attributes meaning to the status difference. When a factory employee with dirty clothes and shoes enters the white-carpeted, walnut-paneled office of a well-dressed executive seated behind a massive desk, it is not surprising that some degree of intimidation occurs. This is especially true if the walls are filled with diplomas, awards, or other evidence of high status. After all, the symbols were carefully selected to show that the office holder is important and powerful.

Time pressure stressful feeling of not having enough time to complete tasks

Time Pressures.   Managers often reflect that their scarcest commodity is time. Most organizations have many deadlines, which create time pressures that constrain an individual's ability to communicate. When people are under time pressures, the sender may not fully develop the message before sending it or may short-circuit the normal channels in hopes of getting a quick response. In addition, the time constraints may not allow the sender to receive feedback on whether the receiver decoded the intended meaning.

Overcoming the Barriers.   How can we improve our communication skills? How can we improve the possibilities that our intended meaning will be understood under these trying conditions? How can we bridge the communication gap that exists in most organizations? Overcoming the barriers to effective communication involves two tasks—improving our encoding of the message and improving our understanding of how others will decode the message.

Are there methods to counteract the barriers to effective communication?

Effective Timing.   Managers may ignore messages or requests simply because other problems are more pressing. Time pressures can reduce a message's impact. Thus you can improve communication through effective timing. One method is to standardize the timing of specific messages. For example, information about a critical project may be distributed every Monday morning until the project is completed. Supervisors and workers affected by the information can expect and be attentive to messages about the project. Another method is to set key staff meetings during periods in the day or week when they will have the attention of the staff members; for instance, Monday mornings might be an attentive time. Also, some companies allow groups to meet away from the facility for important information sharing.

Regulated Information Flow.   One of the most obvious communication barriers concerns the flow of information. For example, the accounting department becomes busier and busier as the April 15 income-tax deadline approaches. Other duties and information exchanges become secondary to getting the tax returns out on time. Management may want to employ certain individuals, called "gatekeepers," to control the flow of information, thus keeping others from being overloaded with information. The assistant to the president serves as a gatekeeper, deciding who will see the president, when, and for how long. The assistant may read reports and other critical information and prepare weekly summaries for the president to review.

Parallel Channels.   When it is crucial that a message be fully understood by both sender and receiver, it may be necessary to provide parallel and reinforcing channels of communication. For instance, a verbal message might be followed up with a memo or letter. The sender not only has gotten the attention of the receiver (through a face-to-face verbal exchange) but also has ensured that both parties will have records for future reference (the memo or letter). Likewise, sending minutes of meetings to the participants is using repetition and parallel channels of communication to ensure understanding.

Empathy.   Empathy is an awareness of the needs and motives of others. Speakers who use words or phrases that the audience feels are offensive are not being empathetic to the audience. Try to know your audience, even though it may be only one person, and to be sensitive to the needs and feelings of your listeners when you speak. Try to place yourself in their shoes and ask yourself, "How would I like to be addressed?"

Feedback.   Individuals give feedback to make sure that the message received was the message sent and to encourage further communication between the parties. When someone says, "What did you hear me say?" or "This is what I heard you say," that person is trying to make sure both parties understand what was communicated.

One form of feedback used in organizations is the performance appraisal. This is one of the more difficult tasks for managers since feedback that is poorly given is threatening to the subordinate.

What rules can help you give effective feedback to another person?

When giving feedback, consider the following suggestions to maximize your efforts:

☐ Be specific rather than general, with clear and recent examples. Statements like "you have good ideas" are less helpful than saying "your ideas for solving yesterday's customer complaints worked well."

☐ Give the feedback at the earliest opportunity that the receiver appears ready to accept it. If the receiver is angry, upset, or defensive, waiting is probably best.

☐ Give only what the receiver can handle at one time. Do not give a list of many items that annoy you all at once. This will make the listener defensive.

☐ State only those things that the listener can correct or do something about.

☐ Check to see if the receiver has really heard you and feels that the items are valid.[10]

Effective Listening.   The ability to listen with understanding is necessary. It has been estimated that as much as 40 percent of a white-collar worker's day is devoted to listening. Yet tests of listening comprehension suggest that these individuals listen at only 25 percent effectiveness.[11] Listening skills affect the quality of boss/subordinate relationships. Effective listening requires careful attention and effort on the part of the receiver. Instead of evaluating the message and its sender or preparing a response, the effective listener attempts to understand both the direct and subtle meanings contained in the message. To understand the total message requires attention to the feelings of the sender as well as the verbal content of the message.[12]

Can listening skills be developed? Some companies that believe they can be developed have set up listening programs for their personnel.[13] Their programs explore various rules and techniques. An example of such rules is the "Ten Commandments for Good Listening"[14]:

1. *Stop talking*
2. Put the talker at ease
3. Show the talker you want to listen

4. Remove distractions
5. Empathize with the talker
6. Be patient
7. Hold your temper
8. Go easy on argument and criticism
9. Ask questions
10. *Stop talking*

Notice that "stop talking" is the first and the last commandment. You *can* learn better listening skills, but no commandments or guides can help unless you *choose* to listen. Effective listening is more a matter of choice than skill.

1. Effective communication results in a shared meaning and a common understanding for both the sender and the receiver. Since managers spend at least 80 percent of their time communicating, effective managers need to develop good communication skills.
2. The model of communication contains intended meaning, encoding, transmission, reception, decoding, and perceived meaning.
3. There are five basic information networks: chain, wheel, Y, circle, and all-channel. The decentralized networks (circle and all-channel) are more satisfying to the members and faster and more accurate on complex problems. Centralized networks (chain, wheel, and Y) are faster and more accurate on simple tasks.
4. Nonverbal behavior can enhance communication if it is consistent with what is being said. Nonverbal behavior includes tone of voice, body language, and physical arrangement of the situation.
5. Certain organizational practices can become barriers to effective communication. Possible barriers include different frames of reference, filtering, in-group language, overload, semantic differences, status differences, and time pressures. These can be addressed and minimized by effective timing, regulated information flow, parallel channels, empathy, feedback, and effective listening.

LEARNING SUMMARY

1. False True communication takes place when the sender and receiver have a common understanding and shared meaning of the message sent.
2. True Studies show that managers spend more than 80 percent of their time in various forms of communicating with others, including meetings, memos, and individual conferences.
3. False We sometimes communicate unconsciously or unintentionally other than what we had hoped to communicate.
4. True There is more intentional altering of communication to the upper levels of management to protect the individuals at lower levels from criticism.

ANSWERS TO "WHAT'S YOUR OPINION?"

5. True   A list of commandments for good listening has the "stop talking" guideline as the beginning and the end.

6. False   Centralized communication works better with simple tasks.

7. True   Nonverbal communication, our behavior, can help us get a message across if we are consistent. If we are inconsistent, such as using an angry voice but such words as "it's OK," the nonverbal communication will confuse the listener.

8. False   Feedback should be specific with clear and recent examples.

KEY TERMS

All-channel network	In-group language
Centralized networks	Lateral communications
Chain network	Nonverbal communication
Circle network	Overload
Decentralized networks	Receiver
Decode	Sender
Downward communication	Semantic differences
Effective communication	Status differences
Encode	Transmission
Empathy	"Y" network
Feedback	Upward communication
Filtering	Wheel network
Frame of reference	

HUMAN RELATIONS APPLICATIONS

It must be obvious by now that communication is a complex task that takes conscious effort to be effective. In this section we will look at some other aspects of communication that the popular literature and our own experiences suggest are important. We have selected only some of the concepts discussed in the chapter to explore. We will cover the environment of communication and translating body language.

The Environment of Communication

Face-to-face communication can have certain problems, depending on the situation. Much depends upon where that communication takes place. A key step in selecting prospective employees is the interview. It is often the deciding point in the hiring process. But the physical environment of the interview can influence the effectiveness of the communication process and, therefore, the interview process.

It is common practice in staffing for sales positions to hold initial interviews in hotel or motel rooms. Such a practice gives sales managers an opportunity to use interview time efficiently. They are not bothered by routine office tasks, and the interviewing site may be convenient to a large number of applicants. In spite of these advantages, there are problems: The *Sloan Management Review* published the results of a survey of college students invited to be interviewed in such settings, which revealed that many individuals feel anxiety concerning such interviews and that some individuals refused to be interviewed in hotel or motel rooms.[15] The study showed that the least popular site was the local hotel, while the best location was the room in a local office building. While these findings held for both men and women, the responses of women were especially striking. While 98 percent indicated that they would appear for an interview in the office building, only 62 percent accepted the local hotel room as a suitable interview site. This survey shows that certain types of environments can be perceived as inappropriate for doing business or interviewing. While the study did not determine the reasons for this anxiety, there cannot be any doubt that it will negatively affect the communications between the interviewer and interviewee. And this is not to the benefit of either party.

Translating Body Language

Many managers want to know how employees are reacting to their styles of management. Employees, asked about their views of the manager's style, may or may not be truthful. But managers can check to see if the employee's body language confirms or denies the verbal message. Learning to read body language is a lot easier than you might think. Some of this skill is common sense. In a manner of speaking, body language is like verbal language—you just need to read it in the same way.

While you take in the verbal language, what do a person's eyes, body position, and tone of voice tell you? Here are some basic things to look for:

Eye contact. If an employee is pleased or is angry with you, she will usually focus directly on you while you speak. If she looks to the side or at the ceiling, she may feel pressured or uncomfortable. If her gaze repeatedly hits the floor, she may need some management support. Rapid eye-blinking often shows anxiety. In summary, a direct contact of eyes indicates fairly straightforward communication, including anger. Other forms of eye contact may mean that you should not just accept verbal statements of "it's OK."

Body position. If an employee feels at ease with your style of management, he will usually face you in a casual and relaxed manner. If he turns away, the meaning is obvious. He is giving you the cold shoulder. If he folds his arms across his chest, he probably is feeling defensive. Finger drumming or other fidgeting indicates nervousness or lack of attention to you.

Nonverbal communication—eye contact or looking away, relaxed or nervous body position, calm or excited tone of voice—can confirm or deny the verbal message.

Speech.   When the person you're with speaks in a steady, calm tone of voice, you know she is at ease and listening. Quick, staccato speech means she is excited. If she's speaking tentatively, it may mean she finds you intimidating.

If any of these signals indicate that you are having a problem, get the problem out in the open. Find out what is wrong before it becomes a bigger problem. Use your insight into another's body language to complement your other communication skills.

PERSONAL GUIDELINES FOR HUMAN RELATIONS SUCCESS

Probably the most difficult yet rewarding skill in communication is the ability to listen effectively. The person who listens better may have an advantage in the communication process because of having more data and because many people feel loyal to a person who listens to their problems. The following guidelines will help you be a good listener:[16]

1. *Learn to tolerate silence.* Many people have a fear of silence, so they either chatter or encourage other people to do so to kill the awful sound of silence. An ability to live with periods of silence in a conversation is helpful in achieving a more complete understanding of what is really taking place.
2. *Look and listen hard.* Observing other people while they speak is an opportunity for understanding them. Watch for facial expressions, gestures, body move-

ments, eye contact, and body language in general. This will help you to understand the real content of the message.

3. *Know your power as a listener.* The listener has real power. A poor listener can destroy the speaker's desire and ability to communicate. Know your power as a listener and use it to your advantage.

4. *Ask questions.* Don't ask questions merely to be polite but to clarify what's going on. Don't be afraid to admit you don't know something. If you're not sure you understand directions, ask for them again.

5. *Reflect feelings.* Indicate through your responses what your feelings are. Similarly, show that you understand the feelings of others in the conversation—that you are aware of more than just the words they are saying.

6. *Give positive and reinforcing nonverbal messages.* Make certain that your body reflects an interest in and understanding of the problem.

7. *Know your emotional biases and try to correct them.* Some of the biggest barriers to effective listening are emotional biases, attitudes, and prejudices within us that distort what we hear. It is impossible to be completely free of such biases, but if we know what our biases are, we will be aware that they may be affecting our ability to understand properly.

8. *Avoid judging.* Probably the single most important key to good listening is to avoid judgments. If you are continually making judgments about what the speaker is saying as it is being said, you will strongly affect the willingness of the speaker to be open and honest with you, whether or not you agree with the comments.

1. Explain the statement, "Words do not substitute for action."
2. How would you respond if someone said to you, "It's up to you to get me to understand you!"
3. Think of a person who is a good communicator. What personal characteristics make that person a good communicator?
4. Why is it so difficult to obtain accurate information from upward or downward communication?
5. How should communication networks be designed?
6. Name the barriers to effective communication and some methods to reduce their effects.

DISCUSSION AND REVIEW QUESTIONS

This exercise illustrates how difficult it is to communicate using one-way communication.

HUMAN RELATIONS EXERCISE

Instructions.

1. Study the following arrangement of boxes. With your back to another person, instruct the person how to draw the boxes. Begin with the top square and

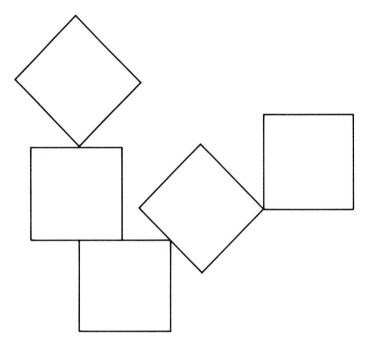

describe each in succession, paying particular note to its relationship to the preceding one. No questions are allowed. Compare the following arrangement with that drawn by the information receiver.

2. Try this same exercise using a two-way communication process that involves face-to-face contact and allows the receiver to ask questions. The results are usually much closer to the original set of boxes.

Adapted from J. William Pfeiffer and John E. Jones, eds., A Handbook of Structured Experiences for Human Relations Training, vol. 1 (rev.) (San Diego: University Associates, Inc., 1974): 13–15. Used with permission.

HUMAN RELATIONS INCIDENT

Mary, the head of Macy's accounting department, feels strongly that subordinates need to know where they stand on all aspects of the job. This has been Mary's guiding principle for many years.

She has recently inherited the boss's son as a subordinate. She has tried to work with him and help him adjust to her expectations of what should be done. She has had numerous meetings over the last four weeks, but it seems to no avail. He just isn't learning as expected, and the other employees are getting angry about the special attention.

Tomorrow Mary must talk to the boss about the situation and try to get his son reassigned to another job that he could handle. Mary stays up late trying to figure out the best way to tell her boss. What should she say?

NOTES

1. Adapted from Jim Muhlstein, ''Gossip, Rumor, Innuendo, Libel—It's All Inder Works,'' *The Everett Herald* (1 April 1986): 1B.

2. S. Chase, *Power of Words* (New York: Harcourt, Brace & Co., 1954): 259.

3. H. Mintzberg, *The Nature of Managerial Work* (New York: Harper & Row, 1973): 38. These findings were supported by Lance B. Kurke and Howard E. Adrich, ''Mintzberg Was Right!: A Replication and Extension of the Nature of Managerial Work,'' *Management Science,* vol. 29, no. 8 (August 1983): 975–84.

4. M. E. Roloff, *Interpersonal Communication: The Social Exchange Approach* (Beverly Hills, CA: Sage, 1981).

5. E. A. Locke and D. M. Schweiger, ''Participation in Decision-Making: One More Look,'' in B. M. Staun, ed., *Research in Organization Behavior,* vol. 1 (Greenwich, CN: JAI Press, 1979).

6. A. Mehrabian, *Tactics of Social Influence* (Englewood Cliffs, NJ: Prentice-Hall, 1972).

7. E. T. Hall, *The Hidden Dimension* (New York: Doubleday, 1966).

8. R. G. Nichols, ''Listening is a Ten-Part Skill,'' *Nation's Business,* 45 (1957): 58–60.

9. J. G. Miller, ''Information Input Overload and Psychopathology,'' *American Journal of Psychiatry,* 116 (1960): 695–704.

10. J. Anderson, ''Giving and Receiving Feedback,'' in P. R. Lawrence, L. B. Barnes, and J. W. Lorsch, *Organizational Behavior and Administration,* 3rd ed. (Homewood, IL: Irwin, 1976): 109.

11. Nichols, ''Listening Is a Ten-Part Skill.''

12. C. R. Rogers and F. J. Roethlisberger, ''Barriers and Gateways to Communication,'' *Harvard Business Review* (July–August 1952): 28–35.

13. J. L. DiGaetani, ''The Sperry Corporation and Listening: An Interview,'' *Business Horizons* (March–April 1982): 34–42.

14. K. Dans, *Human Behavior at Work* (New York: McGraw-Hill, 1972): 369.

15. L. Kaufman and J. B. Wolf, ''Hotel Room Interviewing—Anxiety and Suspicion,'' *Sloan Management Review* (Spring 1982).

16. J. L. DiGaetani, ''The Business of Listening,'' *Business Horizons* (September–October 1980).

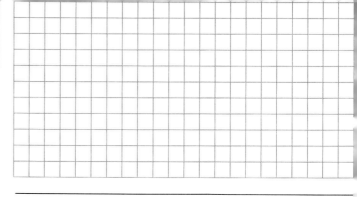

CHAPTER 6
GROUP DYNAMICS

WHAT'S YOUR OPINION? T OR F

_____ 1. A group is a collection of people that come together.

_____ 2. Informal groups are not as important to the supervisor as formal groups.

_____ 3. Small groups can agree more and share more information than large groups.

_____ 4. Turnover and absenteeism increase as the group gets larger, including white-collar workers.

_____ 5. If a group is attacked by an outside force, the group members will become more cohesive to deal with the attack.

_____ 6. Group norms are flexible rules about how members should behave.

_____ 7. Conformity to group rules is a natural and positive force in group development.

_____ 8. As groups grow, they need to develop through certain stages, much as individuals do.

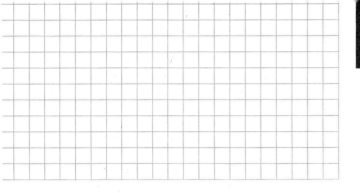

OUTLINE

FUNDAMENTALS OF GROUP DYNAMICS
Nature of a Group
Group Characteristics
Group Development

LEARNING SUMMARY

HUMAN RELATIONS APPLICATIONS
Use of Committees Means Management of Committee
A Novel Way to Teach Managers Group Skills

PERSONAL GUIDELINES FOR HUMAN RELATIONS SUCCESS
Success as a Group Member
Success as a Group Leader

LEARNING OBJECTIVES

☐ Describe a group and identify several types of groups found in organizations

☐ List several characteristics of a group

☐ Discuss the various roles group members can play and the effect of these roles on the group

☐ Describe the positive and negative effects of conformity

☐ Explain the stages of group development

☐ List the major characteristics of an effective group

☐ List and discuss the major human relations applications of group dynamics

☐ Describe a personal approach to more effective group involvement

Can a Group Be Too Much of a Group?

In early August 1981, 12,000 U.S. air-traffic controllers joined in a strike against the federal government. The controllers were confident, dedicated to their cause, and certain they would win. One month later, the controllers' strike seemed to symbolize a suicide march rather than a courageous mission. The controllers' self-confidence was badly eroded. The reaction of the FAA had been miscalculated. The Professional Air Traffic Controllers Organization (PATCO) was frantically seeking a salvage operation that would save the jobs of the controllers and the dignity of the union. One year later the union was dead. Most of its members were fired from their government jobs. The union was found by the courts to have broken the law by striking against the government, and it was decertified.

What happened?

Union members badly overestimated their importance to air travel and their worth to the government. Members genuinely believed that the government could not operate the nation's complex and publicly visible air travel system without them.

While controllers probably endure more stress on the job with early job burnout than most of the general work force, they are also paid more and have job security. An average salary of $33,000 per year with generous benefits didn't seem that low to the general public, and sympathy for their cause did not materialize.

Several other reasons for PATCO's failure need to be considered. One was internal cohesiveness. When the government issued an ultimatum with the backing of the office of the president of the United States, PATCO didn't compromise. Instead, PATCO members pulled together to stick it out. The emotional commitment to union solidarity became "all powerful," even more so than the original logic and rationale of improving working conditions.

Moreover, PATCO didn't listen. They refused to believe President Reagan, who insisted that federal strikes were illegal and would be broken regardless of cost. The general public supported the government position (a rare case at best, considering the times). The controllers were warned that, if a strike were called, the strikers would be dismissed and there would be no amnesty. In addition, their replacements from the military were ready at a moment's notice. The controllers were such a cohesive group that they wouldn't listen to such threats. They felt and knew that they were in the right and it seemed that the more they were threatened, the more cohesive they became and the harder it was to stop their demands.

PATCO also didn't gain the support of other unions, such as the Airline Pilots Association or the mechanics' union. They were overconfident to the point of believing that they could easily shut down the airline system by themselves. Also, they went on strike in the fall when weather conditions and the number of air travelers are moderate. The winter offers a greater challenge because of weather and the holidays. The result of this miscalculation: PATCO is dead and air-traffic controllers are without jobs.

From this opening story we get a glimpse of how important understanding how groups operate is to human relations. Groups can be self-destructive under certain conditions. In this chapter we will explore the nature of groups, some of their characteristics, their stages of development, and some practical uses in managing committees more effectively.

FUNDAMENTALS OF GROUP DYNAMICS

Nature of a Group

Individuals seldom, if ever, act without being influenced by the group to which they belong. Yet most of us are not aware of that influence. Most people spend much of their lives involved with groups—family groups, social groups, professional groups, civic groups, and work groups. For many people, individual success depends on the ability to function effectively within groups. Think about a sports team, a medical team in a hospital, a new small company, or the manager of a work group.

1920's Roethlisberger. Dickson .

In the late 1920s, Fritz J. Roethlisberger and William J. Dickson looked at several work groups at the Hawthorne plant of Western Electric Company.[1] Initially the studies were designed to determine the effect of lighting on the efficiency of the workers. Two groups were studied. The level of lighting for the "experimental" group was varied. The "control" group received the same level of light as they always had in the past. As the light level was increased, so was the production of the experimental group. What surprised the researchers was that the control group's production also went up.

How did the Hawthorne studies help researchers focus on the importance of social interaction to the study of human relations?

Then the experimental group's light was decreased. Production continued to rise. It wasn't until the light reached .06 footcandles, close to moonlight, that the production rate started to fall back slightly, probably because it was so difficult to see.

involving employees in concentration about how conditions affected them.

It became obvious to the researchers that something complex and unexpected had occurred in their study of lighting levels. They pursued other conditions of the workers, such as temperature, humidity, worker diets, and sleeping habits. But, the research data showed *no* relationship between the physical conditions and the production of relay switches. Finally, the researchers realized that because they were often asking the workers for their opinions about the effects of the experiments, they were changing the *social situation* of the workers. They surmised that this interaction was as important or more important than the physical changes.

According to Roethlisberger, "If one experiments on a stone, the stone does not know it is being experimented upon . . . . But if a human being is being experimented upon, he is likely to know it. Therefore, his attitudes toward the experiment and toward the experimenters become very important factors in determining his responses to the situation."[2] Today, this factor is called the "Hawthorne effect."

The social aspects of work were identified in another part of the Hawthorne plant. A group of fourteen workers in three different jobs was observed. The conclusions were that the workers set definitive norms related to output, communications with supervisors, and what was acceptable behavior by the members of the group. This finally destroyed the notion of a "rational economic human" as too simplistic. From that time to the present, researchers and managers have been trying to understand how group dynamics impact the individual members and their overall performance.

What Is a Group? To understand the dynamics involved in a group, we must develop a basic view of what a group is. Suppose that you encounter a construction project that is tying up traffic and you get out of your car to join the other trapped motorists. Or suppose you are in line for several hours waiting to purchase concert tickets. Are these examples of groups? Not in the way we define the term. A *group* is a collection of individuals who interact on a regular basis and see themselves to be mutually dependent with respect to the attainment of one or more common goals.[3]

Group collection of individuals who interact on a regular basis and see themselves to be mutually dependent with respect to the attainment of common goals

Neither the individuals at the traffic jam nor those waiting in the line for concert tickets would meet all of the conditions of this definition. They would be a collection of individuals, not a group. The term *group* is generally restricted to that number of individuals who can be aware of and influence each other. There is no absolute restriction on the size of a group, but usually twenty people is the upper limit of group size. The rationale for this statement is that beyond this number, interaction, mutual influence, and coordination become more difficult, and the group breaks into smaller subgroups.

Can we apply this to any of the previous examples? Although the delayed motorists at the construction site do not meet the definitional requirements of a group, what would happen if an accident occurred at the site, trapping some construction workers? One possible scenario would have the observers organize themselves as a rescue team. A leader or several leaders would emerge and activities would be assumed by or assigned to individuals—remove debris, search for survivors, apply first aid, get professional help, or clear the area for other potential accidents. There would be interaction among observers and a mutual dependence to achieve the goals of freeing trapped workers and supplying medical help.

Thus, a collection of individuals that is not otherwise a group can become a group to deal with a specific problem. At the end of the rescue operation, it is likely that the group would dissolve, with members perhaps not knowing the names of the other rescuers or the workers with whom they had shared an intense experience.

Types of Groups.   Within an organization the most important distinction regarding groups is whether a group is *formal* or *informal.* Employees become members of formal groups because they are assigned to them. Within formal groups people are assigned positions, such as supervisor or chairperson. All members or a particular group share similar activities, skills, responsibilities, and assigned goals. They recognize that they are part of the work group, and the group exists as long as the task or goals exist. Examples of formal groups are a research team, a board of directors, a production committee, and a market research group. Some formal groups, such as a committee or a task force, are temporary in nature. They are created for a specific purpose and typically are disbanded with its accomplishment.

Informal groups emerge naturally from the interaction of the members, who may or may not have purposes related to the goals of the department or the organization. Often the very nature of the organization has a significant influence

Name and describe two types of groups found in most organizations.

At times the goals of an informal group may be opposed to those of the organization, as when having a relaxed atmosphere takes precedence over providing good customer service.

on the formation of informal groups. The physical layout of work areas, type of production process, personal associations and preferences, or management climate of a firm may facilitate the formation of informal groups. Informal groups may emerge to fulfill friend and affiliation needs. Some informal groups emerge because of a common threat that group members face, for example, the establishment of a waste-treatment plant in a residential neighborhood.

An informal lunch group may discuss problems members share on the job and how they might resolve them. At coffee breaks, at lunch time, or after work, informal groups may form to fulfill interest or friendship needs. Common interests, such as age, political beliefs, religious interests, or recreational interests, may result in the formation of interest or friendship groups. But groups may also form simply because people are located close to one another. At times the goals of informal groups may run counter to those of the formal organization. For example, a crew of young waiters and waitresses may be more interested in having a relaxed atmosphere at work than in providing good service to the customers. Individuals who feel frustrated or threatened by a company policy or supervisory practice may form or seek out an informal group for comfort or action to counter the practice. Thus, groups can provide an important support function.

Group Characteristics

What factors can influence the behavior or performance of a group member? Remember the PATCO story and the strength of belief that they would not fail. Here are some of the factors that influence group behavior:

Describe how a group's size can affect its functioning

Size. As a group's size increases, the interaction between individuals becomes more difficult, and it may become harder to influence each other and to see how individual members contribute to the common purpose. In general, studies on group size show the following:

- □ Very small groups (two to four members) show more tension, agreement, and asking of opinions. In small groups it is important that everyone get along.
- □ In larger groups there is more tension release and giving of information because group members can express more differences of opinions.
- □ Groups with an even number of members have a greater difficulty in obtaining a majority and, therefore, create a state of more tension.
- □ The relationship between group size and performance appears to be inconclusive and may depend more on the type of task being performed.
- □ Members of smaller groups report greater satisfaction than those in larger groups. Members of small groups apparently have more freedom from psychological restrictions and thus are more satisfied.
- □ Turnover and absenteeism increase as the group gets larger, especially for blue-collar workers. It seems that, as the group size increases, the tasks become more specialized and communications between members and between members and supervisors become poorer, which may lead to less satisfaction

of higher-level needs. This does not seem to hold for white-collar workers because such workers seem to have more opportunities available outside the group to satisfy their needs.[4]

As groups grow in size, more communication and coordination are required to realize their potential. Although it is difficult to pinpoint an ideal group size, we can offer some ideas about group size when a supervisor forms a group to solve a problem.[5]

Fewer than five members results in:

☐ Fewer people to share task responsibilities
☐ More personal discussions
☐ More participation

More than seven members results in:

☐ Fewer opportunities to participate
☐ More members being inhibited
☐ Domination by aggressive members
☐ A tendency to split into subgroups

While these findings argue for a smaller group size, this must be weighed against the fact that increasing group size offers more ideas and other human resources to achieve the task of the group. The impact of a group's size on the resources available and the effectiveness of a group's communication/coordination is a trade-off that must be considered when staffing a committee or work group.

Cohesiveness. Cohesiveness refers to the amount of attractiveness group members hold toward one another. Cohesiveness means there is a unity in the group and members pull in the same direction. There are differences in cohesiveness among groups of friends, sports groups, and work groups. In some groups, cohesiveness is described as a group spirit or a team spirit. In other groups, members not only seem to lack team spirit, they even seem to dislike one another. Contrast the Japanese style of management, where there is a strong identity between the workers and the firm, and much of American industry, with its 9-to-5, punch-the-time-clock culture.

Group cohesiveness can be increased or decreased under certain conditions.[6] To increase group cohesiveness the attractiveness of the group to group members must increase. This can occur under the following conditions:

☐ Group members have the opportunity to gain prestige or status within the groups.
☐ Group members are in a cooperative relationship rather than in competition with one another.
☐ Group members can fulfill more needs through participation in the group.
☐ An increase occurs in the prestige or status of the group in an organization.

Cohesiveness the amount of attractiveness group members hold toward one another

□ The group is attacked from the outside, causing members to deal with the external threat (this may explain some of PATCO's attractiveness for its members—a threat from the federal government).

To decrease the cohesiveness of a group, the level of attractiveness of the group toward members must decrease. This can occur under the following conditions:

□ Conflict results from members' disagreements over ways to achieve group goals or solve group problems. (Members of highly cohesive groups may often have disagreements, but they try to settle them quickly.)
□ Participation in the group results in an unpleasant experience for an individual.
□ Membership places limits on the individual's participation in individual or group activities outside the group.
□ The evaluation of the group by outsiders who are respected becomes negative.
□ Conditions within the group prevent or restrict effective communication. Reduced communication may result if one or two members dominate group activities and prevent other members from participating.

How can cohesiveness work to the benefit of the organization?

While a cohesive group is good for its members, does that mean it's also good for the manager and the organization? Studies show that it depends on the group's performance norms.[7]

It seems that a basic rule in group dynamics is that the more cohesive a group, the greater the conformity of members to the group's norms. If the performance norm is positive for the organization, high conformity is good as well. If the performance norm is negative (low production or sloppy work), high conformity can work to the detriment of the supervisor or organization. This will be explored more fully in the next section.

Norms   standards of behavior that are expected by members of a group

Norms.   A group norm is a standard of behavior that is expected by members of a group. Norms are often referred to as "rules" that apply to group members.[8] When violated, they may be enforced with reprimands or other group sanctions. In the extreme, violation of group norms can result in social ostracism or expulsion of a member from the group.

What function do norms play in the way a group works?

Norms are developed within a group over time and serve two purposes: First, they identify what behavior is considered appropriate. Exhibiting appropriate behavior leads to group approval and respect. Second, norms define the limits of behavior for group members. As members approach these limits, they are likely to receive signals from other members that they are close to violating group norms. For example, a production unit may have a performance standard set by the industrial engineers of 400 units per day. But the group may establish its own production norm of 325 to 345 units per day. This norm is the expected output for all of its members. If a new group member attempts to show her stuff and increase the number of units above 345, the other members may begin to behave

Thinking Small: Large Computer Firms Create Little Groups

Recently Matt Sanders was kicked out of his office. His belongings and two new workers moved into space at Convergent Technologies, Inc., a computer manufacturer. He had to borrow desks and phones. His boss, Allen Michels, said, "If you get into trouble, call me, and if you get some good news, call me. But I ain't calling you." Needless to say, Sanders was scared.

Sanders was not being fired but in reality had been named the new leader of a strike force to build a new computer that would allow Convergent to enter the market of low-priced personal computers in a short time. The concept was to create an entrepreneurial force of the type that so often in the past had marked the beginning of many a Silicon Valley firm.

Companies in a similar situation believe that small work groups, when given enough freedom, can react better and more quickly to the abrupt changes that constantly confront them. Several examples follow this approach of "smaller is better." Apple Computer, Inc. turned to a small group to help develop its Lisa, an easy-to-use machine for business. Timex Corp. did likewise to get into the computer business quickly with its Timex Sinclair 1000. Vice president Daniel Ross says one of the virtues of the small-group approach is that responsibility gets pushed to lower-level employees. Also, small groups can better focus their energies on a single goal—"Creativity is fostered in this kind of organization," says Ross.

Source: Adapted from Erik Larson and Carrie Dolan, "Large Computer Firms Sprout Little Divisions for Good, Fast Work," *The Wall Street Journal* (19 August 1983): 1. Reprinted by permission of the *The Wall Street Journal*, © Dow Jones & Company, Inc. 1983. All rights reserved.

Michels of Convergent feels that this approach is the only way to compete with the Japanese. He argues that the use of small work groups is more productive for Americans than trying to adopt the Japanese style of management, which depends on the Japanese worker's intense loyalty to the firm. "You keep things small so you can create a culture, the right culture," says Michels.

The machine on which Michels' group worked was presented to the marketplace about nine months after the group started. Karen Toland, the marketing director, says, "I don't have to go through two department heads and write six memos if something needs to be changed. I walk across and say, 'Hey, Charlie, this space bar feels like . . .' and he fixes it." She says that producing the product was an intense process of give and take, made easier because everyone knew each other. She recalls lots of arguments with the engineers when she wanted to call a button on the computer a "Do It" key instead of the more standard, computer-jargon "Execute." "They thought I was nuts," she says. The matter was thoroughly thrashed out, and the machine now has a "Do It" key.

QUESTIONS

1. What norms are present in this organization? How do they support the organization's goal of a new computer?
2. Use the effective group's characteristics to describe this firm.
3. What stage of group development applies here?

in ways that inhibit the new member's action and prevent her reaching a higher number of units.

The more important a norm is to a group the more likely the group is to enforce the norm. Very important norms are termed "pivotal," and acceptance of these is an essential requirement for group membership.[9] An example of a pivotal norm from the opening story might be the requirement of the PATCO union members to honor a picket line while on strike.

Less important norms are called "peripheral"—their violation does not result in loss of group membership, although some lesser penalty may be imposed by the group. An example of a peripheral norm could be the type of language or dress used by the group.

Roles behaviors expected of those in particular positions in a group

Roles.   Roles are the behaviors expected of those in particular positions in a group. This is easy to see in formal groups in which a job description defines what is expected. A leader of an ongoing budget committee, for example, may be expected to call all meetings and arrange necessary paperwork prior to and after a session.

In most informal group situations, that is, when the group has not been established by the organization, role expectations are developed by the group members themselves and may never be formalized. They develop as a result of experiences and interactions in the group.

Both formal and informal groups have role behaviors that can be classified in three areas: *task-related, maintenance-related,* and *self-related* behavior.[10] It must also be remembered that these roles may not be equally played by all groups at any given time. But to the extent that the group does consciously review and modify these roles with certain situations, the better the outcome of the group's efforts.

Task-related roles directed toward establishing and accomplishing the group goals

The following *task-related roles* are directed toward establishing and accomplishing the goals of the group:

- ☐ *The idea initiator* proposes tasks or goals, defines problems, and suggests procedures or ideas for solving problems.
- ☐ *The information seeker* requests facts, seeks information about a group concern, asks for expression of feelings, requests statements or estimates, solicits expressions of value, and seeks suggestions and ideas.
- ☐ *The information giver* offers facts, provides information about group concerns, states beliefs about matters before the group, and gives suggestions and ideas.
- ☐ *The coordinator* pulls together related ideas, restates suggestions after the group has discussed them, and offers a decision or conclusion for the group to consider.
- ☐ *The evaluator* helps assess the group's functioning and evaluates or questions the practicality, logic, or facts of suggestions by other group members.

Maintenance-related roles are directed toward the well-being, continuity, and development of the group. The following are various roles in this area:

- *The encourager* exudes friendliness, warmth, and responsiveness to others and encourages, supports, acknowledges, and accepts others' contributions.
- *The gatekeeper* helps keep communication channels open, facilitates everyone's participation, and suggests procedures that permit sharing of what members have to say.
- *The standard setter* tests whether the group is satisfied with the way it is proceeding and points out explicit or implicit operating norms to see if they are desired.
- *The harmonizer* attempts to reconcile disagreements, reduces tension, and gets members to explore differences.
- *The group observer* stays out of the group's activities and gives feedback on the progress of the group.
- *The follower* goes along in a passive manner and provides a friendly audience.

Self-related roles are oriented only to the individual needs of the members, often at the expense of the group. The following are examples of this category:

- *The blocker* acts negatively and resists most movement that the group proposes.
- *The avoider* maintains distance from the other members and resists interacting with them.
- *The recognition seeker* calls attention to self, boasts about what he or she does or can do, and tries to avoid being placed in an inferior position.
- *The dominator* asserts authority by manipulating the group or certain individuals, by using flattery or asserting a superior status or right to attention, and by interrupting others' contributions.

Effective group functioning rests on a group's ability to utilize and balance both the task-related and maintenance-related roles as the group accomplishes its tasks. Self-related roles are kept to an absolute minimum.

Conformity. Conformity is the degree to which group members adhere to the rules and practices outlined for group members. Conformity in groups is a double-edged sword. Groups need to have a certain amount of conformity to function effectively, yet excessive pressure for conformity can undermine the group's ability to achieve individual or organizational objectives. Either too little or too much pressure to conform can be harmful to a group's functioning. Could this concept begin to explain what happened to PATCO?

The phenomenon of conformity is itself a neutral concept; the degree and type of conformity are the important considerations. On the one hand, it would be impossible to have an effective group without some norms, rules, and procedures. Imagine a newly formed project group that is told to produce a comprehensive plan to introduce a new product within a few days. This group would need time to determine what the norms will be and what roles members will play. Unless these ground rules are defined, there would be no pressure to conform, and the group would be unlikely to perform its assigned task effectively.

Maintenance-related roles directed toward the well-being, continuity, and development of the group

Self-related roles oriented only to the individual needs of the members

Conformity degree to which group members adhere to the rules and practices outlined for group members

Is conformity good or bad for the group?

FIGURE 6-1
Asch's experiment: Confederates were instructed to make inaccurate statements that line C was closest in length to line X.

On the other hand, pressure to conform can be excessive with the group demanding conformity in areas that have nothing to do with achieving individual or organizational objectives. For example, group pressure on members to socialize only with other group members or to dress in a certain way is not legitimate. Extreme pressure to conform can diminish individuality and ultimately the identity of group members, causing the group to become homogeneous and lacking in a variety of skills and abilities.

Can conformity be that strong? A classic study by Solomon Asch provides us with some insights about the nature of group conformity.[11] He gathered eight individuals in a room and showed them three lines of unequal length. He then showed them a fourth line and asked them to say which of the previous lines matched it in length (see Figure 6–1). Their answers were stated in the presence of other participants. The study was a series of these public judgments. In reality, the first seven participants were associates of Asch and had been instructed to answer correctly several times in the beginning. In the last phase of the study, the answers given by the associates were obviously wrong (all gave the same wrong answer), but in about a third of the cases the unknowing participant agreed with the other group members (Asch's associates). When later explaining their choices,

Opening Story Revisited

Returning to the PATCO story, we can now see some of the problems facing this group. One issue is the size of the group—12,000 members. To be effective there must be some clear leadership and smaller groups with which the members can identify. While the story isn't specific in this matter, we can assume that the members weren't closely identified to PATCO's leadership.

Another issue is conformity. We can understand some of their problems as based on excessive conformity, which begins to explain the failure of PATCO members to realistically see what was happening in the support for their cause. As conformity to follow the policy of PATCO became stronger, members who saw the lack of support and tried to voice that concern may have been ignored or punished by other members, depending on how strongly they voiced their opposition to the direction of the union. As the outspoken members were ignored, they may have formed their own groups, and thus cohesiveness would have suffered.

Group Norms Are Sometimes Stressful

Mark Bentlage is a Continental Airlines flight attendant. Prior to a strike against his employer, Bentlage lived a nice, routine life. After the strike was declared, his life became filled with uncertainty and even fear. The uncertainty and fear did not come from lack of income or job prospects, for Bentlage did not join his striking co-workers; he elected to cross the picket lines. In other words, he became a "scab."

His reward from striking peers consisted of threats and obscene language. He parked his car in a secret lot provided by Continental and asked a neighbor to watch his home while he was away. The pressures placed on nonstrikers became intense: Ground communication with a Continental plane was jammed by a mystery radio operator broadcasting the word *scab*. A flight attendant was spat upon and shoved when she crossed a picket line. Strikers took pictures of employees reporting to work. Someone temporarily took over the radio frequency of a Continental flight during a landing approach. At some airports, hoping to avoid confrontations, the company loaded workers onto police-escorted buses that delivered them to flights at the runways.

Other pressures were much more subtle but probably just as intense. Workers reported frequent telephone calls from striking friends entreating them to join the strike. Continued resistance would generally result in the cessation of the telephone calls but at a high price. In the words of one employee, "Some of these people are my best friends, and they won't even talk to me. That really hurts."

Source: Adapted from "Continental Air Workers Crossing Picket Lines Face Rising Hostility," *The Wall Street Journal* (11 October 1983): 35. Reprinted by permission of *The Wall Street Journal,* © Dow Jones & Company, Inc., 1983. All rights reserved.

QUESTIONS

1. Using the theory of norms, explain the behavior of the striking employees.
2. What would be the consequences for those employees who go back to work during the strike?
3. If you were a manager at Continental, what would you do concerning your employees once the strike is over?

the individuals commented that they decided to go along with the group even though they knew the answer was wrong.

As we can see, group conformity is a powerful force in a group's existence. It can get individuals to go against their best judgment. No direct research has pointed to conformity and group productivity, but it seems obvious that a group's productivity can be influenced either negatively or positively. Too much conformity may mean that the group will not be as effective on a task that demands different ideas to solve. It is also obvious that a supervisor must understand the possible results of too much or too little conformity in a work group's make-up.

Socialization: A Human Relations Application of Conformity. One specific application of conformity is the act of socialization. *Socialization* is the process by which employees are transformed from outsiders to participating organizational

Socialization process by which employees are transformed from outsiders to participating organizational and group members

Describe the stages of socialization.

How can an organization use the socialization process effectively?

and group members. As such, socialization is more than a group phenomenon, but much of the influence in the process is exerted by the work group.

Why is this concept important to management? Socialization is important because the outcome of the process can enhance or inhibit the attainment of organizational objectives. It is the same process by which organizational culture is established and passed from employee to employee and work group to work group (see Chapter 14 for details of organizational culture).

The process of socialization happens in stages. Author D.C. Feldman visualizes three stages of socialization: getting in, breaking in, and settling in.[12] *Getting in* occurs before the prospective employee enters an organization, during the acquisition of information on what it would be like to be an employee in a particular firm. Obviously, the organization can influence the results by the amount and type of information it reveals to the individual. *Breaking in* occurs when the individual enters the organization and becomes a member of a work group. The new employee is concerned with gaining acceptance, developing competence in the job, and establishing clear requirements for job and career performance. The organization can effectively influence this stage through a carefully designed orientation plan and structured training programs based on frequent performance evaluations. The final stage, *settling in*, concerns how the employee balances various conflicting demands—organizational life versus family life, and work group expectations versus organizational expectations. The company can positively influence this stage through employee counseling and flexibility in scheduling and work assignments.

Socialization is a good example of a human relations concept that spans several areas of study. It is included in this chapter because the socialization process is heavily influenced by the work group. But the results of socialization and the determination of what direction socialization takes have broader implications. The fact that the socialization process can be influenced by the supervisor and employees outside the immediate work group means that areas such as communication and leadership are also important.

Group Development

Why is it important to understand the stages of group development?

As the previous discussion points out, a manager must try to understand how work groups function and how to positively influence that functioning. One further aspect of this understanding is the developmental stages of a group. As we will see in the following section, groups need to grow and develop much as an individual. If a group gets stuck in one stage, it will be not become as effective as it could be. Supervisors must understand and appreciate the stages through which a group progresses.

Stages of Group Development. Most of us have been in some kind of group from its beginnings to its maturity. We have experienced the subtle influences that change the group from one in which we are at first uncomfortable to one in which we might seek comfort. This is typical in the process of group development.

Yet the changes are usually so subtle and the development so natural that we may be unaware of the process. We rarely try to understand or influence it.

As a group grows and develops it encounters four stages: orientation, differentiation, integration, and maturity (See Table 6–1).[13]

Stage	Group Activity
Orientation	Members get acquainted and size up the situation
	Initial task definition and identification of simple group processes
	First attempts to clarify member roles and authority/responsibility relationship
	Members try to determine how their skills will fit the group task and how the group activity will help group members
	Tentative decision on leadership and behavioral norms
Differentiation	Progress on identifying roles and norms
	Better feel for group task and for composition of group
	Formation of coalitions within the group to promote certain views and interests
	Emergence of interpersonal and subgroup conflicts
	Working through conflicts
	Emergence of competing values and norms for guiding behavior
Integration	Norms operating to obtain conformity
	Procedures established for coping with deviations from norms
	Work flow handled easily
	Development of cohesiveness among group members
	Danger of "groupthink," where loyalty to the group becomes a powerful group norm
	Members perceive themselves as a group
Maturity	Appreciation of group's need for stable norms, roles, goals, leadership, and work processes
	Appreciation of group's need to be flexible about changing demands on group
	Members' awareness of each other's strengths and weaknesses
	Acceptance of individual differences
	Tolerance of conflict over task-related issues, positive approach to conflict management
	Minimal interpersonal conflict

TABLE 6–1
Stages of group development

SOURCE: From *Organizational Behavior: A Managerial Viewpoint* by Robert Albanese and David D. Van Fleet (1983): 259. Copyright © 1983 by CBS College Publishing. Reprinted by permission of Holt, Rinehart & Winston, Inc.

Orientation. During the orientation stage individuals attempt to identify with the group in terms of a give-and-take relationship. They focus on identifying the task of the group, the ways the group will satisfy individual needs, who the leader is, the initial ground rules for acceptable behavior, and how this group fits into the larger organization. During the orientation stage the tone is often one of "niceness" as members test boundaries and seek acceptance.[14] Members introduce themselves and find out about the others in the group. Then they discuss objectives of the group, how they will accomplish those objectives, who will do what and when, and who the leader is.

Differentiation. The differentiation stage reflects the process of getting a better feel for the group itself and its task. Members confront problems arising from the orientation stage and attempt to solve them. During this stage the group tries to nail down the means or methods it will use during the group sessions, such as whether members will vote on issues or if they will try to reach total agreement.

The differentiation stage is characterized by the increased potential for conflict and competition among members. Some of this conflict results from members' past problems with leaders, authority, power, or dependency. For instance, group members who expect autonomy may rebel and become hostile if a leader attempts to exercise strong control. On the other hand, group members who prefer to have authoritarian leadership may be confused, anxious, and hostile if strong direction is not given. Subgroups may be formed to enhance the chances for need satisfaction. Unless these conflicts, issues, and problems are confronted and solved to the satisfaction of members, the group may never advance beyond the differentiation stage.

Integration. The integration stage benefits from the groping and conflict of the previous stage. During integration, problems are resolved as members evaluate their tasks and the frustrations of performing the tasks. Open discussions provide the means for understanding the problems and working out solutions.

The relationships between members are marked by increasing cohesion, sharing ideas, giving and receiving feedback, and exploring ideas and actions related to the tasks at hand. One danger of the integration stage is that members can become enchanted by their "togetherness." This feeling of cohesion can encourage the destructive problem of "groupthink." In groupthink members do not challenge false ideas, negative issues, or destructive norms, thus preventing the group from becoming creative and effective (See Table 6–2).

Maturity. The final stage of group development is maturity. Group maturity refers to the members' integration of flexibility and stability. A mature group recognizes the necessity of a stable system of norms, standards, and practices in regulating the behavior of its members. At the same time, a mature group remains flexible enough that it can adapt to changing conditions. One sign of a mature group is its ability to accept and integrate ideas and individuals from outside the original group into its ongoing activities.

Symptoms	Prevention Actions
1. Illusions of the group as invulnerable	1. Leader encourages open expression of doubt
2. Rationalizing away data that disconfirms assumptions and beliefs	2. Leader accepts criticism of his or her opinions
3. Unquestioned belief in group's inherent morality	3. Higher status members offer opinions last
4. Stereotyping competitors as weak, evil, stupid, and so on.	4. Get recommendations from similar group
5. Direct pressure on deviants to conform	5. Periodically divide into subgroups
6. Self-censorship by members	6. Members to get reaction from outsiders
7. Illusion of unanimity (silence equals consent)	7. Invite outsiders to join discussion periodically
8. Self-appointed "mindguards"—protecting group from disconfirming data	8. Assign someone the role of "devil's advocate"

TABLE 6–2
Groupthink

SOURCE: Adapted from Irving L. Janis, *Groupthink*, Second edition, copyright © 1982 Houghton Mifflin Company. Adapted with permission.

Groups vary in the ability to progress through the stages of development due to their characteristics and situational factors. We would expect rapid progress for groups with mature and experienced members who are motivated toward the group's goals, such as a football team in the Super Bowl. On the other hand, members who have strong ideas about leadership or authority may prevent a group from moving through the differentiation stage.

Leadership, too, can influence the development of a group. Leaders who practice tight control will encounter conflict as the group moves beyond the orientation stage. If these leaders persist in demanding tight control, the group will be unable to progress further. Research studying the effects of leadership style on the rate of development of training groups found that groups developed more rapidly with nondirective leaders.

How can leaders and organizations influence the group's development?

How does the organization influence the development of a group? To develop and progress through the various stages, the groups need to maintain stability in membership for a period of time. To accomplish this the group environment needs security. If the organization is seen as threatening, the groups will not develop in the same manner as a more supportive organizational culture. Therefore, the prevailing managerial philosophy is critical to group development. If top management emphasizes strong authoritarian control, groups, even at the lowest level, will tend to follow this model and remain in the first stages of development. For these reasons, supervisors and managers must recognize the com-

Opening Story Revisited

At which stage of development would you place the PATCO union? It doesn't sound like the maturity stage in which the group can integrate flexibility and stability. Some of their cohesiveness is reflective of "groupthink." For example, how much deviation is allowed? We sense from the story not very much. How much stereotyping? There was a lot of name-calling of the government and President Reagan. How much rationalizing away of outside data about the union's strength? From the story, it seemed that the union was not very aware of the public's and the press's role in portraying the union. Each of these problems suggests that the PATCO group was stuck in the third stage of group development, integration.

plexity of group development and realize that managing groups is a continual process.

Characteristics of Effective Groups.   We stated that groups usually face difficult issues as they develop into mature and effective work groups. In this section, we focus on some of the characteristics of those groups that reach a sufficient level of maturity to warrant being called effective–those that have met the social and task needs of group members and completed the firm's assigned tasks. The following characteristics are not mutually exclusive in nature. Effective groups not only exhibit most of these characteristics, but the characteristics are also additive and complementary in nature.

Clarity of Focus.   Effective groups understand the broad purposes for which they were formed. For instance, a group assigned to develop a new product knows why it exists and what it is trying to do. This is known as _purposing._ Purposing refers to having a direction that is continually referred to and supported by the organization's leadership. A key element is that the group's purpose has a direct relationship to the organization's mission or goals. Purposing allows a clearer commitment to accomplishing the stated goals, resulting in a higher level of motivation and energy. When members are highly motivated, each wishes to be valued by the group and will communicate fully and frankly all relevant information. A good example of purposing is an athletic team who enters a competition and wins at each stage or level. Their commitment and motivation grow as they approach the finals.

Supportive Atmosphere.   An effective work group provides support to its members. Support can take the form of encouraging ideas, listening to a member's problems, or providing help with a knotty technical problem. Group members offer suggestions, comments, ideas, information, and criticism in a helpful manner. Just as important, these contributions are received in the same spirit. This does not imply that there are no differences of opinion about a subject; in fact, there may be more expressions of differences because members feel secure and less egocentric about a problem, a solution, or an idea.[16]

Blending of Task and Maintenance Roles.   We have discussed group behaviors as being task-related, maintenance-related, or self-related. In an effective group, the distinction between "task functions" and "maintenance functions" tends to dissolve. Group members discover that the task requirements demand integrative actions, and they have developed behaviors and attitudes that fulfill these requirements. Much of this blending results from the group members having experimented with various behaviors over a period of time. This is similar to learning to play tennis. At first one makes a series of seemingly unrelated and conflicting moves. But after continued practice, the moves become more natural and flowing. In a similar fashion, group members learn to combine task and maintenance roles in the same communication. What may be a suggestion for a new direction to solve a problem can be viewed as supportive by other group members.

Group Composition.   Another aspect of an effective work group is the composition of membership over time. An examination of the individuals, especially their

A highly diverse group, in which members have different technical, educational, or cultural backgrounds, can bring creativity and fresh perspectives to problems or issues.

skills and personalities, might indicate that they don't seem to fit together. This is not to say that certain groups with members of similar backgrounds aren't effective, but rather that their effectiveness is confined to situations in which group cooperation is important. For example, this homogeneity could be crucial for a group in the public view whose main purpose is to exhibit a cooperative attitude. In contrast, certain situations call for a high degree of creativity and problem-solving ability, which can only be generated in a highly diverse group. People with different backgrounds—technical, educational, or cultural—help to bring fresh perspectives to problems or issues, such as the introduction of a new product.

In effective groups, the membership may change over time to reflect the need for different ideas. New members are accepted and oriented to become effective members of the work group both operationally and psychologically.[17]

Resisting Control.   A final characteristic of effective work groups is the seeming paradox of a group that performs well for the organization's purposes yet is difficult to manage.[18] This occurs frequently in high-technology firms. One such case involved the introduction of computerized axial tomography (CAT) during the mid-1970s. The organization, Picker X-Ray Corporation, established a special group to design and introduce this technology to the medical community. The group itself resisted attempts to control its behavior. Group members had a pay scale higher than the rest of the firm; they appropriated human and technical resources even against the wishes of top management; and they ignored normal channels of communication and formalities required of others in the firm. When the product was introduced the group was quickly disbanded.[19]

The resistance of effective work groups to management control may frustrate the larger system but may be tolerated by management so the group can do what the organization itself cannot do through normal methods.

LEARNING SUMMARY

1. Groups have an important influence on the organization's performance and effectiveness.
2. Groups are usually limited in size and may be informal or formal in nature.
3. Groups influence members through rewards and sanctions.
4. A group's size can affect behavior. Larger groups tend to be less satisfying and can lead to turnover. Smaller groups seem to allow greater participation and satisfaction.
5. Norms and roles are the group's expectations about how individual members should behave. Norms are general expectations about the behavior. Roles can be task-related, maintenance-related, or self-related.
6. Conformity is a powerful influence on group members' behavior. While conformity is needed to get group members to work together, research has shown that conformity can also have a negative consequence in the form of blind obedience.

7. Socialization is a process whereby an employee becomes a fully participating member of the organization. The process includes the stages of getting in, breaking in, and settling in.

8. Groups develop through predictable stages from dependence to independence. Each stage has its own issues to be resolved before the group can move on to the next stage. The stages include orientation, differentiation, integration, and maturity.

9. When a group becomes mature and effective, it exhibits certain characteristics: clarity of purpose, supportive atmosphere, blending of task and maintenance roles, appropriate group composition, and resisting control.

---

1. False   A group is a collection of people who interact with each other on a regular basis and see themselves as mutually dependent to attain some goal.

2. False   Both formal and informal groups are important to the supervisor. While informal groups are not officially sanctioned by the organization, they impose their will on others and can be counterproductive for a supervisor who does not admit their existence and deal with them.

3. True   Small groups share more information and agree with each other more. This is due to the limited number of participants who cannot hide as well as in larger groups.

4. False   This is true for blue-collar workers but not for white-collar workers. White-collar workers apparently can find more opportunities for satisfying higher level needs and therefore turnover and absenteeism do not increase with an increase in the size of the group.

5. True   If a group is attacked by outsiders, the group will become more cohesive to protect itself.

6. False   Norms are standards of behavior that are expected of all members. If the norm is central to the group's successful functioning, the group may censor members who do not follow the rules.

7. True   However, if the group conforms so much that it does not listen to the outside world, it may become less effective, as in the opening story about PATCO.

8. True   Groups do need to grow and develop. Groups can get stuck in one stage of development and not grow, just as individuals can.

KEY TERMS

Cohesiveness	Effective group
Conformity	Formal group
Differentiation	Group development

Informal group	Orientation
Integration	Roles
Maintenance-related roles	Self-related roles
Maturity	Socialization
Norm	Task-related roles

HUMAN RELATIONS APPLICATIONS

Use of Committees Means Management of Committees

Many managers and supervisors approach the conference room with a mixed reaction of fear and frustration before a meeting begins. Part of this reaction is due to pressure over work piling up back in the office and annoyance at yet another meeting.

Some committee leaders attempt to minimize the loss of time by such tactics as arriving late ("Everyone else will be late") or by bringing other paperwork to finish during lulls, or by running out to answer phone calls. These actions are a sure sign of impending failure and the lack of control of another potential management tool. The following are some ideas for supervisors to regain that control.

Is This the Right Method? The first key question to be asked by the supervisor is, "Do I need a group to help me accomplish this task?" A supervisor must determine that a committee is the best approach to the situation. If a meeting is not necessary, do not initiate it; or in the case of a standing committee, *cancel it.* Consider other approaches and methods of communication such as reports, memos, or telephone conversations.

How do you know if a meeting is the best approach? If there is a valid reason for a meeting, you should be able to verbalize a goal for the meeting. Goals should contain action verbs such as "decide," "select," or "recommend" rather than "discuss" or "consider." The goal should be specific enough that the members know when a goal is achieved.

Who Should Attend? The next critical issue is to determine who needs to attend the meeting. There is no right number for a committee, but most authorities agree that the most workable range is three to nine members. More than nine makes it difficult to get participation from all members, so why invite them? Part of the selection involves assessing who has what skills and knowledge to contribute to the session. An important consideration is each member's ability to work in a group setting.

What Advance Work Is Required? Once a meeting has been chosen as the proper vehicle and members have been selected, the leader must begin to prepare for the session. Any information that is critical to the success of the meeting should be forwarded to the members well in advance of the session. In addition to the technical information, a preliminary agenda should be sent. This document will help members know why they have been selected and help them do their homework to make the meeting more effective. This agenda should list the items to be covered, time for the session, goal of the session, other members invited, and location of the meeting room.

A word about the selection of a meeting room: this physical aspect should also receive the attention of the leader before the meeting. Pick a location that is convenient for the members and has the proper tools for a successful meeting. Overheads, flip charts, paper, writing instruments, and proper seating arrangements for face-to-face discussion are some of the items to consider.

Am I Finished Yet? Yes, with the preparation, but the actual meeting is as important as the advance work. A leader must behave as he or she would like the other members to behave. Arrive early enough to prepare and to deal with last-minute changes.

Once a meeting has started, the leader must be an active, involved, and interested party. This will set the tone of the session and some of the expectations for the other members. In some cases, the leader will have to find ways to involve members who are reluctant to participate. This may mean asking questions of those members and seeking out their opinions in an active manner. Likewise, a leader may have to control or direct an overly active member so others can participate, without injuring the offender's pride and, therefore, future participation.

A Novel Way to Teach Managers Group Skills

Many organizations are searching for ways to show managers how building group skills will help the individual manager and the organization become more effective. A novel technique is to conduct this training outside, and we mean outside.

One firm that has tried this approach is Cipher Data Products of San Diego, California. The president, Gary Liebl, and a handful of his top managers have undertaken a unique course developed by Outward Bound.

> "They always told me Cipher Data was an exciting place to work," deadpanned one of the 99 Cipher Data managers and executives who spent the day working through problems, pratfalls, and adventures of a one-day, abbreviated management and group participation skills program . . . .
>
> The expedition by Cipher Data, which designs and manufactures magnetic tape peripherals and controllers used in data storage systems, is evidence of the unusual steps that companies are taking to build team spirit that will help them endure in volatile times.
>
> "To be blunt, this is an experiment," Liebl said, while his Outward Bound team, which had dubbed itself the "Pink Panthers," sat in a sun-drenched field munching bagels stuffed with cheddar cheese and celery sticks coated with peanut butter—all washed down with a container of orange drink.
>
> Outward Bound's nine instructors led the managers through a course that forced participants to rely upon each other's strengths—both physical and mental—and to acknowledge their own weaknesses.

Such exercises as falling backward into the outstretched arms of fellow group members helped the Cipher Data managers develop trust in one another.

> Early exercises—falling backward into the outstretched arms of their fellow patrol members or trying to untie a human knot of executives holding hands—warmed the managers to more complex problems slated for later in the day.[20]

This type of training helps group members deal specifically with the orientation stage and differentiation stage of group development. In orientation, these managers use various personal skills to handle simple tasks, such as to untie the human knot. They develop an appreciation of one another's uniqueness. In the differentiation stage, the group members learn that their task is to develop group skills and that they need to develop trust in one another to accomplish this task, as in falling backward into outstretched arms.

An important lesson is that the group's strength lies in its togetherness. They can accomplish more by working as a cohesive team under certain conditions than by working alone. The conditions are complex, changing, and ones that most of them have never experienced before this training. In a situation of uncertainty (similar to the changing environment of Liebl's computer firm), the members quickly learn to rely on one another and even seek out others to solve a problem or get a different perspective on an issue.

The exercise began unexpectedly when one team member was required to play blind and was blindfolded. The only cure for the "blind" team member was perched precariously in the middle of an imaginary acid-filled pool. To complicate matters, the guide sentenced the blindfolded manager to imaginary death unless he could retrieve the cure in 20 minutes.

The Pink Panthers hammered out a makeshift plan. One woman designated herself as timekeeper, and another team member climbed a nearby tree to fasten a rope to a limb that stretched out over the pit.

The team tied the blindfolded manager to the rope, dangled him over the pit, and shouted directions and encouragement. He safely grabbed the antidote.[20]

This exercise helps the members see the value in developing roles to help the group accomplish its task. The timekeeper is an example of a maintenance role that helps the group monitor its progress.

Cipher Data executives say the Outward Bound program helped them understand how real and imaginary handicaps could be overcome with teamwork.

"We exhibited good, spontaneous teamwork, and it seems that we had to work at it less hard than earlier in the day," Liebl said of the Pink Panthers' successful acid river crossing. "We planned it and leveraged the teamwork that we built earlier in the day."

Liebl said that exercises such as the "acid river" course "stressed the importance of participative management. For a manager to sit behind four walls and to think he's smart enough to know the solution to every problem is horribly naive. I'm always stressing that we go to the hands-on people for those solutions."[20]

From this chapter, we can develop certain suggestions for successfully participating in or managing a group. The group can be a work group or a committee.

PERSONAL GUIDELINES FOR HUMAN RELATIONS SUCCESS

Success as a Group Member

Several suggestions can help you be a more effective group member and have your skills more fully utilized:

- □ *Be on time.* This may sound simple, but being late is a form of nonverbal behavior that is usually read by others as "you don't feel that our time is important." Respect meeting times; if you are late, you waste the time of the other group members.
- □ *Be prepared.* Again, this is a simple rule that assumes you know why the meeting is being called and why you were invited. Both questions should be answered by the group leader if you don't know the answers. Preparation means having studied the material handed out prior to the meeting and having the material you need to answer questions posed by other group members.

☐ *Avoid inappropriate behavior.* By inappropriate behavior we mean doing things that may hamper the group's progress. Some of these behaviors are similar to those of self-related roles. In addition, the purpose and function of a group should be taken as seriously as one's own job.

☐ *Respect others' contributions.* Groups may include members from all parts of the organization, some more involved in the problem at hand than others. Respect all contributions from other areas of the organization. Sometimes these members can see things more clearly because they are not totally involved. Use all expertise by listening to all members.

Success as a Group Leader

The next set of suggestions is meant for leaders of groups or committees.

☐ *Develop and distribute an agenda.* This means that as the group leader you have identified why you need to use a group and who should be invited. After these immediate decisions, you must organize the session to be most productive. Organizing means establishing a series of goals and the necessary steps the group should take. The result of this is an agenda that lists the major activities for this particular session and who is responsible for each. The agenda should be distributed prior to the session for the members to use to prepare their contributions.

☐ *Involve quiet members.* Most groups have members who are not used to being, or do not see themselves as, active members. At the same time, most groups have individuals who are very active and tend to take over a group. A leader must try to balance the participation of all members. In the case of the quiet members, a leader can ask for their opinions about the topic under discussion. Over time the quiet member may begin to contribute voluntarily. Overly active members can be handled by asking them to allow someone else to express an opinion, saying something like, "Thank you for your thoughts on that. . . . We now need to hear from . . . ."

DISCUSSION AND REVIEW QUESTIONS

1. Think of a group with which you are involved. What type of group is it, according to the chapter's material? What stage of development is it presently in?
2. Often a group, such as an athletic team, will lose its cohesiveness. What are some possible causes and what are some possible solutions?
3. What are some examples of group norms? How do groups get members to conform to those norms? What are the implications of such norms for a supervisor?
4. Why is the study of group dynamics important to management?
5. List the characteristics of an effective group. How might a manager use this information to set up a project group to develop a new product?

6. If a work group sets a lower standard of performance than the organization thinks is appropriate, what should the manager of such a group do?

Group Norms

HUMAN RELATIONS EXERCISE

From reading the chapter, you are aware that groups develop norms to control the individual members' behavior. Some of these norms can facilitate the group's accomplishing its tasks. Other norms can hinder a group and keep it from developing. This exercise should help you understand how this happens.

Answer the following questions from your experience as a group member. Use a specific group in which you are (were) an active member and whose membership is (was) important to you. For example, you can use the class in which you are now studying this chapter.

QUESTIONS

1. What are three behaviors expected by the group members that were communicated to you verbally?
2. What are three behaviors expected by the group members that you had to discover on your own?
3. Which expected behaviors from your list of six are the most important to the group? Rank them according to priority.
4. What happened to group members who violated the group's norms by not behaving as expected?
5. Which of the norms help the group? Which hinder the group?

Now share this list with other members in the class. Compare your lists and look for similarities and differences. If you did the class norms, make a composite list for the entire group of class norms.

HUMAN RELATIONS INCIDENT

I arrived at the City Club a little earlier than necessary. Feeling a bit anxious, I decided to remain in my car for just a while. God, I hoped I would see someone I knew!

Maybe I could see what sort of people attend these Junior Club meetings. I noticed that those entering were decked out in fine attire, indeed. I hoped that I fit into the group.

Summoning up my courage, I found myself paying my new member's fee and entering the club room. I received my "write-it-yourself-and-please-be-legible" name tag. My immediate thought was that all these mingling people knew each other and I didn't know anyone. How could I break into a conversation?

Standing near the edge of the room, alone, was an interesting-looking girl who seemed to glance my way shyly. I moved toward her and began the usual, "Hello, my name is . . ."

Conversation was easy with her. She also was new to the group. We provided support for each other during those critical first-night minutes. Eventually, as others filtered by, we began to include them as well.

One generous fellow condescended to offer his opinion of my attire. He said, "*Gentleman's Quarterly* says that your tie should come down just to belt level." Looking down, I noticed that mine hung somewhat longer than preferred. This made me uncomfortable for a bit. But I gave myself the old "this-is-me,-take-it-or-go-fly-a-kite" talking to, which made me feel better.

I began talking to someone about playing squash, a game we both enjoy very much. Then I talked to another person about hiking in the Cascades and fishing.

Suddenly, I realized that I was having a pretty good time. My initial worries had been unnecessary. These people, at least some of them, were a lot like me. Why had I been so worried?

QUESTIONS

1. Describe the group's norms and how the group developed over this brief time period.
2. What suggestions would you make for improving how people meet others?

NOTES

1. F. J. Roethlisberger and W. J. Dickson, *Management and the Worker* (Cambridge, MA: Harvard University Press, 1939): 11.
2. F. J. Roethlisberger, *Management and Morale* (Cambridge, MA: Harvard University Press, 1939): 21.
3. K. N. Wexley and G. A. Yukl, *Organizational Behavior and Personnel Psychology* (Homewood, IL: Irwin, 1977).
4. R. M. Steers, *Introduction to Organizational Behavior* (Glenview, IL: Scott, Foresman, 1981): 188–90.
5. E. J. Thomas and C. F. Fink, "Effects of Group Size," in L. L. Cummings and W. E. Scott, eds., *Readings in Organizational Behavior and Human Performance* (Homewood, IL: Irwin, 1969).
6. Marvin E. Shaw, *Group Dynamics: The Psychology of Small Group Behavior,* 2nd ed. (New York: McGraw-Hill, 1976).
7. L. Berkowitz, "Group Standards, Cohesivenesss, and Productivity," *Human Relations* (November 1954): 405–19.
8. D. Birenbaum and E. Sagarin, *Norms and Human Behavior* (New York: Holt, Rinehart & Winston, 1976): 10–11.
9. E. H. Schein, *Organizational Psychology,* 3rd ed. (Englewood Cliffs, NJ: Prentice-Hall, 1980): 100.
10. L. R. Hoffman, "Applying Experimental Research on Group Problem Solving to Organizations," *Journal of Applied Behavioral Science,* Vol. 15 (1979): 375–91.
11. S. E. Asch, "Effects of Group Pressure upon the Modification and Distribution of Judgments," in H.P. Guetzhow, ed., *Group Leadership and Men* (Pittsburgh: Carnegie Press, 1952): 177–90.
12. D. C. Feldman, "A Piratical Program for Employee Socialization," *Organizational Dynamics* (Autumn 1976): 64–80.
13. J. S. Jacobson and E. Jacobson, "Model of Task Group Development in Complex Organizations and a Strategy of Implementation," *Academy of Management Journal,* Vol. 1 (1976): 98–111.
14. R. B. Caple, "The Sequential Stages of Group Development," *Small Group Behavior,* Vol. 9 (1978): 471.

15. D. C. Lungren, ''Trainer Style and Patterns of Group Development,'' *Journal of Applied Behavioral Science,* Vol. 7 (1971): 689–709.

16. R. Likert, ''The Nature of Highly Effective Groups,'' *New Patterns of Management* (New York: McGraw-Hill, 1961).

17. G. Strauss and L. R. Sayles, *Personnel: the Human Problems of Management,* 2nd ed. (Englewood Cliffs, NJ: Prentice-Hall, 1967): 200.

18. R. E. Callahan and P. Salipante, Jr., ''Boundary Spanning Units: Organizational Implications for the Management of Innovation,'' *Human Resource Management* (Spring 1979): 26–31.

19. Ibid.

20. Greg Johnson, ''Managers Learn Trust, Cooperation in the Mud,'' Los Angeles Times/Washington Post News Service, reported by *The Herald,* (1 April 1986): 01.

PART THREE

ORGANIZATIONAL ASPECTS OF HUMAN RELATIONS

CHAPTER 7
CONFLICT
MANAGEMENT

WHAT'S YOUR OPINION? T OR F

_F_ 1. Conflict is destructive and should always be eliminated.

_F_ 2. Ignoring or avoiding a conflict is a sign of poor management.

_T_ 3. Creating conflict may improve the performance of a department or unit.

_T_ 4. Competition and conflict are different concepts.

_F_ 5. When there is conflict between two groups, conflict within each group generally increases, too.

_T_ 6. The first step in resolving conflict is to separate the opponents.

_T_ 7. If opponents compromise to solve a conflict, they each give up something.

_F_ 8. Young managers are more capable of managing conflict than experienced managers.

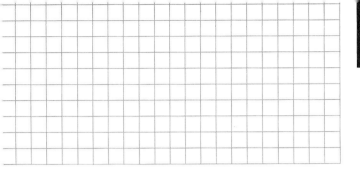

OUTLINE

CHANGING VIEWS OF CONFLICT
  Conflict Defined

HOW CONFLICT WORKS
  Thomas's Structural Conflict Model
  Robbins's Organizational Conflict Model

CONFLICT BETWEEN GROUPS
  Line/Staff Conflict

RESOLVING CONFLICT
  Common Resolution Techniques
  Conflict-Management Style

STIMULATING CONFLICT

LEARNING SUMMARY

HUMAN RELATIONS APPLICATIONS
  Manager/Subordinate Conflict
  Stakes and Conflict of Interest
  How CEOs View Conflict

PERSONAL GUIDELINES FOR HUMAN
RELATIONS SUCCESS

LEARNING OBJECTIVES

☐ Describe and understand two major conflict
   models

☐ Identify conditions where conflict is desirable

☐ Describe the effects of intergroup conflict

☐ Discuss methods for resolving conflict

☐ Describe techniques for stimulating conflict

☐ Understand how personal characteristics
   influence a person's approach to conflict

All in the Family[1]

Perhaps conflict is not worse in family-owned businesses, but it certainly seems like it. Consider the saga of Joe, Max, Bob, and George, four brothers aged 79, 77, 74, and 71.

The brothers are second generation owners of a family business. Their father had said he wanted to ensure continued success of the business and also to treat his sons fairly. In his will he gave each of his sons 25 percent of the voting stock and stipulated that they must be paid equally.

George, the youngest brother, became the chief executive officer when his father died. Now at age 71, still in good health, he continues to work ten-hour days. He discovered that by padding his expense account, he could get around his father's equal-pay decree, giving himself a premium for his active role in the company's management.

Joe, the oldest brother, goes to the office every morning to do only one thing: verify George's expenses. When he discovered that his younger brother was submitting extravagant expense accounts, he decided to monitor the expenses on a daily basis.

Brother Max has no interest in the business but loves the dividends. He shows up at the quarterly brothers' meetings and demands that dividends be increased. George argues that growth of the business requires reinvesting capital, not paying higher dividends.

Bob tries to act as a peacemaker. This has become more difficult since two of the brothers tapped each other's phones. Three of the brothers now want to sell the business, but they can't agree on how to proceed.

CHANGING VIEWS OF CONFLICT

> Conflict takes one-fourth of management time.

Although the conflict among the four brothers is unusual in its intensity, the existence of conflict within organizations is not unusual at all. One survey of executives and middle managers revealed that they spend about 24 percent of their time dealing with conflict. They considered conflict management equal to or slightly higher in importance than planning, communication, motivation, and decision making.[2]

Considering the time a manager must spend dealing with conflict, it seems wise to learn as much as possible about its causes and how to diagnose and manage it.

Conflict Defined

Conflict is best described as a condition of opposition and discord, involving mutual antagonism. Conflict and competition are often confused. The most striking similarity between the two is that in each case goals are incompatible. However, in conflict there is active interference with the other party's attainment of a goal. In most cases, competition involves rules and standards that limit what competitors can do to each other, whereas conflict is unregulated. One authority has described competition as "parallel striving" and conflict as "mutual interference."[3]

Conflict opposition and antagonism

Over the past 70 years, the concept of conflict management has changed significantly three times. These changes represent increased understanding of how conflict occurs, as well as modified philosophies for dealing with it.

Eliminate Conflict. This view is actually quite simple. Since all conflict was seen as destructive, it should be eliminated. The manager was the person charged with getting rid of it. Conflict management therefore referred to the managerial activity of eliminating organizational conflict.

Although this philosophy had undoubtedly been held by many managers decades earlier, writers of the human relations movement defined the view clearly, and it became generally accepted. The central theme of the human relations theory was that of organizational harmony and balance. Writers of this school pointed to a perfect balance between organizational goals and worker needs. It followed naturally that conflict "tended to be viewed as an organizational abnormality, rather than as a natural process in social relations."[4] Conflict and tension were viewed as a deviation from a normal state of cooperation. This deviation could and must be eliminated. This view dominated management literature into the 1940s. Many managers still accept this view, although it has been long discarded by writers as theoretically weak.

Why did early human relations theory recommend the elimination of conflict?

[handwritten note in margin: central theme of human relations was organizational harmony that these people tend to think conflicts but will not create conflict]

Conflict Resolution. A later group of writers broke away from the human relations view of conflict. They recognized conflict as an unavoidable component of social relationships. Completely reversing the earlier view, these writers saw conflict as a normal and natural occurrence in organizations. Further, they emphasized that conflict had different effects on organizations. In some situations, conflict could have good rather than bad effects. Looking on conflict as unavoidable and often helpful was a major revision of the traditional view and had a great effect on management's approach. As one of the pioneers of this theory stated:

> We do not believe that the elimination of conflict is invariably or even typically the desirable goal in wise management of conflict as many who identify consensus with agreement tend to do. Conflicts stem basically from differences among persons and groups. Elimination of conflict would mean the elimination of such differences. The goal of conflict management is, for us, better conceived as the acceptance and enhancement of differences among persons and groups.[5]

The conflict resolution approach is the dominant one in organizations today.

Conflict Stimulation. This third philosophy expands the term conflict management to include the creation of conflict. According to theorists who hold this view, those who advocate conflict resolution admit that conflict can have beneficial results, yet they perceive the manager's task to involve only resolution, rather than creation of conflict:

> Though they recognize that conflict is inherent, (they) give it only superficial acceptance. They grasp for supportive material to defend conflict's existence . . . nowhere is there found the active seeking of conflict, or the positive creation of the conditions that breed conflict.[6]

Proponents of this third view charge that, while those who advocate conflict resolution admit that conflict can be desirable and have beneficial results, they perceive the manager's task to involve only resolution, rather than creation of conflict.

One supporter of conflict stimulation, Stephen P. Robbins, argues that conflict can actually improve performance. While conceding that too much conflict will be disruptive or even destructive, Robbins points out that too little conflict leads to apathy and stagnation. Therefore there is a desirable or optimum level of conflict that will lead to high performance.[7]

How can conflict improve performance?

too little con- flict leads to apathy + stagnation

Conflict can be destructive, as when it produces irresponsible behavior (left), or constructive, as when it results in solving problems (right).

Conflict is constructive when it:

□ Opens up issues of importance, resulting in their clarification
□ Results in solving problems
□ Increases involvement of individuals in issues of importance to them
□ Serves as a release of pent-up emotion, anxiety, and stress
□ Helps build cohesiveness among people by sharing the conflict, celebrating its settlement, and learning more about each other through it
□ Helps individuals to grow and to apply what they've learned to future situations

Conflict is destructive when it:

□ Diverts energy from more important activities and issues
□ Destroys the morale of people or reinforces poor self-concept
□ Polarizes groups, increasing internal cohesiveness while reducing group co-operativeness
□ Deepens differences in values
□ Produces irresponsible and regrettable behavior such as name calling and fighting
□ Increases stress[8]

One need only look at the political sphere to see that conflict can have valuable results. For example, racial minorities made gains in human rights only after the white majority was shocked out of apathy by the civil rights movement in the 1960s and 1970s. People who are satisfied with the status quo may recognize problems and deal with them only when opposition is felt.

A lot of effort has been spent in developing models of conflict. We will briefly review two models and view them in light of the opening story.

HOW CONFLICT WORKS

Thomas's Structural Conflict Model

A structural conflict model describes conditions that lead to conflict and how those conditions shape the behavior of the parties in conflict. The circles in Figure 7–1 represent the parties in conflict. Each party has behavioral predispositions as well as pressures that influence the extent of the conflict.[9]

Each party brings behavioral predispositions to conflict. For example, a highly competitive person might view conflict in terms of a winner-takes-all competition and perhaps be less likely to compromise than a less competitive person. Similarly, a person who is uncomfortable with confrontation might go to extreme lengths to escape a conflict.

Behavior is also influenced by social pressure. As we learned in the preceding chapter on group dynamics, there are norms of behavior for group members.

Behavioral predisposition a tendency to act in a certain way

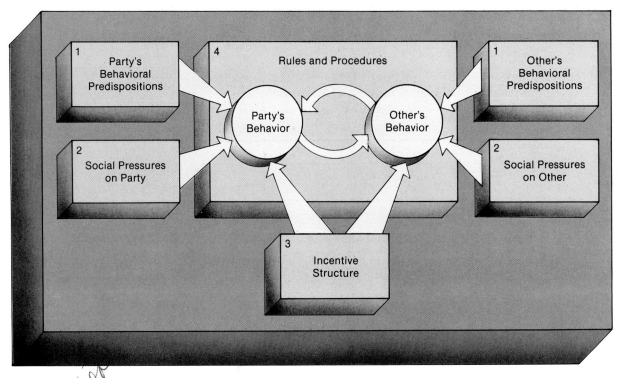

FIGURE 7–1

Thomas's structural conflict model (Source: Adapted from K. W. Thomas, "Conflict and Conflict Management," in M. Dunnette, ed., *Handbook of Industrial and Organizational Psychology.* (Copyright © 1976 by John Wiley & Sons, Inc. Reprinted by permission of John Wiley & Sons, Inc.)

Some of those norms will influence the way people behave in conflict. Norms can even influence the likelihood of conflict. If, for example, the production department supports a norm of noncooperation with the sales force, conflict between the two departments is likely. Further, once conflict between the two exists, cooperation will become even less likely. Union negotiations provide another example of social pressure. Generally, the negotiators for the two sides do not wish to appear too cooperative, since this may be viewed as a sign of weakness by those being represented.

A third source of influence is the incentive structure, or the manner in which the satisfaction of one party depends on the satisfaction of the other party. Two concerns are the size of the stakes, or the importance to each party, and the extent to which there is a conflict of interest. The higher the stakes, the more important an issue is to a party, and the more likely that assertive or even aggressive behavior will occur. Conflict of interest describes the extent to which the concerns of the conflicting parties are incompatible. When the concerns are com-

Let's Find the Guy Who Did This

In 1980, the 2,000 workers of Rath Packing Company, headquartered in Waterloo, Iowa, gave up 30 percent of their wages, half their paid vacation, and part of their holiday and sick pay over an eighteen-month period in return for 60 percent of the company's stock. The exchange was not due to a sudden interest in entrepreneurship: Rath was on the verge of closing, and the employee-ownership plan evolved from an understandable desire to keep its plants open.

Employees hoped for immediate change: new opportunity for promotions, profit sharing, and more efficient operations. The company experienced an almost immediate 10 percent increase in productivity and a 50 percent decline in absenteeism. After five consecutive years of losses, the company had a small profit after only six months of employee ownership.

But by late 1983, the company was on the verge of filing bankruptcy, and Rath's employees—now also Rath's owners—were having trouble figuring out who to blame. In the meantime, there was much dissension, and people found it very difficult to separate the interests of management, the union, and individuals.

Consider, for example, the situation faced by Lyle Taylor, a former butcher. In the 1970s Taylor was the president of a union local and helped negotiate the pork-packing industry's generous medical and dental plans. In March of 1983 Taylor became Rath's president and found himself faced with the need to wrestle away many of those same benefits. To keep the company afloat, the former union leader closed one plant and temporarily suspended operations at two others. To force wage and benefit cuts he endured a three-month strike—from the union he used to lead—at an Indianapolis plant.

Company management felt it must change the expensive seniority system. This left some company directors with a difficult decision, since many board members also belonged to the union.

The following comments by Rath workers characterize the view of employees:

- ☐ "It goes against everything we have fought for all these years."
- ☐ "This company is employee owned, but that doesn't mean much. It is really out of our hands."
- ☐ Employee ownership " . . . is just a piece of paper lying in a safe" that cost some vacations.
- ☐ "It just seems like we're all working against each other. I thought we'd pull together, but the opposite is happening."

QUESTIONS

1. How can the early increase in productivity and the decrease in absenteeism be explained?
2. Are the interests of owners (stockholders) generally in conflict with the interests of workers? Why or why not?
3. Why did many Rath employees feel that employee ownership "doesn't mean much"?

Source: Adapted from B. Morris, "Workers at Employee-Run Rath Packing Are Divided, Bitter After Chapter 11 Filing," *The Wall Street Journal* (14 November 1983): 29. Reprinted by permission of *The Wall Street Journal,* © Dow Jones & Company, Inc., 1983. All rights reserved.

pletely incompatible, the situation is called a "zero-sum game," in which there can be only one winner. Basketball and baseball games are zero-sum games. There are no ties, no "sharing" of a win. One team wins and one loses. There are many parallels in organizations: a desirable promotion that can be won by only

Opening Story Revisited

When we use Thomas's conflict model to look at the opening story, we can clearly describe the behavior of the four brothers. George is trying to pay himself for running the business, Joe is trying to stop him, Max is trying to increase his dividend income, and Bob is trying to make peace among his brothers.

It is more difficult to determine behavioral predispositions since we have little background information on the brothers, but we can make some assumptions. For example, it seems that George is happy running the business (ten-hour workdays) but is concerned about equity (being paid for his extra involvement). Joe seems concerned about equality, as stated in his father's will, and is spending a lot of time to see that the rules are followed. Max might be most interested in security and, therefore, agitates for increased dividends. Bob, as peacemaker, may be uncomfortable with conflict and tries to reduce it in any way possible. We have no information on the social pressures operating here, but we can assume that each brother's spouse and children support his position.

A major factor in this conflict is the incentive structure. The founder of the company, probably unwittingly, dictated a compensation arrangement that led to a serious problem. Despite the different interests and capabilities of the brothers, they were to be paid equally.

There are apparently no formal rules or procedures for resolving the conflict. The brothers cannot even agree on how to proceed in the sale of the company. Before formal rules could be established, the brothers would have to agree on that, too.

one person, recognition as top salesperson of the year, or an award for best group safety record. Of course, there are even more situations where interests are not totally incompatible: budget limitations requiring departments to compete for such resources as a share of available money, priority on the computing system, or access to secretarial support. To a great extent then, the amount of conflict of interest depends on the resources available within the organization.

The final source of influence is the rules and procedures in place for dealing with conflict. These may be either formal or informal agreements. Some union contracts include a clause defining a formal appeal process for workers in conflict with managers. Managers of interdependent departments might agree informally that scheduling conflicts be discussed between them rather than being appealed to the next level of management.

Rules and procedures may be formal or informal.

Robbins's Organizational Conflict Model

Robbins proposed the conflict model shown in Figure 7–2. According to this model, conflict comes from three sources: communication, the organization structure, and personal behavior factors.[10]

We know that much conflict is started by problems in communication. As we discovered in Chapter 5, there are many ways for communication to be misinterpreted or distorted, resulting in serious conflict. However, research also indicates that conflict often stems from things *not* communicated. For example, a manager may place a low priority on a requested revision of departmental budgeting procedures. If other departments place high priority on the revision, the manager may find herself in conflict with other managers or even her boss, because her priorities were "wrong." If a priority is not communicated, people tend to attach their own priorities. Rarely are the priorities the same.

How does poor communication cause conflict?

The organizational structure also can lead to conflict. A high level of bureaucracy may lead to frustration and a search for informal ways of completing tasks. The resulting "rule breaking" may lead to conflict with those who enforce the formal chain of command. Organizational reward systems may lead to conflict

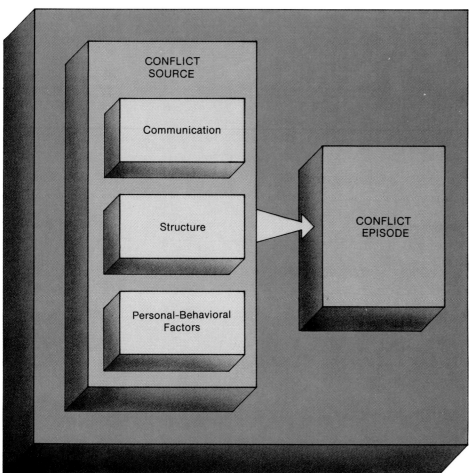

FIGURE 7 – 2
Robbins's conflict model (Source: Adapted from Stephen P. Robbins, *Managing Organizational Conflict: A Nontraditional Approach,* © 1974, p. 99. Adapted by permission of Prentice-Hall, Inc., Englewood Cliffs, NJ.)

Communication
Structure
Personal
Behavioral
Factors

as well. Sales personnel are rewarded for adapting to client needs, including rush orders or other special treatment. Manufacturing personnel are rewarded for being efficient, so they emphasize careful planning and try to avoid rush orders or any special consideration that affects a production run. The more that people or departments depend on one another, the greater the need for cooperation and the greater the potential for conflict.[11]

A major study was conducted of structural conflict in public agencies. Groups that shared clients reported higher levels of conflict than those that did not. Inconsistent priorities and responsibilities between the groups caused disputes as territory overlapped and separating responsibilities became more difficult.[12]

Personal behavior factors include personality, status, and personal goals. Robbins suggested that management has little control over these factors.[13] Personality is formed early in life and substantial change is unlikely, no matter how much the boss desires it! The classic "personality conflict" is difficult to solve. A manager we know fired a highly competent secretary after one month because the secretary's abrasive personality and aggressive stance toward other employees led to undesirable conflict. The problem was discussed with the secretary on at least three occasions, but she was unable or unwilling to modify her behavior sufficiently to reduce the conflict.

As we can see, the choice of a conflict model leads one to a somewhat different perspective on the issue. This can be viewed as a strength rather than a weakness. The value of any model is its use in describing complex situations. As yet there is no general model of conflict, so the wise manager will consider more than one model in the diagnosis of a conflict.

CONFLICT BETWEEN GROUPS

As we learned in Chapter 6, group behavior has different characteristics than individual behavior, and we treat intergroup conflict separately from individual conflict. Group dynamics play an interesting part in conflict. The relationships between departments in an organization can be characterized by the responsiveness of one department to the needs of another, the accuracy of information exchanged, and the attitudes of department members toward other departments and their members.[14] The behavior of groups in conflict parallels that of individuals in conflict: interference with the performance of another group, withholding or distortion of information, overstatement of needs to influence the other department, annoyance, and distrust.

A landmark study in intergroup conflict led to later studies that give us a good picture of what happens within and between competing groups.[15]

Effects within each competing group include:

☐ Each group becomes more closely knit and elicits greater loyalty from its members; members close ranks and bury some of their internal differences.

Opening Story Revisited

When we analyze the opening story using Robbins's model, we see a few different aspects of the problem. Communication, or lack of communication, is certainly a factor in the present conflict. The brothers probably talk to one another only when it is absolutely necessary, and then perhaps only to accuse one another of misdeeds.

Structural variables are an obvious issue. The pay scheme required by the founder's will may have started the conflict. The brothers apparently have the same amount of power as well as the same pay. The president seems unable to make a change in the situation, and there are probably no outside board members to swing the power balance toward any one of the brothers.

Personal behavior factors are a major component of this conflict as well. We speculated earlier about the brothers' behavioral predispositions.

□ Group climate changes from informal, casual, and playful to work- and task-oriented; concern for members' psychological needs declines while concern for task accomplishment increases.

□ Leadership patterns tend to change from more democratic toward more autocratic; the group becomes more willing to tolerate autocratic leadership.

□ Each group becomes more highly structured and organized.

□ Each group demands more loyalty and conformity from its members to be able to present a solid front.

> What are advantages of group conflict for the group's leader?

Effects between competing groups can include:

□ Each group begins to see the other group as the enemy, rather than merely a neutral object.

□ Each group begins to experience distortions of perception. It tends to perceive only the best parts of itself, denying its weaknesses. It also tends to perceive only the worst parts of the other group, denying its strengths. Each group is likely to develop a negative stereotype of the other ("They don't play fair like we do.").

□ Hostility toward the other group increases while interaction and communication with the other group decrease, thus it becomes easier to maintain negative stereotypes and more difficult to correct perceptual distortions.

□ If the groups are forced into interaction, for example, if they are forced to listen to representatives plead their own and the other's cause in reference to some task, each group is likely to listen more closely to its own representative and not listen to the other group's representative except to find fault with the presentation. In other words, group members tend to listen only for that which supports their own position and stereotype.

Job Envy

For most managers, it is traumatic to be passed over for a promotion. For some managers, it is devastating. Skillful executives can soften the blow for those passed over, but many high-level managers don't possess that skill. Consider these two cases that got out of hand:

In the first case, the vice president of a small firm plotted to get even with a colleague who had won a promotion wanted by the vice president. He leaked damaging and false information to a local newspaper indicating that the community had little chance for landing a new plant planned by the company. The leak outraged top executives who initially believed it came from the recently promoted executive. An investigator hired to uncover the leak exposed the vice president, a 16-year company employee. "He was fired and lost everything," the investigator said. "And for what?"

In the second case, a staff manager was the target of a co-worker envious about the manager's recent promotion. The co-worker lied to superiors about how the manager had made work errors and was incompetent. The colleague also made untrue accusations about drinking and carousing. Finally his behavior became so extreme that he was fired, but not before putting the manager through a horrible ordeal. The manager blames what happened on a corporate culture that failed to emphasize teamwork and bred an "each man for himself" climate.

Source: C. Hymowitz and T. D. Schellhardt, "Thy Neighbor's Job: As Insecurities Grow, Office Jealousy Flourishes," *The Wall Street Journal* (17 July 1986): 25. Reprinted by permission of *The Wall Street Journal,* © Dow Jones & Company, Inc., 1986. All rights reserved.

Obviously, such conflict gets out of control quickly, so it should be anticipated and defused before it gets started, as in the following situations:

In a large bank, two managers competing for a promotion began to discredit one another, and their two departments were soon in conflict. The managers' boss, a senior vice president, met with each and informed them that neither would be promoted unless the pettiness stopped. It stopped.

An executive in a communications firm promoted one of two subordinates who applied for a promotion. After making the choice, the executive met with the loser and emphasized that future promotion was entirely possible. The winner and the loser then shared a champagne brunch at corporate expense. They are still friends.

A sales firm addressed the harder aspects of its competitive culture by giving bonuses to high-commission salespeople who helped their less successful colleagues. Rewarding cooperation helps deflect jealousy.

QUESTIONS

1. Which conflict model (Thomas's or Robbins's) better explains the conflict in the first two examples?
2. How would you advise the two organizations to avoid similar situations in the future?
3. What are the major differences between the first two examples and the remaining three examples?

As you can see, conflict can bring both positive and negative behavior among group members. Increased cohesiveness and greater task orientation can lead to improved productivity. Demand for more loyalty and conformity can cut both ways: too much loyalty and conformity can lead to unwarranted feelings of superiority and to groupthink. On the other hand, it is hard to think of anything positive about distorted perception and increased hostility coupled with reduced communication.

If the competition continues to the end, and one group is identified as the winner, we can expect to see the following behavior:

Effects on the winning group:

1. The winning group retains its cohesion and may become even more cohesive.
2. The winner tends to release tension, lose its fighting spirit and become complacent, casual, and playful (the "fat and happy" state).
3. The winner tends toward high intragroup cooperation and concern for members' needs, and low concern for work and task accomplishment.
4. The winner tends to be complacent and to feel that winning has confirmed the positive stereotype of itself and the negative stereotype of the other group. There is little basis for reevaluating perceptions, or reexamining group operations to learn how to improve them.

Effects on the losing group:

1. If the situation permits because of some ambiguity in the decision (say, if judges have rendered it or if the game was close), there is a strong tendency for the loser to deny or distort the reality of losing. Instead, the loser will find psychological escapes, such as "the judges were biased," "the judges didn't really understand our solution," "the rules of the game were not clearly explained to us," or "if luck had not been against us at one key point, we would have won."
2. If the loss is accepted, the losing group tends to splinter, unresolved conflicts surface, and fights break out—all in the effort to find the cause for the loss.
3. The loser is more tense, ready to work harder, and desperate to find someone or something to blame.
4. The loser tends toward low intragroup cooperation, low concern for members' needs, and high concern for recouping by working harder.
5. The losing group learns a lot about itself because the positive stereotype of itself and the negative stereotype of the other group are upset by the loss, forcing a reevaluation of perceptions. As a consequence, the loser is likely to reorganize and become more cohesive and effective, once the loss has been accepted realistically.

Why do losers often learn more than winners?

As painful as loss can be, the losing group stands to benefit a great deal from the conflict. Its perceptions have been challenged, and weaknesses identified. On the other hand, the winning group may simply congratulate itself on being superior and reject any suggestion that its practices could be improved.

Line/Staff Conflict

Conflict is relatively common between certain functional groups or departments in any large organization. For example, one can expect at least occasional conflict between sales and production departments. An even more common conflict is that between the line generalists and staff specialists. Line managers are generally in charge of departments or processes that produce the product or service. Staff managers generally run specialized departments, personnel for example, and provide specialized advice and assistance to line managers.

Line managers sometimes feel that staff people undermine line authority.[16] For example, personnel departments usually specify hiring and firing procedures and are generally heavily involved in the development of performance evaluation and other procedures carried out by line managers.

In a consulting project at a major corporation, we found the following perceptions operating between line and staff managers.

Line managers felt that:

☐ Staff people are "meddlers" who overstep their authority
☐ Staff people suffer from limited perspective; their specialization keeps them from seeing the broad picture
☐ Staff people's advice is frequently naive or unworkable
☐ Staff people frequently complicate inherently simple concepts and procedures

Staff managers felt that:

☐ Line managers resist anything new
☐ Line people call for staff help only when situations become hopeless, then blame failure on advice from staff personnel
☐ Line people treat staff people as second-class citizens
☐ Line managers ignore the advice of staff managers and won't give staff managers authority to implement solutions

The hard feelings between line and staff personnel have been going on for years in this organization and many others. Similar results were reported in studies four decades ago.[17]

[margin note: Why are line and staff groups frequently in conflict? — perceptions]

RESOLVING CONFLICT

The first step in resolving conflict is to determine the nature of the conflict. Classifying the conflict is important to make sure that all parties are dealing with a common denominator. It will also ensure that the problem is unearthed and not just the symptoms of the problem.

Much of the early research on conflict viewed the issue as making a choice between cooperation and competition. In fact there are many options between cooperation and competition, and these are now receiving a great deal of attention. In this section we will describe some of the more widely used methods for dealing with conflict.

In problem solving, or collaboration, the concerned parties come face-to-face to work out a solution together.

Common Resolution Techniques

Problem Solving.   Problem solving, also referred to as collaboration, is one of the most widely used and effective methods for resolving conflict. It involves the concerned parties coming face-to-face to work out a solution together. Essential points of difference are sought rather than a determination of who is right, who is wrong, who wins, or who loses. Through communication and a sharing of feelings, the problem is mutually defined. Similarities are emphasized, and the participants consider a full range of alternatives to solve the problem.

Expanding Resources.   Expanding resources is an obvious approach if that is where the conflict exists. The advantage, of course, is that both conflicting parties achieve victory. Unfortunately, the use of this technique is restricted by the inherent limitation that resources cannot always be expanded. For example, a railroad superintendent of transportation was expected to have the right railcars in the right location when they were needed. Having surplus equipment in a location would be costly, but too few cars would allow an advantage to competitors. Departmental conflict arose when sales wanted adequate cars to meet all cus-

Conflict resolution
problem solving

tomer needs for transportation, while operations viewed the demands as unrealistic and costly.

Avoidance. A useful method for handling conflict is avoidance. While it does not provide a permanent resolution, it can be a successful short-run alternative. The time gained through avoidance can be used for gathering information about the problem. It also can provide a "cooling off" period for the parties involved.

Smoothing. Smoothing, also called accommodating, is a process of playing down differences while emphasizing common interests. Communication revolves around similarly held views, while issues upon which differences exist are not openly discussed.

Why is there no "best" way to resolve conflict?

Compromising. A partial surrender of claims by both parties is called compromise. Like avoidance, it does not result in a distinct loser or a decisive winner. Unlike avoidance, it does result in a decision. Compromise is often used in settling contract disputes with labor unions.

Authoritative Command. Authoritative command may be used when conflicting parties appeal to higher authority to make a decision for them. In essence, they agree to abide by the decision even if they don't agree with it. A weakness of this technique that is shared by compromising is that it eliminates the visible conflict, but almost certainly does not solve the problem that created it.

Altering the Human Variable. Altering the human variable is a slow and costly process to resolve conflict, but can result in long-term solutions. The primary means to achieve this has been through education. Some human relations training seeks to change values and attitudes. With work, the individuals will expand knowledge of self, improve their listening abilities, and improve understanding of others' needs and responsibilities.

Altering the Structural Variable. A quick and sometimes effective resolution technique is to transfer a conflicting member or members out of the unit. Such a member of one group may be a valuable contributor in the next. Creating new "buffer" positions can help, too. An integrator or liaison person can be placed between two conflicting departments, such as purchasing and manufacturing, to coordinate activities and reduce the potential for conflict. Procedures can also be developed for dealing with conflict. A common procedure is a formal system for arbitrating disputes between departments or individuals.

Conflict-Management Style

Thomas developed an important classification of conflict-handling techniques, based on the *intentions* of the parties involved (see Figure 7–3).[18] Two dimensions are used to define five approaches to conflict. The dimensions are cooperativeness (attempting to satisfy the other party's concerns) and assertiveness (attempting to satisfy personal concerns). The five approaches are defined by the amount of emphasis placed on the dimensions.

Competing behavior (assertive, uncooperative) occurs when one party values its own concerns at the other party's expense. The opposite behavior is accommodating (unassertive, cooperative), which satisfies the other party's concerns at the expense of personal concerns. Avoiding (unassertive, uncooperative) neglects all concerns by ignoring the issue or delaying a response. Collaborating (assertive, cooperative) is an attempt to fully satisfy the needs of both parties through problem solving. Compromising is moderate in both cooperativeness and assertiveness. Compromise implies that both parties have some concerns left unsatisfied.

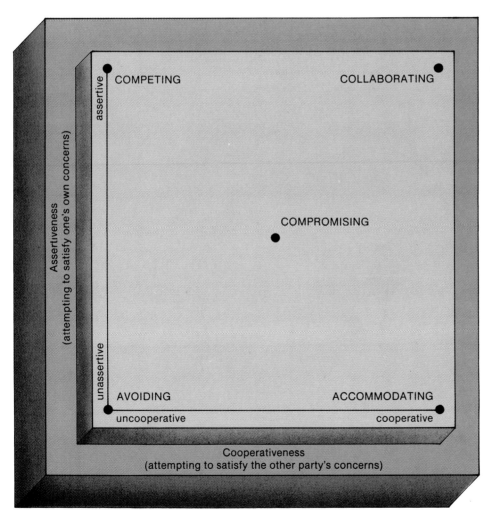

FIGURE 7 – 3
Models of conflict behavior (Source: Adapted from Thomas Ruble and Kenneth Thomas, ''Support for a Two-Dimensional Model of Conflict Behavior,'' *Organizational Behavior and Human Performance,* 1976, 16, Fig. 1, p. 145. Used by permission.)

Opening Story Revisited

What can we say about the conflict styles of the four brothers? Although we don't have a great deal of evidence, we can see that Joe is taking an assertive and uncooperative stance with George, the president. In Thomas's model, Joe would be competing. George seems to have taken an uncooperative and unassertive (avoiding) stance in reply. In demanding higher dividends, Max has apparently adopted a competitive strategy, as has George in his response. Finally, peacemaker Bob is probably trying to compromise. Perhaps phone-tapping is the only means of "communication" left!

Although a manager may prefer one of the five tactics more than the others, there is evidence that people will select the other approaches as appropriate to a particular situation. A study by R. A. Cosier and T. L. Ruble placed subjects in a two-person decision game. Subjects selected one of two possible answers to a question and indicated their confidence in the answer. They were then allowed to select one of five options of how they wished to work with their co-subject to receive a reward. The five options represented the conflict-handling modes of the Thomas model. For example, one option would allow the other subject's decision to be used to determine the size of the payoff (accommodating); another would be to split the payoff evenly (compromising). In every game played, all five conflict-handling styles were used. The results also supported the contention that people perceive a conflict situation in terms of two primary dimensions, as suggested by Thomas.[19]

Is conflict style related to leadership style?

Personal Characteristics and Conflict Style. As might be expected, a manager's personality will influence the choice of conflict resolution. There is evidence that people who have a high need for affiliation prefer smoothing and avoid forcing, while those who are high in Machiavellianism—those who like to manipulate others—prefer forcing and avoid smoothing. People with a high need for deference also prefer forcing, while those with a need for nurturing prefer smoothing.[20]

Interpersonal relationships are important. People who are attracted to each other tend to solve conflict more easily and satisfactorily than parties who have a negative interpersonal attraction.[21]

Management Experience and Conflict Style. At least one study has shown that people may acquire skill at dealing with conflict as they gain management experience. Managers in 240 organizations were placed in four groups: The managers in Group 1 had a high level of responsibility and more than seven years of experience. Group 2 had managers with high responsibility but less than seven years' experience. Group 3 was managers with low responsibility and greater than seven years' experience, while Group 4 held managers with low responsibility and less than seven years of experience.

	Attributed to	
	Self (%)	Other (%)
Collaboration	41	4
Compromise	25	6
Accommodation	8	2
Avoidance	5	16
Competition	21	73

SOURCE: Adapted from K. W. Thomas and L. R. Pondy, ''Toward an 'Intent' Model of Conflict Management among Principal Parties,'' *Human Relations*, 30 (1977): 1094. Used by permission of Plenum Publishing.

TABLE 7–1
Attribution of conflict-handling modes to self and to other party

Group 1 displayed a greater knowledge of the determinants of conflict, and were more effective in the treatment of group conflict than the other three groups. Group 4 had a much lower level of both knowledge and effectiveness. Groups 2 and 3 had similar scores, and were between groups 1 and 4 in knowledge and effectiveness.[22]

Attributing Conflict Behavior to Others. In a conflict, there is an unfortunate tendency to see the other party as being less reasonable. In a survey of managers, Kenneth W. Thomas and L. R. Pondy found that managers felt themselves to desire collaboration and compromise much more frequently than the other party (see Table 7–1).[23]

As you can see, the managers perceived the other party as choosing avoidance and competition much more frequently than themselves. Note also that the managers felt that they chose avoidance the least of the five methods, while the other party chose avoidance second in frequency to competition.

Another study investigated perceptions of interpersonal conflict between supervisors and subordinates. The purpose was to examine relationships between the attributions of conflict management made by one party about another and the other's perceptions of conflict frequency. Where high conflict frequency was perceived, subordinates believed their supervisors were likely to avoid confrontation and compromise, and to use force to settle the conflict. In studying the perceptions of conflict frequency, it was found that the more frequent the conflict, the less the parties liked one another.[24]

We noted earlier that conflict has some benefits. Robbins, one of the foremost proponents of conflict as a management tool, suggests three vehicles for stimulating conflict: communication, organizational structure, and personal-behavior factors.[25]

STIMULATING CONFLICT

Communication. Communication can be used to create conflict in several ways. Messages may be deviated from traditional channels, perhaps by excluding people who had been part of a channel. For example, a medical center had relied on a weekly "managers' coffee" as an important communication device. Suddenly, several managers were excluded from the meeting by a decision to invite only managers who led departments of at least twenty-five employees. The result was an increased level of tension among managers in the institution.

Information can also be withheld from some parties, leaving them at a power disadvantage to those who have the information. For example, the dean of a business school had made a practice of confiding in junior faculty members rather than the senior faculty. The senior faculty felt isolated, and conflict between the faculty levels was significant. By contrast, conflict can be created by providing too much information. Loading people down with information may serve to make them examine their activities critically in an effort to sort out priority items.

Communication that is ambiguous or threatening will also create conflict. In one instance, administrators of a large hospital let it be known that a major realignment of departments was being considered, and that managerial responsibilities could be changed as a result. At once ambiguous and threatening, the message immediately created conflict between some managers and departments.

Organizational Structure. Organizational structure can be used to initiate conflict through changes in size, increase in bureaucracy, leadership styles, alteration of job positions, and changes in interdependence. Research shows that conflict tends to increase with the size of an organization. A larger number of departments, coupled with increased specialization and more levels of authority, leads to separation and problems with communication and coordination. Size generally leads to increased bureaucracy as well, increasing conflict by making coordination and communication difficult, and by creating frustration for many employees.

Transferring a manager with a directive leadership style into a department with a tradition of participative decision making is an example of how leadership style can be used to create conflict. Placing a democratic manager in a department accustomed to autocratic leadership can also cause conflict, by creating uncertainty among the employees and forcing them to consider their work in a new way.

Altering positions is a fairly easy structure change to accomplish. People can be transferred, reporting relationships changed, authority increased or diminished. Another structural method that can cause conflict is the increase of interdependence between units. As we noted earlier, the more units interact, the more likely conflict is. Just as the creation of liaison or "buffer" positions can serve to reduce conflict, the elimination of such positions will serve to increase it.

Personal-Behavior Factors. The most difficult factors to use effectively are personal-behavior factors. Earlier we described how personality affects the choice of conflict resolution. Similarly, personal characteristics will affect the frequency and intensity of conflict. For example, people who have personality conflicts are more likely to engage in conflict than those who are positively attracted to one another.

What are some major risks in starting conflict?

Personality differences can lead to conflict, especially when people share the same work space.

In one company where two people often shared "private" offices, conflicts often occurred over personal-behavior factors. One worker liked to have a radio playing softly in the background, while the other insisted on complete silence. In another instance, conflict occurred over office appearance. One worker was extremely neat while the other was very disorganized (a "slob," according to the office mate). The pair finally had to be separated when Mr. Neat cleared Mr. Slob's desk—into a trash barrel.

LEARNING SUMMARY

1. Once considered to be destructive, conflict is now recognized to have constructive results in many situations.
2. Communication, personal behavior factors, and organizational structure are all common causes of conflict.
3. A group, when in conflict with another group, becomes more cohesive, less casual, more task-oriented, and more organized. It also demands more loyalty and conformity from members.
4. Groups in conflict view one another as the enemy. Each group tends to perceive only its strengths and the other group's weaknesses. As hostility increases between the groups, communication decreases.
5. A certain level of conflict is desirable for organizational effectiveness.

6. Managers generally prefer a particular conflict resolution style but are able to use other styles if necessary.
7. People often consider themselves to be more cooperative than the opposing party.
8. Avoiding conflict will not resolve it but will gain some time to identify the problem more clearly.
9. The stakes involved and the extent of conflict of interest influence the choice of conflict-handling methods.

ANSWERS TO "WHAT'S YOUR OPINION?"

1. False   Conflict can force people to greater creativity, encourage critical examination of their procedures, and cause them to work harder.
2. False   Avoiding conflict can buy time for information gathering and provide a "cooling off" period.
3. True   Conflict can increase effort, as well as improve the group's cohesiveness.
4. True   Competition generally has rules and standards of behavior, while conflict is unregulated.
5. False   Conflict within the group generally decreases, and there is greater conformity to the group's norms.
6. False   The first step is to define the problem.
7. True   Compromise requires that each party surrender part of its claim.
8. False   Research indicates that experience and level of responsibility are positively related to skill in managing conflict.

KEY TERMS

Avoidance	Expand resources
Competition	Intergroup conflict
Conflict	Line-staff conflict
Conflict of interest	Problem solving
Conflict stimulation	Resolution
Conflict style	Smoothing
Constructive conflict	Stakes

HUMAN RELATIONS APPLICATIONS

Resolving conflict is sometimes difficult, and creating conflict is generally risky. In trying to implement any of the strategies listed in this chapter, a manager should never assume that people can be manipulated like pawns on a chess board. People frequently respond in unexpected ways, and a theoretically correct approach might not work for a number of reasons.

Manager/Subordinate Conflict

One of the drawbacks of current conflict theory is that it neglects some important aspects of an individual's relationship to an organization. Conflict between managers and subordinates has been largely overlooked, but one author has proposed some variables to help predict how a subordinate will react in conflict with a manager. The choice of conflict strategy will be based strongly on the subordinate's desire to remain in the organization, the perceived congruence between the attitudes and beliefs of the parties, and perceived safety from arbitrary action by the superior. If all three conditions are positive, the subordinate is likely to choose cooperative strategies. If the conditions are mixed, the subordinate will probably choose less cooperative strategies. Some specific predictions:

1. Problem solving will be chosen only if the subordinate perceives a good working relationship with the manager.
2. Bargaining (compromising) will be chosen only when the subordinate has power to use as leverage, for example the safety of a union contract or the possession of difficult-to-replace skills.
3. Appeasing (accommodating) will be chosen when the employee wants to remain in the organization, but perceives little or no protection from arbitrary action, and believes that the manager holds different attitudes and beliefs.
4. Competing will be chosen only if the employee has a low desire to remain in the organization. Competing refers here to a ''hard'' bargaining position in which the subordinate takes a noncompromising stance in the conflict. This tactic may be successful if the parties share the same attitudes and beliefs, and if the issue is not of great importance to the manager.
5. Avoidance (withdrawing) will be selected if a subordinate has a low desire to remain in the organization, and perceives a low degree of congruence between the parties' attitudes and beliefs.[26]

Stakes and Conflict of Interest

Another consideration in the choice of a conflict tactic is the benefit, or stakes, involved. Thomas observed that the more assertive tactics (competing and collaborating) require a greater investment of time and energy, so they are more likely to be used for issues that are important to at least one of the parties.[27] The extent to which interests are in conflict is also a consideration. Accordingly, Thomas predicted that conflict of interest and the stakes involved will interact to produce the tactics shown in Figure 7–4.

If high stakes are involved and the parties have conflicting interests (that is, the interests cannot both be satisfied), the parties will compete. On the other hand, if stakes are low, the conflict may be avoided, perhaps because the result is not worth fighting for. If the stakes are high but the parties have common interests, they will collaborate (problem solve). If the stakes are low, one party may accommodate the other, again, because the result is not worth a conflict. When

FIGURE 7 – 4
Conflicting behavior as a function of stakes and conflict of interest (Source: Kenneth W. Thomas, "Conflict and Conflict Management" in Marvin D. Dunnette (ed.), *Handbook of Industrial and Organizational Psychology,* Fig. 8, p. 922. Copyright © 1976 by John Wiley & Sons, Inc. Reprinted by permission of John Wiley & Sons, Inc.)

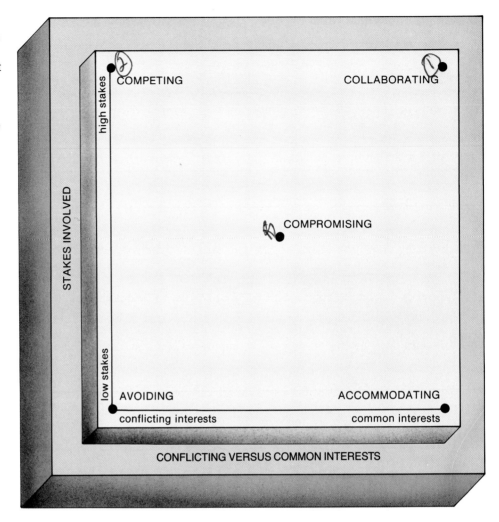

stakes are moderate and the parties' interests overlap to at least some degree, they will compromise.

How CEOs View Conflict

We cited a study earlier that demonstrated that managers with experience and high responsibility knew more about conflict and were more effective in handling it than other managers. Chief executive officers obviously have a great deal of responsibility and experience, so we should be able to learn from their wisdom. A group of chief executives was asked to comment on their use of the five conflict strategies described by Thomas,[28] with special attention to when they would use each of the strategies (see Table 7–2). Note that their responses take into account many of the factors proposed by the theoretical models. Their comments illustrate

TABLE 7 – 2
Uses of the five conflict modes, as reported by a group of chief executives

Conflict-handling Modes	Appropriate Situations
Competing	1. When quick, decisive action is vital—e.g., emergencies
	2. On important issues where unpopular actions need implementing—e.g., cost cutting, enforcing unpopular rules, discipline
	3. On issues vital to company welfare when you know you're right
	4. Against people who take advantage of noncompetitive behavior
Collaborating	1. To find an integrative solution when both sets of concerns are too important to be compromised
	2. When your objective is to learn
	3. To merge insights from people with different perspectives
	4. To gain commitment by incorporating concerns into a consensus
	5. To work through feelings that have interfered with a relationship
Compromising	1. When goals are important, but not worth the effort or potential disruption of more assertive modes
	2. When opponents with equal power are committed to mutually exclusive goals
	3. To achieve temporary settlements to complex issues
	4. To arrive at expedient solutions under time pressure
	5. As a backup when collaboration or competition is unsuccessful
Avoiding	1. When an issue is trivial, or more important issues are pressing
	2. When you perceive no chance of satisfying your concerns
	3. When potential disruption outweighs the benefits of resolution
	4. To let people cool down and regain perspective
	5. When gathering information supersedes immediate decision
	6. When others can resolve the conflict more effectively
	7. When issues seem tangential or symptomatic of other issues
Accommodating	1. When you find you are wrong—to allow a better position to be heard, to learn, and to show your reasonableness
	2. When issues are more important to others than yourself—to satisfy others and maintain cooperation
	3. To build social credits for later issues
	4. To minimize loss when you are outmatched and losing
	5. When harmony and stability are especially important
	6. To allow subordinates to develop by learning from mistakes

[handwritten annotations: "sharing ideas", "problem solving", "developing", "making!!", "actually giving up something"]

SOURCE: Kenneth W. Thomas, "Toward Multi-Dimensional Values in Teaching: The Example of Conflict Behaviors," *Academy of Management Review,* 2 (1977): 487, Table 1. Reprinted by permission.

an awareness of stakes, commonality of interest, different perspectives, personal style, goals, and power, as well as a sensitivity toward the possibility of constructive conflict.

PERSONAL GUIDELINES FOR HUMAN RELATIONS SUCCESS

Managing conflict is one of the most difficult tasks faced by a manager. Conflict generally creates anger and angry people sometimes overreact to situations. The following guidelines may help you:

1. As you begin your management career, don't try to create conflict unless you really know how to do it. Creation of conflict is best reserved for experienced and highly skilled managers.
2. Choose your battles carefully. Before you become personally involved in a conflict, make sure that the stakes are worth it.
3. Realize that all conflict needn't be confronted. Some conflict is desirable.
4. If you must try to resolve a conflict, do the following:
    a. Discover the basic issue in the conflict
    b. Identify the key actors in the conflict
    c. Select a neutral location to reduce the power distance associated with authority
    d. Engage the parties at the level of their values and interests
    e. Allow both parties to express their perceptions without resistance or denial
    f. Practice active listening
    g. Divide large issues into manageable concerns—agree about the agreeable and define areas of disagreement. Uncompromisable, non-negotiable issues should be identified and stated to avoid game-playing and false impressions
    h. Strive for a solution that will allow both sides to "save face."[29, 30]

   Finally, some important do's and don'ts when communicating about a conflict incident:

   ☐ Do present your position logically.
   ☐ Do yield only to positions that have objective and logical foundations.
   ☐ Do encourage participation of all members.
   ☐ Do clarify differences in positions.
   ☐ Do stress similarities.
   ☐ Do keep discussion on the issue.
   ☐ Do seek mutual satisfaction of all parties.
   ☐ Do periodically summarize.
   ☐ Do assign action items to implement the decision.
   ☐ Don't be ambiguous.
   ☐ Don't change your mind just to avoid conflict.
   ☐ Don't assume someone must win and someone must lose.
   ☐ Don't argue blindly, or respond with "yes, but. . . ."
   ☐ Don't resort to majority vote, a coin flip, or ridicule.[31]

1. In what situations would you use conflict stimulation?
2. Why is conflict viewed as "bad" and competition viewed as "good" by most people?
3. From your perspective, which conflict model (Thomas's or Robbins's) is most useful? Why?
4. What can you predict will occur to groups in competition?
5. Describe the major techniques of conflict resolution.
6. Is conflict style related to leadership style? Why or why not?

DISCUSSION AND REVIEW QUESTIONS

Conflict Questionnaire

HUMAN RELATIONS EXERCISE

Step 1: Questionnaire. Complete the following questionnaire. Consider situations in which you find your wishes differing from those of another person. For each statement, think about how likely you are to respond in that way to such a situation. Check the rating that best corresponds to your response.

	Very Unlikely	Unlikely	Likely	Very Likely
1. I am usually firm in pursuing my goals.				✓✓
2. I try to win my position.			✓	✓
3. I give up some points in exchange for others.	✓		✓	
4. I feel that differences are not always worth worrying about.	✓		✓	
5. I try to find a position that is intermediate between his and mine.	✓	✓		
6. In approaching negotiations, I try to be considerate of the other person's wishes.			✓	✓
7. I try to show the logic and benefits of my positions.				✓✓
8. I always lean toward a direct discussion of the problem.			✓	✓
9. I try to find a fair combination of gains and losses for both of us.	✓		✓	
10. I attempt to immediately work through our differences.		✓		✓

	Very Unlikely	Unlikely	Likely	Very Likely
11. I try to avoid creating un-pleasantness for myself.		✓		✓
12. I might try to soothe the other's feelings and preserve our relationships.			✓	✓
13. I attempt to get all concerns and issues immediately out in the open.	✓		✓	✓
14. I sometimes avoid taking positions that would create controversy.	✓			
15. I try not to hurt other's feelings.			✓	

Step 2: Scoring. Assign points to each response as follows:

> very unlikely = 1,
> unlikely = 2,
> likely = 3,
> very likely = 4.

For each mode listed, write the scores under the item number. Then add the scores on the three items for each dimension.

Competing:	Item 1 4	Item 2 3	Item 7 4	Total 11 12
Collaborating:	Item 8 4	Item 10 4	Item 13 4	Total 12 8
Compromising:	Item 3 3	Item 5 2	Item 9 3	Total 8
Avoiding:	Item 4 1	Item 11 2	Item 14 1	Total 4 8
Accommodating:	Item 6 4	Item 12 4	Item 15 3	Total 11 9

Reprinted from J. M. Ivancevich and M. T. Matteson, *Organizational Behavior and Management* (Plano, TX: Business Publications, Inc., 1987), 335–36. This exercise was developed by Arthur Shedlin and Warren H. Schmidt.

Step 3: Discussion. In small groups or with the class as a whole, answer the following questions.

1. What is the most "popular" approach in the class? What is the least popular?
2. Compare the class scores with the "attributed to self" responses in Table 7–1. Discuss similarities and differences.
3. If time allows, break the class into subgroups composed of high and low scores on a particular conflict mode. For example, group people who scored high on competing with people who scored low on competing. Consider a score of 4–8 to be low and a score of 12–16 to be high. Discuss the benefits and drawbacks of both high and low scores for about twenty minutes. Communicate your conclusions to the class.

The Open Budget[32]

HUMAN RELATIONS INCIDENT

Command Press, Inc., manufactures and sells a complete line of greeting cards, invitations, party favors, etc. In 1981, total sales exceeded $100 million and the company employed 360 people.

Preparation of the annual budget for marketing is the combined responsibility of the budget officer, the division sales managers, and the vice president. The budgeting process revolves around a fiscal year that runs from July 1 through June 30 of the following year. Around April 1 of each year, each sales division manager is requested to submit his or her budget proposal for the next fiscal year. After each division manager submits the personnel and financial needs, the budget officer and vice president meet, analyze the requests, and propose a budget.

After the budget is prepared, the president briefs the board of directors. If they approve the budget, the document becomes the new budget for the fiscal year beginning July 1. While the budget is reviewed at midyear (six-month point) and adjusted internally, the general tendency is to leave the budget "as is" once approved.

Linda Seigmiller, sales manager of Division A, prepared her budget proposal on April 6 and submitted it to the vice president. In her budget proposal, she requested one new salesperson because the sales of Division A had increased 7.5 percent during the past year. The unwritten guideline in the company was that a division received an additional person for every 7.5 percent increase in sales. She also requested a proportional increase in supplies, travel expenses, and telephone expenses for Sales Division A. She knew that her division had, by far, the largest sales increase for the year and she felt confident that her requests would be honored.

After preparing and sending her budget proposal to the vice president, Linda received the third-quarter sales figures and observed the following sales increases for each division: A (30 percent); B (6.3 percent); C (4.3 percent); D (8.8 percent). After seeing these figures, she called a staff meeting on May 1. In this meeting, her section managers indicated that they believed the increase in sales would continue for Division A through the next fiscal year. Linda did not inform the vice president of this new projection.

At a staff meeting on June 1, the vice president told the division sales managers that the president had approved the new budget and that it would be distributed within the week. The sales manager of Division C asked a question about new people needed because of increased sales. The vice president responded that Division A would receive 1 additional salesperson, Division B would receive 2.5, Division C would receive 7, and Division D would receive 1. Linda was shocked by the response and immediately requested a reevaluation of the budget because her division had the largest increase in sales and the smallest increase in new personnel.

After leaving the meeting, Linda telephoned the budget officer and asked if he could explain to her the logic for the allocation of new personnel. He replied that she had requested one new position and she received one new position. She countered by informing him of the third-quarter sales figures and said she now needed three new people to meet anticipated sales. She also asked, "Why did Division C receive 7 new authorizations with only a 4.3 percent increase in sales?" The budget officer responded that he didn't exactly know the reasoning behind the allocation of new people; however, he did know that Division A received 100 percent of its requested budget while the other divisions received less than they requested.

After the telephone conversation, Linda felt disgusted because she had been honest during the budgeting process and had requested only those increases that could be documented by increases in productivity, whereas it appeared that other departments had "padded" their budget requests.

QUESTIONS

1. How do you think Linda will approach next year's budget?
2. How should she deal with the present problem?
3. If conflict develops between her division and other divisions, what will be the likely result?

NOTES

1. Adapted from D. A. Vise, "Family Business Can Lead to Family Feuds," *The Washington Post.* Reprinted in *The Seattle Times/Seattle Post-Intelligencer* (18 November 1984): B7. Used by permission of *The Washington Post.*
2. G. L. Lippitt, "Managing Conflict in Today's Organizations," *Training and Development Journal* (July 1982): 67–72.
3. C. F. Fink, "Some Conceptual Difficulties in the Theory of Social Conflict," *Journal of Conflict Resolution* (December 1968): 412–60.
4. A. Etzioni, *Modern Organizations* (Englewood Cliffs, NJ: Prentice-Hall, 1964).
5. W. G. Bennis, K. D. Benne, and R. Chin, eds., *The Planning of Change* (2nd ed.) (New York: Holt, Rinehart and Winston, 1969): 152.

6. S. P. Robbins, *Managing Organizational Conflict: A Non-Traditional Approach* (Englewood Cliffs, NJ: Prentice-Hall, 1974): 13. Used by permission of Prentice-Hall.

7. Ibid.

8. L. B. Hart, "Test Your Ability to Handle Conflict," *Association Management* (August 1984): 70–73. Reprinted with permission of *Association Management* magazine. Copyright August 1984.

9. K. W. Thomas, "Conflict and Conflict Management," in M. D. Dunnette, ed., *Handbook of Industrial and Organizational Psychology* (Chicago: Rand McNally, 1976): 889–935.

10. Robbins, *Managing Organizational Conflict.*

11. J. J. Molnar and D. L. Rogers, "A Comparative Model of Interorganizational Conflict," *Administrative Science Quarterly,* vol. 24 (1979): 405–25.

12. Ibid.

13. Robbins, *Managing Organizational Conflict:* 51.

14. R. E. Walton, J. M. Dutton, and T. P. Cafferty, "Organizational Context and Interdepartmental Conflict," *Administrative Science Quarterly* (December 1969): 522–43.

15. Edgar H. Schein, *Organizational Psychology,* 3rd ed. © 1980, pp 173–75. Adapted by permission of Prentice-Hall, Inc., Englewood Cliffs, New Jersey.

16. J. R. Simon, C. Norton and N. J. Lonergan, "Accounting for the Conflict Between Line Management and the Controller's Office," *S.A.M. Advanced Management Journal* (Winter 1979): 4–14.

17. M. Dalton, "Conflicts Between Staff and Line Managerial Officers," *American Sociological Review* (June 1950): 342–51.

18. Thomas, *Conflict and Conflict Management.*

19. R. A. Cosier and T. L. Ruble, "Research on Conflict-Handling Behavior: An Experimental Approach," *Academy of Management Journal,* vol. 24, no. 4, (1981): 816–31.

20. R. E. James and B. H. Melcher, "Personality and the Preference for Modes of Conflict Resolution," *Human Relations,* vol. 35, no. 8, (1982): 649–58.

21. M. A. Williford, "Relationships Between Interpersonal Attraction and Conflict Management," *Psychological Reports,* vol. 51 (1982): 750.

22. F. Harrison, "The Management of Organizational Conflict," *University of Michigan Business Review,* vol. 31 (1979): 18–33.

23. K. W. Thomas and L. R. Pondy, "Toward An 'Intent' Model of Conflict Management Among Principal Parties," *Human Relations,* vol. 30 (1977): 1094.

24. G. Howat and M. London, "Attributions of Conflict Management Strategies in Supervisor-Subordinate Dyads," *Journal of Applied Psychology,* vol. 65, no. 2, (1980): 172–75.

25. S. P. Robbins, *Managing Organizational Conflict: A Non-Traditional Approach.*

26. S. J. Musser, "A Model for Predicting the Choice of Conflict Management Strategies by Subordinates in High-Stakes Conflicts," *Organizational Behavior and Human Performance* (April 1982): 257–69. Used by permission of Academic Press.

27. K. W. Thomas, "Conflict and Conflict Management."

28. K. W. Thomas, "Toward Multi-Dimensional Values in Teaching: The Example of Conflict Behaviors," *Academy of Management Review,* vol. 2 (1977).

29. D. Sheane, "When and How to Intervene in Confict," *Personnel Journal,* vol. 59 (1980): 515–18.

30. M. Stimac, "Strategies for Resolving Conflict: Their Functional and Dysfunctional Sides," *Personnel,* vol. 59 (1982): 54–64.

31. Adapted from A. K. Hoh, "Consensus-Building: A Creative Approach to Resolving Conflicts," *Management Review,* vol. 70 (1981): 52–54.

32. Case written by Robert A. Zawacki. Reprinted with permission from Dittrich, J. E., and Zawacki, R. A. (1985). *People in Organizations* (2nd ed.) Plano, TX: Business Publications, 261–62.

CHAPTER 8
EVALUATING AND REWARDING PERFORMANCE

WHAT'S YOUR OPINION? T OR F

 1. Performance evaluation must be completely objective.

 2. Employees should participate in the development of standards for measuring their work performance.

 3. Performance should be the only consideration in determining salary raises.

 4. The best way to attract good applicants is to have pleasant working conditions.

 5. A worker's performance should be evaluated only by a manager.

 6. High performers are more likely to quit because of pay than low performers.

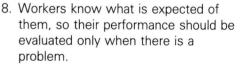 7. Ideally, employee turnover should be nearly zero.

8. Workers know what is expected of them, so their performance should be evaluated only when there is a problem.

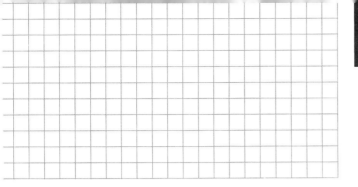

OUTLINE

PERFORMANCE EVALUATION CONCEPTS
  Criteria for Evaluating Appraisal Systems
  Very Subjective Evaluation Methods
  Less Subjective Evaluation Methods
  Rating Errors
  Performance Appraisal and Productivity

EMPLOYEE REWARDS
  The Role of Money
  What Do Rewards Buy?
  Increasing Performance

TYPES OF INCENTIVE PLANS
  Individual Performance Incentives
  Group Performance Incentives

LEARNING SUMMARY

HUMAN RELATIONS APPLICATIONS

PERSONAL GUIDELINES FOR HUMAN
RELATIONS SUCCESS

LEARNING OBJECTIVES

☐ Describe the strengths and weaknesses of performance evaluation systems

☐ Describe major benefits of performance evaluation

☐ Identify common errors made by managers in evaluating employee performance and know how to avoid them

☐ Discuss common types of reward systems and their effects on employee performance

☐ Know how rewards are used to attract, retain, and motivate employees

☐ Ask key questions for determining whether merit pay will affect worker performance

☐ Describe important guidelines for developing performance objectives

Herbie the Waiter[1]

Herbert Pischler is unique in the world of restaurant waiters. His faithful customers, gluttons for exasperation, know him better as "Herbie, the World's Worst Waiter," a title bestowed on Pischler many years ago by the *New York Daily News* and a distinction that Herbie proudly accepts.

Herbie has been around for a long time, and he's been in and then quickly out of the best hostelries in town. Herbie and his current headquarters, Costello's, are a natural match. Situated conveniently for many of New York's more curmudgeonly and card-in-the-hatband sort of newspapermen, Costello's has played host to such people as the late Ernest Hemingway, who used to enjoy fist fights as much as the food and drinks. Herbie-the-World's-Worst-Waiter is a legend still around for us to enjoy.

Legend has it that Herbie first laid claim to his title as worst waiter by spilling a large bowl of soup in the lap of the Prince of Wales many years ago and at some place other than Costello's, where it is highly unlikely that royalty will ever drop by for a few jars on the way home to the castle. Herbie claims that this historic event has been exaggerated over the years. "This I did not do," he says. "I did not spill soup in the lap of the Prince of Wales. Mostly, it went all over the colonel sitting beside him."

Herbie is cherubic and always well-intentioned, but he is also rather absent-minded and prone to sudden naps. Many is the time when a customer, wondering why so much time had passed since asking for the bill, found Herbie sitting at the bar, head in hands and fast asleep.

There was the time, too, when a table full of wagering reporters sent Herbie out to a nearby newsstand for the racing form. When the world's worst waiter failed to return after an hour's time, the reporters formed a posse and went searching for Herbie. They found him curled up on a bench near the newsstand, sound asleep, snoring peacefully beneath the racing form.

Eddie Fitzpatrick, co-owner of Costello's, says, "Everybody loves Herbie. He's an asset." Indeed, it is sometimes difficult to get a table at Herbie's station, even knowing that your meal is sure to come with an imprint of Herbie's right thumb. "Accidents always got to happen," Herbie explains.

It is rumored that Fitzpatrick used to threaten Herbie with dismissal if the world's worst waiter should ever improve.

In recent years, productivity and accountability have become key issues. All organizations face the challenge of achieving a high quality of service or product while maintaining acceptable cost levels. A greater emphasis on accountability creates a need for performance standards that accurately reflect the efficiency and output of employees. A properly administered performance appraisal system can provide the needed standards.

There is no "best" method of performance evaluation, though some designs are better than others. Research shows that work motivation and performance increase when people understand their employer's expectations and performance standards.[2] A good evaluation system makes expectations and performance standards clear and specific. A good system is fair and unbiased and gives employees concrete feedback about their strengths and weaknesses.

Many managers believe that performance evaluation should be objective, but complete objectivity cannot be achieved. How can one be completely objective about another person's willingness to cooperate, his or her planning skills, flexibility, creativity, or cost awareness? Since the manager must evaluate human behavior, judgment will always be required, and the potential for bias or favoritism will always be present. Since complete objectivity is impossible, the task is to create a system that reduces subjectivity to a tolerable level.

Criteria for Evaluating Appraisal Systems

How do you evaluate an evaluation system? We have noted a few important characteristics, but there are other requirements as well. A good system should do the following:

1. Provide useful, accurate feedback to an employee
2. Allow comparisons between employees for administrative decision making
3. Be reliable or consistent in measurement
4. Be valid, that is, clearly related to the job
5. Identify training and development needs
6. Be accepted by both the people being evaluated (ratees) and those who do the evaluating (raters)

Beyond these requirements, there are some additional concerns from an organizational standpoint:

1. Cost of development, in both time and money
2. Cost of administration, in both time and money
3. Skill required of raters

Now let us review some typical methods of evaluation that we have classified as being "very" subjective or "less" subjective.

(margin notes)
PERFORMANCE EVALUATION CONCEPTS

Appraisal standards and measurement

Reliability consistency

This section evaluates the skills, knowledge, and techniques an employee applies in achieving the desired job objective. Using the standards indicated below, rate the employee's performance in the evaluation.

STANDARDS FOR REVIEW

CODE

1. Distinguished: Clearly outstanding—Performance far exceeds the job's requirements in all respects. Only the best belong at this level.

2. Commendable: Above acceptable—Performance is noticeably better than required by the job. Long seasoned and highly proficient employees belong here.

3. Competent: Satisfactory—Performance meets the job's requirements, overall. This is the level of performance expected of most seasoned employees. It implies that the employee achieved all that is expected of the position. A majority of employees belong at this level.

4. Provisional: Improvement needed—Performance falls short of meeting the job's requirements in one or more significant areas. This is normally reserved for inexperienced new incumbents and others who are performing at less than the job's expectations. At this level, there is a demonstrable need for improvement.

A. Work Management Skills

	RATING

Regardless of whether an employee is in a management position, responsible for securing results through the efforts of others, or is in a professional/technical position and is responsible primarily for his or her own results, there are basic work management skills that must be applied in achieving job objectives. Consider the abilities the employee has demonstrated in the following areas.

Planning

—Forecasts and anticipates future conditions and events that will affect work objectives.
—Sets or recommends realistic, measurable, results-oriented objectives.
—Establishes and sequences logical action steps and time schedules for achievement of objectives.
—Determines accurately the necessary manpower, equipment, and financial resources to achieve objectives.
—Analyzes the cost of achieving an objective in relation to the return its accomplishment will bring before making recommendations.
—As required, formulates clear and concise policies and procedures for achievement of objectives.

Comments:

        1   **2**   **3**   **4**

FIGURE 8–1

Example of a criteria-only appraisal form (Source: C. P. Fleenor and M. P. Scontrino, *Performance Appraisal: A Manager's Guide* (Dubuque, IA: Kendell/Hunt, 1982): 33–35. Copyright by C. Patrick Fleenor and M. Peter Scontrino.)

Very Subjective Evaluation Methods

Very subjective systems are the most widely used—and the least useful. Such systems provide the rater with little or no guidance for determining an employee's performance. Following are descriptions of the most common techniques.

Essay. As its name suggests, the essay approach to appraisal requires the rater to respond to one or more open-ended essay questions about the performance of the person being rated. For example, a manager might be asked, "How well did the employee establish and maintain relationships with other people who were necessary to getting results in this job?" A typical essay appraisal includes five or six questions and is two or three pages in length.

This approach is very subjective, since it generally provides few if any guidelines for the rater, who may write as much or as little as desired. Another problem is that raters may not be skilled at describing their opinions in writing.

Ranking. Ranking requires raters to "line up" employees from best to worst. Ranking is frequently used in conjunction with salary decisions to determine how much of a merit increase each employee will receive. Employees might be ranked according to one general criterion, such as overall performance, or according to a number of different criteria, such as quality of work, leadership ability, or coordination skill. The individual rankings are then averaged to arrive at an overall ranking. The ratee generally receives little useful feedback. After all, what does it mean to be ranked twelfth in a department of twenty-seven?

best to worst

Criteria Only. The most commonly used appraisal method is criteria only, sometimes called non-anchored rating scales. Rating factors may include "hard" criteria, such as cost control and return on investment; "soft" criteria, such as decision-making skills and cooperation; and personal traits, such as initiative and creativity. The criteria may be well-defined, but the rater is not given specific standards of performance. Instead, a general rating scale with definitions of different performance levels is provided. Figure 8–1 shows one criterion from a criteria-only form.

Criteria activities to be evaluated

While the form looks very specific, the rater is given no help in determining what the rating should be. Suppose an employee fulfills all six activities listed under Planning in Figure 8–1. Should the employee be judged distinguished, commendable, or merely competent?

How do the three very subjective methods fare against our criteria set forth earlier? Table 8–1 displays their strengths and weaknesses.

The cost of unfair appraisal is very high. That alone is sufficient reason to search for better methods of evaluation, but of course the major reasons are to give employees accurate feedback and to improve performance. To that purpose, let us look at some stronger techniques.

TABLE 8 – 1
Evaluation of very subjective appraisal methods

	Essay	Ranking	Criteria Only
Accuracy/usefulness of feedback	varies	very low	low
Allow comparison among employees	no	yes	yes
Reliability	low	low	low
Validity	varies	low	low
Identify training/development need	varies	low	low
Acceptability to raters	varies	medium	medium
Acceptability to ratees	varies	low	medium
Cost of development	low	low	medium
Cost of administration	high	low	low
Skill required of rater	high	low	low

Less Subjective Evaluation Methods

We will briefly describe three evaluation methods that remove much of the subjectivity that plagues the methods described above.

BARS behaviorally anchored rating scales

Behaviorally Anchored Rating Scales (BARS). BARS require the development of scales, each describing specific work behaviors that have been carefully matched to the job being performed. The development of BARS is straightforward but time-consuming. The first step is to identify groups of similar jobs (job families). People familiar with the job(s) then develop a list of criteria that should be used for evaluation. The final step requires agreement upon performance standards. Each criterion must have performance standards that answer the questions of "how good is good," or "how bad is bad." This final step is called anchoring, since examples of specific job behavior are used to describe good, average, and poor performance. The behavioral examples help raters connect their ratings directly to the job behavior of the person being rated. An example of a BARS is shown in Figure 8–2.

Compare the BARS method of evaluating planning with that of the criteria-only approach in Figure 8–1. The BARS format provides a rater with specific examples of performance that should be rated outstanding, exceeding job standards, meeting job standards, needing improvement, and unsatisfactory. Contrast this with the criteria-only form, which describes planning activities, but offers the rater no help in determining the ratee's level of performance.

The BARS example is a single dimension from a form for evaluating a mid-level manager in a manufacturing firm. There are fifteen criteria in all. Some of the additional criteria are interpersonal communication, cooperation, employee development, budgeting, and client contact and service. Each of the fifteen criteria are anchored with examples of behavior. Note that the rater has the option of *not*

CRITERION ONE—PLANNING

This aspect of the job involves designing, scheduling, and implementing short and long range plans; scheduling workload within plan; anticipating deviations from the plan.

These statements describe persons who are usually rated *outstanding* on planning by most raters.	5. _____ Develops several clear alternative action plans to achieve objectives
	_____ Initiates alternative plans when original objectives are not being met
	_____ Questions current plans against lost or developing opportunities
These statements describe persons who are usually rated *exceeding job standards* on planning by most raters.	4. _____ Anticipates arising problems with prepared contingency plans
	_____ Keeps goals and objectives clearly and frequently in front of subordinates
	_____ Meets with those concerned to review the work situation, asking for inputs in developing problems/opportunities
These statements describe persons who are usually rated *meeting job standards* on planning by most raters.	3. _____ Reviews action plans with superior
	_____ Has plan objectives which fit the needs of other departments
	_____ Completes status reports on time
	_____ Maintains planning process without attempting to improve it
	_____ Has "stretch" in plan but does not indicate how it will be done
These statements describe persons who are usually rated as *needing improvement* on planning by most raters.	2. _____ Completes plan late
	_____ Holds planning meetings only when requested by superior or peers
	_____ Plans do not contain alternatives
These statements describe persons who are usually rated *unsatisfactory* on planning by most raters.	1. _____ Plans only when forced to plan by superior
	_____ Does not involve subordinates in the planning process
	_____ Plans do not include objectives
	_____ Plans contain unrealistic assumptions
	0. _____ This criterion is not applicable or I have not had the opportunity to observe performance on this criterion.

FIGURE 8 – 2

Example of a behaviorally anchored rating form (Source: C. P. Fleenor and M. P. Scontrino, *Performance Appraisal: A Manager's Guide* (Dubuque, IA: Kendall/Hunt, 1982): 37–38. Copyright by C. Patrick Fleenor and M. Peter Scontrino.)

The High Cost of Unfair Appraisal

In the last few years, thousands of employees have filed suits claiming wrongful discharge, and many of the suits were related to employers' methods of performance appraisal. Employees successful in their lawsuits can collect sizable punitive and compensatory damages, as witnessed by the following examples:

☐ A manufacturing executive was passed over for promotion and his performance level began to fall. Although receiving vague signals of dissatisfaction from upper management, the executive received no dismissal warnings and was given no opportunity to improve before his firing. A court awarded the fired manager $360,906 initially, but then reduced the award to $61,000 since he had in fact displayed poor performance in the job.

☐ An IBM sales manager claimed her resignation was forced because the company was unhappy that she was dating a manager from a competing firm. She was awarded $300,000.

☐ Three former executives of I. Magnin were awarded $1.9 million in a suit that claimed unfair dismissal and age bias.

☐ An analysis of forty California jury verdicts showed that the terminated employees won 75 percent of the cases, and the median award was $548,000.

☐ The risk of unfair appraisal reaches beyond the organization itself. According to at least one lawyer, supervisors "may have *personal liability* if they don't give honest appraisals." (emphasis added)

Source: Adapted from J.S. Lublin, "Firing Line: Legal Challenges Force Firms to Revamp Ways They Dismiss Workers," *The Wall Street Journal* (13 September 1983): 1. Reprinted by permission of *The Wall Street Journal,* © Dow Jones & Company, Inc., 1983. All rights reserved.

QUESTIONS

1. In your opinion, why do organizations practice unfair appraisal?
2. Is it fair to hold a supervisor personally liable for unfair appraisal? Why or why not?
3. In the case of the manufacturing executive, why might a court award damages even though the executive was performing poorly before he was terminated?

Opening Story Revisited

How would Herbie fare if the restaurant manager used a BARS for evaluating all of the waiters in the restaurant? Suppose some of the criteria were prompt service, observance of health department rules, and attention to detail. Herbie's naps at the bar, thumb in the food, and soup spilling should result in a very low performance rating. The restaurant owner seems to have one set of criteria for Herbie and another for everyone else. Is such an approach workable, or will it eventually create serious problems?

rating a particular criterion (scale point zero). This avoids the potentially serious problem of raters assigning a rating without actually observing performance on that criterion.

Obviously, substantial time is required to develop criteria for a number of different jobs and to construct anchors for each criterion. BARS are hard to construct for jobs that cannot be easily described in behavioral terms. For example, the job of research scientist involves much mental activity that cannot be observed.

Raters sometimes have trouble equating the examples on a BARS form with the observed behavior of a subordinate, since BARS cannot describe every possibility.[3]

Behavioral Observation Scales (BOS). Behavioral observation scales are constructed in much the same fashion as BARS. The major difference lies in the way the methods are scored by a rater. With BARS, examples of work behavior that might be *expected* of an employee at different performance levels are used to anchor the rating points. By contrast, BOS requires the rater to concentrate on the extent to which the work behavior was actually *observed*. The emphasis on observation gives BOS an advantage over BARS in some applications.[4]

Figure 8–3 shows how some of the BARS statements in the preceding figure would look in a BOS format. The numerical ranges used to assign a performance value are determined by management after the BOS is developed.

How do BARS and BOS differ?

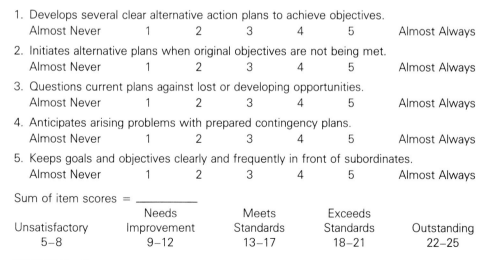

CRITERION ONE: PLANNING

1. Develops several clear alternative action plans to achieve objectives.
   Almost Never   1   2   3   4   5   Almost Always

2. Initiates alternative plans when original objectives are not being met.
   Almost Never   1   2   3   4   5   Almost Always

3. Questions current plans against lost or developing opportunities.
   Almost Never   1   2   3   4   5   Almost Always

4. Anticipates arising problems with prepared contingency plans.
   Almost Never   1   2   3   4   5   Almost Always

5. Keeps goals and objectives clearly and frequently in front of subordinates.
   Almost Never   1   2   3   4   5   Almost Always

Sum of item scores = _____

Unsatisfactory	Needs Improvement	Meets Standards	Exceeds Standards	Outstanding
5–8	9–12	13–17	18–21	22–25

FIGURE 8 – 3
Example of a behavioral observation scale

Management by Objectives (MBO). We use this term broadly, encompassing all approaches that include two major elements. First, at some point in the appraisal process, rater and ratee meet to discuss goals and jointly to establish goals for the ratee. Second, the manager and employee meet later to discuss performance in terms of the previously established goals. Individual employee objectives evolve at least in part from departmental objectives, which in turn reflect total organization objectives.

Objectives goals

The manager's role in MBO is to help the employee set challenging and important, yet realistic goals for the next performance period. During the review period, the manager must monitor employee progress toward the goals, provide feedback as needed, and adjust the goals as necessary. At the end of the review period, manager and employee discuss performance and set goals for the following review period.

Establishing objectives is not always easy. Deciding upon specific areas for setting objectives and determining that those areas are most important to the job may be difficult. Some suggested guidelines appear in Figure 8–4.

Although BARS, BOS, and MBO are different in the ways they are constructed, they share one important similarity: the involvement of the people being evaluated. When ratees are included in the development of their appraisal system, they understand how it works and what its strengths are. In addition, participation reduces employee anxiety and increases the chance that the appraisal tool will accurately reflect the jobs being evaluated.

Table 8–2 describes our assessment of the less subjective evaluation methods.

Rating Errors

Three baseball umpires were talking before a game about their umpiring philosophies:

> Umpire #1: "Sometimes the pitcher throws strikes and sometimes he throws balls, but I call them as I see them.
>
> Umpire #2: "Of course the pitcher throws strikes sometimes, and other times he throws balls, but *I* call them as they *are*.
>
> Umpire #3: "You're both right about the strikes and balls, but they ain't *nothing* until I call them."

That conversation may confirm the suspicions of baseball fans, but more important, it reflects a common problem in evaluating human performance—different values of raters. Imagine the pitcher as a subordinate and the three umpires as supervisors for whom the pitcher works over a period of time. Even if his performance level remains stable, the hapless subordinate might receive three considerably different performance ratings. If the performance is consistent yet the evaluations are not, rating errors are at work.

Rating errors inconsistency or bias

By rating error, we mean any attitude, response tendency, or inconsistency *within* the rater that interferes with accurate performance ratings. The rater may

1 Adapt objectives directly to organizational goals and strategic plans. Do not <u>assume</u> they support higher level management objectives.

2 Quantify and target the results whenever possible. Do not formulate objectives whose attainment cannot be measured or at least verified.

3 Test objectives for challenge and achievability.

4 Adjust the objectives to the availability of resources and the realities of organizational life.

5 Establish performance reports and milestones that measure progress toward the objective.

6 Put objectives in writing and express them in clear, concise, and unambiguous statements.

7 Limit the number of statements of objectives to the most relevant key result areas of the job.

8 Communicate objectives to subordinates so they can formulate their own job objectives.

9 Review objective statements with others to assure consistency and mutual support.

10 Modify statements to meet changing conditions and priorities

11 Do not continue to pursue objectives that have become obsolete.

FIGURE 8 – 4
Guidelines for setting objectives (Source: Adapted from *Managing by Objectives* by A. P. Raia. Copyright © 1974 by Scott, Foresman and Company. Reprinted by permission.

	BARS	BOS	MBO
Accuracy/usefulness of feedback	high	high	high
Allow comparison among employees	yes	yes	no
Reliability	high	high	varies
Validity	high	high	varies
Identify training/development need	high	high	moderate
Acceptability to raters	high	high	high
Acceptability to ratees	high	high	high
Cost of development	high	high	moderate
Cost of administration	low	low	high
Skill required of rater	moderate	moderate	high

TABLE 8 – 2
Evaluation of less subjective appraisal methods

Confronting Employee Behavior

An example of the usefulness of goal setting and feedback comes from a management services firm where a talented computer programmer created tension among co-workers with his behavior. He would demean the intelligence of others, criticize every comment, and otherwise display bad manners. According to a human resources manager, at meetings "he would talk to people like you talk to a computer." His co-workers began to cut meetings short, just to get away from him. One result was that a computer system for another department was behind schedule because the programmer lacked the necessary information to design it.

The programmer's supervisor finally confronted the problem. Over a series of discussions, the programmer wrote out a series of goals: he

would, for instance, substitute the word "customer" or "client" for "user." The idea was that he should view himself as a business supplying a service to customers, rather than as a worker dealing with a "user." He also agreed to "ask more and tell less" at meetings.

Over a period of time, the programmer improved enough that his manager felt he had changed his perception of internal clients. Complaints fell off and cooperation increased. Clearly stated goals and frequent feedback made the difference.

Source: Adapted from L. Reibstein, "What to Do When an Employee Is Talented—and a Pain in the Neck," *The Wall Street Journal* (8 August 1986): 17. Reprinted by permission of *The Wall Street Journal,* © Dow Jones & Company, Inc., 1986. All rights reserved.

QUESTIONS

1. What form of evaluation did the programmer's boss use? Could another form work as well? Why or why not?
2. Refer to Chapter 2. What aspects of perception are involved here?
3. Had the supervisor not acted, what would have happened?

---

not be aware of making an error. The seriousness of rating errors is demonstrated in Table 8–3, which shows actual ratings given to a single worker by two different managers.

Remember that these ratings are for one person, given by two different supervisors observing essentially the same activities. Clearly, at least one of these ratings is completely in error. It is possible that both raters were biased toward the employee, one in a positive direction and the other negatively. How useful is the feedback on these ratings going to be?

Rating errors occur in every performance system. In practical terms it is impossible to eliminate rater errors, though the less subjective evaluation systems make it more difficult for errors to occur. Here are some of the most common rating errors.

Halo Effect. This is a tendency to rate a person who is outstanding on one factor high on all other factors. One very positive trait creates a "halo," blinding the rater to shortcomings in the person being rated.[5] The halo effect is occurring, for instance, when a person who has recently solved an important departmental

TABLE 8 – 3
Ratings of an employee
by two managers

Supervisor A	Supervisor B
Unfavorable toward people	Is open, honest, straight-forward
High and mighty, with superior attitude	Extremely self-confident and knowledgeable
Hard to talk to, gets easily "heated"	Well informed, likes to debate and brainstorm
Tries to solve problems without help	Shows initiative
Knows less than he thinks	Knows more than given credit for
Must be asked twice before anything gets done	Has large volume of work and different priorities than some requesting action

SOURCE: Adapted from C. P. Fleenor and M. P. Scontrino, *Performance Appraisal: A Manager's Guide* (Dubuque, IA: Kendall/Hunt, 1982): 76. Copyright by C. Patrick Fleenor and M. Peter Scontrino.

problem receives high ratings on every factor because of the recent success in problem solving.

There is also a negative halo, which we term the "horns" effect. Here, one very obvious weakness may blind the rater to strengths in the person being rated.

The halo effect occurs when one highly positive trait of the person being rated seems to blind the rater to any shortcomings.

Halo/horns errors often occur when the rater is evaluating employees who have markedly pleasant or unpleasant personality characteristics. If a person is considerate and friendly, perhaps volunteers frequently for special assignments, performance ratings in unrelated aspects of performance may be improperly influenced. Obviously the reverse will tend to be true for the surly, uncooperative employee.

Research has shown that physical attractiveness can influence ratings as well, in ways you might not expect. One study showed that attractiveness was an advantage for women in clerical trainee positions, but a disadvantage for women in managerial trainee jobs. For males, attractiveness had no effect whatsoever in either clerical trainee or managerial trainee positions.[6]

Central Tendency, Leniency, and Strictness. Central tendency errors occur when a rater hesitates to use the ends of a performance scale. Most of the ratings then fall in the middle of the scale. Raters who dislike "grading" people sometimes commit this error. Occasionally the performance system itself encourages central tendency by requiring that all ratings above or below average be supported with essay type information. In such cases some supervisors will give "average" ratings to avoid the need for explanation. The lesson here, of course, is that if ratings are to be supported at all, they should all be supported.

Leniency is a tendency to be overly easy in rating, while strictness is a tendency to be overly severe. Both "easy" and "hard" raters disrupt an evaluation system by making the appraisal process reflect the rater's standards rather than employee performance. The person who tends to rate employees higher than they deserve may wish to avoid disagreement, or may simply have a strong need to be liked by employees. The strict rater often has unrealistically high standards for employees. While high standards are admirable, if all or most employees "need improvement," the rater should carefully evaluate the standards to make sure that they are fair and achievable.

Recency. This error occurs when a manager is influenced by the most recent performance of a subordinate. Most organizations evaluate performance annually, so we would expect ratings to reflect an entire year's performance. Unfortunately, things that happened most recently tend to be remembered more clearly by a manager.[7] The result may be an "annual" review that really covers only the most recent weeks or months. This problem can largely be avoided by encouraging managers to keep written records of employee performance throughout the year, or by conducting formal evaluation more frequently.

Contrast. The contrast error occurs when employees are rated relative to one another rather than to performance standards. Let's suppose that you walk past some automobile dealerships one afternoon. The first showroom you see is filled with Chevrolets. Look at the price of a Chevrolet four-door sedan. On a scale of one to ten, with one being low, rate the price of the Chevrolet. You continue down the street and come to a Mercedes dealership. Look at the price of a

Mercedes four-door sedan and rate the price on a scale of one to ten. Go back to the Chevrolet dealership and rate the price of the Chevrolet sedan once again.

If you changed your rating of the Chevrolet price, you committed a contrast error. Why? Because you changed your "standard" of evaluating price. A flexible standard is not a standard at all. In a work setting, an average (Chevrolet) employee may be punished if compared to an exceptional (Mercedes) employee.

Reducing rating errors takes continual effort. Rating errors occur in every performance system, but there are some steps that can help keep them at a tolerable level:

□ Include the people doing the jobs in the development of criteria and standards.
□ Evaluate existing criteria and standards on a periodic basis. Do they still reflect the most important job activities?
□ Train the managers in the use of an evaluation system. Trained managers are more effective at completing performance appraisal forms, and are perceived by employees to conduct more satisfying interviews than untrained managers.[8] Raters should also receive training in how to recognize and avoid common rating errors.
□ Encourage managers to observe and record observations of employee behavior on a regular basis.[9]

What rating errors have you seen in practice?

Performance Appraisal and Productivity

Can performance appraisal contribute to individual and organizational productivity? We believe that good appraisal systems can. Remember our discussion of goal setting in Chapter 3—challenging yet realistic goals lead to higher performance. A good appraisal system completes the picture by giving employees specific feedback on their progress toward goals. With challenging goals, clear standards, and accurate feedback, productivity will improve.

Who Should Evaluate? The first person who comes to mind is the immediate supervisor of the ratee, who is often in the best position to observe an employee's performance during a review period. In addition, the authority to conduct performance appraisals is an important part of a manager's power, and is considered to be a normal managerial responsibility.

Although a manager usually is and should be involved in appraisals, others may be involved. There are several other potential sources of useful information. Each of them is a supplement to, rather than a replacement for, managerial appraisal. While additional sources can greatly improve an evaluation system, they also complicate it. Whether the value of additional information is outweighed by the cost and effort of collection is an important consideration.

Peer Appraisal. While not widely used, peer appraisal can be an important part of an evaluation system. It requires people to be evaluated by a group of their co-

When should peer appraisal not be used?

workers. This method is quite common among university faculties for the purpose of evaluating performance in research and publication. Naturally, there must be a high level of trust among co-workers for peer appraisal to be used, and the concept is resisted by many employees.[10]

Self-Evaluation. Self-evaluation is popular with many employees and managers, and is valuable for individual development. Self appraisal encourages a person to think realistically about personal strengths and weaknesses. Managers have told us that it also stimulates people to broaden their perspective—to think about their contributions to departmental effort.

Subordinate evaluation. Subordinates are in a good position to observe managerial behavior, and thus can be involved in the evaluation of management ability. Subordinate evaluation is not common, and when used it is generally restricted to providing feedback to a manager rather than influencing the manager's formal evaluation.

Client or customer evaluation. Evaluation by clients is increasingly common in service organizations. The information can be gathered through a questionnaire sent to clients or by personal interview. Many automobile dealerships send questionnaires to their customers, asking them to evaluate everything from the sales force to the garage mechanics. In this case, the data are used for group rather than individual evaluation, but also can be used for individual appraisal. Some organizations are beginning to use client appraisal internally, too. The accounting, security, data processing, and personnel departments, to name a few examples, have "clients" *within* the organization. Those clients can be used to help assess the effectiveness of department services. There is only one requirement that must be met before using a source to supplement appraisal by a manager: the source must have seen the performance of the person or persons to be evaluated.

Which types of appraisal could be used in this class?

Opening Story Revisited

What would evaluations of the world's worst waiter be like if Costello's used several evaluation sources? Client evaluation would be very positive—or would it? What about customers who did not know about Herbie? Would their evaluation of him be good? How would peers evaluate Herbie? If Herbie is so popular, he probably makes quite a bit of money from tips. If peers are a bit jealous, their evaluations would probably be affected. The manager apparently thinks very highly of Herbie, so he probably rates Herbie highly, too.

How to explain such contradictions? Quite simple. Herbie is apparently not evaluated as a waiter. If he were, Costello's would have fired him long ago, as earlier employers apparently did. He is a dismal failure, judged against any usual standards applied to waiters. Herbie is being evaluated as a "character," something he apparently excels at.

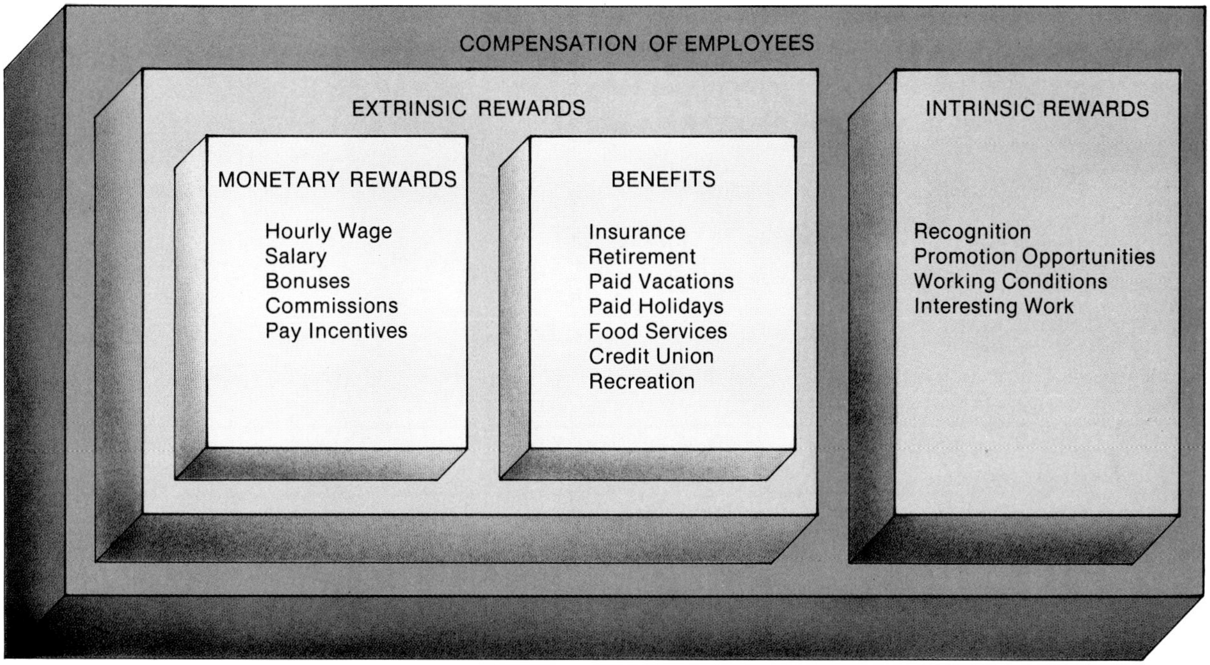

FIGURE 8 – 5
Common employee rewards (Source: M. R. Carrell and F. E. Kuzmits, *Personnel*, 2nd ed. (Columbus, OH: Merrill Publishing Company, 1986): 305.

In our earlier discussion of motivation, the importance of rewards was emphasized. *Intrinsic rewards* are those that occur directly as a result of performing an activity. A feeling of accomplishment upon completing an assignment is an example of intrinsic reward, as is satisfaction with one's working conditions. *Extrinsic rewards* are granted by others, such as the organization, supervisor, and friends. Examples include compliments, salary increases, and promotions.

The potential rewards available to organizations are numerous, but in practice few of them are used in formal reward systems. Figure 8–5 shows some rewards commonly made available to employees. A two-fold problem is faced by managers: identifying what rewards appeal to employees, and determining the best means of delivering the rewards.

EMPLOYEE REWARDS

The Role of Money

In the past, some theorists have argued that money is the most important organizational reward, while others, Herzberg for example, have countered that interesting work is more important. There have been numerous surveys about the importance of pay in relation to other rewards. Pay has been rated first in importance in some studies, but rated much lower in others.[11] No one can seriously argue that money is unimportant, but managers should recognize that it is not always the *most* important reward available to them.

What Do Rewards Buy?

Rewards attract, retain, and motivate employees.

From an organization's perspective, rewards are given for three major reasons: to attract qualified employees, to retain good employees, and to increase performance. We will consider each briefly.

Attracting Qualified Employees. Pay is probably the most important means for attracting a pool of qualified applicants. Job applicants who receive more than one offer can easily compare the pay offers. It is somewhat more difficult to compare the fringe benefit packages offered, and much more difficult to compare the intrinsic attractions of the jobs. It is difficult for an applicant to get an accurate picture of an organization or its management while interviewing, so applicants undoubtedly attach considerable weight to the amount of starting pay.[12]

Job applicants undoubtedly attach considerable importance to the pay offered, while high performers often leave their employers because of dissatisfaction with pay.

Retaining Good Employees. People leave employers for many reasons, but among the most frequent is dissatisfaction with compensation and other rewards. The concept of equity, introduced in Chapter 3, is a critical issue. It has been accepted for years that people develop their view of equity at least partly from information about rewards received by others.[13] Although equity comparison is most frequently made with people inside the organization, outside comparison is not rare, especially among managers.[14] Dissatisfaction occurs when one's reward level lies below the perceived level of equity.

Employee Turnover. Turnover has advantages and disadvantages for an organization. Clearly, zero turnover is not desirable. New ideas and new personalities serve to keep any organization in touch with changing conditions. Zero turnover would also indicate that the organization was doing nothing to get rid of ineffective employees.

When is turnover desirable?

Turnover can be either voluntary or involuntary, desirable or undesirable. Voluntary turnover is initiated by an employee, while involuntary turnover is provoked by the organization. From the organization's perspective, undesirable turnover occurs when good employees must be laid off, are lured away by competitors, or quit because they are dissatisfied. Desirable turnover occurs when poor performers or surplus employees leave. Naturally, managers should try to minimize undesirable turnover and encourage desirable turnover. The general approach would entail creating a working environment and reward structure that encourages and motivates high-performing employees to stay with the organization. This assumes that methods are in place to identify high performers and reward them appropriately. Pay, promotions, and benefits play an important role in keeping good employees. There is evidence that high performers leave because of dissatisfaction with pay, while low performers tend to leave because of dissatisfaction with the job.[15]

Absenteeism. Absenteeism has no advantages for an organization. Absenteeism may be involuntary or voluntary. Since involuntary absenteeism due to illness, accident, or other unavoidable circumstance is beyond the control of both employee and employer, we pay attention here only to absenteeism that is voluntary. Absenteeism is expensive in terms of wages paid to the absent worker, lost productivity, administrative time, and perhaps overtime paid to other workers. In the past few years there has been much attention paid to incentive plans designed to reduce voluntary absenteeism.

Absenteeism time lost from work

One approach is a lottery. In one typical case, employees participated in a monthly drawing for a cash award, provided that they had perfect attendance for the month. Monthly sick leave costs were calculated for the year preceding the lottery and for a year after the lottery's start. Sick leave costs for the lottery year were more than 30 percent lower than in the year before the lottery.[16]

Money is not the only available incentive. One organization began recognizing good attendance with congratulatory letters from supervisors and notations in personnel files. Absenteeism fell from a historical rate of 8.94 percent to 3.91 percent. After a period of time the incentive program was withdrawn and absenteeism rose to 12.99 percent. When the program was reintroduced, absenteeism fell to 5.37 percent.[17]

Increasing Performance

Some managers believe that performance can be raised simply by raising salaries or benefits. It is not nearly so simple, of course. Motivation theory has taught us that people improve performance only if it is rewarding to do so. That means performance must be clearly defined and measured, and rewards that people value must be tied directly to it. None of these are easy to accomplish individually, let alone together. Management must consider several factors when designing an incentive program:

What Performance Can Be Measured? Linking rewards to unmeasured or unmeasurable performance makes allocation of the rewards extremely subjective. If employees do not see a direct link between their performance and rewards, the rewards will have little motivating value.[18]

What Performance Is Important? If a manager is interested in productivity but measures attendance because attendance records are available and productivity records are not, the wrong behavior is emphasized. This is not meant to imply that attendance is unimportant, but it should not be confused with productivity. If the manager ties rewards to attendance, that behavior will receive employee attention. Attendance will almost certainly improve, but productivity might not.

In one city, a manager of an animal control department felt that animal control officers were spending too much time drinking coffee and too little time catching stray dogs and cats. To get the officers out of the coffee shops and into their trucks, the manager announced that the number of miles driven (as measured by the truck odometers) would be recorded daily and used for employee appraisals. Overnight the number of miles driven tripled—and the number of strays collected decreased dramatically. The officers' behavior changed. Unfortunately, attention was focused on the wrong behavior.

Some questions that management should ask before changing or developing a compensation system are:

☐ *Can employees see a link?* If employees believe that their performances will have little or no effect on the way rewards are distributed, the incentives will have little motivational value. An example of weak linkage is the typical organization-wide profit-sharing plan. Many employees believe that they personally can have little impact on profit. For them the profit-sharing plan has little motivating potential.

☐ *Is the incentive plan understandable?* If the incentive scheme is based on "asset turns" and employees do not understand what an "asset turn" is, the incentive is of limited value. Incentive plans should be kept as simple as possible. If they must be complicated, participants should be carefully and thoroughly informed about how the system works.

☐ *Is the plan compatible with values?* If an organization emphasizes teamwork, an incentive scheme that rewards individual initiative may cause serious disruption. If managers or other employees are opposed to a particular incentive plan, it is doubtful that the plan will have the desired effect.

Hundreds of different incentive plans have been developed, most in the hope that they will improve employee performance and productivity. They range from behavior modification plans for improved attendance to organization wide productivity improvement programs. We can catalog the intent of most incentive programs by considering three dimensions: the intended effect on performance (direct or indirect), whether they are aimed at individual or group performance, and whether they have a financial or nonfinancial base. Plans with an indirect impact on performance are used in the hope that they will affect productivity through their influence on some other variable such as employee morale. Figure 8–6 shows an example of an incentive plan for every combination of the three dimensions.

TYPES OF INCENTIVE PLANS

Incentives are financial or nonfinancial, group or individual, direct or indirect.

Individual Performance Incentives

Individual incentives are aimed at changing the behavior of workers individually, though an individual incentive plan, such as merit pay or piece rate, may apply to hundreds or thousands of people in an organization. Here we look briefly at the four examples of individual plans in Figure 8–6.

Financial-Direct Effect: Merit Pay. Sometimes called pay-for-performance plans, these programs involve two components: (1) some method of measuring individual performance, and (2) a financial reward, typically a salary increase or a bonus. From this chapter it should be clear that it can be difficult to measure an individual's performance, and it can be even more difficult to compare performance to determine who should receive the most merit pay.

Financial-Indirect Effect: Cafeteria Fringe Benefits. Cafeteria fringe benefits allow employees to tailor their benefit package to their particular needs. For example, many working couples have medical insurance that covers both the worker and spouse. A cafeteria approach would allow one of the pair to substitute some other benefit for medical insurance. Cafeteria benefit plans are usually not

FIGURE 8 – 6

Examples of incentive plans (Source: Adapted from R. E. Callahan, C. P. Fleenor, and H. R. Knudson, *Understanding Organizational Behavior: A Managerial Viewpoint* (Columbus, OH: Merrill Publishing Co., 1986): 384.)

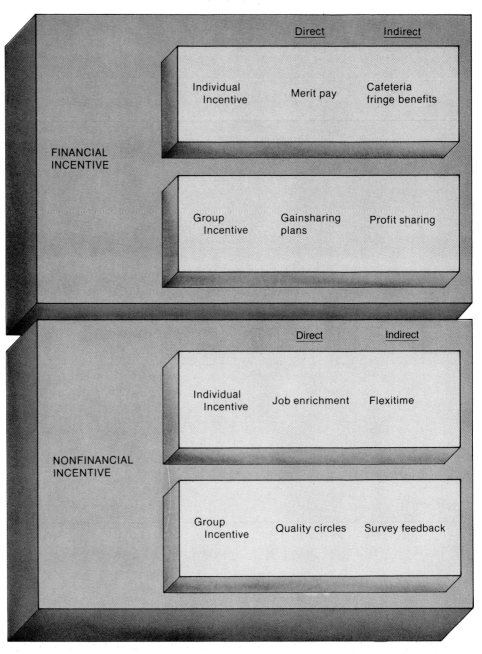

linked directly to performance. Rather they are viewed as a general reward to recruit new employees and to reduce turnover, which should have a long term though indirect impact on productivity.

Nonfinancial-Direct Effect: Job Enrichment. Job enrichment is an approach to job design that creates more challenging work and grants more autonomy to the worker. For many people, the increased challenge and autonomy are motivating factors that lead directly to increased performance.

Nonfinancial-Indirect Effect: Flexitime. Flexitime is a system of scheduling work that allows each employee to select a starting and quitting time that best meets personal needs and preference. Flexitime increases overall job satisfaction for some people, which should lead to lower turnover and absenteeism.

Group Performance Incentives

Some incentives are aimed at improving group rather than individual performance. Such incentives generally encourage greater cooperation and teamwork as a way to increase performance.

Financial-Direct Effect: Gainsharing. Gainsharing includes a variety of group incentive plans sharing the following characteristics: (1) a management style that encourages employee involvement and teamwork, (2) a system that facilitates employee involvement so that all employees have a method for making their ideas and suggestions known, and (3) an organization-wide bonus system that shares productivity improvements with workers.

Financial-Indirect Effect: Profit-Sharing. Profit-sharing plans generally involve an annual sharing of profits with employees. Usually profits must exceed a specified level before any sharing occurs. The payment method ranges from cash awards to delayed compensation (typically a contribution to a pension plan).

Nonfinancial-Direct Effect: Quality Circles. Quality circles create a framework for employee groups to identify and solve productivity problems. The circles meet on a regular basis to discuss productivity and how to improve it. This direct attack on specific productivity problems has been remarkably successful for many organizations.

Nonfinancial-Indirect Effect: Survey Feedback. Survey feedback entails collecting data from work groups and "feeding back" the results for discussion. In discussing the survey results, work groups begin to solve issues identified by the survey that may be limiting their effectiveness. The group's ability to address specific problems leads to increased participation, which in turn may improve satisfaction, thus leading to a desire to improve the group's performance.

Opening Story Revisited

Wﾠhat kinds of rewards go to "the world's worst waiter"? He probably receives the same pay and benefits package as other waiters at Costello's, and he probably collects greater than average tip income. A major part of his reward package is nonfinancial: his reputation as a character, being sought out by customers, the freedom to do things that would get other waiters fired, and being the object of magazine articles and textbook analyses!

LEARNING SUMMARY

1. The increasing emphasis in recent years on productivity has led to a need for clear accountability and well-defined performance standards.
2. Complete objectivity is not possible in performance evaluation, but systems must be made as objective as possible.
3. A performance appraisal system should be reliable and valid, provide accurate feedback, identify training and development needs, and allow comparison among employees. It must also be accepted by both raters and ratees.
4. Behaviorally anchored ratings scales (BARS), behavior observation scales (BOS), and management by objectives (MBO) are "less subjective" evaluation methods. Although they are constructed differently, each requires participation of ratees in development.
5. Rating errors are any attitudes, response tendencies, or inconsistencies within a rater that interfere with accurate ratings.
6. Evaluating performance requires more than common sense or natural ability. Managers must be trained if they are to perform quality appraisal.
7. Possible sources of information for evaluation include peers, superiors, subordinates, self, and clients.
8. Organizations distribute rewards for three primary reasons: to attract qualified applicants, to retain good employees, and to motivate higher performance.
9. Employee turnover is not necessarily undesirable. Turnover can be voluntary or involuntary.
10. Rewards can be classified along three dimensions: financially or nonfinancially based, direct or indirect impact on performance, and aimed at individual or group performance.

ANSWERS TO "WHAT'S YOUR OPINION?"

1. False It is impossible to have a completely objective evaluation system, though it should be as objective as possible.
2. True Employees are often in the best position to describe the most important job activities. Participation is also useful in gaining employee acceptance of work standards.

3. False   There may be other important considerations, such as seniority, working conditions, and cost of living.
4. False   Competitive pay rates are more important in attracting applicants. Pay is one of the few things that can be compared if several offers are being considered.
5. False   A number of sources can be used for evaluation, including self, peers, subordinates, and clients.
6. True   Poor performers are more likely to quit because of working conditions.
7. False   Some turnover is desirable. An organization should strive to get rid of poor performers.
8. False   Workers often feel a lack of direction, especially in terms of what goals are most important. Feedback on performance should be given on a regular basis, not just when required.

<table>
<tr><td>BARS</td><td>Intrinsic rewards</td></tr>
<tr><td>BOS</td><td>MBO</td></tr>
<tr><td>Cafeteria fringe benefits</td><td>Merit pay</td></tr>
<tr><td>Central tendency</td><td>Peer evaluation</td></tr>
<tr><td>Contrast</td><td>Profit sharing</td></tr>
<tr><td>Criteria</td><td>Ranking</td></tr>
<tr><td>Criteria only</td><td>Rating errors</td></tr>
<tr><td>Essay</td><td>Recency</td></tr>
<tr><td>Extrinsic rewards</td><td>Reliability</td></tr>
<tr><td>Gainsharing</td><td>Self evaluation</td></tr>
<tr><td>Halo effect</td><td>Validity</td></tr>
<tr><td>Incentives</td><td></td></tr>
</table>

KEY TERMS

HUMAN RELATIONS APPLICATIONS

In this chapter we have seen how difficult it is to clearly define performance, measure it accurately, and then assemble an incentive program that will lead employees to greater productivity. Sometimes the best of intentions leads to unhappy results.

Such an unpleasant result was observed in a small manufacturing plant. The plant had met an exceptionally heavy production schedule by working all hourly employees an average of sixty-six hours per week over a five-week period. At the end of the period, the plant manager was so appreciative of the effort that he gave each of the employees a $300 bonus.

The hourly employees, who averaged over $4,000 in pay during the period, thought it was nice to get a few extra dollars. The office staff, who had worked

When a plant manager gave each employee a $300 bonus, the office workers were pleased, but the supervisors felt insulted.

limited overtime, thought the bonus was wonderful. The supervisors, who were salaried and not eligible for overtime pay, were furious. They saw the $300 as an insult rather than a bonus. One supervisor commented that the bonus amounted to $2.50 an hour for all of the extra hours he had worked. On hearing of the supervisors' resentment, the manager vowed never to "waste my money on ungrateful employees again." He had spent over $30,000 to upset a key group of employees.

By contrast, an effective and much less costly incentive plan was used by a medical center, where employees of the billing and credit departments were asked to clear up accounting errors on 5,000 accounts. Great amounts of overtime were worked over a two-month period.

Prior to the start of the project, managers held a brainstorming session to develop a motivational scheme (in addition to the overtime pay). A staff meeting was held to explain the need for the project, and how the incentive program was structured. The program as implemented had the following components:

- ☐ The overtime work was voluntary.
- ☐ The overtime could be worked only during two specific periods per week to keep the special project from taking away from the heavy normal workload.
- ☐ Work was conducted in teams of two, with one member from each of the two departments. Each team had one person with experience in account work and one with no experience.
- ☐ Computer pages with twenty-five accounts each were randomly assigned to the teams. A team had to correct all twenty-five accounts before requesting a new list.
- ☐ Each team member received an "auction" ticket for every account completed.
- ☐ At the end of the project, employees were treated to dinner and drinks, served by managers. Following dinner, an auction was held, at which employees could bid on various prizes with the auction tickets they had earned. Prizes included gift certificates to top clothing and department stores, a color TV, a video recorder, and a weekend for two at a nearby resort. Tickets left over at the end of the auction were used for a "grab bag" of small prizes.

The results of the program exceeded management's most optimistic estimates:

- ☐ Over 85 percent of the employees participated.
- ☐ The 5,000 accounts were corrected in one-half the projected time—1,000 accounts were cleared on a single Saturday morning.
- ☐ Teamwork and understanding were fostered via the cross-department teams. Many favorable comments came from employees about this aspect of the project.
- ☐ The cost of the incentive, excluding overtime, was just over $3,000.

What a dramatic difference from the experience at the manufacturing plant! What made the difference? Substantial thought went into the medical center plan *before* it was started. Employees were informed about the project and knew what the "rules" were. Finally, the incentive scheme was based on team performance (number of accounts resolved). Teams with the best performance had the most tickets to use for bidding at the auction, while the grab bag assured that everyone would take home a prize of some sort.

By contrast, the manufacturing manager provided the bonus as an afterthought. There was no incentive value, since employees did not know there would be a bonus. Still, perhaps his greatest mistake was in giving everyone the same reward. It was clear that the bonus was not related in any way to individual or even small group performance. Despite the best intentions of management, such a distribution *always* causes some people to feel cheated.

PERSONAL GUIDELINES FOR HUMAN RELATIONS SUCCESS

In this chapter we have learned how difficult it is to evaluate performance fairly and accurately, and how much thought and care must go into the design of reward systems. Following are some suggestions to help you deal with these difficult matters:

1. Know what you want to reward, then reward it. It is not as simple as it sounds, but some thought will help you avoid the mistake the manufacturing manager made with the bonus.
2. Let employees know what the object of an incentive plan is. Involve them in the design as much as possible. Ask them for ideas.
3. Consider merit pay only if a good appraisal system is already in place.
4. In evaluating performance, critique the behavior, not the employee.
5. Be fair, but don't be afraid to criticize. Most employees don't want a meaningless pat on the back. But remember that a review should include some stroking. Reinforce good habits with praise.
6. Listen. Numerous surveys reveal that employees feel that management doesn't care what they think.
7. Don't wait until the performance review to tell employees what you expect of them.
8. Don't wait until the next performance review to inform employees about how they are doing. Follow up periodically with informal progress reports or mini-reviews.

DISCUSSION AND REVIEW QUESTIONS

1. What should a good performance appraisal system do?
2. What are the major features of BARS? BOS? MBO?
3. List and describe common rating errors.
4. What is the difference between halo effect and contrast?
5. How can rating errors be reduced?
6. What advantages are there in using other raters in addition to the manager? What disadvantages are there?
7. What should rewards accomplish for an organization?
8. What are some examples of financial and nonfinancial incentives aimed at group performance? Individual performance?

HUMAN RELATIONS EXERCISE

Let's Evaluate the Prof

The object of this exercise is to develop a BARS for teaching performance. Break into groups of four to six people.

1. Individually, without discussion, list as many criteria as you can to evaluate teaching. Some example criteria: use of audio/visual aids, lecture delivery, ability to answer questions. Spend five minutes at most on this step.

2. List and briefly discuss the criteria developed by the group. Agree (vote if necessary) on ten to fifteen of the criteria. Allow a maximum of thirty minutes.
3. Reassemble the entire class. Groups list their criteria on the board. Discuss similarities and differences between the group lists. What implications do these have for reliability and validity of the criteria?
4. If time allows, break back to small groups and develop anchor statements for one of the performance criteria.
5. Reassemble the entire class, list and discuss anchor statements. How might they be improved?

Be Punctual or Else!¹⁹

An engineer was assigned to a unit where she had never worked before. The unit had many long staff meetings that could not start until she arrived with the most recent drawings. Punctuality was not her strength—she usually arrived at the staff meetings ten to fifteen minutes late. Her boss mentioned a couple of times that it would be nice if she could arrive at the appointed hour so the meeting could start on time. This went on for about nine months. At the annual performance review covering this period, the boss gave the engineer an *overall* rating of "needs improvement," citing a "refusal to contribute fully to the team effort as evidenced by a continued lack of concern for getting to meetings on time." The engineer was livid when she read this, and complained that punctuality was a completely inappropriate factor for rating a professional engineer.

QUESTIONS

1. What might the manager have done to avoid the disagreement at the appraisal meeting?
2. Was an overall rating of "needs improvement" appropriate?
3. Is punctuality generally a critical performance element for professional employees? Why or why not?
4. How should the manager respond to the engineer?

HUMAN RELATIONS INCIDENT

NOTES

1. Adapted from T. L. Adcock, "They Also Wait Who Only Stand and Serve," *Northwest Orient Magazine* (October 1983): 65.
2. J. Kim and W. Hamner, "Effect of Performance Feedback and Goal Setting on Productivity and Satisfaction in an Organizational Setting," *Journal of Applied Psychology,* vol. 61 (1976): 48–57.
3. W. C. Borman, "Format and Training Effects on Rating Accuracy and Rater Errors," *Journal of Applied Psychology,* vol. 64 (1979): 410–21.
4. G. P. Latham, C. H. Fay, and L. M. Saari, "The Development of Behavioral Observation Scales for Appraising the Performance of Foremen," *Personnel Psychology,* vol. 32 (1979): 299–311.
5. B. R. Nathan and R. G. Lord, "Cognitive Categorization and Dimensional Schemata: A Process Approach to the Study of Halo in Performance Ratings," *Journal of Applied Psychology,* vol. 68 (1983): 102–14.

6. M. E. Heilman and M. H. Stopek, "Being Attractive: Advantage or Disadvantage? Performance Based Evaluations and Recommended Personnel Actions As a Function of Appearance, Sex, and Job Type," *Organizational Behavior and Human Decision Processes,* vol. 35 (April 1985): 202–15.
7. R. L. Heneman and K. N. Wexley, "The Effects of Time Delay in Rating and Amount of Information Observed on Performance Rating Accuracy," *Academy of Management Journal,* vol. 26 (1983): 677–86.
8. B. L. Davis and M. K. Mount, "Effectiveness of Performance Appraisal Training Using Computer Assisted Instruction and Behavior Modeling," *Personnel Psychology* (Winter 1984): 439–51.
9. K. R. Murphy, M. Garcia, S. Kerkar, C. Martin, and W. K. Balzer, "Relationship Between Observational Accuracy and Accuracy in Evaluating Performance," *Journal of Applied Psychology,* vol. 67 (1982): 320–25.
10. A. S. DeNisi, W. A. Randolph, and A. G. Blencoe, "Potential Problems With Peer Ratings," *Academy of Management Journal,* vol. 26 (1983): 457–64.
11. E. E. Lawler III, *Pay and Organizational Effectiveness: A Psychological View* (New York: McGraw-Hill, 1971).
12. L. Dyer, D. P. Schwab, and J. A. Fossum, "Impacts of Pay on Employee Behaviors and Attitudes: An Update," *Personnel Administrator* (January 1978): 51–53.
13. V. H. Vroom, "Industrial Social Psychology," in G. Lindzey and E. Aronson, eds., *The Handbook of Social Psychology,* 2nd ed., vol. 5 (Reading, MA: Addison-Wesley, 1970): 200–208.
14. M. Patchen, *The Choice of Wage Comparisons* (Englewood Cliffs, NJ: Prentice-Hall, 1961).
15. C. M. Futrell and A. Parasuraman, "The Relationship of Satisfaction and Performance to Salesforce Turnover," *Journal of Marketing,* vol. 48 (Fall 1984): 33–40.
16. J. A. Wallin and R. D. Johnson, "The Positive Reinforcement Approach to Controlling Employee Absenteeism," *Personnel Journal* (August 1976): 390–92.
17. F. Luthans and T. Maris, "Evaluating Personnel Programs Through the Reversal Techniques," *Personnel Journal* (October 1979): 692–98.
18. E. E. Lawler III, *Pay and Organization Development* (Reading, MA: Addison-Wesley, 1981).
19. C. P. Fleenor and M. P. Scontrino, *Performance Appraisal: A Manager's Guide* (Dubuque, IA: Kendall/Hunt, 1982): 57. Copyright by C. Patrick Fleenor and M. Peter Scontrino.

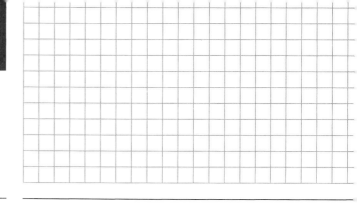

CHAPTER 9
MANAGEMENT OF CHANGE

WHAT'S YOUR OPINION? T OR F

_____ 1. Changes are a constant fact in a manager's life and should be expected.

_____ 2. Managing change in the organization should be as important as managing individuals in the manager's work area.

_____ 3. Often it is better for the manager to wait and inform the workers when it is time to implement a change rather than create anxiety in the workers beforehand.

_____ 4. Change is easily evaluated by management.

_____ 5. Employees have many sources of resistance to change.

_____ 6. One of the most difficult parts of bringing about change is defining the goals of the change.

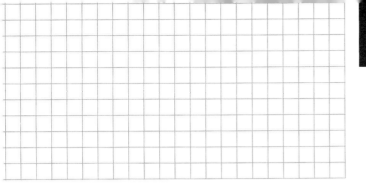

LEARNING OBJECTIVES

- ☐ Identify the major pressures for change facing organizations

- ☐ Describe the steps involved in the change process

- ☐ List the major methods of collecting data about the organization

- ☐ Identify the main sources of resistance to change and how to reduce them

- ☐ List and describe the change strategies for the individual, work group, and the organizational levels

- ☐ Discuss the major human relations applications of the change process

- ☐ Explain several methods for more successful implementation of changes in an organization

Can We Simplify a Worker's Job Too Much?

Dilettante's Chocolate Candy Company had a reputation for high quality candies in the local Seattle marketplace. The candies produced were sold in company-owned stores, and the company was known for its attractive packaging and rich-tasting products.

Production of the candy itself was predominantly automated, but the wrapping and packaging required that the individual pieces be wrapped by hand. The company installed several short conveyor belts where groups of nine to ten employees stood on both sides. As the candy moved along the belt, the employees would remove pieces and place them in small pleated paper cups. The wrapped candy was then placed in appropriate spots in the assortment boxes.

Since the work required relatively little thought, the employees seated at the assembly line chatted and joked with each other during a major part of the day. The foreman who observed this constant chattering felt that since so much time was being used for socializing, the productivity of the employees was not as high as it could be. To reduce this constant socializing, the foreman had partitions installed between the workstations so that the employees were screened off from one another, making it virtually impossible for them to converse while seated at their workstations.

At about the same time, a change in the assortment tray for the candy was made. Rather than merely indicating on the box that an approximate number of jellies, nougats, or caramels were included in a package, the box contained a plastic tray with the indentions of the various candy shapes imprinted on it. The effect of this change was substantial. While the employees previously were able to arrange the candy according to their own preferences (e.g., in circles, rectangles, or just simply sections of nougats, caramels, and jellies), the new change required that a specific piece of candy be included in the particular compartment designated for it. This reduced the employees' flexibility in packing the box. The work was thus limited to merely matching a candy shape with a similar indentation in the tray.

Productivity did not go up as anticipated, but went down 20 percent and absenteeism increased by 25 percent. The foreman was astonished.

<table>
<tr><td>

CONCEPTS OF CHANGE

</td><td>

The opening story suggests that change is not so simple. When a supervisor tries to improve a work group's productivity, sometimes unforeseen negative conse-

</td></tr>
</table>

quences happen. What may be logical in suggesting a change may not be so for those individuals who have to carry out the change. But how can we know this ahead of time? Managers and supervisors must begin to anticipate the results of suggested changes and plan to eliminate some of the problems before they occur.

In this chapter we will look at the reasons changes occur. We will review a model to plan for changes more effectively and two ways to conduct a diagnosis in the organization. We will identify the major reasons people resist change and discuss how to reduce resistance. We will review some of the major methods to successfully deal with changes at the individual, group, and organizational level. Finally, we will see how to apply these ideas.

Pressures for Change

In the case of the opening story, one force creating a need for change is the *market competition*. But, as we shall see, at any one time, firms, groups, and individuals face a multitude of pressures.

It is easy to appreciate the immensity of the forces for change when we read John Naisbitt's *Megatrends*. Naisbitt sees American society evolving and feels that because of these forces for change both organizations and individuals will need to cope differently in the future, if not today.

He suggests several trends that we should understand:[1]

1. Most of us still believe that we live in an industrial-based society; that is, we use mostly mechanical devices. In fact, we have changed to an economy based on the creation and distribution of information. "The new source of power is not money in the hands of a few but information in the hands of many." (p. 16)
2. We are moving in two directions at once—high technology and high touch (high-tech/touch). This means that as we develop new technologies, we must match these with human concern and responsiveness. "We must learn to balance the material wonders of technology with the spiritual demands of our human nature." (p. 40)
3. No longer do we have the luxury of operating as an isolated unit in the world. We must acknowledge that we live in and are a part of a global economy. "Business is replacing politics as the world's gossip." (p. 70)
4. We are redirecting our attention from merely short-term time frames and corresponding rewards to dealing with much longer-term time frames. "Strategic planning is worthless—unless there is first strategic vision." (p. 94)
5. In our private and professional lives, we have rediscovered the need and ability to act innovatively and to work from the bottom up. "The big-business mergers and the big-labor mergers have all the appearances of dinosaurs mating." (p. 87)
6. We are moving from relying on others to self-reliance in many areas of our lives. "We are shifting from a managerial society to an entrepreneurial society." (p. 149)

What are the major forces for change facing most organizations? Describe each.

7. We are giving up our use of hierarchical structures for informal, no-status networks. "The failure of hierarchies to solve society's problems forced people to talk to one another—and that was the beginning of networks." (p. 191)
8. From a black/white society with limited choices, we are exploring the need to have multiple options to create our futures. "In today's Baskin-Robbins society, everything comes in at least 31 flavors." (p. 232)

It is easy to see from this list that change is not merely an occasional evil that supervisors or managers need to face. Rather, change itself has become the norm. It is inherent in a manager's job. Figure 9–1 shows pressures to which managers are having to respond. Managing change and its consequences has become a primary managerial function. It should have the same status as planning, controlling, staffing, and evaluating.

FIGURE 9 – 1
Pressures causing change in organizations

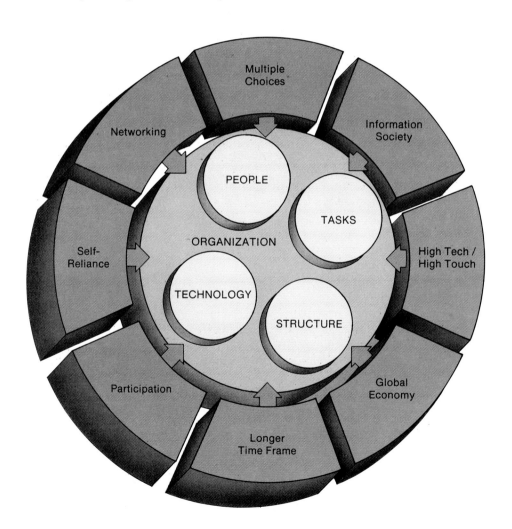

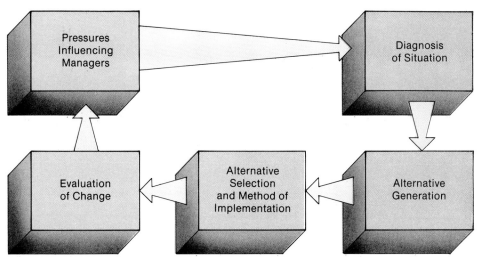

FIGURE 9 – 2
Model for managing change

Model for Understanding Change

To understand how change affects the organization and how managers need to manage changes, we propose the model in Figure 9–2 as a guide. This model will help us understand how the supervisor in the opening story responded to pressures for change.

List and explain the parts of the model for change.

Pressures Influencing Management.   Let us first focus our attention on pressures for change. At any point in time organizations face a multitude of forces that have consequences for the firm if not handled promptly. Examples of these forces are similar to Naisbitt's forces: competition, regulation, technology changes, worker value changes, and other external pressures.

Diagnosis of the Situation.   If the manager decides that the pressures are causing serious problems, a diagnosis of the situation is required to clarify the problem and set change goals. Later in this chapter we will list and explain common methods to collect data for analysis and how to analyze it.

Alternative Generation.   After identifying the problems and the change goals, the manager can focus attention on generating alternatives and techniques to solve the problem. Figure 9–3 shows a continuum of possible changes needed in an organization. Depending on the level of change needed, the manager needs to develop appropriate alternatives.

If the change is slight, such as a new budget format, the alternative can be simple—create and show employees the new format. If the change is complex, such as merging with a new company, the alternatives need to be more detailed— such as new training for employees and the creation of rumor control. The point is to create realistic alternatives based on the needed changes.

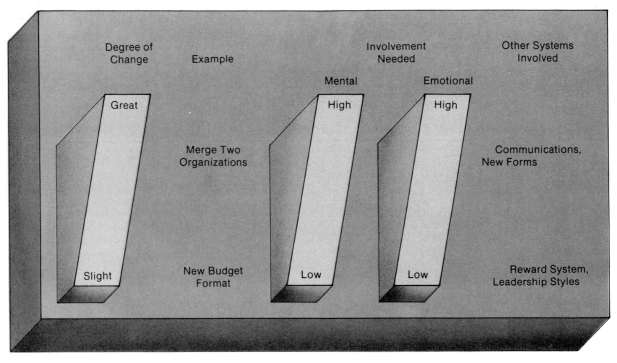

FIGURE 9 – 3
Matching change techniques with needed changes

Opening Story Revisited

The Dilettante Candy Company is probably facing some stiff competition, which means that they must continue to improve operations. Costs need to be watched and quality maintained. The foreman at Dilettante must have centered his diagnosis on how the production employees were working, and then determined that their socializing was limiting their production rate. The firm's management diagnosed that there was too much variation in the placement of candies, which might affect the customer's view of quality. As a result, some production goals were probably set, as for example, the need to increase production 5 percent and reduce customer complaints to only one per week.

In terms of selection of alternatives, we can see that a new production process and the installation of partitions are in the mid-range of Figure 9–3. As a result, the redefining of jobs and the reduction of socialization will mean changes in the emotional and mental reactions of the workers.

Which approach did the supervisor use from Figure 9–4? It seems that a unilateral method was used to design and implement this change. Finally, in terms of evaluation, the results were not as anticipated; production was down 20 percent and absenteeism was up 25 percent. What happened?

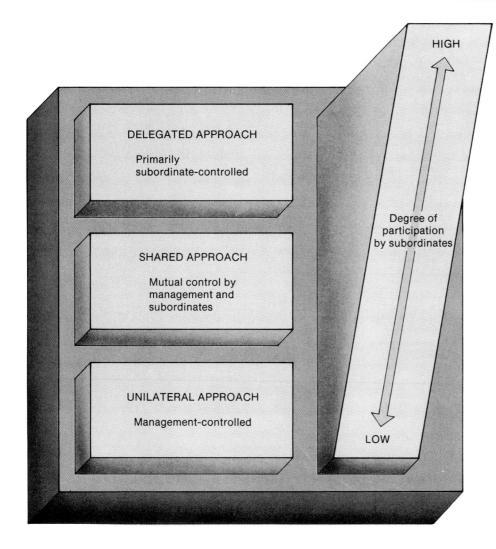

FIGURE 9 – 4
Three approaches to implementing change (Source: Larry E. Greiner, "Patterns of Organizational Change," *Harvard Business Review* (May–June 1967): 122. Copyright © 1967 by the President and Fellows of Harvard College; all rights reserved.)

Selection of Alternative. Having developed a set of alternatives to consider, a manager must decide which technique or combination of techniques to use. In addition, the manager must consider which approach to follow while implementing the solution. Unfortunately, managers are too often very subjective when making this important decision about which alternative to use. Managers have favorite techniques or ideas that may not reflect the change conditions.

Another issue in the selection process is deciding on the approach to use while implementing the alternative. In other words, which form of power should a manager apply when implementing an alternative? One researcher identified three approaches to implementing change.[2] Figure 9–4 summarizes these approaches.

Describe some of the ways to implement change from the manager's perspective.

The first approach a manager could use is to implement the change unilaterally; the subordinate makes little or no contribution. The supervisor, relying on position power and authority, tells the employee what the change is and how to implement it. The worker's responsibility is to follow the manager's instructions.

Another approach recognizes that authority is present in an organization, but that it must be carefully used and shared with subordinates. If the subordinates are mature and capable, there can be a sharing of power in reaching important change decisions and implementing those changes. The chief vehicle for this approach is using a group to solve the problems and make the decisions. The manager and the subordinates equally share responsibility and power to arrive at a method of introducing the needed changes.

A final approach is to delegate power. Under this method, subordinates actively participate in the change program from the onset to the implementation. The subordinates diagnose, analyze, and consider various solutions to the problems. This approach is based on the assumption that the workers know more about the technology and tasks concerning their jobs than does management. Therefore, they should have the most say about the methods of change.

Evaluation of Change.   The last step in any change program should be to evaluate its effectiveness. Did the change result in a more effective organization and more effective employees? In one sense the bottom line for the organization is to survive.

Having presented a conceptual model to understand the manager's role in the management of change, we now consider how to deal with change, including methods to diagnose the situation, dealing with resistances, some change methods, and the human relations applications.

Diagnosing the Situation

Throughout this book, we have stressed how important it is for the manager to understand the uniqueness of each situation. This is especially true when considering changes within the organization. Diagnosis is the first step toward understanding a situation. For example, a manager might complain that first-line supervisors need to be more sensitive to the line workers. A quick suggestion to correct this situation might be to institute communications training. But what is really meant by being "more sensitive" to the workers? Does this mean that supervisors need to listen more to their workers? Does it mean the number of grievances submitted is too high? Or does it mean that management wants more worker suggestions about how to improve operations?

The manager must first diagnose the specific problem before applying a solution. We have found that most situations require more complex solutions than those offered by a simple communications training program.

Traditional versus "Action Research."   Remember that a manager needs to decide whether to share the power during the change program (Figure 9–4). A

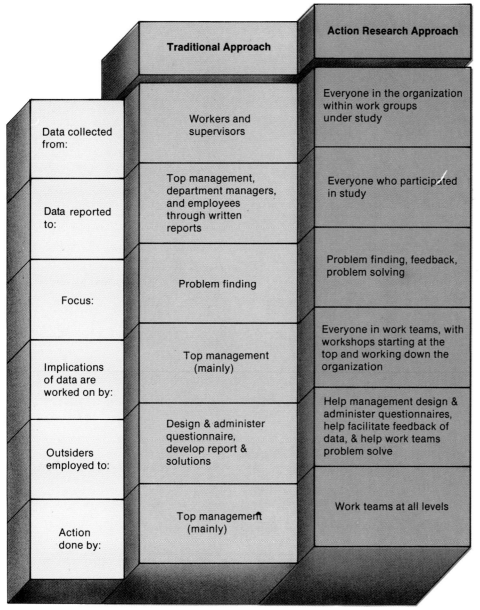

FIGURE 9 – 5
Diagnosis: Traditional approach versus action research (Source: Adapted from A. D. Szilagyi and M. J. Wallace, *Organizational Behavior and Performance,* 3d ed., p. 572. Copyright © 1983 by Scott, Foresman and Company. Reprinted by permission.)

clearer statement of this choice surrounds how the organization approaches the diagnosis of the situation. This is the first stage in which power can be shared in defining the problems. Figure 9–5 summarizes the choice in terms of the "traditional" approach or the "action research" approach to diagnosing the situation. Each approach has different assumptions about why to involve or not to involve workers.

Compare the traditional approach to diagnosis with the "action research" approach.

When Companies Merge

General Foods merges with Philip Morris. R. J. Reynolds takes over Nabisco. During 1985, 3,284 companies were acquired, with a value of approximately $150 billion.

The names and numbers are impressive. But there is more than money involved. When General Electric took over RCA, Samuel W. Murphy, the corporate general counsel for RCA, stated "I was personally dismayed, but I also was upset at seeing something like that happen to a great institution."

Disbelief. Uncertainty. A sense of disaster. We've encountered these reactions again and again in executives whose careers have been stymied by corporate takeovers.

The fear and stress created by a takeover is not limited to top executives. Rumors of mass lay-offs and forced relocations circulate throughout the company. Office workers get the message that their jobs are being reviewed and will depend upon how they fit into the new company, not on their past record. People become rumormongers and pass on worst-case scenarios of plant closing, pay freezes and the loss of benefits.

Nor is the threat limited to hostile and unexpected takeovers. Supposedly friendly mergers of two equal-sized companies or acquisitions of smaller firms by larger ones evoke just as many horror stories. You find bulletin boards filled with cartoons of brides being menaced by dragons and black-robed executioners promising that nothing will change. With individuals preoccupied by the merger and their personal fate, job performance slacks off. Typewriters and copy machines churn out resumes, while company phones are kept busy with calls to recruiters and friends in other firms.

During the merger time, executives develop a crisis-management approach, closeting themselves away from the chaos. They formulate strategies for protecting their company's interests in the merger and start to feel on top of the situation.

The problem with this approach is that the executives have become less accessible, limited their lines of communication, and left their own people uninformed as to what is going on. One employee described this as the "mushroom treatment." "Right after the acquisition we were kept in the dark. Then they covered us with manure. Then they cultivated us. After that, they let us stew awhile. And finally, they canned us."

This mentality is triggered by unsettling events that occur right after the sale of a company and by the multitude of problems involved in combining people from different firms.

If your company is involved in a merger, you are uncertain what it means for your job, your career, and your company. You are afraid of losing your position because it may be duplicated in the other firm or won't fit into the new organization

Source: "The Merger Syndrome," by Mitchell Lee Marks and Philip Harold Mirvis, *Psychology Today* (October 1986): 37–42. Reprinted with permission from *Psychology Today* magazine. Copyright © 1986 American Psychological Association.

Action research approach total organization involved

The *action research* approach was conceived by Kurt Lewin, Ph.D., who was interested in social change and felt that people would feel and respond differently if involved in more of the diagnosis.[3] Specifically, he felt that data collected would have greater meaning if it were interpreted by those who supplied it. He also felt that other issues might be raised that were not previously considered if workers were involved. Finally, he felt it would help the participants to understand the

plan. In addition, you lose your track record and have to prove yourself all over again to a new boss. The merger may also change the entire character and culture of the organization you have lived with for years. Stress is a natural reaction, and as one executive put it, "Merger stress is a 10."

Several common characteristics of mergers add to these problems. First, most merger negotiations center on legal and financial matters, with investment bankers and attorneys leading the way. Scant attention is given to human considerations. Second, premerger negotiations are generally held in secret, and Security and Exchange Commission guidelines limit what can be told, even to employees, before the merger takes place. Third, newspaper and magazine reports focus mainly on the risks and problems of mergers and takeovers, an emphasis that fuels people's worries.

Finally, nobody really has accurate answers to questions about the merger. In most cases, the details have to be worked out in the months after the sale. Reassurances that nothing will change ring hollow. Answers to questions such as who will report to whom, how the organization will be structured, and whether there will be layoffs are bound to change as the merger moves from planning theory to working fact.

As mentioned earlier, top managers usually react to the stress of premerger negotiations by cloistering themselves in crisis-management meetings. As they centralize decision-making and restrict communications, they seem distant and isolated to employees and lose touch with their employees' worries and fears. Formal memos that management has the situation well in hand only rouse suspicion and fuel the rumors of impending disaster. In this environment, the message seems clear: Look out for yourself.

Finally and paradoxically, crisis management is not only natural but essential. Mergers require an enormous amount of work, and a crisis-management team helps accomplish it. Isolating the team and centralizing decision-making ensures that information flows to executives and that plans are coordinated. But the same isolation and centralization can shut team members off from important information elsewhere in the organization and promote a "groupthink" mentality as they consider options and strategies.

QUESTIONS

1. What are some of the resistances that a merger brings to the surface in employees and supervisors?
2. What methods of data collection could help the managers stay on top of the employees' worries and fears?
3. Granted that some form of crisis management is needed and that information about the future will be limited, what can supervisors do on a day-by-day basis to help employees cope better?

nature of the problems more fully and lead to more realistic solutions and action steps.

In contrast, the *traditional* approach usually has an "outsider" or someone in top management work with the data. The data collected may be supplied by workers, but others work with the data. This approach assumes that "experts" have the answers and know what is best.

Traditional approach only management involved

FIGURE 9 – 6

Forces acting on organizations

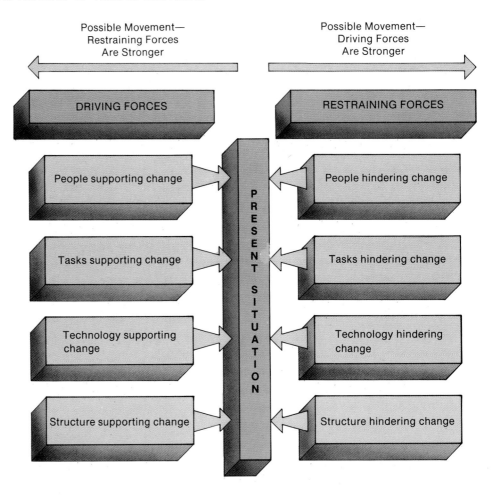

To summarize, the major difference between action research and traditional research is the involvement of those studied in the analysis and interpretation of the data. Action research is based on the assumption that involvement by the collectors will elicit more personal commitment to the needed recommendations and changes.

Force Field Analysis. Having chosen the research approach, the supervisor needs a method to think about the complexities involved. One method is the *force field analysis*.[4] The framework in Figure 9–6 shows that there are two types of forces that pressure an organization. *Driving forces* are those that encourage change, growth, and development. *Restraining forces* are those that resist change and encourage stability or status quo. Both driving and restraining forces can be external or internal to the organization. The figure shows the major types of forces found in most organizations: people, technology, tasks, and structure.

Driving forces pushing for changes

Restraining forces resisting changes

how

Structure refers to the relatively stable set of formally defined working relationships among people, such as changing the number of people reporting to a manager, changing the level to which a department reports, and adding units or work groups to the organization itself.

Technology refers to the equipment and materials, methods of production or operation, and specialized knowledge or experience used to perform tasks. An example of a technology change might be the introduction of computerized automation to an assembly line.

Tasks refers to the actual jobs performed in an organization, which can vary in scope and depth. Changes directed at tasks are attempts to increase a worker's activities, reduce those activities, or change the complexity of those activities.

Finally, *people* refers, of course, to those individuals who make up the organization.

Data Collection Approaches. Before we can proceed in making suggestions on dealing with situations like that in the opening story, we need to collect some data to separate the "real" problems from the symptoms. Many managers and supervisors fail to make this distinction. A good example of this is the statement used earlier that the supervisors aren't communicating well with their employees. To say that communication skills are the problem would be to oversimplify the real issues, such as changing job responsibilities, increased complexity of jobs assigned, or improper tools assigned.

The following are the most commonly used data collection approaches supervisors can use. It should be stated that using more than one approach helps validate the data collected and increases the clarity of what needs to be addressed.

Interviewing. In the interview, the supervisor asks questions directly of the employee. Interviews can be highly structured, using predetermined questions, or unstructured, starting with broad questions and allowing the participant to lead the way. Interviewing is a direct, personal way to get private views and feelings from the employee. The skills needed are discussed in Chapter 10 under employee counseling.

Questionnaires. This is probably the most widely used approach for gathering information. There are a number of predesigned questionnaires available that are useful to managers.[5] Questionnaires can be limited because it is assumed that the researchers know what data they need. This limitation can be reduced if the questionnaire is jointly developed by the supervisor, some employees, and a person from the personnel department. This approach obviously reflects an action research or shared attitude on the manager's part.

Sensing. Sensing is not a common approach used to collect data. However, it does allow the supervisor to informally collect information about the issues, concerns, and needs of the employees. It entails an unstructured group interview in which the manager selects and interviews, usually on a random basis, employees

---

Why is collecting data so important to the change effort?

Interviewing asking employees face-to-face what they think

Questionnaires asking employees to write down what they think

Sensing interviewing employees directly in a group setting

with whom the manager has little or no contact. The types of groups can vary from a unit that works together to members from various levels and functions within the organization. This is a method that can collect rich first-hand information about how the organization is doing internally.

Collages and drawings asking employees to express their thoughts through artistic means

Collages and Drawings. Collages and drawings are simply artistic expressions of problems. For example, we had a client who had an organization undergoing internal conflict between departments. Representing the problems graphically clearly showed the conflict between the departments and some of the issues causing the conflict (different goals and styles of management). Collages may require large sheets of paper, magazines from which pictures and words may be cut, and other materials. Drawings may be in color or in pencil.

While groups are initially suspicious, the richness of the experience is worth the effort. This approach was used with an MBA class that seemed to have lost its motivation. The resulting drawing created tremendous energy among the students and allowed the problem—conflicting needs about testing—to be explored. One MBA student said, "I thought you were crazy to ask us to draw pictures, but

Representing problems graphically through collages and drawings can clarify the nature of the problem and the issues involved.

I'm going to use this with my workers. It helps reduce the barriers between people.''

Observation. One can gather information by watching the activities of people at work or interacting with one another. Observation can be casual (noticing things while walking through a work area) or highly structured (doing a time and motion study). The difference between sensing and observation is that sensing allows the manager to interact with the employees while observation doesn't.

Observation watching rather than asking employees

Dealing with Resistance to Change

As we know from the first sections of this chapter, change forces are continually pushing organizations to change. As a result, management is continually trying to improve its operations and requesting employees to respond to these changes.

How can resistance affect the way people work in an organization?

We also know from the opening story that not all employees embrace changes. Many employees resist changes in damaging ways, such as staying away from work, filing fictitious grievances, sabotaging equipment or performance, or reducing output or productivity. How many forms of resistance occurred in the opening story? Remember that resistances can be overt, such as slowing down production, or covert, such as not clearly "hearing" how to operate a new machine or continually not meeting quality standards.[6]

Opening Story Revisited

W e can now use the force field analysis to understand the situation facing the supervisor in the opening story as he tries to manage the changes in his work group. Figure 9–7 is a summary of those forces. As we can see from the figure, there are several strong forces for increasing production in this situation. But there seems to be just as strong forces limiting production. We come to this conclusion based on the results of the program—productivity is reduced 20 percent and absenteeism is up 25 percent. This indicates that the forces for reducing productivity are stronger. What advice would you offer the supervisor now?

Part of your answer should be based on suggesting to the supervisor and management that they need to diagnose the situation more definitively. They probably used the traditional approach instead of the action research model. Due to the strong reactions of the employees, involvement seems more appropriate at this time. In addition, a variety of data collection methods might help clarify the problems and sort out the symptoms. One could suggest that the supervisor interview individuals about their views of the situation and their ideas for correction. In addition, questionnaires would help clarify how widespread the problem is in the rest of the firm. Even questionnaires to customers might help outline the problems causing complaints. Finally, the supervisor should use his own observations to supplement the other data.

FIGURE 9 – 7
Summary of forces facing supervisor at Dilettante's Chocolate Candy Company

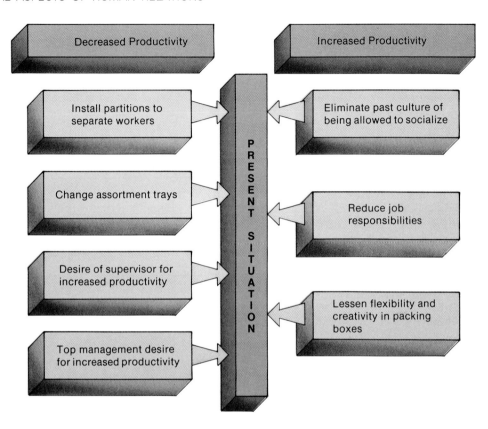

Causes of Resistance.   A simple view of resistance stems from the misperception between what is proposed and how it is accepted. An organization proposes change to become more effective, but individuals whose jobs are affected by the change may not see that view. They see change from their perspective, which may be quite different from management's. To understand this inherent conflict we need to look at some of the common reasons for resistance.

What are the major causes of resistance that prevent changes from being easily implemented?

Economic Loss.   Any change that creates the feeling that jobs will be eliminated and workers will be laid off or demoted to lesser jobs is bound to meet with resistance. Employees naturally fear partial or entire loss of earnings, and even the promise of retraining may not lessen this fear. Consider the typical reaction created by the introduction of computers to many work places: "I wonder how many jobs they can do away with now?"

Knowledge and Skill Obsolescence.   Some organizational changes make individual worker's knowledge and skills, acquired over long periods of time, obsolete. Computers have an image of making past expertise routine. Therefore, it is easy to understand how a bookkeeper whose security and identity is the mastery of a complex accounting system could be threatened by the introduction of computers.

Fear of Unknowns.　Most of us become anxious when confronting a new situation for the first time. The anxiety stems from the unknown factors that may call for new responses. Employees working on a day-to-day basis have some idea about the routine problems that may surface and the reactions of their supervisors to most situations. There is comfort in that knowledge. When a change occurs, such as an office move, the normal pattern is disrupted and the individual must begin to recreate a normal pattern. An employee may wonder: Will I find new friends? Will I have new responsibilities? Who will be my new boss?

Group Resistance.　In Chapter 6, we discussed how groups develop norms for individual behavior within the group setting and how this affects task performance. The more cohesive the group is, the greater the influence the group can exert on members. If management initiates new procedures that are viewed as threatening to a group, the group will likely resist them. This may partially explain "wild cat" strikes by workers when firms introduce changes without proper notification and preparation.

Some employees resist computerization for fear that computers will make their jobs, or their knowledge, obsolete.

Threats to Social System. Most of us work for social needs as well as economic needs. The social relationships that develop in the workplace are often more important to employees than commonly realized. While a firm may be able to ease employees' fears about job loss, there still may be substantial resistance due to the disruption in social relations and friendships. An example of this type of resistance is the introduction of a new office layout that has people face new walls or co-workers.

Threats to Power and Influence. Resistance can also occur because the proposed changes will restructure and potentially reduce one's power and influence. From Chapter 4, we know that one source of power for an individual is the control of something that other people need, such as information or other resources.

In most organizations today, information is being standardized and processed by new functions called "Management Information Systems" (MIS). These new systems are collecting and processing information that many middle managers used to handle. As a result these middle managers are losing some of their power and control to these new departments. It is not surprising that they are finding ways to resist the introduction of MIS.[7]

Reducing Resistance. Once a supervisor has identified potential resistance to planned changes, how can he or she attempt to reduce or avoid that resistance? Figure 9–8, using the force field method, shows both the sources of resistance and some approaches to reducing resistance.

What are the major approaches to reducing resistance to change?

The most popular approaches to deal with resistance to change include education and communication, participation and involvement, facilitation and support, negotiation and agreement, manipulation, and coercion.[8]

Education and Communication. This method deals with the lack of information or inaccurate information about proposed changes. It suggests educating employees before introducing the change. It further suggests openly discussing ideas and issues to help employees see the logic and need for a change.[9]

Participation and Involvement. Using this approach, the initiators of change are able to increase their information level to create a more effective change while allowing those who might resist the change to get involved. As those affected by the change discuss its design and implementation, new ideas and information can be generated. At the same time, this process allows others to develop a sense of "ownership."[10]

Facilitation and Support. In a situation in which workers are resisting change because of problems of adjustment, a simple method is to be supportive. This can include providing emotional support, simply listening, giving the employee time off the job, or providing training for acquiring new skills.

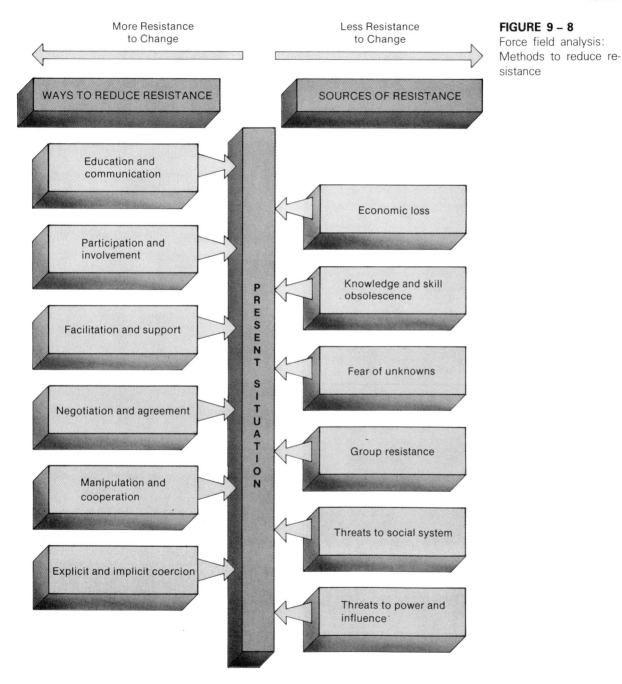

More Resistance to Change

Less Resistance to Change

FIGURE 9 – 8
Force field analysis: Methods to reduce resistance

WAYS TO REDUCE RESISTANCE

SOURCES OF RESISTANCE

Education and communication

Participation and involvement

Facilitation and support

Negotiation and agreement

Manipulation and cooperation

Explicit and implicit coercion

PRESENT SITUATION

Economic loss

Knowledge and skill obsolescence

Fear of unknowns

Group resistance

Threats to social system

Threats to power and influence

Negotiation and Agreement. Certain changes clearly restructure the amount of influence and power that a group may have after the change. Because of this threat of loss, resistance may be reduced only if the firm provides incentives to employees for compliance with the change. For example, in a labor management situation, incentives might involve the trade-offs for instituting a new job classification system with increased future job security or financial benefits. For instance, the Communication Workers of America negotiated with U.S. West, a holding company of regional telephone companies, to set aside $10 million to retain workers displaced by computers.[11]

Manipulation. While we do not advise this strategy for dealing with resistance, we know that it is used in certain situations, and therefore understanding its existence may be important. An example of manipulation would be a manager withholding information requested by another department that is responsible for designing a change, such as a new computer system. The manager may do this to prevent the department from completing its mission and implementing the computer system in the manager's area.

When the previously mentioned approaches do not work or seem too costly, managers may resort to covert methods of influencing employees to accept change. They may choose to be selective about who gets what information and how much information, how accurate the information is, and when to disseminate the information. Another technique would be giving key roles to certain individuals or groups during the design or implementation of the change to gain their cooperation.[12]

Explicit and Implicit Coercion. Another method we do not advise but have seen used is the exercise of raw power. Some changes demand swift implementation to take advantage of benefits. In addition, change initiators might possess considerable power. Both situations lend themselves to managers threatening employees with a loss of job, decreased promotional opportunities, or job changes to gain compliance with change. While one may get immediate results of compliance, a supervisor will most likely face future resistance from those same employees.

Implementing Change

Once an organization or a manager decides that changes are needed and has established the change objectives, several other issues must be addressed before implementation is initiated. This section explores some of these issues, including what type of intervention to choose and how to approach evaluation.

Intervention means or method to implement change more successfully

Types of Intervention. Intervention describes a method or means to manage change more successfully. These means may include either responding to forces for change or creating forces to help prepare individuals to accept change. In our experience as consultants, this last situation is usually the most fruitful. In one sense, supervisors need to create a supportive atmosphere for the change to grow, develop, and be accepted. That is what we mean by creating forces to help prepare people to accept change.

Focus	Type of Intervention
Individual	Training programs
	Job design
	Role analysis
	Coaching and counseling
	Life Planning
Work Group	Team building
	Conflict resolution
Intergroup	Conflict resolution
Total Organization	Survey feedback
	Management by objectives
	Sociotechnical programs

TABLE 9–1
Types of intervention to address resistance to change

As we know from the discussion so far, the organizational change is a complex process. Table 9–1 summarizes the various types of interventions that can address the various parts of changes being proposed. Interventions can focus on the individual, the work group, several work groups, or the total organization.

Life Planning. This intervention consists of a series of activities to help individuals look at their values, life experiences, goals, and action plans to prepare them to achieve their objectives. It can be used effectively in conjunction with other interventions, such as job design, role analysis, and counseling.

Life planning helping employees gain control over their organizational and personal lives

The intervention attempts to help the workers take more control over their work and "outside work" choices.[13] It is based on the assumption that people want to actively plan their future goals. Once a plan is established, the individual is more in control of accomplishing those goals. Feeling in control helps them to better perform in their present position and prepare themselves for future opportunities. The result is more satisfied and realistic employees.

Job Design. This approach entails changing the type or number of tasks an individual performs.[14] It has become increasingly popular in recent years. The most discussed form of job design is job enrichment. Other forms include work simplification, job enlargement, job rotation, and autonomous work groups. The reason for looking at specific jobs centers on the popular notion that reducing job routine will relieve worker boredom and result in a more satisfied and productive worker.

Job design restructuring an employee's job to increase satisfaction and performance

Team Building. Team building is a series of sessions to improve the effectiveness and performance of individuals who work together on a continuing basis, such as a work group or small department.[15] A team building session is more than a typical staff meeting; it may last from two to five days, usually away from the office or plant. The focus of the sessions is on group goals, work distribution, and how the group functions. Each is studied and suggestions for improvement are made by the team members. Most team members feel a deeper sense of commit-

Team building helping a work group function better together

Wrong Number: AT&T Manager Meets Resistance

When William F. Buehler's bosses at AT&T gave him permission to establish his own methods of operation with a new marketing department, Buehler took them literally. Instead of using Bell's standard practice of reams of paperwork, endless meetings, and a strict chain of reporting relationships to get approvals, Buehler discarded the planning manuals and employee tests and put the salespeople on a compensation plan that was unmatched at Bell. Besides using a commission-based system, Buehler fired those who couldn't meet the sales goals.

Did it work? Only too well! Sales of this unit outperformed other units selling larger, more expensive information systems. The term used to describe the energy level of the salesforce was "Buehler Fever."

However, Buehler is no longer head of this group. He still is a vice president but of a planning position. Many of his former subordinates are worried about what is going to happen next to the unit. "We're all upset and worried that we'll lose

Source: Adapted from "Wrong Number: AT&T Manager Finds His Effort to Galvanize Sales Meets Resistance," by Monica Langley, *The Wall Street Journal* (16 December 1983): 1. Reprinted by permission of *The Wall Street Journal,* © Dow Jones & Company, Inc., 1983. All rights reserved.

our new culture," says James Lewis, an account executive.

What happened? Isn't this the kind of innovation that AT&T needs to enter the competitive marketing world that divestiture brought?

The story is complicated, but some comments by various interested parties help clarify it. Robert Cascale, who ran the rival but more traditional sales program and who become the new boss of Buehler's group, states that the change was designed to "integrate the two discrete sales staffs to eliminate duplication in central support services." Lewis speculated that "Bill Buehler ruffled some feathers at the top. I wouldn't rule out that his different style of leadership caused him to be pushed out of a line position." David Nadler of a New York consulting firm said, "Frequently in entrenched organizations where something new and entrepreneurial is tried, the experiment may not survive because it's too threatening to the old line."

What was Buehler's approach? To set up his sales group, Buehler used the book *In Search of Excellence* as a guide. He would use phrases from the book in memos and meetings—"Keep it simple," "Reward results, not progress," "Customer is king." "That little list of points was the

ment and loyalty to the other members and the supervisor because they have a greater appreciation of who the others are personally as well as professionally.

Conflict resolution resolving differences of opinions between work groups

Conflict Resolution. Conflict resolution focuses on getting conflicting groups to bring to the surface the real and imaginary sources of tension occurring between them. Then they test to see which issues can be resolved and propose various solutions to find one acceptable to both groups.

While conflict can and does occur within groups, this intervention is focused on the conflict *between* work groups or units because of their different needs.[16] For example, the manufacturing unit wants to run its production lines as fast as possible and is usually willing to accept a certain amount of below-standard units.

only guide I gave my new work force in January—no detailed plans or directives. I wanted the team to know from the start that this was an entrepreneurial venture, and they were to abide by these points in a way that worked best for them," says Buehler.

He also visited his various branches across the nation rather than having the personnel come to him in New York. "The staffers in my branch have been with Bell for years, but this was the first time any of them had ever seen an AT&T vice president. . . . And then he actually sat down with the billing staff and ate hoagie sandwiches," stated one of those managers he visited.

He also used peer pressure to get results, besides his own authority. Sales results were posted on boards located for everyone to see. "As hokey as it may sound, when a person comes to work every day and sees his red tab isn't the highest one up there, he will work that much harder."

While the initial attempts to change the work methods of his own group weren't smooth, the group eventually got the hang of it and began to make demands on Buehler. As the orders for more products increased, the managers wanted assurances that the products would be available on time from other units responsible for production. When they wanted less paperwork, Buehler reduced the contract from four pages to one. When they wanted quicker approvals of customer designs and bids, Buehler had a committee respond in days rather than the normal months of Bell System deliberation.

But with Buehler leaving his group, the traditional way of doing things—"The Bell Way"—seems to have won this battle. However, we may not have heard the last of Buehler—"I'm meeting with my new planning staff, and. . .we are having a difference of opinion on how we view the world, but I'm used to this kind of resistance. Hey, it's not stopped me before, and it won't now."

QUESTIONS

1. If the programs Buehler is implementing will help AT&T become competitive, why is he meeting resistance from the very people who placed him in that position?
2. What resistances are present in this story? How would you go about dealing with them?
3. Why was Buehler so successful in implementing changes in his own work group?

On the other hand, the sales department wants its customers satisfied so repeat sales occur. Below-standard products may cause customers to buy elsewhere. This situation can easily lead to conflict between the production and sales departments.

Survey Feedback. This approach involves systematically collecting data about the organization, primarily through questionnaires.[17] Occasionally, interviews are used to supplement the questionnaires. This is an example of "action research," which was discussed earlier in the chapter.

Survey feedback collecting, analyzing, and solving problems in work groups

After the data have been collected from the various work groups, the information is returned to those same work groups. Each group and its supervisor do an analysis and propose corrective action, if needed. The two major components of this process are the attitude survey (collecting information through questionnaires or interviews) and the small discussion groups (having the work group analyze and propose solutions). During the small group discussion, an outside person (personnel department) helps the group work together to pinpoint the findings, problems, and solutions.

Management by objectives having all organizational levels create and implement goals

Management by Objectives. The MBO process (discussed in Chapter 8) integrates goals at various levels through the goal-setting process. The process usually requires that managers give their employees some broad direction of where the department is going during the following year. The employee then sets goals that he or she can accomplish during the year and which when added to the other employees' goals will help the manager accomplish the department's goals. As you can see, this is an additive process and one that may require some back-and-forward discussion before the end product is attained. In some organizations, employees are encouraged to set personal goals as well as organizational goals.

Goal setting requires not only determining clear, concise objectives, but also developing realistic action plans and systematically measuring the resulting performance. Finally, there are built-in corrective measures to deal with problems of goal changes. MBO is both a management philosophy and a well-defined process.[18]

Sociotechnical creating a better match between the social and technical aspects of jobs

Sociotechnical. This approach is really a series of various interventions aimed at changing the relationship between social and technical aspects of one's job. A popular title used by companies and union organizations is "quality of work life."[19]

This method looks at several questions. What are the major elements inherent in employees' jobs that cause dissatisfaction and lower performance? How is employee well-being affected by the workplace and changes in the work environment? To what extent are job conditions determined by the technology used and the structure in which jobs exist? Answers to these questions provide the information needed to design tasks and jobs so that the resulting work is more efficient for the company and more satisfying for the worker.

One popular and yet still experimental intervention to improve the quality of work life on the automotive assembly line is autonomous work groups. This method evolved to replace the traditional assembly line with work teams. Instead of each worker doing one or two separate tasks over and over again, the team is responsible for a whole unit of production. Thus, the autonomous work group concept requires individuals to be cross-trained to handle any job within their shift's work schedule. They would also perform some of the supervisor's tasks, such as training new members, scheduling work, and keeping track of who performed which tasks during the shift.

One application of this intervention is used by Saab auto company in Sweden.[20] The automobile engine is assembled by a small group of five to ten work-

The autonomous work group has become popular as a means of improving the quality of work life on automotive assembly lines.

ers. They all have related duties, and they decide among themselves how to assign tasks and distribute work. They rotate jobs; each team member learns how to do all the assembly tasks. The group has broadened responsibilities to include inspection, quality control, housekeeping, and maintenance. Each group puts together the cylinder block, heads, rods, and crankshaft. They work at their own pace and they determine the time they will spend on breaks. The results have been encouraging; there is evidence of higher satisfaction, lower turnover and absenteeism, and improved quality of work.[21]

Evaluation of the Change Process.   A final step in the change process is evaluating the progress or lack of progress that has been made. This is also the most difficult step for several reasons.

What are some of the reasons why it is difficult to evaluate the effectiveness of change?

First, it is difficult to measure change over an extended period of time because other major and often uncontrollable changes influence the effects of the original change effort. For example, the elimination of a major competitor would

Opening Story Revisited

Which resistances do you see in the opening story? Several seem possible. The workers may fear the potential of economic loss if the production process becomes too automated ("They won't need me!"). Group resistance and threats to the social system are strong possibilities. With the partitions, group interaction is virtually eliminated. Therefore, status and friendships are changed without the group members having any say in the results. The increase in absenteeism reflects this reaction.

How would you reduce this resistance? Allowing participation and involvement can benefit this situation, as can negotiation with the workers to find what is important to them and ways to give them what they want while increasing production and reducing customer complaints. Finally, educating the staff and communicating the problems the firm is facing may help explain the need for problem solving on the part of both parties.

What suggestions do you have for implementing changes in the Dilettante situation? It seems that the first problem to be faced is the conflict the previous plans raised. The supervisor should face the group as a whole and try to elicit their feelings about the situation. This probably should be done with an individual from the personnel department who can act as a moderator. Having raised the issues, the group can now address what should be done to increase production and reduce customer complaints. Another alternative is to use the survey feedback approach. Instead of a face-to-face meeting to collect the workers' feelings, a questionnaire could be used. After the information is collected, the group would collectively analyze and suggest solutions.

---

have a significant impact on an organization undergoing internal change to become more effective. It would be difficult to say definitively whether the change effort caused the positive results or whether the elimination of competition made the organization seem more effective.

Second, it is difficult for researchers to gain entry into organizations to perform systematic evaluations. Management is usually concerned about the disruption of normal operations as the researcher tries to conduct interviews or get questionnaires filled out.

Finally, the evaluation attempt is affected by the original clarity of the change goals. As we know from the previous sections on diagnosis, new problems and causes may appear as the organization collects and analyzes data. This can alter the change goals as time progresses and therefore the original goals will be somewhat misleading. If the new change goals are not stated, the evaluation may be incorrect.

While these problems adversely affect evaluation and make it the weakest link in the change process, it is also the greatest source of reinforcement for management to continue its efforts to make the organization more effective. The alternative to one of these measurement procedures is to rely on the "gut feeling" of top management—hardly a strong support or guide during difficult times. As a result, it is important to try to measure in some fashion whether or not the intervention is working. The following are general guidelines:

1. Do *not* establish just one measurement that occurs only at the conclusion of the change. Instead, conduct a series of measurements over an extended period of time. This is important because change does not always take place immediately after the intervention. In some cases there is a lag time, which reflects people learning how to use the new system.

2. Recognize how complex the change process is—cause-and-effect relationships are rarely very direct in nature, much less completely understood by researchers. An intervention may not have a direct cause-and-effect relationship to other factors. For example, implementing an MBO system may not improve coordination between departments immediately. Other factors may hinder the interdepartmental cooperation, and the MBO system may address only some of the issues.

3. Don't be overly dependent on quantitative measures to the exclusion of some qualitative ones. Most managers are more comfortable with numerical signs of progress, such as profits, costs, down time, turnover, and accidents. Yet many interventions will first affect employee feelings and reactions to the intervention itself. These qualitative measures can be effective guides to the depth, speed, and even initial success of a particular change intervention. If positive results are reported, it may provide additional incentive to continue the process even though the quantitative measures haven't yet responded. An example of qualitative measurement is an attitude survey or even testimonials about the change process.

What are some ways to improve how we evaluate change?

Opening Story Revisited

I f anything can be learned from the situation at Dilettante, it is that human responses and reactions are important considerations whenever a change program is designed. In the same sense, measuring the employees' reactions to a change program should also be included. In Dilettante's case, an employee attitude survey should precede any change proposals and should follow the change program. This is in addition to the quantitative measures of production and customer complaints. In addition, the supervisor and management should have done intermediate testing to see how workers were reacting to the changes as they were being implemented. This may have given management clues as to possible future problems.

LEARNING SUMMARY

1. Organizations face many pressures for change, including the need for more information, higher technology, longer time frame, more self-reliance, and multiple choices.
2. One model for the change process includes pressures that influence management to change, diagnosis of the situation, selection of alternatives, and evaluation of the effectiveness of the change.
3. During the diagnosis stage, a manager can use the traditional approach with little employee involvement or the "action research" approach with more employee involvement. Data collection can include interviewing, questionnaires, sensing, collages and drawings, and observations.
4. The change process may meet with resistance caused by the effects of the change. Resistance can stem from several sources: economic loss, knowledge and skill obsolescence, fear of the unknown, group resistance, threats to the social system, and threats to power and influence.
5. The most effective methods to reduce resistance include education and communication, participation and involvement, facilitation and support, and negotiation and agreement. If these do not produce results, management may resort to manipulation, co-optation, and forms of coercion.
6. Interventions are the means to manage the change. The major interventions can be classified by levels—individual, group, intergroup, and organization. They include life planning, job design, team building, conflict resolution, survey feedback, management by objectives, and sociotechnical.
7. While evaluation is difficult because of other uncontrollable events and the potential disruption caused by the evaluation, it should be attempted to help support the change effort and, if necessary, redirect it.

ANSWERS TO "WHAT'S YOUR OPINION?"

1. True   There are many pressures constantly facing a manager that may require action to correct or take advantage of the situation.
2. True   This statement reflects the current trend to become more effective as an organization and as managers in these organizations.
3. False   This a popular notion—to wait and not create stress in workers—but usually the opposite happens: workers resent not being told.
4. False   This is difficult process because of other noncontrollable events and the necessary intrusion that evaluation may require.
5. True   There are six major reasons change is resisted: economic loss, knowledge and skill obsolescence, fear of the unknown, group resistance, threats to social system, and threats to power and influence.
6. True   Many times we quickly grab at the first signs of problems in the organization. These may only be symptoms and not the real causes of the problems needing correction. As a result the change goals may reflect symptoms and not true causes.

Action research

Alternative generation

Collages and drawings

Conflict resolution

Data collection approaches

Diagnosis

Economic loss

Education and communication

Evaluation of change

Explicit and implicit coercion

Facilitation and support

Fear of unknowns

Force field analysis

Group resistance

Intervention

Interviewing

Job design

Knowledge and skill obsolescence

Life planning

Management by objectives

Manipulation

Negotiations and agreement

Observation

Participation and involvement

Pressures for change

Questionnaires

Resistance

Sensing

Sociotechnical

Team building

Threats to power and influence

Threats to social system

HUMAN RELATIONS APPLICATIONS

In this section we will look at one organization that needs to make a major change in its culture and management practices to remain competitive. We will also review how managers use the popular tool, force field analysis. We will use this system to identify what areas the company needs to address. Finally, we suggest a series of guidelines that can help either a supervisor or an employee more successfully deal with changes.

How Difficult Is It to Change an Organization's Culture?

While hard times, such as a recession, force companies to pursue back-to-basics strategies, Emerson Electric Company has taken that approach all along—through the good and the bad times. Its main strategies include reinvesting in basic businesses, relentless cost-cutting, and continual product improvement. Its products range from appliances, pump motors, and heating elements to consumer products such as tools, fans, chain saws, and garbage disposals. In the last twenty-five years, it has consistently outperformed most U.S. manufacturers.

Ironically, though, Emerson's very success in building a corporate culture that focuses so thoroughly on year-by-year returns may hamper its quest to deliver the new technology its markets demand. A culture that was built on cost-cutting and total dedication to the bottom line must be made flexible enough to stimulate the development of technologies and products whose payoff may be years down the road.

Chairman Charles Knight shares this concern, even though under his leadership tight management controls were developed. During the 1980s, Knight is discarding some of his caution. Knowing that Emerson must change, he is spending money where he once conserved it. In contrast to the recessions of the 1970s, Emerson is not reducing its research-and-development expenditures for new products to improve short-term earnings.

But so deeply embedded is Emerson's old culture that some company officials still question whether top management will stick to its new policy if success does not come quickly. For example, managers at one division worry that an important new product might be dropped if profits suffer for any extended period. Their concern is generated from the compensation system that affects division management. While 10 percent to 15 percent of the bonuses awarded is tied to the development of new products, some 50 percent of their bonuses still rides on their bottom-line results.

Another facet of management's concern about Emerson's ability to change is the tradition of being highly decentralized. Emerson must now build a new structure that fosters the sharing of scarce human and financial resources. Emerson had consistently encouraged personnel to identify with their divisions. In fact, divisions kept their own names, and employees' loyalty was to their divisions, not Emerson. Now staff are being asked to contribute engineering, marketing, and manufacturing expertise and resources to interdivisional goals and programs.[22] Where do you begin in this situation? This is reflective of the complexity that managers face as they decide what needs to be done and how to do it.

Using the model presented in Figure 9–2, we can see that Emerson Electric is facing clear external forces of competition. This situation means that some of the past practices of cost-cutting and short-term orientation need to be changed. This situation also shows that the reality of making these changes means more than verbal statements. It is mentioned that incentive programs do not support long-term orientations. Also past relationships between departments do not support cooperation but rather separation.

For Knight to begin making changes a clear diagnosis of the situation needs to be done. Since this is such an important step we will spend time in the next application discussing the use of the force field analysis using Emerson as an example.

Applications of Force Field Analysis

Previously we talked about force field analysis as an analytical tool. Does it really work? Do managers actually use this kind of approach in analyzing change situations? Based on our experience, the answer is ''yes!''

One of the best explanations of force field analysis is in the book *Management: An Experiential Approach.*[23] Using this as a guide, the manager briefly describes the situation as it now exists and the desired situation. Having done this in just a few words, the manager then identifies those forces that are tending to keep the situation as it is and those that are tending to change the situation in the desired direction.

It is suggested that the manager should look in four broad areas for both driving and restraining forces:

□ *Technology forces*—forces that relate to the technology of the change. For example, a manager may desire to increase productivity by 10 percent, but the available equipment can't meet that goal. The fact that the technology isn't available is a restraining force. If it were available, it would be a driving force.
□ *Individual/social forces*—forces related to any of the individuals involved in the situation. For instance, the proposed change may be in the area of greatest interest to the organization's chief executive officer (CEO). The fact that the CEO is interested in the change becomes a driving force. On the other hand, members of a work group see that the change will break up their group and resist this because of the friendships. This becomes a restraining force.
□ *Organizational forces*—forces that relate to the particular organization involved (its culture, management practices, norms, and history). These factors can be either supportive or nonsupportive of the change. For example, a bureaucratic culture usually isn't supportive of an MBO system because of the participatory nature of most MBO programs.
□ *External forces*—any forces outside the organization that relate to the change. For example, a competitor may initiate a new factory rebate program to move products, or the government may institute a new regulation for safety. These types of external forces can be either driving or restraining forces for change in the organization.

After identifying these forces, the manager evaluates the forces according to how strong they are. This is a subjective indication of whether the force is strong, mid-level, or weak. This helps the manager focus on the real issues.

The next step is to evaluate the forces in terms of the ability to control or influence them. Again this evaluation can be quite general, since it is also a subjective judgment. The purpose of this step is to determine the most effective places to apply resources available to implement change. For example, an organizational culture is difficult to influence directly, but an incentive system (which supports the present culture) can be changed and therefore is one possible starting point for the manager. After this analysis, the next step is to develop and implement an action plan based on the strength and influenceability of the various forces.

One limitation of this process is that the resulting analysis is based on the manager's *perception* of the situation. As we know from Chapter 2, this is a tricky area. However, this same problem of perception can become an advantage if the manager decides to share the power and asks subordinates to join the analysis. Then the perceptions become shared and, therefore, influenced by one another. In this manner, the force field becomes a form of communications between individuals. This sharing of information will help the manager know better if more

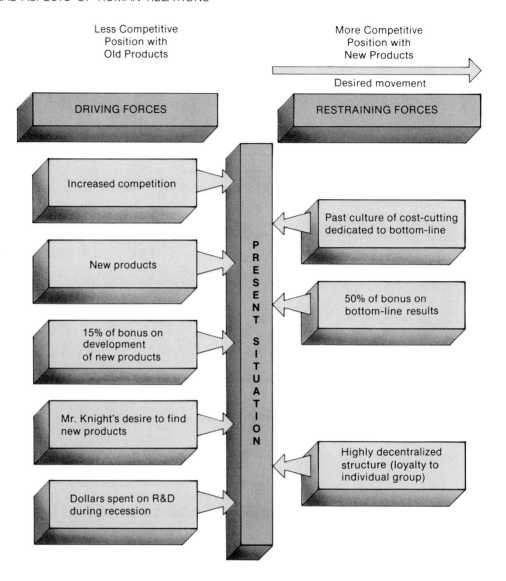

FIGURE 9 – 9
Force field analysis of
Emerson Electric
Company

preparation is needed because workers perceive the situation differently than the manager.

Returning to the Emerson situation, we can now see how Knight and his staff could use the force field analysis to identify key situational variables on which to focus resources. A picture of the possible force field is contained in Figure 9–9. We can see that three of the previous areas—individual/social, organizational, and external forces—are present. At this point, Knight and his staff could evaluate the strength of each force and its controllability. After this analysis, the group can develop appropriate action plans.

In this chapter we saw how universal is the need to manage the change process. The reason is clear—change is continually happening. In some cases we are the initiators of change and in other situations we have to live with changes others have decreed. In either situation, we feel strongly that certain guidelines can improve the chance of success to either live with or initiate changes. The following are our suggestions.

PERSONAL GUIDELINES FOR HUMAN RELATIONS SUCCESS

Resistance is Natural. As managers responsible for creating successful changes, realize that people will resist what they don't know or understand. This is natural. The only way to deal with this issue is knowledge and involvement. As people deal with the same problems or concerns that a manager has, they empathize with the managers and can help in the planning and implementation stages. Simply put, don't hold onto the problems that you as managers are trying to solve; get input and help from those who are also affected by the problem and potential changes before they are set in concrete.

How Do I Know People Are Resisting? Basically you are looking for the degree of commitment to change from others. Commitment is exemplified by those who are pushing for change. While it may be difficult to gauge commitment, there are some behaviors that may provide clues about how others accept the change. Are employees visibly enthusiastic about the change? Are they getting together informally to discuss ways of implementing the change? Does the organization's rumor mill support the change? Is the change seen as a way to become more productive or is it seen as another of management's "bright ideas?" These types of questions can point out potential or actual resistance. Now is a good time to deal with these resistances rather than later when they become more solidified.

Assumptions Limit Our Involvement. As employees, don't assume a negative side to suggested changes. Question the reasons for the change and ask the manager to see if other ideas would be considered. Asking for clarity from the point of view of wanting to implement the changes more efficiently will be appreciated by any supervisor or manager. As a matter of fact, a supervisor will probably seek your opinion out in the future if you are supportive in your questions.

Small Is Sometimes Beautiful. At times, it may be more beneficial to test the changes on a small scale. People accept changes more readily if they see them being used effectively elsewhere. Even if the environment is favorable for the change, people will see its potential success in their own areas and it will reduce the uncertainties involved. It will also allow the bugs and problems to be worked out prior to implementing on a large scale.

Is Timing Critical? Timing is a critical issue for a successful change program. If the organization is facing some external threat, such as market shift or deregulation, organizational members can appreciate the need for changes with proper communication. If the news is public domain (newspapers), the timing might be immediate.

Another point in the timing is taking time to find supporters. Successful change managers will cultivate support of those who have the power to make change happen and let them know the progress. In this manner, the manager uses time to build support for either future changes or expanding the present change.

DISCUSSION AND REVIEW QUESTIONS

1. Why do organizations change?
2. What are the two basic approaches for diagnosing a situation? Describe them.
3. What are the most effective means of reducing resistance? What are some less effective means?
4. Why might people resist change?
5. What approaches can managers use to implement change?

HUMAN RELATIONS EXERCISE

Analyzing Change in Organizations

Change is necessary, yet it is resisted. In this exercise you will be asked to describe some change in an organization of your choice. You will need to determine the reasons for the change and the types of resistance encountered.

The necessity for change is often based on technical factors, while resistance to change is often social in character.

Specific reasons for change may include:

1. Need for increased efficiency
2. Changes in the economic picture
3. Growth or the desire for growth
4. New technology (machines, processes)
5. Appointment of new management
6. New markets or clients
7. Legal changes, new regulations

Reasons for resistance to change are often based on:

1. Fear of economic loss (more work for same pay, loss of overtime)
2. Change in perceived security (possible layoffs, difficulty in learning new routines)
3. Conditions of work (change in hours, procedures)
4. Job satisfaction (less challenge, closer supervision, reduction in authority)

5. Social dynamics (loss of status, group pressure to resist change, requirements to change workmates)
6. Irritation with way change was handled (misunderstood reasons for change, change made too quickly, not being asked for opinion)
7. Cultural beliefs (change not consistent with tradition, deep mistrust of management)

Instructions. Interview a manager about an organizational change he or she has knowledge of. Review the material in this chapter before conducting the interview. Take notes as the manager describes the change, the conditions that precipitated it, and the manner in which the change was accepted or resisted. If possible, also interview a worker who participated in the change and elicit his or her description of the change. Then, using the preceding categories, determine the reasons for the change and the reasons for the resistance. Prepare a report containing your findings, along with some recommendations for avoiding resistance in the future. If no resistance occurred, specify the management actions that made smooth change possible. Compare your findings with those of your classmates.

HUMAN RELATIONS INCIDENT

Frank Carver is the supervisor of a small appliance assembly line with 24 workers. This assembly line was in reality a series of three long tables with a hand-controlled center conveyor belt.

The workers were organized into three groups of eight with each group responsible for assembling a kitchen food mixer. The product had about thirty separate parts that could be assembled in ten minutes. Each table had control over who would assemble which parts for their job on any particular day. Periodically they would change jobs (select a different set of parts to assemble) to prevent boredom. In addition, the three tables would compete with one another to see which group could assemble the most mixers on a particular day and have fun with the job. They were also paid on a group piecework system (pay based on how many mixers produced for an eight-hour shift). It was interesting to note that the groups' pay did not vary except around holidays when they seemed to want to earn extra money.

Frank was just informed by his boss that the company was buying some new technology to modernize his area. He could expect the new equipment in two weeks. Once installed, there would be only one long assembly line with each person assigned to one job (no more shifting around and a limited number of parts to assemble). In addition, ten workers would be reassigned to other parts of the plant since the new line was more efficient and would result in a productivity increase of 40 percent. Upon leaving his boss's office, Frank is clearly confused about what impact this new equipment will have on his job and his workers' jobs. He also is nervous about what the workers are going to say. What would you do in Frank's position during the next several days and after the new equipment is installed?

NOTES

1. John Naisbitt, *Megatrends* (New York: Warner, 1982).
2. Larry E. Greiner, "Patterns of Organization Change," *Harvard Business Review* (May–June 1967): 119–30.
3. Kurt Lewin, "Frontiers in Group Dynamics: Concept, Method and Reality in Social Science; Social Equilibria and Social Change," *Human Relations* (1947): 5–41.
4. Kurt Lewin, "Quasi-Stationary Social Equilibria and the Problems of Permanent Change," in N. Margulies and A. P. Raia, eds., *Organizational Development: Values, Process and Technology* (New York: McGraw-Hill, 1972): 65–70.
5. J. W. Pfeiffer and R. Heslin, *Instrumentation in Human Relation Training* (Iowa City, IA: University Associates, 1973), and *Human Behavior* (New York: Teachers College Press, 1973).
6. Wendell L. French, Cecil H. Bell, Jr., and R. A. Zawacki, *Organizational Development: Theory, Practice and Research* (Dallas, TX: Business Publications, 1978).
7. See M. Lynn Markus, *Systems in Organizations: Bugs and Features* (Marshfield, MA: Pitman Publishing, 1984).
8. J. P. Kotter and L. A. Schesinger, "Choosing Strategies for Change," *Harvard Business Review* (March–April 1979): 111.
9. Vincent E. Giuliano, "Communication Levels Involved in Change," *Financial Executives* (August 1967): 12–26; and Richard C. Huseman; Elmore R. Alexander, III; Charles L. Henry, Jr.; and Fred A. Denson, "Managing Change through Communications," *Personnel Journal* (January 1978): 20–25.
10. Peter Vandewicken, "Collegial Management Works at Jim Walter Corp," *Fortune* (March 1973): 115.
11. Sven Giije, "Boeing Bargaining for Future," *The Seattle Times/Post-Intelligencer* (21 October 1984).
12. Kevin P. Nelliker, "Seiscom Runs into Difficulties, and Some Blame Chairman's Ambitious Expansion," *Wall Street Journal* (5 April 1983): 33.
13. W. L. French and C. H. Bell, Jr., *Organization Development: Behavioral Science Interventions for Organizational Improvement* (Englewood Cliffs, NJ: Prentice-Hall, 1978): 147.
14. J. R. Hackman and G. R. Oldham, *Work Resign* (Reading, MA: Addison-Wesley, 1980).
15. R. Beckhard, "Optimizing Team Building Efforts," *Journal of Contemporary Business*, vol. 1, no. 3 (1972): 23–32.
16. M. Dalton, "Conflict between Staff and Line Managerial Officers," *American Sociological Review*, vol. 15 (1966): 3–5.
17. J. L. Franklin, "Improving the Effectiveness of Survey Feedback," *Personnel* (May–June 1978): 11–17.
18. Stephen J. Carroll and Henry L. Tosi, *Management by Objectives: Applications and Research* (New York: Macmillan, 1973).
19. J. O'Toole, ed., *Work and the Quality of Life* (Cambridge, MA: MIT Press, 1974).
20. Noel Tichy, "Organizational Innovations in Sweden," *Columbia Journal of World Business* (Summer 1974): 18–22.
21. Noel Tichy, "Job Redesign on the Assembly Line: Farewell to Blue-Collar Blues," *Organizational Dynamics* (Autumn 1973): 55–60; and W. A. Pasmore, J. J. Sherwood, eds., *Sociotechnical Systems: A Source Book* (La Jolla, CA: University Associates, 1978).
22. "Emerson Electric: High Profits from Low Tech," *Business Week* (4 April 1983): 58–62.
23. H. R. Knudson, R. T. Woodworth, and C. H. Bell, *Management: An Experiential Approach*, 3rd. ed. (New York: McGraw-Hill, 1979): 209–10.

PART FOUR

SPECIAL TOPICS IN
HUMAN RELATIONS

CHAPTER 10
STRESS MANAGEMENT AND EMPLOYEE COUNSELING

WHAT'S YOUR OPINION? T OR F

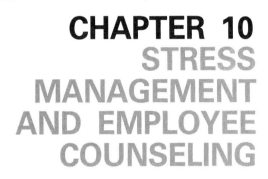

_F_ 1. Stress should be avoided at all costs.

_F_ 2. Stress is a recent event in modern society.

_T_ 3. We can actually identify potentially stressful life events and their levels of stress.

____ 4. Stressors that affect the individual at work are the same areas that make organizations less effective.

_F_ 5. We have not yet been able to link stress to our state of health.

____ 6. Meditation is a specific state of mind that can be described as passive.

____ 7. Giving advice to an employee is a good idea in employee counseling.

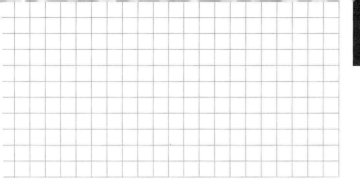

OUTLINE

LEARNING OBJECTIVES

☐ Define the concept of stress and how it affects the body

☐ Describe the major personal and organizational life stressors

☐ Identify and discuss the consequences of stress

☐ Explain personal and organizational methods of handling stress more effectively

☐ List and describe the major functions of employee counseling

☐ Explain the three types of counseling

☐ Describe human relations applications of stress management

☐ List personal steps for more effective handling of stress

Working on Stress

Ah, peace! See that placid, 500-acre vista of tranquil meadows, groves, and streams. Hear the call of a bird. Smell the perfume of hawthorn trees bowed with snowy blossoms. Surely the life of a Discovery Park naturalist is the perfect low-stress job?

Surely not.

We arrived at the park's visitor center on a sodden Saturday morning—just as the naturalist staff was summoning police to arrest a carload of madcap motorists cruising along one of the nature paths. As we left a half-hour later, staffers were responding to another emergency: Vandals had overturned the park's portable toilets.

Finding a low-stress job apparently is not as easy as it might seem.

"This job low stress?" asks Bob McLeod, 24, manager at the Ballard Brown Bear Car Wash. "Ha, ha. You must be kidding! Not when you're busy dashing around trying to gas up some cars and wash others all at the same time. And to cap things off, you may have to replace a radio antenna that's been broken off."[1]

OK, let's try a larger organization. Our next visit is to a large high-tech company making computer equipment.

Tom Van Meter is an executive managing an exciting new product development group. One of his key marketing specialists, Bill McDivit, has become very irritable, and Tom thinks he smells alcohol during meetings when Bill is present. Tom is surprised because he has just offered Bill more job responsibilities and a possible promotion if this product is successful.

Let's visit a production worker. Surely, that job can't be too stressful.

Nancy Collens is a small electronics assembler. She puts two wire packs on a circuit board and uses a special soldering tool that handles eight wires at a time. She can do the entire operation in 20 seconds. Nancy seems to be in a trance. She says it helps her face the job day in and day out. She calls it "spacing out." Her boss says that she is a pretty good worker when she comes to work, but she is on probation for the excessive number of absences.

Our travels seem to continually end in stressful jobs! What is happening here?

UNDERSTANDING STRESS

We all experience stress at some point in our daily lives. To deal with the issue of stress, we need to put it into perspective. Figure 10–1 shows a general model to understand some of the links.

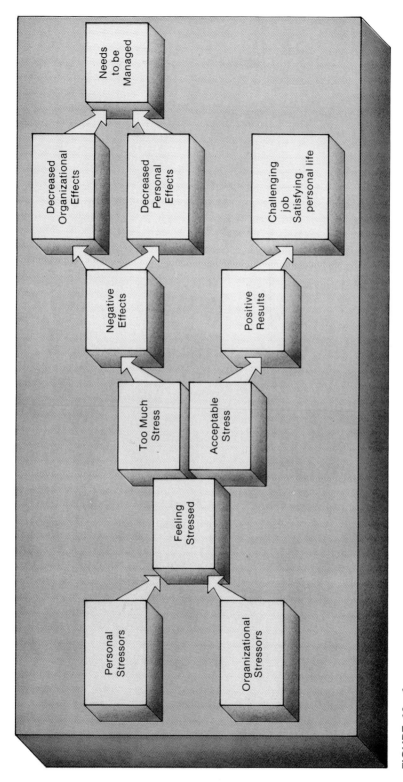

FIGURE 10 – 1
Model of stress links

299

FIGURE 10 – 2
Relationship between stress level and productivity

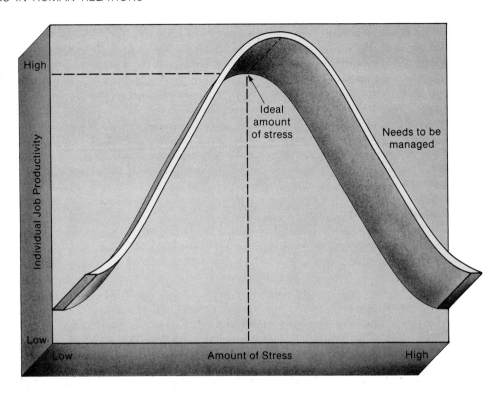

Is all stress bad for the individual?

The causes of stress are problems and issues in either personal or organizational areas. But not all stress is negative. Some level of stress is good for the individual both on the job and personally. Figure 10–2 shows a simple relationship between an individual's productivity and the level of stress. Excessive stress, represented on the high end of Figure 10–2, can affect job performance and personal health. When this occurs, the stress needs to be managed. This can be done individually or through the organization by counseling or other programs.

We can use the model in Figure 10–1 to guide us through some of the topics covered in this chapter. We will first look at the stress, its causes, and consequences. Next we will explore how to manage stress individually and organizationally. Finally we will look at some human relations applications of stress management and counseling.

Nature of Stress

Stress a state of strain on one's physical, emotional, or mental self

What Is Stress? Stress is a state of strain on one's physical, emotional, and mental self. Stress is a consequence of or a response to an action, situation, or force in one's environment. This response or consequence leads to physical and psychological demands.[2] Figure 10–3 shows a basic view of how stress works.

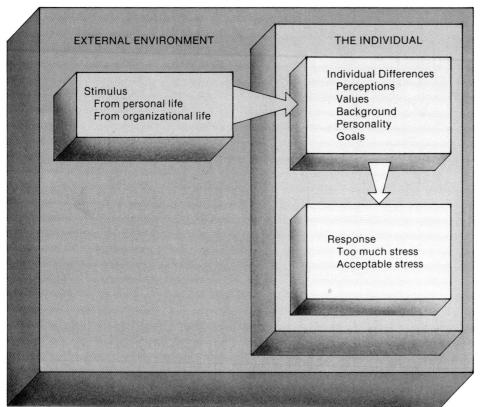

FIGURE 10 – 3
A simplified view of stress

Every day we encounter various stimuli requiring some form of response. The sources are many and various: They can result from our daily activities, such as waking up; our personal lives, such as a fight with a loved one; or our jobs, such as a promotion. These conditions affect us and lead to a certain level of stress, which is influenced by our own individual characteristics and experiences. These individual characteristics include perceptions, values, background, personality, and goals. Any combination of these characteristics can lower or heighten our reaction to the situation. This simply means that each individual will react differently and feel different levels of stress in a given situation. Some of us will view the stress as positive and some of us will view it as negative.

Will everyone experience stress in the same way?

How Does Stress Work? What is stress from a physical standpoint and why should we be concerned about it? The answers to these questions should motivate us to try to manage our individual stress reactions.

How do we know that we are stressed? Figure 10–4 gives us a few of the more typical symptoms of stress. As shown in the figure, people who are stressed may become anxious or nervous, resulting in worry. Constant worry can lead to anger and an inability to relax. Some people may resort to drugs or alcohol.

FIGURE 10 – 4
Symptoms of stress

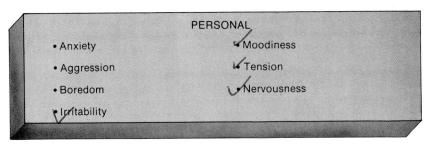

PERSONAL

- Anxiety
- Aggression
- Boredom
- Irritability
- Moodiness
- Tension
- Nervousness

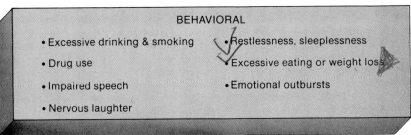

BEHAVIORAL

- Excessive drinking & smoking
- Drug use
- Impaired speech
- Nervous laughter
- Restlessness, sleeplessness
- Excessive eating or weight loss
- Emotional outbursts

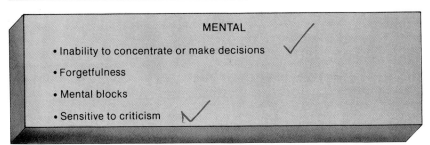

MENTAL

- Inability to concentrate or make decisions
- Forgetfulness
- Mental blocks
- Sensitive to criticism

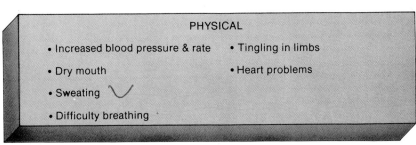

PHYSICAL

- Increased blood pressure & rate
- Dry mouth
- Sweating
- Difficulty breathing
- Tingling in limbs
- Heart problems

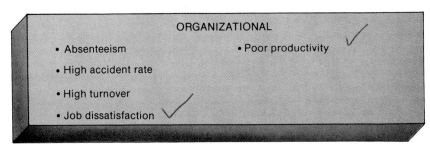

ORGANIZATIONAL

- Absenteeism
- High accident rate
- High turnover
- Job dissatisfaction
- Poor productivity

Stress also can lead to physical disorders if the body does not have time to relax and recover. Some physical problems are of a short-term duration, such as a headache or an upset stomach. Other conditions are long-range and more serious, such as high blood pressure, heart attacks, and stomach ulcers.

Let's look at the process of stress. When an individual faces stressors, the reaction is a "fight or flight" response that includes biochemical and bodily changes. The "fight or flight" reaction results from early times when the choice was either to fight (to kill for food or be killed as food for another) or to run away (escape from the danger). As a result, our nervous systems were conditioned to these two situations, even though modern society has changed. While the saber-toothed tiger is gone, our imaginary saber-toothed boss or even traffic congestion can elicit the same response—fight or flight.

It is beyond the scope of this book to explain the complex physiochemical bodily reactions to stress. But it must be remembered that these responses are the same whether we are fighting for our lives in an auto accident or feeling stress because we have quarreled with the boss. In the physical situation—an auto accident—we would probably relax and turn off the stress reaction once we found out that we were not hurt. But can we as quickly forget about the argument with the boss? If we are still brooding about what the argument may mean to our

What does "fight or flight" mean from a historical perspective?

The "fight or flight" response results from a time when the choice was either to fight (kill or be killed) or to run away in an attempt to escape the danger.

future pay raises or promotions, we are most likely still being stressed bodily with strong chemicals to keep us in a state of readiness. Continual readiness can wear out the body quickly if no period of rest occurs to restore energy.

Sources of Stress

Since stress can have destructive as well as positive consequences for an individual and for an organization, it is important to identify the major sources of stress in our personal lives and at work.

Personal Stressors. In general, personal stressors can be classified as family, financial, marital, legal, or sexual. Each can cause pain for the individual and an unhealthy level of stress to be managed.

In the early 1950s, Thomas Holmes determined that the single common denominator for stress is "the necessity of significant change in the life pattern of the individual."[3] Holmes found that among tuberculosis patients, for example, the onset of the disease had generally followed a cluster of disruptive events: a death in the family, a new job, or a marriage. Stress did not cause the illness, Holmes emphasized—"It takes a germ"—but tensions did seem to promote the disease process.

Holmes found that merely discussing upsetting events could produce physiological changes. An experiment in which sample biopsies were taken before and after discussions of certain subjects showed that tissue damage resulted from talking about, for example, a mother-in-law's upcoming visit.

In an attempt to measure the impact of "life change events," Holmes and Richard Rahe developed a life events scale called the "Social Readjustment Rating Scale" (SRRS). Table 10–1 lists life events and their stress values.

They studied the effects of major life events changes of 5,000 people suffering from stress-related illnesses. After evaluating interviews and questionnaires, they were able to assign a numerical value to each life event. It was found that those who had a high score on the life changes index were more likely to contract illness following the event. Some of the results showed that 80 percent of the people with scores over 300 and 53 percent of the people with scores between 150 and 300 suffered from some form of stress-related illness.

For your own evaluation, check the number of events you have experienced in the last six months and add up the score. Check your scores with the scores cited in the last paragraph and see if you need to reduce your stress levels with the techniques discussed later in the chapter.

Another famous study looked at personality types to see if there was a connection between stress and who we are. Meyer Friedman and Ray Rosenman identified two personality types: Type A and Type B.

The Type A personality is characterized by certain behaviors: "First, there is the tendency to try to accomplish too many things in too little time," according to their study. "Second, there is a free-floating hostility. These people are irritated by trivial things; they exhibit signs of struggle against time and other people."[4]

Describe how stress can be linked to health, according to Thomas Holmes.

What personal characteristic helps individuals cope better with stress?

TABLE 10–1
The social readjust-ment rating scale

Rank	Life Event	Mean Value	Your Score
1	Death of spouse	100	
2	Divorce	73	
3	Marital separation	65	
4	Jail term	63	
5	Death of close family member	63	
6	Personal injury or illness	53	
7	Marriage	50	
8	Fired at work	47	
9	Marital reconciliation	45	
10	Retirement	45	
11	Change in health of family member	44	
12	Pregnancy	40	
13	Sex difficulties	39	
14	Gain of new family member	39	
15	Business readjustment	39	
16	Change in financial state	38	
17	Death of close friend	37	
18	Change to different line of work	36	
19	Change in number of arguments with spouse	35	
20	Mortgage over $10,000	31	
21	Foreclosure of mortgage or loan	30	
22	Change in responsibilities at work	29	
23	Son or daughter leaving home	29	
24	Trouble with in-laws	29	
25	Outstanding personal achievement	28	
26	Wife begins or stops work	26	
27	Begin or end school	26	
28	Change in living conditions	25	
29	Revision of personal habits	24	
30	Trouble with boss	23	
31	Change in work hours or conditions	20	
32	Change in residence	20	
33	Change in schools	20	
34	Change in recreation	19	
35	Change in church activities	19	
36	Change in social activities	18	
37	Mortgage or loan less than $10,000	17	
38	Change in sleeping habits	16	
39	Change in number of family get-togethers	15	
40	Change in eating habits	15	
41	Vacation	13	
42	Christmas	12	
43	Minor violations of the law	11	
		YOUR TOTAL	274

SOURCE: Adapted with permission from T. H. Holmes and R. H. Rahe, ''The Social Readjustment Rating Scale,'' *Journal of Psychosomatic Medicine,* vol. 11 (1967): 213–218. Copyright 1967, Pergamon Journals, Ltd.

Depressed by Success

When Exxon in Houston announced last year that personnel cutbacks were being made in response to the worldwide downturn in the petrochemical industry, Christine L., a marketing analyst, was relieved to find that her job had been spared. During the weeks that followed the layoffs, however, Christine, 34, gained eight pounds and began having trouble sleeping. At work, her productivity slid and she became snappish and forgetful. She grew despondent, even though she had good reason to believe her future with the company was secure.

Christine was exhibiting the classic symptoms of survivor depression, a phenomenon commonly seen in families of the chronically ill, in soldiers in combat, and now in people who work for companies in which personnel terminations have taken place. Survivor depression is a "reactive" or "situational" depression.

Because of the increasing number of mergers and acquisitions and the related layoffs, upheaval in the workplace is now almost a given. In 1985, there were more than 3,000 mergers, buyouts, and takeovers of U.S. businesses; thousands of employees lost their jobs as a result.

It is not unusual for an employee who has been retained to subsequently leave for a position at another company. One study showed that 47 percent of managers leave the companies they work for within the first year of a management change. Some of this exodus is attributed to survivor depression.

Some symptoms of survivor depression include unexplained aches and pains, digestive upsets, changes in eating patterns, patterns that cause significant weight gain or loss, and chronic fatigue or sleep disturbances. Other survivors may have no physical or behavioral symptoms but may suffer changes in their emotions and perceptions.

Survivors of cutbacks often find that they have nobody to talk to. Often their peers have been eliminated, and others won't listen because survivors are not expected to have negative feelings. This isolation and inability to work through depression can be the precursor of self-destructive behavior.

One woman who called a friend after a cutback got this response: "Kathy, you're talking about something that is part of your job—people come and go, sometimes people get fired. What's the big deal?"

Source: Alaina Richardson, "Depressed by Success," *Savvy* (March 1987): 78–79. Reprinted with permission from *Savvy* magazine. Copyright © 1987 by Family Media, Inc.

QUESTIONS

1. Explain how surviving can be stressful for individuals (all stressors)
2. What techniques might help individuals who are facing this form of stress?

Training programs, counselling (on job or of.)

- information to individual to indivdiuate other inappropriate data; doing other job, too much data; doing too many jobs well or wrong job.

Because of the constant stress that they feel, people with Type A personalities are more prone to health problems, such as heart attacks.

The Type B personality is more relaxed and easygoing about life in general. They are more accepting of situations and work within the challenges presented rather than fighting them as Type A personalities will. As a result, they suffer significantly less health problems. Take the brief test later in this chapter to see which type personality you have.

Individual—take action; diet, relaxation,

Organization—address + be sensitive of individuals; right training programs to alleviate it

We must remember, however, that this does not automatically mean that scoring high on SRRS or having a Type A personality will definitely lead to physical problems. One study looked at two groups of middle- and upper-level executives suffering from high stress. They found that the group with little or no illness had some personal characteristics that allowed them to cope better with the large number of stressful life events.[5] These individuals had a high sense of commitment to themselves in terms of a purpose in life, a high sense of control over what occurs in their daily lives, and a view of change as a challenge to be explored rather then a problem to overcome.

Stressors at Work.   Besides having personal sources of stress, individuals face organizational sources of stress. In this area the supervisor may have more control over the causes and methods to help reduce the negative effects of stress. Following are the major sources of stress found in the workplace.

Identify the major sources of stress in the workplace and give an example of each.

Ineffective Communication.   Stress can result from a lack of communication or from a lack of the right kind of communication at the right time. We each see the world differently and we interpret communication attempts differently. For example, there is nothing more stressful than discovering that you have arrived at an appointment with your boss at the wrong time. You misunderstood the appointed time, your boss is upset, and you are edgy.

Information Overload.   This is a frequent cause of stress among individuals. Information overload simply means that an individual is given too much data in a given amount of time and is unable to deal with it. The person is unable to answer letters or return phone calls, must miss or cancel appointments, and experiences stress as a result.

Underutilization of Abilities.   A job may be dull and boring, or the nature of the work does not require use of the individual's full abilities. The degreed engineer who must spend a majority of time doing routine office work and filling out forms may have stress from underutilization. This can also occur for a blue-collar worker who is limited in job tasks.

Role Conflict.   In this situation, stress results from conflicting job demands, expectations, and goals. To do a job both "faster" and "better" may not be possible. For example, the production manager may want more units produced faster while the quality-control manager wants better quality units. An employee caught between the two managers will experience the stress of role conflict.

job responsibilities changed.

Role Ambiguity.   Without clear job objectives, the scope of responsibility is not understood. When an individual does not know what specific job performance is expected, stress is experienced. Role ambiguity also can result from not understanding what part a job plays in meeting organizational objectives. Consider a

— *setting up proper chanels   job duties should be.*

production employee who tightens four nuts on a car, but does not feel any sense of the total car production.

Company Policy, Salary, and Working Conditions. Employees can experience stress when they feel that they should receive more money for their work, or if company policy restricts them from doing things they feel they must do to be effective in their jobs. For example, a manager wishes to assign a few extra duties to an individual for a specific project, but union regulations do not allow it. Stress also can result from such physical conditions as noise, heat, cold, safety hazards, air pollution, and shift work. Continual shift changes are a great source of stress for the employee.

Job Changes. Individuals undergo constant changes when organizations attempt to become more efficient or competitive by requiring different tasks and job responsibilities of workers. These changes can cause stress for the job holder. For example, a firm may computerize its accounting function. As a result, a job that previously required some decisions and calculations may become merely a data-entry position for the individual using a computer. As a result of the computer, the employee now enters only a few numbers in the blank spots showing on the computer screen. As with most changes, job change entails an element of uncertainty and risk that contributes to stress. Change can be especially stressful for individuals afraid of losing their jobs.

Stress Carriers. Many of us come in contact with people who generate stress within us. The angry boss, the dissatisfied customer, or the obnoxious co-worker can increase on-the-job stress. Many stress carriers have no idea of the negative impact they have on others; other stress carriers seem to enjoy the stressful effect they have on others. Type A personalities are good examples of stress carriers who unintentionally and often unknowingly affect those around them.

Opening Story Revisited

From the opening story we can see short-term stress—the vandals and the portable pots—and long-term stress—Bill McDivit's irritable nature and Nancy Collens's excessive absences. Long-term stress is day in and day out without complete rest from the stressful conditions from the individual's point of view.

   Bill's stress could stem from some personal problem as identified by the SRRS. Or it could stem from work conditions, such as the recent job change with more responsibilities. Nancy's stress might be an underutilization of abilities (only simple soldering skills) or personal conditions outside the job. Bob McLeod's stress may be a form of information overload or task overload (gas cars, wash cars, and fix broken antennas all at the same time) and working conditions (noise and unsafe water conditions).

Consequences of Stress

At this point we have some understanding of what stress is and what some of the causes are. We need to review some of the potential effects that should be addressed by the individual or the organization to manage the level and amount of stress.

Let us again point out that not all stress is negative or destructive. But for the purpose of this writing we will discuss the negative effects only.

General Effects. Stress can have a multitude of consequences for people and organizations, many of which are potentially disruptive and dangerous. We can use a classification system to understand the variety of possible effects. This list can also serve as a checklist to indicate how stress is affecting individuals in an organization:

1. *Subjective effects:* anxiety, aggression, apathy, boredom, depression, fatigue, frustration, guilt and shame, irritability and bad temper, moodiness, low self-esteem, tension, nervousness, and loneliness.
2. *Behavioral effects:* accident proneness, drug use, emotional outbursts, excessive eating or loss of appetite, excessive drinking and smoking, excitability, impaired speech, nervous laughter, restlessness, and trembling.
3. *Mental effects:* inability to make decisions or concentrate, frequent forgetfulness, hypersensitivity to criticism, and mental blocks.
4. *Physical effects:* increased blood and urine chemicals, increased blood glucose levels, increased blood rate and blood pressure, dryness of the mouth, sweating, dilation of pupils, difficulty in breathing, hot and cold spells, and tingling in parts of the limbs.
5. *Organizational effects:* absenteeism, poor human relations and poor productivity, high accident and labor turnover rates, poor organizational climate, antagonism at work, and job dissatisfaction.[6]

Name the five possible effects of stress and list several examples of each.

While all of these effects are serious and need to be understood by the supervisor, we feel strongly that the physical and mental effects should receive special attention because of the personal consequences.

Stress and Health. Health consequences of stress are probably more frequently experienced in the work world than any other place. This is due in part to the large amounts of time we spend on the job and on career-related activities. Organizations are becoming increasingly sensitive to quality-of-life issues and the impact these may have on the human costs of doing business.

A long list could be compiled of the possible health effects of job stress: Cardiovascular disease, gastrointestinal disorders, respiratory problems, arthritis, headaches, bodily injuries, skin disorders, physical strain or fatigue, and death have been suggested to be responses to job stress. Medical researchers have also discovered possible links between stress and cancer.[7]

Describe the link between health problems and stress.

Some other interesting studies address a common myth that stress and ulcers are the exclusive domain of executives. A study headed by Robert D. Caplan found links between job characteristics and stress that common sense would probably not support.[8] Caplan et al. found that organizational jobs can be ordered along certain dimensions. They focused on four occupations: blue-collar unskilled, blue-collar skilled, white-collar nonprofessional, and white-collar professional. Figure 10–5 shows the job characteristics and the ordering they used with stressfulness.

How do one's position in the organization and job duties rate in terms of stress level?

The figure shows that more skilled jobs have more task complexity, more social support, more certainty about the future, and more participation in decisions. Not having these job characteristics is associated with a higher level of stress.

One conclusion is that certain working conditions may lead to higher levels of stress and health-related problems. Lower status jobs lead to more stressful conditions because of boredom and dissatisfaction with work roles. This in turn leads to feelings of depression, irritation, and anxiety.[9] Another explanation for the difference is the issue of control. The more skilled and complex the job, the more the individual feels in control of the situation. Earlier we mentioned that individuals who are committed to their own development and success are less stressed by their environment.

Returning to the issue of stress and health, a few statistics can help us appreciate the magnitude of the problem. While stress alone does not cause heart

FIGURE 10 – 5
Job characteristics and how they are ranked for stressfulness

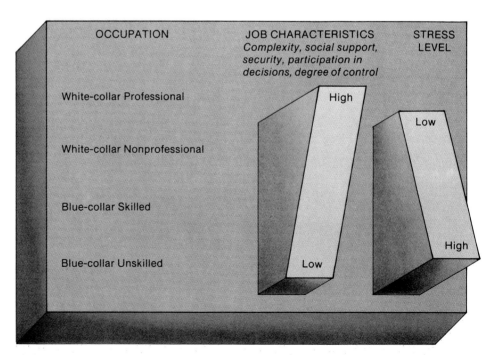

Opening Story Revisited

T he consequences of the stresses in the opening story are varied. Bob McLeod may be experiencing tension from the task overload. This is a subjective effect. Bill McDivit was described as irritable (subjective) and possibly drinking (behavioral). Nancy Collens was "spacing out" (mental effects) and having excessive absences (organizational effects). In addition, Nancy's job is lower in status than Tom Van Meter's and therefore she is more prone to possible stress because of lack of stimulation and control.

While we can't speak with certainty about the health consequences of stress based on this information, alcoholism is a disease that has many health problems associated with it, as well as lost productivity costs for the organization. Nancy's "spacing out" might be drug related and her method of coping with the job and other personal matters.

disease, considerable research links stress and coronary disease.[10] Heart disease by itself accounts for 52 million lost work days annually, representing almost $15 billion in wages.[11] Simply the cost of recruiting replacements for executives lost to heart disease is about $700 million annually. The total bill, just in terms of dollars, is estimated to be close to $30 billion per year in lost productivity, retraining costs, medical care, and premature retirement.

Mental Effects of Stress. In addition to recognizing and understanding stress-related physical illness, we must not underestimate the effects of mental discomfort resulting from stress. While 6 percent of the population are alcoholics, another 10 percent are estimated to be problem drinkers. Add the fact that 6 billion doses of prescription tranquilizers and 9 billion doses of amphetamines and barbiturates are consumed annually, and there is strong evidence that people are experiencing high levels of tension and stress.[12]

But what are the direct psychological consequences of stress? They can include depression, anxiety, nervous exhaustion, disorientation, feelings of inadequacy, loss of self-esteem, lower tolerance for uncertainty, apathy, loss of motivation, and increased irritability. The deadly aspect of these outcomes is that they can form a self-fulfilling loop of increasingly higher levels of stress. While physical illness is more obvious in terms of costs to the individual and the organization, mental effects also have financial consequences. The United States clearinghouse for mental health reports that U.S. industry recently had a $17 billion annual decrease in its productivity due to stress-induced mental-health problems.[13]

Coping with Stress

So far we have explored what stress is and what some of its effects are for the individual and the organization. We now examine some methods of coping with or managing stress.

Any approach to stress management should begin with the individual employee taking responsibility for wanting to reduce the stress. However, when the individual does not assume responsibility for the effects of stress and these effects result in poor job performance, the supervisor has the right to help the individual address the issue of poor performance and its possible causes. We will first explore some of the programs to help reduce individual stress before we look at possible programs for the organization, including counseling and referral.

Personal Stress-Management Programs. There are several possible methods to reduce stress in the individual. However, it is assumed that the individual is aware of the level of stress. We have found that this is a rather large assumption. Individuals need to constantly monitor their own feelings of self-worth, and physical and mental well-being. The brief questionnaire in the Human Relations Applications section is an example of a self-diagnosis.

Exercise. Many physicians believe that the single most important indicator of health is cardiovascular endurance, which can be developed by regular exercise, including jogging, walking, bicycling, and swimming. Research supports this belief. In a study of the effects of exercise, middle-aged men were divided into two

Regular exercise can significantly reduce anxiety, depression, and hostility.

groups, exercisers who completed a jogging program and nonexercisers. Both groups were tested before and after experiencing three stress emotions: anxiety, depression, and hostility. The exercisers showed significantly greater reductions in all three stress emotions as compared to the nonexercising group.[14] The rationale for the stress reduction may be that a person who invests two or three hours per week running slowly and easily for long distances has a handy escape route from the pressures of working and living, at least during the time spent jogging.

Diet. Nutritionists will quickly point out how inadequate the American diet is and point to the need for supplements and special approaches to our diets. The diet should be viewed as the sum total of the substances introduced into the body—drugs, tobacco, and drinks, as well as food.

Relaxation Techniques. Deep relaxation is a highly specific mental and physical state that cannot be reached merely by quietly sitting or lying down. It requires a specific mental approach. There are a multitude of avenues to reach this state— meditation, progressive relaxation, hypnosis, autogenic training (progressive stimulation and relaxation of certain large muscles), and biofeedback.

In the deep relaxation condition, one feels physically relaxed, somewhat detached from the immediate environment, and usually even detached from body sensations. It involves a feeling of voluntary and comfortable abandonment of conscious control over major body functions. This abandonment requires a distinctly passive attitude in which one simply turns over control of the body to its own built-in "autopilot."

Describe the state of mental relaxation.

Mental activity in the deep relaxation state can range from controlled concentration on positive images or messages to drifting free association to the "neutral silence" characteristic of meditation. Deep relaxation is a profoundly restful condition. People who enter this state for fifteen to twenty minutes open their eyes to a feeling of peacefulness and release from tension. Most people report feelings of optimistic cheerfulness, kindliness toward and acceptance of others, and general good humor. Physiologists report dramatic changes in certain key body measurements, such as heart rate, breathing rate, blood pressure, and skin temperature.

Organizational Stress Management Programs. While the previous approaches are geared toward helping the individual reduce or manage perceived stress, organizations also can work to reduce the stress levels.

Change Organizational Systems. Some sources of stress are related to policies, procedures, and practices. Management can be sensitive to employee concerns through interviews, questionnaires, or various observations (see chapter 9 for a more complete list of data-gathering approaches). Once these sources have been identified, supervisors and management can improve systems that not only reduce possible stress conditions but also help make the organization more effective. Examples of areas that address work-related stressors are improving communication

Casino Hits It Big with Employee Hotline

"We're in a high-pressure business," says Arte Nathan, director of personnel at the Golden Nugget Casino in Atlantic City, N.J. Employees see people win and lose large amounts of money every day, he explains. They handle large amounts of cash, and they must deal with customers who demand excellent service. Consequently, many of the casino's 3,500 workers have problems with alcohol, drugs, and unstable marriages.

Two years ago, Nathan researched ways to bring employee counseling programs into the casino. He hired Nechtem and Associates, a New York-based employee relations consulting firm. Nechtem found that employees were afraid to reveal their problems for fear of being fired. So Nechtem and Nathan developed a 24-hour-a-day,

toll-free hotline so that employees and their families could discuss problems anonymously. If a problem is serious, such as drug addiction, the caller is directed to one of eighteen counselors in the area. Nathan says that occasionally hotline operators receive calls from people on the verge of committing suicide, but most callers complain about stress on the job.

The program costs Golden Nugget $125,000 a year. But it's money well spent, says Nathan, because the program has instilled a great sense of loyalty in Golden Nugget employees.

Source: "Casino Hits It Big with Employee Hotline," *Success* (June 1986): 26. Reprinted with permission from *Success* magazine. Copyright © 1986 by Success Magazine Co.

QUESTIONS

1. What are some of the reasons for needing counseling in this type of industry? Can you think of other types of industries that could also benefit from this approach?
2. What type of counseling is best suited to this situation?

(Chapter 5), realistic job performance and goal setting (Chapter 8), improving job design and structural relationships in the organization, designing better methods of implementing change programs (Chapter 9), and managing the areas of organizational conflict (Chapter 7).

How has in-company training in relaxation worked?

Training Programs. Organizations can more directly address the individual's handling of stress levels through training. For example, the New York Telephone Company has instituted a company-wide stress management program designed to teach meditation and relaxation techniques to employees.[15] The employees feel that regular meditation and relaxation techniques help them cope with the work stress and increase their efficiency on the job.

Rigorous research tends to support this method of stress management. One research study looked at a stress training program administered to public agency employees. An experimental group underwent eight weeks of training to help the participants recognize stressful situations and to reorient their personal reactions to stressful events to make them less stressful. This was combined with progressive relaxation techniques to help them manage stress levels. A control group with similar characteristics received no training but were told that they would receive training in three months. The study found that participants who underwent the training experienced fewer physical indications (levels of blood hormones) and fewer reported psychological indicators (less anxiety, depression, and irritation) of stress.[16]

Another area of potential benefit to the individual and the organization is employee counseling by a supervisor or some other professional (either from the personnel department or an outside professional counselor). Counseling is a discussion of a problem that usually has an emotional content and is a source of stress for the employee. Remember the opening story about the irritable McDivit and the "spaced out" Collens.

EMPLOYEE COUNSELING

Need for Counseling

Counseling is undertaken when an employee is experiencing stress because of outside pressures (marital, financial, drug or alcohol, or other personal conditions) or work-related problems that result in impaired performance on the job. This notion of impaired or poor performance is critical to allow a supervisor to intercede with the employee with personal problems. The employee's inability to perform may affect the performance of a unit or department. If left unresolved the problem may spread to other areas of the organization.

Counseling discussion of a problem that usually has an emotional content and is a source of stress for the employee

How widespread is this problem? It is estimated that alcoholics account for $25 billion annually due to lost productivity. This is not the only problem causing organizations to lose productivity. Drug abuse, financial problems, and family problems also reduce a firm's productivity. More than 5,000 companies now offer some treatment and counseling program to return the employee to the job. Many of these programs, called employee assistance programs, are judged to be cost effective.[17]

One study showed supervisors in twenty companies spent 2.5 hours a week counseling employees from moderate to serious personal problems.[18] The supervisors used a variety of techniques to help the employees. Most often they used offering support and sympathy, asking questions, and trying to get the employee to consider alternatives. A positive sign of this study was the opinion of supervisors that they felt positive about this role and considered it an important part of their jobs.

Functions of Counseling

Counseling can perform a variety of functions:

What are the major functions of counseling?

□   *Reassurance* is encouragement by the counselor to face the problem and develop a plan of action. Some examples of reassurance are "Everything will work out;'' or ''Don't worry, you are making good progress.'' This may be fine as a start but it doesn't identify the underlying problem.

□ *Clarification of the employee's thinking* is another function of counseling. In this situation, the employee tries to take responsibility for the problem and design realistic steps for action. As the employee explores the problem, new connections and solutions evolve, helping the employee develop a deeper understanding of the issues causing the problem.

□ *Release of emotional tension* is another function of counseling. Counseling allows the employee to vent the frustrations and other emotions inherent in stress so they don't color possible actions.

□ *Offering advice* to employees helps them develop an understanding of the situation and how to solve it. The supervisor suggests actual solutions and plans of action to reduce or eliminate the employee's problems. Advice should be the last course of action used by the counselor. When advice is given without the employee first trying to solve the problem, the solution is never given the same energy and effort as when the employee develops the solution for himself or herself.

Process of Counseling

Before counseling can be used effectively in a situation involving poor job performance, the supervisor needs to follow a process. This simple process is to identify the deteriorating job performance, document the specifics, confront the employee through counseling, and follow up after the employee begins a program to improve. In some cases the personal problems are beyond the supervisor's expertise and should be referred to a professional in the community.

Types of Counseling

There are basically three types of counseling: directive, nondirective, and cooperative.

*Directive counseling
telling the employee
what to do*

Directive Counseling.   In this form of counseling, the supervisor listens as the employee describes the problem, then decides what action needs to be taken by the employee, and tells the employee what needs to be done. This method, which is similar to advice, can have positive effects. To work properly, the supervisor must listen attentively to the employee's problems and help the employee vent or release emotions. If this occurs, the employee may be ready to accept the advice of the supervisor and resolve the problems.

*Nondirective counseling
active listening*

Nondirective Counseling.   Nondirective counseling requires active listening (this is more fully described in Chapter 5, Communications). It is the opposite of directive counseling. It basically involves the listening to and encouraging of the employee to develop a complete ''picture'' of the situation facing the employee.

Opening Story Revisited

To see the application of some methods of coping with stress for the individuals in the opening story, we will have to use some speculation. The park naturalist may not need a special stress-reduction program other than attention to exercise, diet, or meditation. His stress seems to be situational rather than long term.

Bob McLeod has a recurring form of stress that he can count on each working day, but he sounds as though he is in control of the problem. As a result, he also could use a personal form of stress management. The working conditions could be reviewed to see if special clothing or ear plugs might help him cope with the extremes of noise and dampness. To deal with the constant changes on the job, he might consider a period of time, such as lunch, to remove himself completely from the premises, allowing him to break his stress levels and recoup some energy.

Bill McDivit may need some counseling from Tom as a starting point to reducing his stress. Tom needs to clearly document work performance problems and use that as starting point for the discussion. After listening, Tom may suggest outside help if the problems are more personal in nature, requiring nondirective counseling.

Nancy Collens probably would benefit from a treatment program similar to Bill's. In addition, some changed organizational systems might be considered for this type of worker if the firm's absence rates are considered high. The higher rate could signify a larger problem that needs to be corrected to benefit the organization and the workers. In Nancy's case, the changes may include redesigning the job to involve more of the worker's skills and talents.

follow up!

Once the employee has defined the problem, the counselor encourages the employee to develop solutions and evaluate each to choose one.

This state of active listening is sometimes referred to as "mirroring," in which the supervisor, through empathy, tries to understand what the employee is feeling and then feeds those feelings back to the individual. In this situation, the supervisor accepts the employee's feelings and tries not to judge them. This form of counseling is extremely difficult for an untrained individual to use. It is usually used by mental health professionals from outside of the organization. It is a more costly form of counseling, since the counselor allows the employee to direct the session, which usually is time-consuming.

Cooperative Counseling. In contrast to the previous types of counseling, cooperative counseling involves active participation by both the supervisor and the employee. This give-and-take form of counseling establishes a cooperative exchange between both parties as they explore and solve the employee's problems. This process usually starts with the employee being most involved and the super-

Cooperative counseling combination of active listening and suggestions as to what to do

Cooperative counseling involves a give-and-take exchange between the employee and the supervisor as they explore ways to solve the employee's problem.

visor being an active listener. After the emotions and problems are listed in a rough form, the supervisor begins to play a more active role. At this stage, the supervisor, using his or her own experiences, helps the employee clearly identify the problem needing a solution. Next, the supervisor encourages the employee to suggest initial solutions and helps the employee evaluate them. Again, the supervisor helps by sharing personal experiences to clarify the problem and help the employee develop a realistic solution.

LEARNING SUMMARY

1. Stress can have positive or negative consequences for the individual. A certain amount of stress is beneficial to performance.
2. Stress is a reaction to the environment. Stress places a strain on both body and mind. These reactions are geared toward helping the individual fight or flee from the stressful situation.
3. Personal stressors have been identified in the Social Readjustment Rating Scale. SRRS also shows the level of stress associated with the life events. We can classify personality types into Type A and Type B personalities.

4. Work has many potential stressors for an individual that also can make organizations less effective.

5. Stress can have a multitude of consequences: emotional, behavioral, mental, physical, or organizational. While stress can have negative effects for individuals, people vary in their ability to handle stressful situations.

6. People can cope with stress through a variety of approaches, including exercise, diet, and relaxation techniques. Organizations can help by reviewing internal practices, providing training, and helping through counseling.

7. Counseling is beneficial to the employee and the organization. There are three major approaches: directive, nondirective, and cooperative counseling.

ANSWERS TO "WHAT'S YOUR OPINION?"

1. False Stress at appropriate levels stimulates us to perform at our peak efficiency.

2. False Stress was present from the beginning of the human race. At that time, stress was associated with acquiring food and not being killed by animals.

3. True The Social Readjustment Rating Scale allows us to identify critical life events and how stressful they are.

4. True The areas that cause people stress at work are the same areas that make organizations less effective, such as ineffective communication or poor company policies.

5. False Health issues have been linked to excessive stress, including high blood pressure and heart disease.

6. True Meditation is a mental state characterized as passive and allowing thoughts to pass through the mind without holding onto any particular one.

7. False Giving advice to employees without the employee trying to solve the problems first usually leads to the employee blaming the supervisor if the advice doesn't work. Using active listening with some advice giving is better.

KEY TERMS

Cooperative counseling
Counseling
Directive counseling
Ineffective communication
Information overload
Meditation
Nondirective counseling
Relaxation techniques

Role ambiguity *clear objectives*
Role conflict *production vs. quality*
Social Readjustment Rating Scale
Stress
Stress carriers *generally Type A's*
Stressors *personal/organizational*
Underutilization of abilities

HUMAN RELATIONS APPLICATIONS

Are You Stressed?

Before we look at some of the other human relations applications, it makes some sense to see whether you are experiencing stress and if so, to what degree.

A simple test follows.[19] Check the statements that apply to you and determine your score.

Stress in Your Job

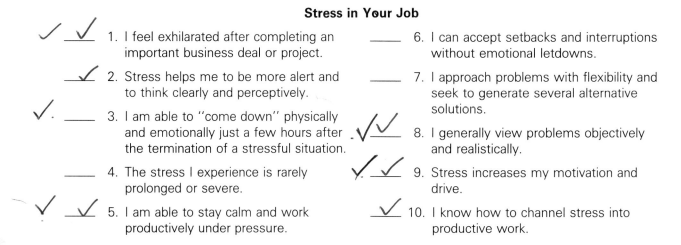

✓ _✓_ 1. I feel exhilarated after completing an important business deal or project.

_✓_ 2. Stress helps me to be more alert and to think clearly and perceptively.

✓. ____ 3. I am able to "come down" physically and emotionally just a few hours after the termination of a stressful situation.

____ 4. The stress I experience is rarely prolonged or severe.

✓ _✓_ 5. I am able to stay calm and work productively under pressure.

____ 6. I can accept setbacks and interruptions without emotional letdowns.

____ 7. I approach problems with flexibility and seek to generate several alternative solutions.

✓✓ 8. I generally view problems objectively and realistically.

✓✓ 9. Stress increases my motivation and drive.

_✓_ 10. I know how to channel stress into productive work.

If you checked seven to ten items in the test, you are at a "comfortable" stress level that probably enhances your performance. If you checked five or six statements, you probably get the job done but are likely to feel tired afterward. If you checked four or fewer items, stress is likely to limit your effectiveness.

You can control stress, but you must first recognize it as a problem. Don't wait for someone you know to recognize it for you—by then it may be too late. Ultimately, it is your responsibility to monitor your own well-being.

What Is a Wellness Program?

From our discussions so far we know that excessive stress impacts our health. This link between stress and health is becoming more important to firms as they realize that health problems cost them money. In 1982, Americans spent $300 billion on health costs with businesses paying $77 billion of this amount. By 2000, health costs are projected to be $1 trillion.[20] Some larger firms are trying to reduce their costs and increase the health of their employees. One consultant to several firms puts this concern into a perspective:

> In order for wellness programs to be effective, you have to get the notion of health in all aspects of corporate culture. Companies have to ask themselves how

they can promote health and prevent illness both off and on site by helping their employees lead healthier lives. But they also have to ask how the corporate culture contributes to unhealthy lifestyles, and how they can encourage wellness through management philosophies. One supports the other. It's useless to have stress management programs if management's policies promote stress. Supportive management is crucial.[21]

One example of this type of program is Control Data Corporation's "Stay Well" program. Employees and spouses are encouraged to enter the program. The first step is to do a medical history and check-up. Using standard risk factors, such as smoking and weight, employees are educated in some of the possible future health problems they might face. After this session, they can choose various programs to reduce risks: how to lose weight, relax, be fit, eat right, quit smoking, protect the back. After the course, employees can join action teams that help them stay on target with good health.

Employee Assistance Programs: Dealing with Tough Problems

When employees experience overwhelming stress from either personal or job-related situations, the employees need some form of help. Enter employee assistance programs (EAP). This program is a structured method of providing counseling to employees.

How would you know that some form of assistance is needed? The following are some indicators:

- ☐ Excessive use of sick leave
- ☐ Coming to work late and leaving early
- ☐ Calling in sick the day before or after a weekend
- ☐ Inability to operate equipment safely
- ☐ Increased number or severity of accidents
- ☐ Customer complaints
- ☐ Red eyes and dilated pupils
- ☐ Excessive crying

EAPs have increased from 600 programs in 1978 to 10,000 programs in 1985.[22] EAPs return an average of six dollars for each dollar invested.[23]

How does the program work? Usually the supervisor notices a steady decrease in the worker's performance. After documenting the specific behaviors that are not productive, the supervisor can approach the employee in a discussion about the job performance. If this discussion suggests that the causes are more than just a misunderstanding, the supervisor can suggest that the employee make use of the firm's EAP. At this point the employee may be referred to the personnel department, which in turn may refer the employee to some outside counseling organization specializing in individual counseling. The result in most cases is that the employee begins to handle the problems and job performance improves.

PERSONAL GUIDELINES FOR HUMAN RELATIONS SUCCESS

The following are some proven stress reducers you might apply:

☐ Be prepared to wait. A paperback book can make a wait in a post office line more pleasant.

☐ For every one thing that goes wrong, there are probably ten or fifty or one hundred blessings. Count them!

☐ Ask questions. Taking a few moments to repeat directions can save hours.

☐ Unplug your phone. Want to take a long bath, meditate, sleep, or read without interruptions? Drum up the courage to temporarily disconnect the phone.

☐ When feeling stressed, most people tend to breathe in short, shallow breaths. Resist that urge, breathe deeply, and relaxation will begin.

☐ Get up and stretch periodically if your job requires that you sit for extended periods.

☐ Make friends with nonworriers. Nothing can get you into the habit of worrying faster than associating with chronic worrywarts.

☐ If an especially "unpleasant" task faces you, do it early in the day and get it over with. Then the rest of your day will be free of anxiety.

☐ Do something that will improve your appearance. Looking better can help you feel better.

☐ Schedule a realistic day. Avoid the tendency to schedule back-to-back appointments; allow time between appointments for a breathing spell.

DISCUSSION AND REVIEW QUESTIONS

1. Discuss how an organization might identify its stressors. What might be done to help employees cope with stress?
2. Identify one situation in which the "fight or flight" response was particularly inappropriate for your behavior. What might you do next time?
3. Describe how individual differences (values, backgrounds, attitudes) can affect how the individual will experience stress.
4. What actions or techniques do you or can you use to cope with stress in your personal life? In work?
5. As a supervisor, how do you know when your subordinate is experiencing appropriate levels of stress for performance? What can you as a supervisor do to help an employee cope more effectively with excessive stress?

HUMAN RELATIONS EXERCISE

What Is Your Personality?

Instructions. As you can see, each scale below is composed of a pair of adjectives or phrases separated by a series of horizontal lines. Each pair has been chosen to represent two kinds of contrasting behavior. Each of us belongs somewhere along the line between the two extremes. Since most of us are neither the most competitive nor the least competitive person we know, put a check mark where you think you belong between the two extremes.

1 2 3 4 5 6 7

1. Doesn't mind leaving things temporarily unfinished — — — 4 — — 7   Must get things finished once started

2. Calm and unhurried about appointments — — 3 — — — 7   Never late for appointments

3. Not competitive — — — — — 6 7   Highly competitive

4. Listens well, lets others finish speaking — — — — 5 — —   Anticipates others in conversation (nods, interrupts, finishes sentences for the other)

5. Never in a hurry, even when pressured — — — 4 — — 7   Always in a hurry

6. Able to wait calmly 1 — — — — — 7   Uneasy when waiting

7. Easygoing — — — 4 — — 7   Always going full speed ahead

8. Takes one thing at a time 1 — — — — — 7   Tries to do more than one thing at a time, thinks about what to do next

9. Slow and deliberate in speech — — — — 5 — 7   Vigorous and forceful in speech (uses a lot of gestures)

10. Concerned with satisfying himself, not others — — — — 5 — —   Wants recognition by others for a job well done

11. Slow in doing things — — — — — — 7   Fast in doing things (eating, walking, etc.)

12. Easygoing — — — 4 — — —   Hard driving

13. Expresses feelings openly 1 — — — — — —   Holds feelings in

14. Has a large number of interests — — — 4 5 6 —   Few interests outside work

15. Satisfied with job — — — — — — 7   Ambitious, wants quick advancement on job

16. Never sets own deadlines — — — — — — 7   Often sets own deadlines

17. Feels limited responsibility — — — — — — 7   Always feels responsible

18. Never judges things in terms of numbers — — — 4 5 — —   Often judges performance in terms of numbers (how many, how much)

19. Casual about work _ _ _ _ _ _ 7   Takes work very seriously 7
                                        (works weekends, brings
                                        work home)
20. Not very precise   _ _ _ _ _ _ 7   Very precise (careful 7
                                        about detail)

Scoring.   Assign a value from 1 to 7 for each score and total them. The categories are as follows:

Total score = 110–140: Type A_1 If you are in this category, and especially if you are over 40 and smoke, you are likely to have a high risk of developing cardiac illness.

Total score = 80–109: Type A_2 You are in the direction of being cardiac prone, but your risk is not as high as the A_1. You should nevertheless pay careful attention to the advice given to all Type A's.

Total score = 60–79: Type AB   You are an admixture of A and B patterns. This is a healthier pattern than either A_1 or A_2, but you have the potential for slipping into A behavior and you should recognize this.

Total score = 30–59: Type B_2 Your behavior is on the less-cardiac-prone end of the spectrum. You are generally relaxed and cope adequately with stress.

Total score = 0–29: Type B_1 You tend to the extreme of noncardiac traits. Your behavior expresses few of the reactions associated with cardiac disease.

This test will give you an idea of where you stand in the discussion of Type A behavior. The higher your scores, the more prone you tend to be. Remember, though, even B persons occasionally slip into A behavior, and any of these patterns can change over time.

HUMAN RELATIONS INCIDENT

John Righter has just been promoted to special products manager of a small appliance manufacturer. He is excited about this new position because it is an opportunity to be creative with a staff whose task is to design new uses for the company's products or suggest other products. Much of their work takes place in creative meetings. His staff is well qualified and very creative.

Within several weeks, John notices that one of his subordinates, Bill, is late to some of the meetings after lunch and seems slightly belligerent with other group members. What is confusing is that the same group member is very congenial at other times and is willing to help anyone with a problem.

This goes on for several sessions until John feels a need to talk to Bill. At the meeting John asks Bill if anything is wrong. Bill says no and asks why John wants to talk to him. Bill feels awkward since he doesn't have any clear facts as yet. They talk in general for a few moments and the session ends. John thinks that he smelled alcohol on Bill's breath but he can't be sure. John asks a group member if Bill is OK. The group member says, "He's always like that." John isn't sure what he should do next.

NOTES

1. Frederick Case, "Working on stress," *The Seattle Times* (19 May 1986): C1.
2. J. M. Ivancevich and M. T. Matteson, "Organizations and Coronary Heart Disease: The Stress Connection," *Academy of Management Review* (October 1978): 14–19.
3. T. H. Holmes and R. H. Rahe, "The Social Readjustment Rating Scale," *Journal of Psychosomatic Medicine,* vol. 2 (1967): 213–18.
4. Meyer Friedman and Ray H. Rosenman, *Type A Behavior and Your Heart* (New York: Alfred A. Knopf, Inc., 1974).
5. S. C. Kobasa, "Stressful Life Events, Personality, and Health: An Inquiry Into Hardiness," *Journal of Personality and Social Psychology,* vol. 37, no. 1 (January 1979): 1–11.
6. T. Cox, *Stress* (Baltimore: University Park Press, 1978).
7. K. Brammer and B. H. Newberry, eds., *Stress and Cancer* (Toronto: C. J. Hofrede, 1982).
8. Robert D. Caplan, S. Cobb, J. R. P. French, R. D. Harrison, and S. R. Pinneau, Jr., *Job Demands and Worker Health: Main Effects and Occupational Differences* (Washington, DC: U.S. Government Printing Office, 1975).
9. D. Katz and R. L. Kahn, *The Social Psychology of Organizations,* 2d ed. (New York: Wiley, 1978).
10. M. T. Matterson and J. M. Ivancevich, "Organizational Stressors and Heart Disease: A Research Model," *Academy of Management Review,* vol. 4 (1979): 347–57.
11. American Heart Association, *Heart Facts* (American Heart Association Communication Division, 1978).
12. J. Follman, *Alcoholism and Business* (New York: AMACOM, 1976).
13. A. Kornhauser, *Mental Health of the Industrial Worker* (New York: Wiley, 1965).
14. S. Lynch, C. H. Folkins, and J. W. Wilmore, "Relationships Between Three Mood Variables and Physical Exercise" (University of Pittsburgh, 1973, unpublished).
15. W. A. McGeveran, "Meditation at the Telephone Company," *Wharton Magazine,* vol. 6, no. 1 (1981): 29–32.
16. D. C. Ganster, B. T. Mages, W. E. Sime, and G. D. Tarp, "Managing Organizational Stress: A Field Experiment," *Journal of Applied Psychology,* vol. 67, no. 5 (1982): 533–42.
17. H. G. Kaufman, *Professionals in Search of Work: Coping with the Stress of Job Loss and Unemployment* (New York: Wiley, 1982).
18. E. M. Kaplan and E. L. Cowen, "Interpersonal Helping Behavior of Industrial Foremen," *Journal of Applied Psychology,* vol. 66, no. 5 (1981): 633–38.
19. Rosalind Forbes, *Corporate Stress* (New York: Forbes Associates, 1979): 14. Reprinted with permission.
20. Michele Salcedo, "The Office Report," *Health and Living* (April 1986): 69–73.
21. Ibid, 69.
22. *EAP Annual Digest,* 1985.
23. Robert Goldman and Jeffery Reyes, "Marketing Employee Assistance Programs to Industry," *Marketing for Mental Health Services* (Sacramento: Haworth Press, Inc., 1984): 92.

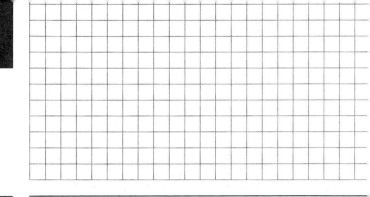

CHAPTER 11
CAREER
DEVELOPMENT

WHAT'S YOUR OPINION? T OR F

_____ 1. Career development is concerned mainly with getting jobs.

_____ 2. Career development generally benefits the organization more than the individual.

_____ 3. Career development programs should be available to all of a company's employees and not restricted to managers.

_____ 4. Career planning always assumes that promotions will result.

_____ 5. Many organizations encourage managers to become mentors to lower-level employees.

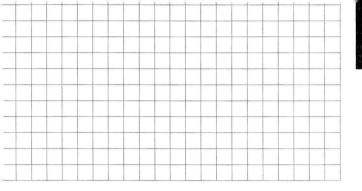

LEARNING OBJECTIVES

- ☐ Describe the major types of career-planning activities
- ☐ Know the basic stages that most careers follow
- ☐ Know whether career counseling will benefit you
- ☐ Describe the role of mentors in career development
- ☐ Identify how the emergence of dual career families has affected career planning

Career Planning Is Easy

Amelia is 31 years old, a single parent, and is returning to college. She graduated from high school in the top of her class thirteen years ago. Bright, attractive, and fascinated by travel, Amelia became a flight attendant for an international airline and flew for eight years. After the birth of her son three years ago, she left the airline for a job in the accounting department of a small company. Amelia has become increasingly aware of the limited opportunities available to her with only a high school diploma. Despite her obvious ability and ambition, she feels thwarted.

Amelia returned to a junior college as a full-time student. She lives on her limited savings. Her mother cares for her son part of the time and the college child-care center attends to him while she is in class. She senses that a two-year degree will offer her only slightly better opportunity than her high school diploma. Some of her friends are transferring to four-year universities and are urging her to do the same. As a young mother, partially dependent again on her mother, and severely handicapped financially and socially, Amelia feels pressured. Should she settle for a two-year degree and its limitations? Or should she endure the hardship for four years and gain the added opportunity and skill that a four-year degree would provide?

Brampton is 45 years old. Ten years ago he became the youngest district manager in his firm. Since then he has watched most of his fellow district managers move on to positions at headquarters—regional directorships, and even vice presidencies. He feels that the brass from headquarters has begun to ignore him, and he doesn't like it. Brampton is not a complainer, but he told his wife, "You know, things aren't like they used to be. John Collins [the company president] was in town last Tuesday and he didn't even call me. I happened to be at the airport and saw him talking to Len [Brampton's assistant]. When they saw me they seemed embarrassed—almost like a couple of conspirators. Or like they'd been talking about me."

The last time Brampton had seen the company president was when they had met for lunch. He had really appreciated that lunch. It had been right after he had missed a promotion that he had really wanted. He had gotten through the screening and finally it was between him and one of those smart-aleck ivy league kids. The kid had gotten the job. That had been a tough time, but then Collins had flown in and taken him to lunch. He would never forget what the president had told him: "Brampton, you're one of our best team players. I know how you must feel, but you've handled disappointments before. You're one of our most dependable managers. You've never been a front runner but you're

always there on the team. Bramwell, the corporation knows and appreciates the job you're doing here. Keep up the good work, my boy!'' Brampton smiled. It was a great compliment, even if old Collins never could keep his name straight.

The opening stories highlight experiences shared by people of different ages, career stages, and personal situations. Our lives have become so entwined with our careers that the two are impossible to consider separately. This blurring of the line between private and work lives has led to an increased importance for career development. Today many organizations have career development programs for their employees. Every worker thinks at least occasionally about the direction his or her work is taking, but only in the past few years have organizations made formal efforts to address the issue.

CAREER DEVELOPMENT

One of the things we have learned in the study of motivation is that people receive rewards and positive reinforcement from their work. Career progress is a powerful reinforcement for many people. Development of skills and increased competence will likely lead to improved self-esteem. In the best of circumstances, an employee enters a career ''success cycle,'' as shown in Figure 11–1.

Career progress acts as reinforcement.

In this cycle, work goals are set to meet challenge from the job. If the worker has some autonomy to set meaningful goals and to determine activities to meet the goals, and receives support from the organization and management, the goals will be attained and lead to a feeling of accomplishment (psychological success). This feeling of accomplishment should lead to increased self-esteem, which in turn will lead to increased job involvement. Involvement then leads to a higher level of aspiration as reflected by increasingly ambitious goals.

While this model is adequate for an introduction to career management, there are additional variables that are worth considering. For example, how a person perceives the availability of career growth opportunities is important, as is the perceived availability of opportunities in other organizations.[1] A person may be happy in a job but leave the organization because a better opportunity is present elsewhere.

Career Categories

Although no two careers are precisely the same, employees can generally be grouped into one of four career categories:[2]

Learners or ''Comers.'' All newly hired or newly promoted employees fall into this category. They are still learning their new jobs and, in the case of the newly hired, have not yet adapted to the organization's culture. They have not yet reached their maximum performance level.

Stars. Employees who display a high performance record over a sustained period are often classified as stars. They are on the fast track—the high potential

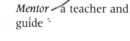
Mentor—a teacher and guide

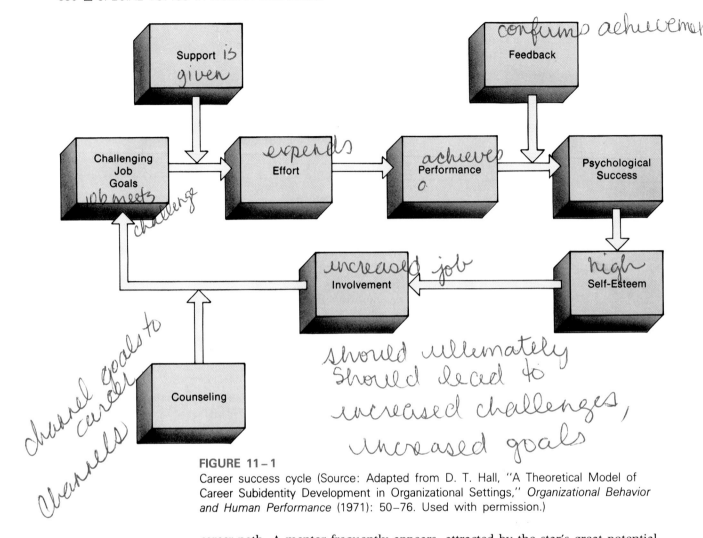

(handwritten annotations on figure: "Support is given", "confirms achievement", "expends", "achieved 0", "job meets challenge", "increased job", "high", "channel goals to career channels", "should ultimately Should lead to increased challenges, increased goals")

FIGURE 11–1

Career success cycle (Source: Adapted from D. T. Hall, ''A Theoretical Model of Career Subidentity Development in Organizational Settings,'' *Organizational Behavior and Human Performance* (1971): 50–76. Used with permission.)

career path. A mentor frequently appears, attracted by the star's great potential. Some organizations have developed formal programs for pairing stars and mentors.

Solid Citizens.   Most of the experienced workers fall into this category. They are satisfactory and, in a few cases, outstanding workers who are seen as having little chance for future advancement. This group performs the bulk of the organization's work, but typically receives little attention. Low morale is a frequent condition within this group.

Deadwood.   These workers have no potential for advancement and work at a marginal or unsatisfactory level. Often they are long-term employees. Sometimes they are the victims of the Peter Principle, which suggests that many people are promoted until they reach a level where they can no longer be effective or "level of incompetence."[3] These employees are recipients of considerable attention either for rehabilitation or dismissal.

Individual Career Stages

There have been a number of descriptions of individual career stages. While no model can perfectly profile the experiences of every worker, the model in Figure 11–2 describes major stages that most of us will go through.

This model proposes that from adolescence into young adulthood people go through a period of exploration. This period will be marked by self-examination and occupational exploration. Some time during young adulthood a field will be selected and a beginning job will be considered for an extended career. This stage may be marked by several job changes as the worker searches for a better fit between occupation and self.

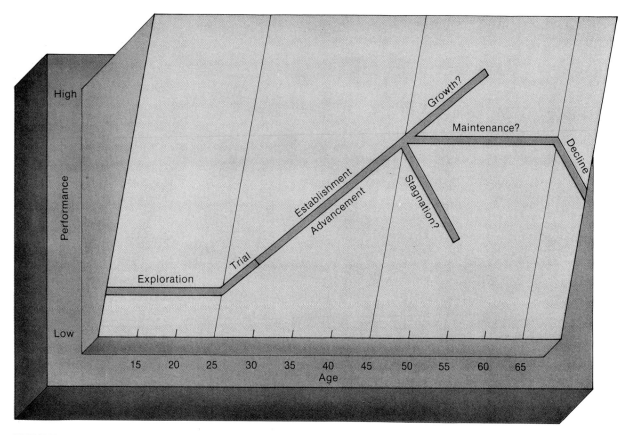

FIGURE 11–2
A model of career stages (Source: Adapted from D. T. Hall, *Careers in Organizations* (1976). Copyright Scott Foresman & Co. Used by permission.)

Many people continue to work beyond the usual retirement age or remain active as volunteers or part-time workers.

The next stage takes place over approximately two decades, into early middle age. Here, the worker becomes established in a career, and if things go well, performance will increase and advancement will occur.

The stage following establishment is crucial, for it marks a turning point. A mid-career plateau may be reached, where the person becomes concerned about maintaining performance level and place in the organizational hierarchy. For many people this period of life is a time for search and re-examination of priorities; for some it is a time of disappointment and depression. Out of this turbulent time may come either continuing growth or stagnation and early decline, depending on how successful the person is in overcoming the mid-life "crisis."

Why do careers fall into stagnation or decline?

The model concludes with a period of decline at about retirement age. While this stage is common, it is certainly not inevitable. Many people work beyond usual retirement age. Significant numbers of retirees even change careers and continue to perform well into their seventies or even eighties. It is important to realize that retirement does not necessarily mean inactivity or low productivity. Many retirees enter local politics, become volunteer workers for various organizations, take part-time jobs or otherwise continue to be active and contribute to their communities.

Opening Story Revisited

Amelia was still in the trial stage of her career, even though she had previously worked at a job for a longer time. What Amelia might not know is that many colleges and universities offer both career and psychological counseling. She should take advantage of this service.

By contrast, Brampton is at a mid-life turning point. In terms of career categories he is probably still a solid citizen, but may soon be viewed as deadwood. Can he or his organization influence what happens next? Will he maintain or improve his level of performance, or will he fall into stagnation and decline?

Career Movement

The model in Figure 11–2 depicted general career movement, but how about movement within an organization? Edgar H. Schein developed the model shown in Figure 11–3.[4]

The three dimensions of the cone represent three types of moves a person may make in an organization. Upward or downward movement along the vertical dimension represents changing rank or level. For example, a product manager who is promoted to the position of director of product development would move from the bottom marketing section of the model to the middle marketing section.

Movement toward the center of the cone represents increasing influence in the specific area. Moving away from the center toward the edge represents decreasing influence. Movement around the edge of the cone represents change to a different function, project, or product within the organization. "Stars" may move rather quickly around the edge of the cone as well as upward. Movement around the edge represents a grooming process in which the star acquires background and experience in several different parts of the business. Because of the relatively rapid movement, stars sometimes do not move toward the center of the cone for some time, simply because they are not in one place long enough to acquire great influence with peers. In essence, their influence rests with someone higher in the organization who is watching out for or acting as a mentor to them.

Which of the three types of movement on the career cone is most important to you?

Career Planning Activities

The amount of career-planning activity varies greatly, but it occurs at least informally in most organizations. Career counseling of subordinates is increasingly recognized as an important management activity. While there are a large number of activities possible, career planning and development tends to fall into the categories of career counseling, career pathing, management or supervisory development, training, or activities for targeted groups. In addition, human resource systems and career information systems may be in place to coordinate career planning and counseling activities. We will look at each in turn.

Career planning is not always formal.

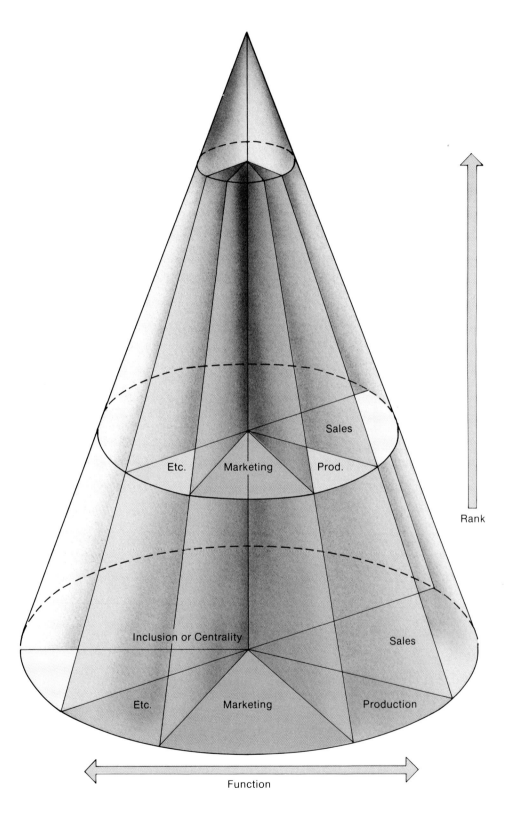

FIGURE 11–3
Schein's model of organization (Source: Edgar H. Schein, "The Individual, the Organization, and the Career: A Conceptual Scheme," *Journal of Applied Behavioral Science,* 7 (1971). Reprinted by permission.)

Rank

Sales

Etc. Marketing Prod.

Inclusion or Centrality Sales

Etc. Marketing Production

Function

Learning and Adapting

Here's how one manager responded to the career development challenge as his company sharply reduced its work force while rapidly automating. This manager of training and development recognized that computer literacy and human resource management were vital to the organization's future. At a staff meeting, the manager reviewed a human resource study that outlined specific skill needs for the future.

Each clerical person in the department was interviewed, and several volunteered to learn new skills. A portable computer was installed, software purchased, and a training schedule was established. Three training directors volunteered to serve new roles as the unit's organizational development specialist, career and human resource specialist, and educational administration specialist. The three enrolled in graduate degree programs in these fields. During their education, the directors began to design and conduct a variety of

Source: Adapted from R. W. Goddard, "Building Careers For Your Employees," *Management World* (June 1985): 14. Used by permission.

new seminars for management and supervisory personnel. The organization's recruiting and training programs were analyzed and new strategies were developed for recruiting and developing employees.

Today the career development cycle is complete. Several clerical staffers have acquired new skills, expanded their jobs, and increased their value to the organization. The three training directors have earned new titles, additional staff, and new responsibilities. The manager has increased the service capabilities of his department. Multiple career goals and organizational objectives have been attained.

QUESTIONS

1. In what ways is this story an example of the management of change?
2. What risks did the training directors take in volunteering for new positions?
3. In what ways does this program fit the model shown in Figure 11–1?

Career Counseling. Career counseling may occur at several points in a person's career. In an organization, some counseling may occur as early as the initial employment interview. Applicants are often asked to talk about their career hopes and plans, and the interviewer may provide both advice and information during the interview. Once an employee is in place, an excellent time for career counseling to occur is at the performance appraisal meeting. Performance appraisal should focus on the future as well as the past, and career counseling is a natural part of such discussion. Counseling can also occur as part of the daily interchange between supervisor and subordinate.

There are more formal procedures for career counseling, including psychological testing, vocational interest testing, and other assessment techniques, as well as techniques for career planning. Formal programs are more likely to be found in large organizations than in small ones. As we noted earlier, most colleges and universities can provide career planning assistance to students.

Career Pathing. Career pathing is a type of career planning in which an organization actively participates in the development of employees' careers. Pathing can take several forms, ranging from programs to help managers acquire necessary experience for future jobs to planned job progression for high-potential employees. Job rotation is sometimes used to prepare first-level supervisors for higher level positions. In this type of job rotation, the supervisors are moved through various departments rather than simply through jobs in one department.

Mentors play four primary roles.

Management or Supervisory Development. There are often two different emphases to management development. One type of development is concerned with identifying and nurturing people who are not yet managers. Many organizations have special programs to identify management potential among hourly workers, coupled with training and development programs to prepare such workers to become supervisors.

The second type of development is aimed at the continuing development of people who are already in management positions. Many companies encourage higher-level managers to spend some of their time developing the managers who report to them. A substantial portion of large companies have in-house management programs. These programs typically have a series of courses designed to sharpen the skills of managers at all levels and to prepare them for added responsibility.

Management development committees are sometimes used to oversee development opportunities with the management group. This is sometimes done by annually reviewing the strengths and weaknesses of each manager. A five-year career plan may be developed in consultation with each manager and the committee will oversee the individual's development in terms of the plan. Such attention is usually reinforcing to the individual. An additional benefit is that there is likely to be great congruence between the individual and organizational goals.

Opening Story Revisited

Amelia could benefit greatly from career counseling. Although she is receiving advice from her friends, she should talk to someone skilled in this type of counseling. Amelia needs help in defining her own desires about a career, and information about the skill and educational requirements needed. Only then can she truly develop a career plan.

Brampton is probably a candidate for targeted group membership, though he apparently doesn't view himself that way. It is obvious that higher-level management feels Brampton has gone as far as he can in the organization. A refresher management course would probably give Brampton the recognition he wants and deserves, and might improve his motivation, performance, and satisfaction.

Training. Training programs are generally not as well coordinated as formal development programs, but can still be instrumental for individual development. The range of possible training experiences is immense, which is both a benefit and a potential liability. If left to choose freely, some people will seek training that is personally rewarding but that may not directly relate to career development. It is common for employees to have access to in-house training programs and outside seminars, as well as tuition-reimbursement programs for local colleges.

Activities for Targeted Groups. These activities may draw on some of the techniques described above, but they are oriented toward the needs of more clearly defined and high-profile groups than simply "managers" or "hourly employees." Some of the more common activities include outplacement programs for terminated employees, preretirement counseling, career counseling and job rotation for women and minorities, and refresher courses for mid-career managers.

Mentoring: Customized Career Development

A dictionary definition of mentor is "a wise and trusted teacher or guide." Informal mentoring goes on daily in most organizations. Supervisors and managers are generally the mentors and most often they initiate the relationship. The mentor becomes an informal advisor to the mentee, answering questions, providing advice, and counseling in the ways of the organization.

Increasingly, organizations are turning to formal mentoring programs. Formal programs can be difficult to administer for a number of reasons: The personal "chemistry" so important to mentoring may not develop, the visibility of the program puts pressure on the participants, and jealousy may develop among those not involved in the program.

Roles Mentors Play. Mentors play a number of roles. Which roles receive the most emphasis depends on the preferences and skills of the mentor, the needs of the mentee, and the character of the relationship between the two people. Researchers C. Farren, J. D. Gray, and B. Kaye describe the primary roles as follows:[5]

Management development is not just for managers.

- □ *Sponsor.* In many ways this is the primary role of mentors—to create opportunities for mentees to develop informal networks and provide situations for them to demonstrate what they have to offer. This may involve helping a mentee with a problem, getting him or her assigned to a special project, providing exposure to top management, and so forth.
- □ *Teacher.* Here the mentor serves as a sounding board and a role model. The mentor can help the mentee to "decode" the organization culture, to learn the unwritten rules, to understand top management philosophy, and to provide the historical basis for important decisions.

A mentor can act as sponsor, teacher, devil's advocate, or coach to a less-experienced employee.

□ *Devil's Advocate.* In this role a mentor challenges and confronts the mentee. The mentee is able to test ideas and assumptions in a low-threat environment. The mentor's greater job experience and understanding of the organization culture provide a valuable test for and sharpening of a mentee's logic and persuasive power.

□ *Coach.* Mentors should be supportive coaches, encouraging where possible, criticizing where necessary. The mentor sets an example for the mentee, helps him or her improve skills and performance, and offers support in defining career direction.

Dual-Career Families

Two-career families are a recent phenomenon, created by the rapid increase in the number of women in the work force. This is a significant social change, caused partly by the women's movement and by changing conditions in the American economy. While two-income families enjoy a higher than average living standard, they must also cope with a number of problems not experienced by most families of previous generations. The employers of these workers are also faced with new problems.

HUMAN RELATIONS FAILURE?

Foreign Intrigue

Not many years ago an overseas assignment was considered to be a desirable or even necessary experience for an aspiring executive. In recent years, the signals have been considerably more mixed. Consider the following:

☐ One young executive left the parent corporation to go with a subsidiary in London. After three years he returned to find the company much leaner and its direction changed. The subsidiary he had worked for was put up for sale. After hanging around headquarters for a few months, he left to join another firm.

☐ Another executive was offered a promotion to a job in London. He was offered the job on a Friday morning and asked for a decision by the end of the day. By the following Wednesday he was in his new London office. Although offered much autonomy, he found that after a year none of his recommendations or requests had been fulfilled. He quit his job and returned to New York.

☐ Expatriate managers sometimes discover that they or their families cannot adjust to a new country and culture. Those who return early from a foreign assignment are now likely to find their careers with their employers to be damaged or even destroyed.

QUESTIONS

1. What career questions would you ask an employer who offered you an overseas assignment?
2. What do you see as the greatest career advantages from a foreign assignment?
3. What are potential career disadvantages from a foreign assignment?

Source: Adapted from M. Salzman, "Pits in the Overseas Plum," *Forbes,* (10 February 1986): 132–33, 135. Used by permission.

The couple faces a series of concerns, depending on their career stages.[6] Early in their careers they must choose where to locate, keeping in mind the availability of job opportunities for both of them. If opportunities are not equal, they may have to decide which career is to be more important.

Even if two careers begin on an equal footing, they will rarely progress at the same rate. By mid-career or even earlier, it is likely that one partner will receive an opportunity greater than that of the other partner. If the opportunity requires a move to a new city, a tough decision must be faced.

Time demands generally increase as a career progresses, frequently while family demands are also increasing. Overload and stress are common problems, especially for professional couples.

Employers also must adapt to the dual-career worker. Offered promotions may be refused, especially if they involve a move. Temporary assignments in other locations may also be resisted.

Many companies have had to relax a prohibition on spouses working in the same office. Couples with highly sought-after skills can, and do, demand special treatment. More flexible work arrangements, along with paternity and maternity leaves are becoming more common. A few organizations now offer counseling and training for dual-career couples.[7]

Dual careers mean opportunity plus stress.

LEARNING SUMMARY

1. Career progress is a powerful reinforcement for many people. While promotions may be involved, career progress can come in other ways, such as changing assignments and more challenging work.
2. A career success cycle begins with challenging goals set cooperatively by employee and employer. Support from the organization leads to high performance, psychological success, and increased self esteem.
3. Most employees can be classified as learners, stars, solid citizens, or deadwood. Solid citizens make up the largest group.
4. Career planning does not end with middle age or even retirement. Many people continue with new careers after retirement from a job.
5. There are a number of formal and informal approaches to career planning. The most common are career counseling, career pathing, management or supervisory development, training, and special activities for targeted groups.
6. A mentor is a wise and trusted teacher or guide. Mentors play several roles, including those of sponsor, teacher, devil's advocate, and coach.
7. Dual-career families have caused both workers and employers to change how they think about careers and career development.

ANSWERS TO "WHAT'S YOUR OPINION?"

1. False   Career development is primarily concerned with creating a good match between people and their careers.
2. False   In the best of circumstances, development benefits both parties equally, but it often benefits the individual more than the organization.
3. True   Managers are not the only employees who have careers.
4. False   Many times career planning results in steps to increase skills in the present job.
5. True   In fact increasing numbers of organizations are developing formal mentor programs.

KEY TERMS

Career counseling

Career development

Career pathing

Career planning

Deadwood

Dual-career families

Learners

Mentor

Solid citizens

Stars

Targeted groups

HUMAN RELATIONS APPLICATIONS

The quality and extent of career development opportunities vary widely. Some organizations have fully developed programs for employees at all levels. Many more have programs available only to management personnel. Most small organizations have no formal program at all. In such organizations, career development is informal, and generally available only if an employee seeks it out.

Career Change Services

The clearest sign that career planning is not adequately addressed by many employers is the emergence of firms that specialize in these activities. Counselors generally offer two services: assessment and training in job-hunting skills.

Assessment usually involves tests and interviews. The tests are generally psychological or vocational interest inventories. The data from the tests serve as a focal point for the interviews. Many people realize clearly for the first time that they are not in a job or even career that is suited to their interests. For example, a successful bank executive discovered after ten years that she didn't like big organizations or being only a small cog. A counselor helped her identify the causes of her dissatisfaction. The executive then began looking for a job in a small company.[8]

Why do some people take years to discover they are in the wrong career?

Once clients have clarified their career interests, career counseling firms provide training in how to sell themselves to potential employers. Counseling packages vary widely in price, but can range up to $5,000 or more. Many colleges and universities offer both testing and training, but generally do not offer a complete package, as do the career counseling firms.

Two-Tier Employment

A rather ominous sign in the late 1980s is the emergence of so-called two-tier staffs.[9] Corporate mergers, slow economic growth, and increased competition have caused many large companies to reduce employment. Mid-level managers have been especially hard hit.

As business fluctuates, newly slimmed-down companies are turning to outsiders for needed help. Some of the outsiders are actually ex-employees who are hired on as temporary help. In essence, these employees serve as consultants and are a "second-tier" of talent. The advantages to the employer are considerable: second-tier employees generally receive no fringe benefits, can be laid off quickly at low cost, and are frequently paid less than if they were permanent staff members. In the future, many people may be managing their careers across several employers at the same time as they serve on a part-time basis at each.

It is never too early—or too late—to think seriously about your career. A first consideration should be whether to use the services of a career counselor. The exercise at the end of this chapter will help you determine that. If you do not seek career counseling, take some time to think about your interests and your skills. What do you really like to do? Are there jobs that are a good match for

PERSONAL GUIDELINES FOR HUMAN RELATIONS SUCCESS

those interests? After you have identified some jobs of interest, evaluate them with the following guidelines:[10]

□ *Costs and benefits.* What is the cost of preparation, in both time and money, for an occupation? Once you know the extent and cost of required schooling you must decide if that job choice is worth the investment to you.

□ *Skills and training.* What are the primary skills needed for success on the job? Are they skills that you have or can acquire? More and more, career opportunities are determined by training received before entry to the labor market.

□ *Salary ranges and career advancement.* Salaries within an occupation often vary by region of the country. The U.S. Bureau of Labor Statistics publishes occupational data on a regional basis. Most college libraries will have a recent copy. Prospects for career advancement can be determined by talking with employers, unions, or professional associations.

Develop a Resume. An attractive, detailed resume is a must for a job hunter. Here are some hints for preparing a resume:

□ *Background data.* Begin with your name, address, and telephone numbers at the top of the resume. Some candidates bury this information in the body of the resume. You want the reader to know your name and how to reach you.

□ *Employment objective.* The title of the position you want to fill, along with a statement of later objectives. For example, "Entry-level position in financial management, which will lead to broad experience and increased responsibility in the field."

□ *Education.* This should be a concise list of schools attended, dates attended, major courses of study, and diplomas or degrees. If you received academic or service awards, mention them briefly in a separate subsection.

□ *Experience.* Note that we did not say "employment experience." Of course, you can label it such if you are now employed or have held a job in the past. Do not simply list your job title or copy your job description. Give specific examples of duties and assignments. If you have held more than one job, describe the most recent one first. Include dates of hiring and leaving, along with reasons for leaving. If you have never worked for pay or have held only part-time jobs, don't overlook other worthwhile experience, for example, work as a volunteer in a hospital gift shop, treasurer of the school investment club, or captain of the volley ball team. Include any activities that will indicate initiative, working in a team effort, leadership, high-energy level, or ability to plan or organize.

□ *Personal data.* This section will generally include your date of birth, height, and weight. Use a separate paragraph to describe personal interests, including hobbies and leisure time activities.

After you have completed your resume, read it carefully. Make sure that it presents you in a favorable but honest light. Then proofread it carefully. Your resume must be neat in appearance and absolutely error-free. Spelling errors, smudges, and obvious corrections will practically guarantee that your resume will be thrown away without being read. Finally, have the resume duplicated or printed on a good quality bond paper rather than standard copier paper.

Dealing with a Job Interview.   Most jobs require an interview of some sort. In some cases, especially in large organizations, an interview will be conducted by a personnel department employee. If you "pass" this interview you will be referred to a manager who has a job opening. The manager will probably interview you as well.

An employment interview is held for two purposes: to let the employer find out about you and to let you find out about the employer. That means there are questions *you* should ask during an interview. Some good questions for you to ask include:

1. How are new employees trained and developed?
2. If hired, what will be my job duties?
3. In your opinion, what kind of person is ideal for this job?
4. What kind of advancement opportunities are there for outstanding performers?
5. How is employee performance evaluated?

Questions Interviewers Ask.   Before going to a job interview it is useful to practice answers to the kinds of questions you are likely to be asked. Every interview is different, of course, but there are some questions that are generally asked in one form or another.

1. What are your particular strengths?
2. In your opinion, what are your weaknesses?
3. What makes you think you will be successful in this job?
4. What are your career goals? (Alternatively, what do you expect to be doing five or ten years from now?)
5. How would other people describe you?
6. Why do you want this job?
7. Why should we hire you instead of another candidate?
8. How would you describe yourself?
9. How much money do you expect to be earning ten years from now?

We advise you to actually rehearse answers to these questions–don't just think about them. Try to answer them fully yet quickly. An answer should not go beyond one minute. One of the best answers we have heard to the question about weaknesses came from a candidate who looked the interviewer in the eyes and said, "I have been told that my biggest weakness is a tendency to work too hard."

DISCUSSION AND REVIEW QUESTIONS

1. Describe the career success cycle (Figure 11–1). How many parts of the cycle can an employee directly control or influence? How can influence be exerted?
2. The model of career stages (Figure 11–2) depicts a choice among career growth, maintenance, or stagnation at about middle age. How can stagnation be avoided and growth encouraged?
3. Someone has said, ''Career counseling is worthless. If you don't know what you want out of life, a counselor can't help you find it.'' Discuss this remark.
4. What are some organizational benefits to be obtained from a formal mentor program? What are the drawbacks, if any?
5. What are the major problems faced by dual-career couples? What are the major problems faced by employers?
6. In your opinion, what are the major problems created by two-tier employment? Are there advantages for second-tier employees, or only disadvantages? Explain your answer.

HUMAN RELATIONS EXERCISE

Do You Need a Career Counselor?

For each item below, decide which of the following answers best describes you and how you feel. Place the number on the line to the left of the item.

1. always   2. usually   3. sometimes   4. rarely   5. never

1. I can identify my best skills.
2. Lack of acknowledgment of my abilities makes me try harder.
3. I participate in a number of activities, both at and away from my work environment.
4. I investigate new concepts in my field and closely related fields and try to learn all I can about them.
5. I am aware of skills that I possess that I haven't yet used.
6. Negative feedback causes me to slow down or stop participating.
7. I often become so engrossed in what I am doing that I lose track of time.
8. I set my goals a little higher than other people do.
9. I want to improve or build on my skills.
10. It is difficult for me to put mistakes behind me and go on to new business.

31   11. I believe I should be rewarded when I do a good job.

31   12. I plan my career and set goals to achieve my plan.

11   13. I know I am able to successfully develop new skills.

42   14. I question the validity or motivation of most work-related compliments.

3 2   15. When I fail to accomplish an assigned task, I believe my supervisor/manager has the right to reprimand me.

4 1   16. I review my accomplishment of personal goals periodically.

Add your total score

     Total = __23 45__

Scores

26–45   You possess basic knowledge and habits to succeed in the organization. If these are correctly applied, along with a good program of networking, success will follow.

46–58   You possess some knowledge of and ability for organizational success; however, they are not fully developed. An influential and skilled mentor, along with a good networking program, will provide a solid foundation for success. If no capable and successful guide is at hand, career counseling should be utilized as a substitute. Without career counseling, undue stress as well as a "spinning wheels" syndrome may occur.

59–64   Career counseling recommended. Your skills are insufficient for organizational success. There is more to being promoted than working harder and being smarter. (And we are not speaking about being manipulative or conniving.) Counseling can provide the necessary answers.

65–80   Definite improvement is required if organizational success is important. Career counseling is a must.

HUMAN RELATIONS INCIDENT

Betty began as a file clerk at Fossil Oil immediately after high school graduation. During her second year she took a Business English course at a local junior college. Four years after being hired she used what she learned in the course and her rusty high school typing training to get a job as a secretary to the president's administrative assistant.

Within five years the company grew from a local operation to a nationally known petroleum company. The original company benefits manager was named to head the newly formed Organizational Development Department. Betty soon went to him and explained that she thought there were many opportunities in the rapidly growing company and that she wanted to pursue some. She mentioned that she was interested in learning something about computers. The OD man told her of a newly created secretarial position in the Data Processing Department. He explained that it would afford someone the opportunity to work with and around computer systems and to learn a lot about information systems.

Betty applied for and got the job. After a year she still had never touched a computer keyboard or terminal nor had she been instructed in any related function.

QUESTIONS

1. What should the OD manager have done when Betty indicated interest in pursuing other opportunities?
2. What should Betty do now? Be specific.
3. Does Fossil Oil have a responsibility to Betty or to people like her? Why or why not?

NOTES

1. S. R. Rhodes and M. Doering, "An Integrated Model of Career Change," *Academy of Management Review,* vol. 8, no. 4 (1983): 631–39.
2. Thomas P. Ference, James A. Stoner and E. Kirby Warren, "Managing the Career Plateau," *Academy of Management Review*, vol. 2, no. 4 (1977): 602–12.
3. L. Peter and R. Hull, *The Peter Principle* (New York: Morrow, 1969).
4. E. H. Schein, "The Individual, the Organization, and the Career: A Conceptual Scheme," *Journal of Applied Behavioral Science,* vol. 7 (1971).
5. C. Farren, J. D. Gray and B. Kaye, "Mentoring: A Boon to Career Development," *Personnel* (November-December 1984): 20–24.
6. F. S. Hall and D. T. Hall, "Dual Career Couples—How Do Couples and Companies Cope With the Problems?," *Organizational Dynamics* (Spring 1978): 57–77.
7. Ibid.
8. "Career-Change Services Spread, Offering Advice on Where—and How—to Job Hunt," *The Wall Street Journal* (22 May 1986): 31.
9. A. Bennett, "Growing Small," *The Wall Street Journal* (4 May 1987): 1.
10. E. Mutari, "Charting Your Future," *Ms.* (November 1985): 91–94.

CHAPTER 12
WORKING WITH UNIONS

WHAT'S YOUR OPINION? T OR F

_____ 1. Unions are responsible for the high prices of many goods made in this country.

_____ 2. Unions protect inefficient workers by making it almost impossible for management to fire anyone.

_____ 3. Union contracts often have such tight rules about what particular jobs a person can do that they force managers to use too many people to get things done.

_____ 4. Many unions are corrupt.

_____ 5. Unions cause a lot of strikes that hurt companies and the country's ability to compete.

_____ 6. Union negotiators are often inflexible, forcing management representatives to agree to demands just to get a contract.

_____ 7. Unions have served their purpose and, in most cases, are obsolete today.

_____ 8. Most union members are not interested in the same work objectives as I am. They are motivated by security and pay, not job advancement and growth.

OUTLINE

UNIONS: WHO LET THE BULL IN THE CHINA SHOP?
Work Rules
What Is a Union?

GAMES NEGOTIATORS PLAY
Making the Contract Work
Union/Management Cooperation

RESOLVING PROBLEMS IN A UNIONIZED ORGANIZATION
Grievances and Grievance Procedures
Right to Fair Representation
Informal Resolution of Grievances
The Written Grievance
Mediation and Arbitration

LABOR LAW TODAY
Who Enforces Federal Union/Management Laws?

UNIONS: YESTERDAY, TODAY, AND TOMORROW
Organizing All Workers
National Union Structure

LEARNING SUMMARY

HUMAN RELATIONS APPLICATIONS
Why Jim Ansara Unionized His Own Company
Can a Quality-of-Work-Life Program Succeed in a Unionized Company?

PERSONAL GUIDELINES FOR HUMAN RELATIONS SUCCESS
Resolving Grievances
Preparing for Collective Bargaining

LEARNING OBJECTIVES

☐ Explain what a union is

☐ Discuss your own attitudes toward unions

☐ Outline the three strategies used by negotiators, and list the advantages and disadvantages of each

☐ Define mediation and arbitration, and identify the differences between them

☐ Explain what an unfair labor practice is, and list unfair labor practices that unions or management might engage in

☐ List common reasons people join unions

☐ Identify the steps in a typical grievance procedure

☐ Design a grievance process for a non-union company

☐ Outline a typical mediation process, and explain what a mediator tries to do.

The Singleterry Division

Perry Pride is plant superintendent of the Singleterry Division of the C. T. Printing Company. Singleterry is a large plant in upstate New York employing 489 people, who normally work on three shifts, Monday through Friday. However, now it is the holiday season and the plant is operating an additional 36 hours on Saturdays and Sundays. This makes an average work week of 52 hours for the production crews.

It is 11:00 Saturday morning and Perry is in his office, worrying. His plant is the least profitable in the company, and there is talk of closing the plant. Still, his cost containment plan seems to be trimming 3.5 percent off total costs—enough to make a large difference in profits. The union has been cooperative in both the cost containment and overtime areas, and seems willing to discuss loosening up some "work rules."

Costs also are helped by the new $16 million press. Nicknamed "The Monster," it consists of eleven units and stands eight feet high and sixty feet long. Most important, it runs three times faster than his next fastest press.

Suddenly Matt, the pressroom supervisor, bursts into his office:

PERRY: What's up Matt?

MATT: Perry, I'm sorry to barge in, but we've got a big problem! The Monster appears to be shaking and the paper coming out is wrinkled. What should I do?

PERRY: Well, let's see if we can find out what the problem is. Corporate headquarters is watching our productivity. Without that new press working all weekend, we can't make it. How about shutting it down and having a couple of our best press operators take a look at it? A couple of them have tinkered with the older presses once in a while. Maybe they can find something.

MATT: I'll get right on it. See you.

Matt went over to the three press operators running The Monster and told them to shut down the machine.

MATT: You three climb up on top of the press. Get on the railing the maintenance people use and hold on. I'll turn the press on slowly and you watch to see what happens. Once we know what's happening, we'll try to fix it.

PAUL (a press operator): No way. I'm not going up there, it's too dangerous. I'm a press operator, not a mechanic.

MATT: This is an order. It comes from the top. Go up there or you're on suspension. You know that an order from Perry must be obeyed.

PAUL: I said forget it!

MATT: Mike? Nat? (indicating the two other press operators.)

MIKE: That's not in my job description.

NAT: Matt, The Monster is too big for us to be fooling around, and. . .

MATT: So, you are refusing my direct order, and a direct order from Mr. Pride? Why, I'll go up there with you if it makes you feel better!

NAT: No, the contract has clear language about the work that press operators are supposed to do, and it does not include walking around the top of The Monster.

MATT: You are all suspended for two days.

Matt walked over to Perry's office.

MATT: Perry, we have to shut The Monster down. The union people won't help. I guess your success at getting them to do things outside their job descriptions only works when it's a little job.

PERRY: Darn it!

Union. The very word produces a strong reaction in many people. In a recent survey by Louis Harris and Associates, Inc., over half of the respondents believed that unions stifle individual initiative and increase the risk of a company going out of business![1] How about your own responses to the questions at the beginning of the chapter? What is your perception of unions? Are you anti-union? Pro-union? Neutral?

Remember the discussion of perception in Chapter 2. How you perceive a subject heavily influences your interpretation of all facts relating to that subject. One person reads the headlines "Flight Attendants Unions Are Losing Strength" and "LTV and Union Meet on Contract Concessions" and thinks, "It's about time those overpaid union people came back to the real world."[2] Another thinks, "The hard won gains of union workers must be given back because of management inefficiencies." Who is right? As a student of human relations, you know that almost never is anyone completely right, while someone else is completely wrong. What is critical is what people believe to be true, and how they act on their beliefs.

Whether you are pro-union, anti-union, or neutral, newspaper headlines over the past fifteen years have identified rapid changes in unionization. Traditionally, union members were white men working in construction crafts or factories. Today, nurses, teachers, baseball players, farm workers in California, and an increasing number of clerical workers are joining unions, while most traditional unions are declining.

While the ultimate impact of these changes is unclear, what is clear is that people in organizations that traditionally have not been unionized must pay close attention to union developments. No longer can anyone totally ignore unions simply because "our type of organization never has a union." In 1952, who would have thought about hospital employees striking?

UNIONS: WHO LET THE BULL IN THE CHINA SHOP?
Unions: Out to ruin the United States?

Unions: The basis for democracy in the workplace?

Today, nurses, teachers, baseball players, farm workers, and clerical workers are joining unions.

Work Rules

Work rule specific language in a contract identifying exactly the type of work a person is supposed to do

The opening story could easily have happened in any unionized environment. It is obviously a case of union members following the exact job descriptions, or work rules, outlined in their union contract—even when their actions may cause a whole plant to close down.[3] Or is it?

In Chapter 3 we saw that people differ in their skills and abilities, and also in their willingness to use their skills and talents. Motivation is a key to effective work performance. Look carefully at the opening story again. What motivational techniques did Matt use on the three press operators? Did he try to motivate them using Maslow's Theory? The equity theory? Goal setting? It certainly appears that Matt used something called K.I.T.A. (Kick In The . . . Ahha). Perhaps we need to look more closely at unions.

What Is a Union?

Union = people

"The Union" does not exist. "The Union" is made up of people—people like you, your parents, and your relatives. When we discuss unions, we are talking about ordinary people doing ordinary jobs (ordinary does not mean simple or easy). When we say that the International Association of Machinists is on strike, we really mean that a lot of individual people are on strike. There is no strike if a majority of people will not go out on strike. A union is merely a group of people who believe they can get more of what they want by bargaining as a group with an organization.

The Collective Bargaining Agreement.   The formal outline of the union/management relationship is contained in the collective bargaining agreement, or contract. The union contract is negotiated by representatives of the union and management representatives. Generally, contracts cover a one- to three-year period. While each contract reflects the particular interests of the company and union involved, Figure 12–1 provides a list of topics contained in a typical collective bargaining agreement.

Collective bargaining agreement   contract

PAY AND WORKING CONDITIONS	GENERAL PERSONNEL PRACTICES	MISCELLANEOUS
Pay rates for regular hours	Hiring policies	Grievance procedures
Allocating overtime and overtime pay rates	Layoff policies and seniority	Duration of agreement
Starting and stopping time for all shifts	Promotions and transfers	Subcontracting out work
Shift differential pay rates	Performance appraisals	No-strike clause
Cost-of-living increases	Pension and retirement plans	Union security and dues check-off
Break times	Sick leave	Time off for union officials to conduct union business
Basic work rules	Vacation times and number of days	Plant visitation by union officials
Safety rules	Holidays	
Determination of work load	Medical benefits	
	Employee insurance	
	Disciplinary procedures	
	Discharge (firing)	
	Arbitration	
	Unemployment benefits	

FIGURE 12–1
Subjects covered in a typical union contract

GAMES NEGOTIATORS PLAY

[handwritten margin note: I win, you lose; you lose, I lose; I win, you win]

Whenever a contract must be negotiated, both management and the union develop a list of "demands."[4] Clearly, neither side can get everything it wants; there must be some sort of process used to achieve an agreement. People negotiating a contract tend to use one of three strategies:

1. *I win, you lose.* This is the most typical strategy in union/management negotiations. On each issue, one side tries to "beat" the other.
2. *You lose, I lose.* This is not typical, but when relationships are extremely bad, one side may want to hurt the other so badly that no attempt at conciliation occurs.[5]
3. *You win, I win.* Both sides try to develop an approach to bargaining that resolves issues so that both "win." This has not been typical of union/management negotiations, but is increasing in popularity.[6]

Opening Story Revisited

When Matt goes back to the pressroom after talking with Perry, he notices a buzz of activity around the old Number Two press. He thinks, "That son-of-a-gun A. K. Nichols is causing trouble again." A. K. has been a press operator for more than 35 years and, in addition to being one of the best press operators in the plant, he is a strong union person. Matt has trouble with A. K. because of A. K.'s "attitude."

Matt immediately goes over to A. K.'s press to find out what is going on.

MATT: OK folks, break it up. Roberts, Fortunato, Goclowski back to work. You know I can write you up for being away from your presses.

A.K.: Hold on, Matt, I was just helping these kids. They are all having trouble getting their presses in register on this job. I was. . .

MATT: Cut it A. K. This job isn't that hard. Everybody back to work.

That afternoon Matt constantly rushed from crisis to crisis. If it wasn't one press having a problem, it was another. What should have been a simple day was turning into a nightmare. With The Monster down, he needed all of his other presses operating at 100 percent, instead they were running far below their normal rates.

Then, at the shift change at 3:30, everything almost ground to a halt. One press ran out of paper, another had its automatic inker develop a kink in the hose and ran out of ink, a third got shut off by mistake. The list of problems seemed endless. By 7:00, Matt and Barb Thomas, the second shift supervisor, had everything running smoothly.

As Matt slumps into the chair in the office the supervisors share, Barb enters.

MATT: What a day! One mess after another. I tell you, some days I think we have a group of kids working for us. They can't do anything on their own.

BARB: Matt, I've been taking a human relations course and I think we have a problem. . . .

There is nothing secret about these strategies, they are ones each of us pursues at various times in our personal lives. The consequences of following the second and third approaches are clear. However, what do you think the consequences are of following the first strategy? Take a few moments to list the advantages and disadvantages. Then see if the advantages outweigh the disadvantages.

Making the Contract Work

The union contract establishes the formal relationship between unionized employees and management representatives. However, it is a mistake to assume that the contract covers everything, or even that it should cover everything. It is the daily interaction between supervisors and union employees that really forms the heart of an effective union-management partnership.

What do you think is going on with the opening story? Remember, back in Chapter 4 you read about the need to carefully find the real problem instead of spending time fixing symptoms. So, what do you think is the *real* problem—the thing or things causing the latest difficulties at Singleterry? If you guessed that the pressroom employees were reacting to Matt suspending the three press operators for two days, we believe you are right. Do you think group dynamics is important here?

What is the real problem?

If it is a fairly cohesive group of union members in the pressroom, there might be a group norm that says, "We will protect each other from what we see as unfair supervisory practices." (Look again at Chapter 6 to review "cohesive group" and "group norm.")

Do group norms affect union members?

If the relationship between supervisor and union members is strained, with hostility and distrust on both sides, the best contract in the world will not lead to high productivity. For example, the story segment above ends with Barb saying she thinks they have a problem. Take a few minutes and jot down some ideas you have about what she might want to say to Matt.

Union/Management Cooperation

Possibly you thought of having Barb ask the union president to tell the union members to get back to full productive work while the problem is worked out. When there is a positive relationship between union and management, frequently union officers do help supervisors work out problems. However, the most helpful union leadership cannot assist management in developing a productive, effective organization in the face of hostility toward management among rank-and-file union members.

Union officers do not have the same control over their members that managers and supervisors have over their employees. As more unions adopt democratic procedures to elect officers, union officers must be receptive to the wishes of their membership. Otherwise, they will not be officers for long.

It is sometimes difficult for supervisors to understand that union officers occupy political positions and, therefore, must respond to political pressures. Unlike a supervisor with one boss, an elected union officer has many people to

Do union officers occupy political positions?

Opening Story Revisited

T he day after Matt suspended the three press operators, Sandra Staples, the union's grievance chairperson, is in his office at 7:15.

MATT: What's up Sandy?

SANDRA: Matt, you know what the difficulty is. I'd like to work it out with you before bringing a formal grievance. I told the three guys to come in, they are in the parking lot. If. . .

MATT: Hold it just a minute. Those three are suspended for two days. Today is day one.

SANDRA: Matt, you know your suspension won't hold water. Let's try for an informal resolution so everyone can get back to work.

MATT: My suspension will hold up. Go ahead and file your grievance; I've talked to management.

report to.[7] What do you think the implications of this are for an effective supervisor?

Certainly one implication is that the supervisor has to be aware that the union officer must sometimes take symbolic (what we often call "political") positions in opposition to management. A second and much more important implication is that the supervisor must occasionally help the union officer. What could Matt do in our case to help Sandra?

RESOLVING PROBLEMS IN A UNIONIZED ORGANIZATION

One of the key ways that a supervisor can help a union officer is to settle complaints rapidly. Of course, that does not always happen, as illustrated by the story segment above.

Grievances and Grievance Procedures

All organizations need some way for employees to complain. In a unionized company, the grievance procedure provides the vehicle for employee complaints. In the past, few non-union companies had a grievance procedure. Today an increasing number of non-union companies are implementing formal grievance procedures. If you work in a non-union company, this section gives you some ideas about what kind of process you may want to consider at your company.

What is a grievance?   The last story ends with Matt telling Sandra to file a grievance. Exactly what happens next is somewhat dependent on their particular contract. However, all contracts provide some way for employees to file a grievance. Technically, a *grievance* is a complaint that management has violated part of the contract, or federal or state law, or has unfairly applied parts of the contract. Read that definition over again, particularly the part that says " . . . or has unfairly applied parts of the contract." That section is especially important today.

If you are in management, it is easy to view a grievance and a formal grievance procedure as a nuisance. After all, you know that neither your company nor its supervisors and managers ever act in an arbitrary or unfair manner. Or do you? Perhaps you are not aware of the way other people perceive your actions. Many progressive companies are teaching supervisors and managers to view grievances as "opportunities to improve."

If we view grievances as opportunities to improve, we can view a grievance procedure as a formal way for employees to raise differences of opinion with management. This does not mean that management must, or even should, view all grievances as identifying things that the company is "doing wrong." It does mean that we need to view grievances as possibly identifying problems that employees and supervisors need to resolve.

> A grievance is an opportunity to improve.

Who Can File a Grievance?   Usually a grievance must be filed by a *grievant*, someone who has been personally affected by some action of a management person. However, in some circumstances, a union itself may file a grievance on behalf of its members.

What Is a Grievance Procedure?   A grievance procedure is the formal process written in a contract for resolving complaints. Figure 12–2 outlines a "typical" grievance procedure. The word "typical" is inside quotation marks because every contract contains wording about what can be grieved and the exact process to use. If you have access to some contracts, compare the grievance section—you may see some interesting differences.

Often, the contract specifies which union official will attempt to resolve the grievance. Usually the local union president, the shop steward, or the grievance committee chairperson is the union official involved. Once Step 6 is reached, the union may also bring in state or regional union officials.

Right to Fair Representation

As soon as our three press operators discuss their situation with the appropriate union official, both federal law and the contract become very important. The United States Supreme Court has ruled on numerous occasions that a union has the duty of fair representation for all people covered by the contract. For grievances, the union must make certain to:

> Unions have a "duty of fair representation."

1. Make a careful investigation of the facts
2. Observe all contractual time limits so that the grievance is not denied because time limits were not observed
3. Present the case to management in a competent manner
4. Process all grievances that have merit
5. Make all decisions regarding the grievance in a nondiscriminatory, nonarbitrary fashion
6. Represent all people covered under the contract, not just union members[8]

FIGURE 12-2

Steps in a typical grievance procedure. The contract will specify an exact number of days—usually 3 to 28—for certain steps, indicated here by the words, "within a certain number of days."

> **1 INFORMAL RESOLUTION**
> Most grievances are settled at this step, sometimes with the help of a union official and someone from the company's personnel or labor relations department.
>
> **2 FILE WRITTEN GRIEVANCE**
> Within a certain number of days after the incident, a written grievance must be filed with the appropriate management person. Union officials usually help the employee prepare the grievance.
>
> **3 FIRST FORMAL GRIEVANCE MEETING**
> Within a certain number of days after receipt of the written grievance, the appropriate management person must meet with the person filing the grievance. A union representative must be allowed at the meeting, and may, in fact, present the case.
>
> **4 MANAGEMENT DECISION ON FIRST LEVEL**
> Within a certain number of days after the meeting, the management representative must send a written decision to the union and the person filing the grievance.
>
> **5 APPEAL TO HIGHER MANAGEMENT**
> If the grievance is denied, the grievance may be appealed to a higher level of management.
>
> **6 FORMAL MEETING AT SECOND LEVEL**
> Top company management, the director of labor relations for the company, and top union officials are now involved. There is generally great pressure to reach an agreement. Both sides may agree to bring in a mediator. A mediator has no connection to either side and no power to make a judgment. The mediator's role is to help the two sides come to an agreement.
>
> **7 ARBITRATION**
> If the grievance is not resolved at step 6, the union usually has the choice of bringing the issue to arbitration.

As a practical matter, what these Supreme Court decisions mean is that many local union officials will pursue most grievances up to arbitration—without trying to get the employees to drop their grievance. This may seem unfair. Clearly, some grievances are unreasonable. Shouldn't union officials exercise some judgment about the quality of a grievance before they "waste" people's valuable time?

In a perfect world, the answer to that question is "yes." However, we are discussing what really happens, not some abstract theory. Imagine that you are Sandra Staples. You know what federal law and court cases have stated because your union has given you training in processing grievances. Do you tell a union member that you are not going to process her grievance and face the possibility that she will sue the union? Imagine how that will look on the front page of the Sunday newspaper.

It is critical for new supervisors, managers, and members of union grievance committees to realize what happens in "the real world." Otherwise, you may become needlessly annoyed with what seem to be nuisance grievances.

In the opening story, the three operators brought their problem to their grievance chairperson, Sandra Staples. Sandra talked to each one individually about exactly what happened, asking specific questions about what was said and taking careful notes as each spoke. She then compared her notes from each person, identified any differences, and met with all three to resolve the differences.

Why did Sandra proceed this way? If you answered that she was protecting the union by making a careful investigation and attempting to build as strong a case as possible for her members, you are right.

In Chapter 5 you read about studies indicating that most people actually remember little of what they hear. By meeting with the press operators immediately, asking specific questions, and taking careful notes, Sandra was practicing effective communications. She will have a written record for the union to refer to throughout this affair.

Informal Resolution of Grievances

After talking with the three press operators, Sandra tried to resolve the problem with Matt directly. In fact, most "grievances" never become formal grievances—

Most grievances are resolved on an informal basis.

Management must pro-
tect management rights.
The union must protect
employee rights.

they are resolved on an informal basis. While it is important for management
representatives to protect the rights of management and for union representatives
to protect the rights of their members, both sides also usually recognize that they
work for the same company.

Recall that in Chapter 7 we indicated that conflict is constructive when it
opens up important issues for review, increases employee involvement, releases
tensions, helps people grow, builds cohesiveness among employees, or results in
solving problems. Far from being nuisances, some grievances indicate opportunities for employees and management to work out differences. When both sides
approach the problem with an open mind, frequently a constructive solution is
possible.

Can grievances repre-
sent constructive con-
flict?

The Written Grievance

If the problem cannot be resolved informally, a written grievance will be filed.
Although grievance forms vary greatly, Figure 12–3 contains the basic types of
information requested on most forms. Once a written grievance has been filed, it
becomes more difficult to solve the problem. The employees and their union on
one side, and management on the other side, have now taken positions. Basically,
each is pointing a finger at the other and saying, "You are wrong."

There is now the strong possibility that the grievance will develop into destructive conflict. If the grievance is not settled at Step 3 (Figure 12–2), it is likely
that mediation or arbitration will be required to settle the conflict.

Mediation and Arbitration

In the private sector, most union contracts provide for both mediation and arbitration of union/management disputes. Mediation attempts to resolve disputes by
getting the two parties to agree on a solution. A mediator doesn't have the power
to impose a solution or to force the two parties to agree. Mediators are the counselors of the business world, trying to get the parties to be open and honest with
each other, deal with any underlying problems, and reach an agreement acceptable to both sides.

What is the difference
between mediation and
arbitration?

Arbitration is different from mediation. First, arbitrators have the power to
issue a final, binding decision. Although some arbitrators run fairly informal hearings, most are quite formal. Each side presents its case, and witnesses are called
to make statements. The arbitrator may ask witnesses questions about the case.
All testimony is recorded. After reviewing the testimony, the arbitrator issues a
decision.

Arbitration meetings
are called hearings.

Because mediation and arbitration are so important, let's explore each in
more depth.

Mediation. Before a mediator can be called in, both the union and management must agree to try mediation. Without agreement on both sides to try, me-

S & S Manufacturing Company
Grievance Form

Please print all information carefully:

Name of grievant _____ Position _____

Plant location _____

Supervisor _____ Department _____

GRIEVANCE INFORMATION

Filed at level _____ To whom submitted _____

Date problem occurred _____

Briefly outline the facts concerning the grievance and explain the nature of the grievance.

Indicate the Article(s) and Section(s) of the Collective Bargaining Agreement which you believe have been violated:

Signature of Grievant _____ Date _____

Signature of Union Representative _____ Date _____

FIGURE 12–3
A sample grievance form

diation cannot be successful. Next, both the union and management must agree on who the mediator will be. Deciding on a mediator may not be easy. Neither side wants to get someone who favors the other. While the mediator has no power to order anyone to do anything, how would you like to be sitting in a room with an "impartial" mediator who really was favoring the other side? Mediators are often selected from among people recommended by either the Federal Mediation and Conciliation Service or individual state labor departments.

Figure 12–4 outlines a typical mediation process. Incidentally, there is no magic number of meetings required in mediation. Sometimes there is only one meeting, sometimes there are several.

What happens in a typical mediation process?

FIGURE 12 – 4
The mediation process

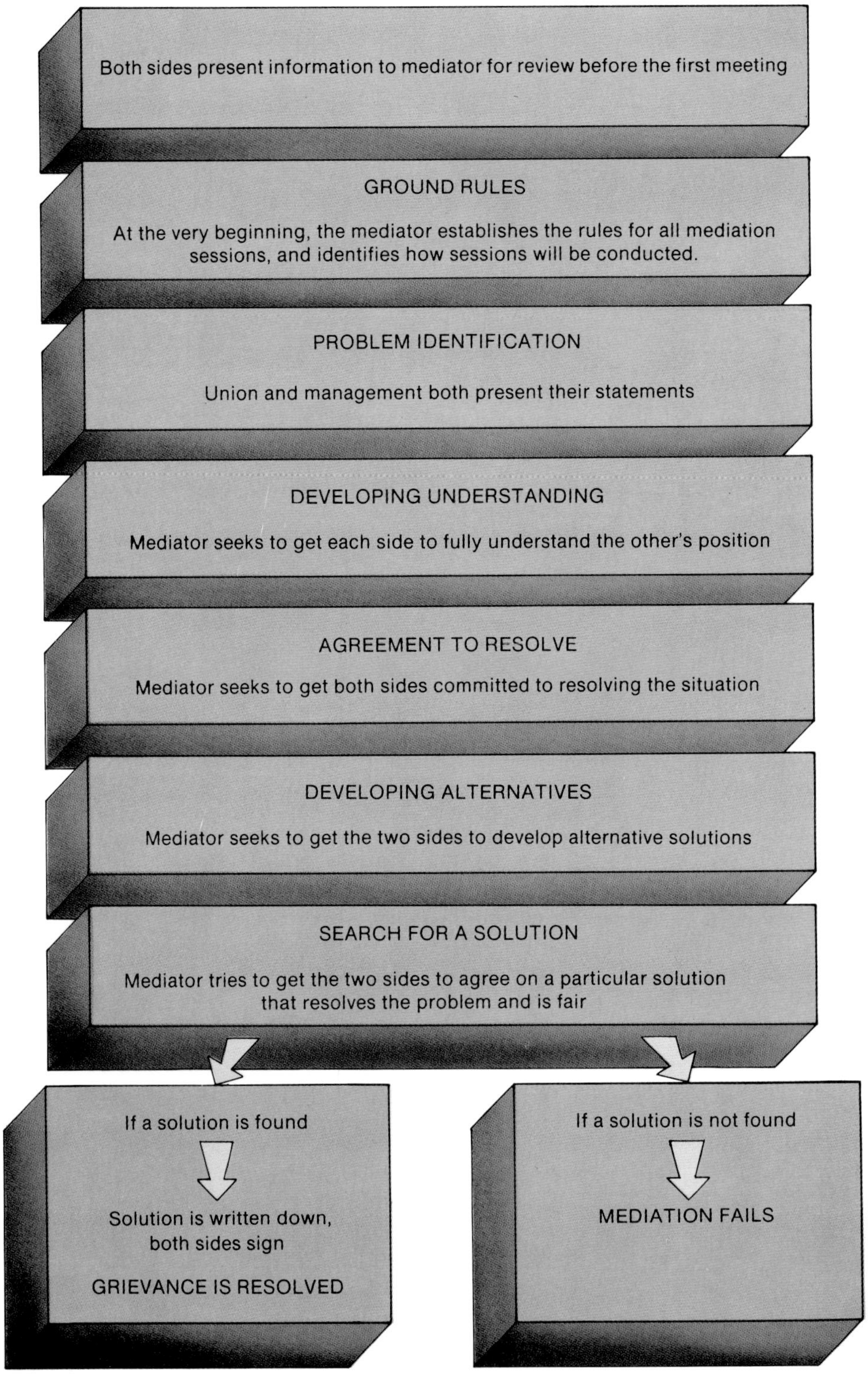

Both sides present information to mediator for review before the first meeting

GROUND RULES

At the very beginning, the mediator establishes the rules for all mediation sessions, and identifies how sessions will be conducted.

PROBLEM IDENTIFICATION

Union and management both present their statements

DEVELOPING UNDERSTANDING

Mediator seeks to get each side to fully understand the other's position

AGREEMENT TO RESOLVE

Mediator seeks to get both sides committed to resolving the situation

DEVELOPING ALTERNATIVES

Mediator seeks to get the two sides to develop alternative solutions

SEARCH FOR A SOLUTION

Mediator tries to get the two sides to agree on a particular solution that resolves the problem and is fair

If a solution is found

Solution is written down, both sides sign

GRIEVANCE IS RESOLVED

If a solution is not found

MEDIATION FAILS

When a union and management agree to try mediation, three results are possible:

1. The two sides agree on a solution to their problem
2. At least one side decides that no agreement is possible, and the mediation process ends
3. The two sides produce an agreement that is later rejected by other union or management officials

Although the third result is unlikely, it is possible. The results of mediation are not binding. Because of this, it is critical that both management and the union always be represented by influential people.

Mediation sessions are usually quite informal. Most mediators try to make the physical setting of the room conducive to open discussion. Even the choice of a room is important. For example, the union representatives probably would not be comfortable meeting in the plant manager's office.

Mediation informal sessions to resolve problems

Arbitration. When an issue goes to arbitration it means that the union and management have not been able to resolve it. It also means that the union feels that it is an important issue. Unless otherwise stated in a particular contract, the decision of an arbitrator is final and binding on both the union and management.

An arbitrator issues a decision that is binding on both union and management.

Eastern Air's Borman Badly Underestimated Obduracy of Old Foe

By late 1985, Eastern Airlines' financial troubles were so severe that without significant cost cutting there was little chance it could survive as an independent company. Frank Borman, Eastern's chairman, felt that he needed wage cuts of approximately 20% from the pilots' union to save Eastern. As the following excerpt illustrates, he did not get all three unions to agree.

When a takeover bid from Texas Air Corp.'s Frank Lorenzo surfaced late Friday, Mr. Borman and other Eastern executives initially seemed convinced that they could use it to force Eastern's three unions to accept management's demands for 20% wage cuts. One director says the offer was seen as a "pincer-play to put the unions under enormous pressure"—by having to choose among the pay cuts, a takeover by Lorenzo, who has a fierce anti-union reputation, or a bankruptcy-law filing.

But as in the past, management seriously underestimated the obduracy of an old foe: Charles Bryan, the leader of Eastern's powerful machinists' union and an Eastern director who has been battling Mr. Borman for more than a decade. At the close of a long evening of tense board meetings, stretching into the early hours of yesterday morning, Mr. Bryan steadfastly refused to join Eastern's two other unions in accepting wage

Source: Excerpt from Gary Cohn, "Eastern Air's Borman Badly Underestimated Obduracy of Old Foe," *The Wall Street Journal* (2 Feb. 1986): 1. Reprinted by permission of *The Wall Street Journal,* © Dow Jones & Company, Inc., 1986. All Rights Reserved.

concessions—even in the face of the takeover threat—without getting in return Mr. Borman's resignation as chairman.

"I've reached the point where I don't think we can do a lot worse than we've been doing," Mr. Bryan said Sunday. . . .

Eastern has been lurching from crisis to crisis for the better part of a decade, and the divisions between labor and management have grown deep and bitter. The atmosphere was captured in an exchange [according to a witness, between Richard Magurno, Eastern's senior vice president for legal affairs, and Charles Bryan]. "Charlie, I'm trying to control my temper, . . . but right now, you just destroyed 40,000 jobs. I want them all to know you're the guy that destroyed their jobs."

Pointing to the room where the [Eastern] directors were still reviewing the Texas Air offer, Mr. Bryan snapped back, "There are 16 guys inside who did it. . . ."

QUESTIONS

1. What would you have done if you had been Frank Borman? Charles Bryan?
2. Under what conditions should union employees accept wage cuts?
3. What can management and a union do to avoid this kind of problem?
4. What has happened to Eastern Airlines since February 1986?

Why have arbitration?

This generally means that one side of the conflict "wins" and the other side "loses."

If there is a possibility of losing, why would either management or the union want to arbitrate anything? Alternatives to arbitration include the union calling either a strike or some form of work slow-down. That is clearly a drastic measure to take, and one that neither managers nor union officials want to happen regularly. Even the prospect of "losing" a case in arbitration is preferable to continually having work slow-downs or strikes over grievances.

Remember the "fair representation" rule mentioned earlier in this chapter? Unions are required to "fairly represent" members in arbitrations also. However, unions also have the right to decide what cases to bring to arbitration.

Arbitration is not cheap. Arbitrators are professionals, frequently from the American Arbitration Association, who receive substantial daily fees for their services. Extensive secretarial services are required. Most contracts require that management and the union evenly share the costs of the arbitration. Also, because the results of the arbitration are often important, both management and the union frequently retain lawyers to advise and represent them. Therefore, the union, especially, must weigh the potential benefits of winning the grievance (and the chances of losing) against the high cost of bringing a grievance to arbitration. Most unions require a vote of an executive board or special committee before a grievance goes to arbitration.

The costs of arbitration can be high.

Establishing Precedents. In addition to arbitration decisions being binding, there is another significant aspect of arbitration. Decisions in arbitration cases help establish precedents. In union/management relations, precedents are important. A *precedent* is a guide for future action. In a grievance, if either management or the union can cite precedents in that company supporting their position, their case is much stronger. Arbitrators pay close attention to any precedents that have been established.

What is a precedent?

Past Practices. *Past practices* are also important in arbitration cases. The term refers to how the organization has handled similar situations in the past. Arbitrators frequently ask both sides if there are any past practices that are relevant to the case. Of course, it is likely that the two sides will not agree on which past practices are important.

What is a past practice?

Do you know much about the law relating to union/management activities? Try answering these questions. Write "yes" if you feel the action is legal, "no" if you feel the action is not legal.

LABOR LAW TODAY

_____ 1. Two unions are seeking to organize workers in a small plant. Since one union is very militant, the owner offers to pay the dues for all employees if they vote for the other union.

_____ 2. During the organizing campaign mentioned above, the company owner passes out literature reminding employees of all the "special benefits" they already have, indicating they are better off than employees in plants the unions represent.

_____ 3. During the same organizing campaign, two employees are highly critical of the union that eventually wins the election to represent the employees. Immediately after the campaign, the new union president tells the two employees that he will get them fired for opposing his union.

_____ 4. While negotiating a contract with management, the union makes a proposal to give employees all days between Christmas and New Year's off. Management refuses to even discuss the proposal.

_____ 5. Management in a company informs employees that anyone conducting union business during scheduled work hours will be subject to disciplinary action. The only exceptions are for two union officers, as provided in the contract.

_____ 6. In the contract for employees in a Boston, Massachusetts, plant, there is a provision that all employees must join the union within 30 days or be discharged from the company.

Wagner Act
Taft-Hartley Act
Landrum-Griffin Act

There currently are three critical federal laws relating to union/management relations. The National Labor Relations Act of 1935 (called the Wagner Act), the Labor-Management Relations Act of 1947 (Taft-Hartley Act), and the Labor-Management Reporting and Disclosure Act of 1959 (Landrum-Griffin Act) form the basis for federal action in union/management relations. Both Taft-Hartley and Landrum-Griffin amended the Wagner Act.[9]

The Wagner Act was pro-union, while the Taft-Hartley Act amendments are generally pro-management. The Landrum-Griffin Act amendments give employees specific rights intended to reduce abuses by both union officials and management. Figures 12–5, 12–6, and 12–7 provide a brief introduction to the key provisions of current federal law.

Examine your answers to the questions at the beginning of this section. Based on the material in Figures 12–5, 12–6, and 12–7, do you want to change any of your answers?

Let's see how you did.

1. Illegal. Violates Point 3 in Figure 12–7.
2. Legal. The owner may present his point of view, as long as he does not use threats.
3. Illegal. See Number 7 in Figure 12–5, and Number 3 in Figure 12–6.
4. Illegal. Management must bargain in good faith, and that means discussing "reasonable" proposals.
5. Legal. Management has a right to demand that people do assigned work during the hours they are being paid. Also, a contract may specifically allow certain union officials time off for union business.
6. Legal. Massachusetts is not a right-to-work state (see the section on State Labor Laws below).

How did you do? Even if you scored 100 percent (congratulations!), be careful. Labor law can change quickly.

1   To organize into unions to bargain collectively with employers over wages, hours, and terms and conditions of employment

2   To be protected against discriminatory acts from management on the basis of their union activities

3   To not have to be a member of a union in order to get a job

4   To bring an unfair labor practice charge against management without fear of retaliatory acts from management

5   To receive financial reports from their union

6   To not be forced to join a union after they are employed, unless they are covered by a valid contract requiring union membership in one of the states that allows such contracts

7   To be protected against discriminatory acts from their union on the basis of exercising their right of free speech in all union affairs and union elections of officers

8   To receive a copy of their collective bargaining agreement from the union representing them

FIGURE 12–5
Employee rights

1   To refuse to bargain with management in good faith

2   To engage in strikes or boycotts to force management into an illegal act

3   To force management to discriminate against employees in violation of the law

4   To require employers to pay for work not done

5   To prohibit employees from engaging in legitimate union activities

6   To force employees to engage in union activities

7   To charge exorbitant initiation fees, or dues, when there is a contract requiring employees to join the union after they are hired

FIGURE 12–6
Union unfair labor practices

FIGURE 12 – 7
Management unfair la-
bor practices

1   To refuse to bargain in good faith with legitimate representatives of its employees

2   To interfere with the right of employees to organize a union and engage in collective bargaining

3   To contribute support to a union

4   To seek either to dominate a union or to organize a union among their employees

5   To either encourage or discourage membership in the union by discriminating for or against union members in hiring or any other personnel action

6   To discriminate against employees for filing an unfair labor practice claim or for testifying under the law

Who Enforces Federal Union/Management Laws?

The National Labor Relations Board enforces federal labor laws.

The Wagner Act created the National Labor Relations Board (NLRB) and gave it jurisdiction over union/management issues. The NLRB has regional offices throughout the United States that work to resolve disputes between unions, employees, and employers. If the NLRB finds that a union or an employer is engaging in an unfair labor practice, it can prosecute the offender in court. The NLRB also has the right to decide which employees are in the bargaining unit—the group of employees the union may bargain for.

What is a bargaining unit?

State Labor Laws.   Your own state has important laws regulating employer/employee relations. For example, one critical provision of the Taft-Hartley Act allows states to pass what are called right-to-work laws. Right-to-work laws forbid contracts requiring workers to join unions and restrict what are called "union security" provisions in contracts. Such laws make it much harder for unions to collect dues and fees from the people in the bargaining unit.

What is a state right-to-work law?

Most people do not think that anyone should be required to join any organization. Yet, most union representatives think that state right-to-work laws are terrible. Why? First, remember that the union must represent all employees in the bargaining unit, whether or not they are union members. The union negotiates pay increases and benefits covering *all* employees in the bargaining unit, and *all* employees have an equal right to union assistance in grievances and arbitration. Second, unions need money to operate. If only half of the eligible employees are union members, they have to pay higher dues than if all employees paid fees.

Should employees be required to pay a fee or join the union that represents them?

Up from the Ashes

The year is 1970—September 14: The Lakewood assembly plant is shut down, having just begun one of the longest strikes in General Motors history. At issue: more than 5,500 grievances, some 1,100 cases of protested discipline. . . . Nothing moves. The strike continues. . . . One hundred and thirty-six days will pass before the membership votes to return to work.

The year is 1983—September 30: The Lakewood plant is again shut down, having been out of production for a year because of declining car sales. Some 40 Lakewood people are gathered in conference room B working out the logistics of a two-week prestartup training program which this group has put together in readiness for returning to production in 1984. They are members of 11 joint committees which have been at work for months on strategies for getting the plant reopened, making it a better place to work and its products competitive in the world market. . . .

A man speaks up. He says he'll have HIS people there. He is chairman of the union shop committee. He's held that position, off and on, for 25 years [and has lead many strikes against the company].

Lakewood, an old inner city plant, a plant notorious in GM for its troubled labor history, and now a model for Labor- Management partnership? . . . Grievances have remained at or near zero, and discipline incidents have declined by 82% . . . Despite the addition of

heavy overtime, . . . absenteeism has declined from 26% in 1981 to 9% . . . Sickness and accident costs have also been cut by two-thirds. . . . Corporate audits have consistently shown Lakewood quality to be at or near the highest levels achieved among conventionally assembled GM vehicles. . . .

All of this didn't just happen. . . . First, we jointly structured and presented a two-week pre-startup training class for all of our employees. . . . [Covering] information sharing, . . . personal development skills, and [the] Pacific Institute video series entitled "New Age Thinking." [Second, voluntary] employee work groups formed on all shifts . . . representing more than 90% of the work force. . . . [Third, we implemented] an extensive ongoing training program for Lakewood employees. . . .

Let me say that Lakewood is NOT mecca. Working together in democratic fashion on a day-to-day basis proved to be the hardest thing most of us had ever done. . . .

QUESTIONS

1. Do you think this can be done at any unionized plant?
2. What are the most important things necessary for successful cooperation?
3. Why doesn't real union/management cooperation happen everywhere?
4. What has happened at GM since this story was written?

Source: Excerpts from "Up From the Ashes," Patricia M. Carrigan, *OD Practitioner*, vol. 18, no. 1 (March 1986): 1–6. Reprinted by prmission.

What do you think about right-to-work laws? Does your state have a right-to-work law?

Labor Law and You. Although there is a complex body of law relating to labor relations, most of us need only a basic understanding of the key concepts. Remember, however, that there are many laws and court cases relating to employers, employees, and union/management relations. If your organization is very large, it will undoubtedly have a labor relations consultant available to management. If you have questions in this area, it may be interesting to talk to that person.[10]

Opening Story Revisited

The day after the three press operators were suspended, Barbara (second shift supervisor) holds a meeting with her crew.

> BARBARA: I just want to say that I hope we can have a productive shift without as many problems as we had yesterday. I know that the difficulty on the first shift bothered a lot of you, but we have to put out top-quality work or we won't keep our customers. We can't have a repeat of all the problems we had yesterday, and I am confident that we won't. We are too good a crew. I'm sure you know that the union has filed a grievance over the suspensions. Let's let the grievance procedure do what it is supposed to do—resolve problems. OK? If anyone has any questions about what is going on, please come to me. I'll tell you everything I can.

Ten minutes later, Sandra corners Barbara.

> SANDRA: I know what you are trying to do, and I won't let you. We've had it with shoddy management tricks around here. I'm filing an unfair labor charge against you, Matt, and Perry.
>
> BARBARA: What? Are you talking about . . .
>
> SANDRA: No whats. You can't run down the union like that, and you can't go around threatening union people just because . . .
>
> BARBARA: Sandy, hold on! I didn't run down the union.
>
> SANDRA: Forget it. We try to work with you folks and what we get are a lot of platitudes about working together when it suits your needs, then attempts to get rid of union people when you get the chance.
>
> BARBARA: Sandy! . . .

As Sandra storms off towards Perry's office, Barbara wonders what an unfair labor practice is.

UNIONS: YESTERDAY, TODAY, AND TOMORROW

Unions: A criminal conspiracy?

It often surprises Americans that in this profoundly individualistic country the first real union activity occurred in 1794 among the shoemakers in Philadelphia. Unfortunately for the union movement, the employers sued the union and the United States Supreme Court said, in effect, that unions were a criminal activity. This rather discouraged early unionism.

The Supreme Court basically reversed itself in a case in 1842, and some early unions began to form. The National Typographical Union, formed in 1852, has existed in some form ever since. Still, there was little significant union activity until the Knights of Labor began in 1869. This was the first attempt at a national union.

Organizing All Workers

The Knights of Labor tried to organize everyone.

The Knights of Labor, emphasizing the solidarity of all labor, attempted to organize people on a city-by-city basis, rather than on the basis of a shared craft. Some of the goals sound pretty tame today: the eight-hour work day, prohibition of child labor, equal pay for men and women, a graduated income tax, and a federal labor department. One hundred years ago, those goals were almost revolutionary. The Knights failed for a variety of reasons, but probably one of the most important was that the individual units failed to significantly address the economic concerns of their membership.[11]

The American Federation of Labor. The American Federation of Labor (AFL) rose out of the failure of the Knights of Labor. The AFL originally took almost an opposite approach to organizing. It focused on forming craft unions (unions organized around people doing similar jobs, such as plumbers, carpenters, or bakers). Rather than emphasizing broad social goals, the AFL concentrated on practical economic gains for its membership. Still, through the late 1920s, unions were not major forces in business.[12]

What is a craft union?

By the 1930s the United States had become a country with massive industrial plants employing thousands of people. Craft unions could not cope with the diversity of occupations concentrated in one location. Walter Reuther with the auto workers, John L. Lewis with the miners, and Sidney Hillman with clothing workers led a movement to form industrial unions—unions including most workers in a particular industry, no matter what specific job the individual had.

What is an industrial union?

The Congress of Industrial Organizations (CIO) was formed by the industrial unions within the AFL. Through a series of sometimes violent confrontations with employers, such as Ford and United States Steel, the industrial unions won the right to bargain for hundreds of thousands of workers at a time. By 1937, when the CIO split away from the AFL, it contained unions with over 3.7 million members.[13]

Why Did People Join Unions? Why did so many people join unions so rapidly? Imagine these working conditions: In the early 1930s there was no Social Security, virtually no company retirement plans, occupational safety was almost unknown, neither the eight-hour day nor the five-day work week was standard, job security was nonexistent, no federal minimum wage existed, and the Depression lowered wage levels throughout the country. A large number of management people were actively hostile toward workers. Under those conditions, might you have wanted to join a union that offered the promise of a different future? Indeed, it might be more interesting to think about why industrial unions did not form earlier.[14]

National Union Structure

Since the late 1930s there have been periodic reorganizations of the national union structure. Today, the AFL and CIO are once again combined. The AFL-CIO includes all major unions. The Teamsters, expelled in 1957 for union corruption, were readmitted in October 1987.

Fastest Growing Unions. From high points in the 1950s and 1960s, traditional industrial and craft unions have generally had declining memberships. But, what are the areas in which union membership has increased? Think of what you know about the 1950s, and the types of people who did not usually belong to unions then. Knowing what you do about unions today, see if you can identify some areas in which union strength is definitely on the increase.

Which unions are increasing their membership?

Did you think of teachers? How many teachers belonged to unions in 1952? A great many belong today. If you thought of teachers, did you include college faculty? There have been dramatic increases in the number of collective bargaining agreements covering college faculty.

What about health-care workers? Who would have thought much about nurses' unions in the 1950s? Today, some of the most aggressive unions in the country are in the health fields.

Did you think of state, county, and municipal employees? Over the past twenty years, the American Federation of State, County, and Municipal Employees (AFSCME) has more than doubled in size. Recently, even office workers, traditionally resistant to unionization, have begun to join unions.

Why Join a Union Today? Why would people join a union today? Reasons include such things as job security, increased pay and benefits, support against arbitrary acts of management, protection against unfair work loads, provision of a way to grieve unfair policies, and because of peer pressure (in an organization where co-workers are union members).

How many things on that list are you not interested in? Most people are interested in most of those. However, perhaps you are thinking, ''Well, I'm interested in all of these, but I think that a union member may be more interested in these than I am.'' You are probably right.

Does Maslow's hierarchy relate to why people join unions?

Do you remember Maslow's hierarchy of needs from Chapter 3? How about Herzberg's two-factor theory? They probably looked pretty interesting to you back then. Take a look at the list of reasons someone may want to join a union and compare the list to Maslow's physiological, safety, and belonging needs. Now, compare Herzberg's dissatisfiers to your list. Are you seeing some direct connections?

Do you suppose that the way unions have functioned in the past fits fairly well with factors surrounding the actual job done? Does this mean we could guess that, as organizations have provided workers with a decent work environment, pay, and related conditions, that traditional unions would decline?

Will Union Membership Increase? What does this mean for the future? As a student of human relations, you need to be on the alert for changes in issues of concern to unions that may make unionization a possibility for more organizations. Also, you must watch for changing conditions in our economy that may make traditional unions more attractive. These changes could produce a rapid increase in union membership.

1. Unions are made up of people who believe they can get more of what they want from an organization by bargaining as a group with management.
2. The collective bargaining agreement, or contract, provides the formal outline of union/management relations. Contracts are negotiated for periods of one to three years.
3. Increasingly, negotiators are trying to structure "win-win" situations, where both sides profit from an agreement.
4. There is an increasing amount of union/management cooperation today.
5. Grievances are formal ways of bringing complaints to management.
6. Most complaints are resolved before becoming grievances. Supervisors and union officials can practice mediation techniques to resolve problems fairly and to the satisfaction of both parties.
7. Arbitration is a quasi-legal process in which both management and the union present their arguments to an arbitrator (a person agreed upon by both sides) who then issues a judgment.
8. Both management and the union may engage in an unfair labor practice. An employee, the union, or management can bring an unfair labor practice charge to the National Labor Relations Board. The NLRB can prosecute an offender in court.
9. The AFL-CIO is the largest single union body in the United States, with most unions belonging to it.
10. Most of the fastest growing unions are in service or professional areas.

There are no clear "right" or "wrong" answers to the self quiz at the beginning of this chapter. However, let's briefly discuss each question:

1. While unions are not responsible for high prices, it is true that unions do tend to increase wages in organizations. The stronger the union is, the more likely it is that contracts will provide significant wage increases.
2. It is almost always more difficult to fire a person covered by a union contract. Supervisors must carefully follow all contract provisions and present a solid case for discharge. Most non-union companies have been able to fire anyone. However, the "employment at will" concept, which states that employees work at the will of the employer and may be terminated at any time, is being severely curtailed in some states. It is possible that in many states in the near future non-union employees will have almost the same employment security as union employees.
3. In the past, many contracts did contain extremely restrictive work rules. Today, many of these provisions are being revised to provide organizations more flexibility in work assignments.

4. Few unions are corrupt. Of course, the corruption cases are the ones that get the headlines.
5. A strike is the union's ultimate weapon. So far, our society has not developed an effective way to give employees as a group an alternate powerful weapon.
6. Contracts require approval by both management and the union. If negative items get into a contract, both sides bear equal responsibility.
7. Traditional unions may be obsolete. That is a question for you to think about.
8. This also is an open question—and a good one to pursue on your own.

KEY TERMS

AFL-CIO	Mediation
Arbitration	National Labor Relations Board
Collective bargaining agreement	Past practice
Craft union	Precedent
Duty of fair representation	Right-to-work laws
Grievance	Unfair labor practice
Grievance procedure	Union
Industrial union	Work rule

HUMAN RELATIONS APPLICATIONS

Why Jim Ansara Unionized His Own Company

Can inviting a union into a company ever make good management sense? An *Inc.* magazine article with the above title argues that it appears to be possible.*

Jim Ansara's construction company in the Boston, Massachusetts, area was in trouble. Projects were taking too long to complete and costs were consistently going over estimates. Too often work was not being done properly and, therefore, had to be redone. Personnel problems were requiring too much supervisory time. According to Ansara, ''Early on, I had personal relationships with all the people, but it became impractical. Meantime, we had a company with no rules or policies. People were happy to work here, but there was too much energy expended on solving problems. Someone was mad at someone else; young people weren't used to showing up with their tools at 7 a.m. . . .'' The list of problems was very long.

But does that mean you invite, yes *invite*, a union in? What about union work rules? What about the union pay scale? What about the risk of a strike or work stoppage? What about union stewards who draw pay but do no actual work? What about the horror stories that everyone has heard?

*Adapted from ''Why Jim Ansara Unionized His Own Company,'' *INC.* (March 1987): 60–66. Reprinted with permission, *INC.* magazine, March 1987. Copyright © 1987 by INC. Publishing Company, 38 Commercial Wharf, Boston, MA 02110.

Well, Jim Ansara checked things out for himself. Ansara thought that jobs with union employees were better organized and cleaner. After working with a unionized subcontractor, Ansara recalled, "He did astounding work, and I was amazed at how organized and knowledgeable his people were on the job. We noticed the amount of production he got out of them, and that his average worker was 35 to 45, not 25 like ours."

Against the advice of almost all of his managers, Ansara approached the union. After talking with union officials, Ansara signed the contract. So far, it has worked. He works hard to respect the spirit of the union rules and, consequently, often gets excused from some of the details. His per hour labor costs have gone up, but it appears that the total labor hours are down because of the more experienced workers. His supervisors indicate that there are far fewer personnel problems on the job. People show up on time—and with their equipment—ready to work.

Will it continue to work? Who knows? Right now, Jim Ansara and the union both have a stake in a strong cooperative relationship. Will they always?

Can a Quality-of-Work-Life Program Succeed in a Unionized Company?

Can significant union/management cooperation ever exist? Yes, but it takes a great deal of effort, support, and planning on both sides. Raymond Williams of AT&T and Glenn Watts of the Communications Workers of America describe one such cooperative effort.[16]

By the mid-1970s both the CWA and AT&T recognized that there were important morale and productivity problems among AT&T workers. In 1980, CWA and AT&T management formed a joint national committee to develop quality-of-work-life programs within AT&T. Throughout the early 1980s there was slow and unsteady progress. Years of treating each other as "the enemy" had caused distrust. Still, the idea spread to include more and more workers and managers.

Whether this particular idea succeeds in the long run, Williams and Watts have identified some areas they believe are critical to successful joint efforts: People on both sides must recognize the need to change traditional relationships. Management must understand that participation is one way to improve quality and productivity. Union members must see that, through participation, they gain a measure of control over their work lives. Top managers and union officers must be personally committed and involved in the process—and support it at every point. The effort must truly be joint, shared equally between the union and management. Joint committees are needed at every level, from the national level down to a local shop.

Intense communication and education are necessary. Often, old conflicts must be dealt with before new relationships can be built. This means that education must be aimed at all levels, not just the top and bottom. Middle managers and local union officials must be actively included so they see the direct benefits of cooperation. Rewards for managers must be revised so they receive proper credit for improving relations.

Developing a joint QWL program takes money—for trained group facilitators, for consultants to set up effective quality groups, for release time for QWL participants to attend workshops. There is a very significant start-up cost.

Finally, a solid evaluation and renewal process is required to keep the project moving. QWL cooperation is a slow and often frustrating process. Mechanisms are needed to evaluate work, support success, suggest ways to improve deteriorating situations, and plan strategy for the future.

CWA and AT&T have proved that, although cooperation is not easy, it is possible. Both sides hope that the successes in this project will outweigh the failures, and show a positive result over the long term.

PERSONAL GUIDELINES FOR HUMAN RELATIONS SUCCESS

Settle fast, settle low, settle fair.

Resolving Grievances

One critical factor affecting organizational productivity, employer/employee relations, and an individual's own career is the ability to resolve complaints. Supervisors who pile up a lot of written grievances, without good cause, rarely rise in the organization. Similarly, union officers who are unable to successfully resolve problems are rarely viewed favorably by either union members or management representatives.

What can you do? Apply the "F-L-F Test" to all grievance situations. The principles behind FLF are simple:

1. Resolve the problem as *fast* as possible. Do not let a small problem become a big one.
2. Settle the complaint at the *lowest* possible level, hopefully before it becomes a written grievance.
3. Be scrupulously *fair* in developing a solution.[17]

Preparing for Collective Bargaining

Most of us never get a chance to serve on a negotiating committee. Yet, if you work in a unionized organization, the contract has direct impact on how your company functions. You can help your organization become more productive and give yourself more visibility as someone who cares by doing a few simple things:

1. Keep careful notes about problems you observe with parts of the current contract.
2. For every grievance you are involved in, keep your own private notes about whether contract provisions made the situation better or worse. Perhaps there are problems with the current contract that are clear only when you review a year's notes.
3. Talk to people in other unionized companies and compare contract provisions, looking for ideas your organization can use.

4. Keep a running list of things you wish were in the contract. Before new contract negotiations start, review your list, talk your ideas over with colleagues, and pick out the best one or two ideas.

Make certain you know exactly when your negotiating team will begin working on new contract "demands." Do not be surprised if you find that people begin working long before new contract negotiations start. Get all of your ideas onto one sheet of paper, and try to arrange a meeting in which you can present them in person.

You may say, "I'm not a supervisor, I'm a union member. This stuff doesn't have much to do with me." Yes, it does. First, isn't it your own contract that we are talking about? Second, you may be a supervisor some day and going through this process will be excellent practice for you.

If you get the opportunity to be on a negotiating committee, either for management or a union, take it! You will probably have quite an experience. Don't assume that you will have a lot of influence, but take careful notes about what each side does that you think is effective or ineffective. Keep all information about the original contract proposals submitted by both sides and then the final document. Also, identify those people on both sides of the table who seem most interested in developing a productive relationship.

Taking careful notes will help your career in several ways:

1. It makes you a potentially valuable member of the next negotiating team, helping you get high visibility in the organization.
2. In interviewing for another job, you can mention—in a positive way—your experience and how it makes you better qualified for the job you want.
3. Identifying who seems most interested in working with "the other side" gives you someone to talk with about problems that may arise after the contract is signed. The more you can talk informally with "the other side," the more you will understand them and be in a position to help resolve conflicts.

DISCUSSION AND REVIEW QUESTIONS

1. What is the difference between mediation and arbitration? Why should an organization prefer one over the other?
2. What does the term "unfair labor practice" mean? Who can an unfair labor practice be filed against?
3. After outlining the steps in a typical grievance procedure, can you identify all the times when mediation might be helpful?
4. What do the terms "precedent" and "past practice" mean? Why are they important?
5. If you work as a supervisor in a non-union organization, would you recommend a formal policy to resolve grievances? Why or why not?

6. What are the advantages to an organization of having a union represent some of its employees?

Negotiation

Negotiating is both a science and an art. Practice your negotiating skills with this exercise.

Instructions. Divide the class into groups of six. Three people in each group represent "management," three represent "workers." Your task is to recommend grades for each of you for today to your instructor. There are to be two A's, three B's, and one C. The "management" representatives hold a great deal of power, since they will be the ones actually making the recommendation to the instructor. However, the recommendation must be signed by *all* six people, so the "worker" representatives hold some power. If the group does not come up with an agreement, all six members get a C.

Should We Go to Arbitration?

Suppose the pressroom in the Singleterry Division had a past practice of having press operators regularly do routine maintenance on the presses. Suppose further, that Matt had been a supervisor in the pressroom for ten years and could cite dozens of cases in which he had worked directly with press operators to diagnose problems with different presses.

Further suppose that the company had an employee time-card situation in which it was noted when an employee was doing maintenance work on a press. This would supply documentary evidence that press operators did maintenance. Matt's case gets a bit stronger, doesn't it? But, let's not jump to a quick judgment.

Let's also suppose that none of the other presses have railings over them, and no press operator has ever been above a press when it was operating. Let's also assume that The Monster really is three or four times bigger than any other press at this location.

So the company has an argument that there is a "relevant past practice" of press operators doing maintenance work. They might also state that the railings are a safe place to be, because the railings are designed for maintenance people to use. On the other hand, the union can claim that this is a totally different type of press than the others in the plant, that the railings may be safe for trained maintenance people but not for untrained people, and that the maintenance done by press operators in the past was minor in relation to what was requested here.

If the issue goes to arbitration, the arbitrator will issue a decision. Suppose he rules that Matt acted within the requirements of the contract, citing the "past practice'' of maintenance by press operators. Not only will the union have lost this particular grievance, but now there also would be a precedent set that allows management to require press operators to do maintenance work on The Monster (and probably any other press that the company installs).

You are the management person who will make the decision whether to pursue arbitration in this case. What are the pros and cons of taking this case to arbitration? What is your final decision?

NOTES

1. Ephraim Lewis, ''BW/Harris Poll: Confidence in Unions is Crumbling,'' *Business Week* (8 July 1985): 76.
2. William M. Carley, ''Flight Attendants Unions Are Losing Strength,'' *The Wall Street Journal* (8 April 1986): 9. Earl Bohn, ''LTV and union meet on contract,'' *The Philadelphia Inquirer* (20 December 1986): 9D.
3. Alex Kotalwitz, ''Work Rules Shape Up As Major Battleground In U.S. Labor Disputes,'' *The Wall Street Journal* (4 June 1986): 1.
4. J. Ernest Beazley, ''U.S. Steel, Union Are at Odds on Eve of Talks,'' *The Wall Street Journal* (11 June 1986): 20.
5. Gary Cohn, ''Eastern Air's Borman Badly Underestimated Obduracy of Old Foe,'' *The Wall Street Journal* (25 February 1986): 1.
6. ''How Power Will Be Balanced on Saturn's Shop Floor,'' *Business Week* (5 August 1985): 65–66.
7. Patricia M. Carrigan, ''Up From The Ashes,'' *OD Practitioner* (March 1986): 1–6.
8. Clyde W. Summers and Robert J. Rabin, *The Rights of Union Members* (New York: Avon Books, 1979).
9. *A Guide to Basic Law and Procedures Under the National Labor Relations Act,* the Office of the General Counsel, National Labor Relations Board (Washington, DC: U.S. Government Printing Office, 1978).
10. *Grievance Handlers and Bargainers Pocket Guide,* The United Auto Workers Education Department (Detroit: United Auto Workers, undated): 75–85.
11. Sidney Lens, *The Labor Wars* (Garden City, NY: Anchor Books, 1974).
12. Thomas R. Brooks, *Toil and Trouble: A History of American Labor* (New York: Dell Publishing Co., 1964).
13. Saul D. Alinsky, *John L. Lewis: An Unauthorized Biography* (New York: Vintage Books, 1970).
14. David Brody, *Labor in Crisis: The Steel Strike of 1919* (Philadelphia: J. B. Lippincott Co., 1965).
15. Raymond Williams and Glenn Watts, ''The Process of Working Together: CWA's/AT&T's Approach to QWL,'' in *Teamwork: Joint Labor-Management Programs in America,* ed. Jerome M. Rosow (New York: Pergamon Press, 1986): 75–88. Used by permission.
16. Steven Briggs, ''The Grievance Procedure and Organizational Health,'' in *Readings in Personnel and Human Resource Management,* eds. Randall S. Schuler & Stuart A. Youngblood (St. Paul, MN: West Publishing Co., 1984): 479–83.

CHAPTER 13
EQUAL OPPORTUNITY ISSUES

WHAT'S YOUR OPINION? T OR F

_____ 1. Part of the manager's job involves using discrimination.

_____ 2. Business owners and managers are usually aware of the adverse impact on minorities of such employment requirements as weight, height, and education.

_____ 3. Nearly half of all Americans belong to a protected group.

_____ 4. Hispanics are the fastest growing minority in the United States today.

_____ 5. Sexual harassment is now considered to be illegal.

_____ 6. Equal employment laws prohibit discrimination only in regard to gaining employment.

_____ 7. Most discrimination problems are the result of unintentional violations of Equal Opportunity legislation.

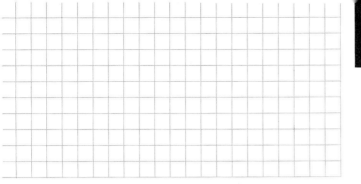

OUTLINE

BASICS OF DISCRIMINATION
  Advantages of Removing Discrimination
  What Are Prejudice and Discrimination?
  Types of Discrimination
  Equal Employment Opportunity and the Law

LEARNING SUMMARY

HUMAN RELATIONS APPLICATIONS
  A Sound EEO Program
  Some Examples of Special Programs for the
  Handicapped

PERSONAL GUIDELINES FOR HUMAN
RELATIONS SUCCESS

LEARNING OBJECTIVES

☐ List several advantages of overcoming
discrimination in the workplace

☐ Define and differentiate between prejudice
and discrimination

☐ Discuss protected groups and their
relationship to reverse discrimination

☐ Discuss four major types of illegal
discrimination

☐ Identify four racial groups facing
discrimination and the special needs and
problems facing these groups

☐ Identify special needs of older and
handicapped workers

☐ Discuss major discrimination legislation and
its implications for management

The Dream Deferred[1]

Bill's division was part of a company newly acquired by a large multinational enterprise located on the West Coast. Hired through a "headhunter" agency by the new parent company, he was the first black manager in his division. Between the time Bill was appointed and the day he walked into his office, an executive who had opposed Bill's selection had been promoted to a vice president—two steps above Bill as his boss's boss. Despite Bill's repeated requests, his immediate superior gave him no written objectives. But all of Bill's colleagues told him they liked the direction he was taking.

The only indication that his race was even noticed was a comment from a sales manager whose performance Bill's division relied on: "I don't normally associate with blacks." Bill learned later that other managers were telling his boss that he was hard to work with and unclear in his plans. His boss did not confront Bill with these criticisms, but just hinted at possible problems.

After six months, out of the blue, Bill was put on probation. According to Bill's superior, the vice president "did not feel Bill could do the job" and suggested to him that Bill accept severance pay and look for other work. Bill decided to stick it out for pride's sake; he knew he could do the job. His work and educational records had proven him to be a winner.

During the following six months, his division performed ahead of plan. Bill was getting compliments from customers and colleagues. His boss assured him that he had proved his worth, and the probation would be lifted. It was. A few months later, Bill's boss finally agreed to set written objectives and scheduled a meeting with him. But when Bill walked into his superior's office, he was surprised to see the VP there, too. The purpose of the meeting was not to set objectives but to place Bill back on probation, or give him severance pay, because he did not "seem to be the right man for the job." Bill left the company and started his own business.

BASICS OF DISCRIMINATION

From reading the opening story we can imagine that Bill's emotions probably ran the gamut from disappointment and dismay to frustration and anger before he finally left the company. Bill was probably a victim of unconscious stereotyping in decision making—a situation that is not unusual. Everyday, intelligent, responsible, and capable people are passed over for promotions because people in decision-making positions are not aware of personal prejudices influencing their decisions.

Prejudice and discrimination have become timely issues in this turbulent and complex era of social and technological change. Anyone making a decision over hiring, firing, demoting, or promoting needs to be aware of the most common types of discrimination and of the laws designed to prevent it. Managers must simultaneously respond to the varying demands of men, women, minority workers, and older workers within a framework of rapidly changing legal pressures and constraints.[2]

In this chapter we will explore topics that managers and supervisors who are concerned with effective human relations practices must know.

Advantages of Removing Discrimination

America is the land of opportunity, but there can be no true equality among its citizens unless there is equal economic opportunity as well. Despite gains since the landmark Civil Rights Act was passed in 1964, today there is still a lot of imbalance in economic opportunity. True equal opportunity would give people a chance to grow toward fulfilling their potential instead of forcing them into idleness, which wastes their time and potential.

Everyone would benefit from removing discrimination in hiring and promoting—society at large, companies and businesses, and the employees themselves. More workers gainfully employed means more taxes being paid and less welfare being distributed. Businesses interested in economic self-interest could fully utilize the talents and abilities of all people. People would become more self-reliant and less dependent. Self-esteem would grow since people who are productive and gainfully employed have better self-images and a more enhanced social status than those who are denied employment.

Removing discrimination ensures that more of the labor force will be employed and hence more contributions to society will be made. Imagine what society would be like if most of America's nearly 50 million working women were to leave the work force. "The country would plunge into an economic state worse than the Great Depression," according to Gay Bryant in *Working Woman Report.* "The money women make keeps a roof over many families. The goods and services women buy with their paychecks keep the economy rolling. Women don't just make a substantial contribution to the economy—they are a central part of it."[3]

Why should we remove all forms of illegal discrimination?

What Are Prejudice and Discrimination?

Derived from the Latin word *prejudicum,* prejudice simply means making a judgment about people without having a knowledge of their personal qualities. Usually it is a highly negative judgment toward a group, focusing on one or more negative characteristics that are supposedly uniformly shared by all group mem-

Prejudice negative judgment toward a group of people

bers.[4] While it is possible to be prejudiced toward a person or group and regard them in a positive light, in this chapter prejudice refers to unfavorable feelings against individuals because they are "different."

Stereotyping   a process of judging a whole group of people by the behavior of a few members

Although there are many social, psychological, and economic explanations for prejudice, it often results from *stereotyping.* Stereotyping is a process in which a group is judged according to the behavior of a few of its members. Since actions of one group member are seen as typical for all group members, stereotypes are overgeneralizations. They are almost impossible to eliminate since they develop over a period of time and since many people share the same stereotypes.

How can stereotyping lead to prejudice?

Stereotypes often lead to a *self-fulfilling prophecy.* This phenomenon occurs when someone's expectation of an event makes the outcome more likely to occur than would otherwise have been true. Self-fulfilling prophecies occur all the time, although you might never have given them that label. For example, you just know that you'll stutter and stammer and really botch that job interview, and sure enough, you do. An expectation that you'll fail helps ensure that you do. Fortunately, the opposite occurs too.

Describe how the self-fulfilling prophecy influences behavior.

There are two types of self-fulfilling prophecies. The first occurs when your own expectations influence your behavior. The second type of self-fulfilling prophecy occurs when the expectations of one person govern another's actions. A supervisor communicates by word or deed that an employee is lazy, ignorant, inferior, clumsy, and inept, and the worker accepts that evaluation and changes his or her self-concept to include that devaluation. Individuals do their darndest to live up—or down—to others' expectations of them. Consequently, the supervisor's stereotyped thinking is reinforced, and he or she thinks, "I knew that person was too 'different' to do the job."

Prejudice is an attitude, but discrimination is an act.

Prejudice is only an attitude, a state of mind, but *discrimination* is an act. It includes any type of behavior in which people are treated differently because of the categories into which they have been conveniently boxed, regardless of their unique attributes and abilities. Discrimination can be intentional or unintentional, subtle or blatant. Examples range from lewd comments and ethnic jokes to refusal to hire and promote certain individuals.

Although prejudice and discrimination are mutually reinforcing, they do not always interact. An employer may hold several biased attitudes toward women, for example, but because of discrimination laws, may not be permitted to keep women in the secretarial pool and exclude them from the managerial ranks. At the same time, a supervisor may be relatively free of prejudices and yet discriminate against certain individuals because of peer pressure.

What type of discrimination is legal and effective for a supervisor to perform?

Part of the job of being a manager includes the necessity to discriminate, but that discrimination must be done on the basis of certain prior and impartial criteria that are relevant to the achievement of overall objectives. This necessary discrimination involves making distinctions and recognizing differences between people. Managers and supervisors must have some way of rewarding superior employees and penalizing marginal ones, but these rewards and punishments should be linked to job performance. Can the person type 70 words per minute? Work weekends and nights? Travel? Drive a truck? If so, the law prohibits dis-

Opening Story Revisited

Bill worked for an equal opportunity employer. Is his case unusual? Was his "evaluation" based on fair and impartial criteria relevant to the achievement of overall objectives?

Although equal opportunity laws have brought women and minorities into positions of responsibility, many feel their careers stymied and their chances for ultimate success frustrated. How can this be when many top executives of large companies say they are committed to fairness and to promoting qualified minorities? Could it be because of the influence of unconscious, unthinking standards? Are prejudice and discrimination interacting regardless of what the laws dictate?

We have to assume that in Bill's case some form of discrimination was present since he was put on probation without any negative feedback about his job performance. In fact, Bill was getting compliments from his customers and colleagues. The statement used the second time he was put on probation was he did not "seem to be the right man."

---

criminating because of age, sex, national origin, or race. The courts have held that race and sex should never be factors used to discriminate.

Most people are aware of the illegal and blatant types of discrimination, but are not so knowledgeable about the subtle forms. Consequently, business owners may discriminate unknowingly and find themselves in court. "No business owner, manager, or supervisor can afford to make a decision or take action without regard to the possible legal consequences."[5] "Neutral" requirements concerning weight and height have been proven to be not so neutral if they exclude women and minorities.

A good example of *unintentional discrimination* is seen in the case of Griggs vs. Duke Power Company.[6] Duke Power required a high school diploma for employment. Griggs, a member of a minority group, had no such diploma. He applied for a janitorial position and was denied employment. An investigation revealed that, since in that geographic area three times as many whites as minorities had diplomas, requiring the diploma was discriminatory. The courts further ruled that educational status had little relationship to the ability of the person to perform the job. Seemingly neutral requirements such as requiring a degree or diploma or maintaining weight or height requirements may be ruled as illegal if they have an adverse impact on a member of a protected group.

Protected Groups. Individuals who are legally protected from discrimination because of the Civil Rights Act of 1964 and subsequent acts are considered to be members of protected groups. Since this protection covers people because of age, sex, religion, national origin, and color, more than three-fourths of all Americans can claim protected group status.[7] In fact, many people belong to more than one such protected group and thus have a "two-fer" status. Some believe this status could put such a worker—an elderly Asian, for example—in double jeopardy.

Margin notes:

Race and sex should never be factors used to discriminate.

What is unintentional discrimination?

Protected groups include more than three-fourths of all Americans and include those protected because of age, sex, race, religion, and national origin.

Double jeopardy does not always result, however. In fact, black women, who have to overcome both race and sex discrimination often experience less discrimination than that experienced by black men. Their situation is unique. Black females apparently are not seen by white men in the same sexual role as white women or in the same racial role as black men. Within a social context black females are more readily accepted in roles of influence than black males. One hypothesis is that white society has historically allowed more assertive behavior from black women than black men because the women are considered to be less intimidating and consequently more acceptable to white male executives.[8]

Nonprotected Groups or Reverse Discrimination. In some cases, people in protected classes have been protected at the expense of others. Some white men between the ages of 20 and 40 feel that they are victims of *reverse discrimination*—discrimination against an employee not included in a protected group. These men claim that it is wrong to end discrimination against some people by practicing it against others.

Discrimination on the basis of age, sex, race, color, religion, national origin, or handicap is illegal; more than three-fourths of all Americans belong to one or more of these protected groups.

Since protected groups feel that past discrimination needs to be corrected, these groups favor parity employment. *Parity employment* means that an organization's employees should approximately represent the proportions of different groups in the local community. For example, if the community has 15 percent racial minorities, the number of supervisors in a firm also should be about 15 percent racial minorities. This can lead to claims by nonprotected groups that reverse discrimination is occurring in the selection of supervisors. Managers sometimes feel that they are walking a tightrope between protected groups and the unprotected majority of white male employees who allege that they are victims of reverse discrimination.

How does reverse discrimination work in a firm?

Types of Discrimination

All people are guilty of prejudging others before gathering all the facts. The prejudices felt and the discrimination demonstrated are multiple and varied. Individuals miss out on job opportunities, training and development, promotions and advancements because of a variety of prejudices, such as those toward people from the South, people who are overweight, or people who belong to "different" religious sects. These types of discriminatory behaviors are unfortunate and difficult to prove. Racism, sexism, ageism, and discrimination against the handicapped are four types of illegal discrimination that are causing a furor in today's work environment. We'll discuss each of them before examining the laws designed to eliminate unequal treatment.

Racism.   A *race* is a group of people defined as socially distinct because of inherited physical characteristics. Racism is prejudice toward a group of people based on race, skin color, or national origin. Racial groups that are most often victims of discrimination today include blacks, Hispanics, Asians, and native Americans. Their physical and cultural differences have often prevented them from being part of the mainstream of American life. Let's briefly examine each of the four major victims of racism in America today.

Racism   prejudice toward a group of people defined as socially distinct because of inherited physical characteristics

Blacks.   Blacks constitute approximately 12 percent of the total U.S. population and have experienced inequalities in both educational and employment opportunities. The unemployment rate for blacks is about twice that of whites, and the average black family income is 60 percent that of the average white family.[9] As a group, blacks have been subjected to great cultural and educational handicaps.

Black employment has recently been worsened by increasing numbers of women and other minorities entering the labor force. From 1976 to 1984, black men lost ground relative to both white women and black women in the professions and officials and managers categories.[10]

While the employment picture still looks bleak, educational levels among blacks have improved. The average number of years of education for blacks increased from 8.0 years in 1960 to 12.2 years in 1982.[11]

Groups most often experiencing racism—prejudice based on race, skin color, national origin—are blacks, Hispanics, Asians, and native Americans.

As a group, blacks have experienced inequalities in both educational and employment opportunities.

Why haven't blacks progressed as far as some other racial groups in the job market?

There are a number of possible explanations for why blacks haven't progressed as far and fast as other groups. Some black Americans may lack knowledge of fundamental job skills needed to be successful on the job. Also, many blacks don't have the advantage of the "buddy system" of finding a job. Many jobs are located through insider sources. For example, a woman tells a friend of an opening in her department. A man tells his sister-in-law of a teacher who's resigning to stay home with her family. Whites are more likely to be aware of and to use this system. For this reason, affirmative action programs advise employers to actively recruit minority workers instead of relying on walk-ins or word of mouth advertising. Think about it. If a business employing predominantly white Anglo-Saxon Protestants does no recruiting and no advertising, who do you think is going to find out about potential job openings?

Colorism an attitude or predisposition to act in a certain way because of a person's skin color

Feeling that racism is too explosive a word, some people believe that blacks have not progressed as far as other racial groups because of "colorism." *Colorism* is "an attitude, a predisposition to act in a certain manner because of a person's skin color."[12] People tend to act unfavorably toward those with different skin color.

Hispanics. Hispanics include individuals from Cuba, Mexico, Puerto Rico, and other Central and South American countries. Hispanics differ greatly among

Slowly but Surely

With more than 6,400 elected officials nationwide, black America boasts more men and women in federal, state, and local offices than ever before. Most of them were elected in predominantly black districts, and many have attained national renown as movers and shakers and makers of public policy. But a slowly increasing number of virtually unknown black officials owe their election victories to a predominantly nonblack electorate. Three examples:

☐ In Anchorage, Alaska, Walter R. Furnace is a Republican state representative. He began a second term in 1987 and hopes to run for governor within 10 years.
☐ Sam Boykin, Jr., is the Democratic mayor of Box Elder, South Dakota, a city of 3,186 people.

Source: Adapted from "Elected Black Officials off the Beaten Path," *Ebony* (March 1987): 54 ff. Reprinted by permission of *Ebony* magazine and Johnson Publishing Co., Inc. © 1987.

☐ Harriet Elizabeth Byrd became Wyoming's first black state representative in 1981. She was serving her fourth term in 1987.

What Furnace, Boykin, and Byrd have in common is their elections from districts where less than 4 percent of the electorate are black. They and many others like them have run on the basis of their qualifications and they have won, often by large margins. Some hold offices in their home towns. Others are transplants who have found off-the-beaten-path communities fertile ground for their political ambitions. All share the experience of winning office where blacks, as one of them puts it, "are almost as rare as unicorns."

QUESTIONS

1. In what ways, if any, has civil rights legislation aided black Americans in their pursuit of public offices?
2. How important do you believe race is in deciding elections?

language barrier the greatest difficulty

themselves and have little in common except the Spanish language, certain historical conditions, the Catholic religion, and traditions such as devotion to God and family.

Today approximately 6 percent of the U.S. population is comprised of Hispanics. Many population analysts predict that because of a young median age and a high fertility rate, this percentage will climb to 18 in only 50 years. If this happens, Hispanics will become America's largest minority.[13]

This rapidly growing minority has traditionally engaged in such low-paying jobs as migrant labor. They've suffered from poor education, a lack of job skills, and a language barrier. On average, Hispanics over the age of 25 have completed 10.3 years of school, compared with 11.9 years for blacks over the age of 25 and 12.5 for whites.[14]

Language is a handicap in the labor force and in the schools. Even so, the average Hispanic family income is about 70 percent of the average white family income, so Hispanics fare better than blacks. One reason for the higher family income is that often recent Hispanic immigrants from low-wage countries are willing to work for less than blacks.

Since language is the most troublesome barrier between U.S. managers and Hispanic workers, why doesn't the Spanish-speaking person learn to speak English? Professor Pastora San Juan of the University of Chicago suggests that since Mexico lies just across the U.S. border and that since Mexicans tend to migrate back and forth in three- to seven-year cycles, the cultural pull is stronger for Mexicans than for other immigrants. Mexicans often think they are in the United States only temporarily and need not bother to learn English. Also, many Mexican Americans who do wish to speak English lack the educational background that would enable them to learn a new language.[15]

Asian Americans. Asian Americans, including Japanese, Chinese, Filipinos, and Vietnamese, accounted for about 1.5 percent of the American population in 1980 and their numbers are likely to double by 2010. Many Asians believe that they are the latest victims of racial prejudice since some highly educated Asians find that degrees that took years to earn may not carry much weight here in the land of opportunity.

Still, Asians are faring better than other racial groups. They are represented far beyond their population percentage at virtually every top-ranking college and university. In fact, with the exception of the Indochinese, the new Asian arrivals are at least twice as likely as native-born Americans to be college graduates.[16] These educational achievements have enabled many Asians to succeed in such professions as medicine and law, and they are well represented in the ranks of managers and other professionals as well. Furthermore, their median income exceeds that of white families.

The reasons for the success of Asian Americans are many. Many are permitted entry to the United States because of a desirable vocational background, and many come from urban middle-class backgrounds with values similar to dominant American values of hard work and diligence. The combination of a reverence for education and a strong achievement drive explains at least part of the success formula.

Native Americans. Native Americans constitute only 0.5 percent of the U.S. population and have fared less well than any of the other minority groups. About 55 percent of the American Indians live below the poverty level, and their rate of unemployment is 50 percent.[17] After more than a century of federal supervision and dashed hopes, the first Americans find themselves still at the bottom of the ladder—high in unemployment, health problems, and alcoholism, low in wealth and education.[18] The per capita income is less than 60 percent of the American average, and the Indian dropout rate from high school is twice the national average.

American Indians who leave reservations hoping for a better life in an urban area find their hopes shattered. They often have limited job skills and education,

Margin notes:

higher median income (as a group discrimination because of success)

Why are Asian Americans more successful, both educationally and economically, than some of the other racial groups?

Native Americans are one of the smallest and poorest racial groups in America today.

least successful

and instead of congregating with other urban Indians who could offer support, they tend to blend in with the rest of the urban poor. The transplanted native American experiences culture shock at the fast-paced city life while being cut off from other Indians who could provide emotional and financial support. Native Americans are one of the smallest and poorest racial groups in America today.

Sexism. As increasing numbers of women enter the work force, discrimination based on gender has become a heated issue. The Women's Liberation Movement has helped bring about an awareness of restrictions based on gender. Sexism is based on widely held beliefs about the abilities, characteristics, and behavior of women and men. Like other prejudices, sexism can limit the opportunities to choose a preferred career or lifestyle. Usually sexism refers to discrimination toward women, but many men feel that they also are victims of it.

Sexism discrimination based on gender

Women constitute a majority of the world population and yet are treated like a minority group. They make up more than 40 percent of the U.S. labor force and their numbers are expected to swell. The Bureau of Labor Statistics predicts that in 1995 the labor participation rate of women will average about 60.3 percent.[19] Today full-time working wives bring home 40 percent of the total earnings in a two-income family.

Many women are pursuing different lifestyles than their mothers and grandmothers did. They've added to their traditional homemaking role and have begun concentrating on profit margins and performance feedback. Unfortunately, even when bright, high-achieving, competent women succeed in academic distinction, status, recognition, and professional advancement, many perceive themselves to be "impostors." "Impostors" acknowledge their competence even as they experience self-doubt and negative evaluation. In the words of a program counselor at a technical training school for women: "The successes are not fully internalized—meaning women don't often take credit for what they've done. So that in a situation where they may have a responsible job, it's emotionally unclear how they got there."[20]

Some positive changes have occurred, but most women still have experienced few visible gains. For many reasons women still tend to cluster in low-paying, "female-intensive" jobs such as nursing, teaching, and secretarial jobs. Education helps but doesn't solve the problem. Female MBAs entering the work force are paid the same starting salaries as men with the same qualifications, but within ten years, women's pay falls behind by 20 percent regardless of the company they work for or their jobs.[21]

Explain why women have not made significant gains in the work place.

In 1980 women earned 50 percent of all bachelor's degrees, but in spite of increased education, there's still a wage gap between the sexes. Women earn 64 cents to every dollar earned by men. The average starting salary for female college graduates is roughly equal to the average starting salary for male high school graduates. Child-care workers (mostly female) earn less than parking lot attendants (mostly male). Librarians (mostly female) earn less than liquor store clerks (mostly male).[21] From Connecticut comes the tale of an illiterate kitchen worker

Abusing Sex at the Office

Sexual harassment, the boss's dirty little fringe benefit, has been dragged out of the closet. Women who have traditionally tolerated harassment just as they have tolerated low wages are beginning to fight back. Many corporations have learned that harassment in the workplace will cost them money. The increase in the number of complaints parallels the upsurge in the number of women working outside the home. An extraordinary number of women are entering the work force, and they aren't as likely to keep harassment to themselves these days.

One result of the new look at sexual harassment is the discovery that women are not the only victims. John, 32, married and a father, wanted to enroll in a federally funded training program. A higher ranking single woman offered to guarantee his admission if he would sleep with her. He did, two or three times, and she pro-

Source: "Abusing Sex at the Office," *Newsweek* (10 March 1980): 81–82. Used by permission.

vided the promised recommendation. But their relationship had other costs. "She made it obvious in the office." John says, "She'd come over and say things like, 'I'm looking forward to tonight.'"

What's a person to do if she or he finds the atmosphere loaded with offensive sexual innuendoes, jokes, or unsought verbal intimacy? What if a person resents being pinched, grabbed, or patted? Workers are legally protected against sexual harassment, but it's best to nip harassment in the bud—in the beginning of a relationship before egos get involved. The best response remains a firm, polite, nonthreatening, "No," especially for verbal harassment unconnected to professional favor.

QUESTIONS

1. Why do you think sexual harassment has become such a hot issue?
2. Why is it so important for allegations to be thoroughly investigated?

---

who was paid $600 more a year than the secretary he asked to help him fill out the application form.[22]

Why does so much inequity exist between the sexes? Cultural conditioning is part of the answer. Men and women have both learned and accepted sexual stereotypes, and a lifetime of conditioning is hard to unlearn in a few short years. Gender-role stereotypes offer mental shortcuts in dealing with others and spill over into the office or factory. Many women feel more comfortable with stereotypically female roles, and many men are content with that arrangement.

How has culture influenced the issue of sexism in business?

Women and men perceive and experience work differently. Women often are unaware of the rules of organizational life that men know and take for granted. Too, women have fewer sexual role models to identify with and fewer mentors to guide them. Without mentors, it is more difficult for women to learn about the opportunities available to them. Poor career planning is also a variable. Some researchers estimate that many women are ten or fifteen years into their careers before they make a conscious career decision.[23] Finally, employers blame sexism on the media, misguided guidance counseling, and the long legacy of women having to take second place in the employment world.[24]

Sexual Harassment.   Sexual harassment is a by-product of sexism. It includes offers of job favors in return for sexual favors, as well as sexually suggestive or offensive speech or conduct. It happens in hospitals, banks, schools, law offices, and factories across the country. Men also experience harassment though not as often as women. Some male supervisors who have control over raises and other working conditions treat sexual favors as another badge of rank.[25]

Sexual harassment job offers in return for sexual favors, or sexually suggestive or offensive speech or conduct.

Ageism.   Ageism is discrimination against people because of age. Those between the ages of forty and seventy are usually thought of as the victims of ageism, but younger workers have claimed to be victims too. Consider this before trying to prevent the promotion of a capable sixty year old: Ageism is the only common prejudice in which those who hold it eventually wind up as the members of the group that they stereotype.[26] With the life expectancy today around 74, your chances of becoming a senior citizen are high.

Ageism discrimination against people because of age

Many people respond to the concept of ageism by thinking of wise and gray oldsters hobbling around with walking canes, yet ageism is experienced by much younger people. Men and women experiencing a mid-life adjustment and subse-

Chronological age is irrelevant to an individual's potential or performance.

quent job change are often surprised and hurt when confronted with prejudiced attitudes. Homemakers who have stayed at home have a difficult time re-entering the work force, especially if their skills are outdated. People who retire after twenty years in the military, employees who get laid off, and other workers whose jobs are replaced by technology sometimes find job-hunting a nightmare.

Chronological age is an invalid and illegal way of assessing an individual's potential. Age does not always have a detrimental effect on capabilities. It's foolish to generalize about older people. *All* people differ in their personalities, physical and mental health, abilities, race, sex, religion, marital status, and life experiences. Age is a relative concept, and the nature of the job can influence appropriate age. Thirty-five is young for corporate presidents and supreme court justices, but old for professional athletes.

Research yields little evidence to link age with incompetence, senility, or lack of worth in the labor market.

A 1959 Department of Labor study of insurance companies, auto dealers, and large department stores suggests that an "older" age is actually an asset in performance. Furthermore, age seems to have little effect on manual workers whose performance remains steady through age fifty, peaking slightly in the thirties. Attendance was not significantly affected, and separation rates (resignations, layoffs, discharges) were high for those under age twenty-five and very low for those over forty-five.[27]

People are living longer and want to continue working for many reasons. Fixed retirement pensions don't keep up with inflation, and many older people need employment to meet financial obligations and acquire necessities. Some have no pensions and rely solely on minimal Social Security benefits. Just as important, all people need social contact and interaction with others. This is especially true for an older person whose family members may be grown and living elsewhere. Finally, no matter what the age, people need to feel productive and useful.

The graying work force has problems not faced by other groups. Obsolescence and job changes are major fears of older workers. No one wants a job with less pay and prestige, but an older worker is often forced into such a situation if earlier acquired job skills are dated. Learning new job skills is sometimes a frightening experience even though older individuals are still quite capable of learning.

Ageism is the only common prejudice in which those who hold it eventually wind up as members of the group they stereotype.

The Age Discrimination Act of 1967, which was amended in 1978, protects individuals from ages forty to seventy from discrimination in employment. Since these people are members of a protected group, employers need to ensure that older employees have equal opportunity. This law also protects employees against mandatory retirement. An employer may not force an employee to retire before the employee reaches seventy years of age except in certain cases—for example, if safety is a factor. This is an especially important act considering the increased longevity and health of Americans.

Discrimination Against the Handicapped. Hiring the handicapped is good business, but unfortunately many employers are reluctant to hire them. In spite of equal opportunity laws, the handicapped continue to be one of our greatest

Opening Story Revisited

Blacks are not the only group suffering from an *invisible ceiling,* that is, they can rise to only a certain level of management and no further. Women managers report that while overt discrimination is almost gone, the real gains in hiring and promotions have leveled off. Women managers find themselves in positions similar to Bill's. They've become a significant part of the corporate pyramid in the past decade but their numbers are still concentrated in its lower half.

Would you guess that there are other forms of discrimination besides race in the problem Bill is facing? In most cases, discrimination is not just localized to one type of protected group. In most organizations, there are multiple forms of discrimination that need to be addressed before there can be true equality.

---

underutilized human resources. It's difficult to say how many handicapped people there are, but researchers suggest 35 million or more. Forcing idleness on the handicapped hurts everyone. Not hiring the handicapped can affect them in adverse ways, and it is a great loss to business and the national economy.

What is a handicapped person? Legally, the handicapped person (1) has a physical or mental impairment that substantially limits one or more of the person's major life activities, (2) has a record of such an impairment, or (3) is regarded as having such an impairment.[28] The impairment may or may not be visible.

The term handicapped is very broad. A handicapped worker can be mentally retarded, blind, deaf, paralyzed, or an amputee; he might have a prison record, cancer, mental illness, epilepsy, or heart disease; she could even be a rehabilitated drug user or alcoholic. The truth is that you might not even recognize a person as handicapped.

Handicaps include visible and invisible impairments.

The keystone law fighting discrimination against the handicapped is the Rehabilitation Act of 1973, which established that handicapped people can't be rejected simply because of their disabilities. While employers should require that the handicapped employee meet the same standards as other employees, there must be a reasonable effort to accommodate handicapped employees on the job, such as lower desks or restructured restrooms.

Excuses, Excuses. Some employers make all sorts of excuses for not hiring the handicapped: that they are more accident prone, that they are offensive to look at, or that having them in the workplace inflates insurance rates. Actually the safety rates are higher among the handicapped, possibly because they are more aware of their limitations and therefore more cautious.

Offensive to look at? Seeing a person with a visible handicap may make co-workers and supervisors uncomfortable. Many times the nonhandicapped don't know how to react to the handicapped, perhaps because of a lack of understand-

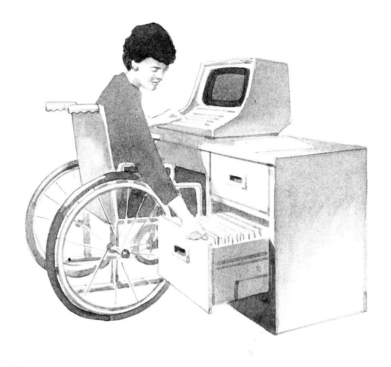

As many employers have discovered, persons with physical or other disabilities are often highly motivated and productive workers.

ing. As with all relationships, people must be exposed to handicapped individuals to get to know them and to learn that there are more similarities than differences between people.

The handicapped are usually highly motivated. As a group, they are efficient, self-reliant, and have low turnover and absentee rates.

Challenges of Working with the Handicapped. Attitudes toward and opportunities for handicapped workers are improving. Supervisors need to be sensitive to the needs of the handicapped and learn to use their special talents and skills. Selective placement is an important step in managing the handicapped worker. This involves matching the physical abilities of the person with the physical demands of the job.

Concentrating on a handicapped person's abilities instead of disabilities is sound advice. Sometimes a seeming disadvantage can actually be an advantage. For example, a deaf person could concentrate and operate quite effectively in an area with loud machinery that may be very distracting to a person without a hearing impairment. A mentally retarded person may be less bored by semiautomated work.

Managers are encouraged to maintain a normal relationship with the handicapped worker. Don't coddle, patronize, or be overprotective. Treat them as you would any other worker.

Equal Employment Opportunity and the Law

No manager can afford to make a decision or take an action without regard to the possible legal consequences. The civil rights legislation of the 1960s was a turning point in the attempt to eradicate inequalities.

Title VII of Civil Rights Act. The Civil Rights Act of 1964 is the landmark legislation that gave impetus to equal opportunity, a concept supported by federal, state, and local laws. Title VII of the Act deals specifically with discrimination in employment and prohibits employment discrimination against individuals because of race, color, religion, sex, or national origin. Title VII is the backbone of most employment discrimination regulations and court decisions. These laws prohibit discrimination in regard to those seeking employment and to the terms and conditions of work after employment.

The Equal Employment Opportunity Commission (EEOC) is the agency primarily responsible for administering and enforcing Title VII. It processes charges of discrimination brought by people and helps organizations establish and imple-

> The Equal Employment Opportunity Commission processes charges of discrimination and helps organizations implement affirmative action programs.

Opening Story Revisited

I f we return to the opening story, we can see a potential area where EEOC could enter the picture. If Bill decided that he was being discriminated against and filed a complaint, EEOC would investigate his situation.

One area to explore is the number of minorities in Bill's division as compared to the local community. If the numbers are too far off, EEOC may ask the company to begin specific recruitment programs to change the numbers.

Another area is Bill's actual situation. Some of the information cites a favorable performance by Bill's group. This seems to indicate that Bill is doing his job and his performance review should indicate these positive results. On the basis of what concrete job performance is Bill being put on probation? We don't have any information except a quote from two levels that Bill "isn't the right man for the job." If this can't be substantiated with facts, EEOC can get Bill reinstated with back pay.

One final set of questions needs to be raised. Is it to Bill's benefit to be reinstated in an organization in which discrimination is deep-rooted? Or does Bill have a responsibility to seek a "correct" action in the form of no discrimination for future employees?

ment affirmative action plans. The commission can also require employers to file reports on the numbers of minority workers holding various types of jobs.

Examples of Title VII violations include refusing to hire, train, or promote protected employees; granting unequal compensation; firing without specific job-related reasons; or practicing any type of segregation or classification that deprives some individuals of employment opportunities.

How does EEOC work with a complaint of discrimination?

If EEOC receives a complaint or has a reason to believe that Title VII has been violated, it conducts an investigation. If there's enough evidence to demonstrate discrimination, EEOC attempts a resolution. The commission tries to get the employer to eliminate the practice in question. If that fails, it's empowered to file suit in federal district court. Guilty employers might have to rehire, pay back wages, or implement an affirmative action program aimed at recruiting minority employees.

Affirmative action employer's effort to increase employment opportunity for groups that appear to be inadequately represented in the company's labor force

Affirmative Action.   Affirmative action is an employer effort to increase employment opportunity (including promotions and all other conditions of employment) for groups that appear to be inadequately represented in the firm's labor force. It forces employers to go beyond simply promising not to be unfair and unjust.

Employers are encouraged to examine their labor force and ensure that all groups are fairly represented. If they aren't, the companies are required to begin a positive effort to provide equal employment opportunities to remedy any alleged past discrimination and prevent it in the future. Affirmative action programs mean that an employer can't passively wait for Puerto Ricans, American Indians, Asian Americans, blacks, women, the handicapped, and workers over forty to apply for jobs, training, or promotions. Usually, there are timetables by which companies plan to accomplish certain goals.

LEARNING SUMMARY

1. Advantages of overcoming discrimination in the workplace are many. The talents and abilities of women and minorities could result in many contributions to the nation. People would become more self-reliant and have better self-images. More taxes would be paid, and less welfare would be distributed.

2. Prejudice is an attitude while discrimination is an act. Prejudice often results from stereotypes—overgeneralizations about a group based on the characteristics of one member. Discrimination ranges from lewd comments and ethnic jokes to refusal to hire and promote certain individuals.

3. Equal Employment Opportunity (EEO) prohibits discrimination against individuals because of age, sex, race, religion, or national origin. Those protected by such legislation are called protected groups. Many not protected by equal opportunity laws feel that they are victims of reverse discrimination.

4. Four major types of illegal discrimination in the workplace are racism, sexism, ageism, and discrimination against the handicapped.

5. Four racial groups who frequently face prejudice and discrimination are blacks, Hispanics, Asian Americans, and American Indians.
6. Workers aged forty to seventy are protected by the Age Discrimination Act. As the life expectancy of Americans increases, more older citizens will desire to be gainfully employed for financial, emotional, psychological, and health reasons.
7. The handicapped are now protected by EEO and include those persons having both visible and invisible handicaps. Employers are required to hire and promote qualified handicapped employees.
8. Major discrimination legislation began in 1964 with the passage of the Equal Rights Act. Since that time, courts have ruled that employers are responsible for subtle types of discrimination, not just blatant types.

ANSWERS TO "WHAT'S YOUR OPINION?"

1. True   This discrimination, however, involves making judgments based on fair and impartial criteria relevant to the job.
2. False   Most managers and business owners are not aware of the adverse impact of "neutral" qualifications on minorities. Most are not even aware of what the subtle, unintentional types of discrimination are.
3. False   Approximately three-fourths of all Americans belong to a protected group. White males between the ages of twenty and forty are about the only ones excluded.
4. True   Hispanics are the fastest growing minority and are expected to be America's largest minority within fifty years.
5. True   Sexual harassment is now considered illegal. The employer's responsibility extends to employees harassing co-workers.
6. False   Equal employment laws prohibit discrimination in regard to recruiting, hiring, promoting, training, demoting, and firing.
7. True   Most discrimination problems are the result of unintentional violations of Title VII.

KEY TERMS

Affirmative action
Ageism
Civil Rights Act of 1964
Discrimination
Equal Employment Opportunity Commission
Handicapped
Prejudice

Protected groups
Racism
Reverse discrimination
Self-fulfilling prophecy
Sexism
Sexual harassment
Stereotyping

HUMAN RELATIONS APPLICATIONS

We strongly believe that dealing with prejudice and discrimination will result in more effective and productive organizations and individuals. In addition, if supervisors strive to improve some of the human relations issues raised earlier in the book (such as communication, motivation, leadership, group dynamics, and conflict resolution), these problems of inequity can be minimized. However, we also know that human nature needs guidance to improve. As a result, the first section of the applications section is our suggestion for creating a sound EEO program. The last section of the application will relate efforts to deal more effectively with the handicapped issue.

A Sound EEO Program

A sound EEO program has a number of basic requirements, as outlined in Figure 13–1. Each requirement is elaborated with specific guidelines.

In the final analysis, the employer's attitudes toward minorities will be known by the employees. For this reason, a positive attitude and approach are necessary for equal opportunity to succeed. There must be strong top management support of affirmative action, and support has to be communicated to all employees. Owners and supervisors alike have to be convinced of the benefits of equal opportunity to make the dream a reality.

Few organizations are perfect; the majority need a little affirmative action. Even though common sense and a desire to be fair will eliminate many of the legal problems that face employers in establishing qualifications, a knowledge of specific guidelines can help assure a sound EEO program.

FIGURE 13–1
A sound EEO program

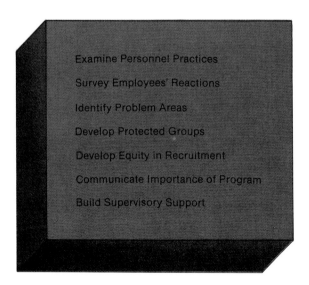

Examine Personnel Practices

Survey Employees' Reactions

Identify Problem Areas

Develop Protected Groups

Develop Equity in Recruitment

Communicate Importance of Program

Build Supervisory Support

Examine Personnel Policies. Management must examine personnel policies to eliminate potentially discriminatory practices. Additionally, managers need to reappraise policies and practices periodically to ensure that guidelines established to create more opportunities for minorities and women do not bring about reverse discrimination.

In the past employers could be arbitrary in deciding what qualifications they wanted in new employees. The so-called qualifications could fit the prejudices and wishes of the employers. If he or she (usually "he" prior to the 1960s) disliked long hair or tall people, then no long-haired, tall applicants need send resumes. Today the employer determines the job qualifications and then asks whether they are fair and whether any prospective employees of protected groups have been eliminated.

The majority of discrimination problems are not the result of deliberate discrimination, but are unintentional violations. Some are obvious, some are not. For example, is refusing to hire women with small children illegal? Yes, if the same requirement is not used for men with small children. What impact will having a good credit rating have on certain protected groups?

Survey Employees' Reactions. One step in any program is to survey employees' reactions to affirmative action guidelines. Some employers think this is a mistake comparable to opening a "Pandora's box" of frustration and dissatisfaction.[29] They fear that polling employees might cause an eruption of latent discontent among unprotected employees. However, the information gleaned is essential for pinpointing departments or areas in which negative attitudes are particularly hostile or intense.

Identify Problem Areas. The employer needs to determine whether or not there are inequalities in salary, education, promotion, and employment of different groups. Statistics are generally used to identify areas of discrimination. Look around. Who does the dirty work? Who performs the menial jobs? Who has the clean, higher status jobs? Who gives orders and who carries them out?

Remember, not every instance of unequal representation necessarily spells discrimination. Maybe some employees aren't motivated toward advancement or don't have the education needed for a highly skilled position.

Develop Protected Groups. Develop those individuals in protected groups that have potential for promotion and are interested in it. Assure them that EEO is available. Employers have found that many women and minorities who were discriminated against in the past have been reluctant to develop themselves or accept promotions. These employees can be helped by specialized training, either in-house or at local colleges.

Develop Equality in Recruitment Practices. If women and minorities are not included in the workplace in proportion to their numbers in the population, recruitment can't be based solely on word-of-mouth. The employer must advertise and do so in such a way to portray equality. Job notices or advertisements must be neutral and cannot indicate any preferences or limitations based on race, sex, or age. Additional means of ensuring equality include recruiting at high schools and colleges having a large number of minorities and women, advertising in newspapers appealing to protected groups, and hiring recruiters who are themselves of protected groups.

Communicate Importance of Program. Within a business or organization, a manager must communicate about equal opportunity to ensure awareness of an EEO program. Supervisors might be given specialized training to make them aware of different work attitudes and values of protected groups. They also need to become aware of their own attitudes and the way in which these same attitudes can influence productivity and the work environment itself. For example, a supervisor might think that older people are not physically able to do a full day's work and might consequently lower the work requirements. The older person's self-concept is affected, and the self-fulfilling prophecy spoken of earlier goes into effect.

Uncertainty and misunderstanding over affirmative action's goals and policies sometimes lead to false expectations among employees. If employees are aware of the legal and social issues surrounding the program, their increased understanding can help change negative attitudes.

Build Supervisory Support. Supervisory support is especially important since supervisors come in direct contact with employees. It's one thing for management to say, "Comply with the law," and another thing for the supervisor to understand the special needs of a mentally retarded employee, be alert to signs of sexual harassment, guard against claims of reverse discrimination, and keep everyone happy and productive.

Work group conflict is increased as new people, especially "different" people, are integrated into the work group. Many supervisors need special training on the laws themselves; others need training on becoming aware of their own attitudes and on how those attitudes can affect workers.

Some Examples of Special Programs for the Handicapped

The efforts of some leading companies to better the lot of handicapped persons provide valuable examples to concerned business people.

Edison. Some of the Edison companies have done an admirable job of upgrading facilities for the handicapped. They have lowered desks, restructured restrooms, cut outside curbs to accommodate wheelchairs, lowered elevator controls and added braille, completely redesigned some furniture and lowered pay phones. Most Edison companies report that these changes have not required excessive funding.

One Edison company has restructured certain jobs, provided special tools and equipment, conducted surveys to learn which employees know sign language, replaced a keypuncher warning bell with a flashing light for hard-of-hearing employees, and adopted a policy permitting handicapped employees to work shorter hours. The company also provides reserved parking close to the place of work for those handicapped employees who use walking aids.

Continental Bank of Chicago. In a major program to eliminate physical barriers to the handicapped, this bank had its large revolving center door replaced by a double air door. The bank works with such agencies as the Chicago Lighthouse for the Blind to pursue its policy of hiring the blind. Continental also has a full-time coordinator of affirmative action for the handicapped.

The bank brags about its handicapped employees, one of whom is Caroline Christ. Christ is blind but has a typing speed that sometimes reaches 96 words per minute—error free. In the past, the normal work load for secretaries combined both transcription typing and "copy" work—retyping written material. Now Ms. Christ types the majority of the dictated material while the other typists do the copy work, and she has been provided desk space to store her seven volume braille dictionary.

The bank's affirmative action program for the handicapped is based on a creative approach, a more realistic evaluation of job requirements, the education of managers and supervisors, encouragement of career planning, hiring of a specialist to implement the program, and involvement in local rehabilitation centers for job training and work orientation.[30]

In this chapter we saw that prejudice and discrimination have no place in the work world. Not only does failure in overcoming discrimination hinder workers, businesses, and the nation as a whole, but the practice itself is illegal. The laws have helped, but the values and the attitudes that determine decision making cannot be so easily legislated.

Certain guidelines can improve your success as a manager in eliminating discriminatory attitudes and practices that hinder the career success of some, cheapen the accomplishments of others, and enforce idleness and a feeling of uselessness in others.

PERSONAL GUIDELINES FOR HUMAN RELATIONS SUCCESS

1. Make it your business to learn about the various discrimination laws. A knowledge of such legislation can save you headaches, hassles, and money down the road. Familiarity with at least the bare bones of the various laws is a must for someone in management.
2. One of the most important things you can do as a manager is to "Know Thyself." You may not be able to overcome your stereotypes, but an awareness of them might be the first step in fighting the negative impact of your faulty overgeneralizations.

3. When you discover your personal prejudices, leave them at home if you don't want to do your company and its employees a disservice.

4. Create a proper work atmosphere within your department so that all employees are fully aware of your company's equal employment opportunity policies. Communicate the importance of the success of the program to all employees and encourage their participation and cooperation.

5. Be alert to possible inequalities of job assignments, advancements, training, or any other aspect of employment. Are white employees considered for promotion after only two years while black employees have to work four years for such consideration?

6. Make every effort to encourage and assist qualified employees from underutilized groups, such as racial minorities, females, older or handicapped workers, to advance within your company. This includes encouraging their participation in training and educational programs, and providing career counseling when necessary.

7. Do not tolerate discriminatory acts. Ethnic jokes, racial slurs, and sexual harassment are illegal.

DISCUSSION AND REVIEW QUESTIONS

1. What is meant by the phrase "people in protected classes have been protected at the expense of others"? Do you agree with this?

2. What are the major advantages of removing discrimination from the workplace?

3. What are some of the problems faced by older people in the labor force today?

4. What are some guidelines to follow in working with the handicapped? Be specific.

5. What are some of the major types of discrimination covered by equal opportunity laws? How does the Equal Employment Opportunity Commission work?

HUMAN RELATIONS EXERCISE

Stereotyping

Instructions. Read the following situation and respond to it as if you were the personnel manager of a large organization. To further test the assumption that decisions are often made on the basis of subconscious stereotyping, ask someone in a management position to read and respond to the incident. Compare your answers and discuss your conclusions.*

---

*Reprinted by permission of Harvard Business Review. "Sex Stereotyping in the Executive Suite" by Benson Rosen and Thomas Jerdee, March–April, 1974. Copyright © 1974 by the President and Fellows of Harvard College; all rights reserved.

Personnel Decisions. Jack and Judy Garrison have been married three years. Jack is an aspiring business executive and Judy is a successful free-lance writer. This is part of a conversation they had after coming home from a cocktail party at the home of an executive in Jack's division.

JUDY: Oh boy, what a bunch of creeps. Do we have to go to these parties, honey?

JACK: Judy, you know we have to. These things mean a lot to me. Tonight I had a chance to talk to Mr. Wilson. On the job it would take a week to get an appointment with him. I was able to get across two good ideas I had about our new sales campaign, and I think he was listening.

JUDY: Is Wilson that fat slob who works in marketing, the one with the dull wife? I spent ten minutes with her and I nearly died! She's too much. Jack, the people there tonight were so dull I could have cried. Why did I major in English Lit. anyway? I prefer to talk to people who know what is going on in the world, not a bunch of half-wits whose main interests are their new cars and spoiled kids. I tried to talk to one guy about Virginia Woolf and he didn't even know who she was. These people are incredible. Do we have to go to another cocktail party again next week? I'd like to see *Look Back in Anger* instead. I've got the tickets. One of my wifely duties is to give you culture. What an uncouth bunch in the business world!

JACK: One of my husbandly ambitions is to get ahead in the business world. You know that these parties are required for bright junior executives coming up in the organization. And I'm a bright junior executive. If we don't go, who knows which of the other junior execs will get to Wilson with their good ideas?

JUDY: Can't you relax and work a 40-hour week? That's what they pay you for.

JACK: I guess I'm too ambitious to relax.

JUDY: I'd still like to go to the play. At least we could think about real problems.

JACK: And I'd be a mediocre, lower-management nobody for the rest of my career.

JUDY: I want you to be a success, Jack. But the idea of spending more evenings talking to idiots is too much.

Choose one of the following responses:

1. The spouse should go to parties and stop making such an issue of it.
2. The junior executive should attend the parties alone.
3. The junior executive should stop attending the parties.

HUMAN RELATIONS INCIDENT

Linda Santiago worked in the secretarial pool of a large corporation for eleven years.* Five years ago, she would have said that she never wanted to be anything but a secretary. She also would have told you that because she had recently had children, she was thinking of quitting. Secretarial work was not a good enough reason to leave her children at a day-care center each day. In fact, the only reason

---

*Reprinted by permission from *People at Work* by Paul R. Timm and Brent D. Peterson; © 1982 by West Publishing Company. All rights reserved.

Linda continued working was that she enjoyed the association with the others in the secretarial pool.

In recent years, the corporation Linda worked for initiated an aggressive affirmative action program. Linda, who had always been a conscientious worker, was offered a promotion. At first, she wavered. It meant leaving her good friends in the secretarial pool for a lonely life among the management, which was predominantly male. Her friends thought she was abandoning them. She worried whether she could handle the new job. But her boss talked her into it and promised to help, reassuring her that he would be her sponsor.

So Linda was promoted, and now she successfully handles a challenging management job. Seeing friends is the least of her many reasons to come to work every day, and her ambitions have soared. She wants to go right to the top. "I have fifteen years left to work," she says. "And I want to move up six grades to corporate vice president at least."

QUESTIONS

1. In what ways has Linda readjusted her expectations? What do you think accounts for this upgrading of goals?
2. What role did Linda's boss play in helping her make the transition from the secretarial pool to management?

NOTES

1. Edward W. Jones, Jr., "Black Managers: The Dream Deferred," *Harvard Business Review* (May-June 1986): 87.
2. Benson Rosen and Thomas H. Jerdee, "Coping with Affirmative Action Backlash," *Business Horizons* (August 1979): 20.
3. Gay Bryant, *Working Woman Report* (New York: Simon & Schuster, 1984): 13–14.
4. Christopher Bates Doob, *Sociology* (New York: Holt, Rinehart, and Winston, 1985): 235.
5. Cliff Roberson, *Staying Out of Court* (Lexington, MA: D.C. Heath Company, 1985): 1.
6. Alfred Blumrosen, "Strangers in Paradise: Griggs v. Duke Power Co. and the Concept of Employment Discrimination," *Michigan Law Review* (November 1972): 59–110.
7. Keith Davis, *Human Behavior at Work: Organizational Behavior,* 6th ed. (New York: McGraw-Hill Book Company, 1981): 380.
8. Edward W. Jones: 91.
9. Rate A. Howell, John R. Allison, and N. T. Henley, *The Legal Environment of Business* (Chicago: The Dryden Press, 1984): 453.
10. Anne B. Fisher, "Good News, Bad News, and an Invisible Ceiling," *Fortune* (9 September 1985): 29.
11. U.S. Bureau of the Census, *Statistical Abstracts of the United States,* 106th ed. (Washington, DC, 1985).
12. Edward W. Jones: 88.
13. Cary Davis, "The Future Racial Composition of the U.S.," *Intercom,* 1985: 8–10.
14. Aaron Berstein, "The Forgotten Americans," *Business Week* (2 September 1985): 55.
15. Mariah E. deForest, "Mexican Workers North of the Border," *Harvard Business Review* (May-June 1985): 151.
16. William R. Doerner, "To America with Skills," *Time* (8 July 1985): 32.
17. Rate A. Howell: 253–54.

18. Steve Huntley, "America's Indians: Beggars in Our Own Land," *U.S. News and World Report* (23 May 1983): 70.

19. Karen Pennar and Edward Mervosh, "Women at Work," *Business Week* (28 January 1985): 83.

20. Lynda L. Moore, *Not as Far as You Think* (Lexington, MA: Lexington Books, 1986): 27.

21. Gay Bryant: 21.

22. Mildred Hamilton, "Measuring Pay Equity," *San Francisco Examiner* (23 April 1984): B10.

23. Margaret Henning and Anne Jardin, *The Managerial Woman* (Garden City, NY: Anchor Press/ Doubleday, 1977): 55.

24. Richard Peres, *Dealing with Employment Discrimination* (New York: McGraw-Hill Book Company, 1978): 34.

25. "Abusing Sex at the Office," *Newsweek* (10 March 1980): 80.

26. Robert Perrucci and Dean D. Knudsen, *Sociology* (St. Paul, MN: West Publishing Company, 1983): 162.

27. Jeffrey Sonnenfield, "Dealing with the Aging Work Force," *Harvard Business Review* (November-December, 1978): 88–89.

28. Rate A. Howell: 483.

29. Benson Rosen: 19.

30. Gopal C. Pati and John I. Adkins, Jr., "Hire the Handicapped—Compliance Is Good Business," *Harvard Business Review* (January-February, 1980): 18–20.

PART FIVE

GLOBAL TOPICS IN HUMAN RELATIONS

CHAPTER 14
ORGANIZATIONAL CULTURE

WHAT'S YOUR OPINION? T OR F

_____ 1. Everything a manager does is influenced by an organization's culture.

_____ 2. Organizational culture is easy to measure.

_____ 3. Stories, myths, and other folklore are an important part of organizational culture.

_____ 4. Philosophy guides policy in most organizations.

_____ 5. Norms are the same thing as rules.

_____ 6. Organizational climate is a more useful managerial concept than culture.

_____ 7. Commitment occurs when people identify with an organization.

_____ 8. Organizational culture can be changed easily.

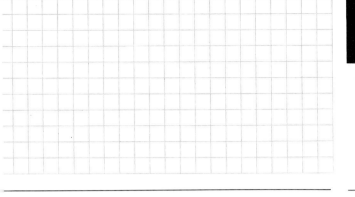

OUTLINE

CONCEPTS OF ORGANIZATIONAL CULTURE
Dimensions of Cultural Fxcellence
The Content of Organizational Culture

ORGANIZATIONAL CLIMATE

ORGANIZATIONAL CULTURE INFLUENCES
ORGANIZATIONAL PROCESS
Culture and Organizational Performance
Maintaining or Changing a Culture

LEARNING SUMMARY

HUMAN RELATIONS APPLICATIONS .
Breaking Up Is Hard to Do
Mapping Organizational Culture

PERSONAL GUIDELINES FOR HUMAN
RELATIONS SUCCESS
Know the Culture You Enter
Know Something About Yourself
Be Culture Aware

LEARNING OBJECTIVES

☐ Identify the dimensions of organizational culture

☐ Describe how dominant values and philosophy are reflected in an organization's policies

☐ Describe why rituals and ceremonies are a part of organizational life

☐ Describe the difference between organizational climate and culture

☐ Identify organizational processes that are heavily influenced by culture

☐ Describe the relationship between organizational culture and performance

☐ Identify the steps in the socialization of new employees

A Tale of Two Companies[1]

Safeco Insurance Company has a rather conservative image. This image stems at least partly from the company's personnel policies. Examples:

- [ ] A dress code, which varies somewhat according to the job, generally requires that men must wear suits and white shirts. Beards are forbidden and hair must be above the collar.
- [ ] Women must dress conservatively, and women executives are expected to wear suits.
- [ ] An extensive interviewing process is used to spot signs of nonconformity in job applicants.
- [ ] Socializing after work is not encouraged, and the company does not sponsor functions outside of work.
- [ ] When employees leave their work floor, they must put on their suit jackets.
- [ ] Having a drink at lunch is grounds for dismissal.
- [ ] The beginning and end of two daily coffee breaks are signaled by music on a speaker system.
- [ ] Everyone, from chairman on down, is expected to work from 8:00 to 4:30 and no more.

A Safeco vice president stated, "We want people who aren't going to be confrontational with authority. People constantly breaking rules are testing the system. We're not interested in them." The firm enjoys a high reputation in the insurance industry and has no trouble recruiting employees, even from the "me" generation.

Microrim, a computer software firm, has policies radically different from Safeco. For example:

- [ ] There is no formal dress code. Jeans are common, and especially among programmers, beards and long hair (including ponytails on men) are not unusual.
- [ ] The company sponsors a monthly beer bust during work hours. Imported beer is provided, and departments take turns providing snacks and "theme" costumes. Off-hours socializing is encouraged, and the company sponsors barbecues and pot-lucks.
- [ ] Programmers sometimes work seven-day weeks for up to three months. It is not unusual for people to be working at 2:00 A.M. simply because they have found something interesting and want to pursue it.

□   The company president regularly takes a few workers and managers to breakfast.

□   Every manager must answer the customer ''hotline'' for two hours each month.

    One employee, describing a common view, said, ''One person is not that much better than another. I hope it stays that way.''

The opening story describes two organizations, both successful in their industries, successful in recruiting quality employees, yet very different in most ways. Most Microrim employees would hate the formality and restrictions of Safeco. Many Safeco employees would feel uneasy with the informality and lack of structure at Microrim. Safeco and Microrim have different cultures.

Organizational culture may be defined as prevailing patterns of values, attitudes, beliefs, assumptions, expectations, activities, interactions, norms, and sentiments that are shared by members of an organization. According to one author-

CONCEPTS OF ORGANIZATIONAL CULTURE

Organization culture shared values and beliefs

Accepted norms of appearance and behavior can vary widely between organizations and reflect the organizational culture.

ity, E. Schein, virtually everything that a manager does or that happens in an organization is influenced by culture.[2] A less elegant definition but one that describes the force of organization culture was expressed by a corporate president. To him, organizational culture is "how we do things in the company."[3] Obviously, such a powerful mechanism is worth studying.

Does the organization's culture really affect the behavior of people who work there? Look again at the opening story. There can be little doubt that the Safeco culture encourages, perhaps even requires, a level of formality that is largely absent at Microrim. Imagine what would happen if we were able to exchange an equal number of Microrim and Safeco employees for one day. They would be dressed "wrong" and act "wrong." We predict that the exchanged employees would be uncomfortable in their new environments. The managers they reported to might be even more uncomfortable.

Many aspects of an organization's culture can be described by careful observation. For example, can't we guess that Safeco and its employees value conservative behavior, "correct" relations between managers and subordinates, adherence to the chain of command, formal communication, and lack of uncertainty? On the other hand, Microrim and its employees appear to value informality, direct access to all levels of management, flexibility in work schedules, and being "creative."

We can make assumptions about the culture of organizations that we are familiar with. For example, wouldn't you guess that meticulous attention to detail and pride in the company product are expected and valued by employees of Rolls Royce? The Boeing Company is another example of an organization that has great pride in its products. A survey taken by Boeing revealed that 98 percent of the employees believed overall product quality to be good or outstanding, and 97 percent rated the company's reputation as good or outstanding.[4] We can assume that product quality and the firm's reputation are important considerations for Boeing employees, a concern encouraged by the organization's culture.

As the Boeing survey showed, dimensions of the organization's culture can be measured and evaluated, providing management with an important administrative tool. We will discuss this issue in some detail later.

Dimensions of Cultural Excellence

One of the best-selling books of the 1980s was *In Search of Excellence*, which popularized the concept of organization culture.[5] In the book, the authors profiled corporations widely believed to be excellent. The list of sixty-two companies studied included IBM, Boeing, Hewlett-Packard, McDonald's, and Eastman Kodak. To be included in the list, the companies had to have at least a twenty-year history of growth and long-term wealth creation, as well as good return on both capital and sales.[6]

After studying the firms, the authors concluded that the companies shared the following cultural elements:

- □ Belief in being "the best"
- □ Belief in the importance of the details of execution, the nuts and bolts of doing the job well
- □ Belief in the importance of people as individuals
- □ Belief in superior quality and service
- □ Belief that most members of the organization should be innovators, and its corollary, the willingness to support failure
- □ Belief in the importance of informality to enhance communication
- □ Explicit belief in and recognition of the importance of economic growth and profits

One might be tempted to turn the list of elements into a prescription, that is, suggest to managers that they need only have a belief in being the best, a belief in informality, and so forth, to run an excellent company. This would be a great oversimplification, since such prescriptions do not tell the listener *how* to foster these beliefs. If your parents ever told you that "to get ahead, you need only to apply yourself," you know what the problem is. Also note that the excellence list presented by the authors lists only "beliefs." Beliefs are only one element of organizational culture, and there are several other aspects that deserve attention.

The Content of Organizational Culture

The content of an organization's culture is composed of a number of different elements:

How do people react when an organizational norm is violated?

- □ *Observed behavioral regularities* when people interact, including the language used and the rituals around both deference and demeanor
- □ *Norms* that evolve in working groups, such as "a fair day's work for a fair day's pay"
- □ *Dominant values* espoused by an organization, such as "product quality," "superior service," or "price leadership"
- □ The *philosophy* that guides policy toward employees and customers
- □ *Rules* of the game for getting along, or the "ropes" that a newcomer must learn to become an accepted member
- □ The *climate* (feeling) that is conveyed by the physical layout and the way in which members interact with customers or other outsiders.[7]

Rituals. Rituals and ceremonies are interesting forms of behavior that can be observed in virtually any organization. These periodic activities communicate important organizational values to the employees. Examples of rituals include the annual Christmas or holiday party, senior "skip" day at a high school, graduation ceremonies, and the award of ten-year service pins.

Why are rituals important?

At a large midwestern firm, the chairman of the board would come down from his office on a day just before Christmas, walk through every department and shake hands with each employee. Of course this was the only time he would

Rituals and ceremonies communicate important organizational values to employees.

be seen by most employees, but this ritual served as a symbol of concern for his "family."[8]

Examples of unusual rituals and ceremonies abound. For example:

☐ At J. C. Penney, those promoted to a certain level are given a shiny black wastebasket, in contrast to the more drab types provided to most employees.
☐ The Reader's Digest Association was founded by people who loved flowers and gardening. To this day, all employees are given Fridays off during the month of May to garden, or anything else they like.
☐ The W. T. Grant retail firm made it a practice to cut the tie of any sales manager who missed his quota.[9]
☐ The same company reportedly humiliated its poor-performing store managers by throwing custard pies in their faces, cutting their ties in half, and inducing them to push peanuts across the floor with their noses.[10] Incidentally, W. T. Grant went bankrupt in 1975.

Although rituals and ceremonies may be more fully developed in older organizations, their importance is recognized in younger, developing organizations as well. Microrim's monthly beer bust with theme costumes is an example. It is important to remember that all rituals contain an important message: they project key values of the organization to the members.

Norms.　Norms are acceptable standards of behavior shared by members of an organization. Every group develops norms, which are "policed" and enforced by group members. Group response to a norm violation depends on the importance of the norm, but the group usually attempts to bring the violator into line, subtly at first, but aggressively if necessary. An automobile salesman was once fired from his job because he drove a foreign car while he worked for an American car dealership. First he was "ribbed" by his co-workers when he purchased the foreign car. When he defended his purchase, the ribbing developed a hard edge. Soon, the sales manager "suggested" that the salesman dispose of his import. A few days went by before the suggestion became a demand. In the meantime, our car salesman felt increasingly lonely. His fellow salesmen always had other plans for lunch and never had time for coffee. Finally, the general manager of the dealership met with the salesman and demanded that the car be sold. The salesman refused and was fired.

Norms shared standards of behavior

We are introduced to the power of norms early in our lives. Families generally hold norms about important aspects of life, including proper behavior, academic performance, importance of religion, and methods of communication. All groups have norms, and group members must pay attention to them. Frequently the norms are not formally stated but are known to group members and communicated in various ways to newcomers.

Why do groups enforce norms?

The dress, speech, and behavior codes of adolescents provide examples of rather strict norms that are rigorously enforced. If the norms dictate that the blouse be worn outside of the skirt, that teachers be "bad-mouthed," and lip gloss *never* be used, members religiously abide or risk embarrassment or even humiliation and expulsion from the group.

The norms of work groups are more subtle but no less important, as the experience of our salesman friend demonstrates. Some norms may be destructive or costly to the organization, for example, "Don't share information with other groups," "Don't trust anything management says," "Don't volunteer for anything," "It is OK to take office supplies home." On the other hand, norms can benefit the organization. A review of the beliefs held by Peters and Waterman's excellent companies suggests that one might find the following norms: "Risk-taking is rewarded," "Think about the customer," and "Management can be trusted to do the right thing." To review a full discussion of group norms, including how they are developed, maintained and enforced, refer back to Chapter 6.

Dominant Values.　Dominant values are the basic assumptions about what ideals are desirable or worth striving for. Corporate values have become a topic of great interest for researchers in recent years. One survey has reported that a majority of employers have addressed the issue of corporate values, with over 40 percent reporting that values have received a great deal of attention in their

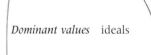

Dominant values ideals

Opening Story Revisited

What norms might be important at Safeco and at Microrim? From the description of Safeco, we can presume that conservative behavior is expected, including strict adherence to rules and regulations. A "professional" appearance is probably valued as well, reflected by a formal grooming and dress code. People are probably expected to remain within their own job descriptions and not be overly creative. By contrast, the norms at Microrim probably require flexibility, creativity and unconventional work habits. Friendly interaction both on and off the job is encouraged.

Can you suggest other likely norms in the two companies?

firms.[11] The executives surveyed also reported that the corporate values usually originated from the corporate founder and top management. The study also presented the executives with a list of ten values to be ranked in importance. The results follow (1 is most important).

example of values team spirit

disregard for human feelings *unethical exploitation*

Rank	Values
1	Performance
2	Fairness
3	Competitiveness
4	Team spirit
5	Corporate family spirit
6	Innovation
7	Entrepreneurship
8	Individual achievement
9	Loyalty
10	Tradition

Are organizational values changing?

Since the executives were given a set of ten values to rank, we cannot assume that the same values would have been listed if a more open question had been asked. Indeed, when asked how their company's values might change over the next five years, the executives foresaw an increased emphasis on performance, entrepreneurship, teamwork, and competitive spirit and innovation. Although a change in emphasis seems reasonable as a response to changes in the corporate environment, let us remember that a dramatic shift is not likely over a short time, since values are strongly held.

The influence on organizational values by corporate founders seems reasonable. After all, it is extremely unlikely that someone would start an organization that espoused values in conflict with his own. The founder's values are often explicitly stated in the charter of the organization. For example, more than seven decades ago, James Cash Penney described the values of his small business as "The Penney Idea," which can be summarized as follows:

1. To serve the public, as nearly as we can, to its complete satisfaction
2. To expect, for the service we render, a fair remuneration and not all the profit the traffic will bear
3. To do all in our power to pack the customer's dollar full of value, quality, and satisfaction
4. To continue to train ourselves and our associates so that the service we give will be more and more intelligently performed
5. To improve constantly the human factor in our business
6. To reward men and women in our organization through participation in what the business produces
7. To test our policy and methods by asking, "Does it square with what is right and just?"[12]

Today of course, the J. C. Penney company is one of the largest and most successful department store chains in the world.

A more recent example of clearly stated values comes from People Express Airlines, founded by Donald Burr in 1980. Burr and the other managing officers spent a lot of time discussing ideas about the "right" way to run an airline. By December 1981, the discussions had resulted in six written "precepts" that were thereafter continually referred to during the growth of the People organization. The precepts:

How do the values of J. C. Penney and People Express differ?

1. Service, commitment to growth of people
2. Best provider of air transportation
3. Highest quality of management
4. Role model for other airlines and other businesses
5. Simplicity
6. Maximization of profits[13]

Philosophy.   The philosophy that guides policy toward employees and customers stems directly from the values articulated by the founders or chief executives. Look again at "The Penney Idea." It should come as no surprise that J. C. Penney provides extensive training to employees, and that it tries to find new jobs for marginal employees rather than firing them. In other words, the philosophy of J. C. Penney management guides important personnel policies. In turn, the management philosophy is rooted in the values of "The Penney Idea."

Philosophy guides policy.

Now look again at the values espoused at People Express. The precepts were translated into policies that resulted in few levels of management (three, initially), broad job descriptions with universal job rotation, the use of work teams rather than individual decision makers, intensive training, and a rigorous hiring process (only one in 100 applicants was hired initially).

Beyond the top 15 officers all remaining full-time employees were either flight managers, maintenance managers, or customer service managers. The titles indicated distinctions in qualifications and functional emphasis rather than orga-

Miracle on 14th Street

A fire swept through a switching center in lower Manhattan. It was the worst single service disaster ever suffered by any single Bell operating company. Before firemen had given telephone repairmen the OK to enter the building, the Bell System had begun one of the typical crisis mobilizations of which it is so justly proud—indeed, it was the largest such mobilization ever. New York Telephone, AT&T long lines, Western Electric and Bell Labs contingents converged on the area. A crisis headquarters—inevitably called a war room—was established in a rented storefront on Fourteenth Street.

Within 24 hours, emergency telephone service had been restored to the medical, police, and fire facilities affected. Shortly thereafter the Bell task force for assessing damage and beginning to restore service had reached its peak strength of 4,000. They worked around the clock in 12-hour shifts of 2,000 each. Except for a few stray problem lines, service was restored just before midnight on March 21, twenty-two days after the disaster.

Source: Adapted from S. Kleinfield. *The Biggest Company on Earth: A Profile of AT&T,* 1981: 307. Used by permission of Henry Holt & Co.

QUESTIONS

1. What appear to be dominant values in this description of AT&T?
2. What norms might be associated with the values?
3. Which is the AT&T culture more similar to—Safeco or Microrim?

nizational authority. Flight managers were pilots. Their primary responsibility was flying, but they also performed various other tasks, such as dispatching, scheduling, and safety checks, on a rotating basis or as needed. Maintenance managers were technicians who oversaw and facilitated maintenance of People Express airplanes, equipment, and facilities by contract with other airlines' maintenance crews. In addition to monitoring and assuring the quality of the contracted work, maintenance managers were utilized to perform various staff jobs.

The vast majority of People's managers were customer service managers, generalists trained to perform all passenger-related tasks, such as security clearance, boarding, flight attending, ticketing, and food service, as well as some staff function activities.[14]

For several years after its incorporation, People Express was a phenomenal success. Its hard-driving staff had succeeded in making the airline the lowest-cost carrier in the country. Productivity figures were approximately double the industry average. The company was featured in stories by major magazines and newspapers and was studied extensively by the Harvard Business School.

In 1985 and 1986, the company suffered serious reverses. It posted its first financial losses and developed serious cash flow problems, due largely to the acquisition of another airline. In early 1986, customer complaints to the Transpor-

420

tation Department were 12.22 per 100,000 passengers, compared to an industry average of 2.22. By late 1986, the company was trying to change some of its operating policies. For example, jobs were becoming more specialized, cost controls were being enhanced, formal lines of authority were developing and standard reporting procedures were put in place. While all of these things conform to "good business practice," note that they are in conflict with the early policies of People Express.[15] The company's financial condition continued to worsen, and in early 1987 it was acquired by Texas Air. The remarkable culture of People Express was not enough to save the company.

Stories and Myths. Stories and myths about dominant personalities seem to be an important part of organizational lore and are part of the cultural fabric. Many of the stories feature a confrontation over rules between a powerful figure and a powerless one. Here are two such stories with very different outcomes.

Thomas Watson, Jr., IBM's chairman of the board, was challenged by a young security guard whose job required inspection of clearances when people entered security areas.

> Surrounded by his usual entourage of white-shirted men, Watson approached the doorway to an area where she was on guard, wearing an orange badge acceptable elsewhere in the plant, but not a green badge, which alone permitted entrance at her door. "I was trembling in my uniform, which was far too big," she recalled. "It hid my shakes but not my voice. 'I'm sorry,' I said to him. I knew who he was all right. 'You cannot enter. Your admittance is not recognized.' That's what we were supposed to say." The men accompanying Watson were stricken; the moment held unpredictable possibilities. "Don't you know who he is?" someone hissed. Watson raised his hand for silence, while one of the party strode off and returned with the appropriate badge.[16]

The IBM story portrays the lowly security guard as a heroine and the chairman as a powerful figure who does not insist upon status prerogatives and rewards people for following job requirements. A Revlon receptionist had a different experience. Charles Revson, head of the Revlon Corporation, insisted that employees arrive at work on time.

> . . . Everyone was required to sign in in the morning. Everyone. Even Charles signed in. One day, . . . Charles sauntered in and began to look over the sign-in sheet. The receptionist, who was new, says "I'm sorry, sir, you can't do that." Charles says, "Yes, I can." "No sir," she says, "I have strict orders that no one is to remove the list. You'll have to put it back." This goes back and forth for a while with the receptionist being very courteous, as all Revlon receptionists are, and finally Charles says, "Do you know who I am?" And she says, "No, sir, I don't." "Well, when you pick up your final paycheck this afternoon, ask 'em to tell ya."[17]

Rules of the Game. The rules for getting along in a company are somewhat different from the formal rules that are a part of every work environment. Here the term is not limited to formal, written rules, but includes all of the unwritten requirements that go with membership in any organization. To become an accepted member of a group or organization, a newcomer must learn the rules of the game and abide by them. In this context, norms become part of the fabric. For example, if the following norm exists: "Don't share information with the quality control department," an associated "rule" for group members might be "Don't sit at a cafeteria table with anyone from quality control."

In our observation of work groups, we have come across many unwritten rules, as well as their direct opposites. Some common ones:

- ☐ Arrive a few minutes early for work / Never arrive early for work
- ☐ Maintain a flexible student advising schedule / Don't advise students outside regular office hours
- ☐ Encourage patients to ask questions about their treatment / Make it clear to patients that the physicians on staff know what is best
- ☐ If you disagree with the boss, tell him or her / Don't disagree with the boss, but go ahead and do it your way
- ☐ Always ask customers if you can help / Make customers approach you if they want help

A friendly and courteous attitude toward customers reflects the norms and unwritten rules of the sales staff.

Newcomers usually learn the rules quickly, though they are rarely written and are discussed only obliquely if at all. Adherence to the rules is a requirement of group membership, and violations will be punished. The extent of punishment depends largely on how important the rule is to the group.

Organizational climate is a description of how people *experience* organization culture. Remember that we defined culture as prevailing patterns of values, attitudes, beliefs, assumptions, expectations, activities, interactions, norms, and sentiments shared by organization members. Organizational climate is described as a set of perceptions concerning the characteristics and quality of the organizational culture. When a worker says "Intergalactic Flange is a great place to work," he or she is making a general statement about the organizational climate at Intergalactic Flange. For example, let's look at some values from a hypothetical organization, and a likely response to an organizational climate survey.

ORGANIZATIONAL CLIMATE

Organizational climate how people experience the organization's culture

Value	Climate Experience
Individualism	People are encouraged to make their own decisions and are rewarded for doing so
Team Spirit	Departments willingly cooperate for the good of the entire organization
Performance	There is competition among individuals and units to be "the best"
Innovation	People can experiment with new techniques without fear of punishment

Organizational climate is a matter of concern and interest for many managers. Surveys of organizational climate are common, and many companies conduct surveys on a regular basis. The elements of climate most often measured include:

1. Organization structure, including reaction to rules, regulations, and procedures
2. Responsibility, making one's own decisions
3. Reward, including perceived fairness of pay and promotion policies
4. Tolerance for risk
5. Warmth, including the extent of informality and feeling of friendliness
6. Support, including the extent of helpfulness by others
7. Standards, including the extent of performance standards, and the importance of goals
8. Tolerance for conflict
9. Identity or sense of belonging[18]

As should be apparent, organizational climate is a more restrictive concept than organizational culture. Indeed, the climate of an organization is described in terms of feelings and perceptions, while culture is the underlying mechanism that is only partly reflected by the climate.

Opening Story Revisited

How might Safeco and Microrim employees respond to the climate elements above? We can speculate that Safeco would probably have a more clearly defined organizational structure than Microrim and much greater reliance on rules, regulations, and procedures. By contrast, Microrim employees would probably feel considerably higher responsibility for making their own decisions and experience a high tolerance for risk. The climate at Safeco clearly is more formal and undoubtedly has more clearly stated performance standards than Microrim. Microrim probably has a higher tolerance for conflict.

It is not so clear how the two companies would be viewed on the remaining elements. Since Safeco emphasizes formal communication and discourages informal gatherings, the climate might well be viewed as less warm and friendly than at Microrim. The same reasoning might apply to support and helpfulness. We do not have enough information to guess how the two companies would rate on reward and identity.

ORGANIZATIONAL CULTURE INFLUENCES ORGANIZATIONAL PROCESS

So far, we have pointed out numerous incidents of how culture affects individual and group behavior. But we also need to emphasize that culture affects how the entire organization operates. In other words, culture has influence beyond the individual or small-unit level. Some of the organization-wide processes affected by culture include cooperation, decision making, communication, and commitment.

Cooperation. Cooperation is a voluntary act and cannot be required. No matter how sophisticated the control system, no matter how elegant the compensation structure, no matter how comprehensive the job descriptions, unforeseen events occur. It is in these unusual and perhaps emergency conditions that cooperation is necessary.

How does culture affect cooperation? Some organizational cultures place great value on being a team player. Cooperation is much more likely in such an organization than one that encourages individual achievement and competition between units. We are not suggesting that emphasis on individual achievement and competition is bad, but high levels of cooperation are not likely in such a culture.

Decision Making. Decision making is also heavily influenced by organizational culture. Remember that culture involves shared beliefs and assumptions. The greater the agreement on and acceptance of shared beliefs, the more likely it is that individuals will make decisions that are consistent with those beliefs.

This is not to say that the decisions will necessarily be of high quality, only that they will be consistent with the culture's assumptions. If the culture has not adapted to a changing environment, some of the shared assumptions may no

When might a strong organization culture be a disadvantage?

longer reflect reality, and decisions based on faulty assumptions will probably not be effective. A strong culture is not always a benefit. Indeed, the stronger the culture, the more important it is to periodically review its central beliefs. Yet this creates a paradox, since the stronger the culture, the less likely people will question the beliefs that they share.

Communication. Communication can be greatly enhanced by a strong culture. Shared beliefs and assumptions allow many things to be left unsaid yet clearly understood. While a benefit overall, this organizational "shorthand" can be confusing to a newcomer. Only experience in the organization gives one the necessary insight for the correct interpretation of subtle cues.

It is also important to remember that, while the potential for good communication is always present, some cultures do not reward openness or honesty. Such cultures are sometimes characterized by what is known as "one-way" communication—reliance on commands and directives rather than discussion and consultation. One manager we know sometimes prefaces his statements with, "This is only a suggestion, but don't forget who is making it." As you might guess, the culture in his organization does not value disagreement with the boss. Communication tends to flow only in one direction.

Commitment. Commitment occurs when people identify with an organization and have some sort of emotional attachment to it. A certain amount of identity can be "bought" with high salaries and attractive benefits, but emotional attachment occurs only when people like and value the organization beyond the aspects of compensation or other tangible rewards.

When People Express was founded, most employees worked more than 50 hours per week, with many working 70 hours or more. There was a sense of belonging to something new and exciting, and a belief that the individual's contribution was important. The story about AT&T's crisis team also shows commitment. Although many workers were paid overtime, an important motivator was undoubtedly the shared value of highly responsive service to customers and the public, as well as a sense of attachment to such a capable "can do" organization.

What does commitment buy an organization? A willingness by individual workers to act in behalf of their employer, to select alternatives that benefit the organization, and to go the extra mile.

Culture and Organizational Performance

It would be easy to conclude that a strong, clearly articulated culture will result in high organizational performance, and indeed this has been suggested by some. *In Search of Excellence* by Peters and Waterman popularized presumed cultural attributes of excellent companies.[19] Others have described traits of "high-performing systems" and "cultures of productivity."

Unfortunately, we believe that the many prescriptions for excellence describe a world that is entirely too simple and the prescriptions are much too

Why aren't strong cultures necessarily effective?

vague. As G. S. Saffold has pointed out, these common features proposed by researchers

> . . . are frequently impoverished generalizations, least common denominators, that do little to illuminate the intricate ways in which culture interacts with organizational processes. For example, Akin and Hopelain report that workers in their highly productive organizations have a good sense of the "right kind of person for the job" and that coal miners describe this person as someone who is "able to work underground." Peters' and Waterman's dictum that excellent organizations are "close to the customer" is a similar finding.[20]

What does it mean that someone is "able to work underground?" How does a company "get close to the customer?" Such questions must be answered directly. It seems that we have much more work to do in describing organizational culture before we can dare to prescribe the cultural elements that promote performance. Indeed, perhaps the elements are different, or at least they are emphasized differently in different industries.

Adding to the confusion is the fact that there is little agreement about what organizational effectiveness is. There are a number of different ways to define effectiveness, largely depending on the perspective of the person promoting the definition. The complexity of this issue was captured by Thomas A. Murphy, then chairman of General Motors:

> If business people have learned one overriding lesson from the '70s, it is that economic success alone is not enough. Important as they are, superior products are not enough; nor are innovations in manufacturing, marketing or service. And certainly, returning a profit on our shareholders' investment, although absolutely necessary, is no longer sufficient to ensure a firm's acceptance . . . [the public] most often uses other scales to weight performance in non-product, even non-business, areas. These gauge the way we respond to society at large. They evaluate the way we relate to our society, its economy, and its physical and social environment.[21]

Maintaining or Changing a Culture

When we think of a strong corporate culture (IBM perhaps), we might be tempted to think that the culture will never change. The truth is that culture does change, however slowly. In our discussion so far, we have emphasized how culture affects behavior. We must acknowledge here that behavior also affects culture. A certain amount of change in an organization's culture is probably necessary over time. The problem facing management is to strike a balance that allows needed change to occur, while maintaining the core elements of the culture. Whether one is primarily interested in changing a culture or resisting unwanted change, Figure 14–1 provides a starting point. According to this model there are five points that managers can change or strengthen: behavior, justifications of behavior, cultural communications, hiring and socialization, and removal of deviant members.

What are the five pressure points for changing organization culture?

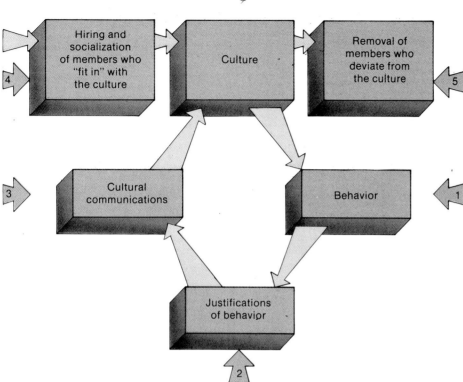

FIGURE 14 – 1
Maintaining or changing a culture (Source: V. Sathe, *Culture and Related Corporate Realities* (© Richard D. Irwin, Inc., 1985): 385.)

Managers seeking to create culture *change* must intervene at these points. Conversely, managers seeking to *maintain* the prevailing culture must counteract any such intervention by others and prevent any weakening of these processes by consciously attending to them.

Behavior. Behavior affects culture and vice versa. Behavior can be changed or reinforced in a number of ways including the organizational reward system, productivity programs, and the performance appraisal system.

Justifications of Behavior Even if we succeed in changing behavior, the values of the old culture may remain, especially if we create behavior change through coercion or manipulation. For example, we may achieve behavior change through threat of termination or, less dramatically, through a generous bonus system that rewards changed behavior.

Although people behave as called for under a new system, they may well continue to share the old values and beliefs. This is the difference between commitment and compliance. While complying with external requirements, one may maintain a commitment to other beliefs. If the organization is trying to change the culture, then attention must be paid to intrinsic motivation (see Chapter 3). On the other hand, if the organization is attempting to strengthen the old culture, the existing values and beliefs should be reinforced.

Cultural Communications.   Cultural communications occur constantly in organizations. They may be part of the formal system of memos, reports, and announcements. They also occur through rituals, ceremonies, stories and other symbolic forms of communication. Here again, the choice involves strengthening of existing cultural communications or de-emphasizing them while developing new messages. For example, the W. T. Grant Company might have taken a different approach toward recognizing managerial performance. Had the company singled out top performers for special rewards rather than selecting poor performers for humiliation, different values would have been communicated.

Why is socialization critical to the maintenance of culture?

What are the seven steps of socialization?

Hiring and Socialization.   The hiring and socialization of newcomers is a powerful tool for maintaining an existing culture, and is useful to some extent in changing a culture as well. Safeco Insurance Company places great emphasis on the selection of candidates who share the values espoused by the company. People Express also knew precisely the type of employees it wanted—remember that only one applicant in 100 was hired. The process of socialization is so important that we will look at it in additional detail.

Organizational socialization can be described in seven steps, beginning with the selection of employees.[22] Figure 14–2 shows the steps in the socialization process.

Selection.   The selection of entry level candidates can vary in rigor from highly selective (People Express, for example) to almost random (the hiring of casual labor at a construction site). The more important culture maintenance is, the more likely that an organization will develop sophisticated methods for hiring new employees. Obviously, a great deal of thought and analysis goes into identifying the "best" traits for selection.

Humility-Inducing Experiences.   These experiences shake the recruit's self-confidence and make him or her more open to indoctrination in company values and procedures. The military boot camp provides a vivid example. The recruits are given short haircuts; thrust into identical, poorly fitting uniforms; and subjected to verbal abuse. Corporations provide humility inducing experiences, too. Some investment banks expect newly hired associates to work up to fourteen hours a day and most weekends. Exhausting travel schedules, impossible assignments, and other "upending experiences" are common. Perhaps Cigna's program (see box, page 430) was intended to be such an experience.

In-the-Trenches Training.   This training involves long hours of hard work mastering the company's business. The humility-inducing experiences have made the recruit more open to indoctrination, and the job training provides intense exposure to the organization's culture.

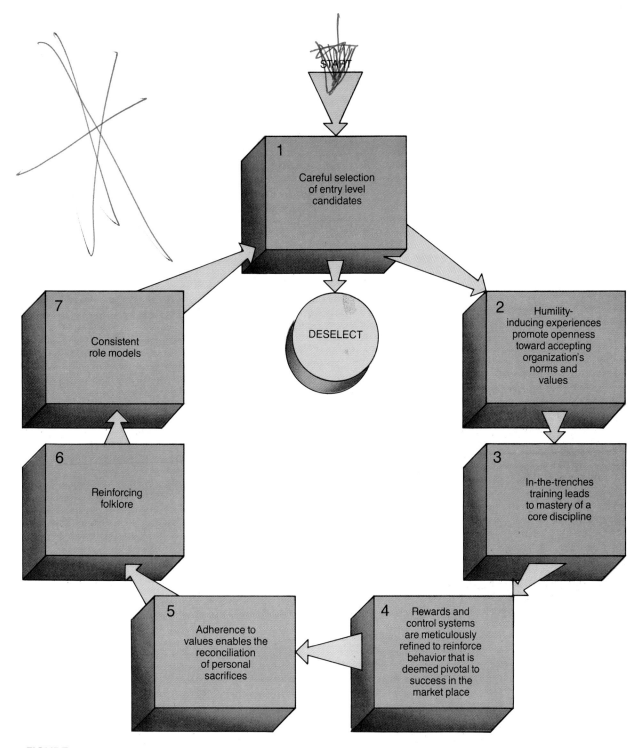

FIGURE 14 – 2
Organizational socialization (Source: R. Pascale, "The Paradox of Corporate Culture: Reconciling Ourselves to Socialization," © 1985 by the Regents of the University of California. Adapted from *California Management Review* (Winter, 1985): 38, by permission of the Regents.)

Attack of the Cignoids

In 1984, Cigna Insurance Company acquired Afia, an international insurance association. The merging of the two companies resulted in extra staff: in fact there were 200 candidates for about 100 key positions. With the help of consultants, Cigna developed a $1 million, 12-week project to evaluate employees and select those who would stay. In the words of one consultant, it became a battle between "The Cignoids and the Afians." A typical week involved interviews, presentations, business planning sessions, and game playing from 8 a.m. until late in the evening. Many candidates reported the psychological interviews to be particularly stressful.

One group of candidates was so numbed toward the end of their week that they couldn't come up with solutions to a problem. Consultants told them the monkey was on their backs—and threw 50 toy monkeys to the startled applicants. Later, a woman dressed as a gorilla entered the room carrying a large stuffed monkey.

Source: Adapted from "Cignoids versus Afians," by John A. Byrne and Richard Morais. Adapted by permission of *Forbes* magazine, September 24,1984. © Forbes Inc., 1984.

At the end of the week, consultants led the executives in a song to Cigna chief executive David (Bill) Schrempf:

"We love you, Bill, oh yes we do,
We love you, Bill, oh yes we do.
When you're not near to us, we're blue,
Oh, Bill, we love you."

Cigna counted the program a success, since the company felt it kept the best executives, and the inevitable merger bloodletting occurred quickly. Some of the managers who won jobs weren't so high on the program. "I found the whole experience demeaning and insulting," recalled one, while another said, "It was humiliating."

QUESTIONS

1. In your opinion, what are some dominant values in the Cigna culture?
2. What do you think the "rules of the game" are for getting along at Cigna?
3. Do you agree with Cigna that the program was a success? Why or why not?

Reward and Control Systems. Reward and control systems reinforce the aspects of the business that are crucial to success, as well as the dominant cultural values. The performance appraisal process is an integral part of this mechanism.

Adherence to Values. Adherence to values implies constant reference to the core values as a basis for identification and evaluation. In *The Miracle on 14th Street*, a core value of AT&T was evident: guaranteeing phone service to customers through any emergency. When employees identify with such a value, they accept personal sacrifices on behalf of their company.

Reinforcing Folklore. Organizational folklore emphasizes the importance of the existing culture. Stories and myths about heroic performances are passed down from one generation to another. The folklore generally reinforces the desired code of conduct.

Consistent Role Models.   Role models are viewed by many strong-culture firms as the most powerful long-term training program available.[23] These "stars" exemplify the best attributes of the culture, and younger employees are expected to pattern their behavior accordingly. These role models may also serve as beacons attracting desirable recruits to the organization.

And finally,

Removal of Deviant Members.   This step involves removing members who do not fit the culture. Despite the most careful selection, a few people who do not fit will be hired. Some people who fit well initially may fit less well later in their careers, due to changing personal or organizational circumstances.

Removal of members implies their departure from the organization. Often, after a company has been acquired, its top management is removed. To a great extent, this is ordered by the new parent corporation because of cultural differences. As such, it sends two powerful messages to the acquired company. First, a change in culture can be expected to bring the acquisition in line with the parent firm. Second, the change will be dramatic, and the old management of the acquired firm can be expected to resist it—in other words, opposition will not be tolerated. Termination is not the only means for removal. Many organizations provide career counseling and outplacement services for employees. Career counseling can be helpful in encouraging employees to examine their relationship to the organizational culture and to explore opportunities available to them. More than one person has left a company voluntarily because of a lack of "fit." Outplacement services help employees who are terminating to find new jobs.

1. Organizational culture is a crucial aspect of an organization's functioning. The culture affects a number of important processes, including cooperation, decision making, communication, and commitment.
2. Organizational culture can be observed and measured.
3. Although some writers propose a culture of excellence, there may be no single set of activities that will ensure high performance.
4. The content of a culture can be described in terms of behavioral regularities, norms, dominant values, philosophy, rules, and climate.
5. Rituals and ceremonies communicate important values.
6. Norms are shared standards of behavior and are enforced by group members.
7. Dominant values are basic assumptions about ideals worth achieving. Philosophy stems from the dominant values and in turn influences policies.
8. Strong cultures do not necessarily result in organizational effectiveness.
9. If a culture is to be changed, the focal points lie in behavior, justifications of behavior, cultural communications, hiring and socialization, and removal of deviant members.

LEARNING SUMMARY

ANSWERS TO "WHAT'S YOUR OPINION?"

1. True   Or at least so the argument goes. Since culture is a dominant feature of the organization, it would be hard to imagine any managerial activity being entirely unaffected by it.

2. True   Aspects of the culture can be measured via questionnaire, but one must not forget that there is not yet a single accepted description of cultural elements.

3. True   Stories, myths, and other folklore serve to communicate important values. They frequently describe some situation in the life of the founder.

4. True   Culture is reflected in the organization's philosophy. Policies should derive from and be consistent with that philosophy.

5. False   Norms are shared standards of behavior. Rules are often developed to enforce those standards.

6. False   Climate and culture are of equal value to a manager. Climate is somewhat more easily changed than culture.

7. False   Commitment occurs only when people have an emotional attachment. Identification can occur without commitment.

8. False   Since culture underlies so many organizational activities and heavily influences how people behave, it is difficult to change.

KEY TERMS

Commitment	Organizational climate
Cultural communications	Organizational culture
Deviant members	Philosophy
Dominant values	Rituals
Humility-inducing experiences	Rules of the game
Justifications of behavior	Socialization
Norms	Stories and myths

HUMAN RELATIONS APPLICATIONS

One of the most dramatic events in American business history was the break up of American Telephone and Telegraph Company. Noted for a distinctive culture that had developed over almost a century, the company was broken into several independent pieces. Here we will look at how the company responded to this enormous challenge.

Breaking Up Is Hard to Do[24]

In 1982, the gigantic American Telephone and Telegraph system signed a consent order with the Department of Justice agreeing to divestiture. Never before had there been such a dramatic change required of a giant enterprise. More than $125 billion in assets were to be spun off, resulting in structural changes of enormous magnitude. For example, the twenty-two Bell operating companies were re-grouped into seven regions and a centralized service staff. The surviving AT&T was reorganized to provide long-distance services and to supply and maintain certain telephone equipment. The seven regional Bell operating companies were severed from the parent AT&T. The regional Bell operating companies are very large companies themselves (assets of $12 billion to $20 billion) and each re-quired major reorganization.

"Culture shock" was apparent throughout the company. After all, the firm had survived and prospered for more than seven decades, finally becoming the largest corporation in the world. The company culture was very strong and had been nurtured for many years. Indeed, an early chief executive had devised a brief mission statement that would guide the company for several generations: "One System, One Policy, Universal Service."[25] Some elements of the Bell culture were:

- ☐ Lifetime careers—many employees spent their entire work lives in the company
- ☐ Intense loyalty to the company. Even retired employees maintain ties through an active retired employees group
- ☐ Perception of fair treatment by the company
- ☐ Management promoted from within
- ☐ Consensus management
- ☐ Dedication to customer service
- ☐ Emphasis on operational efficiency[26]

Divestiture required that the company leave its protected, regulated environment. In fact, the regional operating companies would be directly competing with one another as well as the parent corporation. The "one system, one policy, universal service" prescription no longer applied. Clearly, the old culture would have to change. AT&T management began six sets of activity to launch the change:

1. *Set an example.* In speeches, key executives set aside key symbols, suggesting that "Ma Bell" was no longer an appropriate emblem. Emphasis on the marketplace rather than the regulators was encouraged.
2. *Revamp the system of management.* Thirteen thousand corporate staff employees were redeployed to division or subsidiary staffs, leaving only a few hundred at the AT&T corporate staff level.
3. *Articulate the value system explicitly.* Beginning the day that divestiture was announced, senior officers proclaimed clear messages of expectations and corporate positions. A document, "A Statement of Policy," described the corporation's evolving goals.
4. *Gear training to support cultural values.* Management training began to emphasize topics such as strategic marketing, business strategy formulation, and entrepreneurship.
5. *Revise recruiting aims and methods.* Attention was focused on seeking entry-level managers whose personalities and backgrounds were compatible with the company's aims.

6. *Modify the symbols.* AT&T replaced its famous bell within a circle logo with a globe symbolically ringed by electronic communications.[27]

An earlier attempt to alter the Bell service orientation to give equal weight to marketing failed. In 1961, the company set up a school to teach managers to be more marketing oriented. When managers completed the course, they found that the traditional way of operating still counted in the company. In a fairly short period, 85 percent of the graduates quit and the company disbanded the school. The strong corporate culture had overcome the weak attempt to instill a new managerial orientation. Apparently, a valuable lesson was learned. In addition to the six steps outlined above, the company acknowledged its lack of skills in certain areas and began promoting innovators and changing methods of evaluating performance.[28]

It will undoubtedly take years for the various Bell companies to develop their own cultures, and even then important elements of the old culture will remain. AT&T Chairman of the Board Charles Brown commented on the objective and importance of changing the corporate culture: "If we are able to adapt our marvelous culture to a different environment—and if we remember that the business in the '80s cannot be run by memory—we can set the course for the next century."[29]

Mapping Organizational Culture

Two Swedish banks profiled their organizational cultures prior to merging. A questionnaire developed by Callahan and Fleenor was used to develop the profiles.[30] The questionnaire seeks responses related to ten elements of organizational culture. The elements, along with a sample statement from each element, appears below. Respondents evaluate each statement on a five-point scale ranging from full agreement to full disagreement. Each of the forty-two statements begins with the stem, "People in this (department, company, etc.): . . ."

Element	Sample Question
I. Organizational/Personal Pride	. . . criticize the organization and the people in it.
II. Performance/Excellence	. . . set very high personal standards of performance.
III. Teamwork/Communication	. . . devote extra effort to help co-workers.
IV. Leadership/Supervision	. . . do not hesitate to approach management with a problem.
V. Profitability/Cost Effectiveness	. . . evaluate expenditures in terms of the benefits they will provide for the whole unit.
VI. Colleague/Associate Relations	. . . make an effort to get to know co-workers

VII. Customer/Client Relations	. . . sometimes see customers as a burden or obstruction to getting the job done.
VIII. Innovativeness/Creativity	. . . suggest new ideas or approaches for doing things.
IX. Training/Development	. . . actively look for ways to expand their knowledge
X. Candor/Openness	. . . talk freely and openly about the unit and its problems.

The two banks are regional Swedish banks of approximately the same size, and both were incorporated more than 100 years ago—plenty of time to develop distinctive cultures! What the researchers found was most interesting, as shown in Figure 14–3.

In fact, the bank cultures were similar, but the culture of bank A was stronger. For both banks, the strongest cultural element was customer/client relations.

There were statistically significant differences only on four of the elements: Organizational/Personal Pride, Performance/Excellence, Training/Development,

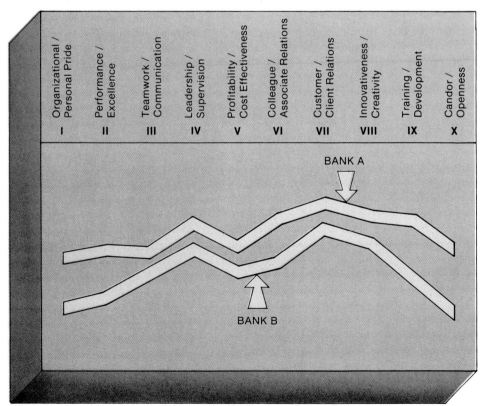

FIGURE 14 – 3

Cultural profiles of two Swedish banks (From a research project under the direction of C. Patrick Fleenor.)

and Candor/Openness. The parallel nature of the curves should be encouraging to management of the banks. The profiles indicate that the cultures differ largely in strength rather than content.

If one should be concerned at all, it would be over the relative weakness of the culture in bank B. Programs for strengthening organizational/personal pride and candor/openness might be considered.

The main point to remember is that organizational culture (and climate) can be measured. Measurement provides a baseline for action. If we know the cultural profile and wish to change it in some way, we can develop programs for the desired change. After the change programs have been completed, another measurement can be taken. Comparison with the baseline measurement will tell us the effectiveness of the change effort.

PERSONAL GUIDELINES FOR HUMAN RELATIONS SUCCESS

In this chapter we looked at the complex topic of organizational culture. One of the most important things you can do, as a manager or as prospective employee, is to understand the culture of your organization. In addition, you should understand yourself, especially your likes and dislikes as related to work and career.

Know the Culture You Enter

Sensible advice certainly, but how does one go about it? Here are some questions that will help you learn about an existing or prospective employer's culture:

1. What does it take to do well in the organization?
2. How is good performance recognized?
3. What is done to help employees improve performance?
4. What are the top managers like?
5. How high is employee turnover? Why do people usually leave?
6. Is there one function (for example marketing) that is considered most prestigious?
7. What does the organization do least well?
8. If the organization advertises, what image does it portray?
9. What are people like to work with here?
10. Are there performance targets and plans?

Know Something About Yourself

What are your own values and beliefs? What kind of environment do you want to work in? Here are a few questions for you to think about:

1. Do you like to take risks, or do you prefer a more cautious approach to life?
2. Do you like surprises and new experiences, or do you prefer stability and certainty?

3. Do you believe that authority should be respected without question, or should it be challenged?
4. Would you rather work alone or be part of a group effort?
5. If you could have any job you wanted, what would it be?
6. What type of job would you dislike the most?

Although these questions will get you started, you can take a much more structured approach. Your school probably has a counselor or a counseling department. Schedule some aptitude and interest tests. There are a number of standardized tests that have proven useful in helping people understand their own preferences.

Be Culture Aware

Sharpen your ability to see an organization's culture. Frequently it is easier to diagnose the culture in an organization other than your own. Look for rituals and norms. If you can describe such aspects of an organization, you may be able to infer a great deal about the dominant values of the organization.

---

1. What is organizational culture?
2. Under what circumstances might you want to measure organizational climate rather than culture?
3. The content of an organization's culture is composed of six elements. Which element would be most visible to the majority of observers?
4. What is the difference between norms and rules?
5. A survey of executives indicated that dominant organizational values may be changing. Discuss how this might be so.
6. Discuss reasons that a strong culture might not result in organizational effectiveness.
7. Why is culture so hard to change?
8. Why is socialization critical to the maintenance of culture?

DISCUSSION AND REVIEW QUESTIONS

Academic Culture

In this exercise we will fill out a brief questionnaire to profile characteristics of the culture in your school or university. The questionnaire is not "scientific," since it is condensed and has not been validated on a larger sample. Its purpose is to give you some data to discuss.

Please respond to every statement in two different ways. For example, one of the statements is: "People who work in this school will keep a student waiting to look after matters of personal importance." Below the statement are two scales:

HUMAN RELATIONS EXERCISE

How much is there now? (min.) 5 4 3 2 1 (max.)
How much *should* there be? (min.) 5 4 3 2 1 (max.)

Circle the appropriate response on each of the two scales. For example, if you think that there is a moderate amount of such behavior among employees, you would circle "3" on the first scale (How much is there now?). If you think this activity should be minimized, you would circle "5" on the second scale (How much should there be?).

1. Students feel comfortable about approaching instructors for advice on both personal and academic matters.
   How much is there now? (min.) 1 ② 3 4 5 (max.)
   How much *should* there be? (min.) 1 ② 3 4 5 (max.)

2. Students take an attitude that one should do only enough to "get by."
   How much is there now? (min.) ⑤ 4 3 2 1 (max.)
   How much *should* there be? (min.) 5 4 3 2 ① (max.)

3. Instructors have a reputation for being fair in grading.
   How much is there now? (min.) ① 2 3 4 5 (max.)
   How much *should* there be? (min.) ① 2 3 4 5 (max.)

4. People who work in this school will keep a student waiting to look after matters of personal importance.
   How much is there now? (min.) 5 4 ③ 2 1 (max.)
   How much *should* there be? (min.) 5 4 ③ 2 1 (max.)

5. Instructors generally demand high standards of performance from students.
   How much is there now? (min.) 1 2 3 4 ⑤ (max.)
   How much *should* there be? (min.) ① 2 3 4 5 (max.)

6. Instructors tend to favor certain students over others.
   How much is there now? (min.) 5 4 3 3 ① (max.)
   How much *should* there be? (min.) ⑤ 4 3 2 1 (max.)

7. Students feel that their opinions are important to instructors and the administration.
   How much is there now? (min.) ① 2 3 4 5 (max.)
   How much *should* there be? (min.) 1 2 3 ④ 5 (max.)

8. The school has a reputation for excellent programs.
   How much is there now? (min.) 1 ② 3 4 5 (max.)
   How much *should* there be? (min.) ① 2 3 4 5 (max.)

9. Who you know and who you are makes a big difference in how well you are treated here.
   How much is there now? (min.) 5 4 3 ② 1 (max.)
   How much *should* there be? (min.) 5 ④ 3 3 1 (max.)

10. Employees at this school try to treat students as well as possible.
    How much is there now?   (min.) 1   2 ③ 4   5   (max.)
    How much *should* there be?   (min.) 1 ② 3   4   5   (max.)

11. Many employees here look upon their jobs as being merely eight hours a day, and the major reward as the paycheck.
    How much is there now?   (min.) 5   4 ③ 2   1   (max.)
    How much *should* there be?   (min.) 5 ④ 3   2   1   (max.)

12. If you are not careful, people will take advantage of you here.
    How much is there now?   (min.) 5   4   3 ② 1   (max.)
    How much *should* there be?   (min.) 5 ④ 3   2   1   (max.)

Instructions.   Three dimensions of organizational culture are represented in this questionnaire: performance/excellence, student orientation, fairness.

Calculating your score: Write your scores from the questionnaire in the table below.

Question Number	Column A *Now* score	Column B *Should be* score	Question Number	Column C *Now* score	Column D *Should be* score	Question Number	Column E *Now* score	Column F *Should be* score
2	5	1	1	2	2	3	1	1
5	5	1	4	3	3	6	1	5
8	2	1	7	1	4	9	2	4
11	3	7	10	3	2	12	2	4
Sum =	13	10	Sum =	9	11	Sum =	6	14
Divide sum by 4 =	3.25	2.5	Divide sum by 4 =	2.25	2.75	Divide sum by 4 =	1.5	3.5

These are the scores for performance/excellence.

These are the scores for student orientation.

These are the scores for fairness.

One additional step is required before discussion—create a "difference score" by calculating the difference between the "now" scores and "should be" scores for each dimension. List your scores on the table below:

Scores for Academic Culture Questionnaire

			Difference:
Performance/Excellence	Now 3.25	Should Be 2.50	(Should Be minus Now) −1.25
Student Orientation	Now 2.25	Should Be 2.75	(Should Be minus Now) −1.50
Fairness	Now 1.50	Should Be 3.50	(Should Be minus Now) −2.00

Discussion. Form into discussion groups with about six people per group. The "now" scores represent your view of the current culture on three dimensions. The higher the score, the more a dimension is valued within the culture. The "should be" scores represent your view of how you would *like* a dimension emphasized. The "difference" score represents the distance between the culture now and how you would like it to be.

1. Compare individual scores on the three dimensions. Discuss similarities and differences. How much agreement is there on the "now" scores?
2. Which of the three dimensions received the highest score? Describe specific examples of events that support the score.
3. Which of the dimensions received the lowest score? Why?
4. Calculate scores for the entire class. To do this, add the individual dimension scores and divide by the number of people in the class.
5. In a meeting of the entire class, discuss the cultural profile. What dimension has the highest score? The lowest? Which dimension has the largest "difference" score? What are implications of that difference for the students? Instructors? Administration?

HUMAN RELATIONS INCIDENT

The Layoff

Walter Ronner started work on a Friday, and within three minutes of arriving received a call from Joseph Danilek, the comptroller of the company, who told him to lay off forty people "today."[31] Ronner asked Danilek, "How do we do this?" "Look, I've got orders from management to lay off forty people," said Danilek. "I don't care how you do it, but get rid of them. By the way, we quit here at 5:15, so don't notify anybody until five o'clock. We want a full day's work out of them."

Ronner thought, "Here I am, coming in as a new man, and the first thing I do is discharge forty people." So Ronner said, "I refuse to do it." Danilek was amazed and said, "Do you mean what you say?" With some trepidation, Ronner answered, "Yes." After all, he and Danilek were on the same level of authority; Danilek was not his superior. "If that's the case," Danilek responded, "I'll have to do it myself."

Forty people were picked at random, and at five o'clock Danilek lined them up on the stairs between the fifth and sixth floors—so the others wouldn't see—and he gave them a lecture about lack of work and handed them their severance checks and let them go.

QUESTIONS

1. What would you say are the dominant values of this organization?
2. Was Ronner right in refusing to fire the people? Why or why not?
3. Why might Danilek have told Ronner to do the firing?

1. Adapted from C. Gelernter, "Corporate Culture," *The Seattle Times* (5 June 1986): D1.
2. E. Schein, "Coming to a New Awareness of Organizational Culture," *Sloan Management Review* vol. 25, no. 2 (1984).
3. W. French and C. Bell, *Organization Development* (Englewood Cliffs, N.J.: Prentice-Hall, Inc., 1984).
4. "Employee Opinion Survey Results Presented," *Boeing News,* vol. 45, no. 25 (27 June 1986).
5. T. Peters and R. Waterman, *In Search of Excellence* (New York: Harper & Row, 1982).
6. Ibid, 22.
7. E. Schein, *Organizational Culture and Leadership* (San Francisco: Jossey-Bass, 1985): 6.
8. R. Ott, *Are Wild Ducks Really Wild: Symbolism and Behavior in the Corporate Environment,* (Northeastern Anthropological Association. Paper presented March, 1979).
9. S. Narod, "Off-Beat Company Customs," *Dun's Business Month* (November 1984): 66.
10. "Grant Managers Risked Pie-in-Face for Failure," *The Wall Street Journal* (4 February 1977): 6.
11. W. H. Mercer, *Employer Attitudes Toward Compensation Change and Corporate Values* (New York: William H. Mercer, Inc., 1983): 1.
12. As cited in "Corporate Culture: The Hard-to-Change Values that Spell Success or Failure," *Business Week* (27 October 1980): 154–160.
13. From Leonard A. Schlesinger and Debra Whitestone, People Express, Case 9-483-103. Boston: Harvard Business School, 1983, p. 8.
14. Ibid. 13.
15. W. M. Casey, "New Flight Plan," *The Wall Street Journal,* (31 July 1986): 1. Also see A. Bennett, "Airline's Ills Point Out Weaknesses of Unorthodox Management Style," *The Wall Street Journal* (11 August 1986): 15.
16. W. Rogers, *Think* (New York: Stein & Day, 1969): 153–54.
17. A. Tobias, *Fire and Ice,* 98–99. Reprinted by permission of Sterling Lord Literistic, Inc. Copyright © 1976 by Andrew Tobias.
18. G. H. Litwin and R. A. Stringer, Jr., *Motivation and Organizational Climate* (Boston: Division of Research, Graduate School of Business Administration, Harvard University, 1968).
19. Peters and Waterman, op. cit.
20. G. S. Saffold, "Culture Traits, Strength and Organizational Performance: Moving Beyond 'Strong' Culture," Unpublished research paper (Institute for Executive Leadership, Trinity Western University, 1986): 8.
21. "1980 General Motors Public Interest Report" (Detroit: General Motors Corporation, 1980): 1.
22. R. T. Pascale, "The Paradox of 'Corporate Culture': Reconciling Ourselves to Socialization," *California Management Review* (Winter, 1985): 29–33. Also see R. T. Pascale, "Fitting New Employees Into the Company Culture," *Fortune,* vol. 109 no. 11, (1984): 28–30, 34+.
23. R. T. Pascale, "Fitting New Employees . . ." p. 34.
24. W. B. Tunstall, "Cultural Transition at AT&T," *Sloan Management Review* (Fall 1983): 16–26, by permission of the publisher. Copyright © 1983 by the Sloan Management Review Association. All rights reserved.
25. Ibid.
26. Ibid.
27. Ibid. 22–24.
28. "Corporate Culture: The Hard-to-Change Values That Spell Success or Failure," *Business Week* (27 October 1980): 148–160.
29. "The Premium Now Is on Leadership," *Bell Telephone Magazine,* no. 1 (1983).
30. R. E. Callahan and C. P. Fleenor, *Organizational Culture Questionnaire,* Copyright 1986.
31. A. Tobias, *Fire and Ice.* Reprinted by permission of Sterling Lord Literistic, Inc. Copyright © 1976 by Andrew Tobias.

NOTES

CHAPTER 15
IMPACT OF COMPUTER TECHNOLOGY

WHAT'S YOUR OPINION? T OR F

_____ 1. Data-entry jobs are more stressful than police work.

_____ 2. Using computers to monitor employee performance reduces the need for direct personal contact by management.

_____ 3. Introduction of computers generally increases worker efficiency.

_____ 4. Workers who use computers in their jobs must be more skilled than those who do similar jobs without computer assistance.

_____ 5. Computers can be used to monitor every aspect of worker performance.

_____ 6. A person must know a lot about computers to use them effectively.

_____ 7. People who fear that their jobs may be lost to computers are not rational.

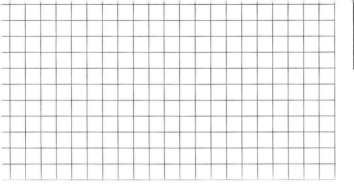

LEARNING OBJECTIVES

☐ Describe how computer technology has changed the definition of work

☐ Understand how computer work creates worker stress and affects employee motivation

☐ Explain how computers can affect the exercise of leadership and power

☐ Describe how communication channels can be changed when computers are introduced

☐ Discuss both opportunities and problems that arise from the computer's ability to monitor work closely

☐ Describe how computers may change managerial decision making

☐ Identify the major causes of resistance when computers arrive in a workplace

A Computer Is My Copilot[1]

The sleek Boeing 767 left the runway at Washington's Dulles Airport and turned toward Los Angeles. At 1,000 feet above the Washington suburbs, the captain pushed a button and removed his hands from the controls. The jetliner, now under the control of its on-board computers, would require no further human intervention until the approach to Los Angeles. The captain actually worked harder than he had to. Computers in high-tech airliners have the capability to roll the craft down the runway, lift it off, reach cruise altitude, direct it to its destination a continent away, calculate the most efficient descent, line up the airport, land the plane, and engage the brakes after landing.

Some pilots love the high-tech jet, but the enthusiasm is not universal. The Airline Pilots Association has a special task force studying cockpit automation. A task force spokesman says: "Today we see engineers deliberately designing automatic systems that deny the crew critical information. . . . For the most part, aircraft designers not only do not design for pilots, they don't even particularly like pilots. The pilots complicate their job. It's a lot simpler to design a system that doesn't have human involvement." One Boeing official has referred to the pilot as "a backup system" to the computer.

COMPUTERS ARE HERE TO STAY[2]

Is there really a computer revolution? Yes, there is. Eventually it may produce change as great as the industrial revolution. Already computers are changing how people work and live. According to sociologist Rosabeth Moss Kanter, ". . . corporate America is living through a transformation as vast and profound as anything since the turn-of-the-century era in which the large corporate organization first took shape."[3]

Surveys have predicted that by 1990 one of four white-collar workers will have an automated workstation, and that by 1992 one-half of all office workers will have personal workstations.[4] Some jobs, including highly technical ones, are being reduced in number or even eliminated. Computer-aided design and manufacturing allowed Chrysler to reduce its engineering group by half, to 4,000 employees, without sacrificing its product development programs.[5]

A revolution indeed—and it is growing at a fast pace. In 1982, there were 5 million personal computers being used in U.S. offices. By 1986, that number had tripled to 15 million. Some observers have predicted that the number of office computers will increase by some 25 percent each year until 1990.

In this chapter we will look at some of the changes occurring in organizations and jobs, and how people are reacting to their new co-worker—the computer.

The Information Society

In the early 1980s, the influential book *Megatrends* described ten major changes taking place in our society.[6] First on the list is the shift from an industrial society to an informational society. In 1950, only about 17 percent of jobs dealt primarily with information. Now more than 60 percent of us work with information as programmers, teachers, clerks, secretaries, accountants, managers, and technicians. Even in manufacturing firms, most of the workers hold information jobs. In other words, most employees spend their time creating, processing, or distributing information. It is the informational aspect of most jobs that is being influenced by computer technology. Computers can speed up the processing of information, increase the accuracy of it, and make it more readily available to people inside and outside of the organization.

Several things are certain about the machines already in place. They are operated by humans, and the linkage between human and machine is not always smooth or effective. Still, many people experience increased productivity, greater creativity, and improved job satisfaction. What makes the difference? In many cases it is the way computers are introduced into the workplace, and how they are related to the work.

Although the computer is a machine, it has achieved a special status in our society. While recognizing the vast potential of computers in the workplace, we must also recognize that the potential can be realized only if the human aspect of the organization is considered first. Most managers have learned that people *always* make the difference between success and failure of any project. Unfortunately, even experienced managers sometimes forget that lesson when computers are involved.

A list of major problems that confront managers as they enter the computer age emphasizes the point that the issues are behavioral in nature:

- □ Problems in work motivation caused by computerization of jobs
- □ Problems involving employee stress due to demands of computerized work
- □ Problems inherent in leadership by remote control
- □ Problems of managerial decision making in the computer age
- □ Problems in adapting to new ways of communicating by computer
- □ Problems of introducing computer technology without meeting intense resistance.[7]

We will consider each of these issues in turn.

In America, work equals information.

In the computerized workplace, the computer terminal eliminates the need to physically handle paperwork.

Computers, Job Design, and Work Motivation

How can computers change core job characteristics?

Work Is Redefined. Computers can drastically change the way work is done. One common occurrence is a restriction of the work experience. Consider a typical secretarial job. The secretary types letters and reports, retrieves and files paperwork, opens and sorts mail, schedules appointments, and answers telephones, along with other activities. With the introduction of a fully automated office system, the secretary has a terminal with video screen and keyboard. The boss has similar equipment. Most of the activities listed above can now be accomplished by interacting with the computer equipment instead of moving paper or dealing personally with other people.

Computers reorganize the relationship between people and their work. An individual must learn to accomplish a task through the medium of an information system rather than by working directly on the object of the task—a product or paperwork.

Opening Story Revisited

The 767 captain's work has been dramatically changed. He has become a "systems manager," entering symbols into the airplane's computers and reading symbols from the computer regarding the flight status. It is no longer necessary to flip through approach maps, calculate fuel reserves, or make minor adjustments to the flight of the aircraft. In fact, during a normal flight, he needn't touch any of the flight controls for the entire trip—approximately six hours from Washington to Los Angeles.

Work Becomes More Abstract. In addition to reorganizing the way work is done, the computer makes the work more abstract and less "real" to employees. A billing clerk in an insurance company now sits before a video display terminal (VDT) most of the day. Before the computer arrived, the clerk maintained customer files, updated them manually, and made frequent decisions on the account status. His desk often groaned under the weight of the papers. Now his desk is clear except for the terminal, and he processes more accounts than ever before. But somehow he misses handling the files, reading them, occasionally putting them aside to think about the best method for dealing with them. There is no time for that now.

How do computers make work abstract?

Social Interaction Is Reduced. In our many visits to computerized workplaces, a common feature was the lack of human voices. Only rarely did we see co-workers talking. Most frequently, the only noise was the clicking of keyboards. Many installations are deliberately designed to discourage employee interaction. Physical separation, placement of partitions, even sophisticated lighting schemes are used to isolate employees. The sense of isolation is not lost on the employees. One worker told us that she felt lonely on the job—yet there were thirty other VDT operators in the room.

How important is social interaction?

Some organizations set performance requirements so high that even if the physical layout allows interaction, there is no time for it. Bell telephone operators are expected to handle calls at an average rate of two per minute. A typical operator will have about 800 contacts per shift. A constant stream of unknown voices and numbers competes for attention as the operators' hands dance over their computer console keyboards. Said one operator:

> "I never hear a word the callers say. As the voices come into my mind, I just freeze the information in one part of my brain and hold it there. Then I pull it out whenever I need it. This allows me to distance myself from my work and ignore the fact that callers treat me like a rock. Who I am and what I do don't meet. My identity is separate from my job. . . . My supervisor once told me, 'We want you to make the right decisions on the job without knowing why.' I'm on automatic."[8]

King of the Road

Forty years ago, when he first steered a big rig onto an open highway, Harley Ewing was proud to work as a truck driver. "It was one of the best jobs on the coast," he recalled. "You were off on your own—no one looking over your shoulder. You felt like a human being."

But today, Ewing says he feels more like "a donkey in the desert" hauling groceries for his employer, the Safeway Company. The change, he says, is symbolized by a black box, about the size of a large paperback novel, that sits on the dashboard of his truck and keeps track of almost everything he does.

When he returns from his trip each day, Ewing plugs the black box (actually a small computer) into a larger computer at Safeway's distribution center. It instantly prints a report that pinpoints

any speeding, improper shifting, or excessive idling. It also tells his supervisor when he stopped for coffee or food and how long he spent on his breaks.

The manager of the distribution center believes the computer will save lots of money by reducing fuel and maintenance costs. But Ewing, 62, says the computer soon will drive him into retirement.

"I'm tired of being treated like an animal," he complained. "They push you around, spy on you. There's no trust, no respect anymore."

QUESTIONS *[handwritten: autonomy length of breaks, schedule, delivery]*

1. In what ways has the "black box" changed Mr. Ewing's job?
2. Is he justified in feeling "spied" upon? Why or why not? *[handwritten: depends · may be type of person who]*
3. If you were his manager, how would you reply to his concerns?

*[handwritten: educate-rationale-cost effective
tip top
- buy more vehicles
- get rid off vehicle]*

Source: Adapted from "The Boss Is Watching," *The Seattle Times* (3 August 1986): A1.

Computer control means loss of job control.

Loss of Mastery of Work. One of the most feared aspects of computer introduction is the potential loss of control, perhaps even loss of understanding, of how one's work gets done. The billing clerk who used to "know" clients by their files, now stares at an amber screen most of the day, occasionally wondering what his job really is. Telephone operators not only work at computer consoles, their performance is monitored by the computer. Their performance rating is determined by the number of calls handled, speed of work, and revenue generated by each call. Only operators with high ratings can be promoted, transferred, or can take advantage of educational benefits.

A telephone-answering service had several district offices in a large city. Each office served about 200 clients and each operator served about twenty accounts, with some sharing of accounts. Then a computerized telephone-switching system allowed the company to consolidate more than 2,000 accounts into a central office. Every operator has access to the full customer database, so calls are now handled on a first-in, first-out basis. Any operator can take a call for any customer.

Although efficiency increased dramatically, the operators felt a tremendous loss of control over the job. Instead of knowing their customers, they now quickly scan a VDT for information or enter messages from callers. The core job dimensions of task identity, autonomy, and feedback from the job have all been weakened.

Decrease in Skill. In a seeming contradiction, the growth of computer-augmented work will probably create a need for less-skilled workers rather than the reverse. While early computers required much knowledge and skill to operate, comprehensive software packages have virtually eliminated the requirement for technical knowledge.

Indeed, advanced software may lead to a decreased need for certain job-related skills. For example, word processing has reduced the need for secretarial typing accuracy, since mistakes can be corrected quickly and easily with no trace of correction. Spell-checking programs can be relied on to prevent common mistakes, thus decreasing the need for that language skill. We have already encountered cashiers who have no need to compute a customer's change. Instead, they merely enter the purchase amount and then the amount offered in payment. The machine calculates the change and, in some cases, automatically dispenses it.

Are any jobs immune to deskilling?

This effect is seen in more complex jobs, too. Nurses in intensive-care units often monitor several patients from a central station. Digital readouts continuously report patients' vital signs. Alarms sound if values exceed an expected range. Despite the obvious advantages computerization has brought to both patient and staff, some health-care professionals are concerned that they may be losing important "soft" skills. The most important of these may be the intuition born of experience acquired in personally observing hundreds or thousands of patients. The look in a patient's eyes, the coloring of skin, and the appearance of pain or restlessness are among many indicators used by medical personnel to anticipate changes in patient condition. These cannot be captured on a digital display.

It cannot be denied that computers have made great contributions to productivity, nor would any reasonable person encourage scrapping the technology. However, we must pay more attention to human needs, and to the long-range effects of making jobs less interesting and decreasing skill requirements.

Opening Story Revisited

An experienced airline pilot would be forgiven for recalling that flying was more fun when the airplane responded to human touch and remembering the satisfaction in making judgments that gave passengers a smooth flight, while saving the company money through skill as an aviator. But more than simply losing the fun of flying, the captain may also be losing some important skills. In an emergency, such as failure of an aircraft system, the solution must come from the brain, eyes, and skill of the human in command. Will a "systems manager" be able to cope?

Computers and Employee Stress

In Chapter 10 we saw that the greatest stress occurs where people face psychological demands, yet have little control over how to get the work done. What happens to workers' sense of control when computers are introduced? The experience varies, of course, but imagine a typical application in an accounting department.

Why are computerized jobs frequently stressful?

Prior to computerization, an accounts-receivable clerk would check in new accounts, complete a brief credit check, review existing accounts for outstanding balances, and prepare and send invoices. After the job is computerized, there is no paper to review. Orders are logged in by the sales department. The computer does a credit check and fills out an invoice with all appropriate discounts included. The clerk is now a VDT operator who simply reviews and enters certain information on the terminal. The flow of tasks is controlled by the computer, not the receivables clerk.

Earlier in this chapter we described how telephone operators are monitored by computers. Telephone operators once used phone jacks to connect with customers and connect customers with one another. Connections are now electronic, automatic, and almost instantaneous. As a result, many senior operators complain about stress caused by loss of job control. As one operator said, "Before, I could choose the speed of plugging in the jacks. If I was tired or not feeling well, I would be able to slow down and plug in the jack a few hundredths of a second later and no one would know. Now the equipment automatically does that and all I do is continue to respond to customers no matter how I feel."[9]

Loss of Control and Stress. There have been a number of studies about the link between stress and work. A study by B. G. Cohen, M. J. Smith, and L. W. Stammerjohn, Jr., investigated three work groups: clerical workers using VDTs, professional workers using VDTs, and a control group of clerical workers using manual methods. While all three groups reported stress, there were significant differences in the amounts reported. The clerical workers using VDTs showed the most stress, followed by the control group and finally the professional group. The clerical VDT workers reported more fatigue than either of the other groups.[10]

Why did professional workers show the least stress and fatigue? Probably because they felt they had control in their jobs. The VDT operators experienced lack of control and the pressure of being constantly monitored by supervisors through the computer system.

A study by Gunn Johannson and Gunnar Aronsson looked at VDT jobs in the insurance industry.[11] The major conclusions from the study:

- [ ] Stress and mental strain were related to delayed response times in the computer system and unpredictable interruptions of system operations
- [ ] Temporary interruptions caused an increase in blood pressure and adrenaline secretion
- [ ] Stress was reported mainly by data-entry workers
- [ ] Data-entry workers reported that their stress continued after work hours

□   A majority of those who worked continuously at a VDT reported feeling physical discomfort within one and a half hours

Clearly, the issue of control may help explain who will feel stress and who won't when work is computerized. As people feel a loss of control over how they work, they may be more prone to experience stress.

Leadership by Remote Control

The computer enables management to apply the techniques of factory production and supervision to office work, a way to enforce discipline and standardization in the office.[12] A bonus of office automation is that "business can finally monitor and measure the clerical function," according to one senior executive. A computer magazine noted that companies can "eliminate unnecessary managerial layers" of supervisors "whose primary activities are monitoring others" by using machines to measure the output, speed, and errors of each employee.[13]

Remote Supervision of Workers.   Many computerized systems are designed to make it easier to enforce production quotas and work speed. Automatic call distributors, for example, are widely used in the insurance industry and in other companies in which clerical workers handle phone calls from customers. The device tallies the number of calls each clerk handles, measures the average delay in answering calls, and counts the calls lost by the switchboard after 30 seconds of ringing. Time standards often set the pace for every clerical job within an insurance company. For example, coding each A-type claim is allotted 4 minutes and a B-type claim 4.7 minutes. Terminals used by data-entry operators record the number of keystrokes per minute and lines processed per day. Many operators are paid piecework rates rather than an hourly wage. The computer rejects inaccurate forms, keeping track of the number of errors, along with volume and speed.

Piecework pay per item completed

The measurements become part of each employee's work record, often without the worker's knowledge. Some programs will even allow a supervisor to record how much time a worker takes for a break. Said one claims processor, "You're paid on production. You know that if you stop to go to the ladies' room it's coming out of your paycheck."[14]

This kind of monitoring is one of the most hotly debated issues stemming from computerization. Many workers complain of stress created by the constant monitoring and pressure to maintain standards of quantity and accuracy. On the other hand, many workers appreciate the availability of an objective record of work performance. The records are also a great aid to supervisors in conducting performance appraisals. A danger is that supervisors may be tempted to focus only on the activities that the computer measures, and to avoid the "softer" interpersonal aspects. In a sense, this can become a form of "remote supervision."

To appreciate just how remote supervision can become, consider this story from a newly hired VDT operator:

"Tuesday, 10:30 P.M.: The lone computer operator comes over to my console and says in a friendly way, 'If you're going to stay here, you'll have to get your productivity up.'

"Oh,' I say, 'what is my speed and what should it be?' 'It's been scientifically set,' he tells me, 'at 15,000 keystrokes an hour.'

"Then he sits down, plays a couple of chords on his control panel and up come my figures. The figures show when I started—to the nearest tenth of a second—when I took a break, and exactly how many keystrokes I'd done all evening. (I am very far below the 15,000 keystrokes an hour.) The real supervisor is inside the machine."[15]

The story of Harley Ewing, the truck driver, is another example of remote supervision. His reaction is that management distrusts him and is spying on him. Although he may be more vocal than most employees, it seems certain that his view is shared by many, and the technology grows ever more sophisticated. Silicon microchips have been developed that can be implanted in a company identification card and used at any time to determine an employee's whereabouts.

Remote supervision means computer control.

There has been little research on the consequences of remote supervision, but we can think of some likely effects. First, remote supervision means less face-to-face interaction between the employee and supervisor. From research into the leadership of successful organizations, we know that employees are more motivated to perform their jobs when they feel some personal attachment to their supervisor and the work being performed. This attachment leads to a commitment and loyalty that is crucial to long-term organizational performance.

Another possible consequence of remote supervision is even higher levels of employee stress. With consistent but remote monitoring, employees are acutely aware of the computer's need for perfection—a standard that cannot be met by humans. But the most potentially damaging result is a loss of trust and respect between employees and their managers.

Remote Supervision at Higher Levels. Remote supervision is not limited to low-level employees. Managers at all levels have commonly gained a certain amount of power and independence by maintaining control of key information. With computer technology, top management can access day-to-day figures on the performance of even distant facilities. The chief executive of a major corporation has a terminal and full access to his company's database. By looking for patterns in the data, he is often able to spot something out of the ordinary, and thus ask searching questions of subsidiary executives.[16]

This increased access to information may be a two-edged sword, according to an article written by S. Zuboff for the *Harvard Business Review:*

It would seem that this new . . . capability would expand top management's opportunities to monitor and direct and, therefore, improve the performance of subordinate managers. But as the on-line availability of information reaches across management hierarchies . . . reduced risk taking and its effects begin to take hold. Managers are reluctant to make decisions on the basis of information that their superiors receive simultaneously. As one plant manager said to his boss in division headquarters: "I'm telling you, Bob, if you're going to be hooked up to the data from the pumps, I'm not going to manage them anymore. You'll have to do it."[17]

Computers and Decision Making

It is clear that computers are changing how decisions are made, but it is less clear whether all of the changes are helpful. The earliest business computer applications were aimed at improving the speed and accuracy of decisions. While computers are now widely used to make routine decisions, their power has only recently been applied to higher-level management decisions.

Decision Support Systems.   Decision support systems (DSS) go a step beyond the traditional corporate database. While most information systems give the user some ability to quantify data, DSS provides the data in a form requested by the user, rather than in an unreadable six-inch-thick printout. DSS provide a set of tools, including programs, database systems, data analysis systems, and data extraction programs, plus a means to integrate those tools into the decision process. In DSS, the end user builds the system, so the tool is coordinated with the thought process of the decision maker.

How can decision support systems improve decision making?

In an unusual application, the Weyerhaeuser Corporation uses a sophisticated simulator to train personnel to make more profitable decisions in allocating raw logs for processing.[18] Logs are crosscut into various lengths and allocated to different mill processes, to be made into different products: paper, plywood, and lumber, for example. The allocation decision is first made in the forest and then by personnel at distribution centers. It's a complicated decision, because there are hundreds of possible length combinations for a single log, and six or more logs per minute may be cut and allocated.

The goal of the decision simulator was to give people inexpensive experience in making the most profitable decision for cutting and allocation. A program was constructed that would make the optimum decision for a log based on the geometry of the log (length, diameter, taper, and curvature) and the quality of the log, including knots and decay. The logs must be matched to the requirements of the various mills. In the simulation, the operator sees a drawing of a log on a video terminal. The log can be rotated and inspected for imperfections. The operator decides where to cut and where to allocate the sections. The computer calculates the profit that would be earned from the operator's decision. The computer then cuts and allocates the hypothetical log, using the allocation that would bring the maximum profit. Finally, the computer displays the profit figure. The object, of course, is for the operator to come as close to the optimum allocation as possible. The simulator clearly improved cutting and allocation decisions, with the net benefit being estimated by the company at $7 million per year.

For many managers, modeling is the most useful aspect of DSS. By providing the ability to simulate decisions and to ask "what if" questions, DSS allows the user to test decisions without implementing them, thus avoiding costly mistakes.

Garbage In, Gospel Out. The term *garbage in, garbage out* has been familiar in computing circles for years. The newer term—*garbage in, gospel out*—refers to the unfortunate tendency of some people to believe that anything from a computer must be correct. It is important for decision makers to recognize that any decision approach is only as good as the data and the assumptions that fuel it. Instead, some accept computer output as the final word about the reality of a situation, sometimes with disastrous consequences. In 1983, a Soviet interceptor shot down a Korean Airlines 747 that had wandered into Soviet airspace, killing several hundred people. Many experts concluded that the 747 crew had entered incorrect coordinates in the computerized navigational system. Their exclusive reliance on that system, with no external verification, may have led to the catastrophe.[19]

Computers and Communication

Computers can greatly change the communication process between individuals and units. An auditor who once visited company branches, where she worked with people and checked their books, now gets needed information from a computer database. A bill collector who knows how to deal with people over the phone, establish relationships, and cajole them into paying must now put less emphasis on the personal touch and pay more attention to the information in computer files.

In many applications, computers have reduced the need for personal contact. From Chapter 5 on communication, we know that nonverbal communication is an important part of communicating. Some research gives us insight into what might happen in the absence of personal contact. Researchers at Carnegie-Mellon University used computer terminals from around the campus to study how electronic contact shapes human communication.[20] Eighteen groups of three students were asked to make decisions about various incidents. In one trial the students talked anonymously by computer. In another trial they identified themselves, and in a third trial they met and talked in person. There was a time limit on all trials.

The computer sessions were stormy. It took the groups longer to come to a decision, arguments were common, and the students frequently used abusive language. On the other hand, when the groups met in person, a single, vocal participant sometimes swayed the group's decision. In the computer groups, participation was more equal, with everyone having some weight in the decision.

Additional research at Stanford University confirms this unruly aspect of computer communication.[21] The investigators found several aspects of "normal" social etiquette to be missing from computer communication. They found that the norms for who speaks to whom, when or whether to interrupt, and how people are to be addressed haven't been worked out yet. Communicating by computer apparently breaks down social barriers that might otherwise inhibit people. For example, students were less hesitant to ask questions of professors through computer networks than in person. A computer network can also overcome status differences (one of the obstacles to effective communication). While discussing issues, people of lower status speak up more and are given more hearing. On a computer network, it is often unclear what a speaker's social status is.[22]

While communicating by computer has some positive aspects, other research indicates that people have some reservations about using the computer and other electronic methods. The transmission of an image, voice, or words is a far cry from sending a sense of a person's presence, and it is that sense that in a large part makes people want to meet in the first place. "Clearly, for purposes of notifying colleagues of bits of news, or circulating long tracts of information, the paper memo, or its electronic equivalent, will do. . . . However, there are times when a bona fide meeting is called for. There are complex issues to resolve, minds to persuade, actions to motivate, ideas to talk through,"[23] according to Valeria Geller of AT&T.

The drawbacks of a lack of face-to-face contact are especially serious for top executives. The generally unstructured nature of their work demands more personal communication than managers at lower levels. Executives typically much prefer the spoken word to the written. According to authority J. P. Kotter, "Most executives don't spend much time dealing with routine, highly verifiable facts, but rather with ambiguities. How do you check out the validity of ambiguous information? By listening to the voice of the person relating it to you, probing away, looking for what's really soft."[24]

Transmission of data and images through videoconferencing allows staff at distant locations to participate in meetings at the home office.

The 500-Mile Lunch Break

While it is easy to connect computers across long distances, Xerox Corporation is going several steps farther in allowing communication between scientists working in company labs located in Palo Alto, California, and Portland, Oregon. The labs are in constant contact with video and speaker-phone connections that are always open. Documents are exchanged with a computer network. The all-day video and audio connections allow the offices to interrelate casually as well as formally. The common area of both labs contains a camera, a big-screen video monitor, and a speaker phone. There are also cameras and monitors in some of the private offices.

In a fairly typical exchange, a scientist in Portland walked into the common area, noticed an engineer in Palo Alto and shouted a quick question about a technical problem. People in the two cities regularly eat lunch on camera, chatting with one another on the screens. One Palo Alto researcher took a break to teach a colleague in Portland to juggle.

Source: Adapted from M. W. Miller, "In This Futuristic Office, Intimacy Exists Between Workers Separated by 500 Miles," *The Wall Street Journal* (27 June 1986: 29). Reprinted by permission of *The Wall Street Journal,* © Dow Jones & Company, Inc., 1986. All Rights Reserved.

The system is not without problems. Being on constant display makes life awkward at times, and before cameras and speaker phones are installed in every office, methods to obtain privacy must be developed. Getting someone's attention over the video link is not always easy—even shouting doesn't always work. So Xerox has put a xylophone in each office and has assigned every researcher a personal melody. When people in Portland want to page a physicist in Palo Alto, they tap out the start of the theme song from a TV series. When a Palo Alto researcher wants to reach Portland's Tom Merrow, the researcher plays the first notes of, naturally, "Tomorrow."

QUESTIONS

1. Why is Xerox spending so much money to connect its scientists by video and audio as well as by computer?
2. Should the video link be used for chatting during lunch or to teach a colleague to juggle? Why or why not?
3. Should Xerox continue with plans to place cameras and speaker phones in every office? Why or why not?

Bell Laboratories confirmed this preference in its own computer networks that link Bell Labs in New Jersey with researchers across the country. It was found that people didn't like to use their terminals for messages of importance. Instead, they would transmit a message on the network requesting a return telephone call or personal meeting.[25]

Computers and Resistance to Change

When an office converts from manual to computer-based systems, or even from an outdated computer system to a newer one, there will usually be some turmoil. We learned in Chapter 9 that resistance to change is common, and introducing a new computer system is generally viewed by workers as a major change.

Computers are usually introduced to improve performance. In successful introductions, productivity gains of 15 percent to 50 percent within the first year are not uncommon. Productivity in tasks such as data entry or bookkeeping can increase as much as 100 percent. On the other hand, managers who are unaware of or insensitive to the effects that computerization may have on people can run into a counterproductive backlash of resentment, jealousy, and resistance.

Such resistance has been likened to the moves and countermoves in a game of chess, where employees develop "counterimplementation strategies."[26] They can be as creative and complex as the implementation strategies planned by management, computer vendors, or systems personnel. Their main objectives include diverting resources from the computer project, deflecting its goals, and scattering its resources. Some of the more common strategies are:

Counterimplementation strategy an attempt to stop change

- [ ] Lay low by declining to participate and by resisting changes proposed by "outsiders"
- [ ] Keep the project complex and hard to coordinate ("I want an integrated-online-real-time-database-management-processing-planning system.")
- [ ] Belittle the system implementor's status and influence
- [ ] Fake interest, but raise objections based on inside knowledge of a unit's operation
- [ ] Divert the system toward some other area ("Maybe marketing could use this.")

Reasons for Resistance.   The general problem is that, while management views computers as a great aid to efficiency and productivity, employees see them as a disruption or threat. We will look at some of the specific causes of resistance.

Fear of Skill Obsolescence.   Computers sometimes change jobs in ways that make a worker's knowledge and skills obsolete. This "deskilling" is not limited to line workers. Managers are subject to it as well. Usually, deskilling reduces the decision making required for the job. As a collection manager put it, "The computer gives us a tighter lock on the [individual] collector, and we can hire less-skilled people. But there's a real loss to the job of skills and know-how. You are being told what to do by the machine."[27]

Fear of Job Loss.   In our experience, this issue has grown because many companies have undergone reduction in force (RIF) programs. If there has been a relatively recent RIF for any reason, workers fear that any change will have the same result. Fear of job loss causes the most emotional response to computers in the workplace.

Feelings of Inadequacy.   These feelings strike many first-time users. This is especially true of people who believe that they are not technology oriented. A computer threatens to confirm their worst fears of incompetence.

Opening Story Revisited

While resistance to the "electronic cockpit" is not universal, the Airline Pilot's Association is clearly concerned. Of the reasons for resistance we listed, which are the most likely to be those of professional pilots? It is likely that resistance would come primarily from fear of skill obsolescence, fear of job loss, loss of control, and lack of identification.

Skills that are not regularly practiced become "rusty." If a computer does all of the flying, including take-offs and landings, some important pilot skills could be lessened.

Job loss is a legitimate concern. The three-person flight crew is apparently a thing of the past—the new generation of jets uses two-person crews.

Finally, if pilots become "systems managers," this will dramatically change the concept of flying and will likely lead to a lack of identification with flying (as it has been done until now) and to a sense of loss of control.

Fear of the Unknown. The fear of the unknown makes most people anxious. Established patterns are reassuring, even if they are inefficient, while new systems pose the threat of ambiguity and uncertainty.

Fear of Failure. Many workers have spent years developing job skills, only to be faced with the need to learn new skills, adjust to unfamiliar methods, and establish new working relationships. They worry that things will move too quickly, and that their performance will never recover.

Loss of Control. Computers and computer systems are often viewed as things over which one has no control. As we noted earlier, workers who perceive a loss of control may develop anxiety, stress, or even depression. At another level, computer systems may threaten an established power structure. Many systems allow top management to analyze data directly, bypassing the traditional method of asking middle management to collect and analyze it. As a result, middle managers may feel threatened. One manager said, "We fear the loss of our jobs or our private information, which can be a source of power. The corporate brass may want faster communication. But, I personally see this (information system) as an intrusion on my productive thinking time."[28]

Threat to Established Relationships. Changes that disrupt existing social patterns or that result in worker isolation are intolerable for many. Many computer jobs require such concentrated attention that rules are established to prevent socializing. In the insurance industry, claims adjusters are commonly forbidden to talk with co-workers except during breaks.

Lack of Identification. A lack of identification with the goals of a system is especially common when the system is installed without consultation with employees who will use it. Computer systems are not normally suggested by lower-level employees. Often their impression is that the system benefits only management. If imposed clumsily from the top, employees are not likely to see any benefit for themselves.

The reasons for resistance are not unique to the introduction of computers, indeed some of them are present with any major organizational change. However, the intensity of resistance can be severe when computers are involved. There is considerable myth about what computers can do, which makes many people nervous. But in addition to myth, there is the clearly documented reality that computers can and have eliminated or dramatically changed jobs in many organizations.

LEARNING SUMMARY

1. Computers have begun to redefine work. More and more employees are handling symbols rather than objects, so their work has become more abstract.
2. Many workers feel a loss of control in their jobs, which may contribute to increased stress. Professional workers are much less likely than clerical workers to feel loss of control.
3. While computers have improved the speed with which information can be communicated, the lack of physical "presence" makes communication of important information difficult; many people would rather make a phone call or conduct a meeting.
4. After computerization, many jobs can be filled by workers with lower skills.
5. Computer monitoring of performance has become a matter of great concern for many workers and for unions. Such monitoring ordinarily emphasizes quantity rather than quality.
6. Decision support systems allow managers to ask "what if" questions and to test some decisions before they are implemented.
7. Computers can reduce the complexity of decision making by establishing logical rules in using data. But this can lead to an over reliance on computer output—"garbage in, gospel out."
8. Middle managers may lose power as operating information becomes readily available to upper-level management.

ANSWERS TO "WHAT'S YOUR OPINION?"

1. True   Data-entry jobs are among the most stressful known; on average they are considerably more stressful than police work.
2. False   Because of the impersonal nature of much computer work, there is frequently a need for increased personal contact between manager and employee.
3. True   Increased efficiency is a major reason for installing computers. An efficiency increase of 100 percent is not rare.

4. False   In fact, many jobs are "deskilled" (require fewer skills) after computers are introduced.

5. False   There are many important performance aspects that computers cannot monitor—politeness, concern for customers, and cooperativeness, just to name a few.

6. False   Comprehensive software programs have made computers easy to use. One needn't be a mechanic to drive automobiles, and one needn't have detailed knowledge of computers to use them effectively.

7. False   Computers have displaced many workers.

KEY TERMS

Decision support systems

Deskilling

Information society

Lack of identification

Loss of control

Mastery of work

Remote supervision

Work abstraction

HUMAN RELATIONS APPLICATIONS

Although the task of introducing or changing computing systems is a difficult one, there are many examples of successful introductions. The successful projects generally apply similar methods, described below.

Education and Communication

This method is aimed at correcting inaccurate information or making up for a lack of information about the change. For example, Washington Natural Gas, with 1,000 employees, has an information center that provides a low pressure setting in which employees can experiment with computers and software. A company brochure describes the center this way:

> The Information Center is a do-it-yourself computer center structured around a combination of hardware, software, and experienced staff support. Its mission is to help . . . employees utilize available computer technology to productively solve daily problems. The Information Center provides services, desk top personal computers, software training, and consultation support to interested employees.[29]

Many organizations have similar programs, including Firestone, First National Bank of Boston, Greyhound Corporation, Frito-Lay Company, Avon Products and the General Services Administration of the federal government.

In addition to resource centers, a number of companies hold internal seminars at various locations for employees who cannot easily reach the resource center.

Facilitation and Support

When people are resisting because of adjustment problems, a simple approach is to be supportive. This can take many forms including providing emotional support, simply listening, or providing training in new skills.

Some companies encourage employees to take hardware and software home to learn and practice. The John Fluke Manufacturing Company, a maker of sophisticated electronic-testing equipment, has such a program. In addition, the company sponsors personal purchases of computer equipment and software with substantial discounts and company financing.

The First National Bank of Boston and Traveler's Insurance have in-house retail stores for purchasing equipment and software. The General Supply Administration of the federal government started a store in 1984 and it had sales of $4 million the first year.

Participation and Involvement

This approach is preached by every management book and management professor—and it really works. The Ciba-Geigy Corporation centralized word processing into one large unit, but was disappointed by a lack of productivity improvement. After three years, the company asked a manager to solve the problem. She asked workers how they would approach the problem of low efficiency. As a result of their ideas, the pool was decentralized in favor of a work-group approach reporting to functional units. According to the manager, "We involved people. It's not something jammed down someone's throat."[30]

Telecommuting: Wave of the Future?

An often discussed use of computers is to allow people to do productive work away from an organization. The University of Southern California's Center for Future Research has predicted that there will be 5 million "telecommuters" by 1995. Telecommuting has some obvious advantages for both employers and employees. The employee avoids the hassle of a physical commute, and the lack of office distractions can lead to greater productivity. Flexibility of working hours can also be a major advantage. For the employer, reduction in office space and parking congestion can be a plus. New labor sources, such as parents at home with small children and the physically handicapped, can also be tapped.

This new form of work has also created some unanticipated problems and some unanswered questions. For an employee, the new-found flexibility may lead to never-ending work weeks. Traditionally, home and work have been in separate locations. Many commuters will confirm that time on a freeway or commuter train allows a psychological transition from job to home. When office and home are one and the same, the transition may be more difficult. Telecommuters have reported feelings of guilt at uncompleted work, and have found it perhaps too easy to get back to the computer in the evening or on weekends. The blurring of

Telecommuting allows an employee to work at home using a computer connected via phone lines to the office system.

the home/office boundary apparently extends to co-workers as well, and a tendency to overwork may be reinforced by colleagues who call at all hours about work-related matters.

Some telecommuters experience the opposite problem. Distractions abound at home, even when one is working alone. At least one telecommuter dropped out of his company's program after gaining 25 pounds. A spouse who works away from the home may add to the problem by asking the telecommuter to run errands during the workday.

A small proportion of telecommuters report feelings of isolation and even loneliness. Some have requested to return to the office because they miss the social contact and the access to informal communication networks. A few have expressed concern that telecommuters are out of sight and therefore out of mind—and are less likely to be promoted or given desirable new assignments. George Chamberlain is a computer programming instructor for Control Data's home-work course. He communicates with his students by computer from his cell at Stillwater State Prison near Minneapolis, where he is serving a thirty-five year sentence. George notes that he wouldn't mind a day at the office.[31]

Unions have become increasingly interested in telecommuting. They are beginning to view clerical telecommuters as an important source of new members. Unions are also concerned that home offices could become the sweatshops of the future—a fear that is not completely unfounded. An insurance company paid clerical home-workers piece rates, offered no paid vacations or benefits, and charged $2,400 per year for equipment rental. Each worker processed more than 200 medical claims a day but netted only about $100 per week.[32]

Telecommuting also raises organizational questions. Two of the more troublesome are how to deal with data security and whether to compensate employees for the use of home space converted to office use. The choice of managerial style and performance appraisal methods will be complicated by any significant movement of work away from company facilities. Insurance will also become problematic—what happens if an employee is injured in the home office?

Professional workers have perhaps been the best served by telecommuting. Professional work tends to be highly individual and generally can be performed at any location. For example, this book was written almost entirely at the authors' homes on personal computers. Our equipment allowed us to communicate with one another, with the publisher, and with data services.

PERSONAL GUIDELINES FOR HUMAN RELATIONS SUCCESS

It is increasingly likely that you and most of your classmates will go to work in organizations featuring moderate to heavy computer use. As a supervisor or "lead," you should find the following advice helpful.

Don't Let the Computer Do Your Dirty Work. An unfortunate consequence of computerizing management information systems is the feeling of some managers that difficult, unpleasant, and undesirable tasks can be done at arm's length. One manager conducted performance appraisal of a problem employee by transmitting the appraisal to the employee's electronic mailbox—no discussion, not even a meeting.

While a computer system can make it easier for managers to escape their more undesirable job responsibilities, only unthinking, insensitive managers will take advantage of it. Granted that such responsibilities can be emotionally draining, but they are often the ones that require human contact.

Maintain Personal Contact. The impersonality of computers makes it important to have frequent face-to-face contact with employees. This means more than just meeting once in awhile so they remember your name. In successful organizations, managers communicate a vision of where the department or organization is going. Even with its colorful graphics, a computer can't communicate that vision. A vision is communicated through a physical presence—employees need to see the excitement and enthusiasm of a leader.

Precise Is Not Necessarily Better.   Computers allow the collection of specific and precise performance measures. This does not necessarily mean the measures are good ones. Consider the job of a corporate telephone operator. Computers make it easy to count the number of calls per hour, the number of rings before calls are answered, even the number of calls lost due to queuing. The computer *cannot* tell management how friendly or helpful the operators are to clients. It cannot tell management whether messages are being taken accurately or if they are being transmitted promptly. Keep in mind that because something can be counted is no guarantee that it is worth counting.

A Computer User's Bill of Rights.   Finally, remember the relative roles of people and computers, and keep in mind this computer user's bill of rights, formulated by S. F. Weinberg and M. L. Fuerst:[33]

1. People have a fundamental right to human companionship. No one should have to work in an all-computer environment. While computers may inevitably replace some workers in some jobs, the remaining employees have a right to interact with fellow human beings.
2. Computers must serve humans, not command them. A computer can advise, suggest, even plead, but it must not command. Final decisions rest with human users, not the machines designed to serve them.
3. Computers should be passive, not intrusive. While a computer may issue warnings when certain dangerous conditions are present, its main function is to respond when information is requested. Humans should not be denied the right to commit errors or make judgments out of ignorance.
4. Programmers must take responsibility for computers' good manners. Programmers should not insult users through innocent computer memory banks.
5. Computers need not be on all the time. Users have the right not to use computers for activities that are more enjoyable without them.
6. Computers should not abridge a person's freedom of speech. Computers should not be programmed to restrict the answers to complex questions. This can frustrate users and lead to inaccurate information in data banks.
7. Computers should not be permitted to be disguised as people. We should know when we're talking to a machine and not a person.
8. Humans will not tolerate computer tyranny. "Because the computer said so" does not lend credibility to an argument. It's not difficult to program a computer to lie. Putting nonsense onto an electronic display does not make it any the less nonsensical.
9. Humans have the right to "down time" as much as machines. Exhaustion comes from constant concentration as much as it comes from physical effort.
10. People should think; computers should help. No computer system should be designed to abrogate the human right to think independently. Their role is to help us be as creative as we can be.

1. What are the major problems confronting managers as they enter the computer age?
2. Describe and discuss common effects on job design when computers are introduced.
3. How does the use of computers increase employee stress?
4. What problems are created by remote supervision?
5. Why do people resist computer systems in the workplace?
6. How might computers change communication in an organization?
7. What methods can be used to increase the chance for a smooth introduction of computers into an organization?

DISCUSSION AND REVIEW QUESTIONS

Computers at Work

From reading this chapter, you are aware that computers can change a number of organizational processes. This exercise will help you understand some of these changes.

HUMAN RELATIONS EXERCISE

Instructions. Using the following set of questions as a guide for constructing your own questionnaire, interview someone who is using a computer on the job now, or who will be doing so. After gathering your data, share your results and identify any general trends or issues that emerge from your discussion. Here is a list of suggested questions:

1. What is your job like using the computer? (What do you think your job will be like after you start using a computer?)
2. How important is it (will it be) for you to understand and be able to use the computer in your job? Why?
3. What difficulties have you experienced (do you expect)? Please give some examples.
4. How are others around you responding to this experience? If it is different, what do you think accounts for the differences?
5. If you performed the same tasks prior to receiving the computer, how does it compare? Harder? Easier? Better? Worse?
6. Has (will) your control of work increased or decreased? How does (will) it feel to have more/less control?
7. Is your performance better or worse as a result of using a computer? Why?
8. What would you do differently if you had a say about how the computer was introduced to your job?
9. Would you recommend that others use computers on their jobs? Why?
10. Do you consider yourself a novice, somewhat knowledgeable, or very experienced with computer use?

HUMAN RELATIONS INCIDENT

The Claims Department

A large insurance company has a department that processes medical insurance claims for 100,000 customers. The department has fifty employees and occupies two floors of a large office building. Before computers, all claims were processed manually. A claims processor checked the forms for mathematical errors, checked that the proper spaces were completely filled in, and made sure the forms were signed by the proper parties before typing up the data.

Now the processors put the claim in front of them, punch a few numbers on a keyboard, and go on to the next claim. They do this all day, day after day. "It's kind of an insult to anyone's intelligence," says one of the processors.

Many processors have complained about backaches, eye strain, and headaches from sitting in front of the terminals all day. In addition, some pregnant women have requested transfers. Finally, sick days, lateness, and grievances have increased dramatically.

Management feels that the higher productivity resulting from computerization is definitely worth the increased employee unrest. However, the supervisors of these groups aren't sure it is worth all of the hassles.

QUESTIONS

1. Why do the supervisors have a different opinion than higher level managers?
2. How should the company respond to these problems—or should it respond at all?

NOTES

1. Adapted from E. J. Hebert, "Too Much Jetliner Automation?," © The Associated Press. Appeared in *The Seattle Times* (12 March 1985): D1.
2. This chapter is based on C. P. Fleenor and R. E. Callahan, *Computers on the Job: Managing the Human Side* (New York: Random House, Inc., 1986).
3. R. M. Kanter, "Office Automation and People: A New Dimension." (Report prepared for Honeywell, Inc., October 1983): 3.
4. R. Mass, "Records, Words, Data, Whatever You Call It, It's Still Information," *Information and Records Management* (June 1982): 18–20.
5. "A New Era for Management," *Business Week* (25 April 1983): 53.
6. J. Naisbitt, *Megatrends* (New York: Warner Communications, 1982).
7. C. P. Fleenor and R. E. Callahan, *Computers on the Job: Managing the Human Side* (New York: Random House, Inc., 1986): vi.
8. Stephen Singular, "A Robot and Liking It, Thanks," *Psychology Today* (March 1983): 22.
9. Personal interview, February 21, 1986.
10. B. G. Cohen, M. J. Smith, and L. W. Stammerjohn, Jr., "An Investigation of Health Complaints and Job Stress in Video Display Operators," *Human Factors,* Vol. 23 no. 4, August 1981: 387–400.
11. G. Johannson and G. Aronsson, "Stress Reaction in Computerized Administrative Work," *Journal of Occupational Behavior,* Vol. 5 (1984): 158–81.
12. *Computer Decisions,* July-August 1979.
13. C. Winier, "Office of the Future May Not Work, Poppel Warns," *Computerworld* (21 May 1979).
14. J. Andrew, "Terminal Tedium: As Computers Change the Nature of Work, Some Jobs Lose Savor," *The Wall Street Journal* (6 May 1983): 1.

15. B. Garson, "Overload in Data Cluster: Vignettes of Life in the Electronic Office," *Mother Jones* (July 1981).
16. "How Computers Remake the Manager's Job," *Business Week,* (25 April 1983): 69.
17. Reprinted by permission of Harvard Business Review. "New Worlds of Computer Mediated Work" by S. Zuboff, September-October 1982. Copyright © 1982 by the President and Fellows of Harvard College; all rights reserved.
18. M. R. Lembersky and U. H. Chi, "Decision Simulators Speed Implementation and Improve Operations," *Interfaces* (July-August 1984): 1–15.
19. V. Belenko, "What Really Happened to KAL Flight 007," *Reader's Digest* (January 1984): 72–78.
20. S. Kiesler, J. Siegel, and T. W. McGuire, "Social Psychological Aspects of Computer Mediated Communication," *American Psychologist* (1986).
21. L. A. Welsch, "Using Electronic Mail as a Teaching Tool," *Communications of the ACM,* Vol. 23 (1982): 105–8.
22. Kiesler, et al., "Social Psychological Aspects."
23. V. Geller, personal communication, September 1983.
24. J. P. Kotter, "What Effective General Managers Really Do," *Harvard Business Review* (November-December 1982): 156–67.
25. V. Geller, personal communication, September, 1983.
26. P. G. W. Keen, "Information Systems and Organizational Change," *Communications of the ACM,* Vol. 24 no. 1 (January 1981): 24–33.
27. J. McNitt, *The Art of Computer Management* (New York: Simon & Schuster, 1984).
28. Personal interview, December 8, 1985.
29. *Information Center,* (Seattle, WA: Washington Natural Gas, October 1984).
30. "The Office of the Future," *Business Week* (30 June 1985): 63.
31. Robert Johnson, "Rush to Cottage Computer Work Falters Despite Advent of Inexpensive Technology," *The Wall Street Journal* (29 June 1983): 37.
32. *In These Times,* (April 1984).
33. Adapted from S. F. Weinberg and M. L. Fuerst, *Computer Phobia* (Wayne, PA: Banbury Books, Inc., 1984): 93–95.

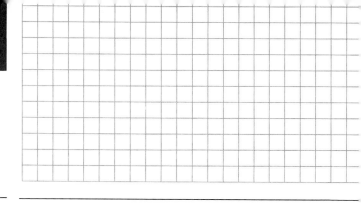

CHAPTER 16
FUTURE DIRECTIONS OF HUMAN RELATIONS

WHAT'S YOUR OPINION? T OR F

____ 1. There are only two or three distinct lifestyles in the United States.

____ 2. Within thirty years, most of us will be working in retail trade or service industries.

____ 3. Immigration will account for most of America's population growth in the next ten years.

____ 4. Attitudes toward work have changed over the past few years.

____ 5. Workers will have more flexibility and control over their work schedules in the future.

____ 6. Managers in the future will have to be computer literate.

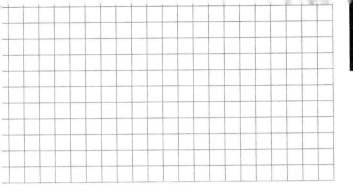

OUTLINE

WHAT LIES AHEAD?
  Trends of the Present

AMERICAN LIFESTYLES

WHERE THE JOBS WILL BE
  The Changing Face of America
  Shifting Values and Work Ethics

HOW WILL MANAGEMENT PRACTICES
CHANGE?
  Management Skills for the Future

LEARNING SUMMARY

LEARNING OBJECTIVES

☐ Compare characteristics of today's organizations with those that may exist in the future

☐ Describe important trends in jobs and labor requirements

☐ Identify major lifestyle categories and characteristics of people who adopt them

☐ Identify specific human relations skills that are likely to be emphasized in the future

A Supervisor in the Year 2020

Mary Barker is a supervisor for Decision Science Services, a firm that provides specialized databases and software support for major corporations. She has been awakened at her apartment by a wake-up call she set last night by dialing her firm's mainframe computer.

When she picks up the telephone, a cheerful synthesized voice announces the time, current temperature, and weather forecast for the metropolitan area. A musical tone follows the forecast, and the personal computer in Mary's home office is turned on by the corporate mainframe. A status report for her department is stored for her review after breakfast.

High on Mary's list of activities for the day is the review of productivity statistics for each of her ten employees. Unlike some managers, Mary likes to talk directly with the employees rather than simply transmitting the statistics to their terminals. Time is always a problem, since the employees work the national average of thirty hours per week, often at home, and they pretty much set their own schedules. Mary, like most supervisors, works about sixty hours per week.

Mary can tell if her employees are working simply by punching a code on her computer keyboard. Her computer then dials the appropriate employee computer. She can even "watch" an employee work by viewing the employee's computer output on her own screen, but she doesn't like to do that without informing the employee.

Mary dials her office number on the nearby video phone, and her secretary's friendly face appears on the screen. While they discuss Mary's schedule for the remainder of the week, a small light flashes on near Mary's computer. She installed it herself when she heard a rumor that upper-level management was monitoring the supervisors. The light indicates that someone has entered the communication link. Mary feels a surge of anger as she continues the discussion with her secretary.

WHAT LIES AHEAD?	How different will work and management be in the year 2020? How will individual performance be evaluated? Will there be new forms of compensation? What will the labor force be like? In what ways will the experience of work change?

Trends of the Present

One of the most talked about books concerning the future of work and society is John Naisbitt's *Megatrends*,[1] which discusses several trends that have consequences for employees and organizations of the future. We will discuss some of these trends.

Megatrends major changes

Informational Society. This trend is the shift from an industrial society to one based on information. This change is concerned with a need for increasing amounts of information in our lives. It is estimated that scientific and technical information, which now increases about 13 percent per year, will jump to an annual rate of 40 percent.[2] At that rate, the amount of such information would double every twenty months.

High-Tech/High-Touch. Another trend associated with increased amounts of information is the need for more technology, which in turn creates a desire for more human contact. As we saw in Chapter 9, people resist change for many reasons, including fear of job loss or skill obsolescence when new technology is introduced. As change occurs ever more rapidly, managers may find a need to spend more time communicating directly with employees.

Decentralization. American society is one of the most diverse in the world, and the country has always been proud of its reputation as a "melting pot." In a society that supports individual rights, groups and individuals strive to be distinct and create choices that reflect their situations. Decentralization is a response to this diversity. Decentralization allows flexibility and decisions made to fit particular circumstances. While this has notable advantages, great energy must be focused on coordination, otherwise perspective on overall goals is lost.

Self-Help. As individuals, we have relied on various institutions to protect us and provide for basic needs. We have relied on the government to help us in retirement (Social Security), the medical profession to provide treatment or cures, and organizations to grow and give us prosperity through increased wages and benefits. But in the past few years there has been a shift away from this form of dependence on institutions. There has been an increase in awareness of the individual's ability to maintain good health. Smoking has decreased substantially, alcohol consumption is down—with wine replacing hard liquor—and health-food products are popular.

This growing self-reliance or self-help affects organizations in subtle ways. People aren't as willing as in the past to move for a promotion. Workers are leaving large organizations and starting their own businesses in record numbers. The trend is toward more self-reliant individuals who will strive to meet their own needs.

What will worker self-reliance mean for employers?

Networks. Networking is the informal sharing of ideas, information, and resources. If reliance on networks increases, the formal pyramid structure of organizations will decrease in importance. Chains of command will be more loosely structured, and people will rely more on their informal associations than on formal hierarchical control to get work done.

AMERICAN LIFESTYLES

Which lifestyle best describes you and your friends?

SRI International, a research and consulting firm, started a "values and lifestyles" (VALS) program a number of years ago to identify major groups of lifestyles among Americans.[3]

The program identified nine distinct lifestyles (figures are from 1984):

1. *Survivors.* Usually poverty stricken and poorly educated. This group totaled about 6 million people.
2. *Sustainers.* Low income, distrustful but, unlike survivors, have not given up hope. About 11 million people.
3. *Belongers.* The largest (60 million) group. Middle class, family-oriented, patriotic.
4. *Emulators.* Very ambitious and competitive, fairly successful. About 13 million people were included in this category.
5. *Achievers.* About 35 million strong, this group represents the establishment. Successful, self-reliant, and hard-working.
6. *I-Am-Me's.* Approximately 6 million people, mostly young, seeking an inner-directed life.
7. *Experientials.* About 11 million people, very well educated, may be deeply involved in ideas and issues.
8. *Societally Conscious.* These 15 million Americans are successful and influential. They are highly concerned with social issues.

Opening Story Revisited

If the trends listed above continue, supervisors like Mary will find themselves in an awkward position. They likely will have employees who are less accepting of authority than those today. Mary will have the added problem of trying to supervise people who are not located in a room together. They may be monitored electronically, but that is not the same as supervision.

---

9. *Integrateds.* Only about 3 million strong, this group reflects both achiever and societally conscious qualities.

SRI researchers further categorized the nine lifestyles into four groups: need-driven (survivor and sustainer lifestyles), outer-directed (belonger, emulator, and achiever lifestyles), inner-directed (I-am-me, experiential, and societally conscious lifestyles), and combined outer- and inner-directed (integrated lifestyle).

The outer-directed and inner-directed groups are by far the largest, and they show signs of rapid change in relative size. While previously comprising 71 percent of the population, outer-directeds had declined to 65 percent by the early 1980s. At the same time, inner-directeds increased from 17 percent to about 27 percent.[4] These survey results tend to confirm the trends toward decentralization and self-help mentioned earlier.

WHERE THE JOBS WILL BE

One forecast of job growth for the years 1982 to 2010 is shown in Table 16–1. The 1995 forecast is from the Bureau of Labor Statistics (moderate projection), while the forecast for 2010 is a rough extrapolation.

According to the predictions in Table 16–1, jobs in manufacturing will remain about 19 percent of the total jobs available, while jobs in trade and services will continue to increase in relative importance. The other sectors will either remain stable or decline in importance.

The Changing Face of America

Employers are facing dramatic changes in the work force over the next few years. Some of the most significant are:

- [ ] The maturing of the baby boom generation. Workers aged 25 to 44 will make up more than half of the work force in the 1990s.
- [ ] Women will represent more than 60 percent of the labor force by 1995, compared with 32 percent in 1960.
- [ ] Husband and wife now work in 40 percent of families, compared with 12 percent in 1959. The figure will pass 50 percent sometime in the 1990s.

TABLE 16 – 1
Job growth from 1982
to 2010

Sector	Jobs (millions)		
	1982	**1995**	**2010**
Mining	1	1	1
Private households	2	1	1
Farming	3	3	1
Construction	5	8	9
Transportation & utilities	6	7	8
Finance, insurance & real estate	6	8	9
Government	16	17	19
Manufacturing	19	23	26
Trade	23	29	31
Services	23	31	35
Total jobs	102	128	139
Labor force	112	130	157
Population	231	256	280

SOURCE: Adapted from A. Porter, "Work in the New Information Age," *The Futurist* (September-October 1986): 10.

□ The number of individuals over 85 years old will increase by 79 percent by 1995. The proportion of Americans over age 65 will increase from 11 percent of the population now to 16 percent by 2020. Many of them will want to continue working past normal retirement age.

□ Immigration will account for most of the population growth in the next decade. Hispanics will come close to overtaking blacks as the largest minority group.[5]

Shifting Values and Work Ethics

The trends described above have led to changes in values and attitudes toward work. The changes do not necessarily mean that people are losing a desire to work, but it is clear that there has been a change in the conditions of work desired by employees.

Writer J. M. Rosow suggests that six categories of attitude change have occurred in the last few years:[6]

□ *Challenge to authority.* Permissive society created a group of people who questioned traditional values and goals. What began as a minority attitude spread to a large portion of the population and subsequently to the workplace, where workers question the authority of managers.

□ *Declining confidence in institutions.* Public scandals such as Watergate and disclosures of unsafe products made by major corporations have reduced trust and confidence in both government and business. This lack of confidence may lead to more frequent challenges to authority.

□ *Resistance to change.* Mistrust of organizations and leadership lead to resistance to technical innovation. Workers begin to rebel against lack of participation in decisions that affect their job security.

□ *Changing attitudes toward work.* Traditional attitudes toward work upheld the notion of work as both a duty and a privilege. Many workers no longer share these attitudes and value leisure activities above work.

□ *Work and family relationships.* The changing nature of marital and family relationships is also having an effect in the workplace. There are more two-income families, more working single parents, and more people who choose to remain unmarried. All of these place stress on traditional work requirements and support services.

□ *Faster changes in society than in the workplace.* Many social changes occurred over a relatively short period. Attitudes toward minorities, civil rights, sexual norms, and other social issues exceeded the ability of organizations to adapt. The "new" attitudes placed considerable pressure on traditional organizational values.

In recent years, many workers no longer share traditional attitudes toward work; they value leisure activities above work.

How will managers cope with changing work attitudes?

Taken together, where do all of the trends lead? Our own predictions follow. As you read them, keep in mind a statement attributed to Pierre DuPont: "One cannot expect to know what is going to happen. One can only consider himself fortunate if he can discover what has happened."

HOW WILL MANAGEMENT PRACTICES CHANGE?

It would be pleasant to predict that managers in the year 2020 will be leading highly motivated, autonomous work groups that are happily engaged in enriched jobs. Some managers undoubtedly will lead such groups, just as some do today. However, we think there will be a strong and probably unthinking shift toward a two-tier work society. One tier will be managers, professional, and highly skilled workers, while the other tier will hold a much greater number of clerical, low-level administrative and unskilled employees. The upper tier will enjoy more flexibility and autonomy in their jobs than today, while the lower tier will have even less than they do presently.

With that prediction as a troubling background, let us imagine how work and management may change in the next few decades.

Nature of Supervision. Supervisors will be relieved of some mundane responsibilities, such as daily scheduling and correcting routine employee errors. Much of that will be done with computer scheduling and monitoring systems. Supervisors will be able, if they choose, to devote more attention to employee feedback and development and to oversee departmental planning.

Performance Appraisal Systems. Managerial and professional jobs will be evaluated almost exclusively with behaviorally anchored scales (BARS), behavior observation scales (BOS), and management by objectives (MBO). Feedback on performance will be much more specific and performance requirements will be more clearly defined than at present. For clerical and other lower-level jobs, there will be heavy reliance on computer programs to monitor work performance. There will be even greater emphasis on quantity than there is today.

Pay and Reward Systems. By 2020, there will be fewer pay systems that are based primarily on seniority. Advanced technology will allow close monitoring of work quantity and perhaps some aspects of quality. Most workers will be rewarded for performance and this emphasis will make jobs more stressful. Profit-sharing plans may be expanded to include loss sharing.

Concept of Work. Even more so than today, highly skilled and knowledgeable people will find work rewarding. Computer technology will allow them to be more productive, and at the same time will grant them greater flexibility. Flexible work schedules will be normal for such employees and many of them will choose to work at home much of the time. For some, it will be possible to go to work for a new employer hundreds of miles away without moving households.

Opening Story Revisited

M ary and supervisors like her will have more time to devote to planning than they do today, but employee supervision will be problematical. Although it will be "easy" to monitor work electronically, there may be legal restrictions on the practice. "Soft" performance criteria, such as cooperation, team effort, and time management, will be difficult to measure for workers located in their homes. Common criteria of today, such as personal appearance, punctuality, and attendance, may be meaningless to Mary's organization.

Less skilled workers will face a different life. Many of them will actually lose some flexibility and autonomy. Continuous monitoring of work output will be common. There will be much pressure for increased productivity. Skills will be engineered out of many jobs, which will make these employees easily replaceable. Stress-related illness will be a major problem for these workers.

Unions.   Unions will enjoy a large increase in membership among white-collar workers who feel threatened by computers and computer monitoring. Labor negotiations will focus less on wages and benefits and more on conditions of work, job security, and employee development. In some respects this represents a full circle to the early days of union formation when workers banded together to improve working conditions.

Government Regulation.   The 1980s trend toward less government regulation in business will be reversed. There will still be regulations requiring fair treatment of minorities. Women will have made great progress in terms of comparable pay and will be proportionally represented in management and executive jobs. Complex regulations will be developed that limit the use of computer monitoring of employee performance and communication. Employee privacy will be safeguarded by law, but workers will still enjoy less privacy than they do now.

Management Skills for the Future

Effective managers in 2020 will use many of the same skills that effective managers apply today, but the emphasis will be different and the cost of mistakes will be higher. Following are our predictions for the most prized skills.

- □ *Communication.* As organizations become more information intensive, increased emphasis will be placed on both oral and written communication skills. People who cannot write well or make clear oral presentations will be at a severe disadvantage.
- □ *Management of change.* It is widely accepted that change is occurring ever more rapidly. Not many years ago, managers could expect stability in their organi-

zations, but no more. The management of change, including methods of reducing resistance to change, will be a major part of any management job.

☐ *Computer literacy.* Computers are already widely used in daily operations at many organizations and are becoming invaluable aids in decision making. Soon managers will be expected to use the machines in many aspects of their work. Computer literacy, by the way, does not require that one become a programmer. It does require an understanding of the basic functions of computers and how relevant applications software is used.

☐ *Cross-cultural perspective.* Expansion into world markets requires an understanding of other values, cultures and political systems. The trend toward global interdependence that has become so evident in the last few years will continue.

Already, unemployment in our automobile and electronics industries is tied to an active Japanese export policy. American farm income is related to Soviet weather and U.S. foreign policy. Even the availability of automobile fuel and heating oil may depend on political stability in the Middle East.

Increasing global interdependence in the future will mean that successful managers must understand and appreciate other values and cultures.

More Companies Are Listening

Employees are becoming more vocal in their opinions about their employers and their work. What does an organization do when there are hundreds or thousands of employees with something to say? Smart employers are responding to this trend by expanding the use of employee surveys. What management hears is not always pleasant, but it is generally useful. Some recent examples:

☐ Leaseway Transportation Corp. truck drivers complained in a survey that their bosses neither encouraged ideas nor were receptive to them. The company offered management-training courses to address the problem.

☐ In an effort to include employee opinions in decisions, Wells Fargo & Co. has surveyed its workers about such things as the effectiveness of the bank's advertising, the quality and innovation of its products, and its responsibility to the community.

☐ In a survey of its 25,000 employees, Hartmarx found consistent complaints about poor feedback from bosses. The company revived a program to teach managers how to conduct performance appraisals.

☐ A survey at Hewlett-Packard found that engineers were concerned about the lack of communication with their peers in other units, prompting the company to accelerate development of an electronic-mail system.

Source: Adapted from L. Reibstein, "A Finger on the Pulse: Companies Expand Use of Employee Surveys," *The Wall Street Journal* (27 October 1986): 27. Reprinted by permission of *The Wall Street Journal,* © Dow Jones & Company, Inc., 1986. All Rights Reserved.

QUESTIONS

1. What risks does a company take in surveying employee attitudes and opinions?
2. If management disagrees with results of a survey, how should they respond to workers?
3. What are some major benefits gained by surveying employee attitudes?

Managers capable of working with a second language will have a significant advantage over monolingual colleagues. Even within the country, there will be a need for managers who can work in both English and Spanish.

☐ *Knowledge of group dynamics.* Increasingly, important decisions are being made by groups rather than individuals. Managers usually supervise small groups. It is important for them to understand how group behavior differs from individual behavior and what forces are at work within and between groups.

☐ *Conflict management.* In the section above on shifting values and work ethics, the predicted changes included challenge to authority, declining confidence in institutions, resistance to change, and changing attitudes toward work. These trends will complicate the exercise of executive power. In addition to skill at resolving conflict, managers will have to be sensitive to personal values and needs.

The human relations concepts discussed throughout this book will help contribute to the attainment of both organizational productivity and individual job satisfaction. None of the applications offer instant results. They take time, money, skill, and commitment.

The challenge is real and so is the opportunity. There has never been a greater need for management talent than now, yet that need will surely increase. Learn as much as you can about the theories presented here, because they represent the best current knowledge about people and work. Armed with knowledge, you can be among the vanguard in this new management era.

LEARNING SUMMARY

1. There are several trends occurring today that may help us predict the future: a shift to an information society, high-tech/high-touch, decentralization, self-help, and networking.
2. The concept of work will continue to change. Professional and other skilled workers will probably have more autonomy and flexibility than they do today. Workers with few skills will have even less autonomy and flexibility than now.
3. The work force will change over the next few years. Young workers and older workers will compose about two-thirds of the work force.
4. Management practice will change in a number of ways: Performance appraisal systems will become more specific, pay and reward systems will change, a "two-tier" work force will emerge, unions will gain strength, and government regulation will increase.
5. Declining confidence in institutions and increased challenge to authority will make it more difficult for managers to manage.
6. In the future, certain knowledge and skills will be critical for managers: oral and written communication, the management of change, computer literacy, a cross-cultural perspective, knowledge of group dynamics, and conflict management.

ANSWERS TO "WHAT'S YOUR OPINION?"

1. False   The values and lifestyles program identified nine distinct lifestyles.
2. True   Based on Bureau of Labor Statistics projections, two-thirds of all jobs will be in trade and service.
3. True   The Hispanic population may overtake blacks as the largest minority group.
4. True   Among other changes, there is less trust in authority and a declining confidence in "the system."
5. False   Management and professional workers will probably have more flexibility, but rank-and-file employees will probably enjoy even less flexibility than they have today.
6. True   Virtually all managers will work with a computer regularly.

Achievers

Belongers

Decentralization

Emulators

Experientials

High-tech/High-touch

I-am-me's

Integrateds

Megatrends

Self-help

Societally conscious

Survivors

Sustainers

VALS program

KEY TERMS

DISCUSSION AND REVIEW QUESTIONS

NOTES

1. Of the predictions in this chapter, which do you believe is least likely to come true? Why?

2. Which of the predictions, if true, will affect you the most? How will it affect you?

3. In what ways will a manager's job be more difficult than today? In what ways will it be easier?

4. The average age of the American population is increasing. How will this affect business and government organizations?

1. J. Naisbitt, *Megatrends* (New York: Warner Books, 1982).
2. Ibid: 24.
3. A. Mitchell, *The Nine American Lifestyles,* (New York: Warner Books, Inc., 1984).
4. A. Mitchell and C. MacNulty, ''Changing Values and Life Styles,'' *Long Range Planning,* vol. 14 (April 1981): 37–44. Also see A. Mitchell, ''Nine American Lifestyles: Values and Societal Change,'' *The Futurist* (August 1984): 4–14.
5. H. Bacas, ''America's Changing Face,'' *Nation's Business* (July 1984): 18–25.
6. J.M. Rosow, ''Changing Attitudes to Work and Lifestyles,'' *Journal of Contemporary Business,* vol. 8 no. 4 (1977).

Creativity

- new ideas, innovative
- more input, opportunities for input.
- some ideas may fael learn from these failures
- persistence → to be able to master
  - can't give up.
- result of improving on other ideas outside of organization.
- development of entrepreneurship (require creating right culture through management beliefs attitudes
  - how to nurture this spirit
  - good reward structure
  - understand other cultures
  - their human relations.

* Privacy
* procedure
* spells out privacy
* Health protection on the
* personnel files
* polygraphs restricted to in house thefts

- amount of uncertainty
- Western no answer to all questions Japs
  - other - numerous peoples view of time - past - present - futuristic
  - know all times

Americans - individuals - collective -

Am/Cana present/ near future - futuristic.
European - past - present
Oriental - futuristic. - past (Meech Lake)

use private/public space
    N/A private (collective)
Jap. public (collective)

Glossary

Absenteeism absence from work, whether voluntary or involuntary.

Achievers self-reliant and hard working persons; a major American lifestyle.

Action research inquiry in which the process of data analysis and solution generation involves those from whom data were collected.

Aesthetic responsive to and appreciative of beauty in art and nature.

Affirmative action an employer's effort to increase employment opportunity for groups that appear to be inadequately represented in the company's labor force.

AFL-CIO American Federation of Labor and Congress of Industrial Organizations; national union organization that includes all major unions.

Ageism discrimination against people because of age.

All-channel network a decentralized communication pattern where each member communicates freely with all others in the network.

Alternative generation a process of creating as many different solutions as possible to a problem.

Anthropology a social science discipline that studies the origins and development of human cultures.

Arbitration the process in which a binding decision is issued after a formal hearing at which each side presents its case.

Attitudes valuative feelings about objects, people, or events.

Authoritarian leader work or job-centered leader who makes decisions without input from others.

Avoidance a short-run conflict-managment tactic that gains time for gathering information and allowing parties to "cool off."

BARS an evaluation method that uses behaviorally anchored rating scales, each scale describing expected work behavior.

Behavior modification the application of operant conditioning to worker behavior in a planned manner.

Behavioral component a set of attitudes that involves a reaction to an object, person, or event; implies a tendency to behave in a certain way.

Behavioral theory focuses on what leaders do and how they do it.

Belongers middle-class and family-oriented persons; the dominant American lifestyle.

BOS an evaluation method using behavioral observation scales, each scale describing observed work behaviors.

Boss-centered leadership characterized by close supervision, negative use of power, emphasis on schedules, and critical evaluation of work performance.

Cafeteria fringe benefits   flexible benefit packages that allow employees some choice in the makeup of their benefits.

Career counseling   a process aimed at helping a person decide upon career direction; often includes formal testing.

Career development   the process of creating a pattern of jobs in a series of steps from the initial job to retirement.

Career pathing   a type of career planning aimed particularly at preparing people for higher level positions.

Career planning   a plan for accomplishing one's goals in a career; may include formal education, on the job training, job rotation, and other programs.

Central tendency   the degree of clustering of ratings to the middle of a performance scale.

Centralized network   a communication network characterized by information flowing through one individual who controls the amount and speed of transmission.

Chain network   a centralized communication network in which information flows upward and downward but not laterally.

Choice theory   focuses on the internal decision that an individual makes about how to behave.

Circle network   a decentralized communication pattern where all members are allowed to interact directly with adjoining members but not with the other members of the same group.

Civil Rights Act of 1964   legislation that protected certain groups of people (age, sex, religion, national origin) from discrimination.

Coercive power   power held by those who can cause others to have unpleasant experiences.

Cognitive component   a set of attitudes that includes the information, beliefs, and ideas that a person has about an object, person, or event.

Cohesiveness   the amount of attraction group members feel toward one another; high cohesiveness can result in group unity.

Collages and drawings   symbols and art work that illustrate a perceived aspect of the organization, used to collect data.

Collective bargaining agreement   a formal contract between the union and the organization.

Commitment   emotional attachment to an organization.

Competition   conflict regulated by rules or standards that limit what antagonists can do to one another.

Computerized work   work previously done by workers either using machines or processing paper, redesigned to be handled by electronic technology. The individual worker now types symbols that instruct the electronic device to machine a part or process information.

Computerphobia   fear of computers; a mental and physical reaction to computer technology.

Conflict   a condition of opposition and discord, involving mutual antagonism.

Conflict of interest   a conflict, usually over jurisdiction, or "turf," that results when the interests of two groups cannot both be satisfied.

Conflict resolution   the active management of conflict through defining and solving unresolved issues between individuals, groups, or organizations.

Conflict stimulation   intentional creation of conflict by a manager to improve organizational performance.

Conflict style   the method of conflict management determined by the intentions of the parties involved, using competition, accommodation, avoidance, collaboration, or compromise.

Conformity   degree to which group members adhere to the rules and practices of the group.

Consideration   a leadership style in which the leader tries to gain the employees' trust and respect and to create a supportive atmosphere for employee development.

Constructive conflict   conflict that helps people clarify issues, solve problems, and improve performance.

Contingency model   a leadership style based on the relationship of three factors: (1) leader/member relations; (2) task structure; and (3) leader positional power.

Contrast   a rating error that occurs when employees are rated relative to one another rather than to performance standards.

Cooperative counseling   involves a combination of a counselor's active listening and suggestions to solve a problem.

Corporate culture   a consensus of beliefs, customs, value systems, behavioral norms, and ways of doing business that are unique to an organization.

Counseling   discussion and suggestions for dealing with a problem that usually has an emotional content and is a source of stress.

Craft union   a union organized around people doing similar jobs, such as plumbers, carpenters, or bakers.

Craft-oriented work work organized according to specific skill categories. Widespread during the Middle Ages, examples included the cobbler guild, furniture guild, and blacksmith guild.

Criteria job standards that are used as the basis for performance evaluation.

Criteria only a subjective type of appraisal in which a rater responds to a general rating scale that contains definitions of different performance standards.

Cultural communications communication that reinforces elements of an organization's culture.

Data collection approaches methods to obtain data, such as interviewing, questionnaires, sensing, polling, and collages and drawings.

Deadwood employees who work at a marginal or unsatisfactory level and have no potential for advancement.

Decentralization in society, a condition that allows flexibility and decisions to be made to fit particular circumstances.

Decentralized network characterized by the absence of a central person through whom communications must flow.

Decision support systems computer-based systems that provide data in a form requested by the user; tools that aid management decision making.

Decode to translate information received by the senses into interpreted or perceived messages.

Delegation leader a leader who gives responsibilities to others and maintains a noninterfering style of leadership.

Deskilling restructuring a job so that less skill is required to perform it; a common result when computers are introduced to certain jobs.

Deviant members group members who violate a group norm or norms.

Diagnosis a systematic method of collecting information and establishing the causes and effects of the situation.

Differentiation a stage of group development that reflects the process of members getting a better ''feel'' for the group and its task.

Directive counseling involves a counselor making decisions and then telling a person what to do.

Discrimination any act or behavior in which people are treated differently because of a category into which they have been boxed regardless of unique attributes or abilities.

Dominant values basic assumptions about what ideals are desirable or worth striving for.

Downward communication the flow of information from a supervisor to a subordinate.

Dual-career families families in which both spouses hold jobs.

Duty of fair representation a union's obligation to process all grievances that have merit in a nondiscriminatory, nonarbitrary way and to represent all persons covered under a contract.

Economic loss lost earnings as a result of losing a job, being laid off, or being demoted to a lesser job.

Education and communication information and discussions about prospective change to employees; used to reduce resistance to change.

Effective communication information flow that results in a shared meaning and common understanding for both an information sender and a receiver.

Effective group a group that exhibits clarity of focus, supportive atmosphere, blending of task and maintenance roles, group composition, and resistance to control.

Emotional component a set of attitudes that refers to the feelings associated with an object, person, or event.

Emotional state a condition that causes one to sense, select, and organize information in a manner consistent with one's feelings.

Empathy awareness of the needs and motives of others.

Employee-centered leadership emphasizes delegation or responsibility and shows a concern for employee welfare, needs, advancement, and personal growth.

Emulators ambitious, competitive, and fairly successful persons; a major American lifestyle.

Encode to transfer one's thoughts, motives, and emotions into symbols that convey meaning to a receiver.

Equal Employment Opportunity Commission an agency primarily responsible for processing charges of discrimination and helping organizations implement affirmative action programs.

Equity theory focuses on an individual's social comparison of an existing condition with an accepted standard.

Essay a subjective method of evaluation that requires a rater to respond to open-ended questions about the performance of an employee.

Esteem needs those needs, valued by oneself or others, that produce feelings of self-confidence, prestige, power, or control.

Evaluation of change a systematic study of the change process to determine the progress or lack of progress that has been made.

Expand resources a technique for resolving conflict by increasing the amount of resources.

Expectancy theory focuses on an individual's beliefs as determined by his or her efforts in relation to job accomplishments and the associated rewards or incentives.

Experientials persons who are well educated and deeply involved in ideas and issues; a major American lifestyle.

Expert power power based on a special ability or knowledge of the power-holder that is needed by the recipient.

Explicit and implicit coercion the act of using some form of power, either overtly or covertly, to get other people to do something.

Extrinsic motivation rewards for doing a good job that are external to the job performer (rewards supplied by the environment), such as wages, working conditions, and job title.

Extrinsic rewards rewards mediated or granted by outside agents, such as the organization, supervisor, or friends.

Facilitation and support emotional support, listening, special attention, or training provided to help employees cope with changes.

Fear of unknowns anxiety felt when an individual confronts a new situation or change for the first time.

Feedback a response initiated by the receiver of a previous communication.

Filtering the passing of incomplete information by a communicator. This may be either intentional or unintentional.

Force field analysis a technique for portraying the conditions that support a change (driving forces) and the conditions that hinder a change (restraining forces).

Formal group a group defined by an organization (for example, a research team), given a specific task or tasks.

Frame of reference the collection of past and present experiences that affect an individual's perception of what is being said. A common experience base increases effective communication.

Gainsharing a group incentive plan in which the savings from productivity improvements are shared with workers.

Goal acceptance degree to which a person accepts a goal.

Goal commitment degree to which a person is dedicated to accomplishing an accepted goal.

Goal difficulty degree to which a goal is easily accomplished through one's own efforts.

Goal setting theory focuses on understanding how individuals set, accept, and accomplish job-related goals.

Goal specificity degree to which a goal is defined.

Grievance a formal complaint against a management activity.

Grievance procedure a formal way for employees to differ with management.

Group collection of individuals who interact on a regular basis and see themselves to be mutually dependent with respect to the attainment of common goals.

Group development progressive stages in a group's existence, including orientation, differentiation, integration, and maturity.

Group resistance the influence that group dynamics can have on members to encourage resistance to change.

Halo effect a perceptual error in which an onlooker evaluates all dimensions of another person according to a single impression; also a tendency to rate a person who is outstanding on one factor as high on other factors.

Handicapped term that describes a person who has a physical or mental impairment that substantially limits one or more of the person's major life activities.

Hawthorne Studies a series of studies done in the 1920s and 1930s that investigated worker reactions to technology and described worker interaction with other workers and with management.

High-tech/high-touch a trend in society. The need for more technology creates a desire for more human contact.

Human relations a discipline concerned with understanding, predicting, and influencing both the individual and the group in organizations.

Humility-inducing experiences activities that shake a new group member's confidence, making the member more open to indoctrination in an organization's values and procedures.

Hygiene factors extrinsically rewarding conditions related to a job environment that can become dissatisfiers if not present to a certain degree.

I-am-me's young people seeking an inner-directed life; a major American lifestyle.

Incentives rewards offered for improved performance.

Industrial Revolution a period of time beginning in the late 1700s when machines and physical power replaced human beings as the main source of power. Breaking jobs down into small elements and assigning workers to perform only small aspects of the work is one consequence of the Industrial Revolution.

Industrial union a union that represents all workers in a particular industry, no matter what specific job an individual has.

Ineffective communication a misunderstanding due to a lack of appropriate information or the timing of the information.

Informal group a group that emerges naturally from the interaction of individuals; may not relate to organizational purpose or goals.

Information overload more data given to an individual in a given amount of time than he or she can effectively handle.

Information Revolution signifies the current period of time when machines and physical power are being replaced by electronic and information technology. Now, much of the mechanized work is being simplified further and controlled by information and computer systems.

Information society a description of American society today, contrasted with its earlier description as an industrial society; a society where more than half of the work force processes information.

Information technology any data processing system including hardware and software. Examples range from simple telephone systems to sophisticated electronic networking systems that use telephones.

In-group language specialized vocabulary used by occupational groups (such as medical, military, or other professions); jargon.

Initiating structure a leadership style in which the leader defines how, when, and where employee activities will be performed.

Integrateds people with qualities of both achievers and the societally conscious group; a major American lifestyle.

Integration a stage of group development where problems are resolved as members evaluate their

tasks and the frustrations of performing them.

Intergroup conflict conflict between two or more groups.

Intervention a method or means to initiate or manage change.

Interviewing gathering information by asking employees face-to-face what they think.

Intrinsic motivation rewards for doing a good job that are internal to the job performer (rewards supplied from the job itself), such as interesting work, work that allows the individual to grow and develop, and work that helps an individual to use all of his or her skills.

Intrinsic reward a reward that occurs directly as a result of performing an activity; an outcome that an individual grants to himself or herself.

Japanese management style characterized by three principles: (1) an emphasis on the group rather than the individual; (2) an emphasis on human rather than functional relationships; and (3) a view of top management as generalists and facilitators rather than as decision makers.

Job design description of an employee's job, may be restructured to increase job satisfaction and performance.

Job satisfaction the degree of positive feeling one has about one's work situation.

Job-centered leadership characterized by close supervision, negative use of power, emphasis on schedules, and critical evaluation of work performance.

Justifications of behavior rationale for behavior; often reflects aspects of an organization's culture.

Knowledge and skill obsolescence occurs when one's knowledge and skills are no longer required or needed to perform a job.

Lack of identification absence of a feeling of association with a job or an organization; occasionally a consequence of computerizing jobs.

Laissez-faire leader a noninterfering type of leader who is neither employee- nor job-centered.

Lateral communication information exchange between peers.

Leader/member relations the degree of confidence, trust, and respect subordinates have in their leader.

Leader position power the extent of a leader's power and influence.

Learners newly hired or newly promoted employees

who have not yet reached their maximum performance level.

Legitimate power power held by individuals because of their position, role, or status in a company that confers a right to direct the actions of others.

Life planning managing change by helping employees gain control over their organizational and personal lives.

Line/staff conflict conflict between line employees, who produce a product or service, and staff employees, who provide specialized advice and assistance to line people.

Loss of control a sense that control of one's work has been taken away, that decisions once being made by the worker are being made by something or someone else.

Maintenance-related roles behaviors directed toward the well-being, continuity, and development of a group.

Management by objectives (MBO) a process in which managers and employees work together to create and implement goals and to evaluate performance.

Manipulation the act of selectively interacting with others in order to obtain desired results.

Mastery of work knowledge of and control over one's work.

Maturity the capacity to set high but attainable goals, the willingness and ability to take responsibility, and the education and experience of an individual or work group; also, a stage of group development in which the group achieves both flexibility and stability.

MBO *See* Management by objectives.

Mechanized work the replacement, during and after the Industrial Revolution, of man and beast as primary sources of physical work. Instead, steam power and various kinds of mechanical equipment were used, and individuals were assigned to assist a machine. As a result, individual workers performed routine repetitive tasks that were machine-determined.

Mediation a process of trying to reach a mutual agreement between labor and management with outside help.

Meditation a type of mental activity used to reach a state of deep relaxation.

Megatrends major trends that are changing American society.

Mentor one who serves as a sponsor, teacher, and coach for a talented junior employee.

Merit pay pay based on performance; requires a method of measuring performance and a financial reward; also called pay for performance.

Moral concerned with the establishment and application of principles of right and wrong.

Motivation factors intrinsically rewarding conditions related to the job itself that meet the needs of employees to use their talents and to grow in their jobs.

National Labor Relations Board a group created by the Wagner Act, which is responsible for resolving disputes between unions, employees, and employers.

Need theory focuses on what inspires individuals to perform certain activities.

Negative reinforcement termination or withdrawal of something unpleasant following a desired response.

Negotiations and agreement a method of sharing influence and power to reach a mutually satisfying solution.

Nondirective counseling involves the use of active listening, or mirroring, by a counselor to help an individual develop solutions to a problem.

Nonverbal communication information transmitted by gestures, body language, and patterns of movement. This information may either reinforce or conflict with the spoken communication.

Norms acceptable standards of behavior that are shared by members of a group or organization.

Norms of reciprocity an exchange between individuals; "I'll do something for you, if you do something for me."

Observation gathering information by watching employees to determine what they think instead of asking them directly.

Operant conditioning conditioning in which a behavior is followed by positive reinforcement, thus producing subsequent behaviors.

Organizational climate perceptions concerning the characteristics and quality of an organization's culture; the *experience* of organization culture.

Organizational culture prevailing patterns of values, attitudes, beliefs, assumptions, expectations, activities, interactions, norms, and sentiments that are shared by members of an organization.

Organizational development activities concerned

with increasing organizational efficiency through employee involvement in the work place.

Orientation   a stage of group development where individuals begin to identify with the group and learn the requirements of membership.

Overload   a condition in which an individual or department becomes bogged down by too much information.

Participation and involvement   allowing individuals to take part in how a change will be implemented, thus reducing resistance to change.

Participative leader   a leader who is more employee-centered than job-centered and encourages employees to help make decisions.

Past practice   the manner in which an organization has handled similar situations in the past.

Paternalistic leader   a leader who is job-centered and also concerned for the welfare of the employees.

Path-goal theory   focuses on how to motivate employees through their association of valued rewards with certain accomplished goals.

Peer evaluation   evaluation of one's performance by co-workers.

Perception   process by which one selects, organizes, and interprets stimuli.

Perceptual errors   factors that shape or distort reality. Common perceptual errors are stereotyping, selective perception, halo effect, set expectations, emotional state, and projection.

Perceptual interpretation   the process of attaching meaning to stimuli. The context in which stimuli appear and the personal characteristics of the interpreter affect this process.

Perceptual organization   grouping of stimuli into patterns based on proximity, similarity, closure, or continuity.

Perceptual selection   process of choosing the stimuli to which one reacts.

Philosophy   a rational explanation for activities upon which an organization's policies are formed.

Physiological needs   those needs concerned with food, clothing, and shelter.

Positive reinforcement   something pleasant that follows a desired behavior.

Pragmatic   the doctrine that ideas have value only in terms of their practical application; emphasis on "facts" and "reality."

Precedent   a past decision from an arbitration case used by arbitrators as a guide for the present decision.

Prejudice   negative judgment toward a group of people.

Pressures for change   the external or internal forces that an organization needs to address in order to be more effective.

Problem solving   a conflict resolution technique requiring cooperation in defining the basis for the conflict.

Profit-sharing   a group incentive plan in which profits are shared with employees, usually annually.

Projection   a tendency to see one's own traits in other people.

Protected groups   individuals who are legally protected from discrimination by the Civil Rights Act of 1964 and subsequent acts.

Psychology   a social science discipline that studies the factors that determine the behavior of individuals.

Punishment   an unpleasant condition produced in an attempt to eliminate an undesirable behavior.

Questionnaires   written questions that seek to measure attitudes, feelings, or opinions.

Racism   prejudice toward a group of people defined as socially distinct because of inherited physical characteristics.

Ranking   a method of evaluation that requires raters to "line up" employees from best to worst in performance.

Rating errors   attitudes, response tendencies, or inconsistencies within the rater that interfere with accurate performance ratings.

Receiver   person to whom a message or information is sent.

Recency   a rating error created when a manager is influenced by the most recent performance of a subordinate.

Referent power   power based on the recipient's identification with the power-holder.

Reinforcement theory   focuses on attempts to structure the environment through various rewards and punishments.

Relationship behavior   emphasizes delegation of responsibility and a concern for employee welfare, needs, advancement, and personal growth.

Relaxation techniques   activities that help an individual experience a specific neurological state of detachment from everyday concerns and a bodily sensation of calm and quiet.

Reliability   the extent to which an evaluation tool is consistent in measuring performance.

Remote supervision   use of computers for monitoring employee output, speed, and errors.

Resistance   behavior, whether overt or covert, that attempts to delay or avoid change.

Resolution   conclusion or end to a conflict.

Reverse discrimination   behavior that seems discriminatory toward individuals who are not in a legally protected status.

Reward power   power based on the ability to provide positive rewards to the recipient.

Right-to-work laws   statutes that forbid union-management contracts requiring workers to join unions.

Ritual   a prescribed form or method for the performance of a solemn ceremony.

Role ambiguity   uncertainty about one's job objectives and responsibilities.

Role conflict   a situation in which an individual is faced with differing job demands, expectations, or goals.

Roles   behaviors expected of persons in particular positions.

Rules of the game   unwritten requirements for "getting along" that reflect group norms.

Safety needs   those needs that include freedom from physical danger or fear of not meeting physiological needs.

Scientific management   an approach to studying and recommending changes based on simplification and standardization of the tasks performed.

Selective perception   the practice of choosing to acknowledge and maybe overemphasize only certain aspects of a situation.

Self-actualization   becoming the best that a person can be; using one's potential to the fullest.

Self-evaluation   appraisal of one's own performance.

Self-fulfilling prophecy   a person's expectation of an event that makes the outcome more likely to occur than would otherwise have been true.

Self-help   an emerging tendency for people to rely less on institutions and more on themselves.

Self-related roles   behaviors oriented only to individual needs of group members.

Semantic differences   different perceived meanings for the same words, often the result of a vague context in which the communication takes place.

Sender   person who sends a message or information.

Sensing   obtaining information by interviewing employees directly in a group setting.

Set expectations   assumptions, based on what a person expects, that distort perception.

Sexism   discrimination based on gender.

Sexual harassment   the offering of job favors in return for sexual favors; also, offensive or sexually suggestive speech or conduct.

Situational theory   focuses on identifying what factors are critical to the leader to influence employees and how to vary the leadership style based on those factors.

Smoothing   playing down differences and emphasizing common interests, sometimes called accommodation.

Social needs   those needs of striving to belong, being accepted, and interacting with others.

Social Readjustment Rating Scale   a measurement of the impact of life events, used in the study of stress-related illnesses.

Socialization   the process by which a person is transformed from an outsider to a participating member of a group; the process of indoctrinating a person to acceptance of an organization's norms and values.

Societally conscious   people who are successful, influential, and highly concerned about social issues; a major American lifestyle.

Sociology   a social science discipline that studies social behavior in groups, organizations, and societies.

Sociotechnical   describes the relationship between the social and technical aspects of one's job.

Solid citizens   the bulk of workers in an organization, who perform satisfactorily or better but have little chance for advancement.

Stakes   benefits to the parties involved in a conflict.

Stars   employees who display a high performance record over a sustained period; sometimes termed to be "on the fast track."

Status differences   a condition which occurs when two parties have unequal power or authority.

Stereotyping   forming an impression of an individual based upon assumptions about a group to which that person belongs.

Stories and myths   folklore about powerful figures in an organization; often tales about heroic performance that are passed down from one generation to another.

Stress a strain on one's physical, emotional, or mental state as a consequence of or a response to an action, situation, or force.

Stress carriers individuals who knowingly or unknowingly create discomfort and concern in others.

Stressors situations or conditions present at work or in one's personal life that may cause discomfort and concern.

Survivors people who tend to be poverty stricken and poorly educated; a major American lifestyle.

Sustainers people who are mostly low income, but who have hope for a better future; a major American life style.

Targeted groups well-defined groups that have been identified (targeted) for special career programs.

Task behavior focuses on explaining what each employee is to do, as well as when, where, and how tasks are to be accomplished.

Task structure the degree of complexity and routineness of a subordinate's activities.

Task-related roles behaviors directed toward establishing and accomplishing group goals.

Team building an approach to managing change by helping group members to function better together.

Theory X and Theory Y a behavioral theory of leadership that compares two sets of assumptions (personal beliefs held by the supervisor) about how and why employees behave.

Threats to power and influence resistance to change that occurs because the proposed change will restructure one's power and influence.

Threats to social system resistance to change that occurs because the proposed change will affect the social relationships between workers.

Transmission action taken to accomplish the sending of information.

Turnover voluntary or involuntary termination of employment. From the organization's perspective, it may be desirable or undesirable.

Underutilization of abilities less than the full use of an individual's abilities and skills.

Unfair labor practice any action by either labor or management that interferes with workers' rights regarding fair representation in job and working conditions.

Union a group of people who feel that they can get more of what they want by bargaining as a group with an organization.

Upward communication the flow of information from one individual to another higher in the organization.

Valence worth or value placed on an outcome.

Validity in performance appraisal, the extent to which an evaluation tool is relevant to the task being evaluated.

VALS program values and lifestyles program; a project that identified major lifestyles among Americans.

Value orientation a personal value that influences behavior.

Values basic convictions about the goodness or badness of conduct or results; rules of right and wrong.

Wheel network a centralized communication network where information flows through one central control point.

Work abstraction a perception by workers that computers make work less "real"; for example, when paper files are replaced by a computer data base, a worker manipulates electronic symbols rather than handling paper.

Work force values the reasons why individuals work and what they want from their jobs.

Work rule specific language in a contract identifying exactly the type of work a person is supposed to do.

"Y" network a communication network where two people transmit information to a central person who then transfers the information to a higher organizational level.

Name Index

Subject Index

WE VALUE YOUR OPINION—PLEASE SHARE IT WITH US

Merrill Publishing and our authors are most interested in your reactions to this textbook. Did it serve you well in the course? If it did, what aspects of the text were most helpful? If not, what didn't you like about it? Your comments will help us to write and develop better textbooks. We value your opinions and thank you for your help.

Text Title _____ Edition _____

Author(s) _____

Your Name (optional) _____

Address _____

City _____ State _____ Zip _____

School _____

Course Title _____

Instructor's Name _____

Your Major _____

Your Class Rank _____ Freshman _____ Sophomore _____ Junior _____ Senior

_____ Graduate Student

Were you required to take this course? _____ Required _____ Elective

Length of Course? _____ Quarter _____ Semester

1. Overall, how does this text compare to other texts you've used?

   _____ Superior _____ Better Than Most _____ Average _____ Poor

2. Please rate the text in the following areas:

	Superior	Better Than Most	Average	Poor
Author's Writing Style	_____	_____	_____	_____
Readability	_____	_____	_____	_____
Organization	_____	_____	_____	_____
Accuracy	_____	_____	_____	_____
Layout and Design	_____	_____	_____	_____
Illustrations/Photos/Tables	_____	_____	_____	_____
Examples	_____	_____	_____	_____
Problems/Exercises	_____	_____	_____	_____
Topic Selection	_____	_____	_____	_____
Currentness of Coverage	_____	_____	_____	_____
Explanation of Difficult Concepts	_____	_____	_____	_____
Match-up with Course Coverage	_____	_____	_____	_____
Applications to Real Life	_____	_____	_____	_____

3. Circle those chapters you especially liked:
1   2   3   4   5   6   7   8   9   10   11   12   13   14   15   16   17   18   19   20
What was your favorite chapter? _____
Comments:

4. Circle those chapters you liked least:
1   2   3   4   5   6   7   8   9   10   11   12   13   14   15   16   17   18   19   20
What was your least favorite chapter? _____
Comments:

5. List any chapters your instructor did not assign. _____

6. What topics did your instructor discuss that were not covered in the text?_____

_____

7. Were you required to buy this book? _____ Yes   _____ No

   Did you buy this book new or used? _____ New   _____ Used

   If used, how much did you pay? _____

   Do you plan to keep or sell this book? _____ Keep   _____ Sell

   If you plan to sell the book, how much do you expect to receive? _____

   Should the instructor continue to assign this book? _____ Yes   _____ No

8. Please list any other learning materials you purchased to help you in this course (e.g., study guide, lab manual).

_____

9. What did you like most about this text? _____

_____

10. What did you like least about this text? _____

_____

11. General comments:

   May we quote you in our advertising? _____ Yes   _____ No

   Please mail to: Boyd Lane
                     College Division, Research Department
                     Box 508
                     1300 Alum Creek Drive
                     Columbus, Ohio 43216

   Thank you!